Masahiro Sakurai

SORA LTD.
TOKYO, JAPAN

Masahiro Sakurai was born in Tokyo in 1970. After joining HAL LABORATORY, INC., he directed and designed the *Kirby* and *Super Smash Bros.* series. After striking out on his own, he founded Sora Ltd. in 2005.

Some of his credits include game design and direction for *Kirby's Dream Land* for the Game Boy system, *Kirby's Adventure* for the NES, *Kirby Super Star* for the Super NES, *Super Smash Bros.* for the Nintendo 64 system, *Super Smash Bros. Melee* and *Kirby Air Ride* for the Nintendo GameCube system, *Meteos* for the Nintendo DS family of systems, *Super Smash Bros. Brawl* for the Wii console and *Kid Icarus: Uprising* for the Nintendo 3DS family of systems. He also supervises the animated Kirby TV show and other Kirby projects.

Thank you very much for playing *Super Smash Bros. for Nintendo 3DS/Wii U.*

Though both games contain massive amounts of content, they're also accessible enough that you can enjoy playing only in a few minutes. We increased the number of fighters, stages, and items significantly, putting more effort and work into these games than any other in the series so far. Furthermore, since the development team had never worked on a *Smash Bros.* game previously, we started the project basically from zero.

On a personal note, during development I cast aside almost everything in my private life, immersing myself in my work. I took no time off, and there were days when I went home only to sleep then return to work again. Indeed, I overdid it and nearly fell apart.

But I'm happy to say we did all this for one person: the player.

Also, I should mention that without the efforts of the development team and the staff at Nintendo, we could never have put so much content into these games.

I think we've made two games that, if you enjoy playing them, will keep you entertained for years to come. After all, this isn't the kind of series where we can release sequel after sequel. I hope you will find something you will like in these two titles and play them in a way that brings you maximum enjoyment.

Thank You,

Masahiro Sakurai

CONTENTS

GAME BASICS

Wii U Menus

MAIN MENU

The game's main menu contains a number of options:

Smash: Straight-up Smash! Play against CPU fighters or people in the same room.

Online: Go online and test your skills against your friends and the world.

Smash Tour: A smashing board game for 1 to 4 players. Collect fighters and prepare for the final battle.

Games & More: Play various game modes, customize a fighter, check out your Vault, and more!

Challenges: Complete Challenges to win prizes!

3DS: Connect to *Super Smash Bros.* for Nintendo 3DS.

Manual: Read the electronic manual.

SMASH

The game's Smash modes focus on pure combat, but you'll find enough settings and options to customize your experience. Choose from Smash, 8-Player Smash, and Special Smash. You can play against CPU fighters or utilize additional controllers to battle it out with friends. The game's Smash modes also offer amiibo functionality. Train your created Figure Players by having them participate in various Smash Battles!

ONLINE

Online allows you to test your skills against your friends and players around the world. With an extra controller, two players can use a single system to participate in online battles! This mode focuses on standard Smash variations, but it also includes some additional options and features:

- **With Friends:** Connect with friends to battle in Smash and Team Smash. The host is able to set the rules for the first match. At the end of each battle, the fighter who finishes in last place chooses the rules for the next match. With Friends is also the only Online mode that allows for customized fighters!
- **With Anyone:** Connect with opponents from around the world. You can play For Fun, in which only your wins will be recorded, or play For Glory, in which your wins and losses will be recorded. For Glory matches are confined to Final Destination form (Ω) stages.
- **Spectate:** Watch replays or bet gold on other players' online battles or view randomly selected matches. You can also review worldwide stats and see how many people are playing online.
- **Conquest:** Participate in special events where up to three teams battle it out. While a Conquest event is active, you can play With Anyone battles as one of the featured characters to earn points for his or her team. The team that gets the most points during the event wins.

For more information about the online features and settings, please refer to the game's manual.

NOTE

SMASH TOUR

Smash Tour is an action-packed board game in which players race to collect fighters, items, and valuable stat boosts. Each time two players bump into each other or someone lands on a Battle Space, the game moves from the Smash Tour board to a randomly selected match type. Collect enough fighters to gain an advantage and power them up to prepare yourself for the final battle!

GAMES & MORE

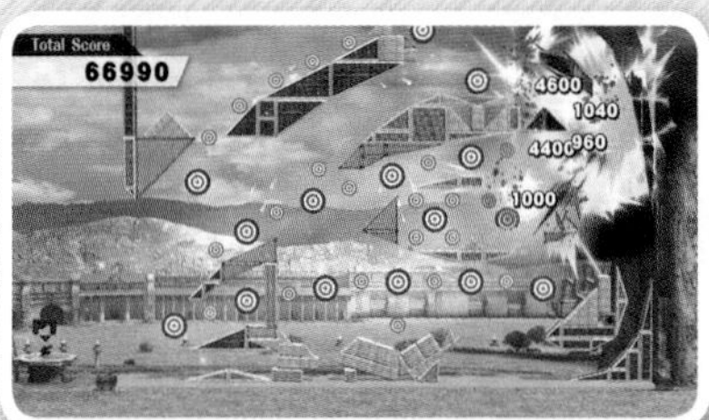

Games & More offers a wide variety of game modes. Put your skills to the test in longer modes like Classic and All-Star or pop in to clear a few Events or Special Orders. You'll also find some fun minigames like Target Blast, Multi-Man Smash, and Home-Run Contest. Create custom fighters and unique stages or head to the Vault to review your trophies, fighter stats, replays, and more!

CHALLENGES

Discover and complete 140 specific Challenges to earn valuable rewards like stages, trophies, equipment, and more! Explore the game to complete some of the easier Challenges and reveal specific details about more complicated tasks. You can even earn special single-use hammers to instantly unlock eligible Challenges!

3DS

You can connect a Nintendo 3DS to your Wii U console for use as an extra controller or to copy custom fighters between your devices! It's important to note, however, that you must own a copy of *Super Smash Bros.* for Nintendo 3DS to take advantage of this feature.

MANUAL

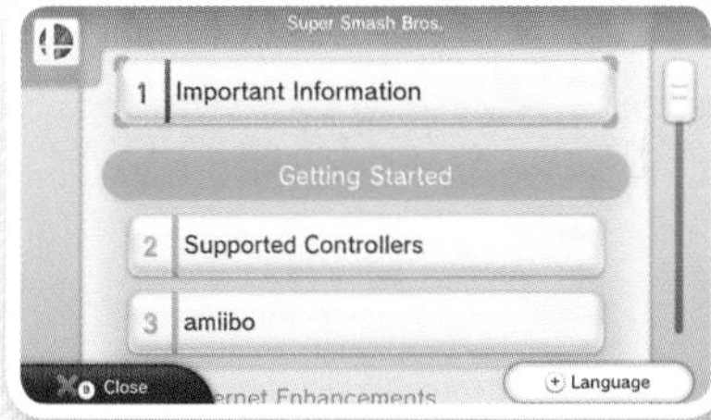

The game's manual contains helpful details about available features, game modes, and fighters. Refer to the manual anytime you need more information about navigating or playing the game.

3DS Menus

MAIN MENU

The game's main menu contains a number of options:

- **Smash:** Test your skills in classic Smash! Challenge the CPU or nearby players.
- **Online:** Connect to the Internet and test your skills against your friends and the world!
- **Challenge:** Take on Challenges and win prizes!
- **Smash Run:** Collect boosts in a vast labyrinth to prepare for an epic final battle!
- **Games & More:** Solo and group games, plus Training, custom fighters, the Vault, and more!
- **StreetPass:** A StreetSmash of epic proportions! Defeat your rivals and win prizes!
- **Wii U:** Connect to *Super Smash Bros.* for Wii U.

SMASH

Smash focuses on pure combat, serving as a great place to practice fundamentals and advanced techniques that apply to virtually all available game modes. You can adjust the settings and match rules to suit your tastes, but the basic objective will always be the same: attack your opponents to deal damage and launch them off of the screen!

NOTE

For more information about the online features and settings, please refer to the game's manual.

ONLINE

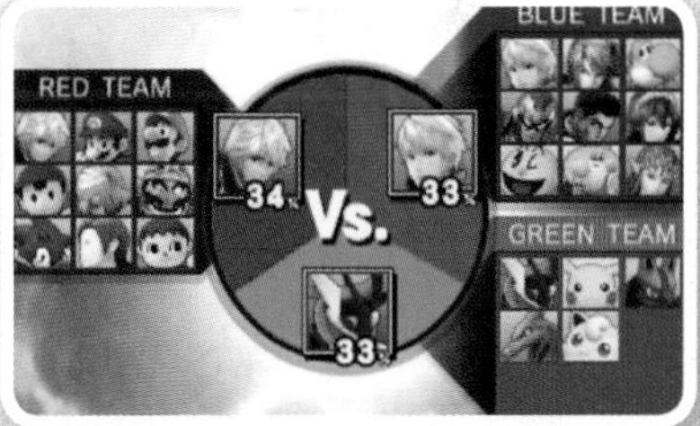

Online allows you to connect with players over the Internet. This mode focuses on standard Smash variations, but it also includes some additional options and features:

- **With Friends:** Connect with friends to battle in Smash and Team Smash. The host is able to set the rules for the first match. At the end of each battle, the fighter who finishes in last place chooses the rules for the next match. With Friends is also the only Online mode that allows for customized fighters!
- **With Anyone:** Connect with opponents from around the world. You can play For Fun, in which only your wins will be recorded, or play For Glory, in which your wins and losses will be recorded. For Glory matches are confined to Final Destination form (Ω) stages.
- **Conquest:** Participate in special events where up to three teams battle it out. While a Conquest event is active, you can play With Anyone battles as one of the featured characters to earn points for his or her team. The team that gets the most points during the event wins.
- **Spectate:** Watch replays or bet gold on other players' online battles or view replays featuring specific characters to research tactics used by other players. You can also review worldwide stats and see how many people are playing online.

CHALLENGE

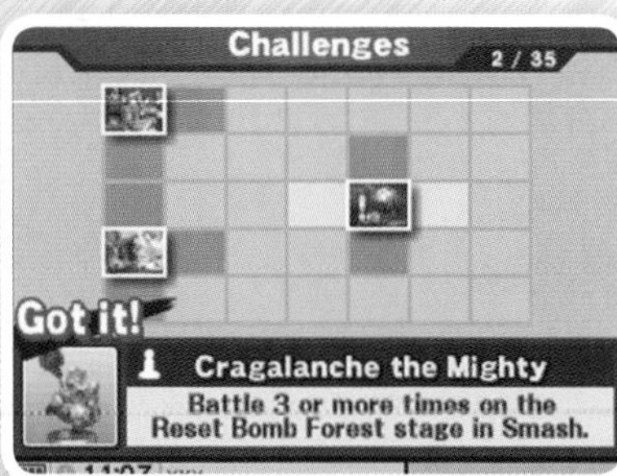

Complete Challenges to earn stages, trophies, equipment, music, and more! There are three Challenge panels, each of which contains 35 tiles. When you complete a Challenge, the corresponding tile is unlocked, and any adjacent tiles display new Challenge objectives.

By default, only the first Challenge panel is unlocked. You must unlock subsequent Challenge panels before you can earn the rewards they offer.

SMASH RUN

Collect stat boosts to power up your character then face off against other fighters in a randomly selected final battle! You have five minutes to build your stats in a massive battlefield; defeat enemies, collect items, and utilize special Powers to improve your chances of victory.

GAMES & MORE

Play a wide variety of game modes. From longer offerings like Classic and All-Star to shorter games like Target Blast and Home-Run Contest, there's something for everyone! You can also create custom sets for your fighters and use the Vault to review your trophies, fighter stats, replays, and more.

STREETPASS

Collect StreetPass tags to battle opponents in StreetSmash. Use your character token to knock your foes right off of the StreetSmash stage! Perform well to earn valuable prizes or use Practice Mode to earn a little gold as you learn the basics of StreetSmash.

WII U

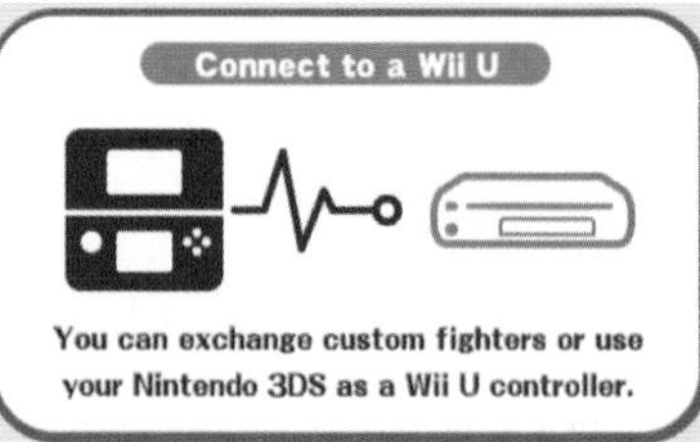

Connect your system to a Nintendo Wii U! This feature allows you to exchange custom fighters between your consoles or even use your handheld system as an extra controller for your Nintendo Wii U! You must own a copy of *Super Smash Bros.* for the Nintendo Wii U to take advantage of this feature.

NOTE

For more information about StreetPass features and settings, please refer to the game's manual and the StreetSmash tutorial.

How to Play

KOS

Super Smash Bros. offers a variety of game modes and match rules. The basics of combat, however, are almost always the same. Attack your opponents to increase their damage percentages—the more damage a fighter takes, the easier it is to launch him or her into the air. Launch an opponent clear out of the stage to earn a KO.

Being launched off of the screen can result in an instant KO, but it's not a certainty. If a small window appears near the edge of the screen, there's a chance the indicated fighter could recover. This often happens when a fighter falls from a platform or fails to keep pace with a scrolling stage, but a window also appears when an off-screen fighter wasn't launched quite hard enough to ensure a KO.

TIP

Fighters with high damage percentages will also find it slightly easier to launch their opponents!

COMBAT ITEMS

Most game modes include various items that can be used during battle. Whenever items are allowed, you can expect to find a variety of weapons, food, gear, and more. Try to grab an available item before one of your opponents has a chance to use it against you.

COLLECTIBLE ITEMS

Collectible items can appear in most game modes. Grab these valuable items to access new features and options:

- **Trophies:** When you spot a trophy, grab it to add that trophy to your collection. Visit the Gallery to view your trophy collection—you might just learn a thing or two about the game's characters, enemies, and items!
- **Custom Parts:** If you spot a sack marked with a wrench icon, you can bet it contains a custom part. Collect these items to unlock equipment, headgear, outfits, and alternate Special moves. Use the custom parts you collect to give your favorite fighters new abilities!
- **Gold:** Grab any coins you spot to increase your available gold. You can use your collected gold to change the intensity of Classic, purchase extra time in Trophy Rush, and buy new trophies from the Shop.

SYSTEM MECHANICS

Despite it's seemingly simple control scheme, the game contains a variety of complicated mechanics and techniques.

SPECIALTY CONTROLLERS

Super Smash Bros. for NIntendo Wii U can utilize a variety of specialty controllers. This section details techniques as they are performed with standard controllers. If needed, please refer to the game's manual or controller options for details about a specialty controller.

If you're playing *Super Smash Bros.* for Nintendo 3DS (or if you're using a Nintendo 3DS as an extra Wii U controller), use the Circle Pad in place of the Left Stick to perform the described techniques.

SMASH RUN POWERS

In *Super Smash Bros.* for Nintendo 3DS, you'll also find collectible Powers. Each of these items appears in a sack labeled with a question mark. Powers can only be used in Smash Run, but they can be found in any mode that drops collectible items. Add Powers to your fighters' custom sets to improve your chances of a Smash Run victory.

DEFAULT WII U CONTROLS

Move	Left Stick
Jump	Ⓨ or Ⓧ (or flick the Left Stick up)
Attack	Ⓐ
Special	Ⓑ
Grab	ZL or ZR
Shield	L or R

NOTE

You can adjust the default control scheme through the "Controls" menu in Smash or through the "Option" menu in Games & More.

DEFAULT 3DS CONTROLS

Move	Circle Pad
Jump	Ⓨ or Ⓧ (or flick the Circle Pad up)
Attack	Ⓐ
Special	Ⓑ
Grab	L
Shield	R

NOTE

You can adjust the default control scheme through the "Options" menu in Games & More.

BASIC MOVEMENT

WALK

Tilt the Left Stick to the left or right to walk. Your speed varies depending on how far you tilt it to the left or right.

DASH

Flick and hold the Left Stick to the left or right to dash. Release the Left Stick to stop dashing.

CROUCH

Tilt the Left Stick down to crouch. Crouching reduces the knockback effects from incoming attacks.

> Some fighters can move while crouching. If your fighter has this ability, tilt the Left Stick down to crouch, then tilt it slightly to the left or right to crawl along the ground.
>
> **NOTE**

DROP

Flick the Left Stick down to drop through thin floors and platforms.

JUMP

Press Ⓨ or Ⓧ to jump. While jumping, use the Left Stick to steer your fighter through the air.

> By default, you can also flick the Left Stick up to jump. This applies to all jump-based techniques.
>
> **NOTE**

AIR JUMP

While in the air, press Ⓨ or Ⓧ to perform an air jump. All characters can perform at least one air jump before they're forced to land, but some fighters can perform a series of air jumps.

SHORT HOP

Quickly tap Ⓨ or Ⓧ to perform a short hop. This technique is especially useful when you want to perform a surprise aerial attack on a standing opponent.

BACK JUMP

Simultaneously press Ⓨ or Ⓧ and flick the Left Stick away from your target to perform a back jump.

FOOTSTOOL JUMP

Hop onto an opponent and press Ⓨ or Ⓧ to perform a footstool jump. This move takes precision timing, but it gives your jump a considerable boost. You can even perform footstool jumps on airborne enemies to send them crashing to the ground!

> Some characters, like Sheik and Lucario, are capable of wall-clinging. To use this technique, jump into a wall, then flick and hold the Left Stick toward that wall to cling for a short time. Flick the Left Stick away from the wall to perform a wall jump!
>
> **NOTE**

OFFENSIVE TECHNIQUES

NEUTRAL STANDING ATTACK

While on the ground, press Ⓐ to perform a neutral standing attack (also known as a "standard attack"). This attack is essentially a quick jab, but it can usually be chained together to perform a fast combo. Depending on your chosen fighter, jab combos can be performed by holding Ⓐ or by tapping the button to perform a series of separate attacks.

TILT ATTACKS

Each fighter has three different tilt attacks (also known as "strong attacks"): Up Tilt, Down Tilt, and Side Tilt. Gently tilt the Left Stick in one of the available directions, then press Ⓐ to perform the corresponding tilt attack.

SMASH ATTACKS

Each fighter has three different Smash attacks: Up Smash, Down Smash, and Side Smash. To perform a Smash attack, flick the Left Stick in one of the available directions as you press Ⓐ. Hold the command to charge a Smash attack for additional power. A successfully executed Smash attack deals heavy damage and launches your opponent.

Depending on your chosen controller, Smash attacks can also be performed by flicking the Right Stick in one of the available directions.

DASH ATTACKS

While dashing, press Ⓐ to perform a dash attack.

AERIAL ATTACKS

Each fighter has five different aerial attacks: Neutral Air, Up Air, Down Air, Forward Air, and Back Air. To perform a Neutral Air attack, press Ⓐ while your fighter is airborne. To perform one of the other available aerial attacks, tilt the Left Stick in the desired direction and press Ⓐ while your fighter is airborne.

SPECIAL ATTACKS

Each fighter has four different Special attacks (also known as "Specials" and "Special moves"): Neutral Special, Up Special, Down Special, and Side Special. Press Ⓑ perform a Neutral Special. To perform one of the other available Special attacks, flick the Left Stick in the desired direction and press Ⓑ. Special attacks can be performed on the ground or in the air.

> **As you play through the game's various modes, you'll collect alternate Specials for your fighters. Each alternate Special can only be used by the specified character and only in place of a specific Special attack (Up Special, Down Special, etc.). Create custom sets to utilize any alternate Specials that match your playstyle.**
>
> **NOTE**

GRAB

Press the Grab button while facing a nearby opponent to perform a grab. Once you've grabbed an opponent, press Ⓐ to attack.

> **You can also perform a grab by holding the Shield button as you press Ⓐ.**
>
> **NOTE**

THROW

Press the Grab button to grab an opponent, then tilt the Left Stick to perform a throw. Each fighter can perform four different throws: Up Throw, Down Throw, Forward Throw, and Back Throw. Tilt the Left Stick in the appropriate direction to perform the desired throw. Use throws give yourself a bit of breathing room or to damage enemies while their shields are active.

FINAL SMASH

If you manage to break open a Smash Ball, press Ⓑ to perform your fighter's Final Smash—an extremely powerful attack that is unique to that character. Different Final Smashes have different ranges and area effects, so make sure you're familiar with your fighter's specific attack!

DEFENSIVE TECHNIQUES

SHIELD

Press and hold the Shield button to activate your fighter's shield. While active, the shield absorbs damage caused by most enemy attacks. The shield shrinks over time, and absorbing damage causes it to shrink much faster. As your shield shrinks, less of your fighter is protected. Tilt the Left Stick to move your shield toward incoming attacks. If your shield breaks, your fighter will be stunned for a short time. Release the button to deactivate your shield. A weakened shield will slowly recharge when it isn't in use. If you manage to activate your shield at the moment an attack lands, however, you'll perform a Perfect Shield. A Perfect Shield blocks the attack without the usual shrinking penalty!

NOTE

Shields cannot protect fighters from throws, and some attacks are able to penetrate a shield without breaking it.

SPOT DODGE

Press the Shield button as you flick the Left Stick down to perform a spot dodge. This move allows you to avoid taking damage without moving or compromising your shield. It only lasts a short time, however, so it's best to use it against quick attacks.

AIR DODGE

Press the Shield button while your fighter is airborne to perform an air dodge. While air dodging, you can use the Left Stick to steer the fighter just as you would at any other point in a jump. This move allows you to avoid damage for a short time, so use it wisely!

FAST FALL

While your fighter is dropping or falling,, flick the Left Stick down to perform a fast fall. This allows your fighter to land as quickly as possible. Fast falling is a good way to avoid aerial attacks, but it's particularly helpful when your fighter is suffering from a fall state.

NOTE

A "fall state" describes an inability for your fighter to perform aerial moves. Fall states most often occur after performing Up Specials while your fighter is airborne. A fall state only ends when your fighter lands, so the sooner you can get back to solid ground, the better!

DODGE

Press the Shield button as you flick the Left Stick to the left or right to perform a dodge. This evasive roll allows you to avoid taking damage without compromising your shield, but it can also be used to slip behind an enemy for a well-timed counterattack.

AIR CONTROL

When you're launched into the air (or if you're hit when an air dodge fails), you have a small amount of control over your trajectory. For example, you can flick the Left Stick in the direction you're moving to travel slightly farther. Flicking the Left Stick in the opposite direction will slow you down a bit.

SUPER ARMOR

Most attacks will be interrupted when a fighter takes damage—this mechanic is known as "flinching." Some attacks, however, have an added effect called "super armor." Super armor allows a fighter to continue his or her attack while taking damage. Unlike invincibility, this effect does not prevent a fighter from taking incoming damage, and there's always a limit to how much damage super armor can withstand. Once a fighter's super armor is broken, he or she will flinch as usual.

ADDITIONAL TECHNIQUES AND COMMANDS

RECOVERY

Each fighter has a combination of moves that can be used to recover from falls or from being launched. Recovery moves vary between fighters, but air jumps and Up Specials are usually your best options. It's not always possible to recover from a big hit, but the right technique will improve your odds of success.

> Please refer to this guide's character descriptions for recommended recovery moves.
>
> **NOTE**

TAUNT

Each fighter has three different taunts: Up Taunt, Down Taunt, and Side Taunt. Press the +Control Pad in one of the available directions to perform the corresponding taunt. Taunting leaves your fighter vulnerable to attacks, so taunt wisely!

ITEM USE

You'll encounter a variety of items during combat, and individual items can have wildly different effects. Approach an available item and press Ⓐ to pick it up. Some items will be automatically consumed or activated, but many items can be used manually by pressing Ⓐ while your fighter is holding them. Press the Grab button to drop an unwanted item, or simultaneously press the Grab button and flick the Left Stick forward to throw the item. Press the Grab button while dashing to throw an unwanted item even farther!

EDGE MOVES

> Only one fighter can grab a single edge at one time. When a fighter grabs an occupied edge, the previous occupant is knocked loose.
>
> **NOTE**

Your fighter will automatically grab the platform's edge if he or she gets close enough to it during a recovery attempt. This triggers a brief period of invincibility and presents a few tactical options. Some fighters can even utilize moves or tools to grab platform edges from greater distances.

While grabbing the ledge, you can:

- Edge Roll: Press the Shield button to roll back onto the platform as you dodge enemy attacks.
- Edge Attack: Press Ⓐ to attack near the edge of the platform as you pull yourself up.
- Edge Climb: Tilt the Left Stick toward the edge to climb up.
- Edge Jump: Press Ⓨ or Ⓧ (or flick the Left Stick up) to propel yourself over the platform. This option does not count toward your fighter's air jump limit.
- Release: Flick the Left Stick down or away from the platform to release the edge. This option counts toward your fighter's air jump limit, but it also allows you to follow up with a quick aerial attack or recovery move.

amiibo

amiibo™ figures

are a brand new way to interact with your favorite Nintendo characters and games.

Tap amiibo figures to the Wii U™ GamePad controller (no portal required!)

and watch them come to life and affect different games in surprising ways.

See http://www.nintendo.com/amiibo for more information.

From amiibo™ Figures to Figure Players!

In *Super Smash Bros.* for your Nintendo Wii U, you can use amiibo figures to create and train Figure Players—intelligent fighters that learn new tactics as they battle! With the game's amiibo functionality, activating your personalized fighter is as simple as tapping an amiibo figure to the Wii U GamePad.

Your Figure Players can be used as allies, or they can serve as particularly challenging opponents. The more you interact with one of these fighters, the more it learns. Your amiibo Figure Players can use this knowledge to emulate your fighting style and to determine the best counters for your preferred habits. The more time you spend with a Figure Player, the more it knows you!

Feed your Figure Player any equipment to alter its stats and grant it special abilities. But choose wisely! Any resulting effects will be permanent, and once a piece of equipment is consumed, it's gone for good. You can also equip your amiibo Figure Players with any of the alternate Special moves you've managed to collect for that character.

Challenge your friends to an amiibo figure battle and let your Figure Players duke it out! Has your Figure Player learned enough to be victorious? There's only one way to find out, and your effort is sure to be rewarded—using your amiibo figure on a friend's Nintendo Wii U allows your respective Figure Players to exchange helpful gifts!

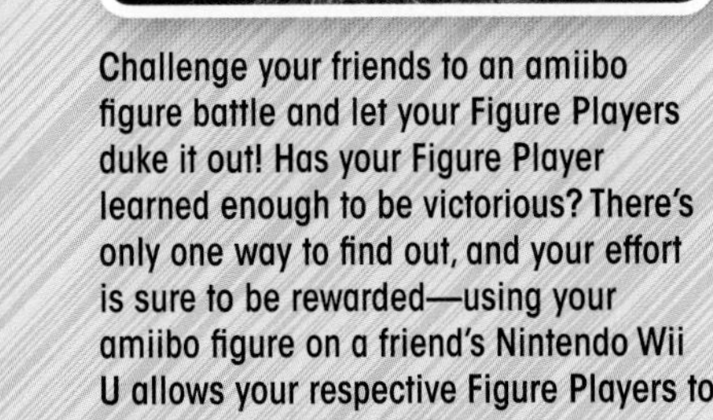

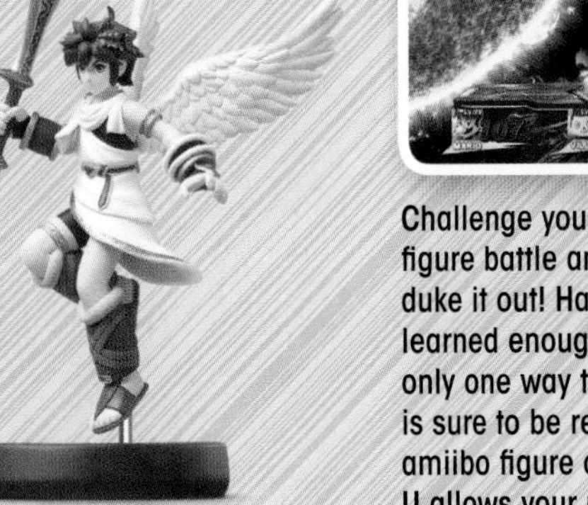

BOWSER

Trophy Description

Mario's archnemesis and the reason Peach spends more time in "another castle" than in her own. His plans almost never work out, and occasionally he even finds himself on Mario's side. In *Smash Bros.*, he's a serious heavyweight who laughs off weaker attacks. Hit him hard to send him flying!

STATISTICS

MAXIMUM NUMBER OF JUMPS: **2**

CAN WALL JUMP: **No**

CAN WALL CLING: **No**

CAN CRAWL: **Yes**

Alternate Colors

Smash Attacks

SIDE SMASH DAMAGE 14~23%

Bowser performs a massive dropkick to your opponent! During the attack, the ends of Bowser's feet are both invincible.

DOWN SMASH

DAMAGE 1~9% MAX DAMAGE 16% : 7 HITS

Bowser tucks into his shell and spins, hitting your opponent multiple times. Bowser's torso has some invincibility during this attack.

UP SMASH DAMAGE 6~20%

Bowser ducks down before jumping upward. This attack hits on the way up and again as Bowser comes back down.

Basic Attacks

STANDING ATTACK DAMAGE 5%, 6.5%

Bowser strikes at your opponent twice. Fairly decent range and damage for a poke. His attacking hands are invincible.

UP TILT DAMAGE 10%

Bowser swings his arm over his head and attacks *behind* him. Be sure you're facing the right way before using this attack! His outstretched arm is invincible during the attack.

DASH ATTACK

DAMAGE 8~10%

A surprisingly fast attack given Bowser's size, this jump kick can catch your opponents off guard.

SIDE TILT DAMAGE 12%

Bowser extends his claw for a strong attack. His claw has some invincibility. You can angle this slightly upward or downward.

DOWN TILT

DAMAGE 11~14% MAX DAMAGE 25% : 2 HITS

This double low strike combos for a ton of damage, if you can land it. His attacking hands are invincible.

EDGE ATTACK

Bowser returns to the stage with a solid punch sweep.

Air Attacks

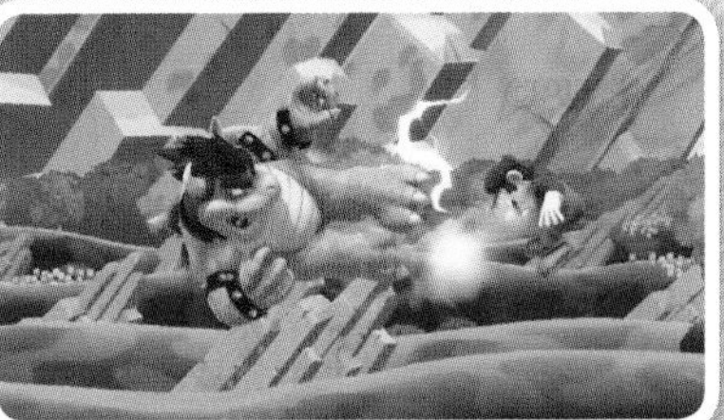

NEUTRAL AIR ATTACK

DAMAGE 5% MAX DAMAGE 20% : 4 HITS

Bowser's new cartwheel attack. Useful to hit opponents in front, above, and below you.

DOWN AIR ATTACK

DAMAGE 2~16% MAX DAMAGE 18% : 2 HITS

Bowser boosts a little higher before plummeting down again, spiked shell first. Be careful how you use this if the stage isn't below you!

BACK AIR ATTACK DAMAGE 19%

One of Bowser's best knockout moves, this dropkick is deadly.

UP AIR ATTACK DAMAGE 15%

Bowser uses his head as he executes a vicious headbutt. His head is invincible throughout the attack.

FORWARD AIR ATTACK

DAMAGE 11~13%

This overhead, downward strike has good range and is solid when chasing opponents or keeping them out.

Special Attacks

FIRE BREATH (Neutral Special)

DAMAGE 1.2% MAX DAMAGE 4.8% : 4 HITS

Bowser breathes fire onto his opponents. The longer you hold the button, the more this attack's range and power reduces. The end of its range has a small push effect, and you can vary the angle of the attack a little bit. It takes about 10 seconds to regain its full power from minimum.

Fire Shot

DAMAGE 4~5%

Bowser shoots a fireball from his mouth. As it travels farther, its damage drops a little.

Fire Roar

DAMAGE 1.8~2.7% MAX DAMAGE 18.9% : 7 HITS

Significantly more damaging, this flame is also much larger. To get it to maximum strength from its minimum takes about 20 seconds!

FLYING SLAM (Side Special)

DAMAGE 18%

Bowser swings his arm and, on contact, grabs your opponent and leaps into the air to bodyslam that opponent! After grabbing an opponent and jumping, both Bowser and the opponent can press left or right to alter the location they where they fall. If the opponent has less damage, that opponent has more effect on the movement. With the right amount of damage and timing, though, you can dive off stage to sacrifice yourself and get a knockout in exchange!

Dash Slam DAMAGE 12%

Though the damage on this variation is lower, the grab range is larger. Additionally, Bowser cano move left and right significantly more, but his jump height is not as high.

Dash Slash DAMAGE 6~8%

Bowser charges at the opponent and slashes with his claws. Good knockback but deals the least damage of all of Bowser's Side Specials.

WHIRLING FORTRESS (Up Special)

ON LAND 1~4% MAX DAMAGE 11% : 8 HITS

IN AIR 2~10% MAX DAMAGE 35% : 11 HITS

Bowser ducks into his spiked shell and performs a spin attack. He can move horizontally during the spin, and if you hit the button repeatedly, Bowser can gain some extra height.

Flying Fortress

DAMAGE 2~4%

When used in the air, Bowser gets much higher with this variation. From the ground, Bowser jumps high vertically. This attack sends opponents flying in one hit and you have some control over Bowser's horizontal momentum.

Sliding Fortress

DAMAGE 6%

This variation allows Bowser to move horizontally a lot when used in the air; his vertical recovery, however, is reduced. He moves faster and hits opponents away in a single hit. There is a lot of recovery from this attack, regardless of whether it was used on the ground or in the air.

BOWSER BOMB (Down Special)

DAMAGE 4~20% MAX DAMAGE 24% : 2 HITS

Bowser jumps into the air, horns first, before returning with a stomp! This attack can hit on the way up and again as Bowser comes back down. If used in the air, Bowser immediately drops.

Turbulent Bomb

DAMAGE 4~9% MAX DAMAGE 13% : 2 HITS

When Bowser lands from this, wind from the force of his stomp shoves opponents away. Bowser jumps less high when using this on the ground, and the damage is less overall. The closer opponents are to Bowser's landing, the stronger they are pushed away.

Slip Bomb

DAMAGE 2~18%

This variation sends Bowser high into the air before he returns very quickly. The force of this drop shakes the ground, causing nearby opponents to fall down. Notethis version loses the upward attack of the default Bowser Bomb.

Final Smash

GIGA BOWSER

Bowser transforms into Giga Bowser for about 15 seconds! That's right: a GIGANTIC version of Bowser! In this form, Bowser still takes damage but will not flinch when he gets hit. Most of Giga Bowser's attacks are the same as regular Bowser's but most do more damage. One notable exception is SIDE SMASH, which is a headbutt for Giga Bowser but a dropkick for regular Bowser. Giga Bowser's regular attacks are claw swipes instead of Bowser's double punch, and his dash attack leaves him grounded in an unfavorable position. Yes, you will be a big target, but opponents will run away from you in fear of your knockout power!

Strategy

While Bowser is the heaviest character in the game, he is also one of the slowest. At a low percentage, he can absorb lower-damage attacks without flinching, so use this to your advantage—try to exchange hits because you will almost always win the trade in damage output. Bowser also has some armor on his Whirling Fortress and Flying Slam, and this armor makes it generally easier to connect with your opponent. With Bowser's large size comes extended range with his Tilt attacks. Bowser's Forward Tilt and Up Tilt should be incorporated when spacing your opponent. Take your time and remember you will almost always be able to reach your opponent before your opponent can reach you!

When considering Bowser's Special attacks, note some of the differences between air and ground functionality. When performed on the ground, Whirling Fortress stays grounded, and while Bowser can still control it horizontally, he can't move to fall off the stage. When he performs Bowser Bomb in the air, it will go directly down from his current position, and he will also no longer perform his upward headbutt before descending. Bowser Bomb can be particularly useful in free-for-all battles thanks to its large hitbox, but note that Bowser can be hit out of it from below! Given its long recovery, you'll want to use this sparingly, as your opponents will definitely be on the lookout for it. If you can hit it just right, though, Bowser Bomb will do a lot of damage to your opponent's shield!

In the air, Bowser's Back Air is definitely his primary knockout attack. His Neutral Air attack can keep opponents off you, hit opponents below you, and allow you to chase with Up Air. Bowser's Forward Air attack is good to chase opponents off stage, and his Down Air sends opponents up and away on a direct hit. If your opponents are shielding a lot, remember to throw! The more scared they are of Bowser's throws, the easier it will be to hit them with your other heavy-hitting attacks! Against opponents who like to counter, use Bowser's Down Smash. The first hits are light, so the amplified counter damage won't hurt Bowser much, but if you connect, they will be in a world of pain. When edge-guarding, use Bowser's Fire Breath or consider going off-stage with Back Air! Even after a Back Air attempt, you should be able to recover with the aerial version of Whirling Fortress.

Recovery

Bowser's main recovery option is Whirling Fortress. This gives him good vertical recovery, plus he can recover horizontally with it. Be sure to hit the button repeatedly to gain as much extra height as possible. Fire Breath is also useful as you make your way back to the stage—it can push opponents away from the edge, making it difficult for them to edge guard optimally. If approaching from high above the stage with an opponent waiting to punish your landing, you might want to Bowser Bomb to grab the edge. This strategy is risky because you have to get the spacing right or you'll plummet to your doom, but if done correctly, this should get you to the edge sooner than your opponent expects while giving you some invincibility on the edge.

BOWSER JR.

Trophy Description

Bowser's beloved, spoiled son sports a bandanna with a large mouth drawn on it. Like his father, Bowser Jr. longs to take Mario down. In *Smash Bros.*, he'll fight from inside his heavily armed Junior Clown Car. The Clown Car takes less damage than Bowser Jr., so mind your positioning.

STATISTICS

MAXIMUM NUMBER OF JUMPS: **2**

CAN WALL JUMP: **No**

CAN WALL CLING: **No**

CAN CRAWL: **No**

Alternate Colors

Smash Attacks

SIDE SMASH

DAMAGE 1~11% MAX DAMAGE 16% : 6 HITS

Bowser Jr. uses the Junior Clown Car's drill arms to drill his opponents with this multi-hit attack. It can also be aimed slightly up or down.

DOWN SMASH DAMAGE 18%

Bowser Jr. drops two giant cannonballs out of each side of the Junior Clown Car. Opponents hit by the cannonballs are blasted diagonally away.

UP SMASH

DAMAGE 1~6% MAX DAMAGE 13.2% : 7 HITS

Bowser Jr. flips and uses the Junior Clown Car's spinning propeller to attack! Hits multiple times before launching the opponent upward.

Basic Attacks

STANDING ATTACK

DAMAGE 3%, 2% RAPID STRIKES 15% : 7 HITS

The Junior Clown Car puts on its boxing gloves and punches twice before going into rapid punches and launching opponents diagonally away.

UP TILT **DAMAGE 6%**

Bowser Jr. scoops opponents up into the air with the fork from the Junior Clown Car.

DASH ATTACK

DAMAGE 1.5~4% MAX DAMAGE 11.5% : 6 HITS

Two spinning blades come out of the Junior Clown Car's mouth and move side to side to find anyone nearby.

SIDE TILT **DAMAGE 8%**

A giant fork stabs out of the Junior Clown Car. You can aim this up or down.

DOWN TILT

DAMAGE 1.5~5% MAX DAMAGE 8% : 3 HITS

The Junior Clown Car's mouth opens and a giant tongue comes out to deliver a licking! Hits multiple times and launches opponents horizontally away.

EDGE ATTACK

Chained cannonballs shoot back onto the stage, attacking anyone nearby before the Junior Clown Car flips itself back up with the chains.

Air Attacks

NEUTRAL AIR ATTACK

DAMAGE 3~6%

The boxing gloves come out, and the Junior Clown Car spins in the air.

DOWN AIR ATTACK

DAMAGE 1.3~2% MAX DAMAGE 12.4% : 9 HITS

A drill comes out of the bottom of the Junior Clown Car to drill into the opponent multiple times.

BACK AIR ATTACK **DAMAGE 8~14%**

A cannonball comes out the front of the Junior Clown Car before it swings around to strike behind itself.

UP AIR ATTACK **DAMAGE 6.5~10%**

Bowser Jr. reaches up and swings a hammer above his head.

FORWARD AIR ATTACK

DAMAGE 2~11% MAX DAMAGE 13% : 2 HITS

A giant cannonball hangs out of the Junior Clown Car and bounces up and down

Special Attacks

CLOWN CANNON (Neutral Special)

NO CHARGE 4.9~7% MAX CHARGE 12.6~18%

Bowser Jr.'s primary projectile, this fires a slow-moving cannonball. Holding down the Special button increases the cannonball's speed and strength. If it is shielded, it continues through and keeps going.

Piercing Cannon

NO CHARGE 2~4% MAX CHARGE 5~10%

This cannonball is smaller and less damaging, but it pierces through multiple opponents. When used from the air, you immediately begin to fall.

Air Cannon DAMAGE 0%

Instead of shooting a cannonball, this version just blows out air, so it deals no damage. The longer you charge it, the longer the duration of the attack but not of the blowing power. When used in the air, this pushes Bowser Jr. back.

MECHAKOOPA (Down Special)

DAMAGE 2~7% MAX DAMAGE 9% : 2 HITS

The Junior Clown Car spits out a Mechakoopa, which ticks back and forth along the ground. It explodes if thrown, if attacked, or after a set amount of time. Only one Mechakoopa can be out at a time. Mechakoopa can also be picked up by Bowser Jr. or an enemy.

Impatient Mechakoopa

DAMAGE 1~4% MAX DAMAGE 5% : 2 HITS

Fire a lightweight Mechakoopa farther than usual. The Mechakoopa does not move, but it explodes quicker than usual.

Big Mechakoopa DAMAGE 15%

Fire a large, powerful Mechakoopa that explodes if it hits an opponent. When it doesn't hit an opponent, it walks around but does not detonate until its timer runs out. The damage and range of the explosion is much larger than normal.

CLOWN KART DASH (Side Special)

DASHING 4~7.4% SPINNING 8~12.3%

The Junior Clown Car sprouts wheels and takes off toward opponents. The faster it moves, the more damage it deals. If you change directions, the car spins. The Junior Clown Car can take some damage without flinching, but if Bowser Jr. is directly hit, the move ends.

Koopa Drift DASHING 2% SPINNING 1~2% MAX DAMAGE 12% : 11 HITS

The dash portion of this version is less damaging with less range, but when you spin, the Junior Clown Car goes into a drift that hits opponents multiple times. After hitting multiple times, it knocks opponents away with its final hit.

Grounding Dash DASHING 8% SPINNING 0%

This dash is shorter, but if you hit opponents with it, they are buried. As you back up to dash, you have some super armor. Doing a spin causes you to stop abruptly, pushing opponents out of the way without damaging them.

ABANDON SHIP (Up Special)

DAMAGE 5~13% MAX DAMAGE 18% : 2 HITS

HAMMER 10~15%

Bowser Jr. ejects himself out of the Junior Clown Car. Moments later, the car explodes, damaging nearby opponents! Without the car, Bowser Jr. can also attack while in the air. Don't worry about the car, though—it will respawn under Bowser Jr. when he lands!

Meteor Ejection

DAMAGE 3~10% MAX DAMAGE 18% : 2 HITS

Bowser Jr. jumps out of the Junior Clown car and sends it downward. Opponents hit by this are meteor smashed. When used on the ground, the explosion occurs at the same time as you eject. You have some super armor during this attack.

Koopa Meteor

DAMAGE 10~17% MAX DAMAGE 27% : 2 HITS

The Junior Clown Car launches high into the air before exploding. When it explodes, Bowser Jr. is shot downward. You cannot grab onto edges while the Junior Clown Car is ascending.

Final Smash

SHADOW MARIO PAINT

Bowser Jr. gets in disguise as Shadow Mario and paints an "X" on the screen with his Magic Paintbrush. This is a stage-wide attack that hits opponents when they touch the paint. Bowser Jr., however, is free to move around and attack during it. When this move is activated, Bowser Jr. is teleported to the top left of the screen, so you can use this to save yourself from self-destructing as well. While this racks up damage well, it isn't particularly great at knocking opponents out, so it's important to use Bowser Jr. to get the KOs while opponents are taking damage from the paint.

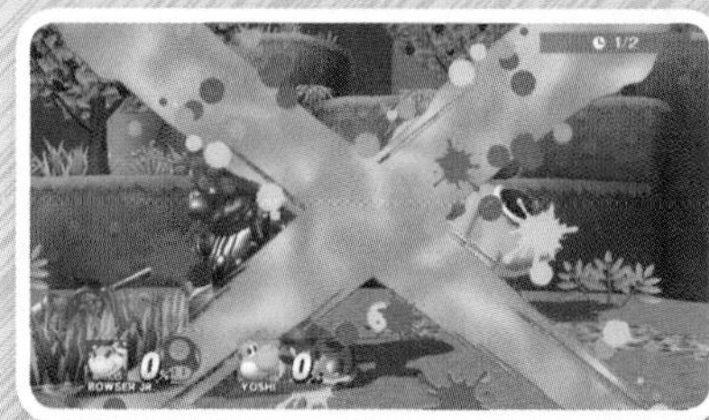

Strategy

Bowser Jr. is one of the few heavy characters in the game that also has good mobility and recovery. Since the Junior Clown Car takes reduced damage compared to Bowser Jr., it's even more difficult for opponents to knock this character out! Once Bowser Jr. is KO'd, he has the means for both vertical and horizontal recovery, so he always has an option. The main thing to watch out for are moves with a lot of recovery, like his Down Smash, that leave you open to enemy attacks if opponents shield or evade you. With his Clown Cannon, Mechakoopa, and Clown Kart Dash, Bowser Jr. has options to effectively rack up damage from a distance, and up close, his Down Tilt, jabs, and Dash attack are good options.

You can charge up the Clown Cannon from a distance, as it has better damage and knockout potential when charged. And when playing at a distance, you can send out Mechakoopa to run interference while you charge up the Clown Cannon. Use the Clown Kart Dash to create distance when being harassed, or use Bowser Jr.'s heavy weight to your advantage to go in with it and deal damage. Bowser Jr.'s Dash attack is particularly useful as well; the hitbox is far from him, and it leaves the car more exposed than Bowser Jr. This works well when you are above a group of opponents. And because Bowser Jr. still has an aerial attack available while making his way to the ground, you aren't completely vulnerable in this situation.

In fact, this aerial attack has tremendous KO potential, making it one of his best moves. A good way to combine special attacks is to send out a MechaKoopa and chase after it with Clown Kart Dash. If the MechaKoopa hits, charge into them with Clown Kart Dash, then Abandon Ship!

Bowser Jr.'s aerial attacks are also all useful. Use his Down Air for shield pressure or to rack up damage. His Back Air and Forward Air are both effective, but they do start up a little slow. Neutral Air attack is fantastic, as it covers both sides. When airborne, Up Air is your only option against characters above you. On the ground, Side Smash is great, and Down Smash works well against players who like to roll a lot. When opponents are trying to return to the stage, stay roll distance from the edge and time a Mechakoopa to reach the edge a little after your opponent. The Mechakoopa will limit an opponent's options in returning immediately. Use this opportunity to charge up a Smash attack and limit that opponent's options even further! Additionally, you can use the Clown Cannon, as the cannonball will drop after some distance and still deal damage. This makes it a great tool against enemies who are trying to recover.

Recovery

Bowser Jr. has some of the best recovery tools in the game. His Clown Kart Dash gives him decent horizontal recovery while his Abandon Ship launches him very high vertically. Additionally, you can jump from Clown Kart Dash even after using your double jump! This gives additional recovery height as well. Used in combination with each other, these should give you a fairly easy time getting back to the edge. Don't forget that with the Abandon Ship, you can slightly control the horizontal trajectory Bowser Jr. uses. You can also use his Forward Air attack to bring him back horizontally a bit to throw off your opponent's timing.

CAPTAIN

Trophy Description

In the *F-Zero* racing scene, Captain Falcon uses his Blue Falcon to win big. His origin largely a mystery, he's made his way to the *Smash Bros.* battlefield to prove his worth outside the cockpit. He's got speed and power, and his distinct Falcon Punch leaves a dent. Start it in the air to surprise your foes!

STATISTICS

MAXIMUM NUMBER OF JUMPS: **2**

CAN WALL JUMP: **Yes**

CAN WALL CLING: **No**

CAN CRAWL: **No**

Alternate Colors

Smash Attacks

SIDE SMASH DAMAGE 19%

Captain Falcon attacks forward with a powerful elbow strike. This can be aimed up or down.

DOWN SMASH DAMAGE 14~18%

Captain Falcon kicks forward then backward. These two hits do not combo.

UP SMASH

DAMAGE 6~13% MAX DAMAGE 24% : 2 HITS

Captain Falcon jumps into the air and spins while kicking vertically. This attack has good vertical KO power.

Basic Attacks

STANDING ATTACK

DAMAGE 2%, 2%, 5% RAPID JABS 7% : 6 HITS

Two punches followed by a knee. Hitting the button repeatedly will do two punches followed by a flurry of rapid strikes that ends with an uppercut.

UP TILT **DAMAGE 11%**

A downward heel kick attack that has a meteor effect, bouncing opponents off the ground.

DASH ATTACK **DAMAGE 6~10%**

A running shoulder charge.

SIDE TILT **DAMAGE 8~9%**

Captain Falcon kicks forward horizontally. This can be aimed up or down.

DOWN TILT **DAMAGE 10%**

A sweep attack with decent range and damage.

EDGE ATTACK

Captain Falcon pulls himself back up then sweeps the opponent's legs.

Air Attacks

NEUTRAL AIR ATTACK

DAMAGE 4~6% MAX DAMAGE 10% : 2 HITS

Captain Falcon performs two spinning kick attacks in front of him.

DOWN AIR ATTACK

DAMAGE 14%

Captain Falcon stomps downward with both feet. This attack has a meteor effect.

BACK AIR ATTACK

DAMAGE 8~14%

Captain Falcon rotates to attack behind him with his arm.

UP AIR ATTACK

DAMAGE 10~13%

A big flipkick attack.

FORWARD AIR ATTACK

DAMAGE 3~19%

This jumping knee attack has some good launching power when you see it sparkle!

Special Attacks

FALCON PUNCH (Neutral Special)

ON LAND 25~28% IN AIR 22~25%

Captain Falcon charges up for a moment before releasing his trademark punch. You can swap directions of the punch for extra damage by hitting the opposite direction early in the charge up animation.

Falcon Dash Punch

ON LAND 11~22% IN AIR 11~20%

As the name implies, a dash precedes this punch. In general, damage is a little lower than the default version. You can still reverse the direction of the punch for slightly more damage.

Mighty Falcon Punch

ON LAND 6~25% IN AIR 6~22%

Increases the knockback power of the Falcon Punch. The hitbox is larger, but it has a longer startup.

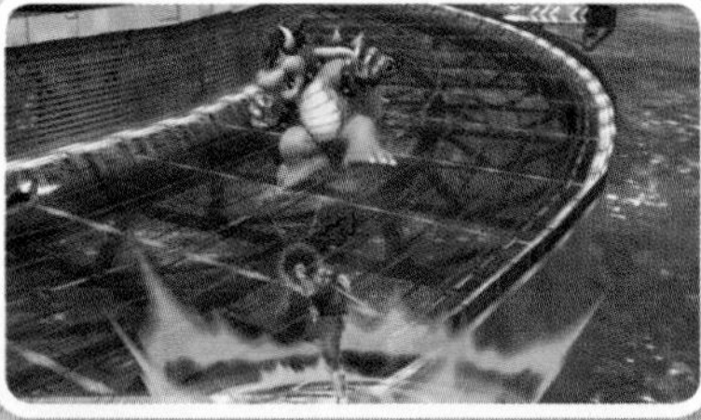

FALCON DIVE (Up Special)

DAMAGE 5~12% MAX DAMAGE 17% : 2 HITS

This jumping attack turns into a throw attack if you connect with an opponent. Useful for both recovery and attacking, but you are in a fall state on whiff. On hit, you can perform the attack again without waiting to land first.

Falcon Strike DAMAGE 8%

Captain Falcon raises his fist overhead and jumps to punch. The jump is high, but this doesn't turn into a throw attack on hit. You are still left in a fall state on whiff.

Explosive Falcon Dive

DAMAGE 10~15% MAX DAMAGE 25% : 2 HITS

This is a much higher damage version of the Falcon Dive. The jump height is less, but the knockback from the attack is significant.

RAPTOR BOOST (Side Special)

ON LAND 9% IN AIR 8%

Captain Falcon dashes forward to launch his opponents with an uppercut. If he doesn't make contact with anyone, he falls to the ground. If you do this while airborne, be sure to land on a stage because you enter a fall state on whiff. When used in the air, if the move hits an opponent on the top of his or her head, it will have a meteor effect.

Heavy Raptor Boost

ON LAND 12% IN AIR 12%

This customization flexes Captain Falcon's muscles as he gains super armor to not flinch while he delivers a massive blow to knock opponents away. The attack is slower than the default version.

Wind-Up Raptor Boost

ON LAND 8% IN AIR 7%

Captain Falcon quickly sways back before stepping in to uppercut the opponent. This is the weakest of the three options, but it's also the fastest.

FALCON KICK (Down Special)

ON LAND 7~13% IN AIR 9~15% MAX 24% : 2 HITS

This jumpkick attack differs greatly depending on whether it's used in the air or on the ground. In the air, Captain Falcon kicks downward diagonally. From the ground, Captain Falcon kicks sideways.

Falcon Kick Fury

ON LAND 1~7% MAX DAMAGE 11% : 5 HITS

IN AIR 2~5% MAX DAMAGE 23% : 10 HITS

A multi-hitting variation in which Captain Falcon attacks with a series of strong kick attacks. K.O. power is slightly reduced, as is the distance covered with the grounded version.

Lightning Falcon Kick ON LAND 6~12%

IN AIR 4~14% MAX DAMAGE 18% : 2 HITS

An electrified version of the Falcon Kick. Captain Falcon pushes through opponents, but the speed of the attack does not slow down. The distance covered is farther for the grounded version. When used from the air, this can also stun the opponent momentarily.

Final Smash

BLUE FALCON

Captain Falcon calls in his vehicle, the Blue Falcon. The Blue Falcon swoops in from the screen and hits all characters in its path, sending them to a track. Captain Falcon is then shown driving the Blue Falcon to run over his opponents, blasting them into the air. The move deals about 40% damage to everyone it hits and knocks them back upward in the direction Captain Falcon is facing. Generally, use this when a character is closer to the side of a stage or else the knockback won't be enough to get the KO. The range on the Blue Falcon arriving is fairly limited, but it is still able to hit at least three characters if they are bunched together.

Strategy

While Captain Falcon is a medium-weight character, the damage and recovery on some of his attacks might make you believe he is a heavyweight. He has a fast run speed on the ground, good air mobility, and decent range on his attacks. His aerials are fairly quick and have good range and power as well. A lot of his attacks have unfavorable recovery, however, as well as a dependency on hitting the sweet spots of moves to be most effective. For example, his Forward Air attack can deal 19% damage and knockback far if you hit it perfectly. But if you don't hit it perfectly, this can be as low as 3%! Fortunately, this is the most extreme example, and the rest of his aerial attacks have a smaller range of damage output. Overall, Captain Falcon must rely on timing, spacing, and his survivability to do well.

Falcon Punch is one of the most iconic moves in the series and can deal a lot of damage and knockback. Just be sure you have sufficient time to pull off this attack. Unlike Ganondorf's version, Captain Falcon's version doesn't have any sort of super armor, so you can easily be hit out of the startup of this attack. Raptor Boost is great at closing distance and can even go through some projectiles. But it is fairly slow, so players can see it coming. When used in the air, though, its meteor effect can be useful, especially when edge-guarding. Edge-guard while on stage because you are in a fall state after using this in the air. Similarly, use Falcon Kick to close distance on the ground. From the air, use Falcon Kick's downward trajectory to edge-guard as well. Falcon Dive is best used for recovery but can also be used as an air grab to surprise opponents. If off-stage with multiple opponents, hit and repeat this, as you can use it again when you connect with it in the air.

In the air, Captain Falcon has a variety of options. His Up Air is a huge flipkick attack that has good range and knockback. His Forward Air has incredible knockback and damage potential, but as previously mentioned, you have to hit on the sweet spot. It also has a lot of recovery when used low to the ground and starts up a little slowly, so consider this before using it. Down Air is best used for its meteor smash, especially when you're off-stage. On the ground, Captain Falcon's best options are Side Smash for horizontal KOs and Up Smash for vertical KOs. When edge-guarding, you can also use Falcon Punch against returning opponents. In general, use your speed to approach opponents, the range on your Neutral Air to keep opponents away, and close distance with Raptor Boost or Falcon Kick. Find opportunities to land your Falcon Punch, Forward Air, Side Smash, and Up Smash to rack up damage with throws when possible.

Recovery

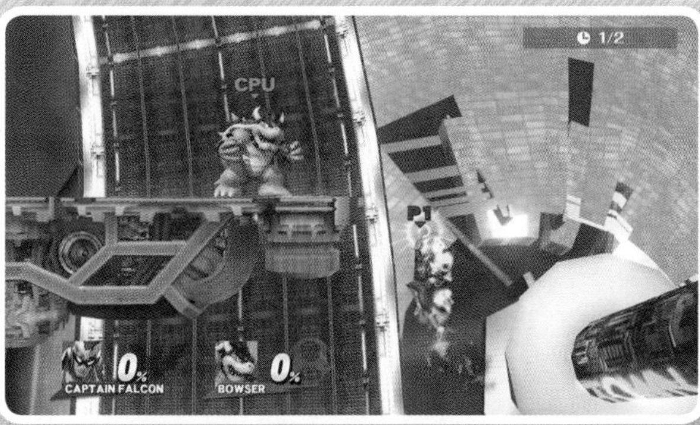

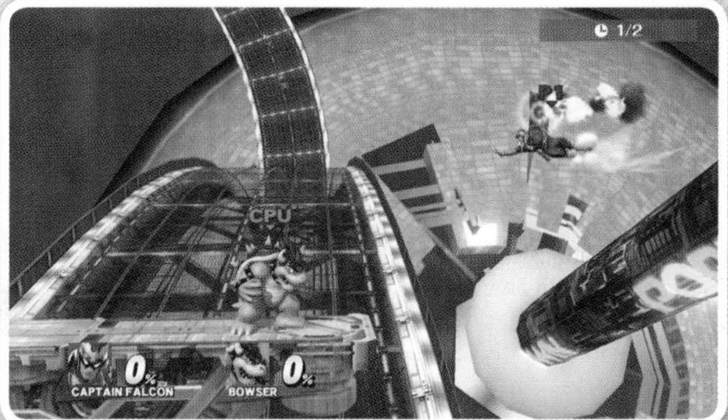

Captain Falcon has an average set of recovery options. For horizontal recovery, use his Raptor Boost, but note that you enter a fall state if it fails to reach the stage. For vertical recovery, use his Falcon Dive. You can aim it a bit to the left or right once it begins but not by much. Don't forget he also has a wall jump, which can come in handy to gain an extra jump. Finally, use Falcon Kick when returning to the stage from high above, but it's risky because you can self-destruct if you miss the stage.

CHARIZARD

Trophy Description

The iconic Fire/Flying-type Pokémon. Charizard's scorching breath can melt anything in its path. It soars through the air, seeking only worthy foes to test itself against. In *Smash Bros.*, Charizard unleashes the destructive Flare Blitz Special move—a move so strong, it even injures the user!

STATISTICS

MAXIMUM NUMBER OF JUMPS: **3**

CAN WALL JUMP: **No**

CAN WALL CLING: **No**

CAN CRAWL: **No**

Alternate Colors

Smash Attacks

SIDE SMASH DAMAGE 14~17%

Charizard winds up then uses its long neck to attack with this headbutt. This attack has some invincibility.

DOWN SMASH DAMAGE 16%

Charizard stomps the ground while flapping both wings down to attack.

UP SMASH

DAMAGE 5~11% MAX DAMAGE 16% : 2 HITS

Charizard uses each wing to attack in an upward motion. The second attack pops opponents up into the air.

Basic Attacks

STANDING ATTACK

DAMAGE 3%, 4%, 5%

A three-hit attack string where Charizard claws at your opponent before knocking that opponent up and away.

UP TILT DAMAGE 8%

Charizard hops and attacks upwards with its wings. The wings do not take damage here, so this is especially useful against airborne opponents.

DASH ATTACK DAMAGE 8~11%

Charizard lifts its foot while running to boot opponents into the air.

SIDE TILT DAMAGE 7~10%

Charizard whips its tail around to hit the opponent. This can be aimed up or down.

DOWN TILT DAMAGE 10%

Charizard uses its long neck to headbutt opponents out of the way.

EDGE ATTACK

Charizard returns to the stage with a headbutt attack.

Air Attacks

NEUTRAL AIR ATTACK

DAMAGE 7~10%

Charizard performs a front flip while attacking with its tail.

DOWN AIR ATTACK DAMAGE 8~14%

Charizard kicks downward with one foot. This attack has a meteor effect.

BACK AIR ATTACK DAMAGE 10~15%

A strong tail attack with long range.

UP AIR ATTACK DAMAGE 13%

Charizard swings its head upward to hit opponents above it. This attack has some invincibility.

FORWARD AIR ATTACK

DAMAGE 11~12%

Charizard claws forward in the air.

Special Attacks

FLAMETHROWER (Neutral Special)

DAMAGE 1~2% MAX DAMAGE 8% : 4 HITS

Charizard breathes fire onto nearby opponents. You can aim it up and down, but the longer you use it, the shorter its range. If you use it up all the way, it takes about 10 seconds to fully recharge its range.

Fire Fang

DAMAGE 2~8% MAX DAMAGE 10% : 2 HITS

Charizard breathes a smaller flame continually.

Fireball Cannon

DAMAGE 2~3% MAX DAMAGE 9% : 3 HITS

Charizard shoots balls of fire that travel far but deal less damage. This will fire three fireballs at a time.

FLY (Up Special)

DAMAGE 2~5% MAX DAMAGE 17% : 6 HITS

This attack spirals upward, hitting the opponent multiple times. Charizard is super armored from the moment he jumps and only hits opponents in front of its face.

Rising Cyclone

DAMAGE 2~6% MAX DAMAGE 22% : 8 HITS

This version sucks in opponents and launches them out, but Charizard does not jump as high. This attack hits both in front of and behind Charizard.

Fly High DAMAGE 0%

Charizard flaps its wings to instantly launch itself even higher. This is not an attack, and you cannot control Charizard horizontally.

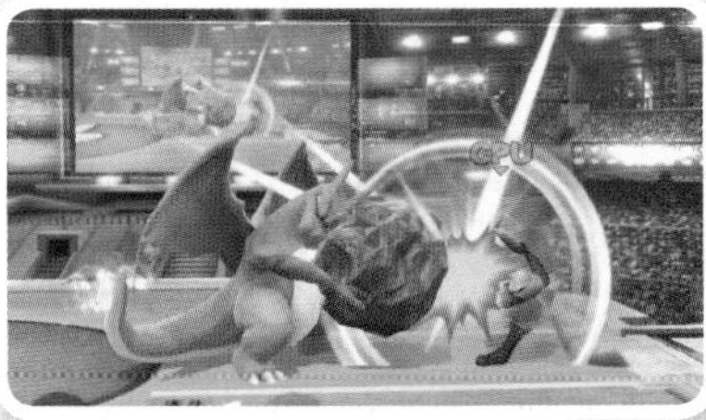

ROCK SMASH (Down Special)

DAMAGE 3~14% MAX DAMAGE 29% : 6 HITS

Charizard headbutts a rock so that its fragments hit the opponents. The fragments fly out in random directions, so be close to maximize efficiency. Charizard has some super armor here and will not flinch if hit during this attack.

Sinking Skull DAMAGE 9~12%

This headbutt buries opponents into the ground, leaving them open to follow-up attacks. Charizard has no super armor on this variation. It also has a meteor effect when hitting airborne opponents.

Rock Hurl

DAMAGE 2~8% MAX DAMAGE 16% : 5 HITS

Similar to the original Rock Smash except it starts up a little faster and the rock fragments go faster and farther than usual. Additionally, the damage is reduced in this version.

FLARE BLITZ (Side Special)

DAMAGE 4~15% MAX DAMAGE 19% : 2 HITS

Engulfed in flames, Charizard flies far forward in a damaging attack. Striking an enemy or obstacle results in a small explosion that can also cause damage. Charizard takes damage from this, even when it doesn't connect with anything.

Blast Burn

DAMAGE 4~9% MAX DAMAGE 28% : 5 HITS

This version doesn't travel as far or as fast, but it's more explosive than the original. It deals more damage to both Charizard and whomever it hits.

Dragon Rush

DAMAGE 1.2~4% MAX DAMAGE 13.6% : 9 HITS

This less powerful, shorter-range version does not deal damage to Charizard. There is no explosion at the end, but you still hit opponents multiple times.

Final Smash

MEGA EVOLUTION

Charizard transforms into Mega Charizard X. In this form, it can continuously fly in all directions, you can press the Special button to shoot fireballs, and Charizard has super armor for the duration of the transformation. Damage taken during this transformation is reduced. Pressing the Attack button does an attack similar to Charizard's Up Special, except you can do it in any direction and it knocks the opponent away horizontally. Each fireball does about 16% damage, while each spiral attack does about 24% damage. The fireballs temporarily trap the opponent in a Fire Blast, giving you a chance to hit with the spiral attack. Be sure you're over ground before the transformation wears off!

Strategy

Charizard is a heavier character with below-average mobility and attack speed. It makes up for this with above-average damage output and long range on its attacks and throws. Its Flamethrower and Flare Blitz can be useful in wearing down faster opponents from a distance. To compensate for its slower attack speed, Charizard also has various invincibilities and super armor to use with Side Smash, Up Air, and Rock Smash.

From a distance, Charizard can pressure opponents to approach by using its Flamethrower attack. This doesn't do much damage, but it's very disruptive, so use it mainly to set up additional offense. It's also useful for dealing with projectiles or when edge-guarding. Flare Blitz is useful for punishing opponents at a distance, for backing away from opponents, or for just crashing into groups of opponents and dealing damage to everyone. Charizard takes about 4% damage for using this, even if Charizard doesn't make contact for the explosion. You can also make contact and explode if you merely crash into a wall or a steep slope, so take care when these obstacles are nearby. Rock Smash is best used up close or at a small distance away from opponents. Its super armor allows this attack to complete and damage opponents, even if they're hitting you. This is particularly useful if opponents have high damage and you're looking for a KO. (Note that the headbutt is the primary damage, not the rock pieces.) Fly has some super armor at the beginning, making it more viable as an attack as well, but its primary use is still for recovery. You can also control Fly a bit to the left or right.

In the air, Charizard is a little more of a threat because of its extra jump. Back Air is Charizard's best aerial to get KOs, and Down Air gives an excellent meteor smash. Up Air is more useful lower in the air, thanks to the invincibility it has on Charizard's head. For KOs on the ground, use Side Smash for its awesome damage with invincibility. Down Smash and Flare Blitz can be good for horizontal KOs; Up Smash, Up Air, and Fly can be used for vertical KOs. When edge-guarding, use Flamethrower, Side Tilt, and Down Tilt. Use Charizard's range to your advantage, and grab opponents to pressure them into jumping so you can hit them with your Up Tilt or Up Air! When you are at a higher percentage and therefore at a higher risk of being KO'd, consider using Fire Blitz more! Though damaging to Charizard, the move has priority as well as a high KO potential.

Recovery

Charizard has a couple of good tools for recovery. Flare Blitz is its best option for horizontal recovery, but be aware it will always damage you, even if it doesn't make contact with an opponent. You are not put into a fall state after Flare Blitz, but if you crash into a stage with it, then you end up in a fall state. For vertical recovery, Charizard's best option is its Fly Special. Finally, don't forget that Charizard has three jumps instead of two like everyone else!

DARK PIT

Trophy Description

Pit's mysterious, black-clad doppelgänger, Dark Pit. (Some call him Pittoo, but he really doesn't like that.) When he first appears, he immediately goes after both Pit and the Underworld Army. In *Smash Bros.*, he uses moves a lot like Pit's, though both his bow and his Sacred Treasures are different.

STATISTICS

MAXIMUM NUMBER OF JUMPS: **4**

CAN WALL JUMP: **No**

CAN WALL CLING: **No**

CAN CRAWL: **No**

Alternate Colors

Smash Attacks

SIDE SMASH

DAMAGE 5~10% MAX DAMAGE 15% : 2 HITS

Dark Pit strikes forward with each of his blades. The second attack deals more damage and knocks your opponent away.

DOWN SMASH DAMAGE 10~12%

Dark Pit slashes his blade at your opponent's feet. Sends the opponent diagonally away. This attack hits in front of Dark Pit, then behind Dark Pit.

UP SMASH

DAMAGE 2~8% MAX DAMAGE 13% : 3 HITS

Dark Pit swings his blades around as he leaps into the air, hitting your opponent multiple times. The last hit sends the opponent upward.

Basic Attacks

STANDING ATTACK

DAMAGE 2%, 2%, 5% RAPID STRIKES 9% : 8 HITS

Dark Pit strikes forward with his blades in this three-hit attack. The last hit knocks the opponent up into the air.

UP TILT

DAMAGE 2~5% MAX DAMAGE 10% : 3 HITS

A flipkick attack followed up by two additional kicks. The last kick launches opponents vertically.

DASH ATTACK DAMAGE 11%

Dark Pit dashes forward with both blades extended in front of him.

SIDE TILT DAMAGE 7~10%

Dark Pit swings his blades together like a pair of scissors. Fairly quick with good range.

DOWN TILT DAMAGE 6%

Dark Pit sweeps his opponent with one of his blades.

EDGE ATTACK

Dark Pit swings himself back up to the stage and kicks your opponent away.

Air Attacks

NEUTRAL AIR ATTACK

DAMAGE 0.7~4% MAX DAMAGE 8.9% : 8 HITS

Dark Pit spins his blades around his body, hitting opponents multiple times. Only the last hit knocks the opponent away.

DOWN AIR ATTACK DAMAGE 10%

Dark Pit swipes a blade in an arc below him. This has a meteor effect at the start of the move.

BACK AIR ATTACK DAMAGE 8~12%

Dark Pit quickly thrusts both blades behind him. Great range and knockback.

UP AIR ATTACK

DAMAGE 2% MAX DAMAGE 10% : 5 HITS

Dark Pit spins his blades above his head like a helicopter. Hits multiple times and knocks the opponent upward.

FORWARD AIR ATTACK

DAMAGE 1.5~4% MAX DAMAGE 7% : 3 HITS

Dark Pit spins his blades in front of him. Opponents caught in this attack are hit multiple times and are launched away diagonally.

Special Attacks

SILVER BOW (Neutral Special)

DAMAGE 3.9~10.5%

With this primary projectile attack, Dark Pit fires an arrow of darkness. Charge it to add strength, range, and speed to the arrows. You can also move the arrows up or down after firing but not by much. Hold Up while charging to aim upward.

Piercing Bow DAMAGE 6.1~13%

This arrow pierces opponents and deals more damage, but it cannot be curved. It takes longer to charge up to maximum, and it has a longer recovery period after firing.

Guiding Bow DAMAGE 2.6~6.9%

This arrow is much more maneuverable than normal. While the power and speed are decreased, its lifespan is longer. You can only have one arrow out at a time, and the recovery period is longer.

PANDORA WINGS (Up Special)

DAMAGE 0%

Dark Pit launches himself extremely far, thanks to his wings. You can aim this in any upward direction, but it's a recovery tool only, not an attack. You are in a fall state after using this move.

Striking Flight

DAMAGE 6.5~9.5%

Deal damage and knock away nearby enemies. You can't control the angle at which Pit flies as much.

Breezy Flight DAMAGE 0%

With a slightly slower startup but a quicker launch, this version creates a wind around Pit that pushes opponents out of the way.

GUARDIAN ORBITARS

(Down Special) DAMAGE 0%

Bring out shields to reflect projectiles and block attacks. The shields also push away any opponents who are too close. This only protects Dark Pit from the sides.

Impact Orbitars DAMAGE 5%

The Impact Orbitars damage opponents and knock them away; however, they don't shield you or reflect projectiles.

Amplifying Orbitars

DAMAGE 0%

Any projectiles reflected are returned faster and more powerful. The shields can be kept out much longer, but they break much easier as well. This version doesn't push away nearby opponents.

ORBITARS DATA

	STARTUP	SHORTEST DURATION	LONGEST DURATION	DAMAGE SCALING	SPEED SCALING
GUARDIAN ORBITARS	9th frame	20 frames	**80 frames**	1.5x	1.7x
AMPLIFYING ORBITARS	11th frame	16 frames	150 frames	2x	2x

ELECTROSHOCK ARM

(Side Special)

ON LAND 11.5% IN AIR 9.5%

Dark Pit charges forward before releasing an uppercut to his opponent. This attack launches the opponent diagonally away.

Electrocut Arm

ON LAND 13.5% IN AIR 11.5%

Dark Pit holds a pose with super armor then uppercuts anyone who attacks him. This functions similarly to a counter, as he doesn't dash forward.

Quickshock Arm

ON LAND 9.2% IN AIR 7.2%

The startup of the dash is slower, but this variation travels farther and faster. This also deals less damage.

Final Smash

DARK PIT STAFF

Dark Pit fires a beam from his staff that launches anyone in its path. This directional Final Smash has incredibly long range, able to reach nearly all the way across Gerudo Valley! As this has minimal vertical range, line up as many opponents as possible. The camera will zoom in on anyone hit by the beam, unless they are off screen.

Strategy

Dark Pit is an average-weight character with great air mobility, thanks to his multiple jumps. Overall, the main difference between Pit and Dark Pit is in the arrows they shoot with their Neutral Special. The angle at which opponents are launched with their Side Special is also slightly different. They suffer from the same weakness in that their KO power is lacking. Both must rack up damage with their multi-hitting attacks before trying to KO opponents. On the ground, your multi-hitting options are rapid jabs, Up Tilt, Side Smash, and Up Smash. In general, your ground options start up quickly, have decent range, and recover fairly quickly. For ground-based pokes, try Side Tilt, Down Tilt and Dark Pit's three-hit jab string.

Compared to Pit's Palutena Bow, Dark Pit's Silver Bow's main differences are that the arrows are more damaging and curve less. This means they are slightly easier to avoid because they are a little easier to predict. If they do hit, though, they do a little more damage. It's still important to move them up and down when fighting at a distance, especially from the air. Electroshock Arm launches less vertically than Pit's similar Special, but it also does slightly more

damage and is a good horizontal approach option. To aid in your defense, Guardian Orbitars are useful to push out close opponents, shield Dark Pit from attacks, and reflect projectiles.

Dark Pit's main strength is in his aerial mobility. Use his four jumps to be less predictable in approaching enemies while harassing them with Silver Bow. All Dark Pit's aerial attacks except Back Air and Down Air will hit multiple times to rack up damage. Since they all use his blades, they extend Dark Pit's range, keeping him a little safer. Back Air is your best option to KO opponents when airborne, and Down Air's meteor effect can be useful against opponents off-stage. Down Air is also useful when it doesn't meteor smash, though, because it launches opponents up and away.

Recovery

Dark Pit has a bunch of great options for recovery. First, he has four jumps, but vertically the third and fourth jumps gain less and less height. You can still use the four jumps to cover great horizontal distance. And for horizontal recovery, Dark Pit can use Electroshock Arm, which sends him flying across the stage but doesn't put him in a fall state! Finally, for vertical recovery, Dark Pit has Pandora Wings, which is one of the longest-reaching tools in the game. The only downside to it is that it is not an attack. Still, you can also use it as either a horizontal or a diagonal recovery. Between Dark Pit's four jumps, Pandora Wings, and Electroshock Arm, you shouldn't have too much difficulty getting him back to the stage.

DIDDY KONG

Trophy Description

Red cap? Red T-shirt? Rocketbarrel Pack? Yep, it's Diddy Kong. His agility lets him get attacks in quickly in this game. Fire up his Rocketbarrel Pack and keep the button held down to fly further. You can even steer him in the air! Tip: If you don't mind fighting dirty, make your opponent slip on a Banana Peel, then hit 'em while they're down.

STATISTICS

MAXIMUM NUMBER OF JUMPS: **2**

CAN WALL JUMP: **Yes**

CAN WALL CLING: **Yes**

CAN CRAWL: **Yes**

Alternate Colors

Smash Attacks

SIDE SMASH

DAMAGE 5~11% MAX DAMAGE 16% : 2 HITS

Diddy Kong performs a spinning two-hit attack.

DOWN SMASH DAMAGE 12~15%

A wide, circular sweep attack.

UP SMASH

DAMAGE 2.5~6% MAX DAMAGE 11% : 3 HITS

Diddy Kong flips upward, hitting multiple times and ending with an uppercut that sends opponents upward.

Basic Attacks

STANDING ATTACK

DAMAGE 1.5%, 1.5%, 2%

RAPID STRIKES 9% : 7 HITS

Diddy Kong performs two punches and a tail strike before going into rapid strikes with his tail.

UP TILT DAMAGE 6%

Diddy Kong hops and swings his arm in an arc overhead. A hit sends opponents upward.

DASH ATTACK

DAMAGE 2~3% MAX DAMAGE 7% : 3 HITS

A cartwheeling multi-hitting attack!

SIDE TILT DAMAGE 7~10%

Diddy Kong leans forward and strikes with both arms outstretched. Can be aimed up or down.

DOWN TILT DAMAGE 6%

A double-handed attack toward your opponent's feet.

EDGE ATTACK

Diddy Kong hops back to the stage while swinging his tail around to hit anyone nearby.

Air Attacks

NEUTRAL AIR ATTACK DAMAGE 6%

A jumping flip attack that can hit both in front of and behind Diddy Kong. This is best used when you are above your opponent. Try to chase afterward with Up Air.

DOWN AIR ATTACK DAMAGE 10~13%

A huge double overhead strike that bounces opponents off the ground.

BACK AIR ATTACK DAMAGE 9%

Diddy Kong kicks way behind him. This is one of his best aerial attacks.

UP AIR ATTACK DAMAGE 8%

Diddy Kong shows his flexibility by kicking over his head. Try to use it after hitting a Neutral Air Attack. It is also a fairly good KO move.

FORWARD AIR ATTACK

DAMAGE 10~12%

A spinning dropkick attack that sends opponents away from Diddy Kong.

Special Attacks

PEANUT POPGUN
(Neutral Special)

DAMAGE 3.4~12.3% EXPLOSION 23%

Diddy Kong's primary projectile, his peanut shooter. Charging it up will shoot farther and cause more damage, but overcharge it and it can explode in your face! Watch for Diddy Kong grabbing his hat, as this is the sign the Popgun is about to backfire!

Exploding Popgun

DAMAGE 1% EXPLOSION 18~25%

This popgun does not shoot peanuts! Instead, it charges up to the explosion in about half the time. The explosion has more range than usual, is most powerful in the center, and pushes Diddy Kong back a bit. If you release early, the pogun just fires a puff of air that does 1% damage.

Jumbo Peanuts

DAMAGE 7.6~11.4% EXPLOSION 18%

A slower variation of the popgun that shoots giant, stronger peanuts. These giant peanuts do not travel as far, but they certainly deal more damage.

ROCKETBARREL BOOST
(Up Special)

FLYING DAMAGE 6~10% EXPLOSION DAMAGE 18%

Allows Diddy Kong to rocket through the air while you steer. Charging it allows you to travel farther. While charging, you can choose a direction to fly in.

Rocketbarrel Attack

FLYING DAMAGE 15~18% EXPLOSION DAMAGE 20%

This heavier version of Rocketbarrel deals more damage on hits and during explosions. The downside, though, is it is a bit more difficult to fly. It also has more recovery time than the regular version.

Rocketbarrel Kaboom

FLYING DAMAGE 5~7%

EXPLOSION DAMAGE 11~17%

This Rocketbarrel charges to full in about half the time and has higher manueverability. One major difference, though, is that any impact with the ground causes the Rocketbarrel to explode. The size of the explosion is larger than normal.

BANANA PEEL (Down Special)

DAMAGE 4.7~6.2%

Toss a banana peel into the air behind you to slip up your enemies! Only one banana peel can be out at a time. You can also pick it up off the ground to throw it again, but it will vanish after being thrown twice, after hitting an opponent, or after being slipped on.

Shocking Banana Peel

DAMAGE 4.4~5.4%

This banana peel shocks and paralyzes opponents. Banana peels that are stepped on paralyze opponents longer. You can't toss this banana peel as high as the regular version.

Battering Banana Peel

DAMAGE 5.4~7.1%

Diddy Kong throws this banana peel straight up into the air. If it hits any opponents, they aree knocked upward. If it's stepped on, this banana peel also knocks opponents into the air.

MONKEY FLIP (Side Special)

GRAB DAMAGE 1% MAX DAMAGE 3% : 3 HITS

THROW DAMAGE 5~7% MAX DAMAGE 12% : 2 HITS

STOMP DAMAGE 5% MAX DAMAGE 10% : 2 HITS

KICK DAMAGE 12~14%

Diddy Kong leaps forward at your opponent. On a hit, he grabs the opponent, and you can either hit the Attack button to launch that opponent sideways or press Up to jump off the opponent's head. If you grab an opponent in the air, that opponent will break free quicker than an opponent you grab on the ground. Alternatively, instead of going for the grab, you can hit the Special button again to have Diddy Kong kick while jumping.

Back Flip KICK DAMAGE 8~17%

Diddy Kong backflips, and his only attack option out of this is a flying forward kick. This kick is stronger than the default kick and is also quicker.

Flying Monkey Flip

GRAB DAMAGE 1% MAX DAMAGE 3% : 3 HITS

THROW DAMAGE 3~5% MAX DAMAGE 8% : 2 HITS

STOMP DAMAGE 7.5% MAX DAMAGE 15% : 2 HITS

KICK DAMAGE 8~10%

Diddy Kong jumps higher in this variation and gains extra damage and a meteor smash effect during his stomp. His horizontal movement is slightly reduced as well.

Final Smash

ROCKETBARREL BARRAGE

Diddy Kong straps on his Rocketbarrel and takes flight! While this is active, he can fly continuously through the air for about 14 seconds before the Rocketbarrel explodes. Each peanut shot does about 5% damage while the explosion of the Rocketbarrel does about 20% but doesn't harm Diddy Kong. You can also ram into opponents while flying for about 12% damage. One strategy might be to fly along the top of the stage, out of reach of opponents, while raining peanuts on them from above! You have invincibility during this Final Smash, so don't be afraid to get close if necessary!

Strategy

With impressive speed, Diddy Kong is one of the lighter medium-weight characters in the game. His mobility is a notch above other characters as he can also crawl, wall cling, and wall jump. He has a strong projectile game with his Peanut Popgun, his Banana Peel, and good range on most of his attacks. Use his speed and projectiles to fight from a distance. When you have a Banana Peel out, try to stay nearby—if someone slips on it, or even goes to pick it up, you can use this as an opportunity to attack with your Dash attack or Monkey Flip. Or if you are closer, go for a Side or Down Smash! With his tilt attacks, Diddy's Kong's Side Tilt has great range and damage while his Up Tilt knocks opponents fairly high. Down Smash, Side Smash, and Forward Air are his strongest attacks for KOs.

In the air, Diddy Kong also has good options. His Forward Air has great range and does good damage. Down Air has a meteor effect, which can be very useful earlier in matches. And Back Air, while not particularly damaging, has great speed, range, and recovery, allowing you to use it multiple times in a single short hop. Aside from his average weight, one of Diddy Kong's weaknesses is that all of his projectiles can be caught or picked up! Banana Peels can be picked up and thrown back at Diddy Kong, and peanuts he fires can be caught and thrown back, too! Note that if you attack a peanut shell, sometimes you'll get a peanut you can eat to recover health. If an opponent is waiting for your peanut, consider charging it up all the way! This is risky because the backfire will leave Diddy Kong extremely vulnerable, but it does no damage to him, and if it hits an opponent, it delivers a whopping 23% damage! In general, though, be sure to mix up how long you charge it so it will be harder for opponents to catch.

Monkey Flip has a variety of uses, as it covers great distance and has a multitude of options. If you use the Up or Jump option after catching an opponent in the air, it actually gives you a small meteor effect. When using the jump kick out of Monkey Flip while you still have your double jump available, you can use double jump to follow up with a Forward Air as well! Rocketbarrel Boost gives much more control to you than ever before—now you can even use it go horizontally! If it's fully charged, though, take care not to blast yourself off the stage!

Recovery

Diddy Kong has two good recovery tools. First, he has his Monkey Flip for horizontal recovery. This swings Diddy Kong forward a considerable distance. If you still have your double jump, use it; otherwise, you'll be in a fall state. Second, Diddy Kong has his Rocketbarrel Boost, which allows him to steer while flying. Rocketbarrel Boost should be his main vertical recovery tool—he has Monkey Flip to cover horizontal ones, though charging Rocketbarrel Boost up in time is sometimes difficult. Note that if Diddy is attacked while using his Rocketbarrel Boost, the pack breaks free and flies off on its own. To cover a lot of distance, do one jump, Monkey Flip, double jump, charge Rocketbarrel Boost, and then take off!

DONKEY KONG

Trophy Description

The king of the jungle really, *really* loves bananas. His adventures usually start with people stealing his hoard of them. In *Smash Bros.*, he's known for his incredible strength and long reach. Despite his size, he's still pretty quick. He can even jump carrying heavy items! Use this knowledge well.

STATISTICS

MAXIMUM NUMBER OF JUMPS: **2**

CAN WALL JUMP: **No**

CAN WALL CLING: **No**

CAN CRAWL: **No**

Alternate Colors

Smash Attacks

SIDE SMASH DAMAGE 19~20%

Donkey Kong pulls his arms back before clapping on anyone in front of him.

DOWN SMASH DAMAGE 14~18%

Donkey Kong raises his arms before slamming them down on both sides of him. The arms are invincible during the downward swing.

UP SMASH DAMAGE 18%

Donkey Kong claps his hand above his head. Covers less horizontal range than you might expect, but both his head and arms are invincible during this attack.

Basic Attacks

STANDING ATTACK DAMAGE 4%,6%

A strong two-punch attack.

UP TILT DAMAGE 9~11%

Donkey Kong swings his arm in an arc over his head to the ground on the other side of him. This hits most of the way through the arc, not just at the destination. The arm used is invincible during this attack.

DASH ATTACK DAMAGE 8~10%

With this new attack, Donkey Kong rolls himself at the opponent.

SIDE TILT DAMAGE 10%

Donkey Kong swipes forward with his impressive reach. You can aim this slightly up or down. The arm used is invincible during this attack.

DOWN TILT DAMAGE 6~7%

Donkey Kong ducks while swinging at an opponent's feet. The arm used is invincible during this attack.

EDGE ATTACK

Donkey Kong returns to the stage with a clobbering overhead strike.

Air Attacks

NEUTRAL AIR ATTACK

DAMAGE 8~11%

A spinning attack that hits opponents away.

DOWN AIR ATTACK DAMAGE 13~16%

A downward strike with Donkey Kong's foot. Cause a ground bounce when hit in the air.

BACK AIR ATTACK DAMAGE 8~13%

This jumping back kick is fantastic. Use it often.

UP AIR ATTACK DAMAGE 13%

This headbutt attack knocks opponents up into the air. His head is invincible during this attack.

FORWARD AIR ATTACK

DAMAGE 13~16%

A double axe-handle overhead strike. Also bounces the opponent off the ground when hit in the air.

Special Attacks

GIANT PUNCH (Neutral Special)

DAMAGE 10~12% MAX DAMAGE 18~28%

Donkey Kong winds up for a massive punch. The more spins on his wind-up, the stronger the punch is. Press the Special button at any point while spinning to release the punch. Use Left or Right to cancel on the ground and use air dodge to cancel in the air. When used in the air, it deals slightly less damage.

Lightning Punch

DAMAGE 10~12% MAX DAMAGE 8~15%

Donkey Kong spins his arms faster, generating electrical energy. This charges to maximum power up to four times faster than the regular version, but it deals less damage. The attack is a little quicker but does not give partial invincibility or super armor effects.

Storm Punch

DAMAGE 0~8% MAX DAMAGE 0~18%

In this variation, the force of the punch sends out a tornado that blows the opponent back. The more you charge it up, the larger the tornado is. This charges to maximum twice as fast as the regular version.

HEADBUTT (Side Special)

DAMAGE 8~10%

Donkey Kong performs a massive headbutt on his opponent. If the opponent is grounded, that opponent is buried in the ground temporarily. In the air, this performs a meteor smash. This is very damaging to shields.

Jumping Headbutt **DAMAGE 5~10%**

In this variation, Donkey Kong jumps before headbutting. Opens are buried a shorter duration, and it does not have meteor smash properties in the air.

Stubborn Headbutt **DAMAGE 9~13%**

Gains super armor when you begin the attack so you don't flinch from enemy attacks! This is slower but more powerful.

SPINNING KONG (Up Special)

DAMAGE 2~10% MAX DAMAGE 36% : 8 HITS

Spinning like a tornado with his massive arms outstretched, Donkey Kong can cover a lot of horizontal distance with this Special. You can move him left or right while he uses this attack. This has super armor on the ground before he starts spinning then brief invincibility on his arms as he starts spinning. In the air, you have only the invincibility, not the super armor.

Chopper Kong

DAMAGE 0%

For recovery, this version sends you higher faster but does not attack the opponent. You are also limited in how much you can move side to side. This version has no invincibility during its startup.

Kong Cyclone

DAMAGE 3~12% MAX DAMAGE 15% : 2 HITS

Draws in opponents as Donkey Kong spins. As opponents are drawn in, you have super armor and do not flinch from their attacks. The arms do not have invincibleity while spinning, and for recovery purposes, this is about the same as the regular version. This version deals more damage on land than in the air compared to the regular version, which does more damage in the air than on land.

HAND SLAP (Down Special)

DAMAGE 14%

Donkey Kong slaps the ground, creating shockwaves that pop opponents into the air. This doesn't affect characters already in the air, however. You can continue slapping by repeatedly hitting Special without holding Down any longer after the first slap. You can even do this move in the air!

Focused Slap

DAMAGE 7~14% MAX DAMAGE 21% : 2 HITS

Paralyzes opponents with your right hand then knocks them away with the left hand. The impacted area is smaller, but it deals more damage. The paralyzing blow only works on grounded opponents. When used in the air, the damage is higher than the regular version; however, you don't get any ground bounce or meteor effects.

Hot Slap

DAMAGE 4~12% MAX DAMAGE 16% : 2 HITS

Donkey Kong slaps pillars of fire out of the ground! The second pillar rises higher and deals more damage. Unlike other variations, this attack can hit airborne opponents while you are grounded.

Final Smash

KONGA BEAT

Donkey Kong whips out his bongo drums and bangs them, sending out shockwaves to hit your opponents. This includes a music minigame in which you hit the Attack button when the red-and-white circles cross over the target. You get an indicator saying GREAT, GOOD, or BAD. The better you do, the stronger your shockwaves are. Donkey Kong doesn't take damage during this Final Smash, and he can't move once he starts it. Be sure to position yourself close to your opponents, and try to use Konga Beat when your opponents are close to an edge.

Strategy

Being one of the heavier characters in the game, Donkey Kong can withstand some punishment before being in danger of being KO'd. Despite his huge size and weight, his mobility is impressive. Strong KO power, good throws, and a multitude of spikes combined with the excellent range on his attacks make him a threat at all times. His large size, however, makes him an easy target. Couple this with slow recovery on some of his attacks, and you'll have to make sure your attacks count! His most notable attacks are his Back Air, Forward Smash, and his throws. Back Air's hitbox and hurtbox make you feel somewhat invincible, so use this where you can to rack up damage. His Forward Smash does a huge chunk of damage, so try not to use it too much, and it'll catch opponents off guard when they get blasted off the stage! Giant Punch is a great intimidation tactic when fully charged, so be sure to charge it whenever possible. Each arm spin adds an additional 2 points of damage to it, and hitting at the top will net you extra damage.

After burying an opponent with Headbutt, you can immediately charge up at least two spins on Giant Punch. A safer and easier option is to follow up with the two jab attacks. The higher percentage the opponent is at, however, the longer that opponent will be buried, and the longer you can charge up Giant Punch. Alternatively, you can attack with the grounded version of Spinning Kong. Use Hand Slap when you anticipate your opponent might spot dodge or roll, but note this is vulnerable to air attacks. Note when Giant Punch is fully charged, you have super armor and do not flinch from attacks when performing the attack. If it is not fully charged, you do not have super armor, but the arm used is invincible. Down Air, Forward Air, and Headbutt in the air all give you meteor effects or ground bounces with various strengths. Up Tilt is an important tool to cover the area immediately above Donkey Kong as well as behind him.

Donkey Kong's long arms means increased throw range. Couple this with his good throw game, and it becomes something you should always try to use. During Donkey Kong's Forward Throw, he can walk around while carrying the opponent! Use the Forward or Down options while carrying to throw opponents farther away from you in those respective directions. At low percentages, use Down Throw instead to set up better follow-up options. Donkey Kong's Back Throw hurls the opponent a decent distance. Try to use this from the side of a stage, then follow up with a couple of Back Air attacks. You can then use Spinning Kong to knock opponents farther, while also getting Donkey Kong back to the stage.

Recovery

Donkey Kong is limited when it comes to recovery options. His main recovery tool is his Spinning Kong. This is extremely useful for horizontal recovery but gives him very little lift vertically. Donkey Kong will be left in a fall state after this move. So, to maximize your recovery, your best option is to double jump and then Spinning Kong. But if you land on the ground before this move is ready to complete, Donkey Kong will be vulnerable to attacks!

DR. MARIO

Trophy Description

In the 1990 puzzle game *Dr. Mario,* Mario threw on a white coat and decided to take a shot at that whole "medicine" thing. In this game, he's a balanced fighter who can throw Megavitamin capsules and nimbly deflect blows with his Super Sheet. He's not quite as quick as normal Mario, but his attacks deal a bit more damage.

STATISTICS

MAXIMUM NUMBER OF JUMPS: **2**

CAN WALL JUMP: **Yes**

CAN WALL CLING: **No**

CAN CRAWL: **No**

Alternate Colors

Smash Attacks

SIDE SMASH DAMAGE 15.7~19%

Dr. Mario unleashes a blast immediately in front of him. This can be aimed up or down.

DOWN SMASH DAMAGE 11.2~13.4%

Dr. Mario swings his legs around his body to sweep the opponent.

UP SMASH DAMAGE 15.7%

An overhead smash that starts behind Dr. Mario.

Basic Attacks

STANDING ATTACK

DAMAGE 2.8%, 1.7%, 4.5%

Dr. Mario punches twice then kicks the opponent away.

UP TILT DAMAGE 7.1%

A jumping spinning uppercut useful for combos.

DASH ATTACK DAMAGE 6.7~9%

Dr. Mario runs at the opponent then does a baseball slide attack.

SIDE TILT DAMAGE 7.8%

Dr. Mario kicks forward horizontally. This can be aimed up or down.

DOWN TILT DAMAGE 5.6~7.8%

A spinning sweep attack that pops opponents up.

EDGE ATTACK

Dr. Mario quickly returns to the stage and dropkicks your opponent's shins.

Air Attacks

NEUTRAL AIR ATTACK

DAMAGE 5.6~9%

Dr. Mario does a jump kick attack that stays out for awhile.

DOWN AIR ATTACK

DAMAGE 1.6~3.6% MAX DAMAGE 15% : 8 HITS

Dr. Mario drills down into the opponent while spinning rapidly. This attack hits multiple times.

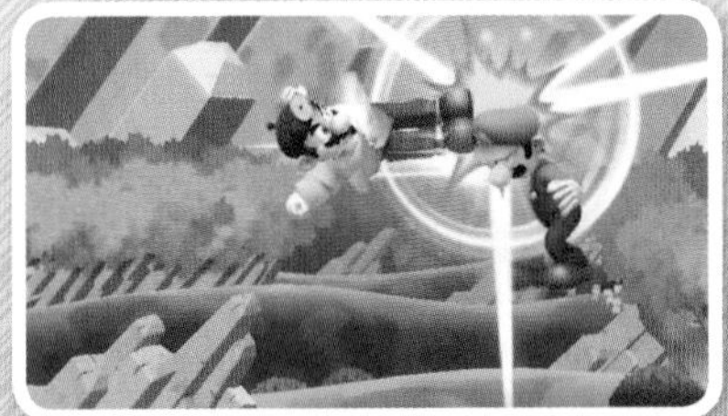

BACK AIR ATTACK

DAMAGE 7.8~13.4%

A reverse dropkick with good knockback.

UP AIR ATTACK DAMAGE 7.8%

Dr. Mario does a flipkick attack midair!

FORWARD AIR ATTACK

DAMAGE 10.1~15.7%

An overhead punch that is useful off-stage.

Special Attacks

MEGAVITAMINS

(Neutral Special) DAMAGE 4.5~5.6%

Bounce a vitamin capsule off the ground. These bounce higher than Mario's and cannot be absorbed.

Fast Capsule

DAMAGE 1.7~3.4%

These capsules are shot much faster, but they aren't as strong. The range is also slightly less.

Mega Capsule

DAMAGE 1.7% MAX DAMAGE 16.8% : 10 HITS

Throw a large capsule that moves slowly. The range is very short, but it can hit opponents multiple times.

SUPER SHEET (Side Special)

DAMAGE 7.8%

Use this to sheet swing and reflect projectiles or to turn your opponents around. The horizontal range is limited, but the vertical range is good.

Shocking Sheet DAMAGE 12.5%

This launches opponents with an electrified sheet, but it does not reflect projectiles.

Breezy Sheet DAMAGE 0~5.6%

Blow opponents away with a swipe of this sheet that also deals damage. The closer the opponent is, the farther that opponent is pushed away.

SUPER JUMP PUNCH

(Up Special) DAMAGE 6.7~13.4%

This leaping uppercut differs from Mario's in that it only hits once and has no invincibility on startup. To make up for this, this version is more powerful at the start of the jump.

Super Jump DAMAGE 0%

This slower jump travels higher, but you do not attack during it. You have more control of your horizontal movement, however.

Ol' One-Two

DAMAGE 9~14.6% MAX DAMAGE 23.5% : 2 HITS

A burning uppercut that doesn't travel as high but that has a strong explosion at its peak. This attack only hits at the beginning and peak of your jump. Your horizontal movement is limited as you ascend.

DR. TORNADO (Down Special)

DAMAGE 1.3~3.4% MAX DAMAGE 8.7% : 5 HITS

Dr. Mario spins like a tornado with arms outstretched. Hit the button repeatedly to rise higher into the air. You can also move left or right during this attack. Horizontal movement speed is about half of Luigi's, but vertical movement is much faster.

Soaring Tornado

DAMAGE 6.7%

Dr. Mario spins so fast that he creates a wind to blow opponents away. It rises high but can't move much horizontally. The damage from the attack comes when Dr. Mario extends his arms at the end.

Clothesline Tornado

DAMAGE 9% MAX DAMAGE 17.9% : 2 HITS

This spin launches any opponents it comes in contact with. It spins much slower and takes awhile to startup. Recovery after spinning is also longer than usual.

REFLECT DATA

	STARTUP	DURATION	DAMAGE SCALING	SPEED SCALING
SUPER SHEET	6th frame	17 frames	1.5x	1x

Final Smash

DOCTOR FINALE

Dr. Mario unleashes a vitamin barrage with vitamins growing in size as they get farther away from him. The attack starts narrow immediately beside Dr. Mario and gets more vertical range as it extends horizontally away from him. Opponents caught in the barrage get pushed horizontally away, so use this on opponents who are closer to the sides of a stage.

Strategy

While his basic moveset is similar to Mario's, Dr. Mario's has some important differences. Dr. Mario's attacks are about 10% stronger, but his movement speed is about 20% slower and his jump height is about 10% lower. His Megavitamins are useful to harass opponents from a distance while his Super Sheet is great against projectiles or opponents with longer range. Dr. Tornado is good for shield pressure and combos, and Super Jump Punch deals good damage out of shield.

Megavitamins are your main projectile to deal damage at a distance. Using it on your way down from a jump allows you to chase after it to pressure your opponent. If your opponent opts to shield, be prepared to throw that opponent. This projectile is not energy based, so characters with an absorb like Ness aren't able to absorb these capsules! Dr. Mario's Super Sheet is excellent to deal damage while turning opponents around. It has a slightly larger reflection window than Mario's Cape, and it doesn't have the same hitbox. Dr. Mario's has less horizontal range but more vertical range. Super Jump Punch is good for Dr. Mario out of shield, as it deals consistent damage. The biggest difference from Mario is that Dr. Mario has Dr. Tornado instead of F.L.U.D.D. It doesn't move as much horizontally as Luigi's, but its still useful to deal damage and pressure shields.

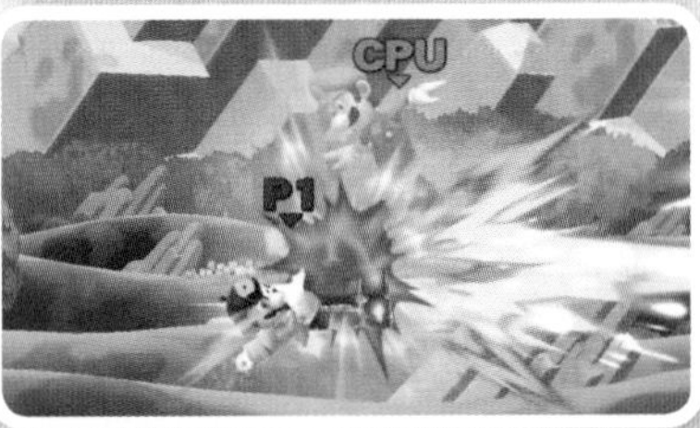

In the air, Dr. Mario's best KO options are Forward Air, Back Air, Up Air, and Super Jump Punch. On the ground, Forward Smash is your best bet. Build up damage using Dr. Mario's jab and tilts, but be careful against opponents with longer range. Use your Neutral Air out of short hop to force opponents to shield, then mix them up with lots of throws or cross them up and attack their shield from behind. Dr. Mario's Back Air is also incredibly useful out of short hop as well. Short hop, then Back Air, and fast fall while drifting away from opponents to recover more safely while still keeping the pressure on. For edge-guarding, use Super Sheet to turn opponents around, and harass them with Megavitamins. Super Sheet doesn't stall Dr. Mario in the air, so you have to be more careful off-stage with this.

Recovery

Dr. Mario has pretty decent recovery options. He has Super Jump Punch as his primary vertical recovery. Like Mario's, you can aim it to the left or right slightly when inputting the direction, and it leaves you in a fall state. Dr. Mario, however, also has his Dr. Tornado for horizontal recovery. The faster you hit the button, the more he spins, allowing you to move left or right to position yourself. Although this doesn't put you in a fall state, it gives you a slight vertical boost only the first time you use it per jump. Also note Dr. Mario's Super Sheet doesn't stall him in the air like Mario's Cape does to Mario.

DUCK HUNT

Trophy Description

You could call these two the stars of the NES 1985 launch title *Duck Hunt*. The goofy dog would chase down any ducks hit by the Zapper. In *Smash Bros.*, these two work as a team to fight. When a can or clay pigeon is in play, hit the button again to fire at it. Show your foes how the ducks felt!

STATISTICS

MAXIMUM NUMBER OF JUMPS: **2**

CAN WALL JUMP: **Yes**

CAN WALL CLING: **No**

CAN CRAWL: **Yes**

Alternate Colors

Smash Attacks

SIDE SMASH

DAMAGE 4~9% MAX DAMAGE 17% : 3 HITS

Fires multiple shots horizontally in front of Duck Hunt. A longer charge has more range than the quickest version.

DOWN SMASH

DAMAGE 5~6% MAX DAMAGE 16% : 3 HITS

Alternating shots immediately in front of and behind Duck Hunt. Landing the first shot will launch opponents into the second shot, which will launch them again into the third shot.

UP SMASH

DAMAGE 2~10% MAX DAMAGE 14.4% : 3 HITS

Multiple shots close above Duck Hunt's body with the last shot knocking opponents high vertically.

Basic Attacks

STANDING ATTACK

DAMAGE 2.5%, 2.5%, 4%
RAPID STRIKES 6% : 4 HITS

The dog has a three-hit string with its paw, head, and hind legs while the duck comes in for the rapid strikes.

UP TILT DAMAGE 7%

The dog kicks its hind legs up while the duck swings upward with its wings.

DASH ATTACK DAMAGE 7~10%

The dog slides forward while the duck attacks out in front with its beak.

SIDE TILT DAMAGE 8%

While the dog crouches, the duck flies out horizontally to attack the opponent with its beak. This can be aimed up or down.

DOWN TILT DAMAGE 8%

The dog swings its hind legs toward the opponent while the duck flies out to attack the opponent's feet with its beak.

EDGE ATTACK

The dog climbs back up to the stage while the duck strikes forward for covering fire.

Air Attacks

NEUTRAL AIR ATTACK

DAMAGE 5~11%

The dog does a cartwheel attack midair!

BACK AIR ATTACK

DAMAGE 10~12.5%

The dog kicks back with its hind legs while the duck attacks with its beak.

DOWN AIR ATTACK

DAMAGE 5~10% MAX DAMAGE 15% : 2 HITS

The dog kicks downward with one of its hind legs before the duck swings around and also strikes the opponent downward. There is a meteor smash when the duck's attack hits an airborne opponent.

UP AIR ATTACK

DAMAGE 3~6% MAX DAMAGE 12% : 3 HITS

The duck flaps its wings and strikes upward with its beak to hit multiple times.

FORWARD AIR ATTACK

DAMAGE 6.5~10%

The dog kicks forward above its head with its hind legs while the duck attacks with its beak.

Special Attacks

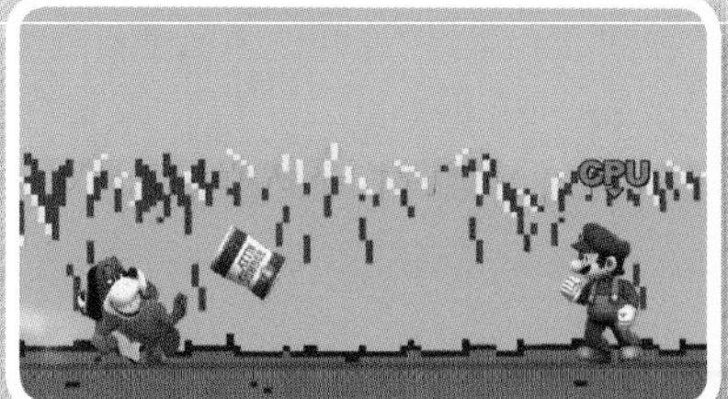

TRICK SHOOTING

(Neutral Special) CAN BODY 1.3~4.4%

CAN EXPLOSION 8% SHOTS 1.8%%

Kick out a can that explodes after about 10 seconds or on contact with an opponent. Pressing the button again shoots the can, causing it to bounce higher into the air. After eight shots, the can drops from its current position and explodes. The faster the can is moving, the higher its damage on contact.

High-Explosive Shot

CAN BODY 1% CAN EXPLOSION 7% SHOTS 5%

This variation kicks the can out much quicker and explodes after just one shot. If the can is not shot, the duration before it explodes is also shorter.

Zigzag Shot

CAN BODY 2~4.3% CAN EXPLOSION 6% SHOTS 6%

This can bounces back and forth as it is shot. Opponents hit by the shots are blasted upward. This can does not explode from your opponents' hits.

CLAY SHOOTING (Side Special)

CLAY BODY 2% CLAY EXPLOSION 5%

SHOTS 1.8% MAX DAMAGE 5.4% : 3 HITS

Throw a clay pigeon out horizontally. Smash the input to send it out even farther. Hitting the button again fires three shots at it. The clay pigeon can also hit an opponent before it has been shot. If this happens, timing your shot immediately after gives you a small combo. Shooting the clay from this attack takes priority over shooting the can from Trick Shooting.

Rising Clay CLAY BODY 2~8%

This clay pigeon can't be shot. The farther it travels, the more damage it delivers. If used while a can from Trick Shooting is out, shots go to the can.

Clay Break CLAY EXPLOSION 6% SHOTS 7%

These shots deal much more damage, but the clay pigeon does not deal any if it hits an opponent. The three shots are fired at the location of the clay pigeon when you press the Special button.

DUCK JUMP

(Up Special) DAMAGE 0%

The duck flaps its wings to fly up, lifting the dog to safety. This is only a recovery, not an attack. You can control the direction the duck is flying by hitting Left or Right, but you can't cancel this move once it begins.

Duck Jump Snag

DAMAGE 1~2% MAX DAMAGE 8% : 7 HITS

As the duck flies up, the dog bites at nearby opponents. You can't fly as high with this version.

Super Duck Jump DAMAGE 0%

The duck flaps its wings with such force that it launches you high up and pushes opponents aside. You can't move horizontally much during this attack.

WILD GUNMAN (Down Special)

DAMAGE *SEE GUNMAN DATA TABLE*

Duck Hunt spawns one of five gunmen to fire a shot. Some gunmen fire quicker than others, but all can be destroyed before firing their shots. You can only have one gunman out at a time. The sequence of gunmen is random, but the same gunman does not appear twice until all five have appeared. These gunmen can shoot the can and the clay pigeons as well.

Quick Draw Aces

DAMAGE *SEE GUNMAN DATA TABLE*

These gunmen fire quicker but have less range on their shots. Damage is slightly increased, but the gunmen have less stamina.

Mega Gunman

DAMAGE *SEE GUNMAN DATA TABLE*

Call out a giant, slower gunman. These gunmen take much longer to shoot, but they have a lot of stamina, so they are useful as shields.

GUNMAN DATA

	SPEED RANK	RANGE RANK	WILD GUNMAN	QUICK DRAW ACES	MEGA GUNMAN
MOUSTACHE	5	2	4%	6%	3%
BEANPOLE	4	1	4%	6%	3%
BLACK SUIT	2	2	5%	7%	4%
SOMBRERO	3	3	7%	9%	6%
BOSS	1	2	6%	8%	5%

Final Smash

NES ZAPPER POSSE

A flock of ducks fly through the battlefield immediately in front of Duck Hunt, striking anyone in their path. Opponents struck by the ducks enter a cinematic where they get to meet all of the Wild Gunmen at the same time, along with a bunch of exploding cans! This Final Smash has great damage and explosive power.

Strategy

Duck Hunt is one of the most versatile zoning characters in the game, thanks to a variety of projectile options. While these projectiles make for a great long-range game, Duck Hunt also possesses some long-range attacks whenever the duck flies out to strike. Though Duck Hunt is two characters, they are below-average weight and if either gets hit, that hit deals damage to both, so be sure to keep opponents away with their projectiles! Always try to have a can from Trick Shooting out, as it gives you more options in how to attack your opponent. As for weaknesses, Duck Hunt's weight and, surprisingly, Duck Hunt's recovery and KO power can be issues. While Duck Jump can recover very high, you can't cancel it, it isn't an attack, and you can be hit out of it. While all of the Smash attacks deal good damage, they are all multi-hit. Because the shots are so quick, it can be difficult to time them to get all hits out of them.

Trick Shooting is an essential projectile for Duck Hunt because the can explodes on contact with an opponent and has good knockback. Note that the can hitting an opponent deals damage, the shots at the can also hit other opponents, and the explosion damages anyone around it. The faster the can is traveling, the more damage it deals on impact. Experiment with different timings for shooting the can—or even leave it as a trap and don't shoot it! You can also move while advancing the can, which allows you to use it as a shield of sorts during your approach! Clay Shooting is another good projectile for Duck Hunt, as you can choose when you want to shoot the clay pigeon. If you use Clay Shooting when Trick Shooting's can is out, hitting the Special button focuses on the clay pigeon before returning to the Trick Shooting can. The shots at the clay pigeon can also advance Trick Shooting's can, so try to combine these attacks! Because each of the gunmen can be defeated, be ready to attack your opponent if they choose to attack the gunmen! The Wild Gunman spawns one of five gunmen that fires a single shot at the opponent. They have different attack speeds, ranges, and damage on their shots, and their shots can also hit the clay pigeons from Clay Shooting and the can from Trick Shooting! Duck Jump is mainly used for recovery and is not an attack.

Back Air and Forward Air have the best range and are your best options to KO opponents while in the air. With the Forward Air, try to hit at maximum range for best results. Down Air is also very good for its meteor smash. For Smash attacks, Side Smash is your best option. Down Smash and Up Smash can be very difficult to time, but with practice, you will learn to land them more consistently. Side Tilt is a great poke, and Up Tilt is a good option to cover opponents approaching from above you. Though KO power can be an issue, Duck Hunt has excellent edge-guarding capability, thanks to its Trick Shooting can and Clay Shooting. Use a throw to get opponents off-stage, then bombard them with your projectiles!

Recovery

Duck Hunt really only has one good recovery tool, the Duck Jump. Duck Jump is your only way of getting back up to a stage. You can move the duck left or right as it carries the dog and flies back up. Once this recovery starts, you can't stop it, and it isn't an attack. This means you have to avoid enemy contact altogether. The lesser but more obvious recovery tool is Duck Hunt's double jump. The second jump is considerably higher than most characters' as the duck flaps its wings to get you as high as possible. Consider using this before using the Duck Jump if you really need to get a lot of height because you are in a fall state after Duck Jump.

FALCO

Trophy Description

A talented pilot and part of the Star Fox team, Falco can be a bit rough around the edges. He once led his own galactic gang before joining up with Fox. In *Smash Bros.*, his ability to jump high and deal damage in the air makes him a powerful threat, and his thrown Reflector can catch foes by surprise.

STATISTICS

MAXIMUM NUMBER OF JUMPS: **2**

CAN WALL JUMP: **Yes**

CAN WALL CLING: **No**

CAN CRAWL: **No**

Alternate Colors

Smash Attacks

SIDE SMASH DAMAGE 10~15%

Falco swings both wings down in front of him with this overhead attack.

DOWN SMASH DAMAGE 12~15%

Falco does the splits, hitting opponents both in front of and behind him. Both feet are invincible during this attack.

UP SMASH

DAMAGE 4~12% MAX DAMAGE 16% : 2 HITS

This backflip attack hits twice before knocking your opponent vertically.

Basic Attacks

STANDING ATTACK

DAMAGE 3%, 2% RAPID STRIKES 4.6% : 5 HITS

Two punch attacks before Falco goes into a rapid spin attack and a final punch to send opponents away horizontally.

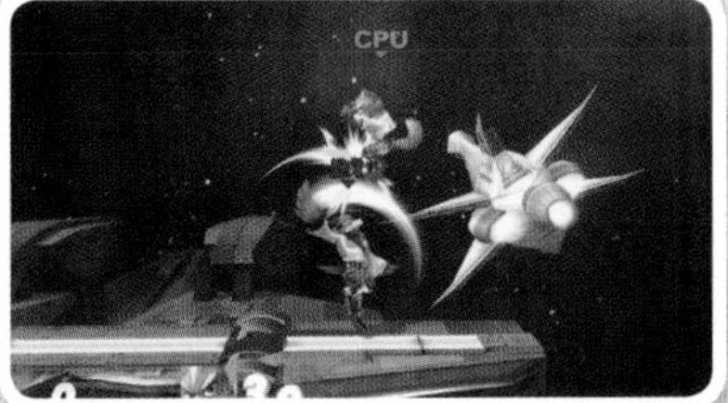

UP TILT

DAMAGE 3~5% MAX DAMAGE 9% : 2 HITS

A jumping, spinning uppercut attack that hits twice.

DASH ATTACK DAMAGE 6~9%

A running jump kick attack that has good range.

SIDE TILT DAMAGE 9%

Falco kicks forward a good distance. This can be aimed up or down.

DOWN TILT DAMAGE 9~12%

A crouching, spinning attack in which Falco uses his tail to attack.

EDGE ATTACK

Falco returns to the stage with a spiral dropkick.

Air Attacks

NEUTRAL AIR ATTACK

DAMAGE 2~4% MAX DAMAGE 12% : 4 HITS

Falco spirals in the air with wings outstretched to attack. His feet can hit as well.

DOWN AIR ATTACK DAMAGE 8~13%

Falco drills down into the opponent with his feet. There is a meteor effect at the start of the move.

BACK AIR ATTACK DAMAGE 7~13%

Falco turns and kicks horizontally behind him.

UP AIR ATTACK DAMAGE 11%

A reverse flipkick attack in which Falco strikes with both feet.

FORWARD AIR ATTACK

DAMAGE 1~4% MAX DAMAGE 10% : 6 HITS

A spiral attack in which Falco attacks with his beak. This hits multiple times.

Special Attacks

BLASTER

(Neutral Special) DAMAGE 3%

Falco's primary projectile attack, this blaster isn't as fast as Fox's but each hit makes enemies flinch. Slightly faster when used in the air.

Explosive Blaster

DAMAGE 1~2% MAX DAMAGE 0% : 5 HITS

This fires a blaster shot that slows down and explodes. Enemies hit by this explosion are knocked back.

Burst Blaster DAMAGE 1~2%

This version of the Blaster fires shots faster but has less power and range. Additionally, opponents don't flinch on hit.

FALCO PHANTASM

(Side Special) DAMAGE 6~7%

Dash forward at high velocity, knocking anyone caught in your path upward. Hitting airborne opponents with this sends them straight downward, making this great over any abyss.

Falco Phase DAMAGE 0%

Falco dashes incredibly fast while he's invincible. This is not an attack and has a bit more recovery at the end of it.

Falco Charge DAMAGE 4~12%

This is a shorter version of the Falco Phase; it deals more damage but only travels about half the distance. This move is strongest at the start of the attack. The airborne version does not have a meteor effect against airborne opponents.

FIRE BIRD (Up Special)

DAMAGE 2~3% MAX DAMAGE 31% : 15 HITS

Falco engulfs himself in flames before blasting off through the air. You can choose which direction you want to fly. You are in a fall state after this attack.

Fast Fire Bird DAMAGE 2%

This version requires no charge time but doesn't travel as far. Additionally, the damage is reduced, and it only hits opponents once.

Distant Fire Bird

DAMAGE 2~8% MAX DAMAGE 20% : 10 HITS

It takes longer to fully charge this, but it flies farther and does more damage to opponents. Its speed is a little slower than usual, but it can hit opponents multiple times.

REFLECTOR

(Down Special) DAMAGE 5%

Falco kicks out an energy shield that reflects projectiles and attacks opponents. The shield only hits on its way out, not on its return to Falco.

Accele-Reflector DAMAGE 2%

This reflector speeds up projectiles as it returns them, but it doesn't increase their damage. This only reflects when moving forward.

Reflector Void DAMAGE 9%

Instead of reflecting projectiles, this reflector destroys them. Hitting opponents with this version deals the most damage of Falco's Reflector alternate Specials.

	STARTUP	DURATION	DAMAGE SCALING	SPEED SCALING
REFLECTOR	1st frame	33 frames	1.2x	1.3x
ACCELE-REFLECTOR	10th frame	7 frames	1x	2.1x
REFLECTOR VOID	7th frame	37 frames	N/A	N/A

Final Smash

LANDMASTER

Falco jumps straight off-stage and returns in the Landmaster vehicle; the upward jump off-stage is also a small attack. The Landmaster vehicle itself has a few ways to attack. First, it has its main cannon, which can be fired with any attack button. The attack also hits anyone standing on the cannon itself. You can also perform a roll attack with the Landmaster by hitting Down. Of course, you can also drive over opponents or land on them to cause damage. Jumping in the Landmaster uses the ship's thrusters to push you upward. Use this to lift opponents up past the blast line to KO them if they don't hit Down to pass through the ship. Be careful not to go so high that you

self-destruct, though! Also avoid falling off the stage while in the Landmaster, as there's no way to cancel out of the ship! While your thrusters can lift you for a while, if you get part of the ship stuck under the stage, you're going to be in trouble quick! Finally, if opponents attack the ship enough, it reduces the amount of time you get to spend in it!

Strategy

Falco is one of the lightest characters in the game and has a very high first-jump height. On the ground, his speed is average, but his Blaster and Reflector allow him to fight at more of a distance. With this jump, he can chase opponents into the air and combo with his Down Air, Forward Air, and Neutral Air to rack up damage. His KO power is below average, but he still has good options once he gets an opponent's damage up. On top of this, his recovery has been buffed because Falco Phantasm doesn't leave him in a fall state.

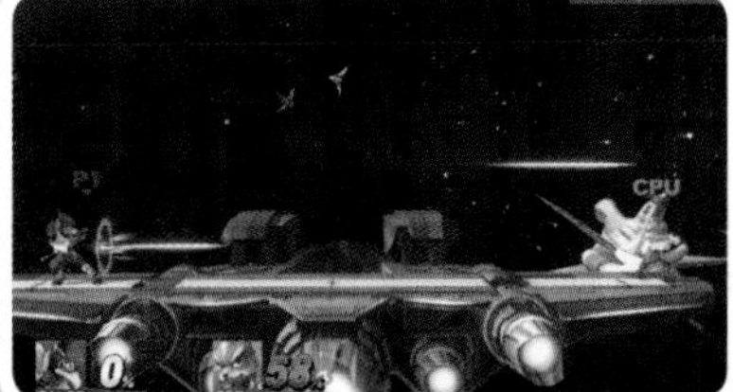

This update to Falco Phantasm is significant because the move also has a meteor effect on airborne opponents. This means you can use it to edge-guard against opponents and still have a chance to recover! Falco's Blaster is much slower than Fox's, but it has the added benefit of making opponents flinch on hit. Using it in the air is recommended, as it is slightly faster in the air than on the ground. As with Fox, if you shoot again while the gun is still out, you get a consecutive blast without putting the Blaster away. This allows for faster shots when opponents are farther away. Firebird hits multiple times as an attack, but since it leaves you vulnerable in a fall state, it's better used as a recovery tool. Falco's Reflector is one of his best tools—it has a fast startup and covers a lot of distance in front of him. Not only does it reflect projectiles with more speed and damage, but it can also hit and push opponents. If opponents are close to the edge, you can actually push them off the stage with this!

In the air, Falco has a bunch of good tools. Neutral Air and Forward Air help rack up damage, and Down Air has a quick meteor effect. Up Air can be useful for vertical KOs when combined with Falco's jump height. The best aerial tool he has, though, has to be Back Air with its impressive range and KO power. On the ground, Falco's Side Smash is very strong and has decent range. His Down Smash also has good range, starts up fairly quickly, and has invincibility on Falco's feet. Save his Up Smash for vertical KO opportunities. Falco's Up Tilt has good vertical range, while his Side Tilt has good horizontal range. Additionally, his Down Throw leaves opponents fairly close for easy pressure and follow ups. For edge-guarding, stop opponents with Falco Phantasm's meteor effect and your Blaster. Down Smash can also be useful in this situation, thanks to its invincibility.

Recovery

With Falco's fast fall speed you are going to have to be ready to recover as soon as possible. Don't forget to use your wall jump as well since it essentially gives you an extra jump. For horizontal recovery he has his Falco Phantasm which covers a lot of distance. For his vertical recovery, Fire Bird is his main option. Once you input the notation for Fire Bird, you can hit any direction to send Falco flying in that direction, however he will be in a fall state afterwards. One thing to note is that Falco Phantasm does not leave you in a fall state, so you are actually able to follow it up with Fire Bird as well! This greatly helps his recovery game. When approaching the stage from above try to use Fire Bird, Down Air, or Forward Air.

FOX

Trophy Description

Fox McCloud is the leader of the mercenary flight team Star Fox, often enlisted to defeat the evil Andross. His piloting skills are top notch, but in *Smash Bros.* his strength is sheer speed. His Reflector move allows him to turn projectile attacks against his foes, increasing their power for a punishing blow.

STATISTICS

MAXIMUM NUMBER OF JUMPS: **2**

CAN WALL JUMP: **Yes**

CAN WALL CLING: **No**

CAN CRAWL: **No**

Alternate Colors

Smash Attacks

SIDE SMASH DAMAGE 11~14%

Fox hurls himself towards the opponent with this acrobatic kick.

DOWN SMASH DAMAGE 12~14%

Fox drops into the splits, kicking both in front of and behind him. During the attack, both of Fox's feet are invincible.

UP SMASH DAMAGE 11~16%

A flipkick attack that launches opponents vertically. For a little while after the start of the move, Fox's head has some invincibility.

Basic Attacks

STANDING ATTACK

DAMAGE 2%, 1% RAPID JABS 5.5% : 6 HITS

Fox does two jab attacks into rapid kick strikes before kicking the opponent away.

UP TILT DAMAGE 5~9%

Fox bends forward and flips a leg up behind him to kick above and in front of him!

DASH ATTACK DAMAGE 4~6%

Fox runs and does a flying jump kick toward your opponent.

SIDE TILT DAMAGE 6%

A quick front kick attack. This can be aimed up or down.

DOWN TILT DAMAGE 6~8%

Fox spins around while crouching, using his tail to sweep the opponent, popping that opponent into the air.

EDGE ATTACK

Fox flips back to the stage and uses both of his legs to sweep the opponent.

Air Attacks

NEUTRAL AIR ATTACK

DAMAGE 6~9%

Fox sticks out his leg in a jump kick attack that has good startup and stays out for a long time.

DOWN AIR ATTACK

DAMAGE 1~3% MAX DAMAGE 12.4% : 8 HITS

Fox spins and drills his way down into the opponent. This attack hits multiple times.

BACK AIR ATTACK DAMAGE 13%

Fox turns and does a spin kick attack behind him.

UP AIR ATTACK

DAMAGE 5~11% MAX DAMAGE 16% : 2 HITS

Fox uses both legs to do a backward flipkick attack. This attack has very small horizontal range.

FORWARD AIR ATTACK

DAMAGE 0.6~3% MAX DAMAGE 7.4% : 5 HITS

Multiple spinning kicks! Can hit up to five times.

Special Attacks

BLASTER (Neutral Special)

DAMAGE 1.4~3%

Fox rapid-fires lasers at his opponent. They deal damage but do not cause the opponent to flinch. Be sure to use this at a distance.

Impact Blaster DAMAGE 2~4.3%

These stronger shots cause opponents to flinch, but you can't fire multiple shots rapidly. Each shot moves slower than the original version, but those shots stay on-screen longer as well.

Charge Blaster DAMAGE 10.5%

An even stronger but slower shot than the Impact Blaster. Firing this pushes Fox back slightly, and you can't fire multiple shots rapidly.

FOX ILLUSION (Side Special)

DAMAGE 3%

A lightning-quick dash that sends Fox through opponents, knocking them upward. If used on the ground, you don't fly over the edge of a stage. When used in the air, however, you fly over an edge.

Fox Burst DAMAGE 13%

At the end of the burst is an explosion that deals damage, but the dash itself does not. Fox also has some invincibility during the explosion.

Wolf Flash DAMAGE 3~10%

Similar to Fox Illusion, this version angles upward instead. If the attack hits an airborne opponent after the dash, it has a meteor effect.

FIRE FOX (Up Special)

DAMAGE 2~14% MAX DAMAGE 28% : 8 HITS

Fox charges up before blasting off in a direction of your choosing. Great for both horizontal or vertical recovery.

Flying Fox DAMAGE 0%

This uses a jetpack to move Fox quickly, but it has attack. The distance is shorter, but the startup is much quicker.

Twisting Fox

DAMAGE 1~2% MAX DAMAGE 13.4% : 11 HITS

Fox dashes into a tailspin to hit enemies multiple times. The speed is slower, but it does startup faster. Through the dash, your speed does not decrease, and unlike Fire Fox, you do not crash into the stage, no matter what angle are at when you hit it.

REFLECTOR (Down Special)

DAMAGE 2%

This move reflects projectiles while increasing their speed and power. It can also damage opponents who are close enough to get hit by it. On hit, it pushes the opponent back pretty far. Hold the button to continue reflecting. After a successful reflection, you can input a direction to jump or evade.

Big Reflector DAMAGE 0%

This larger reflector covers a wide area but doesn't attack the opponent. Instead, the opponent ispushed by wind toward Fox.

Amplifying Reflector DAMAGE 0%

This reflector has a longer startup, but reflected projectiles are even faster and more damaging. Using this version in the air does not stall Fox in the air.

REFLECTOR DATA

	REFLECT STARTUP	DAMAGE SCALING	SPEED SCALING
REFLECTOR	4th frame	1.4x	1.4x
BIG REFLECTOR	7th frame	1.2x	1x
AMPLIFYING REFLECTOR	11th frame	2.1x	1.8x

Final Smash

LANDMASTER

Fox jumps straight off-stage and returns in the Landmaster vehicle; the upward jump off-stage is also a small attack. The Landmaster vehicle itself has a few ways to attack. First, it has its main cannon, which can be fired with any attack button. The attack also hits anyone standing on the cannon itself. You can also perform a roll attack with the Landmaster by hitting Down. Of course, you can also drive over opponents or land on them to cause damage. Jumping in the Landmaster uses the ship's thrusters to push you upward. Use this to lift opponents up past the blast line to KO them if they don't hit Down to pass through the ship. Be careful not to go so high that you self-destruct, though! Also avoid falling off the stage while in the Landmaster, as there's no way to cancel out of the ship! While your thrusters can lift you for a while, if you get part of the ship stuck under the stage, you're going to be in trouble quick! Finally, if opponents attack the ship enough, it reduces the amount of time you get to spend in it!

Strategy

Fox is one of the fastest characters on the ground or in the air with incredible falling speed, given his average weight. With short hops and fast-fall, Fox can usually pull off multiple jumps and aerials in the time slower characters take to do one. While this can be a benefit for combos, it also works in reverse, allowing opponents to combo him easier on the ground with tilt combos and rapid strikes. His speed is counterbalanced by his generally short-ranged attacks. The main exception to this is his long-range Blaster. It doesn't cause opponents to flinch, however, so they can choose to ignore it and attack Fox.

Learning to shoot Fox's Blaster as fast as possible is a good way to rack up damage on your opponents. You can easily do three Blaster shots in a full jump, so try to do three in a short hop! Even though opponents won't flinch, it will try their patience and eventually force them to approach you. Also, when Blaster hits, it refreshes your stronger attacks. Fox Illusion is a quick long-range attack that can catch opponents off guard, but its slow startup and landing lag make it more useful as a recovery tool. Fire Fox allows you to blast in any direction, but generally you want to use this for recovery as well. The flames around Fox can hit opponents, but Fox can also be hit by projectiles to cancel this out. Against projectile-heavy opponents, Fox can also use his Reflector, which returns projectiles at increased speed and damage, but it's a little slower to start up than in previous games.

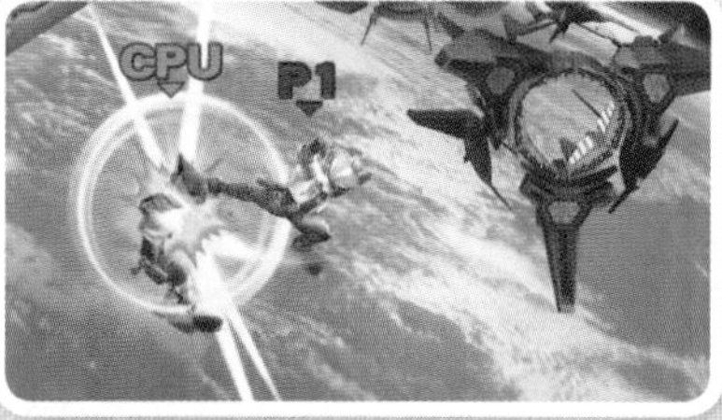

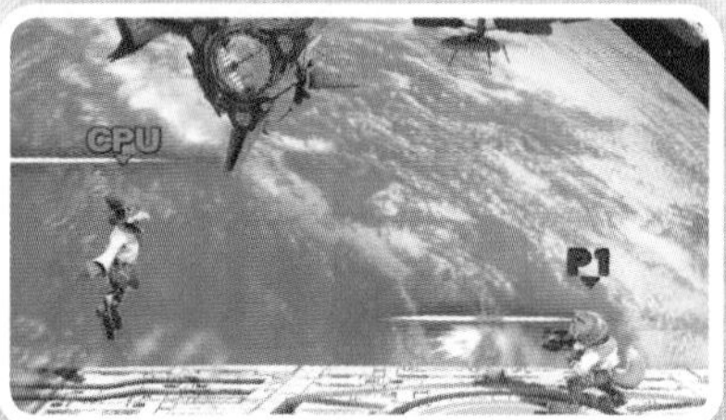

For KOs in the air, Back Air is your best horizontal option while Up Air is your best vertical option. From the ground, Up Smash is good, as Fox's head is invincible, and Down Smash is good because Fox's feet are invincible. Side Smash is still your best longer-range attack option, though. Use Fox's ground speed and fast falling speed to combine your attacks and rack up damage with combos. Forward Air, Down Air, and his Up and Down throws are good ways to start racking up damage.

Recovery

With Fox's fast fall speed, be ready to recover as soon as possible. Remember to use your wall jump when necessary; it basically gives you an extra jump. For horizontal recovery, Fox has his Fox Illusion, which covers a lot of distance. For vertical recovery, Fire Fox is his main option. Once you input the notation for Fire Fox, you can hit any direction to send Fox flying in that direction, but he is in a fall state afterward. Note that Fox Illusion doesn't leave you in a fall state, so you are actually able to follow it up with Fire Fox as well! This greatly helps Fox's recovery game. When approaching the stage from above, use Fire Fox, Down Air, or Forward Air. Additionally, use Fox's Reflector to slow his fall and stall.

GANONDORF

Trophy Description

Ganondorf, the King of Darkness and owner of the Triforce of Power, is bent on plunging the kingdom of Hyrule into ruin. Thankfull, he's usually stopped by Link before this happens. In Smash Bros., he makes up for his low speed with devastating power. The strength of his blows can knock back most opponents. Rush in when the enemy's open and strike hard!

STATISTICS

MAXIMUM NUMBER OF JUMPS: **2**

CAN WALL JUMP: **No**

CAN WALL CLING: **No**

CAN CRAWL: **No**

Alternate Colors

Smash Attacks

SIDE SMASH DAMAGE 24%

Ganondorf steps forward with a big-damaging elbow strike. This can be aimed slightly up or down.

DOWN SMASH

DAMAGE 6~15% MAX DAMAGE 21% : 2 HITS

Ganondorf kicks forward and then backward. The first kick can combo into the second kick. The second kick launches opponents away.

UP SMASH DAMAGE 21~24%

Ganondorf kicks vertically, punting his opponents into the sky.

Basic Attacks

STANDING ATTACK DAMAGE 4~8%

A single strong jab that has a sweet spot at the tip. This jab has a lot of knockback as well.

UP TILT DAMAGE 18~28%

Ganondorf lifts his leg and charges up before unleashing a downward kick. Though it has ridiculously long startup and charging times, this attack also has ridiculous KO potential! While Ganondorf's leg is up, it pulls in nearby opponents.

DASH ATTACK DAMAGE 10~14%

Ganondorf tucks his head and shoulder-charges anyone in his path, popping them into the air.

SIDE TILT DAMAGE 12~13%

Ganondorf delivers a strong kick forward. Good range and damge.

DOWN TILT DAMAGE 13%

A slow low kick that deals decent damage and knocks opponents into the air.

EDGE ATTACK

Ganondorf hops back to the stage and sweeps opponents upward with a swing of his arm.

Air Attacks

NEUTRAL AIR ATTACK

DAMAGE 5~12% MAX DAMAGE 21% : 2 HITS

A spinning double-kick attack.

DOWN AIR ATTACK DAMAGE 17~19%

Ganondorf stomps downward with both legs. Ganondorf tucks his body a bit before attacking, so it's actually easier to hit with this, even when enemies aren't entirely below you. Meteor smashes and ground bounces as well.

BACK AIR ATTACK DAMAGE 16~17%

Ganondorf turns midair and swings his arm behind him for decent damage and high knockback.

UP AIR ATTACK DAMAGE 6~13%

Ganondorf does a quick flipkick attack.

FORWARD AIR ATTACK

DAMAGE 16~17%

An overhead downward punch strike that deals good damage.

Special Attacks

WARLOCK PUNCH (Neutral Special)

ON LAND 30% TURN AROUND 37%

IN AIR 38% TURN AROUND 40%

Charges up with dark energy before unleashing a devastating punch. You can turn Ganondorf to face the opposite direction by hitting in that direction during the startup of the move. When used on the ground, this move is difficult to interrupt, as it has some Super Armor.

Warlock Blade

ON LAND 15~22% TURN AROUND 17~24%

IN AIR 17~24% TURN AROUND 19~26%

Ganondorf charges his sword with dark energy before thrusting it forward. The range of the attack is fairly good, and the tip of the sword deals the most damage. This attack is very good at breaking down shields. You can break weaker shields in a single hit with the tip of the sword.

Warlock Thrust

ON LAND 9~16% TURN AROUND 12~19%

IN AIR 9~16% TURN AROUND 12~19%

This is a faster Warlock Punch that has an explosion at the end of it. The center of the punch is the sweet spot for damage. The damage is the same regardless of whether it was started from the ground or the air. This version has no super armor.

DARK DIVE (Up Special)

DAMAGE 1~7% MAX DAMAGE 11% : 5 HITS

A jumping swing to grab an opponent before shocking and exploding off of that opponent. On a successful hit in the air, you can use any attack as you descend, including this attack.. If you don't grab anyone, Ganondorf swings with a punch attack at the peak of his jump.

Dark Fists

DAMAGE 6~11% MAX DAMAGE 17% : 2 HITS

Ganondorf punches opponents into the air then hits them again to send them higher. Opponents won't be grabbed in this version. Ganondorf has some super armor during this attack as well.

Dark Vault

DAMAGE 1~3% MAX DAMAGE 4% : 2 HITS

Ganondorf jumps much higher than usual, but he only grabs opponents at the beginning or end of this jump. You have a little control over Ganondorf's horizontal motion, and on a successful grab, you ascend a little higher than usual. If you don't connect with the grab, there is no separate attack afterward.

WIZARD'S FOOT (Down Special)

ON LAND 10~12%

IN AIR 8~15%

When used on the ground, this is a horizontal flying kick attack. Each opponent you hit slows Ganondorf down. In the air, this is a kick that goes diagonally downward. The airborne version has a meteor effect at the start of the attack.

Wizard's Dropkick

ON LAND 7~9%

IN AIR 6~11%

Ganondorf jumps low into the air before doing the flying kick. When used from the ground, Ganondorf's feet have some invincibility, and there are no meteor effects.

Wizard's Assault

ON LAND 7~10%

IN AIR 6~14%

This is a faster flying kick that can go through groups of opponents. Attack power decreases the farther Ganondorf travels. When used in the air, the tip of Ganondorf's feet deliver a meteor smash.

FLAME CHOKE (Side Special)

ON LAND 12% IN AIR 15%

Dash forward to choke your opponent before dropping that opponent to the ground. When used in the air, Ganondorf grabs the opponent before slamming that opponent to the ground. This move has a meteor effect when used in the air. Ganondorf has super armor while grabbing opponents if this was started from the ground.

Flame Wave

ON LAND 8~10% MAX DAMAGE 18% : 2 HITS

IN AIR 10% MAX DAMAGE 20% : 2 HITS

Ganondorf dashes forward to grab opponents then blasts them upward. Opponents near the blast take damage as well. The dash distance is shorter than usual.

Flame Chain

ON LAND 1.2~5% MAX DAMAGE 15.8% : 10 HITS

IN AIR 1.2~5% MAX DAMAGE 12.2% : 7 HITS

In this variation, Ganondorf strikes opponents repeatedly while dashing forward. You can hit multiple opponents, but Ganondorf does not have any super armor. This also differs from the regular version in that you can use it on land, and it won't send you over an edge.

Final Smash

BEAST GANON

Ganondorf transforms into Beast Ganon and charges forward with this directional Final Smash across the length of the stage. Beast Ganon always charges in the direction Ganondorf is facing when the Final Smash is activated. After this move ends, Ganondorf reappears in the spot where he activated the Final Smash, and if he was in the air then he performs an additional jump. Beast Ganon has a decent vertical size and is not be affected by platforms. Anyone caught in the area where Ganondorf transforms will be buried and stomped on, taking an additional 20% damage.

Strategy

Along with Bowser, Ganondorf is tied for being the heaviest character in the game. Naturally, this means it's harder for other characters to knock him off the stage, so to balance this, Ganondorf has below-average mobility, recovery, and attack speed. The flip side of this, however, is that pretty much any attack Ganondorf lands is going to hurt—a lot! To land these attacks requires patience and good defense. Using your shield, spot dodges, and air dodges effectively will help immensely. To assist with Ganondorf's mobility, use Flame Choke and the grounded version of Wizard's Foot. Also be aware that Dark Dive does not leave Ganondorf in a fall state when it hits the opponent! This can come in handy when battling off-stage!

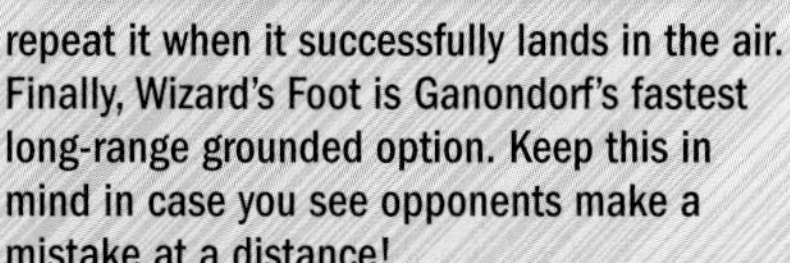

Warlock Punch deals insane damage, especially if you turn it around before it strikes. Additionally, starting it while Ganondorf is high in the air will yield even more damage! So, for maximum damage, start it in the air, and turn it around! With Flame Choke, Ganondorf has some Super Armor once you grab an opponent, so don't be scared to use this. Flame Choke also does a bit more damage in the air than it does on the ground. With Dark Dive, you can actually control it a bit to the left or right to improve your chance of hitting. Don't forget you can repeat it when it successfully lands in the air. Finally, Wizard's Foot is Ganondorf's fastest long-range grounded option. Keep this in mind in case you see opponents make a mistake at a distance!

For aerial attacks, your fastest options are Ganondorf's Neutral Air and Up Air attacks. If you can land it, Down Air has a very strong meteor smash. Forward Air and Back Air deal good damage but are a little harder to land. If you use Wizard's Foot from the air, it has a meteor effect and lets out a shockwave when Ganondorf lands, pushing opponents away and dealing some damage. It should be noted that Flame Choke in the air can be useful for a suicide KO. Ganondorf has ridiculous power in his grounded strikes, but your best bets to KO opponents are Side Tilt and all of Ganondorf's Smash attacks. If you want to get a little crazy, go for his Up Tilt! It takes a long time to come out, but when it hits perfectly, it is Ganondorf's most damaging attack!

Recovery

Ganondorf's recovery tools are fairly limited. For horizontal recovery, he has Flame Choke, but it doesn't cover much distance and puts him into a fall state after use. For vertical recovery, he only has Dark Dive. You can angle Dark Dive slightly during the input of the attack by hitting more of a diagonal direction than directly up. This will help you get to the edge as soon as possible. Dark Dive also goes into a fall state afterward, so you can only choose one of these options. If Ganondorf is returning to the stage from above, use Wizard's Foot to attack on the way down, but it's fairly steep and if you miss the edge, you will self-destruct.

GRENINJA

Trophy Description

This Water/Dark-type Pokémon is the fully evolved form of Froakie. It's just as fast and dangerous as any other ninja, and the throwing stars it can make out of water can shear metal. In *Smash Bros.*, as well as being a graceful, speedy fighter, it can also use moves like Hydro Pump that let it travel through the air and avoid falling.

STATISTICS

MAXIMUM NUMBER OF JUMPS: **2**

CAN WALL JUMP: **Yes**

CAN WALL CLING: **Yes**

CAN CRAWL: **Yes**

Alternate Colors

Smash Attacks

SIDE SMASH DAMAGE 14%

Greninja slashes horizontally with a blade made of water.

DOWN SMASH DAMAGE 9~11%

Greninja swings downward on either side of itself with blades of water.

UP SMASH

DAMAGE 5~14% MAX DAMAGE 6% : 5 HITS

Greninja stabs upwards with blades of water before swinging them downward on either side of itself.

Basic Attacks

STANDING ATTACK

DAMAGE 2%, 1.6%, 3.5%

RAPID STRIKES 6% : 5 HITS

Multiple jab strikes before going into rapid strikes.

UP TILT DAMAGE 4.5%

Greninja swings its extremely long tongue in an arc over its body, hitting anything in its path.

DASH ATTACK DAMAGE 7%

While running, Greninja spins around and sweeps the opponent!

SIDE TILT DAMAGE 6.5%

Greninja kicks forward horizontally. This can be aimed up or down.

DOWN TILT DAMAGE 7%

Greninja crouches down then kicks out low, sending opponents back horizontally.

EDGE ATTACK

Greninja pulls itself back up then swings both legs at the opponent to trip that opponent up.

Air Attacks

NEUTRAL AIR ATTACK

DAMAGE 6~11%

Greninja lets out a burst of water all around itself.

DOWN AIR ATTACK DAMAGE 8%

Greninja dives downward to stomp on the opponent. The meteor effect on this attack allows you to combo into itself. Greninja recoils on hit and jumps back up.

BACK AIR ATTACK

DAMAGE 2.5~4% MAX DAMAGE 9.5% : 3 HITS

Multiple rapid kick strikes behind Greninja that knock opponents back horizontally.

UP AIR ATTACK

DAMAGE 1.3~3% MAX DAMAGE 9.5% : 6 HITS

A spiraling upward series of kicks. This hits multiple times.

FORWARD AIR ATTACK

DAMAGE 14%

Swing forward horizontally with Greninja's water blade.

Special Attacks

WATER SHURIKEN
(Neutral Special) DAMAGE 3%

CHARGED 0.7~9% MAX DAMAGE 12.5% : 6 HITS

Shoot a water shuriken at your opponent. Press the button to charge and increase the damage and size of the shuriken. Note that this charge can't be canceled, so you must release the shuriken. At maximum charge, it does not disappear on hit.

Stagnant Shuriken
DAMAGE 1% MAX DAMAGE 6% : 6 HITS

CHARGED 2% MAX DAMAGE 12% : 6 HITS

These water shurikens are larger and hit multiple times, even if you don't charge them all the way to maximum. They hover in place wherever they are created.

Shifting Shuriken
DAMAGE 3% CHARGED 3%

These water shurikens behave differently depending on whether you charge them or not. If you do not charge them, they knock opponents straight up on hit. If charged, they pull in the opponent. Both versions deal the same amount of damage.

HYDRO PUMP (Up Special)
DAMAGE 2% MAX DAMAGE 6% : 3 HITS

Shoots water to propel you in two directions. After inputting Up Special, immediately input two additional directions. The water deals a bit of damage to your opponents and can also push them.

High Capacity Pump
DAMAGE 0%

Greninja fires off a lot more water to fly a longer distance at a slower speed. Any opponents hit by the water are pushed around but don't take any damage.

Single-Shot Pump
DAMAGE 5%

A single shot that launches Greninja much higher upward. Opponents hit with the water take damage, but Greninja can't move horizontally or change course.

SUBSTITUTE (Down Special)
DAMAGE 11~14%

Greninja evades the opponent's attack with a substitute, then teleports and counterattacks. This also counters attacks that originate behind Greninja. On a successful counter, you can input the direction you want Greninja to attack the opponent.

Exploding Attack
DAMAGE 8~10%

A teleport attack with an explosion when Greninja reappears. You don't have to successfully counter an opponent's attack to use this, so Greninja doesn't have invincibility during the startup of the teleport. The explosion is strongest at its center.

Substitute Ambush
DAMAGE 15~18%

This counter is slower, but it has a much more powerful counterattack. This counterattack is also useful for breaking down shields.

SHADOW SNEAK
(Side Special) DAMAGE 10~12%

Sneaky, indeed! Send your shadow along the floor by holding the button. While holding the button, you are still free to move and jump. When you release the button, Greninja teleports with a flipkick to wherever the shadow is and at whatever height Greninja is. While teleporting, Greninja is invincible.

Shadow Strike DAMAGE 15~17%

This is a slower version of Shadow Sneak but delivers a much stronger attack. The time between warp and attack is longer than usual.

Shadow Dash DAMAGE 6~7%

Instantly sends Greninja a set distance ahead to deliver a weaker attack. Though the damage is lower, it still knocks opponents away.

Final Smash

SECRET NINJA ATTACK

Greninja drops a mat in front of itself, and if the opponent is there, Greninja flips that opponent up into the night sky. Then Greninja rapidly attacks them against the silhouette of the moon before spiking them back down toward the stage. This does about 52% damage! The only downside is it has very limited range compared to most Final Smashes in the game.

Strategy

Greninja is one of the fastest characters in the game and has good jump height and recovery options. Combine this with its average weight and good range—thanks to Greninja's water blades—and you can see why Greninja can be quite capable in battle! Use your charged-up Water Shuriken to fight from a distance, and punish from a distance with your ground speed or Shadow Sneak! Don't get carried away with your speed, though, as your weight is your weakness.

As a projectile, the Water Shuriken is effective at interrupting the opponent and dealing some damage. Even the smallest of shurikens causes the opponent to flinch. Since there is a lot of recovery, it is best to use the uncharged version of Water Shuriken from a short hop. The largest shurikens can hit multiple times and carry opponents off the stage. Shadow Sneak is one of the most interesting special moves in the game. The teleport uses Greninja's current vertical position but has Greninja appear horizontally wherever its shadow is. When Greninja reappears, it flipkicks the opponent. When knocked vertically away from the stage, you can use this to change your horizontal position during your descent to throw off your opponent's expectations. On stages with darker ground, it's increasingly difficult to keep track of the shadow, so opponents will find it harder to keep track of you! While the shadow is moving, you can still control Greninja as well, so you can fake out opponents by jumping toward them so they expect an attack as your shadow teleports to the other side! Similar to Pikachu's Quick Attack, Hydro Pump allows Greninja to fly in two directions while simultaneously attacking the opponent. Hydro Pump, though, is more to push opponents and allow Greninja to escape than it is to damage opponents. Substitute is Greninja's counter, which can be good for edge-guarding along with Hydro Pump and Water Shuriken.

In the air, Forward Air stands out for its impressive range, speed, and damage while Neutral Air can be useful to protect you around multiple opponents. Back Air and Up Air are useful for racking up damage, and Down Air is great because of its meteor smash. For KOs, Forward Air and Up Air are your best options. For ground-based attacks, Side Smash is great, and Up Smash can hit multiple times for tons of damage but less knockback. Side Tilt, Down Tilt, and Greninja's Dash Attack have great range and speed. Remember to use Greninja's extra mobility like crawl, wall cling, and wall jump!

Recovery

Greninja has a variety of useful recovery attacks. His main tool is definitely Hydro Pump. Similar to Pikachu's Quick Attack, Hydro Pump allows Greninja to fly in two additional directions to get back to the stage. Additionally, the water it spits out can push opponents and deal damage. For horizontal recovery, Greninja can also use his Shadow Sneak. When you see the shadow get onto the stage, let it go to return to the stage with a flipkick. Because Shadow Sneak retains your current vertical height, however, you need to be above the stage to land on it. Since Shadow Sneak doesn't put you into a fall state, you can still use Hydro Pump if you don't quite make it to the stage. Use Greninja's Substitute Special to slow your fall and try to counter. To slightly stall, you can throw Water Shuriken as well, but you probably won't want to use this more than once.

IKE

Trophy Description

One of the main character from the *Fire Emblem* series. Having fought in the Mad King's War, restored the fallen nation of Crimea, and taken on the Begnion Empire, Ike is rightly called a hero. He has the strength to back the title—one good swing of his blade can launch the heaviest of foes.

STATISTICS

MAXIMUM NUMBER OF JUMPS: **2**

CAN WALL JUMP: **No**

CAN WALL CLING: **No**

CAN CRAWL: **No**

Alternate Colors

Smash Attacks

SIDE SMASH DAMAGE 17~22%

Ike slams down his huge sword with this overhead downward strike directly in front of him. Sends opponents diagonally upward.

DOWN SMASH DAMAGE 8~17%

Ike strikes low in front of and then behind him.

UP SMASH DAMAGE 10~17%

Ike swings his sword in arc over his head, starting in front of him and ending on the ground behind him.

Basic Attacks

STANDING ATTACK

DAMAGE 3%, 3%, 5%

This jab series starts with a punch, then an advancing kick, and concludes with a downward sword strike. You can delay each hit.

UP TILT DAMAGE 10~14%

Ike lifts his sword horizontally over his head and jumps upward. Pops your opponent up vertically.

DASH ATTACK DAMAGE 5~10%

Ike swings his sword upward directly in front of him as he slides forward.

SIDE TILT DAMAGE 12~14%

A far-reaching horizontal sword slash. This can be aimed up or down.

DOWN TILT DAMAGE 7%

A long-range one-armed sword sweep.

EDGE ATTACK

Ike pulls himself back up to the stage and swings his sword horizontally with one arm.

Air Attacks

NEUTRAL AIR ATTACK

DAMAGE 6~9%

Ike swings his sword downward and around his body, starting in front him.

DOWN AIR ATTACK DAMAGE 15%

Ike flings his sword downward between his legs. This attack can meteor smash.

BACK AIR ATTACK DAMAGE 13%

Ike whips his sword behind him. This is his fastest aerial attack.

UP AIR ATTACK DAMAGE 11%

Ike whirls his huge sword above his head in one big spin.

FORWARD AIR ATTACK

DAMAGE 12%

This overhead downward strike is similar to Marth's except it's larger, slower, and heavier.

Special Attacks

ERUPTION (Neutral Special)

DAMAGE 10% CHARGED 26~35%

A fiery strike with Ike's sword into the ground. This can be charged up through three stages to deal more damage and increase its range, but at full charge, the blast will hurt Ike as well.

Tempest DAMAGE 0~5% CHARGED 0~14%

The force of Ike's sword plunge creates a strong wind. When charged, it knocks opponents away farther and takes less time to fully charge. When going from stage 2 to stage 3, the damage, range, and wind power are increased.

Furious Eruption

DAMAGE 7% CHARGED 25~32%

The longer you charge this, the wider area it covers, but it also hurts Ike. Charging from stage 2 to stage 3 increases damage and range. From stage 2, Ike receives 10% damage, and at stage 3, he receives 15% damage.

QUICK DRAW (Side Special)

DAMAGE 6% CHARGED 13%

Ike lunges at his opponent with a sword slash. Charge this up for increased range and damage. You cannot cancel the charge on this attack. You enter a fall state after using this in the air, so stay over the stage!

Close Combat

DAMAGE 3~4% MAX DAMAGE 7% : 2 HITS

Instead of using his sword, Ike instead rams through opponents with a body blow. Charging this up increases the speed and range, but not the power, of this attack.

Unyielding Blade

DAMAGE 7% CHARGED 19.1%

Ike is super armored for about 2 seconds while charging up and lunging. It takes about 50% longer to charge up to maximum, but your attack damage increases as well. The lunge itself is slower with less range than the regular version.

AETHER (Up Special)

DAMAGE 1~6% MAX DAMAGE 20% : 7 HITS

Ike throws his sword up, leaps to grab it, and swings it on his way back down. Ike will not flinch from damage while the sword is going up. Hitting opponents on the way down causes a meteor attack. Make sure you're over solid ground before using this or you'll plummet to your demise!

Aether Drive

DAMAGE 1~9% MAX DAMAGE 27% : 7 HITS

Ike throws his sword up at an angle diagonally away from him before catching it in midair and then slashing straight down. The jump height is lower than usual, but the damage is higher. You can only grab the edge three times with this before you need to return to the stage.

Aether Wave

DAMAGE 1~10% MAX DAMAGE 13% : 2 HITS

This attack sends out a shockwave upon landing from the Aether. The shockwave knocks back opponents, but the attack isn't very strong. Ike has super armor when landing (in addition to the super armor he has when he starts the attack).

COUNTER (Down Special)

DAMAGE *SEE COUNTER TABLE*

Ike counters incoming attacks with his sword before retaliating with a counterstrike. The counterstrike's damage depends on the opponent's attack strength.

Paralyzing Counter

DAMAGE *See Counter Table*

This counter stuns your opponent and inflicts 1% of damage. Missing this counter leaves Ike very vulnerable.

Smash Counter

DAMAGE *SEE COUNTER TABLE*

This counter has a much stronger counterattack and is slower than the regular counter.

COUNTER DATA

	STARTUP	DURATION	DAMAGE SCALING	MIN DAMAGE	MAX DAMAGE
COUNTER	9th frame	26 frames	1.2x	10%	50%
PARALYZING COUNTER	11th frame	13 frames	-	1%	1%
SMASH COUNTER	11th frame	27 frames	1.5x	15%	50%

Final Smash

GREAT AETHER

Similar to his Aether attack, Ike uses Great Aether to swing his sword upward, catching all nearby opponents. Whoever is caught is sent up into the air, where Ike joins them with his sword and boots before bringing them all back down with a powerful sword slam. Any opponents below can be hit by this last downward attack as well. The Great Aether does about 50% damage on all opponents caught in it and has average KO potential.

Strategy

Ike wields a huge two-handed sword, and he's known to swing it with one arm! He's incredibly powerful with lots of range, but his weakness is his mobility and attack speed. His above-average weight helps balance his slow attack speed by keeping him in the fight, but he still has trouble against faster or projectile-heavy opponents. Ike's jab series can be useful for keeping up with faster opponents, though, so use it when fighting up close. When opponents start getting to high percentages, Ike becomes notably deadly, as many of his attacks can KO them. His Side Tilt and Up Tilt do as much damage as a lot of other characters' Smash attacks! For Smash attacks, Side Smash and Up Smash are your best bets. And even though Down Smash covers both sides, Up Smash does the same thing with higher damage, making it the better option against players who like to roll.

There are three phases to Ike's Eruption attack. Ike's body begins to flash rapidly in the second phase, indicating the move has increased range and damage. In the third phase, damage and range are the same as in the second phase, but the tip of Ike's sword will glow, and the attack will damage Ike. Additionally, Ike has some super armor during Eruption. To close distances quickly, Quick Draw is one of Ike's best tools, though it has a lot of recovery, and it doesn't do much damage uncharged. Still, if the opportunity presents itself, Quick Draw is worth going for. Aether is Ike's most fun tool to use in groups of opponents and also his main recovery tool. It has super armor, so even though you take damage, the move continues through the attacks. You can be KO'd if in the air, so this isn't foolproof. When it does work, you deal a lot of damage on everyone around Ike. Counter can be used even when you aren't facing the opponent and can be useful when edge-guarding or being pressured. Ike's Counter starts up a little slowly but has a big counter window and a high minimum amount of damage.

Though Ike's aerials are slower than other characters', the range of his sword makes them incredibly deadly. For KOs, Forward Air and Back Air are your best options, while Down Air is best used for its meteor smashes. Overall, pick and choose your spots to attack with Ike carefully. Going in recklessly can certainly deal a lot of damage, but this is very risky because of the long recovery Ike has after attacking with his sword. You can mitigate this by fighting up close using his jab string, Side Tilt, and throws.

Recovery

For recovery, Ike has two main options. First, he has Quick Draw for his horizontal recovery, but this leaves him in a fall state. For vertical recovery, Ike has Aether, but you have to land on the stage or edge with this or you will self-destruct. You can control this a bit to the left or right on the way up. Be sure you're facing the right way! Another interesting thing to note about Aether is you can do it from far under a stage like Final Destination, but it still sends Ike to the edge to grab on! If you're high up on your way back to the stage, you can Counter to slow your fall a little before using Aether to get back to the edge. If you repeatedly drop from an edge and use Aether to re-grab the edge, you can only do this five times. After the fifth time, Ike won't grab the edge from Aether, and you need to return to the stage before being able to do so again.

JIGGLYPUFF

Trophy Description

This Normal/Fairy-type Pokémon is best known for its soothing singing, which can put foes to sleep. In *Smash Bros.*, it fights best in the air and can even jump six times in a row. The downside, though, is that Jigglypuff's so light, most opponents could launch it in their sleep!

STATISTICS

MAXIMUM NUMBER OF JUMPS: **6**

CAN WALL JUMP: **No**

CAN WALL CLING: **No**

CAN CRAWL: **No**

Alternate Colors

Smash Attacks

SIDE SMASH DAMAGE 12~15%

Jigglypuff lunges forward with a front kick! This is Jigglypuff's longest forward range and highest damage Smash attack.

DOWN SMASH DAMAGE 11%

Jigglypuff's feet stretch out, attacking opponents on both sides. This attack also pushes opponents away, making it great for edge guarding.

UP SMASH DAMAGE 12~14%

Jigglypuff headbutts forward!

Basic Attacks

STANDING ATTACK DAMAGE 3%, 3%

Jigglypuff quickly jabs forward twice.

UP TILT DAMAGE 8~9%

Jigglypuff quickly leans forward and kicks up from behind its body, launching opponents upward.

DASH ATTACK DAMAGE 8~12%

Jigglypuff dashes forward with a flying headbutt attack!

SIDE TILT DAMAGE 10%

A spinning horizontal kick attack. This can be aimed up or down.

DOWN TILT DAMAGE 10%

Jigglypuff crouches and kicks out a leg toward your opponent.

EDGE ATTACK

Jigglypuff returns to the stage with a surprisingly long-range kick attack.

Air Attacks

NEUTRAL AIR ATTACK

DAMAGE 6~11%

Jigglypuff does a jumpkick attack. This stays out for a long time and does less damage if it hits later.

DOWN AIR ATTACK

DAMAGE 1.5~2% MAX DAMAGE 14% : 9 HITS

Jigglypuff drills down into the opponent, hitting multiple times.

BACK AIR ATTACK DAMAGE 13%

Jigglypuff kicks backward while spinning to face that direction.

UP AIR ATTACK DAMAGE 9%

Jigglypuff swings an arm overhead, knocking opponents higher up. Can be useful for combos.

FORWARD AIR ATTACK

DAMAGE 6~9%

A dropkick attack that has good knockback.

TIP

All of Jigglypuff's Air Attacks have good damage with very low knock back. Coupled with Jigglypuff's multiple jumps, this greatly increases your combo opportunities and overall effectiveness while airborne!

Special Attacks

ROLLOUT (Neutral Special)

DAMAGE 6~14%

This rolling attack can be charged for greater speed and damage. You can control the direction and cause a spinout by hitting the opposite direction you are traveling. You can only change directions twice. If you are hit by an opponent, you stop rolling, but if you run into a shield, you pass through.

Relentless Rollout

DAMAGE 1~7% MAX DAMAGE 4% : 4 HITS

With this variation, you don't stop if you are hit by an opponent. Rolling time is longer than normal, and speed is slightly higher as well. The downsides are it's slightly harder to change directions, and the damage is lower.

Raging Rollout DAMAGE 7~23%

Charge up and roll straight ahead with this rolling attack that pierces through shields! You can't turn around, and the duration of the move is shorter. This is the most damaging of the rollout attacks, but it also takes the longest to charge to full power.

POUND (Side Special) DAMAGE 11%

A stiff forward-moving slap that causes the opponent to pop vertically into the air. It has deceptive range and stays out for a long time. This attack is strong against shields. When you use it while airborne, you can hit up or down to move a little in that direction. This is very useful to stall or extend your time in the air.

Sideways Pound DAMAGE 7%

Jigglypuff stomps opponents with its feet, launching them sideways. Jigglypuff does not advance forward during this attack. Hitting up or down doesn't move you, and this version is not as strong against shields.

Pound Blitz

DAMAGE 1~5% MAX DAMAGE 9% : 5 HITS

Jigglypuff punches the opponent while sliding across the ground. This version hits multiple times.

SING (Up Special) DAMAGE 0%

Jigglypuff sings nearby opponents into a drowsy state, leaving them vulnerable for free followups. This only hits on grounded opponents. The higher the opponent's damage, the longer that opponent will be asleep. This attack has more range as the animation progresses.

Hyper Voice DAMAGE 4~6%

Instead of putting opponents to sleep, this version knocks opponents away. Unlike Sing, this attack can hit airborne opponents. The final sound wave has more range than the rest.

Spinphony

DAMAGE 0.5~1% MAX DAMAGE 4% : 6 HITS

This melody spins opponents around in place and deals some damage! It doesn't put opponents to sleep, but the range is much larger than the other versions.

REST (Down Special) DAMAGE 20%

Jigglypuff takes a nap, and anyone who is making contact at that moment is in for a rude awakening. If any opponents survive the hit, they have a flower on their head that does damage over time. This move has a very small hitbox and should only be used when you are close enough to move an opponent or if opponents are attacking you and about to make contact. Jigglypuff has a little bit of invincibility during the startup of this move.

Leaping Rest DAMAGE 10~15%

Jigglypuff launches upward while sleeping. At startup, there is some invincibility, but the damage and knockback are lowest during the beginning of the attack. You cannot grab onto edges or move horizontally while ascending, so you can't use this as a recovery move.

Wakie Wakie DAMAGE 15%

Jigglypuff takes a very short nap and then explodes after waking up! While Jigglypuff is asleep, a breeze pushes opponents away. The explosion deals 5% damage to Jigglypuff, but it deals more damage to anyone else it touches. While this explosion can't be countered, it can be absorbed.

Final Smash

PUFF UP

Jigglypuff wills its body to get larger and larger, eventually pushing opponents off-screen. When it's at its peak size, anyone touching Jigglypuff is blasted off farther. Jigglypuff can't be harmed during this attack. If used while airborne, you don't fall down. This is much more effective if you can catch opponents close to the stage edges or on smaller stages.

Strategy

Jigglypuff is the lightest character in the game, known for its multiple jumps and superior air mobility. Jigglypuff is so light that if its shield is popped, it results in a KO, regardless of Jigglypuff's damage percentage. Additionally, Jigglypuff is extremely small, so the reach of its attacks is limited. If you keep the battle in the air, though, Jigglypuff can still decimate opponents by chasing them off-stage with its multiple jumps. Half of Jigglypuff's Special attacks can help it approach opponents, but the other half have you gambling with your life!

Rollout is a great tool against approaching opponents. If an opponent shields, always change directions to hit them again. Hitting a shield with all three hits can cause it to break! Try not to fly off-stage with it, or you may have a hard time getting back if your speed was too high! Pound is an amazing Special for two reasons. First, it's active for a long time and advances Jigglypuff forward. More important, though, when used in the air, it won't drop Jigglypuff vertically. This lets you combine Pound with your multiple jumps to stay in the air even longer! Sing and Rest are where you begin to risk your lightweight life. Sing causes Jigglypuff to sing a song that puts opponents to sleep. The song has three parts, and the third part has the most range, but this attack only works on ground opponents. The closer someone is to Jigglypuff when falling asleep, the longer that opponent will be asleep, so charge up your Smash attack to punish accordingly! Of course, if you miss, it's fairly obvious what you were trying to do, and you immediately become a huge target for anyone wanting to get a KO. Rest is a single hit that deals a solid 20 damage and knocks the opponent vertically. If that opponent isn't KO'd, the

opponent has a giant flower on its head that does a ton of damage over time. Rest has a bit of invincibility at startup, so you can use it like a counter. The hitbox is very small, and you practically have to be inside another character for it to hit, which is why it's best used as a counter. Of course, if you miss it, Jigglypuff is asleep and vulnerable for about three seconds, giving opponents plenty of time to charge up their heaviest attack to knock you out! Even on a successful hit with Rest, Jigglypuff is vulnerable for so long that you should really only try to hit Rest if it is going to result in a KO. A good way to land Rest is to use Pound to pop the enemy up, then use short hop into Rest!

In general, you want to stay in the air with Jigglypuff. When jumping, don't remain stationary. Jigglypuff is able to move back and forth a lot in the air. Use this to your advantage, and be unpredictable in your movements! You can use Rollout occasionally to try to get damage, but most of the time you will be out-ranged and less mobile while you are on the ground. When fighting on the stage, a combination of short hops with Forward Air can be quite strong. Use it to knock enemies off the stage, then follow them down for a quick KO. If you land a Sing, then definitely charge up a Smash attack to go for a KO! Alternatively, you can go for a throw to get your opponent into the air and start pressuring that way, too. Once enemies are off-stage, Jigglypuff really shines. Chase after them, and use your Forward Air and Back Air to push opponents farther off-stage. After each hit to push them away, use your extra jumps and air mobility to avoid any retaliation attempts. Similarly, you can push opponents higher and higher off-stage while using Jigglypuff's Up Air attack. If opponents are trying to return from below the stage, Down Air is particularly useful for edge-guarding.

Recovery

The first thing to learn about Jigglypuff is to *never* use Up Special! While this works for most other characters, with Jigglypuff you plummet to your doom! Jigglypuff's main tool for recovery is going to be its six jumps. With Jigglypuff being floaty, you can use these jumps to travel great distances horizontally as well as vertically. You can also use Pound to move horizontally. This Special attack moves Jigglypuff forward considerably while stopping your vertical momentum temporarily. Use this multiple times in combination with your jumps, and you can recover ridiculous amounts of distance. Remember not to be predictable in your return pattern with your jumps. Because you have so many jumps, you don't need to come directly back to the stage. Take your time, and move left and right with each jump to throw off your opponents. You can also use Rollout to cover horizontal distance—just be sure you're facing the right way! If an opponent is standing at the edge and you hit that opponent with Rollout, Jigglypuff will actually be left in a special fall state, as it is stuck in the Rollout spin. So when using Rollout, be sure you either connect with the edge itself or go over your opponent to land on the stage.

KING DEDEDE

Trophy Description

He calls himself the King of Dream Land, but he doesn't have a lot of interest in ruling. He really loves to eat, so it's no surprise that he's a heavyweight fighter. Despite his size and low speed, he can easily recover with his four jumps. His Jet Hammer will leave a mark on everyone he meets.

STATISTICS

MAXIMUM NUMBER OF JUMPS: **5**

CAN WALL JUMP: **No**

CAN WALL CLING: **No**

CAN CRAWL: **No**

Alternate Colors

Smash Attacks

SIDE SMASH DAMAGE 6~24%

Dedede slowly lifts his huge hammer before swinging it down in front of him.

DOWN SMASH DAMAGE 13%

A spin attack with the hammer down by his feet to hit anyone nearby.

UP SMASH DAMAGE 9~14%

Dedede whips his hammer around to hit down behind him.

Basic Attacks

STANDING ATTACK

DAMAGE 4%, 4% RAPID STRIKES 8% : 6 HITS

Dedede swings his hammer horizontally then upward before spinning it for rapid strikes into an upward ender.

UP TILT DAMAGE 10~12%

Dedede hops a little then headbutts your opponent. King Dedede's front arm and head are invincible during the attack.

DASH ATTACK DAMAGE 13~16%

Dedede runs toward his opponent and then falls on that opponent, using his size as a weapon!

SIDE TILT

DAMAGE 2~3% MAX DAMAGE 9% : 4 HITS

Dedede spins his hammer forward in front of him.

DOWN TILT DAMAGE 6~10%

Dedede looks tired as he rolls forward before dropping to the ground for a nap. Repeating this attack will force him to continue to roll or cartwheel over. This can combo against opponents who are at a low percentage and allows King Dedede to move forward while attacking

EDGE ATTACK

Dedede return to the stage and then kicks out toward the opponent.

Air Attacks

NEUTRAL AIR ATTACK

DAMAGE 7~12%

Dedede spreads his limbs, hitting anyone around him.

DOWN AIR ATTACK DAMAGE 8~15%

Dedede swings his hammer downward to meteor smash opponents. This hits under the rear half of Dedede's body.

BACK AIR ATTACK DAMAGE 16%

An upward hammer strike toward Dedede's back.

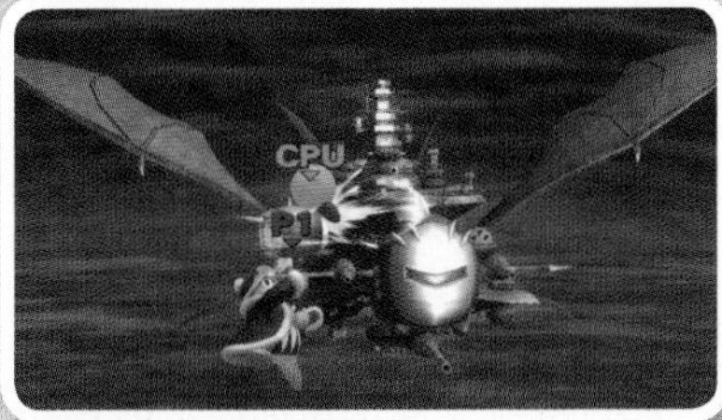

UP AIR ATTACK

DAMAGE 1~5% MAX DAMAGE 12% : 8 HITS

Dedede extends his hammer high up and spins it in an attack.

FORWARD AIR ATTACK

DAMAGE 13%

A downward hammer strike immediately in front of Dedede.

Special Attacks

INHALE (Neutral Special)

DAMAGE 10% STARS 10~20%

King Dedede sucks his opponent into his mouth. He can continue to move and jump around, but he can't attack or shield. Attacking spits the opponent out as a star, which can be used to attack other opponents. The heavier the inhaled opponent, the stronger the attack power when that opponent becomes a star. You can also inhale items and projectiles. Healing items heal 50% more than normal this way.

Dedede Storm

DAMAGE 2~3% MAX DAMAGE 21% : 9 HITS

King Dedede creates a cyclone from his mouth that pulls opponents in and hits multiple times before launching them upward. Holding the button continues the attack. You can't inhale projectiles or items with this variation.

Taste Test **DAMAGE 12% STARS 10~20%**

King Dedede inhales opponents slightly faster than usual before spitting them back out as stars. You can't contain the swallowed opponents, but they can't escape before being spit out as a star.

SUPER DEDEDE JUMP (Up Special)

DAMAGE 5~15% MAX DAMAGE 26% : 2 HITS

A huge jump into the air, followed by a huge splash attack! You can hit Up during the animation to cancel it, but this leaves you in a fall state. The later you cancel it, the worse the landing! This attack has invincibility on startup and on King Dedede's feet during his descent. Additionally, King Dedede has super armor while rising and during the splash attack. Hitting airborne opponents has a meteor effect while opponents hit on the ground are buried.

Rising Dedede **DAMAGE 6~15%**

King Dedede attacks only on the way up in this variation. After the peak of the jump, he is in a fall state. You can't grab the edge during the start of this fall state.

Quick Dedede Jump

DAMAGE 5~10% MAX DAMAGE 21% : 3 HITS

This variation sees King Dedede jump and splash much faster; however, he doesn't jump as high or hit as strong.

JET HAMMER (Down Special)

ON LAND 11% MAX CHARGE 28~38%

IN AIR 10% MAX CHARGE 16~27%

King Dedede charges up his hammer before delivering a massive swing. You can walk around and even single jump while charging the hammer. Be careful—if you charge it for too long, it will start dealing damage to King Dedede unless your damage is already 100% or more. At full charge, the center of the hammer has the highest attack power.

Armored Jet Hammer

ON LAND 9% MAX CHARGE 20~24%

IN AIR 8% MAX CHARGE 15~22%

This variation has super armor throughout charging, so King Dedede won't get interrupted while delivering this massive blow. The trade-off is that the overall damage output is lower. Additionally, at full charge, King Dedede takes damage twice as fast as normal.

Dash Jet Hammer

DAMAGE 6~7% MAX CHARGE 16~18%

The force of the jet pushes King Dedede back as he charges up but sends him dashing forward when swinging the hammer.

GORDO THROW (Side Special)

DAMAGE 9.5~14% MAX DAMAGE 24% : 2 HITS

Throw a Gordo at the opponent. Hit up, down, or forward after inputting this attack to change how the Gordo bounces. Only one Gordo may be out at a time, but a Gordo bounces three times if it doesn't make contact with any opponent or wall. With the right timing, though, opponents can hit the Gordo back! For maximum damage, hit the opponent with both King Dedede's hammer and the Gordo!

Topspin Gordo

DAMAGE 11% MAX DAMAGE 21% : 2 HITS

This Gordo is slow to fall, but once it hits the ground it picks up a lot of speed! Note this Gordo only bounces once if it doesn't strike an opponent.

Bouncing Gordo

DAMAGE 6~10% MAX DAMAGE 16% : 2 HITS

A Gordo that bounces back and forth up to 5 times. Each hit does less damage than the regular version, but this Gordo can't be hit back by opponents!

Final Smash

DEDEDE BURST

King Dedede inhales his opponents into a spinning vortex. He then pummels them with his hammer before lobbing a bomb at them for the final blow, launching everyone in an upward diagonal direction. This does about 46% damage to everyone caught in the vortex. The range on the Inhale is about half of the Final Destination stage.

Strategy

King Dedede is one of the heaviest characters in the game and as such has some extremely heavy-hitting moves. One thing that separates him from other heavyweights is that he has multiple jumps, allowing him a better recovery. Overall he has good range on his attacks, massive damage, a good throw range, and decent aerial mobility for a heavyweight. His Side Smash has a long startup, but it's one of the hardest-hitting Smash attacks in the game. Even his Dash attack can KO lighter opponents under 100%. A good place to grab an opponent is after the first two hits of King Dedede's Standing Attack. Use a Down Throw, then chase with a Forward or Back Aerial Attack.

Opponents will be scared of Dedede's damage and range, so get ready to initiate. Dedede's Inhale attack has some invincibility when sucking opponents in, so you can use it like a ranged counter. Once you've inhaled someone, your best options are to jump off-stage before shooting them out or to shoot them at other opponents. If opponents are just trying to camp you, Dedede has the option of throwing a Gordo at them. Because this can be hit back, it isn't the best projectile, but you can mix up its timing and set up obstacles with the different variations. This makes Gordo Throw particularly interesting when edge-guarding. The Super

Dedede Jump is Dedede's main recovery tool but only on its way up. On its way down, it does have some super armor, invincibility, and the ability to meteor smash. Finally, his Jet Hammer attack can be charged up to deal ridiculous amounts of damage. While charging, you can still move and jump, so don't be afraid to let it damage you a little if you're close to an opponent. This is best used in free-for-all situations against groups of opponents. One-on-one it is easier to see coming.

In the air, Back Aerial and Up Aerial are your best attacks to KO opponents. They are a little slow, but their KO power makes up for it. Down Air is also good for meteor smashing opponents who are in the air, but you have to be significantly above them to do so. For KOing opponents from the ground, your best bets are Down Smash, Side Smash, Dash Attack and the Gordo Throw. Up Tilt has some invincibility that gives it extra versatility. When edge-guarding, Down Tilt and Forward Tilt come in handy, as does Gordo Throw. Take your time, use your throws, and make opponents pay for their mistakes!

Recovery

King Dedede's main recovery tools are his five jumps and his Super Dedede Jump. Super Dedede Jump can be aimed to go in a left or right parabola with an accurate diagonal input using the Special button. Be sure to land on the stage with this, or King Dedede will self-destruct. If you use it from under a stage like Final Destination, King Dedede pushes his way up and finds the edge. If you're going to miss the edge while using this attack, you can always hit Up to cancel the fall, but it leaves you in a fall state. With enough space, though, even during a fall state you may be able to float yourself back to an edge. As with all characters possessing multiple jumps, don't be predictable on your return—move left or right while jumping to confuse your opponents. You can also attack with the Gordo Throw towards the stage to occupy your opponent, then use Super Dedede Jump to recover from below the stage.

KIRBY

Trophy Description

Round little Kirby lives in the peaceful hills of Dream Land on the Planet Popstar. He can inhale things with his big mouth, either copying their abilities or spitting them out again. In *Smash Bros.,* Kirby can inhale opponents and copy their standard Specials. He gets launched easily but recovers well.

STATISTICS

MAXIMUM NUMBER OF JUMPS: **6**

CAN WALL JUMP: **No**

CAN WALL CLING: **No**

CAN CRAWL: **No**

Alternate Colors

Smash Attacks

SIDE SMASH DAMAGE 11~15%

Kirby charges forward with a kick attack. This can be aimed up or down.

DOWN SMASH DAMAGE 10~14%

Kirby spins, attacking with his feet. This hits both in front of and behind Kirby. When Kirby begins rotating, both feet have a little invincibility.

UP SMASH DAMAGE 4~5%

Kirby launches himself up and does a flipkick attack. The foot that goes above his head is invincible.

Basic Attacks

STANDING ATTACK

DAMAGE 2~3% RAPID JABS 7% : 6 HITS

Kirby quickly jabs in front of him. Leads into rapid jabs with an ender.

UP TILT DAMAGE 4~5%

Kirby shows his flexibility by bending forward and sending his leg up behind him to kick forward! This foot has some invincibility.

DASH ATTACK

DAMAGE 1~4% MAX DAMAGE 9% : 6 HITS

After running, Kirby flips onto his hands and spins himself, kicking anyone around him. Hits multiple times and pops the opponent up.

SIDE TILT DAMAGE 7~8%

Kirby spins and kicks horizontally. This can be aimed up or down.

DOWN TILT DAMAGE 6%

Kirby gets low and performs a leg sweep.

EDGE ATTACK

Kirby pops back up to the stage and delivers a kick to the opponent.

Air Attacks

NEUTRAL AIR ATTACK

DAMAGE 4~10%

Kirby spins vertically multiple times in the air, hitting anything around him.

DOWN AIR ATTACK

DAMAGE 1~2% MAX DAMAGE 9% : 7 HITS

Kirby kicks downward multiple times. This has a small meteor effect.

BACK AIR ATTACK

DAMAGE 8~13%

A reverse dropkick that deals solid damage for Kirby.

UP AIR ATTACK DAMAGE 9%

Kirby does a flipkick attack similar to his Up Smash.

FORWARD AIR ATTACK

DAMAGE 3~5% MAX DAMAGE 12% : 3 HITS

Kirby does three quick spinning kicks forward.

Special Attacks

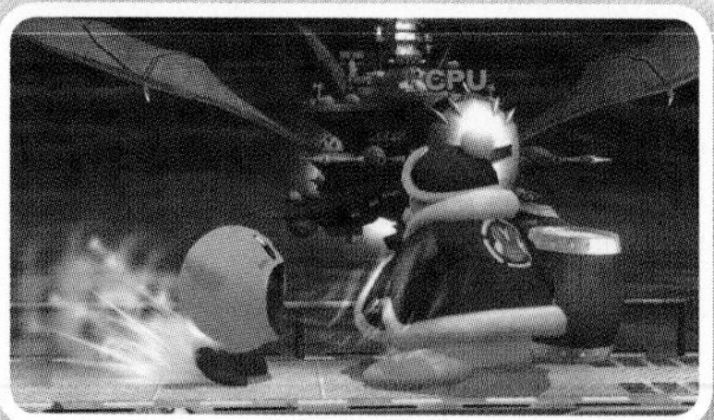

INHALE (Neutral Special)

DAMAGE 6~20%

Kirby sucks his opponent into his mouth. Hit the Special button to copy your opponent's Neutral Special ability and deal 10% damage or hit attack to spit that opponent out as a star that can hit other opponents! Spitting out the opponent deals 6% damage to that opponent. The heavier the opponent, the higher damage they deal to others when spit forward. You can use the copied ability by using the Special button. Use Kirby's Taunts to toss away the copied ability quickly. Down Taunt is your fastest option to toss it away.

Ice Breath

DAMAGE 1.2~6% MAX DAMAGE 14.4% : 5 HITS

Instead of inhaling opponents, Kirby instead blows cold breath and freezes his opponents in ice to stop them. The closer to Kirby's mouth an opponent, the higher the damage is. This move recovers slower than the regular version.

Jumping Inhale DAMAGE 5~8%

Kirby jumps and inhales his opponent but doesn't have the strong vaccuum effect. Stars that are spit out do not deal damage, but copying behaviors works the same. This is most useful for its ability to hold opponents in Kirby's cheeks longer. Jump off-stage with this and drop opponents far away before using your multiple jumps to get back up.

STONE (Down Special)

ON LAND 14% : IN AIR 18%

Kirby transforms into one of three heavy objects and drops to the ground. In this form, he does not flinch or take damage up to a certain limit (approximately 25%). Kirby can be thrown out of this form, so try not to stay in it too long. Once you reach the damage limit, the transformation is canceled, and you receive half the additional damage. These objects can push opponents, if they're close enough.

GROUNDING STONE

ON LAND 6% : IN AIR 10~12%

Opponents hit by this stone are buried in the ground. Opponents hit by the shockwave or when this is used on land are not buried. These stones can withstand less punishment (approximately 15%) before having the transformation canceled.

Meteor Stone DAMAGE 12%

These stones have a meteor effect. When Kirby uses this from the ground, he rises up before transforming and dropping. These stones can take up to 20% damage before the transformation is canceled.

FINAL CUTTER (Up Special)

DAMAGE 2~6% MAX DAMAGE 12% : 3 HITS

Kirby swings his sword upward before leaping into the air, then striking downward to the ground with a shockwave upon landing. This will meteor on the way down, so be sure you are over the stage when using it. You can move this left or right while attacking.

Wave Cutter

DAMAGE 5~10% MAX DAMAGE 15% : 2 HITS

This variation doesn't attack on the way up or down. The strike to the ground, though, is much stronger and sends rocks flying up!

Upper Cutter DAMAGE 10%

Swing up with a higher jump, but you are defenseless as you fall back down. During your ascent, you have some invincibility.

HAMMER FLIP (Side Special)

ON LAND 19~35% : IN AIR 15~27%

This hammer attack can be charged up to unleash massive damage and launch opponents. When fully charged, however, Kirby continuously takes damage, so be aware of this! If you are over 100% damage, though, you won't be damaged any further! At full charge, the swing is super armored, so you won't flinch.

Hammer Bash

ON LAND 18~21% : IN AIR 4~17%

This version slams the opponent straight up with the hammer. This has high damage, but you cannot charge it up. When you use this in the air, you can time it to swing once in each direction.

Giant Hammer

ON LAND 22~40% : IN AIR 20~32%

This hammer is enormous and deals incredible damage. Though it is slower to startup and to swing, the damage potential is incredible. Additionally, while charging the hammer, Kirby will be super armored and will not flinch. While charging, Kirby retains the super armor while walking and jumping, though both movements are slower than normal. Note this racks up damage at a faster rate than the regular version and doesn't have any invincibility at the start of the swing when grounded.

INHALE

You can hold the Special button to increase the duration of the Inhale. While inhaling an opponent, Kirby has some invincibility until that opponent is in Kirby's mouth. Once inhaled, the opponent can get out quicker by jiggling the controller. The jiggles of the controller force Kirby to slightly move involuntarily in those directions. Characters whose Neutral Specials do not copy over exactly are Olimar, Lucario, Rosalina & Luma, Robin, and Duck Hunt.

Final Smash

ULTRA SWORD

Kirby pulls out the Ultra Sword and swings at your opponent. All opponents caught by the initial swing are pulled in and trapped for the onslaught. The range on the first hit is just under half of the Final Destination form. After the initial swing, the range of the attack extends and hits other opponents who are nearby. If you are immediately beside your opponent when starting the attack, that opponent receives a few extra percentage points of damage. If they're at the side of a stage, most characters will be KO'd after about 40% damage, so look for this opportunity!

Strategy

Tied for lightest character in the game, Kirby is also one of the smallest. So, while he will be launched away relatively easily, it's also a little harder to hit him! When he does get knocked off-stage, his multiple jumps assist greatly in his return. With these multiple jumps and good aerial attacks, his air game is above-average. In the air, though, he moves slowly, so you don't have a ton of control over maneuverability. Because of his small size, Kirby's primary issue is his attack range. Against characters who rack up damage from a distance or have good long-range attacks, this could pose a problem.

Because one of Kirby's offensive weaknesses is his range, try to use Inhale on an opponent who has a good ranged attack or projectile: Palutena, Robin, Mario, Link, Fox, etc. If you inhale someone whose ability you don't want, shoot that character out at another opponent for more damage. Alternatively, if that character has weak recovery, consider jumping off stage and shooting that character out then! Inhaling items can restore some health, but if you inhale explosive items, they hurt! Hammer Flip does a lot of damage, and if you charge it up all the way, it gains some super armor and invincibility, but you take damage. Since Kirby is so light, added damage is not the safest route to go! Final Cutter is fairly useful, as it doesn't leave you in a fall state, but it does meteor, so you must be

over the stage when using it. Final Cutter also has fairly good mobility to the left and right, so you can use it upon landing to push opponents away with its shockwave. Finally, Kirby's Stone is a great way to prevent taking damage, but remember that Kirby can be grabbed from this form. Again, because Kirby is tied for lightest character, the less damage you take, the better off you are.

When looking to KO opponents, Kirby's best options are his Back Air attack and his Side Smash and Up Smash. Additionally, Hammer Flip and Stone can also be used to KO opponents. Down Air has a small meteor effect, but if you're looking to meteor smash, your best bet is Final Cutter, as long as you're still going to land on the stage. On the ground, his attacks are quick with good recovery, and he has decent throws, so don't be afraid to fight on the ground. His Up Tilt, Up Smash, and Down Smash all have some invincibility. In the air, Down Air and Forward Air are good for pressure, especially when combined with Kirby's multiple jumps. When edge-guarding opponents, don't be afraid to chase off the stage with your Back Air, Forward Air, and Up Air. Most characters won't be able to recover as well as you do, so just save enough jumps to get back to the stage!

Recovery

Kirby's primary recovery tool is his multiple jumps. Additionally, for vertical recovery, Kirby can use his Final Cutter, which can be aimed slightly to the right or left during the input. If you don't reach the stage with this attack, though, Kirby will self-destruct! Horizontally, you have to rely on Kirby's jumps. Remember not to be too predictable with your jumps. Use as many as you can, and be sure to move left and right with each jump!

LINK

Trophy Description

Green clothes? Pointy hat? Yep, it's Link, all right! In this game, his sword and shield make for effective attacking and blocking, and his bow, bombs, and boomerang will spice up any battle. He's even brought his Clawshot for grabbing enemies and edges. Jeez, just how much stuff can Link carry?

STATISTICS

MAXIMUM NUMBER OF JUMPS: **2**

CAN WALL JUMP: **No**

CAN WALL CLING: **No**

CAN CRAWL: **No**

Alternate Colors

Smash Attacks

SIDE SMASH DAMAGE 7~14%, 12~13%

Link swings his sword downward and then horizontally. Press the button again for the second attack, which is a stronger launcher.

DOWN SMASH DAMAGE 10~17%

Link sweeps with his sword in front of and then behind him. The first hit launches more vertically while the second hit launches more horizontally.

UP SMASH

DAMAGE 3~11% MAX DAMAGE 18% : 3 HITS

A three-hit attack string using Link's sword. The last hit does the most damage and launches your opponent vertically.

Basic Attacks

STANDING ATTACK

DAMAGE 2.5%, 2.5%, 5%

A three-hit attack string using Link's sword. Decent range and a true combo at lower percentages.

UP TILT DAMAGE 9%

Link swings his sword in an arc over his body and can hit opponents behind him. Knocks opponents away vertically.

DASH ATTACK DAMAGE 13~14%

A leaping downward sword strike. This is almost as strong as a Smash attack, with the tip of the sword actually being even more powerful!

SIDE TILT DAMAGE 13%

A downward sword swing similar to Link's Side Smash.

DOWN TILT DAMAGE 12%

Link swings his sword toward your opponent's feet.

EDGE ATTACK

Link returns to the stage and stabs his sword at your opponent's feet.

Air Attacks

NEUTRAL AIR ATTACK

DAMAGE 6~11%

A jump kick attack that stays out a long time and has decent range.

DOWN AIR ATTACK

DAMAGE 15~18% MAX DAMAGE 26% : 2 HITS

Link uses his sword as a pogo stick, stabbing opponents below him. At lower percentages, this can combo for two hits and has good knockback. At the beginning of the attack, there is a meteor effect.

BACK AIR ATTACK

DAMAGE 3~5% MAX DAMAGE 8% : 2 HITS

A spinning double back-kick attack.

UP AIR ATTACK DAMAGE 13~15%

Link thrusts his sword upward. This attack stays out fairly long and sends your opponent spiraling into the air.

FORWARD AIR ATTACK

DAMAGE 8~10% MAX DAMAGE 18% : 2 HITS

This spinning sword attack hits twice for good damage.

Special Attacks

HERO'S BOW (Neutral Special)

DAMAGE 4~12%

Link fires an arrow at an opponent. The longer you charge it, the farther it will fly and the stronger it will be. At full charge, the arrow will fly straight.

Power Bow DAMAGE 1~19%

This stiffer bow doesn't shoot arrows as far, but when fully charged the arrows are much more powerful and launch opponents away.

Quickfire Bow DAMAGE 2~7%

These magic arrows pierce your opponent. They aren't as damaging and don't go as far as the original arrows, but they do go faster and always straight.

GALE BOOMERANG (Side Special) DAMAGE 0~7%

Link chucks his boomerang at the enemy. It deals some damage while moving forward and can pull opponents toward you when it returns. No damage is dealt during its return.

Boomerang DAMAGE 3~9%

This "normal" boomerang deals damage in both directions but does not create a tornado, so it doesn't pull in opponents. On its way out, it does 5~9%, and on the return, it does 3% damage.

Ripping Boomerang

DAMAGE 0.7~4% MAX DAMAGE 8.2% : 4 HITS

This boomerang hits multiple times. It doesn't travel as far and will continue on its path after hitting an opponent. This means you can use it to hit groups of opponents where the other versions of Boomerang return after hitting one enemy.

SPIN ATTACK (Up Special)

DAMAGE 5~19.2%

When used in the air, this is a jumping spinning sword attack used mainly for recovery that can deal up to 20% damage in 8 hits. On the ground, though, Link spins in place with a sword attack that hits once. You can charge it up to deal more damage with the grounded version.

SHOCKING SPIN DAMAGE 5~22.4%

This more powerful version uses an electrified sword. When you're airborne, it only hits in front of you, and you don'trecover as high vertically. This also has more recovery than the normal version.

WHIRLING SPIN DAMAGE 0%

Used primarily for recovery, this version is not an attack. You have more control of your horizontal motion and jump much higher. Even when you use it from the ground, you perform the jump.

BOMB (Down Special) DAMAGE 5~9.2%

Link pulls out a bomb to throw that explodes on impact or when its fuse expires. You can throw it up, down, or sideways. Its explosion when hitting an enemy won't hurt Link, but if it explodes only on Link then Link takes damage.

Giant Bomb DAMAGE 8~13.3%

This bigger bomb is much stronger and has more range than the regular Bomb. It doesn't explode on contact with the enemy, but it can explode if hit with a strong attack. It explodes after a fixed amount of time, which is shorter than the normal Bomb. Note that this explosion can damage Link.

Meteor Bomb DAMAGE 5~9.2%

This bomb has less range and a quicker fuse, but if it hits an opponent midair, it delivers a meteor effect.

Final Smash

TRIFORCE SLASH

Link sends out a beam of light across the stage directly in front of him. The first opponent it makes contact with is stunned, and Link dashes in to unleash an incredible sword combo that ends with a giant swing. This last hit has more horizontal range than any of the previous hits and catches anyone who stays too close. This Final Smash has great range and can reach across the Final Destination form.

Strategy

Link has above-average weight and decent range on all of his attacks, thanks to his sword. He also has a variety of projectiles he can use to attack characters from afar. This means he can easily switch between playing a ranged game or an up-close game. Along with his sword, he also carries his Hylian Shield, which blocks projectiles as long as you are not attacking. Link reacts when blocking a projectile, but this only works when projectiles make contact with his shield, so he can still be hit with projectiles from behind. His weaknesses are his overall speed and his horizontal recovery.

Link's projectile game can be hard for an opponent to get around. His Hero's Bow fires quickly, and if you charge it up first, it fires extremely far. His Bomb attack deals decent damage, and as long as you successfully hit your opponent, Link will not take damage from it. This allows you to use Bomb for close combat as well. If you throw a bomb vertically, you can pull out a second bomb, too! And while holding a bomb, you have a bit of time before it explodes, so use this time to send out your Gale Boomerang or use the Hero's Bow. The Gale Boomerang deals damage on the way out, and on its way back it pulls opponents in, giving you opportunities for free attacks. Note that when Gale Boomerang pulls opponents in during its return, it does so for no damage. Not catching the boomerang can be useful to push opponents off or farther from the edge—even more so because you can also aim this diagonally! Mixing up this assortment of projectiles will cause havoc for any opponent, especially for those who do not have projectiles or projectile counters.

For grounded attacks, Link's Dash attack, Side Tilt, and Down Tilt are all relatively strong attacks. His Up Smash attack hits multiple times, the last hit launching opponents upward. His Down Tilt attack actually has a bit of a meteor effect, but it's hard to make this hit consistently. For Link's aerial attacks, his Neutral Air stays out for awhile and has decent range. Both his Up Air and Down Air attacks are also active for a long time, with the Down Air having a meteor effect as well. To KO opponents, though, Down Air and Forward Air are your best bets. Don't forget you can also use Link's grapple in the air as an attack—it doesn't do a ton of damage, but it is effective for longer range aerial battles. When edge-guarding, use all of the projectiles at your disposable. Bombs thrown downward at recovering enemies are particularly useful. As mentioned previously, you can throw Gale Boomerange toward the stage, then not catch it, so it pushes recovering enemies away from the stage. For enemies with worse horizontal recovery, keep them out with charged-up arrows from the Hero's Bow.

Recovery

Link's Spin Attack is his main tool for vertical recovery; it has great range and protects you from nearby opponents. Where Link is lacking, though, is in his horizontal recovery. His main option for this is to use his grapple/throw. You can use this to grab onto the edge, but you have to time it correctly and be facing the right way. Press the Throw button again to pull yourself up or hit Up to return to the edge. Note that Link's Spin Attack leaves him in a fall state. If you are holding onto a bomb that explodes while you're in fall state, you can use Spin Attack again! And if opponents are waiting for you, it might help to throw out a Gale Boomerang before attempting your recovery.

LITTLE MAC

Trophy Description

This little boxer from the *Punch-Out!!* series makes up in heart what he lacks in height. He wasn't afraid to take on the boxing champs, and he's not afraid of the Nintendo stars, either. In *Smash Bros.*, he packs a serious punch. When his KO Meter fills up, wade in and trigger a devastating uppercut.

STATISTICS

MAXIMUM NUMBER OF JUMPS: **2**

CAN WALL JUMP: **Yes**

CAN WALL CLING: **No**

CAN CRAWL: **No**

Alternate Colors

Smash Attacks

SIDE SMASH

DAMAGE 17~19% : ANGLED DOWN 22%

Little Mac lunges forward with a straight punch. Press Up during this Side Smash to transition into an uppercut that launches opponents upward. Press Down for a lower-hitting Smash that is strong against shields and deals more damage! Little Mac has super armor during this attack.

DOWN SMASH DAMAGE 12%

Little Mac briefly winds up, then punches at the feet of the opponent, sending that opponent horizontally away. Note that this is two hits: first in front and then behind Little Mac. Little Mac has super armor during this attack.

UP SMASH DAMAGE 15~20%

With this overhead punch, Little Mac swings his fist in an arc over his head. When performed up close, this becomes a fire overhead punch and deals more damage! Little Mac has super armor during this attack.

Basic Attacks

STANDING ATTACK

DAMAGE 2%, 3%, 8% RAPID STRIKES 11% : 9 HITS

Little Mac can do three punch attacks before turning his opponent into a punching bag with his rapid strikes and then ending with an uppercut.

UP TILT DAMAGE 9%

Little Mac attacks behind him with a wild overhead swing of his fist.

DASH ATTACK DAMAGE 10%

This running overhead downward punch has good knockback and can catch opponents off-guard.

SIDE TILT

DAMAGE 4~8% MAX DAMAGE 12% : 2 HITS

Little Mac steps forward and delivers a one-two combination of straight punches.

DOWN TILT DAMAGE 8%

A crouching long-range punch that knocks your opponent into the air.

EDGE ATTACK

Little Mac hops back on stage and swings at the opponent's feet.

Air Attacks

NEUTRAL AIR ATTACK DAMAGE 2%

Little Mac does a single punch directly in front of him.

DOWN AIR ATTACK DAMAGE 4~5%

This downward punch attack has a meteor effect at the tip.

BACK AIR ATTACK DAMAGE 4~6%

Little Mac swings an arm behind him as he spins around.

UP AIR ATTACK DAMAGE 4~5%

Little Mac reaches up and forward as he does this overhead downward punch.

FORWARD AIR ATTACK

DAMAGE 4~5%

A jumping hook punch toward the opponent.

Special Attacks

STRAIGHT LUNGE (Neutral Special)

ON LAND 9~14% : MAX CHARGE 20~25%

IN AIR 7~10% : MAX CHARGE 15%

KO PUNCH ON LAND 35%

KO PUNCH IN AIR 13%

A long, lunging, powerful punch. Press once to start charging it up and then again to release it. The longer you charge it, the more range and damage it delivers. During the charge and the dash, Little Mac has super armor. When your KO Meter fills up from dealing or receiving damage, this attack transitions into the KO Punch attack. Note the KO Punch is also super armored.

Flaming Straight Lunge

ON LAND 9~14% : MAX CHARGE 20~25%

IN AIR 7~10% : MAX CHARGE 15%

Little Mac charges forward with a flaming punch that hits opponents multiple times before launching them.

Stunning Straight Lunge

ON LAND NO CHARGE 7~10% : MAX DAMAGE 6% : 3 HITS

ON LAND MAX CHARGE 10~18% : MAX DAMAGE 16.8% : 7 HITS

IN AIR NO CHARGE 1.2~3% : MAX DAMAGE 5.4% : 3 HITS

IN AIR MAX CHARGE 1.4~5% : MAX DAMAGE 13.4% : 7 HITS

When this variation is fully charged, it delivers a punch that stuns the opponent. It charges to full a little quicker than the regular version, but there is no super armor at all on this version.

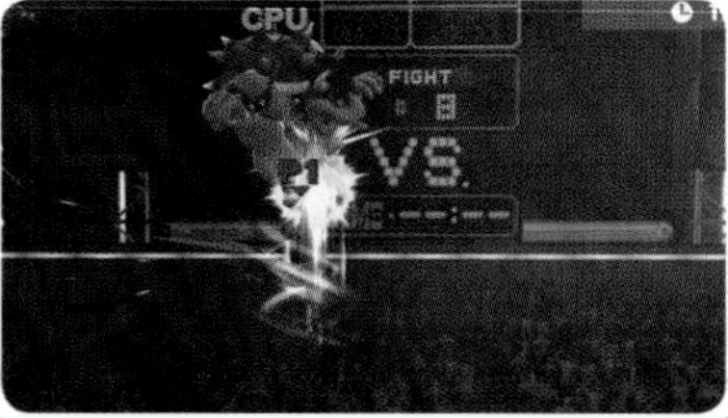

RISING UPPERCUT (Up Special)

DAMAGE 1~3% MAX DAMAGE 10% : 6 HITS

This spinning uppercut sends Little Mac spiraling upward while striking opponents multiple times. You can control it a bit to the left or right.

Tornado Uppercut DAMAGE 3~4%

Little Mac jumps even higher with this version, and nearby opponents are blown away by the power of the wind. It only hits opponents once before knocking them away. The final hit at the peak is stronger than usual,

Rising Smash

DAMAGE 4~16% MAX DAMAGE 20% : 2 HITS

Launch opponents up into the air then jump after them to deliver a damaging punch. Little Mac doesn't jump as high in this alternate Special, and you can't move him horizontally while he is ascending.

SLIP COUNTER (Down Special)

DAMAGE *SEE COUNTER DATA TABLE*

Little Mac puts his guard up in anticipation of an enemy attack. If he catches an attack, he doesn't receive any damage and counters with an uppercut. You are invincible during the counterattack.

Compact Counter

DAMAGE *SEE COUNTER DATA TABLE*

A weaker counterattack that leaves your opponent in range for you to follow up with additional attacks. Even if an opponent's damage is very high you won't knock that opponent back as far as normal.

Dash Counter

DAMAGE *SEE COUNTER DATA TABLE*

This counterattack sees Little Mac dashing farther to retaliate. The counter window duration is smaller, but the counter also starts up a little quicker. The dash distance is longer when used from the ground than it is from the air.

COUNTER DATA

	STARTUP	DURATION	DAMAGE SCALING	MIN DAMAGE	MAX DAMAGE
SLIP COUNTER	5th frame	25 frames	1.3x	10%	50%
COMPACT COUNTER	5th frame	25 frames	0.8x	4%	50%
DASH COUNTER	4th frame	21 frames	1.1x	7%	50%

JOLT HAYMAKER (Side Special) DAMAGE 14%

Little Mac performs a leaping overhead punch that jumps over low attacks. To cut his range shorter or to punch earlier, simply press the button again. You get a little invincibility when this is used from the ground but not from the air. Be careful how close you are to the edge before using this!

Grounding Blow DAMAGE 9%

This variation has a meteor effect against airborne opponents and buries grounded opponents on hit.

Guard Breaker DAMAGE 18%

A slower Jolt Haymaker attack that pierces through shields! It has no invincibility but does have super armor during the jump. Pressing the Special button again while you are airborne doesn't cause the punch to come out any faster.

Final Smash

GIGA MAC

Little Mac transforms into Giga Mac! In this form, he still has access to his same moves, including Smash attacks, tilts, throws, Specials, and aerials. The difference is that damage is increased, and he has increased range because of his size. Additionally, his KO Meter temporarily disappears while he is Giga Mac, so no KO Punch is available. His fully charged forward smash uppercut variation is a one-hit KO against most of the cast. Giga Mac still takes damage, but he doesn't flinch when getting hit. Use this to your advantage and as soon as they hit you, punish attacks with attacks of your own!

Strategy

Ground-based combat is the name of the game for Little Mac. He has super armor on all of his Smash attacks, and his KO mechanic gives him an even stronger attack from the ground. Little Mac has very good ground speed, but he's also below average in terms of weight. Boxers aren't using to jumping while fighting, though, and Little Mac highlights this weakness with his poor jump height, aerial attack range, and damage. This is balanced by his impressive jab speed, KO Punch, and one of the best counters in the game. Keep the fight on the ground, and use your KO Punches wisely.

Little Mac's KO Meter is filled up whenever he receives or deals damage. When his KO Meter is full, you will see a KO symbol by health percentage. Wait for the right opening, then hit your Neutral Special attack to unleash the KO Punch, which has huge damage and launching potential. In general, Straight Lunge is a good way to close distance and deal a lot of damage, but opponents can see it charging from a mile away. Luckily, it has super armor, but since Little Mac is lighter than average, you have to make sure not to take too much damage! Jolt Haymaker takes some getting used to, as it travels ridiculously far. Practice shortening its range to hit opponents by hitting the Special button again early. Also, use it from the ground to take advantage of its invincibility that the air variation doesn't have. Rising Uppercut is useful against opponents jumping in; it has some invincibility, but you are in a fall state afterward. When opponents are being predictable or using slow attacks, be sure to use the Slip Counter. It's one of the best counters in the game—it has a faster startup, a longer window of opportunity, and higher damage potential than even Marth's Counter!

For KOs, of course your best option is going to be Little Mac's KO Punch, if you have it available. Treat it like a Final Smash, and try to hit multiple opponents with it. Otherwise, Side Smash and its Up variation can be useful for KOs, as can Side Tilt. Little Mac's dash attack can be very surprising and useful for KOs as well, but it's usually safer to approach with your jab or Side Tilt. In the air, your best KO option is to Down Air and get a meteor smash. Little Mac's Back Air has the best range out of all of his aerials, but it's still relatively weak, so focus on your ground game. Don't forget to mix your opponents up by using Little Mac's throws as well. When edge-guarding, stay on stage and use his Down Tilt, Side Smash, charged Straight Lunge, and Slip Counter.

Recovery

Little Mac's best vertical recovery option is his Rising Uppercut. This recovery gains a lot of vertical height but accepts very little directional influence left or right. It also leaves you in a fall state if it doesn't connect with the stage. For horizontal recovery, Little Mac has Jolt Haymaker, which sends him soaring through the air to attack. You can shorten the range of this attack by hitting the Special button again earlier. If you miss the stage, though, this also leaves you in a fall state. When approaching the stage from high above, use Slip Counter to slow your fall and still recover with Rising Uppercut or Jolt Haymaker afterward. And don't forget to use your Wall Jump if the opportunity presents itself! In general, Little Mac's recovery is lacking, so it is best to position yourself far from edges whenever possible

LUCARIO

Trophy Description

A Fighting/Steel-type Pokémon that excels in combat through the reading and manipulation of Aura. As Lucario takes more damage, its attacks grow in strength. At maximum power, Lucario deals triple damage and its Aura Sphere is particularly devastating! Foes won't even know what hit them!

STATISTICS

MAXIMUM NUMBER OF JUMPS: **2**

CAN WALL JUMP: **Yes**

CAN WALL CLING: **Yes**

CAN CRAWL: **Yes**

Lucario's attack damage is affected by his aura level. At 190% and higher, Lucario's attacks are at maximum damage, though attack properties like knockback, size, and distance may still be affected beyond this value. Damage values included indicate the smallest and largest aura levels (Lucario at 0% and at 190% or higher).

NOTE

Alternate Colors

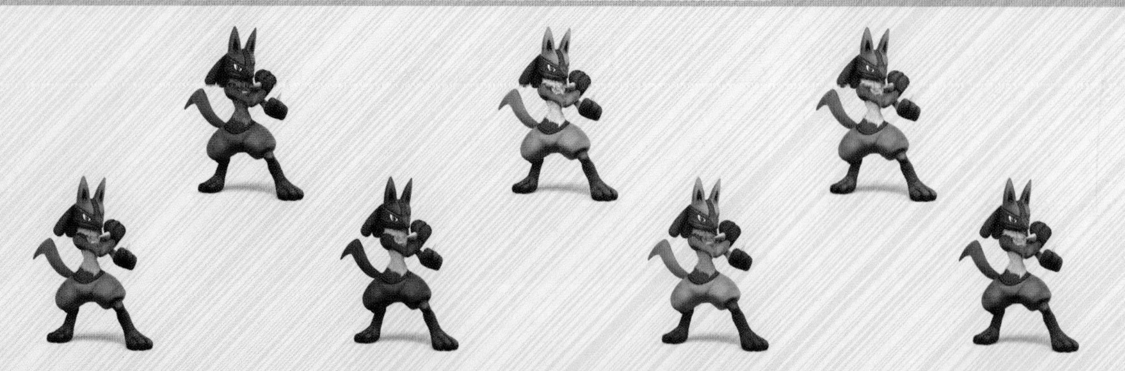

Smash Attacks

SIDE SMASH

AURA LEVELS	DAMAGE
Smallest	8.6~10.6%
Largest	22.1~27.2%

Lucario attacks directly in front of itself with an Aura blast.

DOWN SMASH

AURA LEVELS	DAMAGE
Smallest	9.2%
Largest	23.8%

Lucario strikes out with both hands, sending an Aura blast in each direction.

UP SMASH

AURA LEVELS	DAMAGE	MAX DAMAGE
Smallest	2.6~9.2%	11.9% : 2 Hits
Largest	6.8~23.8%	30.6% : 2 Hits

Lucario uses an Aura attack to lift your opponent directly in front of it.

Basic Attacks

STANDING ATTACK

AURA LEVELS	DAMAGE
Smallest	1.7%, 1.3%, 2%
Largest	4.3%, 3.4%, 5.1%

Lucario does a three-hit combo, ending with a kick that sends your opponent diagonally away.

UP TILT

AURA LEVELS	DAMAGE
Smallest	3.3~4%
Largest	8.5~10.5%

Lucario swings its leg in a roundhouse kick that lands on the ground in front of it. Pops your opponent up and can combo into itself at low percentages.

DASH ATTACK

AURA LEVELS	DAMAGE
Smallest	4~5.3%
Largest	10.2~13.6%

A running jump kick attack from Lucario.

SIDE TILT

AURA LEVELS	DAMAGE	MAX DAMAGE
Smallest	2.6~4%	6.6% : 2 Hits
Largest	6.8~10.2%	17% : 2 Hits

Lucario steps forward and punches with an Aura blast at the end of its hand. This can be aimed up or down.

DOWN TILT

AURA LEVELS	DAMAGE
Smallest	3.3%
Largest	8.5%

Lucario crouches and kicks out one leg to sweep the opponent, knocking that opponent away horizontally.

EDGE ATTACK

Lucario hops back onto the stage and blasts the opponent with Aura.

Air Attacks

NEUTRAL AIR ATTACK

AURA LEVELS	DAMAGE	MAX DAMAGE
Smallest	4~5.3%	9.2% : 2 Hits
Largest	10.2~13.6%	23.8% : 2 Hits

Lucario unleashes a spinning Aura attack in front of and behind itself that has surprisingly good range. This can hit multiple times.

DOWN AIR ATTACK

AURA LEVELS	DAMAGE	MAX DAMAGE
Smallest	3.3~4%	7.3% : 2 Hits
Largest	8.5~10.2%	18.7% : 2 Hits

Lucario kicks downward twice.

BACK AIR ATTACK

AURA LEVELS	DAMAGE
Smallest	9.9%
Largest	25.5%

Lucario turns midair and strikes backward with one arm.

UP AIR ATTACK

AURA LEVELS	DAMAGE
Smallest	4~7.3%
Largest	10.2~18.7%

Lucario gets vertical and kicks upward with one leg.

FORWARD AIR ATTACK

AURA LEVELS	DAMAGE
Smallest	4%
Largest	10.2%

This high kick attack sends opponents diagonally upward.

Special Attacks

AURA SPHERE (Neutral Special)

Charges a ball of energy that can cause damage even while it's charging. Store your charge by hitting Left or Right to use your evasive roll. Press the button again to launch it. Store your charge while airborne by air dodging. The higher your Aura, the more damage it deals and the bigger the charged energy ball gets.

AURA LEVELS	DAMAGE
Smallest	4.6~11.4% : While Charging 0.5%
Largest	11.7~29.3% : While Charging 1.2%

Snaring Aura Sphere

AURA LEVELS	DAMAGE
Smallest	1.7~9.6% : While Charging 0.3%
Largest	4.3~24.7% : While Charging 0.9%

This Aura Sphere is slow moving but draws opponents in. The longer you charge it, the slower it moves. Additionally, this Aura Sphere doesn't disappear once it hits an opponent.

Piercing Aura Sphere

AURA LEVELS	DAMAGE
Smallest	2~4.5% : While Charging 0.5%
Largest	5.1~11.5% : While Charging 1.3%

A faster, weaker Aura Sphere that pierces through opponents and continues traveling forward. It takes about half the time of the regular version to charge to full.

FORCE PALM (Side Special)

AURA LEVELS	DAMAGE	GRAB	GRAB ALOE
Smallest	5~7.8%	8.6%	6.6%
Largest	12.9~20.2%	22.1%	17%

This punch uses Lucario's Aura for its range and damage to knock your opponent back. If used up close, Lucario will grab the opponent before punching and knocking that opponent diagonally upward.

Advancing Force Palm

AURA LEVELS	DAMAGE	GRAB	GRAB ALOE
Smallest	4~6.6%	6.6%	4.6%
Largest	10.2~17%	17.9%	11.9%

Lucario dashes forward as he uses the Force Palm. Range is slightly shorter and does not get larger with higher Aura levels.

Long Distance Force Palm

AURA LEVELS	DAMAGE	GRAB	GRAB ALOE
Smallest	2.8~4.9%	8.6%	4~5.3%
Largest	7.2~12.6%	22.1%	10.2~13.6%

A longer range Force Palm that deals less damage.

EXTREME SPEED (Up Special)

AURA LEVELS	DAMAGE
Smallest	4%
Largest	10.2%

Lucario's Aura is used to blast Lucario through the air in the direction of your choosing. The higher your Aura, the farther you fly. You also have some control over Lucario's movement through the air. The move ends with a small kick attack upon landing. Lucario is in a fall state if this move ends while you are still in the air.

Ride the Wind DAMAGE 0%

Lucario soars through the air for a longer period of time. This doesn't deal any damage and Lucario travels through the air slower.

Extreme Speed Attack

AURA LEVELS	DAMAGE	MAX DAMAGE
Smallest	2.6~4.6%	7.3% : 2 Hits
Largest	6.8~11.9%	18.7% : 2 Hits

This variation hits and causes damage to any opponents in Lucario's path. It is slower to startup and Lucario doesn't travel as far compared to the regular version.

DOUBLE TEAM (Down Special)

AURA LEVELS	DAMAGE
Smallest	7.3%
Largest	18.7%

Lucario waves its hands around and prepares to counter your opponent's next strike. If successful, Lucario counters with a side kick. You can enter the opposite direction of the countered attack to change the direction of Lucario's attack. Lucario is invincible during its counterattack.

Glancing Counter

AURA LEVELS	DAMAGE
Smallest	6.6%
Largest	17%

In this variation, Lucario dodges briefly then strikes back with a strong punch. This occurs even if Lucario does not counter or dodge any incoming attack.

Stunning Double Team

AURA LEVELS	DAMAGE	MAX DAMAGE
Smallest	0.6%	1.9% : 3 Hits
Largest	1.7%	5.1% : 3 Hits

Instead of being hit by a counterattack, the opponent is paralyzed, and Lucario reappears for you to retaliate! The higher the opponent's accumulated damage, the longer that opponent is paralyzed.

COUNTER DATA	STARTUP	DURATION
Double Team	5th frame	35 frames
Stunning Double Team	5th frame	35 frames

Strategy

Lucario's defining aspect is its Aura mechanic. The more damage Lucario takes or the more behind in a match it is, the larger its Aura will be. When its Aura is larger, Lucario will deal more damage and some of its Special attacks are also affected in strength, size, or range. As Lucario is average weight with average ground speed and good air mobility, Aura requires a lot of risk and reward management. The risk comes from Lucario having to be close to KO'd or losing a match before becoming super effective! Your reward is easier come-from-behind victories because of Lucario's growing strength!

Aura Sphere is useful in multiple ways. First, use it completely uncharged to harass opponents. It's fairly fast and wobbles up and down a little when it's uncharged. When used in the air, it isn't affected by gravity, which is useful in zoning your opponents to limit their approach options. The move has a long recovery, so the uncharged version is best used in the air. As you charge it up, Aura Sphere can actually damage opponents around it or wear down their shield. It charges fairly fast, making it useful as an attack, and once it's fully charged, it does a lot more damage and knockback. The higher your Aura, the larger the sphere gets and the more damage it does. Force Palm also extends Lucario's range and does extra damage when used up close, as it becomes a grab. This grab can also damage other opponents around its impact area because Lucario hits the grabbed opponent with an Aura blast that sends that opponent flying up and away. With higher Aura, Force Palm's range and damage increases, but the grab range up close remains the same. Lucario's Extreme Speed sends it blasting through the air and can end with a kick attack at the end of its animation. The higher your Aura, the farther Lucario flies through the air! Double Team is a quick counter that stays active a good amount of time and can be useful against slower opponents.

Lucario's air mobility is good, given its solid jump height and aerial attacks, but it lacks a true meteor smash. Down Air works well, especially for edge-guarding, but you might want to use the generic foot stool as well. Neutral Air has good range, Up Air is useful for vertical KOs, and Back Air is a good choice when going for horizontal KOs. Forward Air and Up Air are your popular choices for combos. On the ground, Lucario's Smash attacks are all fairly slow, and you need to have Lucario's Aura up before those attacks have any KO power. Use Lucario's jab, Side Tilt, and Up Tilt if you're forced to fight up close at low percentage. Lucario's grab range is pretty good. Use Down Throw and follow up with air attacks to rack up damage. While higher Aura is important, don't let opponents damage you for free just to obtain a higher Aura level! Always deal damage, so when your Aura is higher, it's even easier to get a KO!

Final Smash

MEGA EVOLUTION

Lucario transforms into Mega Lucario. Mega Lucario has super armor so doesn't flinch from being hit but still takes damage. Taking damage reduces the time Lucario spends in this transformed state. In this form, Lucario's Aura will be at maximum level, regardless of Lucario's current damage. This means its Aura Sphere is larger and causes more damage. This also affects Lucario's Force Palm's range, damage, and knockback. Additionally, this give Lucario ridiculous recovery with Extreme Speed flying very far and very fast. Be careful with the Extreme Speed, though, because it can be a little hard to control.

Recovery

Lucario's main recovery option is its Extreme Speed. With this attack, you can send Lucario blasting off both horizontally or vertically, but it will be in a fall state afterward. Additionally, once Lucario takes off, you can control it through the air, almost in a full circle. The more damage Lucario has taken, however, the further Lucario flies with this recovery. For instance, when you have Lucario's Final Smash active, this is at max distance, and you can even blast yourself off the stage to self-destruct! When returning to a stage from high above, use his Double Team to slow Lucario's fall while trying to counter. Also remember that Lucario is one of the few characters with both a wall cling and a wall jump. Use these to time your return to the stage better, especially when things are hectic above!

LUCINA

Trophy Description

Chrom's daughter and the future Princess of Ylisse. When she arrives from a doomed future seeking to prevent it from ever happening, she goes by the name Marth before her identity is revealed. She fights much like her adopted namesake, but more than just the tip of her sword is powerful.

STATISTICS

MAXIMUM NUMBER OF JUMPS: **2**

CAN WALL JUMP: **No**

CAN WALL CLING: **No**

CAN CRAWL: **No**

Alternate Colors

Smash Attacks

SIDE SMASH DAMAGE 14.7%

Lucina swings her sword downward immediately in front of her.

DOWN SMASH DAMAGE 9.5~13.8%

Two sword sweep attacks, first in front of and then behind Lucina.

UP SMASH

DAMAGE 3~14.3% MAX DAMAGE 17.3% : 2 HITS

Lucina steps forward and thrusts her sword upward. This can hit grounded opponents in front of her as well as airborne opponents above her.

Basic Attacks

STANDING ATTACK

DAMAGE 4.8%, 4.8%

Lucina swings her sword upward in front of her up to two times.

UP TILT DAMAGE 6.7~7.1%

Lucina launches opponents vertically with an upward swing of her sword.

DASH ATTACK DAMAGE 10%

Lucina slides forward and attacks horizontally with her sword, knocking opponents away diagonally.

SIDE TILT DAMAGE 10%

Lucina uses a diagonal swing of her sword in front of her.

DOWN TILT DAMAGE 8.1%

Lucina crouches down and stabs her sword at your opponent's feet.

EDGE ATTACK

Lucina returns to the stage and quickly strikes toward your opponent's shins with her sword.

Air Attacks

NEUTRAL AIR ATTACK

DAMAGE 2.4~6.7% MAX DAMAGE 9% : 2 HITS

Lucina swings her sword twice horizontally. This can combo and is best utilized with her air mobility.

DOWN AIR ATTACK

DAMAGE 11.4~13.5%

Lucina swings her sword in an arc below her. This attack has a meteor effect.

BACK AIR ATTACK

DAMAGE 10%

Lucina swings her sword behind her as she spins to face the same direction.

UP AIR ATTACK DAMAGE 10%

Lucina does a backflip while swinging her sword upward. Opponents are launched vertically on contact.

FORWARD AIR ATTACK

DAMAGE 8.1%

Lucina swings her sword downward immediately in front of her.

Special Attacks

SHIELD BREAKER (Neutral Special)

DAMAGE 8.1% MAX CHARGE 21.9%

Lucina stabs her sword forward to pierce and break through shields. This attack can be charged to do more damage.

Storm Thrust

DAMAGE 0~3.8% MAX CHARGE 0~10.4%

As Lucina thrusts her sword forward, she creates a gust of wind that knocks opponents back. The longer the charge, the faster the wind. This version of the attack deals less damage and doesn't work well to break shields.

Dashing Assault

DAMAGE 2.8~5.7% MAX CHARGE 8.6~15.2%

In this variation, Lucina dashes forward as she thrusts her sword. For increased range, Lucina sacrifices a bit of damage. This attack is strongest at the beginning of the dash and takes a bit longer to fully charge. The longer you charge it, the farther she will dash, but the speed is the same. This version has less potential to break shields than the regular version does.

DANCING BLADE (Side Special)

LOW COMBO 3.3%, 3.3%, 3.3%, 2~4.8% MAX DAMAGE 12.8% : 5 HITS

MEDIUM COMBO 3.3%, 3.3%, 4.3%, 5.7%

HIGH COMBO 3.3%, 3.3%, 4.3%, 6.7%

This is a four-hit sword string. Keep hitting the button to continue the string. You can hit Up or Down to vary the hit range on individual hits of the string. Hits 2, 3, or 4 can be modified with Up, and hits 3 or 4 can be modified with Down.

Effortless Blade

DAMAGE 2.4%, 2.4%, 2.4%, 4.3%

There are no Up or Down variations within this attack string. The first hit is a bit slower to startup, and you have more time to input the next attack between hits. The damage for each hit is less in this version.

Heavy Blade

LOW COMBO 7.6%, 9.5%, 10.4%, 2.1~11.4%

MAX DAMAGE 19.8% : 5 HITS

MEDIUM COMBO 7.6%, 9.5%,10.4%, 13.3%

HIGH COMBO 7.6%, 9.5%, 10.4%, 14.3%

In this sword combo, each strike is stronger but launches the opponent. This makes it harder to land all of the hits, even though the range on each hit is slightly increased. Each additional strike is slower than it usually is.

DOLPHIN SLASH (Up Special) DAMAGE 6~11%

Lucina swings her sword upward as she rises through the air. This can be angled slightly to the left or right during the input of the attack but not after. So, to rise to the left, enter the attack as Up + Left with the Special button. This attack does more damage at the beginning of its animation.

Crescent Slash DAMAGE 6~12%

Lucina rises in an arc as she strikes. The most damaging part of this attack is around the midpoint of the arc. As a recovery tool, this doesn't travel as high up, but you can move more horizontally on your way back down. This version has a lot of recovery upon landing.

Dolphin Jump DAMAGE 0%

There is no attack in this version, but Lucina jumps higher than usual! Similar to Crescent Slash, this version has a lot of recovery upon landing.

COUNTER (Down Special)

DAMAGE SEE *COUNTER DATA TABLE*

Lucina readies her sword to counter an incoming attack. The strength of the counter depends on the attack being countered. Lucina can counter while her back is to the opponent!

Easy Counter

DAMAGE SEE *COUNTER DATA TABLE*

The window to counter attacks is larger, but\ the attack power is lower than usual.

Iai Counter

DAMAGE SEE *COUNTER DATA TABLE*

After a successful counter, the opponent is knocked behind you. The minimum counter does less damage; however, when countering more damaging attacks, it deals more damage. The counter window is smaller than the regular version as well.

COUNTER DATA

	STARTUP	DURATION	DAMAGE SCALING	MIN DAMAGE	MAX DAMAGE
COUNTER	6th frame	22 frames	1.2x	8%	50%
EASY COUNTER	6th frame	29 frames	0.7x	4%	50%
IAI COUNTER	3rd frame	14 frames	1.3x	6%	50%

Final Smash

CRITICAL HIT

Lucina dashes incredibly far across the screen to deliver a critical blow to the first opponent she runs into. Any enemies caught nearby will also be hit. This move has enough knockback to take out the heaviest opponents, even at 0%! You can cancel this attack by hitting any attack button. This can be useful to stop yourself from flying too far off-stage and save you from a self-destruct.

Strategy

Lucina is a lightweight sword fighter who relies on up-close combat to be most effective. Sharing the same moveset as Marth, Lucina's play style is very similar. The one factor truly separating them, however, is that Lucina does not rely on hitting with the tip of her sword to maximize damage output. Across the board, her attacks deal *less* damage than Marth's tip versions but deal *more* damage than Marth's non-tip versions. Essentially, this means Marth has more potential but requires much more precision. While this means Lucina should theoretically have an easier time—as KOing heavier characters may be an issue—she may have to battle longer to get the KOs, so this isn't clearly an advantage. If you're interested in learning Marth, though, Lucina is a good way to start.

Similar to Marth, Lucina has to use her mobility and range to get in on opponents. Against projectile-heavy characters, focus on shielding, dodging, and rolling to make your way in. Use short hop with Forward Air and Neutral Air to pressure opponents. Additionally, poke them with Side Tilt and Down Tilt. When they are pressured by your offense and you notice them shielding a lot, this is your time to throw! Shield Breaker can deal significant amounts of damage when fully charged, and as its name implies, it can even completely break weaker shields in a single full charge! If you break a shield, either fully charge another Shield Breaker as an attack or follow up with a charged Side Smash that will hit at the tip. Dancing Blade is a multi-hit attack you can use to keep your opponents on their toes or to choose how you want to launch an opponent. Ending with Forward sends opponents horizontally while ending with Up can get you a KO at high percentages. More important, because Dancing Blade counts as multiple hits, it's a good way to refresh your stronger KO options! Dolphin Slash is extremely fast and high for an attack, but it leaves you in a fall state. You have some invincibility at the start of this move, though, so it's particularly useful to beat out incoming attacks. This is much better used in a one-on-one situation where landing the attack won't leave you vulnerable to other opponents during your fall state. As for Counter, Lucina shares Marth's fast counter startup speed and increased damage return.

When using Smash attacks for KOs, Up Smash and Side Smash are your best bets. Up Smash is Lucina's one attack that actually does more damage than Marth's version when both hits connect. From the air, finish with Forward Air and Neutral Air for KOs or Down Air for meteor smashes. KOing heavier characters may be difficult, so maximize your edge-guarding potential. Try to meet opponents off-stage with Neutral Air or Forward Air, and Counter if they attack their way back to the stage. Since you don't have to use the tip, Down Tilt at the edge can also be very annoying for opponents returning to the stage. For projectile characters focus on shielding, dodging, and rolling to make your way in.

Recovery

Lucina's recovery tools are fairly straightforward. Her primary recovery tool is Dolphin Slash. This reaches extremely high, but you have to aim it accurately to reach the edge, plus it leaves you in a fall state. For horizontal recovery, Lucina really doesn't have a good fast option, though uncharged Shield Breakers do move her slightly forward. A fully charged Shield Breaker in the air launches you horizontally, though it takes a while to charge up. If knocked away very high, follow up a fully charged Shield Breaker with Dolphin Slash for best results! Finally, to stall in the air a little, use the first hit of Dancing Blade.

LUIGI

Trophy Description

Luigi recently celebrated his 30th anniversary with the Year of Luigi, but all that attention just made him even more shy and awkward. In *Smash Bros.* (as in life), Luigi tends to follow his brother's lead. but he adds his own flair to moves like Super Jump Punch. His taunts, however, are 100% Weegee.

STATISTICS

MAXIMUM NUMBER OF JUMPS: **2**

CAN WALL JUMP: **No**

CAN WALL CLING: **No**

CAN CRAWL: **Yes**

Alternate Colors

Smash Attacks

SIDE SMASH DAMAGE 14%

Luigi takes a step forward and delivers a swift strike with his fingers, but the range on this is quite limited. You can aim this slightly up or down.

DOWN SMASH DAMAGE 14~15%

Luigi performs a double-legged sweep attack that pops your opponent up off the ground.

UP SMASH DAMAGE 12~14%

Luigi swings his body forward as he delivers a massive headbutt. His head is invincible during the attack.

Basic Attacks

STANDING ATTACK

DAMAGE 3%, 2%, 5%

Luigi's standing jab leads into a three-hit string that does a total of 10 damage and pops your opponent up into the air and away.

UP TILT DAMAGE 6%

Luigi clubs his opponent with an overhead downward strike. Not much damage but fast recovery.

DASH ATTACK

DAMAGE 1~2% MAX DAMAGE 8% : 7 HITS

Luigi delivers a flurry of punches while running forward! The last hit will launch opponents forward.

SIDE TILT DAMAGE 8%

Luigi kicks forward. This can be aimed slightly upward or downward, but all variations deliver the same damage.

DOWN TILT DAMAGE 8%

Luigi crouches and kicks out a low attack directly in front of him, popping your opponent up into the air.

EDGE ATTACK

Luigi pulls himself up from the edge while simultaneously performing a double-legged sweep.

Air Attacks

NEUTRAL AIR ATTACK

DAMAGE 6~12%

Luigi's standard jump kick attack lasts for a long while, making it fairly useful. Use it early in your jump arc.

DOWN AIR ATTACK

DAMAGE 8~10%

A drillkick attack best used when approaching opponents from above. You can meteor smash opponents by hitting them right on top of their head.

BACK AIR ATTACK DAMAGE 8~14%

This reverse dropkick is great, as it has great range and keeps the rest of Luigi's body away from your opponent. It is also one of Luigi's best attacks for knockouts.

UP AIR ATTACK DAMAGE 7~11%

This flipkick is best used against opponents above Luigi and deals solid damage.

FORWARD AIR ATTACK

DAMAGE 9%

Another overhead punch attack, this time from the air. Use this with fast fall against grounded opponents.

Special Attacks

FIREBALL (Neutral Special)

DAMAGE 6%

Luigi hurls his Fireball straight ahead. The fireball rotates through the air and bounces off walls. It differs from Mario's fireball in that it's not affected by gravity.

Bouncing Fireball DAMAGE 4~6%

This fireball travels farther than normal and also bounces. After it's fired, its damage steadily drops. There is also a larger recovery period after using this.

Iceball DAMAGE 6%

Instead of fire, this is an iceball that moves slower but can freeze opponents. The opponent's damage must be 40~45% or higher to be able to freeze them.

GREEN MISSILE (Side Special)

DAMAGE 6.2~21% MAX DAMAGE 25%

Luigi charges up before blasting himself headfirst toward your opponent. The longer his Green Missile is charged, the farther Luigi is launched. If Green Missile is charged for too long, however, Luigi gets tired and needs some time before he is able to use this attack again. Additionally, there is a 1 in 8 chance this move will blast extra far (and deliver extra damage). But if Luigi uses it with a wall nearby, he might get his head stuck in that wall, so use with caution!

Floating Missile

DAMAGE 4.3~18% MAX DAMAGE 23%

This variation flies straight forward and charges to full power in about half the time. The damage and flying speed of the attack are reduced.

Quick Missile

DAMAGE 5.1~20% MAX DAMAGE 20%

Here Luigi will fly farther and faster than in the normal version. If the attack misses, you also end up in a slide. It takes longer to fully charge, has a lower chance of randomly exploding, and a higher chance of getting stuck in walls.

SUPER JUMP PUNCH (Up Special)

ON LAND 1~25% IN AIR 1~20%

Luigi's Super Jump Punch is similar to Mario's except when it comes to damage—it does the most damage at the very beginning, so he needs to be extremely close to your opponent for Super Jump Punch to deal a lot of damage. If he's farther away, it will deal only 1 point of damage! It has some invincibility, and you can control a bit to the left or right.

Fiery Jump Punch

ON LAND 1~18% IN AIR 1~15%

With this version, it's easier to get a clean hit for maximum damage; however, the attack and jump are slightly weaker. It has slightly more invincibility than the regular version, and you can control it left or right more than the default version. Additionally, there is a lot of recovery after landing.

Burial Header

DAMAGE 1~8% MAX DAMAGE 17% : 3 HITS

This headbutt smacks and buries your opponents into the ground on the way back down from the punch. While ascending, though, you can't get a clean hit with the initial punch. This move jumps higher than the regular version and it has decent recovery. Using this on an edge, Luigi is still able to grab onto the edge during his descent.

LUIGI CYCLONE (Down Special)

DAMAGE 1.5~3% MAX DAMAGE 9% : 5 HITS

With both arms outstretched, Luigi spins around. You can control Luigi horizontally during his animation. Tapping the Special button repeatedly causes Luigi to rise vertically during this attack.

Mash Cyclone DAMAGE 0~6%

Luigi spins fast to create a cyclone that blows opponents away. He rises higher but is not able to move as much from side to side. The attack is only after he is done spinning and when he holds his fists out.

Clothesline Cyclone

DAMAGE 8% MAX DAMAGE 16% : 2 HITS

This much more damaging customization launches everyone it hits while Luigi spins. The speed is slower, but the launching power is strong. It doesn't rise much vertically, and there is a lot of recovery after spinning.

Final Smash

POLTERGUST 5000

—Luigi whips out his Poltgergust 5000 vaccuum and begins sucking up nearby opponents. Anyone sucked into the vaccuum takes damage the entire time they are trapped within, so the earlier you get someone in, the better! After Luigi is done sucking opponents in, he blows them out for additional damage.

Strategy

Luigi has good mobility, good Air attacks, good Tilt attacks, and great recovery options. Because Luigi is an average weight character, all of this definitely comes in handy. Use his mobility to avoid larger, stronger characters while simultaneously using his Fireballs to tack on damage whenever possible. Also note that Luigi slides after dashing—you can use this slide to quickly turn around and Side Tilt in the opposite direction while sliding away, to keep your opponents at bay. You can also slide and charge up his SIDE and UP SMASH attacks. The SIDE SMASH must be done in the opposite direction that Luigi is sliding. Luigi's Air attacks are each named to fit their actions appropriately. So, although it may seem obvious, when you are airborne, it's important to use his Back Air attack against opponents behind you, his Down Air attack against opponents below you, and his Up Air attack for opponents in front of you. If he's surrounded, go for the Luigi Cyclone instead.

When playing Luigi, you always have to weigh the risks and rewards of using Green Missile and Super Jump Punch. While Green Missile is an effective long-range attack, if you catch it on a bad charge, Luigi may overshoot his target and fly off the stage or collide with a wall. If you try to use his Super Jump Punch to KO an opponent, you have to be sure you're close enough for the attack to deal its full damage or you will only deal 1 point of damage before leaving yourself completely vulnerable. So, set up your opponent with one or two jab attacks to get in range, letting you deal the full damage of Super Jump Punch! Out of shield, your best bet is to go with an UP SMASH attack.

Luigi is one of the only characters in the game who has taunts that do damage. For style, use Luigi's down taunt on an opponent holding onto the edge to send that opponent meteoring to his or her doom!

Recovery

The three main choices Luigi has for recovery are Green Missile, Super Jump Punch, and Luigi Cyclone. Green Missile is best for a horizontal recovery, as the longer you charge it, the more Luigi can recover. If spaced and timed correctly, when Luigi glides over a small platform with Green Missile, he can actually land normally and avoid his recovery. You must land on the platform, but have enough momentum that Luigi slides off the platform. So, on stages like Battlefield, try recovering to one of the upper platforms. Super Jump Punch is great for a vertical recovery, especially if you are concerned about an opponent attacking you on your way up. And finally, because Luigi Cyclone can lift Luigi vertically and allows you to control him horizontally, it's one of his best tools to recover without being predictable. You can even use Luigi Cyclone multiple times in a row to bait your opponent into attacking prematurely.

MARIO

Trophy Description

As iconic as iconic gets, this gaming celebrity is known for saving the world from Bowser. He's got amazing jumping skills and makes use of a wide range of transformations. In his free time, he plays too many sports to count. In *Smash Bros.*, he's a well-rounded fighter you can rely on. Say it with me: "It's-a me, Mario!"

STATISTICS

MAXIMUM NUMBER OF JUMPS: **2**

CAN WALL JUMP: **Yes**

CAN WALL CLING: **No**

CAN CRAWL: **No**

Alternate Colors

Smash Attacks

SIDE SMASH DAMAGE 14~17%

Mario unleashes an explosive blast immediately in front or behind him. You can guide this slightly up or down.

DOWN SMASH DAMAGE 10~12%

Mario swings both legs around in a double-leg sweep attack that sends your opponent to the side. This can be useful when your opponent is trying to grab onto the edge or when you want to catch opponents rolling behind you.

UP SMASH DAMAGE 14%

This overhead smash is best used to catch opponents falling directly above you. Mario's head is invulnerable during this attack, making it the perfect choice to use against airborne opponents. On a hit, this sends your opponent upward.

Basic Attacks

STANDING ATTACK
DAMAGE 2.5%, 1.5%, 4%

Mario's standard attack can be used repeatedly and goes into a three-hit attack string. The third hit pops your opponent up.

UP TILT **DAMAGE 6.3%**

This jumping spinning uppercut does decent damage and knocks your opponent into the air, allowing for further follow-ups! Use this when your opponent is jumping at you or if your opponent is on a ledge above you.

DASH ATTACK **DAMAGE 6~8%**

During Mario's running animation, this attack does a running slide. This move has a lot of recovery, however, so try to use it only in situations where it is guaranteed to succeed.

SIDE TILT **DAMAGE 7%**

Mario kicks forward. You can guide this slightly upward or downward. Try to connect using this after knocking your opponent into the air!

DOWN TILT **DAMAGE 5~7%**

Here Mario performs a sweep attack with decent range. This also pops the opponent up into the air.

EDGE ATTACK

Mario swings himself back up to the ledge with his arms and kicks at your opponent's feet. Use the invincibility from your first edge grab to make this move more effective.

Air Attacks

NEUTRAL AIR ATTACK
DAMAGE 5~8%

Mario performs a jump kick attack. This is especially useful out of a short hop rather than a full jump.

UP AIR ATTACK **DAMAGE 7%**

Mario performs a flip kick. Be sure to use this only when you are facing your opponent!

DOWN AIR ATTACK **DAMAGE 1~5%**
MAX DAMAGE 12% : 7 HITS

Mario stretches out both arms and performs a multi-hitting spinning attack. This move follows Mario's jump momentum, so it works well in both the rise and the fall of his jump arc. You can also move Mario horizontally while he is performing this attack. Note this attack can hit a maximum of seven times and passes through some projectiles.

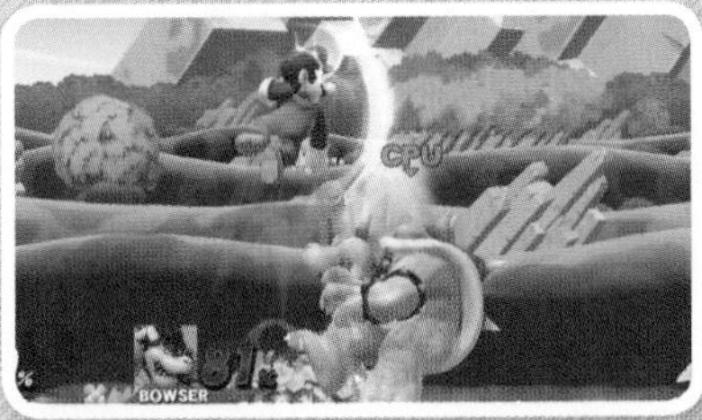

FORWARD AIR ATTACK
DAMAGE 10-14%

This overhead punch knocks opponents downward on impact. This can be very useful when used on airborne opponents trying to get back to the stage as it gives a meteor effect.

BACK AIR ATTACK **DAMAGE 7-10.5%**

This reverse dropkick can be very useful to keep opponents away. It also recovers very quickly, allowing you to string together multiple Back Air attacks from a short hop before landing. It is also very safe, making this one of Mario's best aerial attacks.

Special Attacks

FIREBALL (Neutral Special)

DAMAGE 4–5%

This is Mario's primary projectile attack. It deals 5 damage per hit and bounces twice before fizzling out. Note that each Fireball is affected by gravity and requires a floor to bounce.

Fast Fireball DAMAGE 1.5~3%

This variation shoots fireballs forward very quickly. They deal less damage and have less range, but they make up for this in speed. As with the regular Fireball, the damage decreases after being fired.

Fire Orb

DAMAGE 1.5% MAX DAMAGE 13.5 : 9 HITS

These large fireballs move slowly and have less range, but they hit multiple times, leaving oppponents open for follow up. Note the fire does not disappear on contact with an enemy, and it does not cancel out enemy projectiles.

SUPER JUMP PUNCH (Up Special)

DAMAGE 1~5% MAX DAMAGE 12% : 6 HITS

This jumping uppercut is Mario's main recovery move to get back to the ledge when he's below the stage. It is also a multi-hitting attack that knocks coins out of your opponent, so the earlier it strikes the opponent, the more damage it inflicts.

Super Jump

This variation removes the attack but gives you more range and control over your recovery. It is a little slower and does not have invincibility on startup, but you can move left or right a lot easier.

Explosive Punch

DAMAGE 8~13% MAX DAMAGE 21% : 2 HITS

A jumping punch attack that launches opponents with a fiery fist on startup. At the peak of the jump is an explosion that also deals damage. Moving left or right during ascent does not change course at all. There is no invincibility on startup.

CAPE (Side Special) DAMAGE 7%

Mario swings his cape to attack your opponent and spin that opponent around! With proper timing, this attack can also be used to reflect projectiles. Additionally, you can use this attack to slightly stall while airborne and throw off your opponent's timing.

Shocking Cape DAMAGE 11,2%

Mario strikes opponents with an electrified cape. While dealing the most damage out of Mario's Cape variations, it loses a lot of the standard Cape's versatility. It does not reflect projectiles, does not stall when used midair, and does not turn opponents around on hit.

Gust Cape DAMAGE 0-5%

This Cape variation creates a gust of wind with Mario's swing of the cape. The closer the opponent is, the stronger that opponent is pushed away. This also deals a bit of damage but does not allow you to stall when used midair. As a reflect tool, it starts up a little slower than the standard Cape but has a bigger window to reflect projectiles.

CAPE DATA

	REFLECT STARTUP	DURATION	DAMAGE SCALING	SPEED SCALING
CAPE	6th frame	15 frames	1.5x	1x
GUST CAPE	8th frame	22 frames	1.5x	1x

F.L.U.D.D. (Down Special)

DAMAGE 0%

The Flash Liquidizer Ultra Dousing Device (better known as F.L.U.D.D.)! This move inflicts no damage, but it can be used to push your opponents away or off the stage. Press once to begin charging up the F.L.U.D.D.—the longer you charge it up, the farther it shoots! Because you are vulnerable while charging the F.L.U.D.D., you have to be decide carefully when to charge it. Additionally, you can hit Left or Right to roll out of charging; you can hit Block to cancel charging as well. To unleash the F.L.U.D.D., hit the Special button again while charging!

Scalding F.L.U.D.D.

DAMAGE 1.2% MAX DAMAGE 9,6% : 8 HITS

Though it does not spray as far, this variation damages the opponent! It does not push back opponents and charges up to maximum about 40% faster. Note charging up the attack does not increase the damage, and the spray does not push back Mario.

High-Pressure F.L.U.D.D. DAMAGE 0%

A much higher- powered version of the F.L.U.D.D., this version really sends opponents reeling. The tank is much larger, though, so it takes about 60% longer to fill it up. While spraying opponents, Mario is also pushed back farther than usual.

While the F.L.U.D.D. is firing, you can aim it up and down—this can be very useful when fighting multiple opponents! Additionally, F.L.U.D.D. can also cancel out a variety of projectiles if you don't want to risk trying to time your Cape attack!

NOTE

Final Smash

MARIO FINALE

Mario releases a flurry of fireballs horizontally at everyone in his path. Because the vertical range on this is limited, however, you want to line up directly beside your opponent(s) for the best results. The closer you are horizontally, the more hits you'll be able to land as well. The best time to use this is when you can catch an opponent already off stage—the farther to the side, the better!

Strategy

Mario is a mix of a gunner and a brawler—he has some decent projectiles as well as some fair up-close fighting abilities. His toolset allows him to be most effective with a defensive play style, but that requires a lot of patience. Use his Fireball attacks to add damage from a distance to your opponent. If you use it during the descent of your jump, you can dash to follow the Fireball. If your opponent blocks the Fireball, you can mix that opponent up with a grab or any other attacks. Be sure to charge up your F.L.U.D.D. whenever you can so it will be completely ready when you need it. This is particularly useful in free-for-all battles where you can push multiple opponents with it.

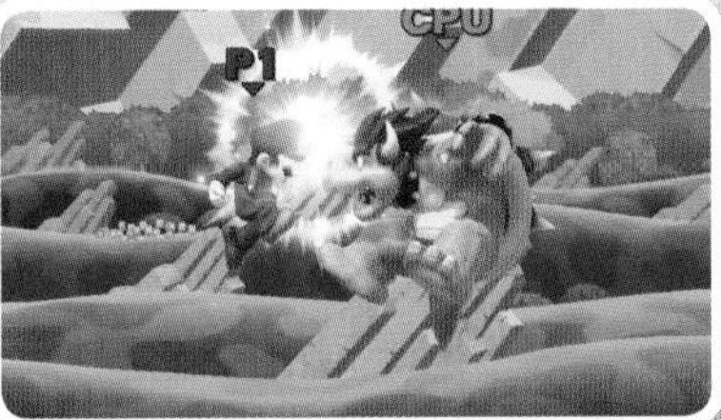

Mario's main weaknesses are that his attacks don't have a lot of range and that he is an average-weight character, so once he racks up damage, his knockback increases quickly. So, if you have an opponent using a lot of projectiles against you, be sure to use Mario's Cape to reflect them. The Cape is also good for doing damage, for turning your opponent around, and for helping with Mario's ranged weakness, as it counters longer-ranged attacks. Additionally, his Cape can be especially useful for edge guarding. So, yes, definitely use the Cape! Fireball is also a great tool when edge guarding and can open up more opportunities for the Cape.

When opponents are above you, use your Up Tilt attack or UP SMASH attack for its invincibility. In general, you want to stay away from Mario's Super Jump Punch here because of its bad recovery, but this attack does have invincibility on start-up as well and deals solid damage. Still, try to save your Super Jump Punch to punish out of shield instead. When approaching enemies air to air, use Mario's Down Air or Back Air attacks. Down Air is also useful for shield pressure, especially if your opponents are shielding a lot of your Fireballs. Mario's Forward Air is a meteor attack, so use this to spike your opponents when they are no longer over the stage. And when approaching enemies on the ground, stick to Mario's short hop neutral attack with fast fall and mix your opponent up with a grab or another short hop neutral attack! Finally, with fresh opponents, throwing an opponent downward can often combo into multiple Up Tilt attacks followed by Up Airs and Super Jump Punch!

Recovery

When it comes to recovering from being off the stage, Mario has very few options. His main attack is going to be his Super Jump Punch, which launches him upward. Aiming slightly to the left or right with the Super Jump Punch sends Mario in that direction, so be sure to aim accurately for the edge. Additionally, Mario can use his Cape attack to slow down his fall and move him forward a little. Use this so you aren't predictable about when you are coming back to the ledge. Mario's Down Air attack can also be used to gain some horizontal recovery.

Lastly, remember to use his Fireball attack to keep opponents occupied while you return from high above the stage.

MARTH

Trophy Description

Marth, the prince of Altea, is the hero of the first ever *Fire Emblem* game and its remake, Fire Emblem: Shadow Dragon. In this game, his graceful sword skills are what set him apart. Strike with the tip of his blade to deal extra damage, and use his Counter skill to defend yourself, no matter which direction you're being attacked from.

STATISTICS

MAXIMUM NUMBER OF JUMPS: **2**

CAN WALL JUMP: **No**

CAN WALL CLING: **No**

CAN CRAWL: **No**

Alternate Colors

Smash Attacks

SIDE SMASH DAMAGE 13~18%

Marth swings his sword over his head and down in front of him, sending opponents diagonally away. Hitting with the tip of the sword deals 18% damage.

DOWN SMASH DAMAGE 8~17%

A low sword attack first in front of and then behind Marth. Hitting with the tip of the sword deals 17% damage and sends opponents diagonally away.

UP SMASH

DAMAGE 3~17% MAX DAMAGE 16% : 2 HITS

Marth thrusts his sword upward. Hitting with the tip of the sword deals 17% damage in a single hit and launches opponents vertically.

Basic Attacks

STANDING ATTACK
DAMAGE 4~6%, 4~6%

Marth can slash up to two times with his sword.

UP TILT DAMAGE 5~9%

Marth uses a backhand upward sword swing that pops opponents up.

DASH ATTACK DAMAGE 9~12%

Marth slides and swipes his sword horizontally at anyone in front of him.

SIDE TILT DAMAGE 9~12%

Marth swings his sword diagonally in front of him.

DOWN TILT DAMAGE 7~10%

A crouching low sword stab.

EDGE ATTACK

Marth returns to the stage and attacks at your opponent's shins with his sword.

Air Attacks

NEUTRAL AIR ATTACK
DAMAGE 2~8% MAX DAMAGE 11% : 2 HITS

Two horizontal sword slashes that can combo. Works well when advancing or retreating in the air.

DOWN AIR ATTACK DAMAGE 11~14%

Marth swings his sword in an arc below him. This attack also has a meteor effect.

BACK AIR ATTACK DAMAGE 9~12%

Marth turns around in the air and swings his sword in an upward arc in front of him.

UP AIR ATTACK DAMAGE 9~12%

Marth does a backflip as he swings his sword upward.

FORWARD AIR ATTACK
DAMAGE 7~10%

A downward strike of the sword directly in front of Marth. Hitting early against a grounded opponent can bounce that opponent off the ground!

Special Attacks

SHIELD BREAKER (Neutral Special)

DAMAGE 8~9% MAX CHARGE 22~24%

Marth thrusts forward with his sword to stab his opponent. You can charge this up to do a lot more damage! If it's charged up, you can break some shields in a single hit! Using this while Marth is airborne moves Marth forward slightly.

Storm Thrust

DAMAGE 0~4% MAX CHARGE 0~11%

As Marth thrusts his sword forward, he creates a gust of wind that knocks opponents back. The longer the charge, the faster the wind. This version of the attack deals less damage and doesn't work well to break shields.

Dashing Assault

DAMAGE 3~6% MAX CHARGE 9~16%

In this variation, Marth dashes forward as he thrusts his sword. For increased range, Marth sacrifices a bit of damage. This attack is strongest at the beginning of the dash and takes a bit longer to fully charge. The longer you charge it, the farther he will dash, but the speed is the same. Note that this version has less potential to break shields than the regular version.

DOLPHIN SLASH (Up Special)

DAMAGE 6~11%

This upward strike is primarily in front of Marth. It's his main recovery tool and deals the most damage when the attack begins.

Crescent Slash DAMAGE 6~12%

Marth rises in the path of an arc as he strikes. The most damaging part of the attack is around the midpoint of the arc. As a recovery tool, this doesn't travel as high up, but you can move more horizontally on your way back down. This version has a lot of recovery upon landing.

Dolphin Jump DAMAGE 0%

There is no attack in this version, but Marth jumps higher than usual! Similar to Crescent Slash, this version has a lot of recovery upon landing.

COUNTER (Down Special)

DAMAGE *SEE COUNTER DATA TABLE*

Marth lifts his sword to counter his opponent's attacks. The amount of damage returned in the counterstrike depends on the strength of the strike being countered. Countering a Smash attack can KO an opponent.

Easy Counter

DAMAGE *SEE COUNTER DATA TABLE*

The window to counter attacks is larger; however, the attack power is lower than usual.

Iai Counter

DAMAGE *SEE COUNTER DATA TABLE*

After a successful counter, the opponent is knocked behind you. The minimum counter does less damage, but when countering more damaging attacks, it deals more damage. The counter window is smaller than the default version as well.

COUNTER DATA

	COUNTER START	DURATION	DAMAGE SCALING	MIN DAMAGE	MAX DAMAGE
COUNTER	6th frame	22 frames	1.2x	8%	50%
EASY COUNTER	6th frame	29 frames	0.7x	4%	50%
IAI COUNTER	3rd frame	14 frames	1.3x	6%	50%

DANCING BLADE (Side Special)

LOW COMBO 3~4%, 3~4%, 3~4%, 2~6%

MAX DAMAGE 14% : 5 HITS

MEDIUM COMBO 3~4%, 3~4%, 4~5%, 5~7%

HIGH COMBO 3~4%, 3~4%, 4~5%, 6~8%

Marth performs a multi-hit sword combo as you repeatedly hit the Special button. Pressing Up or Down will also change the attacks you see from this combo. Red indicates medium, blue indicates high, and green indicates low. Blue knocks up higher and red knocks back farther. The second hit can only be high or medium while the third and fourth hits can also be low. Use the first hit in the air as a stall tactic.

Effortless Blade

DAMAGE 2~3%, 2~3%, 2~3%, 4~5%

There are no Up or Down variations in this attack string. The first hit is a bit slower to startup, and you have more time to input the next attack between each hit. The damage for each hit is less in this version.

Heavy Blade

LOW COMBO 7~9%, 9~11%, 10~12%, 2.2~13%

MAX DAMAGE 21.8% : 5 HITS

MEDIUM COMBO 7~9%, 9~11%, 10~12%, 14~16%

HIGH COMBO 7~9%, 9~11%, 10~12%, 13~15%

In this sword combo, each strike is stronger but launches the opponent. This makes it harder to land all of the hits, even though the range on each hit is slightly increased. Note that each additional strike is slower than it usually is.

Final Smash

CRITICAL HIT

Marth dashes incredibly far across the screen to deliver a critical blow to the first opponent he runs into. Any enemies caught nearby will also be hit. This move has enough knockback to take out the heaviest opponents, even at 0%! You can cancel this attack by hitting any attack button. This can be useful to stop yourself from flying too far off-stage and save you from a self-destruct.

Strategy

Marth is a lightweight swordsman who must get in on his opponent and force an up-close fight. He has above-average ground speed and decent mobility in the air. Thanks to the range of his sword, up-close fighting is usually in his favor. The biggest challenge in using Marth is learning to hit with just the tip of his sword to maximize damage and knockback potential. All of his attacks are improved by hitting with the tip! Use short hop Forward and Neutral Air to pressure opponents and poke with Side Tilt and Down Tilt. When opponents are pressured by your offense and are trying to shield a lot, this is the time to use throws. Against projectile-heavy characters, focus on shielding, dodging, and rolling to make your way in.

Marth's Shield Breaker can deal significant amounts of damage if fully charged, and as its name implies, it can even completely break weaker shields in a single hit! If you happen to break a shield, either fully charge another Shield Breaker as an attack or follow up with a charged Side Smash that will hit at the tip. Dancing Blade is a multi-hit attack you can use to keep your opponents on their toes or to choose how you want to launch an opponent. Ending with Forward sends opponents horizontally while ending with Up can get you a KO at high percentages. More important, because Dancing Blade counts as multiple hits, it's a good way to refresh your stronger KO options! Dolphin Slash is extremely fast and high for an attack, but it leaves you in a fall state. You have some invincibility at the start of this move, though, so it's particularly useful to beat out incoming attacks. This is much better used in a one-on-one situation where landing the attack won't leave you vulnerable to other opponents during your fall state. Marth's Counter starts up quickly and returns more damage than it originally received, so look to counter larger, slower attacks!

When using Marth's Smash attacks for KOs, Side Smash is your best bet, as it does the most damage even without hitting the tip. From the air, finish with Forward Air and Neutral Air for KOs or Down Air for meteor smashes. KOing heavier characters may be difficult, so maximize your edge-guarding potential. Try to meet opponents off-stage with Neutral Air or Forward Air and Counter if they attack their way back to the stage. Using Down Tilt at the edge can also be very annoying for opponents returning to the stage.

Recovery

Marth's recovery tools are fairly straightforward. His primary recovery tool is Dolphin Slash. This reaches extremely high, but you have to aim it accurately to reach the edge, plus it leaves you in a fall state. For horizontal recovery, Marth really doesn't have a good fast option, though uncharged Shield Breakers do move him slightly forward. Charging the Shield Breaker is best used immediately after using your second jump for the extra height and momentum. A fully charged Shield Breaker in the air launches you horizontally, though it takes a while to charge up. If knocked away very high, follow up a fully charged Shield Breaker with Dolphin Slash for best results! Finally, to stall in the air a little, use the first hit of Dancing Blade.

MEGA MAN

Trophy Description

The main hero from Capcom's 1987 action game, *Mega Man*. He travels from stage to stage, defeating Robot Masters to obtain new weapons. He uses this vast arsenal in *Smash Bros.* in a variety of ways. Metal Blades, for example, can be fired in eight directions and picked up off the ground!

STATISTICS

MAXIMUM NUMBER OF JUMPS: **2**

CAN WALL JUMP: **Yes**

CAN WALL CLING: **No**

CAN CRAWL: **No**

Alternate Colors

Smash Attacks

SIDE SMASH DAMAGE 11.5%

Mega Man charges up his blaster and fires it horizontally. When this is charged, it increases distance, size, and damage output.

DOWN SMASH DAMAGE 9–17%

Mega Man blasts pillars of flames up on either side of him, knocking opponents up into the air.

UP SMASH

DAMAGE 1.5–6% MAX DAMAGE 15% : 7 HITS

Mega Man raises both hands and electrocutes opponents above him, knocking them away vertically.

Basic Attacks

STANDING ATTACK DAMAGE 1~2%

Mega Man can fire his blaster up to three times before putting his blaster down.

UP TILT DAMAGE 8~17%

A jumping spinning uppercut attack that has some invincibility.

DASH ATTACK

DAMAGE 1~3% MAX DAMAGE 10% : 8 HITS

While moving forward, Mega Man spins like a top, hitting multiple times.

SIDE TILT DAMAGE 2%

While advancing forward, Mega Man can fire his blaster. Again, you can fire up to three shots before putting his blaster down.

DOWN TILT DAMAGE 5~8%

Performs a slide attack that has good range, knocking opponents away horizontally. Mega Man's feet have some invincibility.

EDGE ATTACK

Mega Man pulls himself up and then does a small slide attack similar to his Down Tilt to strike the opponent.

Air Attacks

NEUTRAL AIR ATTACK

DAMAGE 2%

Mega Man fires his blaster in the air. He can fire up to three times before putting his blaster down.

DOWN AIR ATTACK DAMAGE 12~14%

Mega Man shoots a hand as a missile downward. This move has a meteor effect.

BACK AIR ATTACK

DAMAGE 3~5% MAX DAMAGE 12% : 3 HITS

Mega Man uses the Slash Claw to attack behind him. This can hit multiple times.

UP AIR ATTACK

DAMAGE 1~3% MAX DAMAGE 20% : 11 HITS

Launches a mini-tornado upward. If it hits an opponent, it carries that opponent upward.

FORWARD AIR ATTACK

DAMAGE 5~8.5%

Mega Man swings a Flame Sword forward in front of him.

Special Attacks

METAL BLADE (Neutral Special)

DAMAGE 3% MAX DAMAGE 6% : 2 HITS

Pull out Metal Man's spinning saw. You can choose the direction you want to throw it by inputting a direction after hitting the button—even behind you! If you throw it at the ground, anyone can pick it up. This projectile can pass through opponents and continue hitting other opponents.

Hyper Bomb DAMAGE 6~8%

Use Bomb Man's weapon! This bomb is thrown in an arc, and when it makes contact, it explodes. This bomb can be caught and thrown back! The explosion does not hurt whoever threw the bomb.

Shadow Blade

DAMAGE 2% MAX DAMAGE 4% : 2 HITS

Throw Shadow Man's spinning blade. It flies a set distance, piercing opponents along the way, until it makes a u-turn and comes back. It also hits opponents on its way back. Shadow Blade cannot be caught by opponents. Like Metal Blade, Shadow Blade can be thrown in any direction.

CRASH BOMBER (Side Special)

DAMAGE 1~4% MAX DAMAGE 8% : 5 HITS

Use Crash Man's weapon and fire a bomb that sticks to walls, floors, and opponents. Opponents can transfer the bomb by running into one another.

Ice Slasher DAMAGE 4%

Shoot Icc Man's weapon to fire an ice projectile that can freeze opponents on contact. The opponent must have high accumulated damage before that opponent freezes; Mario at 20% or higher freezes. This move can pierce opponents along the way.

Danger Wrap

DAMAGE 3~7% MAX DAMAGE 13% : 3 HITS

Use Burst Man's weapon and fire an explosive projectile that arcs upward. This explosion does not harm Mega Man.

RUSH COIL

(Up Special) DAMAGE 0%

Your trusty dog, Rush, shows up to boost you up into the air. Opponents can use him as well, though! Mega Man has some invincibility at the start of the jump.

Tornado Hold

DAMAGE 1~2% MAX DAMAGE 0% : 5 HITS

Use Tengu Man's weapon, a tornado-blowing fan, to send you upward. You can't move horizontally while ascending.

Beat

DAMAGE 0%

Summon the bird-type robot Beat to pull Mega Man up through the air. You rise slowly, but you can move horizontally very well.

LEAF SHIELD (Down Special)

SPINNING 2% MAX DAMAGE 8% : 4 HITS

THROWN 3.8% MAX DAMAGE 7.6% : 2 HITS

Summon Wood Man's rotating shield. It damages opponents who come into contact with it. Pressing the button again allows you to throw it at your opponents.

Skull Barrier

SPINNING 0%

THROWN 2% MAX DAMAGE 4% : 2 HITS

This rotating barrier of skulls is Skull Man's weapon. It reflects enemy projectiles unless it's sent out as an attack. If the skulls touch an opponent it pushes them back instead of dealing damage. The only time this move deals damage is if it's thrown out as an attack.

	STARTUP	DURATION	DAMAGE SCALING	SPEED SCALING
SKULL BARRIER	11th frame	100 frames	1.2x	1.2x

Plant Barrier

SPINNING 3% MAX DAMAGE 12% : 4 HITS

THROWN 4.2% MAX DAMAGE 8.4% : 2 HITS

Use Plant Man's weapon for protection and more damage. Petals surround you, and they must be hit twice by opponents to be destroyed. They deal the most damage of Mega Man's Down Special options, but they don't travel as far when thrown.

Final Smash

MEGA LEGENDS

Mega Man shoots out the Black Hole Bomb across the stage. On impact or after a second, the bomb explodes, creating a black hole that sucks opponents in. Anyone sucked in meets the five Mega Legends as they all charge up and fire energy beams from their blasters! The combo does about 40% damage to whoever is hit first, 39% to anyone else, and knocks everyone up and away. For range, the Black Hole Bomb travels just over half of Final Destination before it explodes, and it can suck in opponents from the opposite end of Final Destination.

Strategy

Mega Man is a gunner-based character, as he relies more on his weaponry than on hand-to-hand combat. He has slightly above-average weight and average mobility. His Standard Attack, Side Tilt, and Neutral Air all fire his blaster to harass opponents. The blaster shots don't travel very far, but every bit of damage helps! Also note his Side Smash is actually a projectile. The longer you charge it up, the larger the projectile becomes, the farther it travels, and the more damage it deals.

With Metal Blade, you have two opportunities to throw it. First, you can throw it immediately in any of eight directions: up, down, forward, backward, and all four diagonals. If you throw it at the ground or a wall, you can pick it up. Once picked up, it functions as an item and can only be thrown forward, backward, up, or down. Crash Bomber travels very far and deals decent damage to opponents caught in its blast. Use this from a distance and fire it into groups of opponents. Because opponents can pass it off on one another, use this to predict their movements. The explosion can hurt Mega Man and can transfer to Mega Man as well, so use this from a distance! Leaf Shield doesn't stay up for very long, but while it does, it can block projectiles. Grabbing an opponent while you have the Leaf Shield allows you to combo, including the damage of the leaves. You can still use your dodges and shield while you have the Leaf Shield up. Rush Coil is never an attack, so it's mainly used as a recovery tool. Note that other opponents can also use Rush!

In the air, Mega Man's main option for KOs is his Back Air for horizontal KOs, Down Air for meteor smashes, and Up Air to push opponents out of the ceiling. On the ground, his best options are charged-up Forward Smash and Up Smash. Use his projectiles and ranged attacks to build up damage before going for these options. When fighting up-close, Up Tilt is useful because of its invincibility, and Down Tilt is useful because of its range. Down Tilt can be avoided fairly easily because the move is slow, though, so use it sparingly. When you knock away an opponent, take this opportunity to shoot a projectile, bring up your Leaf Shield, or charge up your Side Smash. Take advantage of Side Smash's range as much as you can. For edge-guarding, Side Smash, Forward Air, Metal Blade, Crash Bomber, Leaf Shield, and all of Mega Man's blaster attacks are useful. Keep opponents out with these and try to catch them coming in with a Down Air meteor smash.

Recovery

Mega Man has average vertical recovery but poor horizontal recovery. His Rush Coil boosts him very high into the air, and if you use it a second time in a row, it sends you even higher, though you aren't able to do this from the air. Horizontally, though, you can't move very far left or right after using Rush Coil. Additionally, use Mega Man's Down Air to slow your descent while simultaneously attacking below you. Though it doesn't help Mega Man's horizontal recovery much, don't forget you have access to a wall jump!

META KNIGHT

Trophy Description

Kirby's mysterious rival, this masked swordsman appears in several *Kirby* games. His cape transforms into wings to grant him flight. In *Smash Bros.*, his quick sword skills and aerial agility set him apart. He can jump up to five times in a row, and he has a Special move to soar higher.

STATISTICS

MAXIMUM NUMBER OF JUMPS: **6**

CAN WALL JUMP: **No**

CAN WALL CLING: **No**

CAN CRAWL: **No**

Alternate Colors

Smash Attacks

SIDE SMASH DAMAGE 16%

Meta Knight slashes his sword horizontally in front of him.

DOWN SMASH DAMAGE 7~10.1%

Meta Knight swings his sword quickly around his body. Hits both in front of and behind him.

UP SMASH

DAMAGE 2~4% MAX DAMAGE 9% : 3 HITS

Meta Knight slashes furiously upward as he leaps into the air. Can hit up to three times before sending the opponent upward.

Basic Attacks

STANDING ATTACK

DAMAGE 1~2% MAX DAMAGE 7% : 6 HITS

Meta Knight goes straight into his rapid slashes! Letting go of the Attack button causes Meta Knight to end with a jumping uppercut with his sword.

UP TILT DAMAGE 5~7%

A jumping spinning uppercut attack with Meta Knight's sword fully extended upward.

DASH ATTACK DAMAGE 5~6%

Meta Knight delivers a long-range jump kick to your opponent.

SIDE TILT DAMAGE 2%, 2%, 3%

This leads into a three-hit attack if you continue to hit the Attack button. Two horizontal sword slashes followed by an upward slash. The third hit has good launching power.

DOWN TILT DAMAGE 5%

Meta Knight crouches down and quickly stabs forward a good distance with his sword.

EDGE ATTACK

Meta Knight slowly pulls himself back to the stage before swinging his sword forward.

Air Attacks

NEUTRAL AIR ATTACK

DAMAGE 5~7%

Meta Knight flips multiple times, striking anyone in his path.

DOWN AIR ATTACK DAMAGE 6%

Another quick sword slash, this time in an arc below Meta Knight's body.

BACK AIR ATTACK

DAMAGE 1.5~4% MAX DAMAGE 8.4% : 3 HITS

Three quick sword strikes behind Meta Knight.

UP AIR ATTACK DAMAGE 5%

A very quick sword slash in an arc over Meta Knight's body.

FORWARD AIR ATTACK

DAMAGE 1.5~3% MAX DAMAGE 7.4% : 3 HITS

Meta Knight strikes forward with three quick sword slashes.

Special Attacks

MACH TORNADO (Neutral Special)

DAMAGE 1~3% MAX DAMAGE 8% : 6 HITS

This spinning attack hits multiple times. Hitting the button repeatedly increases the number of spins and lifts Meta Knight higher. The tornado can also destroy weaker projectile attacks. You are in a fall state when this move completes.

Entangling Tornado DAMAGE 9%

This tornado sucks opponents in then knocks them straight up into the air. It doesn't move as much horizontally, but it has more horizontal range.

Dreadful Tornado

DAMAGE 1.5~6% MAX DAMAGE 13.5% : 6 HITS

While you can't increase the number of spins in this version, it is much more damaging. Horizontally, you can't move as far, and there is more recovery at the end of this attack.

DRILL RUSH (Side Special)

DAMAGE 1~3% MAX DAMAGE 11% : 9 HITS

Meta Knight flies forward, drilling his sword into his opponents. You can control the angle of the Drill Rush. You are in a fall state after this move.

High Speed Drill

DAMAGE 0.8~3% MAX DAMAGE 8.6% : 8 HITS

Drill farther but only in the forward direction. It is slightly faster but also less damaging than the regular version.

Shieldbreaker Drill

DAMAGE 1~2% MAX DAMAGE 11% : 10 HITS

This variation chips away at shields, but it's weaker at the end of the attack. The distance you travel is shorter, the damage is less, and you cannot control the angle of the move.

SHUTTLE LOOP (Up Special)

DAMAGE 6~9% MAX DAMAGE 15% : 2 HITS

This jumping upward strike is followed by a looping second strike. It has more range than you might expect, but you are in a fall state after this move. You have a little horizontal control over the second part of this attack.

Blade Coaster

DAMAGE 5~8% MAX DAMAGE 13% : 2 HITS

Meta Knight flies forward instead of upward. Any enemies hit are launched at a lower angle. Compared to the regular version, this travels farther but is weaker in damage.

Lazy Shuttle Loop DAMAGE 6~9%

The first part of the loop has no damage, and the second part has more damage than usual. You have a bit of invincibility during the startup of this move.

DIMENSIONAL CAPE (Down Special) DAMAGE 14~16%

Meta Knight teleports in the direction of your choosing. If you hold the button, he attacks when he reappears. With or without attacking, though, you're in a fall state after this move.

Shield Piercer

DAMAGE 1~9% MAX DAMAGE 11% : 3 HITS

In this variation, the attack penetrates shields, but the overall power and range are less. The distance Meta Knight travels is also shorter than usual. You can do up to 3 hits. While this pierces shields, it doesn't break them. You can also use this to pass through counterattacks!

Stealth Smasher DAMAGE 15~17%

Meta Knight travels farther while invisible but is not invulnerable. You can be hit by attacks while hidden, but you will have some invincibility when reappearing before your attack. The attack itself does much more damage and knockback than the original version.

Final Smash

GALAXIA DARKNESS

Meta Knight waves his cape over his opponents. The range on this cape is much farther than one would expect. You can see the range with the swipe and sparkles that follow along with the cape. Opponents who are hit flinch as the screen fades to black, and then Meta Knight strikes with a massive blow, sending them upward for 40% damage. All other characters on-screen who were not hit by the cape take about 10% damage. Because this launches more vertically than horizontally, use it closer to the tops of stages when possible.

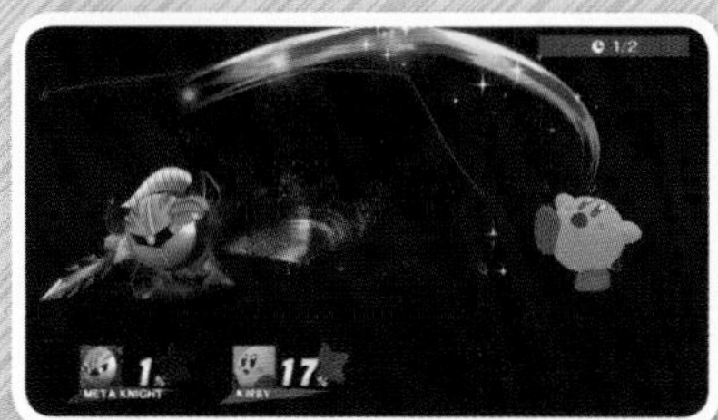

Strategy

Meta Knight is one of the lightest and smallest characters in the game. His armor and cape make him a bit heavier than Kirby. He is also incredibly fast, both with his ground movement and his attack speed. All of his Special moves are attacks that can also be used for recovery in some way. Combine this with his multiple jumps ,and it makes his edge-guarding very strong—he can meet opponents off-stage while still retaining good recovery options. Aside from his lightweight status, his weaknesses are his aerial movement speed and his overall damage output. This makes him less effective in free-for-all settings but more viable in one-on-one modes. Overall, though, he has multiple tools to approach unpredictably, to KO opponents, and to recover.

Since Meta Knight is a lightweight and doesn't have any projectiles, opponents may try to use projectiles against him to rack up damage. Use your Mach Tornado to blow out weak projectiles while controlling your spacing from the opponent at the same time. Because you have so much control over Mach Tornado, this makes it harder for opponents to predict when Meta Knight is actually approaching. Another approach tool and long-range punish is Meta Knight's Drill Rush. Use it to punish opponents at range and carry them upward or downward over stage edges! Finally, for an unpredictable approach, keep opponents guessing with Dimensional Cape. Use it to move farther away or nearby to keep your opponent off guard. Try to catch opponents committing to long-range attacks, then teleport in and attack! Shuttle Loop does decent damage, but its flight path can be a little hard to hit opponents who aren't immediately above or beside you. And it leaves you in a fall state afterward, so make sure you land this attack or catch an edge with it!

To rack up damage, Meta Knight has a bunch of options. First, he doesn't even have a standing jab—it just goes straight into rapid jabs! Additionally, his Forward Air and Back Air both start up quickly and do decent damage. Use his Drill Rush and Mach Tornado punish long-range mistakes. Meta Knight's Up Air is very quick, but it lacks damage. His Down Air is also fairly quick, but it also lacks damage and doesn't have a meteor effect. In general, this makes his best aerial options Forward or Back Air for KOs. From the ground, use his speed to your advantage along with grabs, Dash Attack, Side Tilt, and Down Tilt. Side Smash is his best option for KOs, but it isn't as fast as his Down Smash, which also hits on both sides. All of his Special moves deal decent knockback as well and can be used to KO opponents.

Recovery

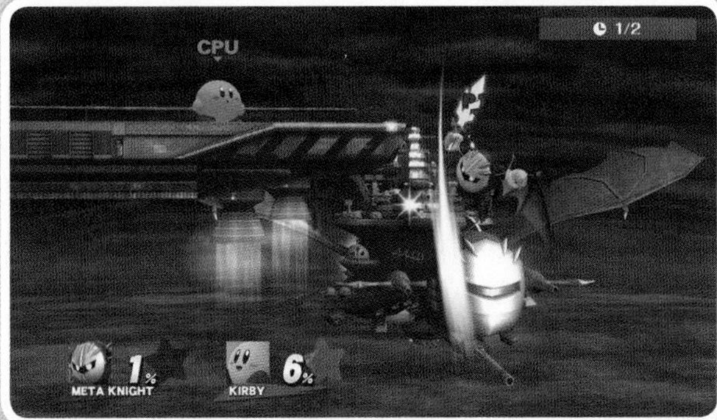

Meta Knight has a variety of recovery options in addition to his six jumps! All of his Special attacks can be used for recovery in some form, but all of them leave Meta Knight in a fall state! With Mach Tornado, you can recover horizontally while attacking. Drill Rush lets you control some horizontal and vertical recovery. Shuttle Loop is Meta Knight's highest vertical recovery tool. Dimensional Cape allows for both horizontal and vertical recovery. In general, you should try to get back to the stage using your jumps and aerials before relying on your Specials.

MR. GAME & WATCH

Trophy Description

Game & Watch was first released in 1980, making the series the father of the Game Boy and Nintendo DS. Or maybe an older sibling? Anyway...in *Smash Bros.*, Mr. Game & Watch uses distinct retro-moves to damage his foes. However, he's only two dimensional, so he's pretty easy to send flying.

STATISTICS

MAXIMUM NUMBER OF JUMPS: **2**

CAN WALL JUMP: **No**

CAN WALL CLING: **No**

CAN CRAWL: **No**

Alternate Colors

Smash Attacks

SIDE SMASH DAMAGE 14~18%

Mr. Game & Watch lights a torch before swinging it down at the opponent.

DOWN SMASH DAMAGE 13~15%

Mr. Game & Watch pulls out two hammers and slams them down on either side of him.

UP SMASH DAMAGE 16%

Mr. Game & Watch dons his diving helmet before headbutting the opponent!

Basic Attacks

STANDING ATTACK

DAMAGE 3% RAPID STRIKES 4% : 3 HITS

Mr. Game & Watch uses a Bug-Spray Gun to spray the opponent multiple times. The puff of air can cancel out some projectiles!

UP TILT

DAMAGE 7% MAX DAMAGE 14% : 2 HITS

Raise a flag out of the ground, and hit opponents standing in its way.

DASH ATTACK **DAMAGE 6.5~10%**

Mr. Game & Watch looks like he might have tripped and fallen, but this dive deals decent damage and knockback.

SIDE TILT **DAMAGE 4~10%**

Whip out a chair, and swing it down onto your opponent!

DOWN TILT **DAMAGE 1~6%**

Reach down and flip up a manhole cover immediately in front of Mr. Game & Watch. Nearby enemies will be hit by the manhole cover.

EDGE ATTACK

Mr. Game & Watch returns to the stage, and then he swings a bell at opponents.

Air Attacks

NEUTRAL AIR ATTACK

DAMAGE 4~5% MAX DAMAGE 17% : 4 HITS

Hold up a bowl of fish above your head. The fish will jump out of the bowl and can deal damage to enemies!

DOWN AIR ATTACK

DAMAGE 3.5~11% MAX DAMAGE 14.5% : 2 HITS

Mr. Game & Watch pulls out a key and rides it down into the ground. Can meteor smash and ground-bounce opponents, but it has a lot of recovery!

BACK AIR ATTACK

DAMAGE 2~3% MAX DAMAGE 12% : 5 HITS

Mr. Game & Watch attacks behind him with a turtle that can hit multiple times!

UP AIR ATTACK

DAMAGE 0~9% MAX DAMAGE 16% : 2 HITS

Shoot air upward at opponents. The outline of the puff of smoke deals damage, but anyone around the outline will still be pushed.

FORWARD AIR ATTACK

DAMAGE 6~11.5%

Swing a box downward onto nearby opponents.

Special Attacks

FIRE (Up Special) DAMAGE 0~6%

One of the best recovery moves in the game: firefighters appear with a trampoline to launch Mr. Game & Watch high before he parachutes down. You can control his descent slightly by moving him to the left or right. Hitting Up or Down closes the parachute, forcing him to fall faster. While descending, you can use any attack except this one.

Heavy Trampoline DAMAGE 10~16%

In this variation, the damage you do while ascending is increased, but the height you travel is lower. Your fall speed with the parachute open is slower than usual. There is a lot of recovery when you land from this attack.

Trampoline Launch DAMAGE 8~12%

This trampoline launches you higher up than any other. It also launches nearby opponents! You won't have a parachute for your descent with this version.

JUDGE (Side Special)

DAMAGE *SEE JUDGE DAMAGE TABLE*

A number between 1 and 9 appears above your head, and then you swing your hammer. The higher the number, the higher the power! Getting a 1 deals 12% damage to yourself! Getting a 7 leaves an apple behind to recover 4% health. Getting an 8 freezes an opponent in ice!

Extreme Judge

DAMAGE *SEE JUDGE DAMAGE TABLE*

In this version, the gavel swings faster and only gives you a 1 or a 9. There is an 80% chance you will get a 1 and a 20% chance you will get a 9. Getting a 1 also deals 5% damage to yourself. Note that getting a 9 isn't as strong as in the regular version.

Chain Judge

DAMAGE *SEE JUDGE DAMAGE TABLE*

The number shown indicates the number of continuous hits by the gavel! Stronger numbers have a lower chance of appearing compared to the regular version.

CHEF (Neutral Special)

DAMAGE 4~5% MAX DAMAGE 9% : 2 HITS

Fling food from your frying pan at the opponent! Hold down the Special button to fling five in a row. Hitting opponents with your frying pan deals damage and will knock back much farther.

XXL Chef

DAMAGE 2~9% MAX DAMAGE 11% : 2 HITS

In this variation, you fling gigantic food at the opponent. The food has less range but more power. Each piece of food takes some time to throw, so you can't throw multiple foods at a time.

Short-Order Chef

DAMAGE 0.5~2% MAX DAMAGE 2.5% : 2 HITS

Quickly fling smaller bits of food at the opponent. They don't travel as high, but they do travel farther. The food is also flung out a little faster, so you can have up to three bits out at a time. The angle the foods travel is different than the regular version. Some food, like fish, is so weak that it won't make opponents flinch on hit.

OIL PANIC (Down Special)

DAMAGE *SEE PANIC DATA TABLE*

Mr. Game & Watch absorbs energy-based projectiles, though not physical ones like Link's arrows. Notice the bucket filling up with each catch? Once filled, unleash its power against your opponents! The stronger the projectiles you absorb, the faster the bucket fills, and the more damaging the attack is.

Efficient Panic

DAMAGE *SEE PANIC DATA TABLE*

This bucket fills up very quickly but doesn't deal as much damage or have as much range.

Panic Overload

DAMAGE *SEE PANIC DATA TABLE*

This bucket has a smaller absorption area, but the resulting attack is much larger. The damage from this version is also slightly lower than the regular version.

PANIC DATA

		DAMAGE NEEDED TO FILL UP THE BUCKET			OIL DAMAGE	
Move	Startup	Level 1	Level 2	Level 3	Minimum	Maximum
OIL PANIC	7th frame	< 10%	> 10%, < 20%	> 20%	18%	60%
EFFICIENT PANIC	5th frame	-	-	> 1%	10%	24%
PANIC OVERLOAD	7th frame	< 10%	> 10%, < 20%	> 20%	15%	45%

JUDGE DAMAGE

	JUDGE		EXTREME JUDGE	CHAIN JUDGE	
NUMBERS	DAMAGE	MAX DAMAGE	DAMAGE	DAMAGE	MAX DAMAGE
[1]	2%	-	5%	1%	-
[2]	4%	-	-	2~3%	5% : 2 Hits
[3]	6%	-	-	3%	9% : 3 Hits
[4]	8%	-	-	2~3%	11% : 4 Hits
[5]	3%	12% : 4 Hits	-	3%	15% : 5 Hits
[6]	12%	-	-	2~3%	17% : 6 Hits
[7]	14%	-	-	2.5~4%	19% : 7 Hits
[8]	9%	-	-	2.4~4.2%	21% : 8 Hits
[9]	32%	-	23%	2.3~10%	28% : 9 Hits

Final Smash

OCTOPUS

Mr. Game & Watch transforms into a giant octopus. Each hit of his tentacles deals about 15% damage. Opponents landing on top of or on the back of the octopus also take damage. Hitting any attack button extends the front tentacles farther to attack. While the octopus looks like it's floating, it must have ground below it. You have a decent double jump to help reach airborne opponents and to survive if you fall off edges, but you can't grab onto edges.

Strategy

Mr. Game & Watch can catch opponents off guard with his retro-animation style, and he has excellent tools as well as great recovery. His light weight, however, means you have to be a little more careful about taking damage. Use Chef to fire off food and keep opponents away. When they get in close, look for opportunities to use both Judge and Side Smash. Because Judge is random, you have to hope for a good result; if you get the opportunity, however, you have to go for it. If you're going up against a projectile-heavy character, try to use Mr. Game & Watch's Oil Panic, but remember that it only catches energy-based projectiles. When opponents start feeling defeated because their projectiles keep getting caught, that's the time to harass them with more of your own projectiles! Remember, though, that Chef is just for racking up damage and annoying your opponent into making mistakes. See how your opponents react to it, and you'll be able to better counter them. If they're shielding a lot, go in for throws! Mr. Game & Watch's down throw is particularly useful, but the range on his throws isn't the best.

In the air, Mr. Game & Watch has a lot of good tools. His Neutral Air, Forward Air, and Back Air have a large hitbox away from him, which makes them very useful. His Down Air can meteor smash, but don't use this too much as it has a ton of recovery when it hits the ground. Note that both his jab and his Down Tilt are capable of canceling out some projectiles, so you have these options, along

with Oil Panic, to deal with projectile-happy opponents. For knocking opponents out, all of Mr. Game & Watch's Smash attacks have good potential, but Up Smash is your best bet if you get to charge up. Down Smash is good against opponents who roll a lot, as it covers both sides, and Forward Smash is good to guard the edge. Be sure to cycle through the Smash attacks to keep them all fresh!

Recovery

Mr. Game & Watch is a fairly floaty character, which makes returning to the stage with him a little easier. He doesn't really have any Special attack to advance him horizontally, so you have to rely on him being floaty to move him left and right as he falls. His vertical recovery tool is his Fire Special, where firemen launch him up extremely high before he parachutes down again. The parachute slows his fall even more, so you have to use this time to move him left and right. You can also use his Oil Panic as a small stalling tactic to throw off your opponent's timing; however, it takes awhile for Oil Panic to complete before you can use

Fire to continue your recovery. More important, though, Oil Panic can be used to cancel your horizontal knockback and send Mr. Game & Watch straight down immediately! This can save you from being KO'd! After using Fire, be ready to attack with your Down Air or Forward Air as you float back down, though, because opponents have plenty of time to prepare for your return!

NESS

Trophy Description

Hailing from Onett, a small town in Eagleland, this young boy's ordinary looks hide his psychic powers. Ness fought against the evil Gigas in *EarthBound*, and in *Smash Bros.*, he unleashes some of the same PSI moves. Watch out for the PK Thunder, a guided attack that can also launch Ness like a rocket!

STATISTICS

MAXIMUM NUMBER OF JUMPS: **2**

CAN WALL JUMP: **No**

CAN WALL CLING: **No**

CAN CRAWL: **No**

Alternate Colors

Smash Attacks

SIDE SMASH DAMAGE 18~22%

Ness swings a baseball bat at the opponent horizontally. This baseball bat has insane launching power and can also be used to reflect projectiles!.

DOWN SMASH

DAMAGE 1~10% MAX DAMAGE 12% : 3 HITS

Ness sends his yo-yo backward before rolling it forward with the "walk the dog" trick. This knocks opponents away horizontally.

UP SMASH

DAMAGE 9~13%

Ness swings a yo-yo at your opponent. This attack actually starts behind Ness before swinging it all around him with the "around the world" trick

REFLECT	STARTUP	DURATION	DAMAGE SCALING	SPEED SCALING
Side Smash	19th frame	13 frames	2x	2.5x

Basic Attacks

STANDING ATTACK

DAMAGE 2%, 2%, 4%

Ness jabs forward twice then kicks the opponent away.

UP TILT DAMAGE 5~7%

Ness lifts both hands into the air before blasting the opponent with his psychic powers.

DASH ATTACK

DAMAGE 2~7% MAX DAMAGE 10% : 3 HITS

Ness rushes toward the opponent, with both arms outstretched, while creating a PSI force in front of him. This attack hits multiple times.

SIDE TILT DAMAGE 9%

Ness kicks forward horizontally. This can be aimed up or down.

DOWN TILT DAMAGE 2~4%

While crouching, Ness quickly kicks out at the opponent. This can trip opponents when used at max range.

EDGE ATTACK

Ness returns to the stage and does a quick sweep attack.

Air Attacks

NEUTRAL AIR ATTACK

DAMAGE 7~11%

A spinning attack with both arms outstretched.

DOWN AIR ATTACK

DAMAGE 10~12%

Ness kicks downward with one leg. This attack can meteor smash your opponent.

BACK AIR ATTACK

DAMAGE 8~15%

A reverse dropkick attack with decent knockback.

UP AIR ATTACK

DAMAGE 13%

Ness flips his body while simultaneously unleashing a massive headbutt that can launch opponents upward.

FORWARD AIR ATTACK

DAMAGE 1~4% MAX DAMAGE 7% : 4 HITS

Ness reaches forward to blast opponents with his psychic powers. This can hit multiple times.

Special Attacks

PK FLASH
(Neutral Special) DAMAGE 9~37%

This electrical blast rises vertically out of Ness before descending. You can control its downward arc either to the left or right. Hold the button to increase the damage and range of the explosion and to extend the amount of time you have to control it. Once you release the button, the blast explodes. It also explodes after about three seconds.

Rising PK Flash DAMAGE 6~24%

This PK Flash continues to rise. You cannot move it much horizontally, and it deals less damage.

PK Freeze DAMAGE 10~19%

Much less damage, but the hit itself freezes opponents in their tracks! The falling speed is slightly slower than the regular version.

PK FIRE (Side Special)
DAMAGE 1~4% MAX DAMAGE 22% : 10 HITS

Ness throws a lightning bolt that explodes into a pillar of flames once it connects with an opponent. When Ness is grounded, he throws the lightning bolt horizontally, but when he's airborne, he throws the lightning bolt downward at an angle.

PK Bonfire

DAMAGE 2~5% MAX DAMAGE 52% : 11 HITS

In this variation, the range is much shorter on the lightning bolt, but the flame pillar sticks around for much longer. The bolt travels slightly slower and the flame pillar doesn't shrink over time.

PK Fire Burst

DAMAGE 1~8% MAX DAMAGE 9% : 2 HITS

This lightning bolt bursts into a single flame on contact with an enemy. The single flame knocks back opponents much more strongly than in the other versions. This version travels slightly farther than the default version.

PK THUNDER (Up Special)
DAMAGE 1~8% MAX DAMAGE 9% : 2 HITS

BODY BLOW 21~25%

Ness releases a ball of lightning that you have total control over. Hitting your opponent with this nets you some damage. If you can steer it back into Ness, it shoots Ness off in the direction it was last traveling; Ness takes 0 damage. If you hit Ness with the lightning and he then hits an opponent, it results in massive damage to the opponent only! Ness cannot move during this attack. If used in the air, Ness will fall slowly.

Lasting PK Thunder

DAMAGE 1~7% MAX DAMAGE 11% : 5 HITS

BODY BLOW 1.5~10% MAX DAMAGE 25% : 11 HITS

This ball of lightning pierces through opponents and doesn't disappear, which allows it to hit multiple times. Even if you hit it into Ness, the resulting body blow can hit multiple times. Another difference is Ness's speed doesn't decrease much after hitting someone with the body blow.

Rolling PK Thunder

DAMAGE 1~12% MAX DAMAGE 13% : 2 HITS

BODY BLOW 30%

A stronger but slower version of PK Thunder. The damage on the body blow is also increased, but Ness's speed does not decrease after hitting an opponent.

PSI MAGNET (Down Special)
DAMAGE 0%

Ness surrounds himself in a giant magnet bubble that absorbs energy-based projectiles to heal his damage. Hold the button to extend the duration of the bubble. When you release the button, it has a push effect on anyone else inside or near the bubble.

PSI Vacuum

DAMAGE 5~10%

Ness pulls in opponents then damages them at the end of the move. The closer opponents are to Ness, the stronger they are knocked away. In this variation, projectiles are not absorbed.

Forward PSI Magnet

DAMAGE 9%

Ness creates a PSI Magnet field in front of him. When the move completes, it deal damages and knocks away anyone who is too close. It also absorbs projectiles.

ABSORB DATA	STARTUP	DURATION	RECOVERY RATE	MAX RECOVERY
PSI MAGNET	10th frame	35 frames	1.6x	30%
FORWARD PSI MAGNET	12th frame	32 frames	1.2x	30%

Final Smash

PK STARSTORM

Ness calls down a rain of stars to the center of the stage. You can control the PK Starstorm by angling it left or right, but its origin point is over the center of the stage. Each hit does about 8% damage and knocks the opponent away more horizontally than vertically. You are invincible during the attack, and if it's used while airborne, you do not fall.

Strategy

Despite Ness's compact size, he is actually an average-weight character! He has a variety of projectile attacks to protect himself at range, and he has some devastating throws and Smash attacks. His mobility and jump height are average, but he has a unique double jump that sends him higher than most. His weaknesses are in his recovery and Smash attack range. With quick attacks, a decent projectile game, and surprise KO power, though, he's a force to be reckoned with. For surprise KOs, master using PK Thunder to hit Ness into opponents and learn the range on Ness's Side Smash!

PK Thunder is Ness's primary projectile, as it is his most versatile projectile. Because you have total control over its path, you can use it to attack at range, zone out opponents, edge-guard, or blast it into Ness to KO opponents! Blasting it into Ness is your main recovery tool, so be sure to practice this technique. PK Fire is best to trap opponents for combos and to keep them out. PK Flash is best used for edge guarding since it has a long startup and recovery. Using it for edge guarding will allow you to better position yourself and charge it up. Make sure you have enough space before attempting to use this. PSI Magnet heals Ness when used against projectile-heavy characters. Note, however, that this only absorbs energy-based projectiles. So, while this absorbs Mario's fireballs, it does *not* absorb Dr. Mario's capsules!

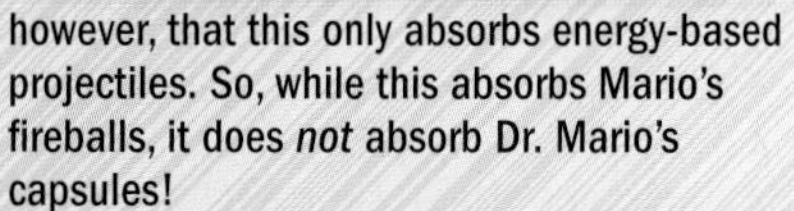

In the air, Ness has many quick aerial attacks. Forward Air has the best range because of the psychic blast in front of Ness, but other characters can still outdistance you. Up Air and Back Air are good for KOs, while Down Air is good for its meteor smash. On the ground, range is still an issue, but your tilt attacks are fairly fast. Smash attacks have poor range, but Up Smash can actually cause damage while being charged. Ness's throws are also particularly good if you can reach your opponent, particularly with Ness's Back Throw. The Side Smash baseball bat has awesome KO power, so this is definitely the option you want to look for. When edge-guarding, use your PK Thunder and PK Flash to make it difficult for opponents to return. PK Fire is a good trap on-stage and can also be thrown at opponents as they try to make their way back to the stage.

Recovery

Ness is one of the most difficult characters to recover with in the game. While his double jump gets him fairly high, none of his Specials move him vertically or horizontally. Instead, master PK Thunder to circle around yourself then hit you in the correct direction you want to recover in. After this hits Ness, though, you are left in a fall state unless you collide with a stage floor or an opponent. If approaching from above the stage, hitting yourself into the stage floor is usually your best option. The best way to hit this is to control PK Thunder up and away from Ness then down and toward him. If opponents are hitting you with projectiles, use PSI Magnet to absorb them before using PK Thunder to get back to the stage.

OLIMAR

Trophy Description

A veteran spaceship pilot for Hocotate Freight, Captain Olimar partners with Pikmin in *Smash Bros.* to help him in battle. Olimar is much stronger when he's got Pikmin with him, so keep them plucked and good to go. Pikmin abilities are based on their color—learn what each is best at!

STATISTICS

MAXIMUM NUMBER OF JUMPS: **2**

CAN WALL JUMP: **No**

CAN WALL CLING: **No**

CAN CRAWL: **No**

NOTE

The majority of Olimar's attacks vary in damage based on the Pikmin that Olimar has available for the attack. Damage values are shown with their associated Pikmin color

Alternate Colors

Smash Attacks

SIDE SMASH

Olimar throws a Pikmin forward at the opponent.

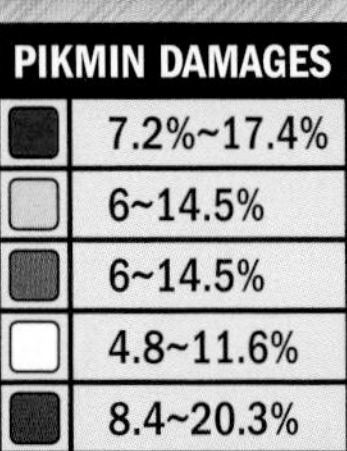

PIKMIN DAMAGES	
	7.2%~17.4%
	6~14.5%
	6~14.5%
	4.8~11.6%
	8.4~20.3%

DOWN SMASH

Olimar sends out a Pikmin to either side of him. This uses the next two Pikmin you have queued up, making it useful for a quick Pikmin shuffle as well.

PIKMIN DAMAGES	
	10.8~13.2%
	9~11%
	9~11%
	7.2~8.8%
	12.6~15.4%

UP SMASH

Olimar swings a Pikmin upward to launch opponents upward.

PIKMIN DAMAGES	
	12~15.6%
	10~13%
	10~13%
	8~10.4%
	14~18.2%

Basic Attacks

STANDING ATTACK

DAMAGE 3~4%, 3~4%

Olimar punches forward twice for a two-hit combo.

UP TILT

DAMAGE 0.6~4% MAX DAMAGE 7.6% : 7 HITS

Olimar jumps and extends both arms as he spins through the air. This attack hits multiple times.

DASH ATTACK

DAMAGE 4~7% MAX DAMAGE 11% : 2 HITS

A running cartwheel attack.

SIDE TILT **DAMAGE 11%**

Olimar winds up and then leans forward for a big punch.

DOWN TILT **DAMAGE 6%**

A head-first slide attack at the opponent's feet.

EDGE ATTACK

Olimar hurls himself back up to the stage as he punches forward.

Air Attacks

NEUTRAL AIR ATTACK

DAMAGE 1.5~2% MAX DAMAGE 8% : 5 HITS

This jumping spiral attack is Olimar's only air attack that doesn't involve or require a Pikmin.

DOWN AIR ATTACK

Olimar strikes downward with a Pikmin.

PIKMIN DAMAGES	
	10.8%
	9%
	9%
	7.2%
	12.6%

BACK AIR ATTACK

Olimar swings a Pikmin horizontally behind him to hit opponents away.

PIKMIN DAMAGES	
	13%
	10.8%
	10.8%
	8.6%
	15.1%

UP AIR ATTACK

Olimar swings a Pikmin above his head. On contact, this knocks opponents vertically away.

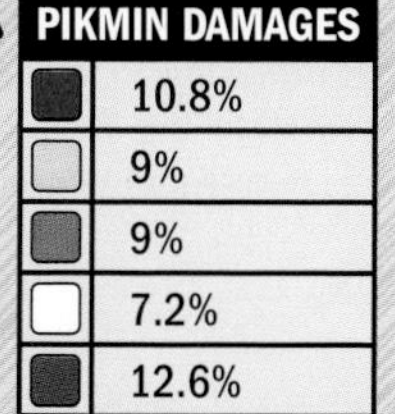

PIKMIN DAMAGES	
	10.8%
	9%
	9%
	7.2%
	12.6%

FORWARD AIR ATTACK

Olimar swings a Pikmin in a downward arc to strike anyone in front of him.

PIKMIN DAMAGES	
	10.2%
	8.5%
	8.5%
	6.8%
	11.9%

Special Attacks

PIKMIN PLUCK (Neutral Special)

DAMAGE 0%

Olimar plucks Pikmin out of the ground in the following order: red, yellow, blue, white, purple. You can have a maximum of three Pikmin at any given time, and you must be on the ground for this to succeed. Doing this in the air only leaves you vulnerable.

Hardy Pikmin Pluck DAMAGE 0%

These Pikmin have much more durability than regular Pikmin; they are roughly ten times as durable as their regular counterparts. It takes longer for Olimar to pluck them from the ground, and they move a bit slower, making it easier for them to get separated from Olimar.

Explosive Pluck

These Pikmin explode when plucked, damaging opponents and launching them in different directions. Generally, these Pikmin have lower durability and die off much faster.

PIKMIN DAMAGES	
■	8%
■	8%
■	8%
□	5%
■	10%

WINGED PIKMIN (Up Special)

DAMAGE 0%

Winged Pikmin arrive to carry Olimar up to safety. The more Pikmin with Olimar, though, the heavier he is to carry. You can control the direction they fly. Olimar can cancel the flight by using one of his aerial attacks.

Winged Pikmin Jump DAMAGE 0%

Winged Pikmin pull Olimar up so quickly that a blast of wind knocks nearby opponents away. It is much quicker than the regular version, but you can't move horizontally as much.

Mighty Winged Pikmin DAMAGE 0%

With this variation, it doesn'tmatter how many Pikmin you have tagging along with Olimar; you get to roughly the same height and movement with 1 Pikmin or 3 Pikmin. The downside to this is that the flight time, height, and movement speeds are all reduced from the regular version.

PIKMIN ORDER (Down Special)

DAMAGE 0%

Olimar blows his whistle to re-order his Pikmin or to recall them quickly. Use this to make sure your Pikmin are in the order you expect them to be. Olimar's body has super armor as he bends backward to make this call.

Order Tackle

PIKMIN DAMAGES		MAX DAMAGE
■	1~3%	4% : 2 Hits
■	1~3%	4% : 2 Hits
■	1~3%	4% : 2 Hits
□	2~3%	5% : 2 Hits
■	5%	10% : 2 Hit

Pikmin returning to Olimar deals damage to opponents. Olimar is left vulnerable after this call, as it takes longer to recover.

Dizzy Whistle

DAMAGE 0.1~1% MAX DAMAGE 1.1% : 2 HITS

The force of this whistle spins nearby opponents as your Pikmin are recalled. Opponents take a little bit of damage, but Olimar does not have any super armor in this variation.

PIKMIN THROW (Side Special)

PIKMIN DAMAGES		MAX DAMAGE
■	1.3%	10.4% : 8 Hits
■	1.3%	10.4% : 8 Hits
■	1.3%	10.4% : 8 Hits
□	2.6%	20.8% : 8 Hits
■	6.5%	6.5% : 1 Hit

Olimar throws the lead Pikmin at the opponent. Most Pikmin latch on to deal damage, but the purple one only hits hard on impact. The lower your opponent's percentage, the longer the Pikmin can stay latched on.

Sticky Pikmin Throw

PIKMIN DAMAGES		MAX DAMAGE
■	1%	16% : 16 Hits
■	1%	16% : 16 Hits
■	1%	16% : 16 Hits
□	2%	32% : 16 Hits
■	5%	5% : 1 Hit

This variant makes the Pikmin much harder to shake off. Theydeal less damage when they hit; however, because they cling on longer, the maximum damage possible is much higher. The purple Pikmin is an exception, as it deals less damage and does not cling to the opponent.

Tackle Pikmin Throw

All Pikmin follow the purple Pikmin's lead and don't latch on to the opponent. Instead, all of them will just hit the opponent to deal damage and knock them away.

PIKMIN DAMAGES	
■	5%
■	5%
■	5%
□	3%
■	8%

PIKMIN ATTRIBUTES

RED Deal good damage and have good knockback.

YELLOW Deal average damage but have good range and hitbox size. Immune to electric attacks while able to deal those attacks, allowing for combos.

BLUE–The most durable of Pikmin, these have more health. Average damage but great for throws.

WHITE Least durable but deal a lot of poison damage, making them good when thrown or during pummels. Can be thrown the farthest.

PURPLE–Usually the most damaging Pikmin. Use it for Smash attacks or throw it at opponents to knock them away.

Final Smash

END OF DAY

Olimar blasts off in his rocket before crash-landing it back down into his opponents. While he is up in his rocket, Bulborbs arrive and damage your opponents as well. When the rocket returns, anyone around the impact area takes damage. Watch the lens at the bottom of the screen to keep track of where your opponents are so you can guide the rocket to the optimal spot. You can guide the rocket quite a bit, as long as you start moving it early in its descent. Opponents are knocked up and away from the rocket impact. If you activated the Final Smash on top of an enemy, that enemy is buried for the duration of the Final Smash!

Strategy

Nothing is more important to Olimar than having Pikmin plucked and ready to go! Olimar's tilt attacks, Dash Attack, Edge Attack, Neutral Attack, and Neutral Air Attack are his only attacks that don't require Pikmin. All of his Smash attacks and other aerial attacks require Pikmin to deal any damage! With below-average weight and mobility, Olimar needs Pikmin available to keep opponents away. Luckily, plucking Pikmin with Pikmin Pluck is fairly quick. Keep in mind that plucking Pikmin always pulls them in the same order, so memorize that order. Note that whichever Pikmin is in the front of the line is the one you will use for your Pikmin-based attack. The Pikmin do varying amounts of damage and have different attributes.

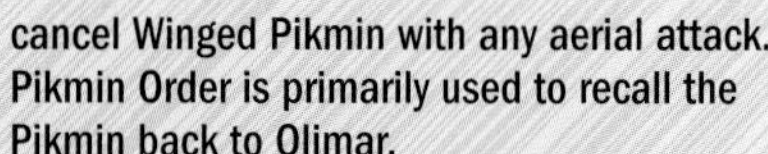

Pikmin Throw is Olimar's main projectile and farthest reaching attack. All Pikmin except the purple one latch onto opponents and deal damage over time until they are knocked off. The purple one does a single hit that knocks opponents back. The white Pikmin deals the most significant damage, up to 20%, while red, yellow, and blue deal about 10% maximum. It should be noted that although their damages are the same, blue is the most durable of these Pikmin. Winged Pikmin is mainly a recovery tool for Olimar; it also allows him to move horizontally. The more Pikmin you have in line with you, the slower you rise, so try to use Pikmin Throw before activating Winged Pikmin. You can cancel Winged Pikmin with any aerial attack. Pikmin Order is primarily used to recall the Pikmin back to Olimar.

Smash Attacks and aerial attacks are Olimar's primary method to rack up damage. For Smash Attacks and aerial attacks, Pikmin deal damage from highest to lowest in this order: purple, red, a tie between yellow and blue, then white. Most of Olimar's aerial attacks are quick and, as long as you are using the appropriate Pikmin, can knockback very far. Down Air in particular has good spike effect and Forward Air knocks back horizontally quite well. Using the right Pikmin for the right situation is important. For Smash attacks, use purple. The red, yellow, and blue Pikmin are also useful for Smash Attacks because of their extra range, but they deal a little less damage. For aerials, use red, purple, or yellow. For throws, use blue or white. And when throwing at opponents, use purple to knockback, white to damage, or yellow to electrocute. Remember, if all three of your Pikmin are latched on to opponents, you can't pull anymore, but you can still use your non-Pikmin-based attacks! Without Pikmin, Up Tilt and Neutral Air can be useful to rack up some damage while Forward Tilt can be good for damage and knockback.

Recovery

Olimar's only recovery tool is his Winged Pikmin, which allows him to recover both horizontally and vertically. Once you call the Winged Pikmin, immediately input the direction you want to go or Winged Pikmin allow Olimar to drop farther. How fast Olimar moves, though, is affected by how many Pikmin he has with him. With three Pikmin, Olimar rises very slowly while having none allows him to rise very quickly. If you are very far from the stage, use your Pikmin Throw to get rid of Pikmin before using the Winged Pikmin to recover! This is especially useful when returning to the stage from high above. The thrown Pikmin will keep your opponents occupied, making your recovery a little safer.

PAC-MAN

Trophy Description

The yellow, circular hero of the game *PAC-MAN*, which is recognized as the "Most Successful Coin-Operated Arcade Game" by Guinness World Records. In *Smash Bros.*, he uses several moves inspired by the original PAC-MAN. Wakawaka your foes by charging up the Power Pellet move and aiming at them.

STATISTICS

MAXIMUM NUMBER OF JUMPS: **2**

CAN WALL JUMP: **Yes**

CAN WALL CLING: **No**

CAN CRAWL: **Yes**

Alternate Colors

Smash Attacks

SIDE SMASH DAMAGE 9~16%

PAC-MAN attacks forward with a Ghost in hand.

DOWN SMASH DAMAGE 7~13%

PAC-MAN charges up and then pushes a Ghost out on either side of him. This hits opponents horizontally away.

UP SMASH

DAMAGE 3~14% MAX DAMAGE 17% : 2 HITS

PAC-MAN swings a Ghost overhead as an attack to knock opponents upward.

Basic Attacks

STANDING ATTACK

DAMAGE 3%, 2%, 4%

This three-hit attack string has PAC-MAN doing two punches then a flipkick to knock opponents up and away.

UP TILT DAMAGE 7%

PAC-MAN clobbers the opponent on top of the opponent's head with this overhead strike. This attack has some invincibility.

DASH ATTACK

DAMAGE 2~5% MAX DAMAGE 9% : 3 HITS

PAC-MAN goes retro and chomps at the opponent multiple times.

SIDE TILT DAMAGE 8%

PAC-MAN does a powerful side kick. This can be aimed up or down.

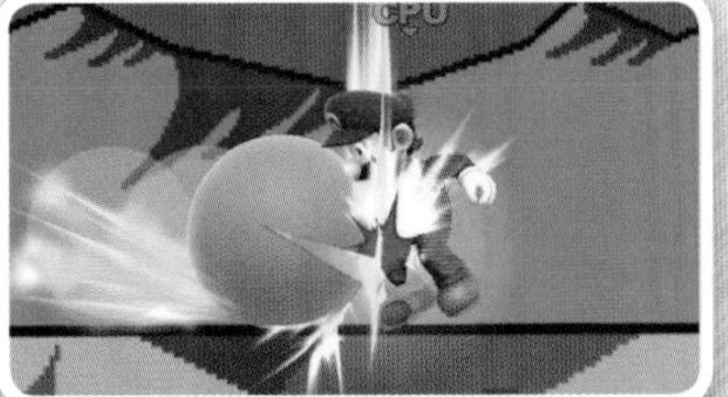

DOWN TILT DAMAGE 6%

Transforms into retro PAC-MAN and chomps forward suddenly. This has good range and is quite surprising.

EDGE ATTACK

PAC-MAN hurls himself up and then kicks the opponent away with a sweep attack.

Air Attacks

NEUTRAL AIR ATTACK

DAMAGE 3~10%

Transforms into retro PAC-MAN and spins rapidly to hit the opponent.

DOWN AIR ATTACK

DAMAGE 1.5~6% MAX DAMAGE 10.5% : 4 HITS

PAC-MAN kicks downward multiple times, hitting up to four times.

BACK AIR ATTACK

DAMAGE 7~11.8%

This reverse dropkick has good damage and knockback.

UP AIR ATTACK DAMAGE 10%

A flipkick attack in the air.

FORWARD AIR ATTACK

DAMAGE 5.3%

PAC-MAN kicks out horizontally in front of him. This attack doesn't do much damage but recovers very quickly.

Special Attacks

BONUS FRUIT (Neutral Special)

DAMAGE ***SEE BONUS FRUIT TABLE***

PAC-MAN summons fruit to throw. As the fruit cycles in his hand, you can hit Left or Right to evasive roll or shield to store that item. Once stored, if you hold the button again, PAC-MAN will continue charging to cycle through the remaining fruit. When you tap the button again, it throws that fruit. You can also pick up fruit to throw again if you are quick enough. See the sidebar for more information.

Freaky Fruit

DAMAGE ***SEE FREAKY FRUIT TABLE***

These fruits move differently than the original fruit; motion, speed, and damage are different.

Lazy Fruit

DAMAGE ***SEE LAZY FRUIT TABLE***

PAC-MAN summons slow-moving fruits that stick around a lot longer.

BONUS FRUIT	DAMAGE	DESCRIPTION
CHERRY	4%	Tossed low to the ground and only bounces once.
STRAWBERRY	6%	Thrown a little farther than the Cherry and bounces twice.
ORANGE	8%	Thrown straight at higher speed with decent damage.
APPLE	9%	Bounces multiple times, covering a lot of distance.
MELON	12%	Slowly floats through the air, but if it hits, it deals a good chunk of damage.
GALAXIAN SHIP	11%	Flies through the air and loops back to strike again. Can hit twice for twice the damage. Note that it will not disappear upon hitting an opponent.
BELL	8%	Bounces very high and doesn't deal much damage, but if it connects, it stuns the opponent, allowing for followups.
KEY	15%	Thrown very fast and deals the most damage but takes the longest to charge up. Note that it will not disappear upon hitting an opponent.

FREAKY FRUIT	DAMAGE	DESCRIPTION
CHERRY	2%	Bounces back and forth in opposite directions.
STRAWBERRY	4%	Bounces back and forth in opposite directions. Travels farther than the Cherry.
ORANGE	2%	Thrown straight and faster than usual but with less damage.
APPLE	9%	Moves forward little by little while bouncing. As it bounces, it will also accelerate.
MELON	13%	Slowly floats through the air in an arc before bouncing back in the opposite direction.
GALAXIAN SHIP	9%	Flies through the air, but after turning it will return at an angle, going up into the air.
BELL	6%	Follows the same trajectory as original, but when it rings, it goes straight upward.
KEY	10%	Can blast opponents away, but it needs to be used very close as it disappears quickly after being thrown.

LAZY FRUIT	DAMAGE	DESCRIPTION
CHERRY	2%	Bounces forward very slowly.
STRAWBERRY	5%	Slowly bounces forward before bouncing higher vertically.
ORANGE	8%	Flies directly forward very slowly. Does not go very far.
APPLE	9%	Moves like the Strawberry but farther and bounces higher at the end.
MELON	12%	Moves like the Strawberry, but travels farther than the Apple.
GALAXIAN SHIP	27% : 9 Hits	Flies forward then loops multiple times.
BELL	10%	Slowly ascends straight up before dropping straight down.
KEY	10%	Flies directly forward very slowly while spinning rapidly.

POWER PELLET (Side Special)

NO CHARGE 4.1~10%
MAX DAMAGE 16% : 2 HITS
FULL CHARGE 4.1~12%
MAX DAMAGE 22% : 2 HITS

PAC-MAN summons Pac-Dots that end with a Power Pellet, and he chases after it. You can aim the pellets upward or downward, but if you bounce off the ground you stumble and are left vulnerable. Hold the button down to summon more Pac-Dots! If an opponent hits the final pellet, the move ends, and the pellet is on the floor as an item to restore 2% health.

Distant Power Pellet

NO CHARGE 1.8~10%
MAX DAMAGE 15.7% : 3 HITS
FULL CHARGE 1.8~12%
MAX DAMAGE 20.3% : 4 HITS

These Pac-Dots move farther out faster, but PAC-MAN himself dashes slower. Overall damage is reduced, but PAC-MAN attacks more times along the way.

Enticing Power Pellet

NO CHARGE 3.3~10% MAX DAMAGE 16% : 2 HITS
FULL CHARGE 3.3~15% MAX DAMAGE 25% : 2 HITS

These Pac-Dots are placed slower, but they can pull opponents toward them. The damage is slightly higher, but you don't have as much control over the placement of the Pac-Dots.

PAC-JUMP (Up Special)

DAMAGE 5~10.1%

Set up a trampoline to launch yourself high into the air. The trampoline can be used three times. The first bounce leaves it blue, second bounce leaves it yellow, and the third bounce leaves it red, indicating it has expired. Each jump is higher than the last, and opponents can use the trampoline, too!

Power Pac-Jump

DAMAGE 1.5~3%
MAX DAMAGE 9% : 5 HITS

This trampoline can only be used once, but it sends PAC-MAN much higher into the air. During his ascent, PAC-MAN attacks opponents multiple times and knocks them straight upward.

Meteor Trampoline

DAMAGE 3~5%

This trampoline attacks from below when people jump on it. Once the trampoline is red, anyone who jumps on while it's on land is buried, and anyone who jumps on it in the air is knocked down with a meteor smash. The first jump is the highest while each of the following jumps is lower.

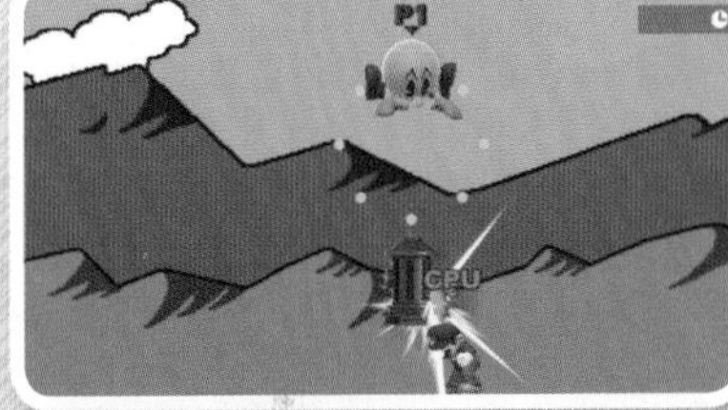

FIRE HYDRANT (Down Special)

DAMAGE 9~13%

Throw down a fire hydrant that blasts jets of water. The hydrant shoots water out both sides or out the top. The hydrant drop deals damage, but the water jets only push opponents; the jets don't damage them. If the hydrant takes enough damage, it is knocked free, dealing damage to anyone it comes in contact with.

On-Fire Hydrant

DAMAGE 4~15%

This hydrant blasts fire instead of water and can damage PAC-MAN as well! Damage is higher than normal, and the hydrant shoots flames three times.

Dire Hydrant

DAMAGE 9%

This hydrant explodes after awhile or when it hits the ground. When it's used from the air, PAC-MAN has some invincibility during the startup of this attack. The explosion does not hit PAC-MAN.

Strategy

PAC-MAN has slightly above-average weight and average mobility. Despite being a smaller character, he has decent range, which is also helpful whenever he transforms into retro PAC-MAN. His Smash attacks all use the Ghosts, so they extend out farther from his body, making them safer to use. In the air, he has a lot of good options, including his Power Pellet and Fire Hydrant. His throw has a longer startup than most, but it has good range as well. Overall, PAC-MAN is well rounded and quite capable; his biggest weakness is punishment out of shield and slower heavier attacks, despite his average weight.

Ranged fighting is where PAC-MAN excels. His Bonus Fruit gives him multiple options for projectiles. Galaxian Ship has the most damage potential by itself because it can loop and hit again, but Bell's stun is useful to combo for more damage. Many of the Bonus Fruit projectiles can be picked up or caught after they've been thrown, allowing you to throw them again if you're fast enough. If the Bell doesn't make contact with anyone and you're able to pick it up off the floor, throwing it an opponent can still stun that opponent! When using Power Pellet offensively, aim your trail of Pac-Dots upward after the point at which it will hit the opponent. This way you are more likely to combo into the second hit. Hitting opponents as PAC-MAN bites down on the big Power Pellet knocks back farther as well. To use Power Pellet a little safer, end your Pac-Dots immediately in front of your opponent. This way PAC-MAN's attack will still reach and he will recover a little quicker. Fire Hydrant is another long-range fighting tool when you drop it while airborne. Additionally, PAC-MAN can hit opponents above him when he throws the Fire Hydrant downward. You can attack the Fire Hydrant to send it flying toward opponents as well! With Pac-Jump, you can only grab onto the edge three times. You must return to the ground to reset this, or PAC-MAN can't grab the ledge from trampoline jumps again.

Your best options for KOs in the air are Back Air and Up Air. Forward Air is amazing; you can use it multiple times per jump. Down Air is good for racking up damage, but it doesn't meteor smash. On the ground, Forward Smash, Up Smash, Side Tilt, and Dash Attack have great knockback, and Up Tilt has some invincibility while Down Tilt's sudden dash forward will catch opponents off guard. For edge-guarding, PAC-MAN has a bunch of great options. Use the Fire Hydrant against opponents far from the stage, then use Power Pellet to get back to the stage yourself. On the stage itself, set up the Fire Hydrant to push opponents from the stage with its blasts of water or set up the Pac-Jump trampoline to force them into a jump. When they try to get back, use Bonus Fruit, and stop them from advancing with your Forward Air, Up Air, or Back Air.

Final Smash

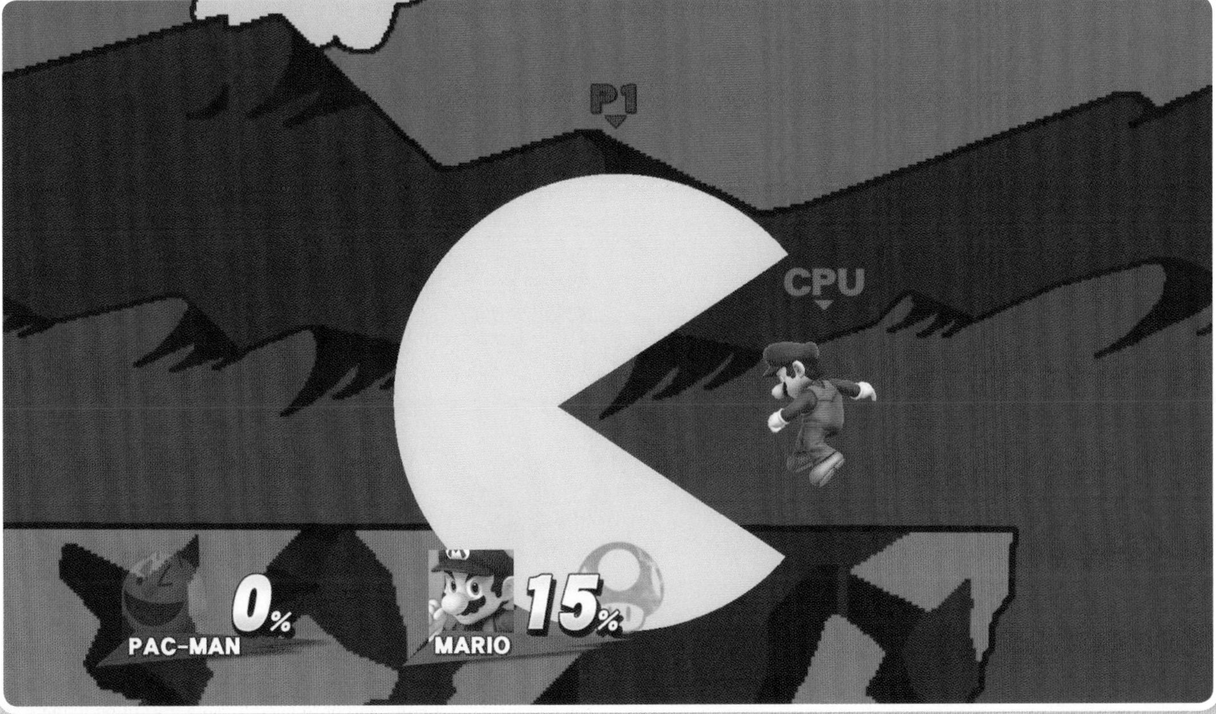

SUPER PAC-MAN

PAC-MAN transforms into a giant version of his retro self and goes on a chomping spree! Retro PAC-MAN can only move Up, Down, Left, or Right. Hitting a direction sends him chomping in that direction. You can hold down the Special button to increase his movement speed! Additionally, moving off-screen causes you to reappear on the opposite side of the screen! Each chomp he lands on an opponent deals about 15% damage and turns the opponent into a pair of eyeballs. Follow the eyes to increase your chances of chomping them again and knocking them farther off-stage.

Recovery

PAC-MAN has some great recovery tools. For vertical recovery, he has his Pac-Jump Special that basically adds a trampoline to any part of a stage. The more you jump on it, the higher you get, but if you use it you enter a fall state. For horizontal recovery—as well as some vertical recovery—use PAC-MAN's Power Pellet. The good thing about Power Pellet is you can control it so PAC-MAN moves in an arc upward or downward. Additionally, you enter a unique state after Power Pellet that allows you to use any other aerial attack or any other Special (although not Power Pellet again). To slow your fall, use Bonus Fruit, but you need to cancel out of it by using an air dodge. Don't forget to use your wall jump as well!

PALUTENA

Trophy Description

In *Kid Icarus: Uprising,* the goddess of light uses telepathy to communicate and grants miracles to support Pit on his adventure. In *Smash Bros.,* Palutena has special moves like Warp and Heavenly Light at her disposal. She's very adaptable—you can customize her into a long- or close-range fighter!

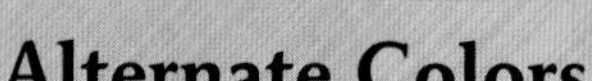

STATISTICS

MAXIMUM NUMBER OF JUMPS: **2**

CAN WALL JUMP: **No**

CAN WALL CLING: **No**

CAN CRAWL: **No**

Alternate Colors

Smash Attacks

SIDE SMASH DAMAGE 13~16%

Giant wings flap forward to strike anyone in front of Palutena. Opponents just outside the range of this attack are pushed back.

DOWN SMASH DAMAGE 13~15%

Giant wings slam down on either side of Palutena, hitting anyone in the path. Opponents just outside the range of this attack are pushed back.

UP SMASH DAMAGE 9~16%

Palutena summons a pillar of light immediately in front of her that blasts opponents upward. The pillar is extremely tall!

Basic Attacks

STANDING ATTACK

DAMAGE 3% RAPID STRIKES 5.8% : 5 HITS

Palutena lowers her staff to hip level to attack opponents multiple times. After the rapid strikes, a final hit launches opponents away.

UP TILT

DAMAGE 1~2.5% MAX DAMAGE 8.5% : 7 HITS

Palutena spins her staff above her head. Hits multiple times and launches opponents vertically.

DASH ATTACK

DAMAGE 5~9%

Palutena charges her opponent with her shield. During this dash attack, she has partial invincibility. This attack also reflects!

SIDE TILT

DAMAGE 4~6% MAX DAMAGE 18% : 3 HITS

Palutena sends her staff spinning in front of her. Best used against groups of opponents.

DOWN TILT DAMAGE 5~8.5%

Palutena spins her staff on the ground in front of her. Can launch opponents diagonally away.

EDGE ATTACK

Palutena swings herself back up to the stage and performs a long-range leg sweep.

Air Attacks

NEUTRAL AIR ATTACK

DAMAGE 1.5~4% MAX DAMAGE 11.5% : 6 HITS

Palutena spins her staff around her body. Hits multiple times.

DOWN AIR ATTACK DAMAGE 9%

Palutena kicks downward and then to the side. Has a meteor effect when hitting opponents in the air.

BACK AIR ATTACK

DAMAGE 9~12%

Using her shield, Palutena strikes behind her. During the attack, the upper half of her body has some invincibility.

UP AIR ATTACK

DAMAGE 1~5% MAX DAMAGE 9% : 5 HITS

Palutena raises her staff up to hit opponents above her multiple times. Decent horizontal hitbox, but it's difficult to land because of her height and jump distance.

FORWARD AIR ATTACK

DAMAGE 7%

A very quick jump kick attack that does not stay out for very long.

Special Attacks

AUTORETICLE (Neutral Special)

DAMAGE 2.9% MAX DAMAGE 8.7% : 3 HITS

Targets an opponent and fires three energy blasts from Palutena's staff. You must be facing the opponent, and there must be no obstacles in the way. If obstacles are in the way or if the target is out of range, then no shots are fired.

Explosive Flame

DAMAGE 0.6~4% MAX DAMAGE 7.6% : 7 HITS

Palutena creates a blast in front of her that can hit opponents multiple times.

Heavenly Light

DAMAGE 1% MAX DAMAGE 4% : 4 HITS

Palutena surrounds herself with rays of light that damage opponents. Holding the button extends the duration of this attack.

REFLECT BARRIER

(Side Special) DAMAGE 0~5%

Palutena casts forward a reflective wall. It reflects projectiles and pushes opponents out of the way.

Angelic Missile DAMAGE 13%

Palutena launches herself forward to collide with opponents and knock them away. When used in the air, Palutena can use it repeatedly before landing.

Super Speed DAMAGE 0~7.8%

Palutena shows off her speed as she dashes headfirst toward opponents. Attack power scales with the distance you travel. You can cancel the dash by hitting the Special button again or by hitting Back. You will have to wait a short time before you can use the move again. If used in the air, you can use your aerial attacks with the appropriate directional inputs and the Attack button. Your vertical height will not be maintained when you use this in the air, so you will continue to fall throughout the dash.

WARP (Up Special) DAMAGE 0%

Palutena teleports in any direction of your choosing. You can't attack or be attacked while teleporting. Be sure not to land off-stage, or you will fall to your doom!

Jump Glide DAMAGE 0%

After jumping, Palutena glides down, allowing you to control her horizontal movement. You can cancel the glide by hitting Down. You can also perform any aerial attacks with the appropriate directional inputs and the Attack button. Palutena is in a fall state if you attack or if the moves duration expires.

Rocket Jump DAMAGE 10~12%

An explosion at Palutena's feet sends her flying straight upward. The explosion is a bit stronger on land, but when used in the air, it has a meteor effect against airborne opponents. Palutena is in a fall state after this attack.

COUNTER (Down Special)

DAMAGE *SEE COUNTER TABLE*

Palutena raises her staff and shield to counter incoming attacks before retaliating with her staff. This counter has good range. Palutena is invincible during her retaliation.

Lightweight DAMAGE 0%

Palutena becomes lighter and faster, but this also makes her easier to launch. Her walk speed, run speed, and jump height are all increased temporarily. Once the move ends, her walk speed, run speed, and horizontal air movement speed are slower than usual for a little while. Once this penalty period is over, Palutena's body glows and you can use Lightweight again.

Celestial Firework

DAMAGE 1.2~3.2% MAX DAMAGE 8% : 5 HITS

Palutena launches a firework into the air. It detonates on contact or after a set time. This move has some invincibility on startup.

	STARTUP	DURATION	DAMAGE SCALING	SPEED SCALING
REFLECT BARRIER	9th frame	58 frames	~1.2x	~1.2x

	STARTUP	DURATION	DAMAGE SCALING	MIN DAMAGE	MAX DAMAGE
COUNTER	10th frame	22 frames	1.3x	10%	50%

While other characters' alternate Special attacks have modified attributes of the regular Special attacks, Palutena's are all unique. Her regular set of Special attacks is quite defensive; however, her alternate choices open up her offensive options.

NOTE

Final Smash

BLACK HOLE LASER

Palutena summons a black hole to pull opponents in before she jumps backward to unleash a huge laser beam attack on them. The laser beam lowers over the duration of the attack. While the black hole reaches about half of Final Destination form, the laser beam makes it most of the way across Gerudo Valley. Since Palutena jumps back before using the laser beam, it has the potential to hit opponents that were behind her when she started the black hole. Overall, this has good damage and KO potential, launching opponents diagonally away.

Strategy

Palutena is one of the lighter characters in the game, but she's also one of the fastest! Her ground speed, air speed, and fast fall speed are surprisingly high, given her height. Her weakness, though, is she can't really fight from range because most of her Special attacks are defensive. To be most effective, go on the offense while using all of your defensive tools to keep you safer. Palutena's Smash attacks are quite damaging with excellent range; Up Smash in particular has a very high hitbox and is useful to prevent opponents from approaching you. Forward Smash has great KO potential and can push away opponents who are just outside of its hitbox, similar to Down Smash. Her Tilt attacks start off a little slow but cover a good amount of ground.

Autoreticle is Palutena's sole long-range projectile attack. She must be facing the opponent, and the opponent must be in range for the autoreticle to target and fire. This targets the closest opponent who is not in an invulnerable state. Once fired, the blasts head toward the reticle. Damage on this is fairly decent, but it takes some time to pull off, so make sure you're in a safe position. Reflect Barrier is useful to push opponents away and to reflect projectiles. Reflected projectiles are faster and stronger on return. Use this near the edge to make life difficult for opponents off-stage. Palutena's Counter is her next defensive tool, returning damage stronger than it was originally dished out. As a bonus, it also attacks in the correct direction, so use this in the air or against opponents behind you. Warp is fast and can get you out of trouble quickly, but be sure not to land off-stage, as you will be in a fall state! Also note that Palutena briefly turns invisible when using spot dodge or evasive rolls; this can confuse opponents up close.

For aerial offense, Palutena has some good options as well. Forward Air is extremely quick and has a sweet spot just on top of Palutena's foot. Neutral Air is useful to keep opponents off of you. Palutena's Back Air is her best option to KO opponents, and it has some invincibility as well. Lastly, her Down Air has a meteor effect against airborne opponents. To punish long-range on the ground, don't be afraid to try a Dash Attack—it has partial invincibility! This can be effective for edge-guarding along with Palutena's Autoreticle, Counter, and Reflect Barrier. Overall, use her speed to your advantage to deal some damage, then use your Smash attacks and Back Air to knock opponents out!

Recovery

Palutena has one main tool for all of her recovery: her Warp Special. It covers an impressive distance both horizontally and vertically, but it leaves her in a fall state. Fortunately, Palutena has a couple of Specials to slow her fall by a little bit. First is her Autoreticle attack, which will also fire at any nearby opponents. Her other Special that can slow her fall is her Counter—use this when you see someone coming to attack you air-to-air.

PEACH

Trophy Description

Princess of the Mushroom Kingdom, Peach continues to prove that "powerful" and "cute" are not mutually exclusive. In *Smash Bros.*, Peach uses her dress to float above the fray, suddenly descending and attacking with numerous weapons. A frying pan? An umbrella? TOAD?! Where does she keep it all?

STATISTICS

MAXIMUM NUMBER OF JUMPS: **2**

CAN WALL JUMP: **No**

CAN WALL CLING: **No**

Can Crawl: **No**

Alternate Colors

Smash Attacks

SIDE SMASH TENNIS RACKET 13%, GOLF CLUB 15%, FRYING PAN 18%

Peach's SIDE SMASH rotates between three weapons in order: a tennis racket, a golf club, and a frying pan. The tennis racket launches farthest, the golf club has the most range, and the frying pan does the most damage. Launch angle increases from tennis racket to golf club to frying pan.

DOWN SMASH

DAMAGE 2~3% MAX DAMAGE 14% : 5 HITS

This low attack hits multiple times as Peach spins while crouching.

UP SMASH DAMAGE 10~17%

Peach whips a ribbon around herself as she twirls. Both her arms and her head are invincible during this attack.

Basic Attacks

STANDING ATTACK DAMAGE 2%, 3%

Peach's Standing attack is a very quick two-slap combo that pops the opponent up into the air. Use the speed of the first hit by itself to interrupt your opponent, but be careful when commiting to both strikes.

UP TILT DAMAGE 8~10%

This uppercut releases a heart at its peak. It has enough forward range to hit a standing opponent in front of Peach and pops your opponent up in front of her, allowing for follow-ups.

DASH ATTACK

DAMAGE 4~6% MAX DAMAGE 10% : 2 HITS

Peach lunges forward with boths arms outstretched with this two-hit dash attack. The second hit releases a magic attack that pops opponents up even higher.

SIDE TILT DAMAGE 6~8%

A high forward kick with very good vertical range.

DOWN TILT DAMAGE 7%

Here Peach sweeps your opponent with a single swipe in front of her with her arm, popping your opponent up into the air. Her swinging arm is invincible during this attack.

EDGE ATTACK

Peach returns to the stage with a low arm sweep similar to her Down Tilt.

Air Attacks

NEUTRAL AIR ATTACK

DAMAGE 5~13%

Peach twirls in the air to perform a single slap. Use this out of Gliding or from short hops. This is more powerful at the beginning of the attack.

DOWN AIR ATTACK

DAMAGE 1~5% MAX DAMAGE 11% : 4 HITS

One of Peach's best aerial attacks, as it can lead to combos that rack up tons of damage or to wear down an opponent's shield. This multi-hitting attack can be very frustrating for opponents and is especially strong when used out of Gliding.

BACK AIR ATTACK DAMAGE 7~12%

This reverse hip bump can travel quite far and deliver solid damage, so be sure not to underestimate its utility.

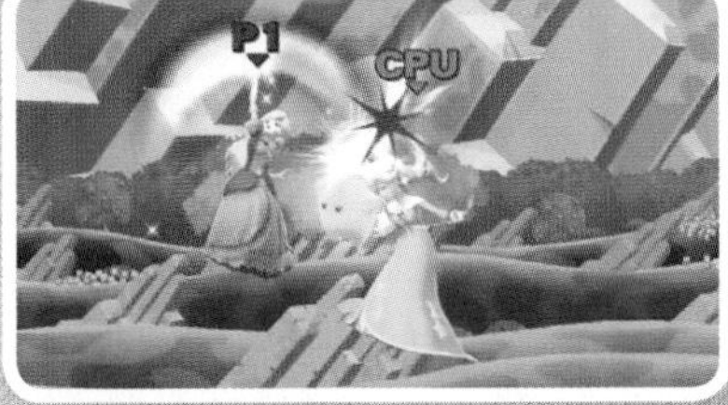

UP AIR ATTACK

DAMAGE 4~6% MAX DAMAGE 10% : 2 HITS

This rainbow attack covers the area above Peach's head. Use it against opponents above you.

FORWARD AIR ATTACK

DAMAGE 15%

This forward swinging attack has great range and does a lot of damage.

Special Attacks

PEACH BOMBER (Side Special)

DAMAGE 10%

Peach bombs the opponent with an explosive hip bump. On a successful hit, Peach can immediately float if she still has it available. This will allow you to chase down opponents that were knocked away by Peach Bomber.

Flower Bomber DAMAGE 4%

Hitting with this attack causes flowers to sprout from your opponents head to deal damage over time. The distance covered is shorter in this version, and it has more recovery when it misses.

Flying Peach Bomber DAMAGE 12%

A flaming hip attack that sets your opponents aflame and knocks them away. This is quite strong but also has a large recovery when it misses.

PEACH PARASOL (Up Special)

DAMAGE 1~4% MAX DAMAGE 11% : 6 HITS

Primarily used as a recovery tool, Peach Parasol is also an attack! Peach jumps and opens her parasol to slow her fall. You can tap Down to attack with the parasol during the fall, but this will make you fall faster. You can hit Up to reopen the parasol as well. You can also move left or right as she comes down.

Parasol High Jump DAMAGE 0%

This customized version is not an attack. Instead, Peach jumps very far away very quickly and falls without opening her parasol.

Light Parasol DAMAGE 3%

This variation of the parasol allows Peach to open the parasol and float upward! Her initial jump isn't as high, and you can still open and close the parasol to attack or control your vertical movement. Overall, though, you have less time to use this parasol than with the default version.

TOAD (Neutral Special)

DAMAGE 2% MAX DAMAGE 18% : 9 HITS

Toad can be used to counter your opponent's attacks and inflict some damage. This can be a good option when your shield is wearing thin or as a stall tactic to stay in the air longer. The strength of your opponent's attack does not affect the power of Toad's counterattack. You also have some invincibility when pulling out Toad.

Sleepy Toad DAMAGE 3%

This counterattack by Toad puts opponents to sleep! This only puts grounded opponents to sleep; airborne opponents are knocked away. This version starts up a little slower.

Grumpy Toad

DAMAGE 1~2.5% MAX DAMAGE 8% : 4 HITS

This variation is an attack by itself, not a counter. It's weaker, you are not invincible when bringing out Toad, and you can't use it to stall while airborne.

TOAD DATA

	COUNTER STARTUP	DURATION
TOAD	11th frame	21 frames
SLEEPY TOAD	13th frame	14 frames

VEGETABLE (Down Special)

DAMAGE *SEE VEGETABLE TABLE*

Peach reaches into the ground and pulls out a Vegetable.Use the Attack button to throw the Vegetables up, down, forward, or backward. Smash the direction to throw it farther. Vegetables vary in damage, and sometimes Peach can even pull out rare items like Bob-ombs, Beam Swords, and Mr. Saturn! The more damaging an item is, however, the less chance Peach has of pulling it out! Keep pulling to see what you get!

Light Veggie

DAMAGE *SEE VEGETABLE TABLE*

Light Veggies are pulled much faster and travel lighter through the air. Their strength is weaker, and you are not able to pull Special items. When hitting an opponent, Light Veggies float back farther than regular Vegetables. There is a limit to the number of Vegetables you can have out at any given time.

Heavy Veggie

DAMAGE *SEE VEGETABLE TABLE*

Peach uses her strength to pull Heavy Veggies out of the ground. She can't throw them as far, but they hit a lot harder! You cannot pull Special items. There is a limit to the number of Vegetables you can have out at any given time.

VEGETABLE DAMAGE DATA

FACIAL EXPRESSION	VEGETABLE DAMAGE	LIGHT VEGGIE DAMAGE	HEAVY VEGGIE DAMAGE
GRIN	2~13.4%	7.5%	15%
STARE	2~13.4%	7.5%	15%
CLOSED EYES	2~13.4%	7.5%	15%
SURPRISE	2~13.4%	7.5%	15%
SMILE	2~13.4%	7.5%	15%
WINK	6~17.4%	10.5%	18%
DOT-EYES	12~23.4%	15.5%	24%
WRINKLED FACE	23~34.4%	25.5%	37%

FLOATING

Peach can float in the air if you hold the Jump button—she will float from the peak of her jump. She can also move horizontally while floating. Further, she can float at any point of a jump by hitting Down while holding the Jump button. She can float off the ground immediately by holding Down then hitting and holding the Jump button. This gives you access to her Air attacks while she is on the same level as a grounded opponent. While floating, Peach can use aerial attacks even while holding items! However, this also means that she cannot throw items while floating.

Final Smash

PEACH BLOSSOM

Peach's Final Smash causes giant peaches to fall from the sky. Anyone caught nearby is put into a special Deep Sleep state. They will be completely vulnerable in this state, so be sure to target whomever has the highest health percentage! As soon as you hit anyone, they will wake up, so you have only one good shot! You can also eat the peaches to restore health—each peach returns 10% health to Peach. Try to eat as many as possible before going for a KO blow against your opponents.

Strategy

Peach's main strengths are her projectiles, her horizontal recovery, her combo potential, and her versatility, thanks to her float ability. Her weakness is that she's a lightweight character who doesn't have very strong knockout options. You'll have to use her projectiles and her float ability to build up damage on your opponents while outspacing them to deal additional damage. Her jab is also a very useful interrupt tool and will get you out of trouble, and her Forward and Back Air attacks are her better knockout tools. While she's floating, it can be very tempting to use her Forward Air Attack a great deal; however, you want to save its strength to try knocking out opponents later in the match. Float can also be used slightly above an opponent's head level to threaten that opponent's shield with Peach's Down Air Attack. You can also use float to do Forward Air attacks while moving backward or Back Air attacks while moving forward! You can even chain together multiple Back Air attacks by doing one from float, then releasing float, and then doing it again!

The second technical part about Peach's game is her Vegetables. Keep an eye out for the more damaging ones and then hope you get one of the rare items! Pull Vegetables as often as possible to find these rare ones.

Throw them up, down, forward, or back, and pull another one in the process. Note that if you connect with a thrown Vegetable, you can catch it again to re-use it! And definitely try this if you pull one of the rarer Vegetables! If you throw one very high up, you can pull another, throw it forward, catch the first one on its way down, and then throw that as well! This will give you two Vegetable tosses in quick succession!

When it comes to using Toad, you need to be very careful, as Peach is left vulnerable on whiff. Don't forget you can also use Toad in the air, which can be especially fun after being popped off the edge if your opponent tries to immediately attack you. When Peach is edge guarding, Toad can also be useful in stopping your opponents from attacking their way back onto the edge. Another surprise edge guarding tool is Peach's Peach Bomber, which travels a good distance in a short amount of time. Of course, throwing Vegetables at opponents as they are trying to recover is always a good option, too. And don't forget you can also throw Vegetables downward at opponents trying to get back up to the stage as well.

Recovery

As Peach is a lightweight character, you will need to master her recovery options. In general, her vertical recovery isn't the strongest, but her horizontal recovery options are amazing. Her main vertical recovery tool is the Peach Parasol, as she jumps higher into the air before slowly descending. During her descent, she can also move horizontally left or right. Another option she has is to float when you hold the Jump button—this also allows her to recover horizontally, allowing her to move left or right and giving her access to her attacks at the same time. Her Peach Bomber travels far horizontally and is a good horizontal recovery option as well. You can also use Toad as a slight stall tactic to throw off your opponent's timing. But in the end, Parasol is Peach's only real vertical recovery option—and its slow descent allows opponents to catch up to you quickly, so try to get to the edge with it to gain some invincibility. Note, that with the parasol open, Peach only grabs the edge if she's facing forward. If she's facing the wrong way, close the parasol to enter a fall state and grab the edge.

PIKACHU

Trophy Description

Recognized the world over, Pikachu is an Electric-type Pokémon that stores energy in its cheeks for use in battle. In *Smash Bros.*, Pikachu is a well-rounded fighter with speedy, powerful electric attacks. Quick Attack can be used twice in a row if two directions are input, one after another.

STATISTICS

MAXIMUM NUMBER OF JUMPS: **2**

CAN WALL JUMP: **Yes**

CAN WALL CLING: **No**

CAN CRAWL: **Yes**

Alternate Colors

Smash Attacks

SIDE SMASH DAMAGE 12~18%

Pikachu leans forward, releasing electricity from its cheeks.

DOWN SMASH

DAMAGE 2~3% MAX DAMAGE 13% : 6 HITS

Pikachu spins on the ground, hitting opponents with its tail and electricity.

UP SMASH DAMAGE 7~14%

Pikachu uses its tail in this jumping flipkick attack.

Basic Attacks

STANDING ATTACK

DAMAGE 1~1.4% MAX DAMAGE 7.8% : 6 HITS

Pikachu looks down and rapidly rams its head into the opponent.

UP TILT **DAMAGE 5%**

Pikachu's whips its tail over its body to hit the ground in front of it.

DASH ATTACK

DAMAGE 6~10%

Pikachu pounces at your opponent and attacks with a headbutt.

SIDE TILT **DAMAGE 8~10%**

Pikachu stands on its hands and kicks out with its legs. This can be aimed up or down.

DOWN TILT **DAMAGE 6%**

Trip the opponent using Pikachu's tail.

EDGE ATTACK

Pikachu flips itself back on-stage, attacking with its tail.

Air Attacks

NEUTRAL AIR ATTACK

DAMAGE 5.5~8.5%

Pikachu spins forward in the air, using its tail to attack while spinning.

DOWN AIR ATTACK

DAMAGE 4~12% MAX DAMAGE 16% : 2 HITS

Pikachu spirals down toward the ground with electricity shooting out of its cheeks. This hits once in the air for 12% and can deal an additional 4% with a shockwave upon landing.

UP AIR ATTACK

DAMAGE 4~5%

Pikachu flips in the air to strike upward with its tail.

FORWARD AIR ATTACK

DAMAGE 1.7~3% MAX DAMAGE 9.8% : 5 HITS

Pikachu spirals forward with electricity shooting out of its cheeks. This attack can hit multiple times.

Special Attacks

THUNDER JOLT (Neutral Special)

DAMAGE 3~6%

Shoot off a bouncing ball of electricity. This follows the contour of a stage, even over edges.

THUNDER WAVE DAMAGE 1~3%

This ball of electricity is slightly weaker but stuns your opponents, leaving them open to followup. The higher an opponent's damage, the longer the duration of the stun.

THUNDER SHOCK DAMAGE 3~10%

Fires a ball of electricity that goes straight forward and does not bounce. After some time or if it hits something, it gives off a strong jolt of electricity. While Pikachu is moving, it's weaker than normal, but the discharge does much more damage. Note the distance traveled by the ball of electricity is shorter than normal.

SKULL BASH (Side Special)

DAMAGE 6.2~21.4%

Pikachu blasts forward, spiraling headfirst. Charge this move longer to increase its range and damage. Perform this with a Smash input and it is partially charged.

SHOCKING SKULL BASH

DAMAGE 0.9~4.3% MAX DAMAGE 19.7% : 10 HITS

In this version, Pikachu is covered in electricity and hits the opponent multiple times before blasting them away. This travels slightly less distance and does slightly less damage. It makes up for this with its multiple hits and knockback potential.

HEAVY SKULL BASH

DAMAGE 0.9~32.1%

This version hits a lot harder, dealing most of its damage closer to its startup. The farther it goes, the weaker it gets.

QUICK ATTACK (Up Special)

DAMAGE 2~3% MAX DAMAGE 5% : 2 HITS

This two-part attack allows Pikachu to dash attack in any two directions. After inputting the Up Special, immediately hit the control stick in the two directions you want Pikachu to travel. If the first one hits, you have to slightly delay your input for the second directional attack.

METEOR QUICK ATTACK

DAMAGE 2~3% MAX DAMAGE 6% : 2 HITS

Moves even faster and also gives a meteor effect on hit. The overall distance is shorter than usual, but both hits are equally damaging.

QUICK FEET DAMAGE 5%

Travels much farther, but you can't change direction. It deals more damage and the hitbox is slightly larger on this attack.

THUNDER (Down Special)

DAMAGE 6~15% MAX DAMAGE 23% : 2 HITS

Pikachu calls down a bolt of lightning that has a huge meteor effect when it hits near the cloud. Combo into this from your Up Throw. If the bolt hits you as well, Pikachu discharges additional damage while being temporarily invincible, and it does even more damage to your opponent. The lightning is initially pretty low in damage, but it quickly ramps up and stays at a fixed level during its descent.

THUNDER BURST

DAMAGE 2~15% MAX DAMAGE 19% : 3 HITS

Lightning does not strike in this customization, but Pikachu releases electrical energy all around itself. This hits opponents multiple times before blasting them away. The more hits opponents take before the last attack, the farther they are blown away. Pikachu has no invincibility in this version.

DISTANT THUNDER

DAMAGE 5~13% MAX DAMAGE 11%, 13%

This lightning strike originates higher than usual and is very powerful. This version starts very strong then gradually decreases in strength. You can also use this to strike Pikachu to discharge additional damage, but this discharge is weaker than normal, and Pikachu is not invincible.

Final Smash

VOLT TACKLE

Pikachu transforms into a giant ball of electricity you can control around the stage, even through platforms. Bumping into opponents deals a little bit of damage but doesn't cause much knockback. Hitting the Attack button makes the electricity ball pulse and discharge additional damage. Hitting an opponent with that pulse grants much more damage and knockback. Each time you use the pulse, though, there's a short cool-down time where the ball becomes darker and smaller before you can use it again. During this time, the attack power isslightly less. When the ball regains its original size, the pulse is ready to be used again. This is great for stages with multiple platforms and multiple opponents. Use it to juggle opponents through the air to guide them off-stage!

Strategy

Pikachu is a quick, lightweight character that relies on its speed to rack up damage on opponents before going for KOs. Increasing its mobility options, Pikachu can also crawl and wall jump. In the air, mobility isn't Pikachu's strong point, but Thunder helps with its tall vertical hitbox. Pikachu can also surprise opponents from a distance with Skull Bash and Quick Attack. Pikachu's main weaknesses are its light weight, short range, and aerial attacks. Use your Thunder Jolt to harass opponents, and keep the pressure on with your speed, throws, and multi-hitting aerials like Forward and Back Air. Note that Back Air and Down Air have an extra hit upon landing, so practice using these from the right height to maximize damage. Because your aerials have short range, consider fighting from higher platforms.

Pikachu's main projectile attack is Thunder Jolt. This ball of electricity is affected by gravity, so if you throw it from the air, it continues downward at an angle. Once it connects with the stage, it continues to bounce along the ground and over the edges of the stage. This makes it particularly useful for edge-guarding on certain stages. To attack opponents from great distance, charge up Skull Bash to blast Pikachu toward them. This move doesn't leave you in a fall state, so you can use it to edge-guard while still having your Quick Attack available to recover. Quick Attack is very versatile—you can use it in two directions. You can use it to quickly run away from an opponent or you can use it to attack opponents. If platforms are nearby, Quick Attack gives you even more options. Generally, though, this is your best recovery option. Thunder comes down at the location where Pikachu calls it, and it has a meteor effect when it hits near the cloud. If you use it while moving forward, it actually arrives behind you, which can be useful when opponents are chasing you. If the bolt hits Pikachu, it deals even more damage to anyone around. In free-for-all modes, use Thunder and Thunder Jolt as much as possible, but watch out for opponents who have a reflect ability!

For KOs, Pikachu's best options are Side Smash, Up Smash, and Neutral Air. Down Smash can be useful to rack up damage and refresh other attacks while having decent vertical knockback. Because Pikachu isn't the strongest in this area, edge-guarding can help you get KOs earlier. Use Skull Bash to connect with opponents off-stage. Other good off-stage options are Thunder, Down Air, and Forward Air. If you're on the stage defending, use Side Tilt and Down Tilt to prevent opponents from grabbing onto the edge.

Recovery

Pikachu has some of the best recovery tools in the game. Horizontally, you have Skull Bash, which can be charged to take Pikachu even farther horizontally. While this is a great recovery tool, it pales in comparison to Pikachu's other recovery tool, Quick Attack. This attack lets you quickly dash in two separate directions for recovery! Practice the timing to get both dashes in. Because Skull Bash doesn't leave you in a fall state, you can easily combine these two Specials to travel fully under Final Destination and back up! Just jump off, charge Skull Bash, use your double jump, then Quick Attack back to the opposite ledge.

PIT

Trophy Description

Pit is the captain of Palutena's royal guard. Despite the wings on his back, Pit needs the Power of Flight from Palutena in order to truly fly. In *Smash Bros.*, he can still get more air than most with four jumps and a special move that boosts him higher. He also has a new reflect move—it protects both sides!

STATISTICS

MAXIMUM NUMBER OF JUMPS: **4**

CAN WALL JUMP: **No**

CAN WALL CLING: **No**

CAN CRAWL: **No**

Alternate Colors

Smash Attacks

SIDE SMASH

DAMAGE 5~10% MAX DAMAGE 15% : 2 HITS

Pit slashes forward twice with his blades. The second hit is much more damaging.

DOWN SMASH DAMAGE 10~12%

A sweep attack with the blades that sends opponents up and away.

UP SMASH

DAMAGE 2~8% MAX DAMAGE 13% : 3 HITS

Pit spins his blades as he leaps into the air. This hits multiple times and sends your opponent upward.

Basic Attacks

STANDING ATTACK

DAMAGE 2%, 2%, 5% RAPID STRIKES 9% : 8 HITS

A three-strike attack with the third hit launching opponents away.

UP TILT

DAMAGE 2~5% MAX DAMAGE 10% : 3 HITS

A flipkick attack that goes into two additional kicks with the last kick launching opponents upward.

DASH ATTACK DAMAGE 11%

Pit dashes forward and strikes with one blade in front of him.

SIDE TILT DAMAGE 7~10%

Pit uses his blades like a pair of scissors and swipes them together in front of him.

DOWN TILT DAMAGE 6%

A long-range single-blade sweep.

EDGE ATTACK

Pit handstands his way back to the platform before striking with a low kick attack.

Air Attacks

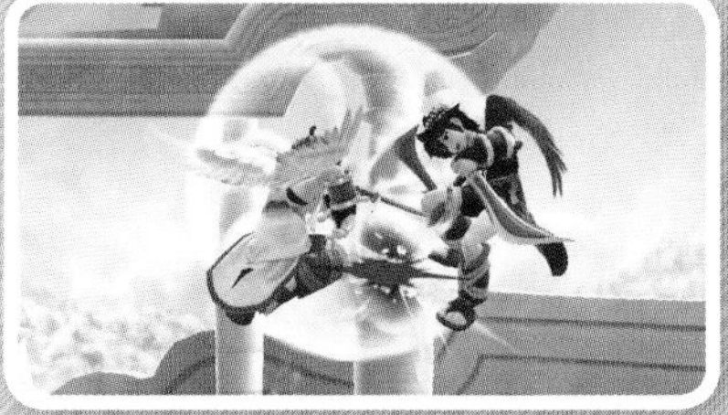

NEUTRAL AIR ATTACK

DAMAGE 0.7~4% MAX DAMAGE 8.9% : 8 HITS

Pit spins his blades rapidly around his entire body. Hits multiple times, and the last hit knocks opponents away. Despite its appearance, it doesn't really hit behind Pit.

DOWN AIR ATTACK DAMAGE 10%

Pit swipes downward with a single blade. This has a meteor smash effect at the start of the attack.

BACK AIR ATTACK

DAMAGE 8~12%

Pit uses both blades and stabs directly behind him.

UP AIR ATTACK

DAMAGE 2% MAX DAMAGE 10% : 5 HITS

Pit spins his blades above him as if they were helicopter blades. Hits multiple times and knocks opponents upward.

FORWARD AIR ATTACK

DAMAGE 1.5~4% MAX DAMAGE 7% : 3 HITS

Pit spins his blades in front of him. This hits multiple times.

Special Attacks

PALUTENA BOW
(Neutral Special) DAMAGE 3.3~8.6%

Pit fires an arrow that you have some control over. You can charge up the arrow to increase its speed. You can aim the arrow straight up or back by hitting Up or Back, respectively.

Piercing Bow DAMAGE 5.1~11.7%

This arrow pierces opponents and deals more damage. It takes longer to charge up to maximum, and there is a longer recovery period after firing.

Guiding Bow DAMAGE 2.1~6%

This arrow is much more maneuverable than normal. While the power and speed are decreased, its lifespan is longer. You can only have one arrow out at a time, and the recovery period is longer as well.

UPPERDASH ARM
(Side Special) ON LAND 11% IN AIR 9%

Pit dashes forward and uppercuts. During the dash, this also deflects projectiles, and Pit has super armor and doesn't flinch. Some deflected projectiles, like Mario's Fireball, will not deal damage, while others, like Pikachu's Thunder Jolt will deal damage.

Interception Arm ON LAND 13% IN AIR 11%

Pit holds a pose with super armor then uppercuts anyone who attacks him. This functions similarly to a counter, as he does not dash forward.

Quickdash Arm ON LAND 9% IN AIR 7%

This variation travels farther and faster but deals less damage. The startup is a bit slower, and there is a bit more recovery as well.

POWER OF FLIGHT (Up Special)
DAMAGE 0%

Pit soars through the air. You can control the upward direction Pit flies. This is purely a movement or recovery tool, not an attack.

Striking Flight DAMAGE 6~9%

Deals damage to nearby enemies during takeoff! You can't control the angle at which Pit flies as much.

Breezy Flight DAMAGE 0%

Slightly slower startup but a quicker launch, this version creates a wind around Pit that pushes opponents out of the way.

GUARDIAN ORBITARS
(Down Special) DAMAGE 0%

Shields come down on both sides of Pit, shielding him from enemy attacks and reflecting projectiles. Additionally, it pushes back opponents who touch them. You are still vulnerable from above, but Pit has super armor and doesn't flinch. Holding the button keeps the shields out longer.

Impact Orbitars DAMAGE 5%

The Impact Orbitars come down to damage opponents and knock them away; however, they don't shield you or reflect projectiles.

Amplifying Orbitars DAMAGE 0%

Any projectiles reflected are returned faster and more powerful. The shields can be kept out much longer, but they break much easier as well. This version does not push away nearby opponents.

ORBITARS DATA

	STARTUP	SHORTEST DURATION	LONGEST DURATION	DAMAGE SCALING	SPEED SCALING
GUARDIAN ORBITARS	9th frame	20 frames	80 frames	1.5x	1.7x
AMPLIFYING ORBITARS	11th frame	16 frames	150 frames	2x	2x

Final Smash

THREE SACRED TREASURES

Pit equips the Three Sacred Treasures and takes aim at opponents all around him, though mainly at those in front of him. He shoots a multitude of homing arrows before calling down beams of light from the sky. Optimally, you want to make sure opponents are in front of you when using this, as very few of the attacks go behind Pit. While this Final Smash has a lot going on and racks up damage fairly well, it doesn't seem to have significant KO power.

Strategy

Pit is an average-weight character with fantastic air mobility and recovery, thanks to his multiple jumps. His ground speed is average, and most of his ground-based attacks have decent startup and recovery. Overall, his KO potential isn't great, so use his Palutena Bow, air mobility, and multi-hit attacks to rack up as much damage as possible. To aid in defense while building up damage, his Guardian Orbitars creates space, absorbs hits, and reflects projectiles. Multi-hitting attacks on the ground include his jab series, Up Tilt, Up Smash, and Side Smash. To KO opponents from the ground, Pit's best options are Upperdash Arm and his Smash attacks. Side Smash is good, but remember the second hit is the one that has the most damage and knockback.

Firing arrows from a distance is an important part of Pit's game to build damage and frustrate opponents. Arrows fired from Palutena's Bow can travel very far, but they fade out after a time. Charging longer increases the distance arrows can travel and their speed. You have a lot of control over each arrow, so move them around as much as possible. This makes you less predictable and gives your opponent fewer options to approach. Pit's Upperdash Arm is a great way to approach horizontally with its forward motion. It's particularly useful against projectile characters because it deflects projectiles, and it has some super armor as well. Guardian Orbitars are a great way to defend against projectile-heavy characters, as Guardian Orbitars reflect projectiles back faster and stronger. The duration of the Guardian Orbitars can be extended by holding down the button longer. The shields have limited endurance, however, so they can be broken! If they're broken, they require some time to recover.

Fighting in the air is one of Pit's strengths because his blades extend his range. Most of his aerial attacks hit multiple times and have decent knockback, but they are slightly lacking in KO power. When you get an opponent's damage up high enough, however, simply pick the correct option to make contact. In general, Pit's Back Air is best for KOs in the air. His Down Air also has a meteor effect. Interestingly, Back Air and Down Air are his only aerial attacks that are not multi-hitting. Remember to use his multiple jumps to position yourself and fake out opponents.

Recovery

Pit has some of the strongest recovery options in the game. First, he has four jumps, but vertically the third and fourth jumps gain less and less height. You can still use the four jumps to cover great horizontal distance. And for horizontal recovery, Pit can use Upperdash Arm, which sends him flying across the stage but doesn't put him in a fall state! Finally, for vertical recovery, Pit has Power of Flight, which is one of the longest vertical recovery tools in the game. The only downside to it is that it's not an attack. Still, you can use it as either a horizontal or a diagonal recovery. Additionally, Power of Flight has a small bit of invincibility! Between Pit's four jumps, Power of Flight, and Upperdash Arm, you shouldn't have too much difficulty getting him back to the stage.

R.O.B.

Trophy Description

This NES accessory was released in 1985, a groundbreaking system that controlled the robot via a game on the screen. In *Smash Bros.*, R.O.B. has two projectile weapons and can use his rocket base to fly through the air. If you let his Robo Beam charge over time, it'll make for a powerful blast.

STATISTICS

MAXIMUM NUMBER OF JUMPS: **2**

CAN WALL JUMP: **No**

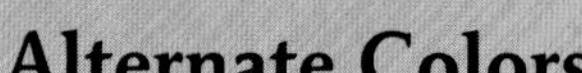

CAN WALL CLING: **No**

CAN CRAWL: **No**

Alternate Colors

Smash Attacks

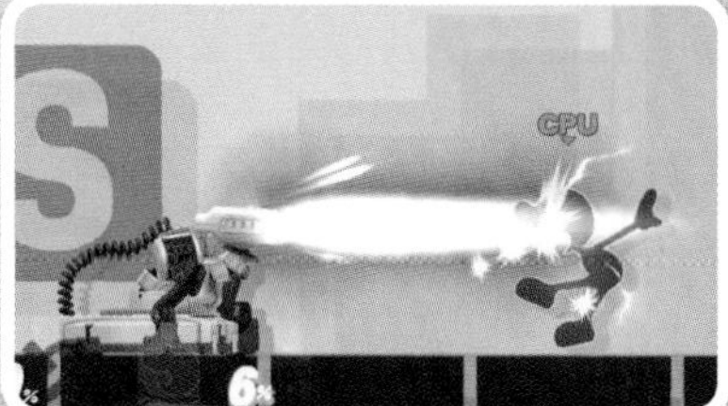

SIDE SMASH DAMAGE 6~15%

R.O.B. leans forward and blasts opponents with a medium-range beam. This can be aimed up or down.

DOWN SMASH

DAMAGE 1.5~5% MAX DAMAGE 13% : 5 HITS

R.O.B. extends his arm and does a spin attack. This can hit multiple times.

UP SMASH

DAMAGE 3~14% MAX DAMAGE 17% : 2 HITS

R.O.B. does a handstand and uses his rocket base to blast opponents upward.

Basic Attacks

STANDING ATTACK DAMAGE 3%, 3%

R.O.B. swings forward in this two-punch attack string.

UP TILT

DAMAGE 3~6% MAX DAMAGE 9% : 2 HITS

Using both of his long arms, R.O.B. strikes upward. Useful to combo at low percentage.

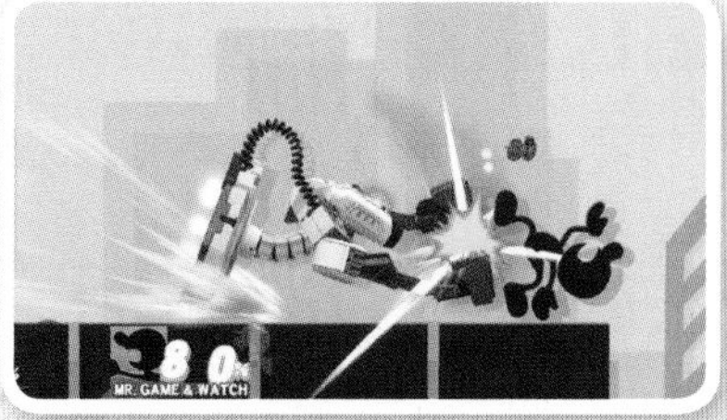

DASH ATTACK DAMAGE 7%

R.O.B. rolls on forward then suddenly strikes downward with both arms.

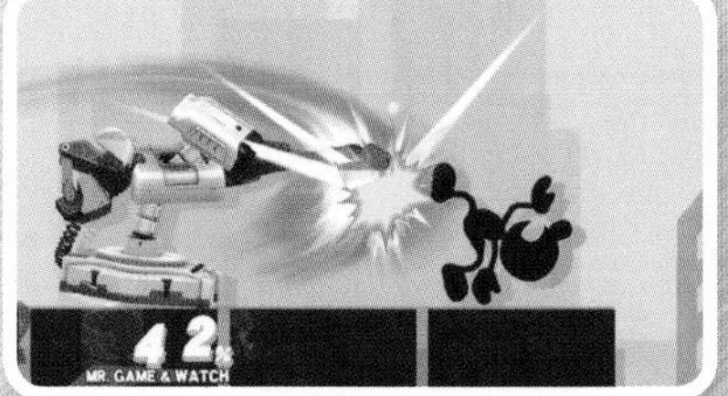

SIDE TILT DAMAGE 5~8%

R.O.B. delivers a solid hook punch. This can be aimed up or down.

DOWN TILT DAMAGE 5%

While crouching down, R.O.B. does a quick jab toward the opponent's feet.

EDGE ATTACK

R.O.B. pulls himself up and swings his rocket base at the opponent.

Air Attacks

NEUTRAL AIR ATTACK

DAMAGE 6~8%

R.O.B. uses his rocket base to blast himself around in this strong front-flip attack.

DOWN AIR ATTACK DAMAGE 6~12%

R.O.B. shoots the burners on his rocket base to hit opponents from above. This can also meteor smash opponents.

BACK AIR ATTACK DAMAGE 4.5~12%

R.O.B. briefly tucks in before extending and exploding the blaster on his rocket base behind him. Note that using this attack boosts R.O.B. forward.

UP AIR ATTACK

DAMAGE 1.5~4% MAX DAMAGE 10% : 5 HITS

Using his robotic joints, R.O.B. spins his arms rapidly upward, striking opponents multiple times. The last hit launches the highest vertically.

FORWARD AIR ATTACK

DAMAGE 7%

R.O.B. swings both arms forward in a clobbering downward strike that knocks opponents diagonally away.

Special Attacks

ROBO BEAM (Neutral Special)

NO CHARGE 4.5~7% MAX DAMAGE 11.5% : 2 HITS

FULL CHARGE 7~10% MAX DAMAGE 17% : 2 HITS

MISFIRE 7%

R.O.B. fires a laser beam from his eyes. This beam can be angled up or down and can bounce off the floor. After using the beam, you need time to recharge before it regains its full range. R.O.B.'s charge level is indicated by the flashing light on top of his head. Once the light is pulsating, you can fire a massive beam for more damage.

Wide-Angle Beam NO CHARGE 3.5~7% MAX DAMAGE 10.5% : 2 HITS FULL CHARGE 7~8% MAX DAMAGE 15% : 2 HITS MISFIRE 7%

This beam can be aimed in a much wider range, but the damage is a little bit lower. Charging up between levels is slightly faster, as is the beam itself.

Infinite Robo Beam

NO CHARGE 2~4% MAX DAMAGE 7% : 2 HITS

FULL CHARGE 4~10% MAX DAMAGE 14% : 2 HITS

This laser beam never runs out of charge, so you can keep firing it. The range is shorter, the damage is lower, and you can't change the angle of the shot as much. This version does not bounce off the floor, and it doesn't pierce opponents like the regular version. The laser itself is a bit slower, and it takes longer to charge to maximum.

ARM ROTOR (Side Special)

DAMAGE 0.7~3% MAX DAMAGE 13.4% : 12 HITS

R.O.B. spins with arms outstretched and finishes with an uppercut attack. You can tilt and control R.O.B. left or right during this attack. While spinning, this also reflects projectiles. Repeatedly hit the button for extra hits, damage, and farther travel distance.

Reflector Arm DAMAGE 2~4%

R.O.B. spins with a longer arm extension, making it easier to reflect projectiles. You can't move R.O.B. left or right during this version of the move. This version starts reflecting much sooner than other versions.

Backward Arm Rotor

DAMAGE 2~4% MAX DAMAGE 6% : 2 HITS

R.O.B. spins opponents around while knocking them away. The duration of this attack is less, and it doesn't slow your fall when used in the air.

GYRO (Down Special)

NO CHARGE 2~8.3% FULL CHARGE 2~10.7%

R.O.B. fires a spinning top at the opponent. The longer you charge the button, the stronger the top is if it hits an opponent, the farther it flies, and the longer it spins. The spinning top can be picked up to throw. Only one top can be out at a time.

Fire Gyro

NO CHARGE 3~9.2% FULL CHARGE 3~12.4%

R.O.B. fires a flaming top that deals more damage but doesn't travel as far. The top's spin time is also shorter than normal.

Slip Gyro

NO CHARGE 1~4.8% MAX DAMAGE 5.8% : 2 HITS

FULL CHARGE 1~7% MAX DAMAGE 10% : 2 HITS

R.O.B. fires a slippery top that slides around instead of bouncing. The speed of the top is much faster, and if it hits an opponent, it continues sliding.

REFLECTION DATA	STARTUP	DURATION	DAMAGE SCALING	SPEED SCALING
ARM ROTOR	16th frame	30 frames	1.5x	1.3x
REFLECTOR ARM	9th frame	20 frames	1.8x	1.5x
BACKWARD ARM ROTOR	12th frame	5 frames	1.5x	1.3x

ROBO BURNER (Up Special)

DAMAGE 0%

Use your thrusters to boost up into the air. After the initial input, tap Up to use the thrusters intermittently and hover until your next attack. R.O.B. can only use Robo Burner when he has enough fuel, and fuel only recharges when R.O.B. is on the ground.

Robo Rocket DAMAGE 5~8%

This variation launches you high into the air, but you can't hover. Fuel recharges much faster when you are on the ground. After takeoff, there is a small attack from the thrusters that has a meteor effect on it.

High-Speed Burner DAMAGE 0%

This allows R.O.B. to fly around much quicker, but it uses up fuel extremely fast. This means the amount of time you can spend flying is considerably less.

Final Smash

SUPER DIFFUSION BEAM

Fires a huge beam that branches into four smaller beams at the end. You can slightly move the beams up or down. If an opponent is caught in one of the smaller beams, that opponent is sucked into the bigger beam. After the beam charges to max power, it fires an additional shot that has much more vertical range. For optimal damage, catch an opponent in the area where the beam branches. Doing so gets you 5–10% more damage.

Strategy

As a heavier character, R.O.B. has heavier attacks with slower startup in addition to a couple of strong projectiles to keep opponents at bay. His long robotic arms give him excellent range for his tilt attacks, Smash attacks, and Arm Rotor. While he has a good number of aerial attacks, his weakness is that his stronger options tend to start up slower. So, while he can do massive amounts of damage and blast opponents off-stage, it requires good timing and spacing. Given his heavy weight, he has fantastic recovery options with Robo Burner and his Back Air attack; however, Robo Burner's duration shortens with consecutive uses, requiring recharge time in order to be most effective. His projectiles are useful and deal decent damage, but Robo Beam requires recharge time as well. As you can see, R.O.B. has a lot of great tools, but they generally have some sort of drawback. This means minimizing drawbacks and maximizing strengths is even more important to play R.O.B.

The Robo Beam is R.O.B.'s main projectile attack in which he fires a laser beam from his eyes. You need to pace yourself when using this attack because its strength lies in how long it's not used. The LED flashing on R.O.B.'s head shows how far along he is in recharging the beam. When fully charged, the beam passes through other beams and projectiles, so use it whenever you have a good opportunity to land it. R.O.B.'s other projectile attack is his Gyro. Charging this attack allows you to throw it farther and allows the top to spin longer. You can cancel out of the charging animation while maintaining the charge by rolling, shielding, or grabbing. Attack opponents with this directly, or set it as a trap on-stage. If you try to use it again while it's already out, R.O.B will go through an animation in which he tries to throw one out, leaving him vulnerable. Arm Rotor is a good tool to hit opponents multiple times with its long range, so use it to rack up damage on opponents. It can also be used to reflect projectiles, but the reflection window does not start up immediately, This comes in handy against projectile-heavy characters.

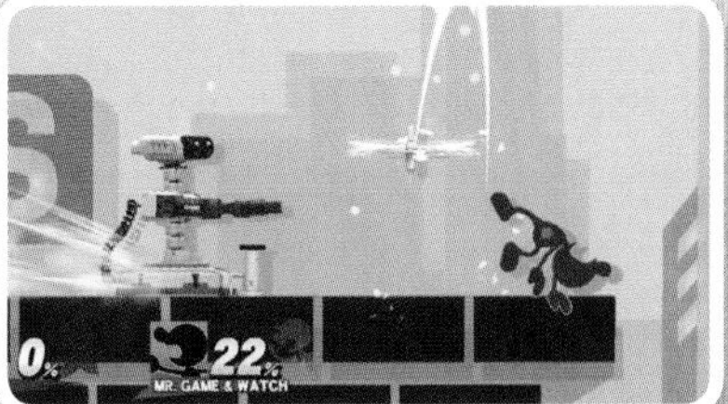

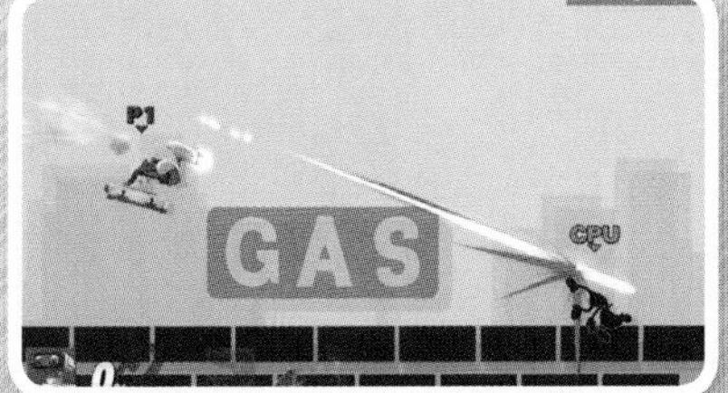

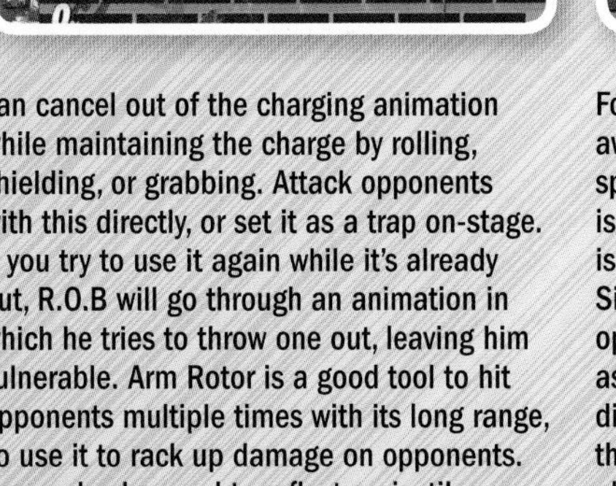

For KOs in the air, Back Air is your best choice. Down Air is useful for meteor smashes, and Up Air is useful for racking up damage and launching opponents vertically. Forward Air is decent at knocking opponents away diagonally and forward because of its speed. For ground attacks, R.O.B.'s Side Tilt is particularly quick for its range, and Up Tilt is good for combos. For KOs on the ground, Side Smash and Up Smash are your best options. When edge-guarding, use your Gyro as a trap to make opponents' returns more difficult. If you have Robo Beam available, the higher the charge, the better. You can also chase opponents off-stage with your Robo Burner and Back Air or Forward Air. Just make sure you have enough fuel before attempting this!

Recovery

R.O.B. has quite a few options for recovery. For vertical recovery, use his Robo Burner thrusters to boost into the air. Using Robo Burner leaves you in a fall state, so be sure to use your double jump beforehand. Once you've started Robo Burner, press the Special button to use R.O.B.'s thrusters. This also allows you to move R.O.B. horizontally by hitting Left or Right, making Robo Burner good for horizontal recovery as well. You can only use thrusters if R.O.B. has enough fuel, so don't stay up there too long! Additionally, fuel only replenishes when R.O.B. is on the ground, so don't jump too much if you think you might need fuel. For horizontal recovery, you can also use R.O.B.'s Back Air attack to move forward. Finally, when you use his Arm Rotor in the air, R.O.B. gets a bit of height and moves forward. Don't expect to grab the edge after this spin, though, because of the uppercut after the spin! The best way to use this is to land on the edge of the stage while attacking.

ROBIN

Trophy Description

This is the male Robin, your avatar in *Fire Emblem Awakening*. The goal of this adventure doesn't change much because of your gender choice, but Robin's marriage options do. In *Smash Bros.*, Robin brings powerful magic and swordplay to bear. He can exhaust his moves, but they'll be restored over time.

STATISTICS

MAXIMUM NUMBER OF JUMPS: **2**

CAN WALL JUMP: **No**

CAN WALL CLING: **No**

CAN CRAWL: **No**

TIP

LEVIN SWORD

If Levin Sword is available, all Smash attacks use it. If it is not available, they are performed with the Bronze Sword. Smashing your aerial inputs uses the Levin Sword, if it is available.

Alternate Colors

Smash Attacks

SIDE SMASH

	DAMAGE
BRONZE SWORD	9.6%
LEVIN SWORD	5~16%

Robin stabs forward with his sword.

DOWN SMASH

	DAMAGE
BRONZE SWORD	8%
LEVIN SWORD	8~15%

A downward swing of the sword all the way to the ground. The Levin Sword version sends out an electric current that can also hit opponents who are immediately in front of, or behind, Robin. This electric current only hits opponents who are on the ground.

UP SMASH

	DAMAGE
BRONZE SWORD	9%
LEVIN SWORD	5~15%

An upward thrust of the sword.

Basic Attacks

STANDING ATTACK

DAMAGE 3%, 3%

ARCFIRE 5% RAPID STRIKES 9% : 7 HITS

Two quick Bronze Sword strikes followed by either a fire blast that combos when the move is input slowly or rapid strikes when the move is input quickly.

UP TILT DAMAGE 6%

A jumping uppercut with the Bronze Sword that pops opponents up.

DASH ATTACK DAMAGE 6~10%

Robin slides in with his Bronze Sword extended horizontally.

SIDE TILT DAMAGE 7.5%

A quick forward slice with Robin's Bronze Sword.

DOWN TILT DAMAGE 6%

A quick sword sweep with the Bronze Sword.

EDGE ATTACK

Robin pulls himself up and lies down on the stage then stabs the opponent's feet with his Bronze Sword.

Air Attacks

LEVIN SWORD AERIALS

If Robin has Levin Sword available, you can perform all aerial attacks, except Neutral Air, with the Levin Sword. If Levin Sword is available but is not out yet, then you can Smash input your aerial attacks to bring out Levin Sword and use it for the aerial attack. With the Levin Sword, you have more damage and range.

NOTE

NEUTRAL AIR ATTACK

Robin swings downward in front of and behind himself. This is the only aerial attack that cannot be done with the Levin Sword.

	DAMAGE
BRONZE SWORD	7%
LEVIN SWORD	N/A

UP AIR ATTACK

Robin does an uppercut attack with his sword as he spins in the air.

	DAMAGE
BRONZE SWORD	7.8%
LEVIN SWORD	5~13%

DOWN AIR ATTACK

A quick downward strike with his sword. With Levin Sword, this can meteor smash.

	DAMAGE
BRONZE SWORD	7.2%
LEVIN SWORD	5~12%

FORWARD AIR ATTACK

Robin strikes in front of himself using his sword.

	DAMAGE
BRONZE SWORD	6.6%
LEVIN SWORD	5~11%

BACK AIR ATTACK

Robin swings back with his sword. This attack stays out for a while.

	DAMAGE
BRONZE SWORD	9%
LEVIN SWORD	5~15%

Special Attacks

THUNDER (Neutral Special)

DAMAGE *SEE THUNDER DAMAGE TABLE*

Robin casts a bolt of lightning magic. This attack can be charged to cast Elthunder, Arcthunder, and Thoron. You can cancel into evasive rolls by hitting left or right during charging. If charged in the air, you carry momentum. The only way to cancel in the air is to air dodge or release it. You only need one point to begin charging to any of the above levels. This means if you only have one point available, you can still charge to Thoron!

Thunder+

DAMAGE *SEE THUNDER DAMAGE TABLE*

All lightning magic is greatly strengthened; however, each use consumes more points out of each tome. The charging time is also longer than the regular version.

Speed Thunder

DAMAGE *SEE THUNDER DAMAGE TABLE*

In this variation, all lightning magic charges up quicker and travels faster and farther. The downside is damage is reduced across the board, and Thoron only hits once.

ELWIND (Up Special)

DAMAGE 5~7% MAX DAMAGE 12% : 2 HITS

Robin casts wind magic downward twice to boost into the air. Each casting deals damage, and the second launches you much higher into the air. On hit, this has a meteor effect against opponents, and you are always in a fall state after using this move. A single blast of Elwind consumes one point. If you have 0 points available, Elwind can't be used, and you fall.

Soaring Elwind

DAMAGE 5% MAX DAMAGE 10% : 2 HITS

The first blast of Elwind only floats you, but the second blast sends Robin soaring. In this variation, you can't move as much horizontally, and there's no meteor effect on hit.

Gliding Elwind

DAMAGE 4~7% MAX DAMAGE 12% : 2 HITS

The first blast of Elwind shoots you at an angle, and the second blast sends you straight up.

NOSFERATU (Down Special)

DAMAGE 0.8% MAX DAMAGE 15.2% : 19 HITS

This curse drains the life of enemies! Add damage to your opponent while reducing your own damage! You can be hit out of this attack. The more accumulated damage Robin has over his opponent's accumulated damage, the more Robin heals for! Additionally, grabbing opponents from behind with Nosferatu also heals Robin more than usual.

Distant Nosferatu

DAMAGE 0.6% MAX DAMAGE 11.4% : 19 HITS

This variation has more range but deals less damage and heals for less. Additionally, it doesn't take into consideration the difference in accumulated damage to heal Robin for more.

Goetia

DAMAGE 1% MAX DAMAGE 19% : 19 HITS

Robin captures his opponents by pulling them in and trapping them. This doesn't heal Robin, but it does a lot of damage. The range is much larger; roughly double that of Nosferatu."

ARCFIRE (Side Special)

DAMAGE 1~4% MAX DAMAGE 13% : 9 HITS

Casts a fireball diagonally toward the ground. On impact, the flames erupt, catching opponents inside it and leaving them open for followup. This Special and all variations of it consume one point on use.

Arcfire+

DAMAGE 2~8% MAX DAMAGE 10% : 2 HITS

This spell causes a large fireball to erupt when the fireball hits. It takes a bit longer to cast and travels a bit farther than the original.

Fire Wall DAMAGE 7%

Robin casts a large flame pillar to protect against enemy attacks. This only makes contact with the terrain, not fighters.

THUNDER DAMAGE TABLE

	THUNDER	ELTHUNDER	ARCTHUNDER	THORON (TAP)	THORON (HOLD)
Thunder	3% (1)	9% (3)	10% : 8 Hits (5)	10.4% : 4 Hits (8)	18.2% : 7 Hits (8)
Thunder+	5% (2)	11% (5)	13.4% : 8 Hits (8)	17.5% : 5 Hits (20)	31.5% : 9 Hits (20)
Speed Thunder	2% (1)	5% (3)	7.5% : 6 Hits (5)	10% (8)	10% (8)

**Numbers in parenthesis indicate the number of points consumed*

TIP

Robin has a limited number of times to use the Levin Sword and tomes. Using either consumes one point. When you run out of points, the tome or item is discarded. If the Levin Sword is out of points, Robin only has access to the Bronze Sword. Knocking out opponents reduces the restore time, and if you are KO'd or land your Final Smash, they are fully restored.

	LEVIN SWORD	THUNDER	ARCFIRE	ELWIND	NOSFERATU
Points	8	20	6	18	4
Restore Time	10 sec	12 sec	12 sec	8 sec	40 sec

THUNDER TOME

Robin's Neutral Special upgrades to different attacks based on the length of time you charge the attack. The first level is Thunder, which deals low damage but is the fastest. As you charge it, the color of the tome changes to yellow and to red before it reaches its max potential. When yellow, Thunder charges into Elthunder and deals more damage but is slower. When red, it charges into Arcthunder, which throws a rod projectile with high-launching power. When fully charged, it becomes Thoron, a yellow beam that can damage multiple opponents at once. Hold the button when using Thoron to extend its range.

Final Smash

PAIR UP

Chrom appears on stage to assist Robin and dashes in at the opponent. If Chrom connects, they both take to the skies before unleashing a massive team combo on everyone who was hit by the dash. The first opponent hit will take slightly more damage than the others—about 45%, while the others get 43% each. The final blow will bounce those opponents back up near Robin, close enough to attack, so be prepared! The range on this attack is a little less then half of Final Destination, so you have to be fairly close to use it.

Strategy

Robin is an average-weight character with features of both a swordfighter and a projectile-based character. On top of this, Robin also has resource management thrown in, as his tomes and Levin Sword have limited uses. They respawn in time, but you have to be prepared to fight with or without these tools. His sword-fighting range and damage is greatly increased, both on the ground and in the air, when he has his Levin Sword. Levin Sword requires some precision, however, to maximize its damage and effectiveness. His Bronze Sword has less range and deals less damage, but its damage is consistent for aerials and Smash attacks.

Robin's primary projectiles are his Thunder and Arcfire. Depending on the matchup you're facing, you should know what level of Thunder you want to charge up to. You can store your current charge by shielding, using your evasive roll, or by using your air dodge. In a free-for-all setting, charge up Thoron and line up multiple enemies. If in a one-on-one situation where your opponent is at a high percentage, you should probably charge up to Arcthunder for its launching power. If you're just trying to harass from range, then Thunder or Elthunder are good options, but both use up your tome faster. Arcfire is an important projectile, as it traps opponents and leaves them open for combo. If you can

land it, follow up with a dash attack. If you already have the Levin Sword out, then follow up with a Levin Sword attack.Nosferatu is an interesting life-stealing attack that damages the opponent and heals Robin. t is a little difficult to land, but it heals for a ton of health. Since it is considered a grab, it can be used against shielding opponents! Land it on an opponent's back, and it's even stronger! Elwind is Robin's primary recovery tool, but as an attack, its first blast also has a meteor effect that might come in handy.

On the ground, Robin's best options to KO an opponent are his Levin Sword Smash attacks. In the air, his Levin Sword Back and Up Airs are your best bets while the Down Air can meteor smash. It's also important to note that Robin's jab series consumes uses of his tomes, depending on which ender you do. If you use the third hit that blasts opponents away, it uses one point of the Arcfire tome; if you use the rapid-fire strikes, it uses one point of your Elwind tome. As with Robin's other tomes, when it runs out, you are temporarily unable to use that tome and its associated attack until it respawns.

Recovery

For recovery, Robin's main tool is Elwind. You can choose the direction of Elwind when you input the direction of the attack to make sure Robin heads in the correct direction. After the second hit of Elwind, which sends Robin much higher, you have more horizontal air control of Robin. Be careful, though—if you use Elwind too much, the tome runs out, and the attack does nothing, leaving Robin with no recovery option!

ROSALINA & LUMA

Trophy Description

The mysterious Rosalina lives in the Comet Observatory with the Lumas. She first traveled with them in search of their mother. In *Smash Bros.*, Rosalina and Luma can fight in different places at the same time. If you can trap someone between Rosalina and Luma, you'll be able to unleash incredible damage!

STATISTICS

MAXIMUM NUMBER OF JUMPS: **2**

CAN WALL JUMP: **No**

CAN WALL CLING: **No**

CAN CRAWL: **Yes**

Alternate Colors

Smash Attacks

SIDE SMASH

	DAMAGE
ROSALINA	12%
LUMA	5~7%

Rosalina leans forward and casts a galaxy in front of her. Luma surges forward horizontally. This can be aimed slightly up or down.

DOWN SMASH

	DAMAGE
ROSALINA	7~9%
LUMA	4~5%

Rosalina spins and casts galaxies at the ground in front of and then behind her. Luma strikes behind and then in front.

UP SMASH

	DAMAGE
ROSALINA	12%
LUMA	4~6%

Rosalina arches her back as she swings upward. Luma does an upward flip attack.

Basic Attacks

STANDING ATTACK

	DAMAGE	RAPID STRIKES
ROSALINA	2%, 1%, 3%	9% : 4 Hits
LUMA	2%, 2%, 4%	5.4% : 3 Hits

A multi-hitting attack in which Rosalina attacks with her wand while Luma swings. When doing rapid hits, Luma spins while Rosalina continues attacking with her wand.

UP TILT

	DAMAGE
ROSALINA	8%
LUMA	3~8%

A halo emits upward out of Rosalina, and Luma swings upward.

DASH ATTACK

	DAMAGE	MAX DAMAGE
ROSALINA	3~4%	7% : 2 Hits
LUMA	3%	3% : 1 Hit

Rosalina swoops forward and attacks with her wand while Luma swoops forward. The opponent is launched up and away.

SIDE TILT

	DAMAGE
ROSALINA	5~6%
LUMA	4.3%

Rosalina swings both legs around and Luma swings out horizontally in a wide arc.

DOWN TILT

	DAMAGE
ROSALINA	4.5%
LUMA	3.5%

Rosalina trips far out in front of her, and Luma dives downward toward the opponent's feet. When Luma is close, this is a 2-hit combo.

EDGE ATTACK

Rosalina pulls herself up and performs a trip attack similar to her Down Tilt.

Air Attacks

NEUTRAL AIR ATTACK

Rosalina performs a forward flip, attacking with her legs. Luma attacks forward and then behind.

	DAMAGE
ROSALINA	6~10%
LUMA	3~4%

FORWARD AIR ATTACK

Rosalina backflips with a galaxy in front of her, while Luma swings forward. This multi-hitting backflip is best used when Luma is close in order to maximize damage.

	DAMAGE	MAX DAMAGE
ROSALINA	1~4%	7% : 4 Hits
LUMA	5%	5% : 1 Hit

UP AIR ATTACK

Rosalina emits a ring upward and Luma flips.

	DAMAGE
ROSALINA	2~10%
LUMA	4%

BACK AIR ATTACK

Rosalina gets horizontal with a galaxy and kicks out directly behind her while Luma dashes in to kick in the same direction.

	DAMAGE
ROSALINA	11%
LUMA	4%

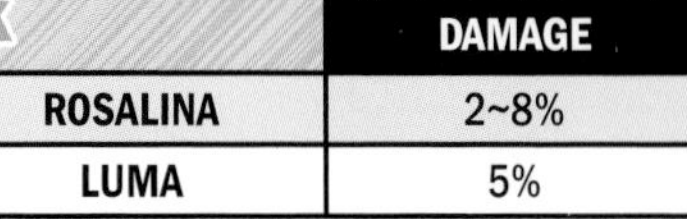

DOWN AIR ATTACK

Rosalina emits a ring from the bottom of her dress directly below her that hits multiple times while Luma kicks down.

	DAMAGE
ROSALINA	2~8%
LUMA	5%

Special Attacks

LUMA SHOT (Neutral Special) DAMAGE 5.2~16%

Use this to send Luma forward, ahead of Rosalina. The longer you hold the Special button, the farther Luma will go, dealing more damage to anything in its path. At full charge, Luma is invincible during the dash forward. Press the button again to recall Luma.

Luma Warp DAMAGE 1%

Luma warps a set distance in front of Rosalina. There is a small bit of damage when Luma appears, but this version is mainly for its speed in moving Luma forward.

Power Luma Shot DAMAGE 3.2~22%

Luma spins while traveling forward. Luma's movement speed is very slow, but the damage is much higher. It takes about 50% longer to charge this version up to its maximum.

LAUNCH STAR (Up Special) DAMAGE 0%

Rosalina's primary recovery tool, this launches her upward at an angle. You can control the angle a bit to the left or right. Rosalina is in a fall state when this move completes.

Launch Star Plus DAMAGE 0%

This variation sends Rosalina flying through the air much faster, but she can't control the angle of her ascent.

Launch Star Attack DAMAGE 1~5% MAX DAMAGE 13% : 7 HITS

This is the only version in which Rosalina attacks the opponent as she ascends. The downside is she doesn't get as high into the air.

STAR BITS (Side Special)

DAMAGE 2.8% MAX DAMAGE 8.4% : 3 HITS

Rosalina commands Luma to fire three Star Bits forward. They are fired in three directions. These Star Bits pierce through opponents and cannot be deflected or absorbed.

Floaty Star Bits

DAMAGE 1.2~2.8% MAX DAMAGE 6% : 3 HITS

A much larger Star Bit that flies slower and doesn't travel very far but lasts longer. The startup is a little slower on this version.

Shooting Star Bit DAMAGE 4~5%

This Star Bit travels straight forward at high speed. It travels farther but gets weaker the farther it goes. This version doesn't pierce opponents and can be deflected or absorbed.

GRAVITATIONAL PULL (Down Special) DAMAGE 0%

This Special draws in surrounding items and projectiles toward Rosalina. The projectiles and items that are pulled in will briefly spin around Rosalina. While spinning around Rosalina they can cause damage to nearby opponents.

Catch & Release ROSALINA DAMAGE 6%

Rosalina pulls in opponents to damage them but doesn't pull in projectiles or items. If Rosalina takes damage, this move is canceled.

Guardian Luma LUMA DAMAGE 3~5%

Luma temporarily grows extremely large to protect Rosalina from damage. This Luma is invincible and does a bit of damage as well.

Strategy

The duo of Rosalina & Luma makes for one of the more interesting characters in the game, as you really have to manage them as a unit to maximize their potential. Damage that Luma takes will not be added to Rosalina's percentage, making Luma an effective shield. Additionally, for some Final Smash attacks, if Luma gets hit but Rosalina doesn't, Luma will take the damage, and Rosalina will be left unscathed. If Luma takes too much damage, however, Rosalina will have to fend for herself for a while, but Luma will respawn eventually. Note that Luma destructing does *not* cost Rosalina any stocks. So, use Luma as a shield as much as possible, but remember that Luma's attacks do less damage than Rosalina's do. If your opponents decide to focus on Luma, use that opportunity to go in with Rosalina! If they try to avoid Luma and make a beeline for Rosalina, recall Luma and be prepared with your Smash attacks! Though Luma respawns quickly, Rosalina's overall effectiveness drops without Luma around. For this reason, it is important to protect Luma with Rosalina and vice versa.

Luma Shot is your primary way of setting Luma's distance away from Rosalina, and it's also a great long-range attack. After a short amount of time, Luma will slowly return to Rosalina, if you don't decide to use Luma Shot again to recall Luma. If a lot of opponents are near you, be sure to keep Luma close. Against projectile-heavy characters, use Luma as a shield at a distance while still attacking! Don't forget that against projectile characters, you can also use Gravitational Pull to draw in projectiles or other items. Star Bits is a great way to rack up damage on opponents while preferably keeping Rosalina at a safe distance. Rosalina's Up Tilt and Forward Tilt are good tools to keep opponents out. Her Down Air and Back Air are her stronger options while her Forward Air is active the longest. Don't underestimate her jab as well, since the wand extends this farther than expected. Be sure to use Luma's Tilt and Aerial attacks to rack up damage before using your Smash attacks to get the KO. When going for KOs, try to use her Smash attacks instead of aerials, and use a charged-up Luma Shot for long-distance KOs.

One of the more advanced strategies for this character is to send Luma past your opponent, then sandwich that opponent between Rosalina and Luma. Dash attack behind Rosalina to make Luma attack forward at the opponent! Another interesting option to try is their Down Smash as they attack in opposite directions. As the game progresses, these sandwich strategies will undoubtedly separate average Rosalina players from great ones. Additionally, when guarding the edge, Luma can cause all sorts of problems for returning opponents. Lastly, note that Luma can attack even while Rosalina is sleeping, buried, or stunned. This can save you from many attacks in the game, even if you break your own shield!

Final Smash

POWER STAR

Rosalina summons a Power Star, which shoots out multiple smaller stars across the stage. The Power Star grows larger and larger, damaging players in its vicinity. When it reaches its peak size, it lets out one more explosive burst with a lot of knockout potential. While the Power Star is growing and shooting out smaller stars, Rosalina & Luma are free to move around and attack. Try to hit opponents into the star to rack up damage. This works better on stages with platforms, as the Power Star always spawns above Rosalina. Placing it beside opponents who are close to an edge can force them out and over.

Recovery

Rosalina's only real tool for recovery is her Launch Star. This Special has fantastic range and can be used for both horizontal and vertical recovery. If you want to use it to go directly vertical, you can do so by hitting back after inputting the Launch Star. You'll be in a fall state after Launch Star ends, so you'll want to use it to grab onto an edge or to get as far from opponents as possible. This move can cover the Final Destination form horizontally, so be prepared for it. Remember that Rosalina is invisible when she uses an air dodge; this can come in handy to create space for yourself while recovering. If you use Luma Shot to send Luma far out over the edge, Luma will only have three jumps to get back to the platform before falling. Be sure to recall Luma by hitting the Special button again to prevent Luma from self-destructing.

SAMUS

Trophy Description

Samus Aran has fought her way across a variety of planets in the *Metroid* series. She wears a Power Suit designed by the Chozo, giving her incredible versatility in a fight. She can wade in with kicks and punches,, but she favors beams and missiles. A fully charged Charge Shot packs a serious punch!

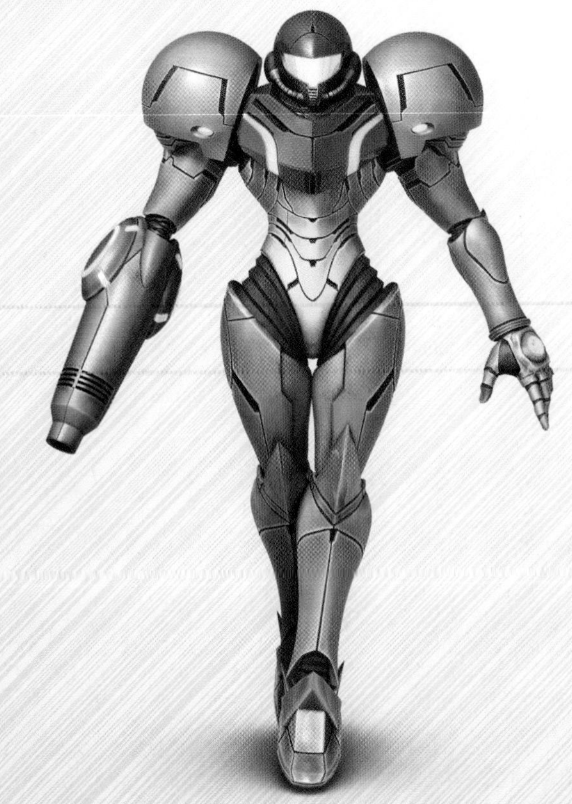

STATISTICS

MAXIMUM NUMBER OF JUMPS: **2**

CAN WALL JUMP: **Yes**

CAN WALL CLING: **No**

CAN CRAWL: **No**

Alternate Colors

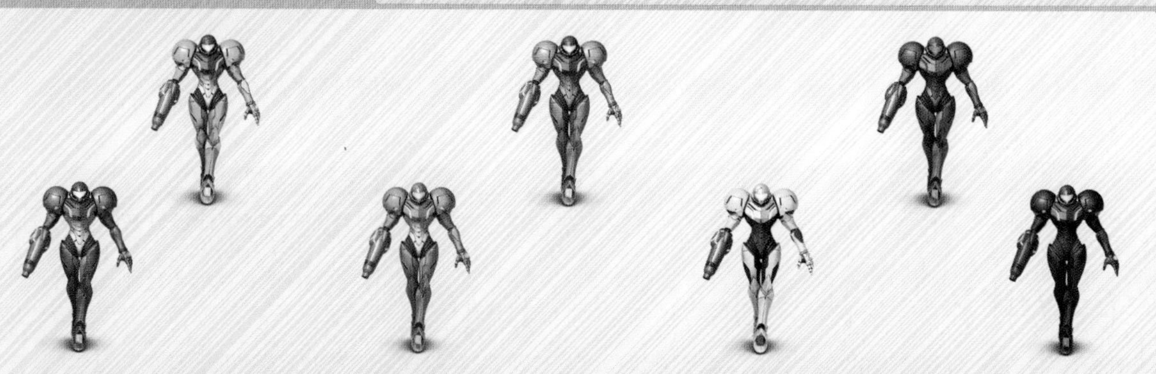

Smash Attacks

SIDE SMASH DAMAGE 12~14%

Samus jabs her arm cannon into your opponent to blast that opponent. You can angle it up or down.

DOWN SMASH DAMAGE 10~12%

A quick sweep attack that hits both in front of and behind Samus.

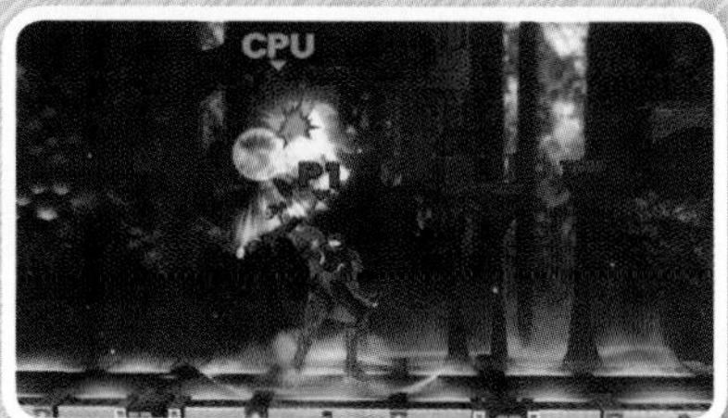

UP SMASH

DAMAGE 3~6% MAX DAMAGE 18% : 5 HITS

Samus uses her arm cannon in an arc above her head. This can hit grounded opponents but more often hits multiple times against airborne opponents.

Basic Attacks

STANDING ATTACK DAMAGE 3%, 8%

A jab that goes into a downward swing of her arm cannon that pushes opponents back.

UP TILT DAMAGE 12~13%

Samus raises her leg before bringing it down on anyone in front of her. When this hits grounded opponents who have very low damage, it leaves them open to follow-up attacks.

DASH ATTACK DAMAGE 6~10%

Samus tucks her head and plows into your opponent shoulder first. Comes out fairly quick and has decent range as well.

SIDE TILT DAMAGE 5~7%

This spinning horizontal kick attack has good range and is fairly quick. You can angle it up or down. For the most damage, try to hit with the tip of this attack.

DOWN TILT DAMAGE 12%

Samus fires her arm cannon at the ground in front of her. Launches opponents up and away.

EDGE ATTACK

Samus returns to the stage with a long-range trip attack.

Air Attacks

NEUTRAL AIR ATTACK

DAMAGE 6~8% MAX DAMAGE 15% : 2 HITS

Samus performs a spinning kick that hits in front of and behind her.

DOWN AIR ATTACK DAMAGE 10~14%

Samus swings her arm cannon in an arc below her. This attack can have a meteor effect.

BACK AIR ATTACK DAMAGE 9~14%

A reverse back kick that has a lot of range.

UP AIR ATTACK

DAMAGE 1~4% MAX DAMAGE 11% : 6 HITS

A spiraling upward drill-kick attack. Good for racking up damage.

FORWARD AIR ATTACK

DAMAGE 1~5% MAX DAMAGE 11% : 5 HITS

Samus blasts her arm cannon in a downward arc in front of her. Can hit multiple times for a lot of damage.

Special Attacks

CHARGE SHOT (Neutral Special)

DAMAGE 3~25%

While grounded, Samus charges up her projectile attack. Hitting Left or Right gives you an evasive roll to continue charging from where you left off. You can also Shield to stop and store your charge. Pressing the button again releases the shot. When used in the air, Charge Shot fires from whatever level you've charged to.

Dense Charge Shot DAMAGE 4~27%

This more powerful variation has greater knockback but takes 30% longer to fully charge. Its travel speed is slower, but it stays out twice as long as the regular version.

Melee Charge Shot DAMAGE 5~18%

Release a shot immediately in front of you. The longer you charge it up, the wider the attack is. Note this version can hit multiple opponents; however, it can't reflect or absorb.

MISSILE (Side Special) DAMAGE 5~10%

Fires a homing missile at the closest opponent. If you input the attack as a Smash attack, it fires a Super Missile. The Super Missile launches higher, travels farther, and deals more damage, but only travels horizontally. Note, you can only have one Super Missile out at a time or Samus will misfire.

Relentless Missile DAMAGE 3~12%

These missiles stick around much longer, deal more damage, and travel slower. The Homing Missile sticks around three times longer and the Super Missile stays out 60% longer. Note you can only have two Homing Missiles or 1 Super Missile out out at any given time.

Turbo Missile DAMAGE 4~9%

This variation has the missile staying put before rapidly speeding forward. Before speeding up, it focuses on one opponent, but once it begins speeding up it flies straight.

SCREW ATTACK (Up Special)

DAMAGE 1~12% MAX DAMAGE 12% : 12 HITS

Samus balls up and spins into the air, striking anyone caught in her tracks multiple times. You can control this a bit to the left or right. This attack has some invincibility on startup.

Screw Rush

DAMAGE 2~5% MAX DAMAGE 15% : 6 HITS

This version rushes to the side and hits multiple times. You don't recover as high vertically.

Apex Screw Attack

DAMAGE 2~9% MAX DAMAGE 11% : 2 HITS

This version hits twice, once at the beginning and once at the peak. The first hit will knock players into the second stronger hit.

BOMB (Down Special)

DAMAGE 4~5% MAX DAMAGE 9% : 2 HITS

Samus drops a bomb from Morph Ball form. The bombs explode on impact or after a short time. These bombs do slightly more damage if they hit an opponent directly. If Samus is hit by the explosion, it sends her upward a bit but does not deal damage to her.

Slip Bomb DAMAGE 2.5~3.5%

Though this bomb deals less damage, it gives a meteor effect against airborne opponents and trips grounded opponents.Additionally, the bomb's fall speed is faster, the explosion is larger, and the fuse is shorter.

Mega Bomb

DAMAGE 4~9% MAX DAMAGE 13% : 2 HITS

This bomb is much more damaging, but it takes longer to explode. Only one can be out at any given time. Because the explosion is higher, you can use it to bomb-jump higher as well.

MISSILES

You can fire multiple homing missiles simply by holding a side direction and repeatedly hitting the Special button.

Final Smash

ZERO LASER

Samus charges up and fires her giant Zero Laser at all opponents. She can aim it up or down a bit while firing. This attack also has a vacuum effect, pulling in players around Samus and bringing them into the laser beam. Opponents who are immediately in front of the Samus receive a little bit of extra damage during the startup of the beam. Range-wise, it has no problem crossing Gerudo Valley, so you won't have any issues using it on other stages. Overall, it has great range, damage, and KO potential for opponents with some damage who are near the side of a stage.

Strategy

Samus has a variety of projectiles to attack opponents from long range and some good tools to rack up damage in the air. She is somewhat unique in that she is a fairly heavy character with decent ground speed who is also rather floaty. While she has a strong long-range game, she can also be effective up close. Her main weaknesses are her horizontal recovery and her KO power. She does have a few good tools that rack up damage well enough, so this helps address her KO power.

For Samus's long-range game, you have a lot of choices. You have Charge Shot, which you can use in quick bursts or fully charged up, and you have two Missile variations. Since a fully charged Charge Shot has good KO potential, consider keeping it fresher by using it less. Mixing up Homing Missile and Super Missile will throw off your opponent's timing. If you ever hit with a Super Missile, immediately send out more Homing Missiles or charge up your Charge Shot. (When it comes to knockback, Super Missiles are much more effective than Homing Missiles.) If playing in free-for-all modes, use a lot of Bombs around you as small traps to keep you safer while using your projectiles. Since the bombs don't damage Samus, it literally doesn't hurt to have one around. You can even use the blast from one to bounce Samus and make her stay in the air longer.

Screw Attack has a tiny bit of invincibility and is a decent out-of-shield option, but it's primarily used for Samus's vertical recovery. Don't forget you can also shoot these projectiles in the air to create a vertical minefield for your opponents to avoid!

Up close, Samus's Side Tilt attack is very quick, given its excellent range, but its damage output is fairly low. Down Tilt is also good for its speed and knockback. You can also use Samus's long-range grapple to throw opponents while on the ground, as it prevents opponents from approaching recklessly. For KOs, go with Side Smash, Down Tilt, or a fully charged Charge Shot. Up Smash can work for KOs as well, but because it's hard to use against standing opponents, use it against airborne opponents instead. In the air, Samus has a couple of good damage-racking options with Up Air and Forward Air. For KOs in the air, however, go with Back Air. When opponents are off-stage, use your missiles to edge guard, as this may interrupt their recoveries. If you successfully interrupt them, try to follow up with Down Air for a meteor smash.

Recovery

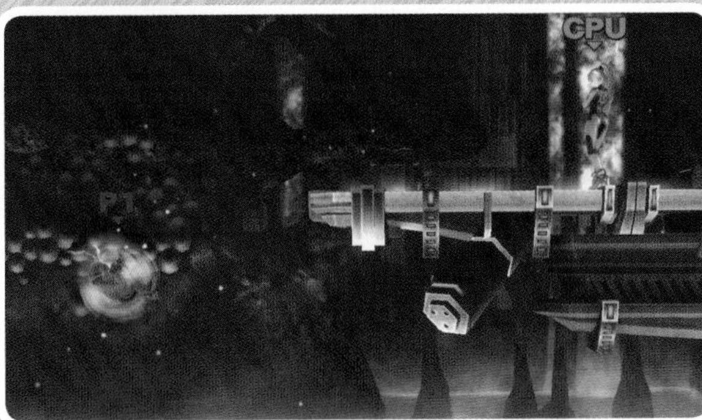

Samus's main recovery option is her Screw Attack for vertical recovery. You can aim this a little to the left or right during the input of the attack. Horizontally, Samus doesn't have a lot of options outside of her grapple. Use the grapple when off-stage to catch onto the edge, and press Up to pull yourself back up. Additionally, you can use Samus's Bomb to stall temporarily. Moving left or right while dropping bombs will help keep you afloat awhile. This is especially useful when other opponents are off-stage with you.

SHEIK

Trophy Description

In *The Legend of Zelda: Ocarina of Time*, Sheik claimed to be a surviving Sheikah. This was just a cunning disguise for Princess Zelda, however, so that she could escape Ganondorf. In *Smash Bros.*, she's the complete opposite of Zelda, striking with fast attacks that can keep an opponent off-balance.

STATISTICS

MAXIMUM NUMBER OF JUMPS: **2**

CAN WALL JUMP: **Yes**

CAN WALL CLING: **Yes**

CAN CRAWL: **Yes**

Alternate Colors

Smash Attacks

SIDE SMASH

DAMAGE 5~8% MAX DAMAGE 13% : 2 HITS

An advancing two-hit kick attack with decent knockback.

DOWN SMASH

DAMAGE 3~6% MAX DAMAGE 9% : 2 HITS

A flaring multi-hit leg sweep.

UP SMASH

DAMAGE 11~15% MAX DAMAGE 26% : 2 HITS

Sheik lifts her hands as an attack before striking down to either side. Combos for big damage, but the first hit does significantly more damage.

Basic Attacks

STANDING ATTACK

DAMAGE 2%, 3% RAPID JABS 7.8% : 7 HITS

Sheik strikes twice, and if you rapidly hit the button, Sheik will go into rapid punches before launching the opponent away.

UP TILT

DAMAGE 5~6% MAX DAMAGE 11% : 2 HITS

Two kicks in one! First, Sheik kicks upward before swinging the same leg down at opponents in front of her.

DASH ATTACK DAMAGE 4.5~6.5%

Sheik dashes forward and swings her arms apart at anyone in her path.

SIDE TILT DAMAGE 4%

Sheik kicks forward and upward. This kick is very useful for combos.

DOWN TILT DAMAGE 7.5%

A compact sweep attack.

EDGE ATTACK

Sheik returns to the stage with a long-range dropkick.

Air Attacks

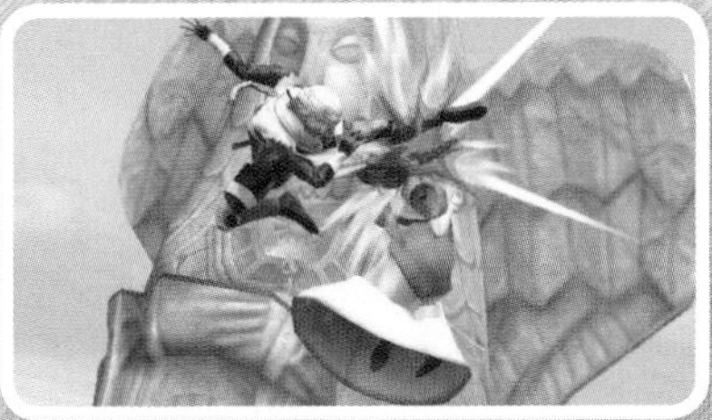

NEUTRAL AIR ATTACK

DAMAGE 4~8%

A jump kick that stays out for a very long time and has very good reach.

DOWN AIR ATTACK

DAMAGE 2~8% MAX DAMAGE 10% : 2 HITS

Sheik plummets to the ground with this quick spiking kick attack. Has a meteor effect at the start of this attack.

BACK AIR ATTACK DAMAGE 5~11%

This reverse jump kick has incredible range. Sheik kicks fairly high here, so you'll need to make sure your opponents are higher than Sheik when using this attack.

UP AIR ATTACK

DAMAGE 1~4% MAX DAMAGE 8% : 5 HITS

Sheik flips and kicks while spiraling into the sky! Hits multiple times before the last hit launches the opponent upward.

FORWARD AIR ATTACK

DAMAGE 6~6.8%

Sheik attacks to her side with a downward punch.

Special Attacks

NEEDLE STORM (Neutral Special)

DAMAGE 1.2~1.9% MAX DAMAGE 11.4% : 6 HITS

Throws needles at the opponent. While Sheik is grounded, the needles fly forward. While she's airborne, she throws the needles diagonally downward. Charge it to send more needles farther for more damage.

Penetrating Needles

DAMAGE 1.6~2.2% MAX DAMAGE 6.6% : 3 HITS

As the name implies, these needles penetrate enemies and continue traveling. You can only throw three at a time. The charge time is less and the range is shorter than normal.

Paralyzing Needle DAMAGE 1%

This throws a single poisoned needle that paralyzes the opponent. The higher the opponent's accumulated damage, the longer that opponent paralyzed. The range is shorter than normal.

BURST GRENADE (Side Special)

DAMAGE 0.1~12.6% MAX DAMAGE 15.8% : 8 HITS

Throws a grenade that sucks opponents toward it before it explodes. If Sheik is hit before the grenade explodes, the grenade becomes an item where it was left behind.

Gravity Grenade DAMAGE 3.6%

The grenade has a smaller explosion, but opponents hit by this explosion are knocked toward Sheik. Hold the button to delay the explosion. This grenade does not detonate while it is moving, and it doesn't pull in enemies before exploding.

Skimming Grenade

DAMAGE 2~4.6% MAX DAMAGE 8.6% : 3 HITS

Sheik throws a small, bouncing grenade. The farther it travels, the less damage it deals.

VANISH (Up Special)

DAMAGE 0~12% MAX DAMAGE 17% : 2 HITS

With this teleport, Sheik throws a bomb to the ground before warping to another location of your choosing. When Sheik uses this in the air, she jumps higher before teleporting. This deals damage both on exit and re-entry of the teleport.

Gale DAMAGE 0%

This faster teleport sees Sheik disappear into a puff of smoke. It is faster, and Sheik can travel farther during the teleport, but it does have a longer recovery period. This teleport deals no damage..

Abyss DAMAGE 4~5%

Sheik stays hidden longer during this teleport, but her teleport distance is shorter; however, a meteor effect occurs when she reappears.

BOUNCING FISH (Down Special)

DAMAGE 12%

A flipping heel kick attack. If it hits, Sheik bounces back away from the opponent. During the bounce, you can hit the button again to kick again. This is limited to three heel kicks, but you can use it from one opponent to the next! Note you can control the jump's distance by hitting forward or back. You can also use the kick attack sooner by hitting the button earlier.

Jellyfish

DAMAGE 8~10.5% MAX DAMAGE 18.5% : 2 HITS

Sheik flips higher in this version, and if she lands the kick, she bounces straight up. When you hit a grounded opponent, hitting the button again performs a second heel kick on the same opponent.

Pisces DAMAGE 15.5%

Sheik flips quicker and lower in this version, and if the kick lands, she can control her movement. There is no option for a second kick, as the first knocks opponents back.

Final Smash

LIGHT ARROW

Sheik pulls out a large bow and fires an arrow across the stage. It hits all targets in its path, but the damage and knockback decrease after each target. The first opponent receives 45% damage, the second receives 34%, and the third receives 25%. The range is incredible, reaching across Gerudo Valley. This Final Smash differs from Zelda's in that the knockback is much more horizontal, and the damage is much higher. This makes Sheik's version a little more useful when trying to push players off a side.

Strategy

Sheik is an incredibly fast, average-weight character—she weighs more than Zelda now! Her mobility is increased with Vanish, allowing her to teleport while still inflicting damage to those around her. Bouncing Fish can be useful for air mobility as well. Additionally, Sheik can crawl, wall cling, and wall jump, giving her options most other characters don't have. With these options, plus Vanish and Bouncing Fish, Sheik has fairly good recovery. With her speed and mobility, she has no problem racking up damage on opponents, but she lacks strong options to KO them.

Needle Storm is an interesting projectile because it beats out a lot of other attacks. Rather than using it for camping or zoning, consider using it to interrupt your opponents as they approach. This can leave them open for Side Smash or Dash Attack. Burst Grenade is also interesting because it creates a bit of a vortex, sucking opponents in. Of course, if your opponent is sucked toward you, be sure to keep your offense up with your jab, Forward Tilt, throws, or aerial attacks. From Down Throw or Up Throw, chasing your opponents with Up Air is a strong option. While Vanish is good for distancing yourself from opponents or for recovering, it can also be used offensively. Try using it close to the ground and do it downward. If you're able to combo it into itself, you can get up to 17% damage!

For Sheik's ground game, Side Tilt and Up Smash are some of her best options: Side Tilt can combo into itself in many situations, and Up Smash is by far Sheik's most damaging attack. Additionally, Up Smash has invincibility on Sheik's head and arms while attacking. For aerial attacks, Down Air is of note because of its meteor effect at the start of the attack. The majority of its damage is done when hitting opponents in the air, not during its landing. Sheik's Back Air is also notable, as it has great range and comparatively high damage. Up Air is useful if you find opponents up near the top of a stage, but in general use it for racking up damage instead of knocking opponents out. For edge-guarding, Sheik's best options are to chase off-stage with her aerial attacks. Back Air is your best bet, but look to use Neutral Air and Forward Air as well, depending on your positioning. Since Sheik's recovery is above average, you can afford to be more aggressive while chasing off-stage. If you prefer a safer but less effective approach, use your Needle Storm and Burst Grenades to disrupt your opponent's recovery.

Recovery

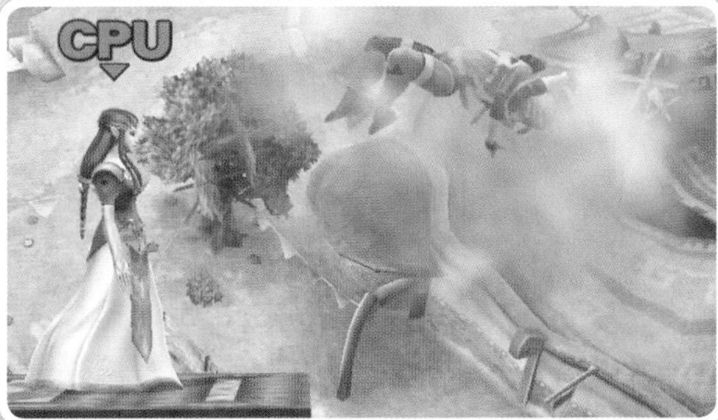

Sheik's two primary recovery options are her Vanish and Bouncing Fish. Vanish is the most useful, as it allows both horizontal and vertical recovery. And dealing damage both before and after the teleport is a great option. Sheik's second option is Bouncing Fish, which is a flipkick attack that covers good horizontal distance—just make sure you're facing the right way! Don't forget to use wall jump or wall cling when possible as well.

SHULK

Trophy Description

In *Xenoblade Chronicles*, this young lad's colony is attacked by the Mechon, so he and his friends set off to take them down. In *Smash Bros.*, his Monado Arts let him change his specialization during battle. You can choose to boost a stat—his jump or attack, for example—but other stats might drop as a result, so choose wisely.

STATISTICS

MAXIMUM NUMBER OF JUMPS: **2**

CAN WALL JUMP: **No**

CAN WALL CLING: **No**

CAN CRAWL: **No**

Alternate Colors

Smash Attacks

SIDE SMASH

DAMAGE 5~12% MAX DAMAGE 17.5% : 2 HITS

Shulk stabs forward then extends the beam of his Monado sword to hit even farther. This can be aimed up or down.

DOWN SMASH

DAMAGE 3~13% MAX DAMAGE 33% : 3 HITS

Shulk spins multiple times while swinging his Monado out in a sweeping motion around. Long range but long recovery as well.

UP SMASH

DAMAGE 4~13% MAX DAMAGE 17% : 2 HITS

Shulk slams the Monado into the ground while it points upward. The beam then blasts upward, knocking opponents vertically.

Basic Attacks

STANDING ATTACK

DAMAGE 3%, 3%, 3.2~4.3%

A three-hit attack string with a jab, kick, and then sword uppercut.

UP TILT DAMAGE 6~7%

A jumping spinning uppercut attack with the Monado sword.

DASH ATTACK DAMAGE 10%

A horizontal sword slash as Shulk slides forward.

SIDE TILT DAMAGE 10.5~12%

Shulk swings the Monado sword horizontally.

DOWN TILT DAMAGE 6~8%

Shulk crouches down then sweeps the opponent with his sword.

EDGE ATTACK

Shulk returns to the stage with a sweeping sword strike similar to his Down Tilt.

Air Attacks

NEUTRAL AIR ATTACK

DAMAGE 6~7%

Shulk swings his sword upward in a wide arc in front of him.

DOWN AIR ATTACK

DAMAGE 4~10% MAX DAMAGE 16% : 2 HITS

With his sword pointed downward to the ground, Shulk extends the beam of the Monado. This attack has a meteor effect.

BACK AIR ATTACK

DAMAGE 7~11%

Wind-up then stab backward behind Shulk. This attack has good range and power but a slow startup.

UP AIR ATTACK

DAMAGE 4~9% MAX DAMAGE 13% : 2 HITS

Shulk strikes upward with his sword then extends the beam to hit even farther.

FORWARD AIR ATTACK

DAMAGE 5~6.5%

Shulk swings his sword downward directly in front of him.

Special Attacks

MONADO ARTS (Neutral Special)

DAMAGE N/A

Shulk activates one of his five Arts for Jump, Speed, Shield, Buster, or Smash. See sidebar for more information. You can cancel out of a Monado Art by either hitting the Special button quickly three times or by holding the Special button.

Decisive Monado Art DAMAGE N/A

Shulk chooses Monado Arts as usual, but he can't cancel out of them. They also last a bit longer and have increased statistics.

Hyper Monado Arts DAMAGE N/A

In this variation, each Monado Art attribute goes to its extreme. Any attribute that was increased gets increased more, but any attribute that was decreased gets decreased more!

BACK SLASH (Side Special)

FROM FRONT 9~10% FROM BEHIND 13~16%

A huge forward-leaping sword slash. If you hit the opponent's back, it deals way more damage. Be sure to land on the stage or Shulk continues downward!

Back Slash Leap

FROM FRONT 8~10% FROM BEHIND 11~16%

Shulk jumps higher than usual to deliver this strong slash.

Back Slash Charge

FROM FRONT 3~6% FROM BEHIND 6~15%

Shulk is super armored until he attacks in this version. The tradeoff is that this version deals less damage.

AIR SLASH (Up Special)

FIRST SLASH 4~5% ADDITIONAL SLASHES 5.5%

This jumping sword attack launches your opponent into the air. It can be followed up by a second horizontal attack in the air by hitting the Special button again. You can move Shulk a little to the left or right.

Advancing Air Slash

FIRST SLASH 4~5% ADDITIONAL SLASHES 8%

Instead of launching straight up, Shulk launches diagonally upward for the first slash. The second slash deals more damage than usual.

Mighty Air Slash

FIRST SLASH 6~8% ADDITIONAL SLASHES 10%

A much more damaging version of Air Slash. Shulk trades increased damage for decreased range and decreased horizontal mobility.

VISION (Down Special)

DAMAGE *SEE VISION DATA TABLE*

Shulk brings down his sword to counter incoming attacks. The counterattack is a large wind-up sword swing. Hold the direction towards your opponent while countering and Shulk will dash past the opponent and swing behind himself. This counter attack launches farther. The more you use this counter, the less effective it becomes. Each time you use it, the counter window shrinks to about 2/3 of its original size.

Dash Vision

DAMAGE *SEE VISION DATA TABLE*

Shulk counters incoming attacks with a farther-reaching retaliation. The counter window is slightly smaller than usual and decreases at the same rate as the original; however, the counter window does recover slightly quicker.

Power Vision

DAMAGE *SEE VISION DATA TABLE*

This version has a much larger window to counter attacks and deals much more damage. When you use it, however, the counter window shrinks to about 1/10 of its original size! If you rarely use counterattacks and have a high rate of landing them when you do, this is the version for you.

MONADO ARTS

JUMP Increases your jump and allows you to move quicker in the air, but you take more damage.

SPEED You do less damage and have a lower jump height, but you can move faster.

SHIELD You have a stronger shield, but you move slower, jump lower, and have lower damage output. Additionally, you take less damage and will not be launched as far.

BUSTER You deal and receive more damage but cannot launch opponents as far or as high.

SMASH You can launch opponents easier, and you yourself get launched easier, but you deal less damage.

VISION DATA

	STARTUP	LARGEST DURATION	MINIMUM DURATION	DAMAGE SCALING	MINIMUM DAMAGE	MAXIMUM DAMAGE
Vision	7th frame	35 frames	5 frames	1.3x	7%	50%
Dash Vision	7th frame	25 frames	5 frames	1x	5%	50%
Power Vision	7th frame	45 frames	3 frames	1.5x	14%	50%

Final Smash

CHAIN ATTACK

Shulk calls in Dunban and Riki to join him for a devastating chain attack. Stunned opponents are obliterated by the ensuing team combo before returning to the stage and exploding up and away from Shulk. The opponent closest to Shulk takes an extra 10% damage from Shulk's Neutral Special Jump Art for a total of 40% while everyone else takes 30%. The damage changes during Shulk's Monado Arts applies to the Final Smash as well: Buster Art does 55% damage and 41% to everyone else; Speed Art does 28% and 21% to everyone else; Shield Art does 27% and 20% to everyone else; and Smash Art does 20% and 15% to everyone else but launches much farther. The range on the initial strike is about 1/4 of the Final Destination stage, so be close to your opponents to use it. If you're going for a KO, use the Smash Monado Art, but choose your art before even getting the Smash Ball, which makes this a little more difficult to do.

Strategy

Shulk is a sword-based fighter with extreme versatility, thanks to his ability to switch between his Monado Arts. Choosing the right Monado Art at the right time against your opponents is vital to maximizing Shulk's potential. Shulk has slightly above-average weight with great range and decent damage but slow startup and recovery on most of his attacks. Compared to other swordfighters, he is somewhat of a cross between Ike and Marth. Regardless of Monado Art, his general weakness is the speed and recovery of his attacks, which he makes up for with range and damage output. While he has good vertical recovery, his horizontal recovery is a little lacking. Forward Tilt, Up Tilt, and back throw are also useful in battle. Note that you can also use Shulk's jab string for up-close battle—you can delay each hit and don't suffer too much recovery after the first two hits.

Shulk has five Monado Arts to choose from: Jump, Speed, Shield, Buster, and Smash. Hitting the Special button by itself cycles between these options, and whichever one you leave it on last is the one that gets activated. Once a Monado Art is activated, you can cancel out of it by quickly hitting the Special button three times. Once you use a Monado Art, it's on cooldown and appears gray, leaving you unable to select it again for about 10 seconds. Picking the best Monado Art for the moment depends on many factors: your current damage percent versus the opponent's damage percent, your mobility versus the opponent's mobility, and how far ahead or behind you are in a match. Study the strengths and weaknesses of each to make it easier to decide which you need in battle. Back Slash is a good damaging attack, but it can leave you open for retaliation as well. Jump into groups of opponents from behind with this for maximum effectiveness. Air Slash can be useful out of shield against slower attacks and knocks horizontally away with its second hit. The Vision counter has a dynamic window to counter attacks. Each time you use it, the counter window gets smaller, down to a minimum. That counter window slowly gets larger, back to its initial size, as long as you aren't using it.

In the air, Shulk's fastest attack is his Forward Air. For you to land his Up Air, opponents need to be very high in the air, but it does good damage and knockback. Down Air is very slow to start up, but it has incredible range below Shulk and also has a meteor smash. Neutral air is a little slow but can hit behind Shulk and covers good space in front of him. Back Air is his best KO option, but again, it requires some time to start up. On the ground, Shulk's Forward Smash and Up Smash are his best options for KOs. Forward Smash has impressive range, thanks to the beam firing from the tip of the Monado. Hit with this tip for additional knockback. Down Smash is best used to damage groups of opponents who are closing in on you. For edge-guarding, use Shulk's Forward Smash, Down Smash, Forward Air, and Back Air. Additionally, if you have the Jump Monado Art active, you will be able to chase farther off-stage!

Recovery

Shulk's recovery options are fairly limited but straightforward. Vertically, you can recover with his Air Slash, but if you miss it, Shulk enters a fall state. Even when deep under a stage, it pushes its way up to the edge. Don't forget to use both hits of Air Slash, as it can get you that little bit of extra height you might need. You can also aim Air Slash to the left or right a little bit. For horizontal recovery, Shulk can use his Back Slash, but if you miss, you plummet to your destruction! You also need to land on the stage because Shulk does not grab the ledge while using Back Slash. To slow your fall, use his Vision counter. If available, you also have time to activate Shulk's Jump Monado Art, as it boosts the height on his double jump and Air Slash! This greatly increases your recovery while leaving the more combat-appropriate Monado Arts available when you return to the stage.

SONIC THE HEDGEHOG

Trophy Description

The main star of the *Sonic the Hedgehog* series. He's an easygoing hedgehog who blows past the competition with his speed. Seriously, on the ground he's faster than anyone else in *Smash Bros.* Use this to your advantage, avoiding blows while landing lightning-fast attacks.

STATISTICS

MAXIMUM NUMBER OF JUMPS: **2**

CAN WALL JUMP: **Yes**

CAN WALL CLING: **No**

CAN CRAWL: **No**

Alternate Colors

Smash Attacks

SIDE SMASH DAMAGE 14%

Sonic winds up and unleashes a straight punch attack. This can be aimed up or down.

DOWN SMASH DAMAGE 12%

Sonic drops into the splits, kicking both in front of and behind himself.

UP SMASH

DAMAGE 1~5% MAX DAMAGE 14% : 8 HITS

Sonic balls up and jumps at your opponent, spinning while hitting that opponent multiple times.

Basic Attacks

STANDING ATTACK

DAMAGE 2%, 2%, 4%

Two punches followed by a kick that knocks opponents away.

UP TILT

DAMAGE 2~6% MAX DAMAGE 8% : 2 HITS

Sonic jumps and spins while kicking vertically, launching the opponent vertically as well.

DASH ATTACK

DAMAGE 1~3% MAX DAMAGE 6% : 4 HITS

Sonic balls up to strike multiple times before ending with a kick attack.

SIDE TILT

DAMAGE 4~7% MAX DAMAGE 11% : 2 HITS

Sonic planks and kicks out his legs at the opponent. This can be aimed up or down.

DOWN TILT DAMAGE 6%

Sonic crouches then whips his leg around in a sweep attack.

EDGE ATTACK

Sonic returns to the stage balled up to strike the opponent.

Air Attacks

NEUTRAL AIR ATTACK

DAMAGE 5~12%

Sonic balls up while moving in a small circle to hit opponents. This is active for quite awhile.

DOWN AIR ATTACK DAMAGE 7~8%

This divekick attack moves at a sharp angle toward the ground. It has a meteor effect if it hits airborne opponents.

BACK AIR ATTACK DAMAGE 10~14%

Sonic winds up then quickly kicks behind him.

UP AIR ATTACK

DAMAGE 3~6% MAX DAMAGE 9% : 2 HITS

Sonic gets upside down and claps his feet together, hitting opponents above him.

FORWARD AIR ATTACK

DAMAGE 0.8~3% MAX DAMAGE 7% : 6 HITS

Sonic spins at your opponent headfirst, hitting multiple times.

Special Attacks

HOMING ATTACK

(Neutral Special) DAMAGE 5~12%

Sonic homes in on the closest opponent. Make sure Sonic is in range, otherwise Sonic bounces into the ground.

Stomp DAMAGE 5%

Sonic jumps into the air before slamming straight downward. There is a meteor effect from this attack.

Surprise Attack DAMAGE 8%

Similar to the regular version except much faster and with less range. The downside is that the damage is also lower.

SPIN DASH (Side Special)

DAMAGE 4~11% MAX DAMAGE 18.6% : 3 HITS

Sonic spins up as you hold down the button then rolls around when you release it. The longer you charge, the faster Sonic rolls. You can control him, and if he collides with the enemy, he deals damage. You can cancel this into Homing Attack or Spring Jump. While charging, you can cancel by hitting Shield or Grab.

Hammer Spin Dash

DAMAGE 3~7% MAX DAMAGE 16% : 3 HITS

Sonic hops high off the ground and buries any opponent he hits on the way down. Changing directions while rolling stops the move instead of changing directions.

Burning Spin Dash

DAMAGE 4~13% MAX DAMAGE 19% : 1 HITS

This Spin Dash deals slightly more damage and does not have a hop at the beginning. All jumps during the dash are also lower than normal.

SPRING JUMP (Up Special)

DAMAGE 4%

Sonic launches himself up from his spring. The spring sticks around for a while for anyone to use. If dropped from the air, it causes a little damage to whomever it hits below. While falling from the air, you can use aerial attacks or air dodge but not Specials. Sonic has a bit of invincibility after the jump.

Double Spring DAMAGE 2%

This version does not launch Sonic as high, but Sonic can use it twice! When used on the ground, the first spring instantly disappears. When used in the air, the first spring disappears once you use the move again.

Springing Headbutt DAMAGE 1~7%

Sonic headbutts opponents above him after he launches off the spring. When used on the ground, the spring quickly disappears and nearby opponents are knocked away. Jump height is slightly less than normal, and Sonic doesn't have any invincibility.

SPIN CHARGE (Down Special)

DAMAGE 1~6% MAX DAMAGE 16% : 5 HITS

Sonic dashes forward in a ball. This can be powered up by rapidly pressing the Special button while holding Down to make it faster and stronger. When you release Down, Sonic moves forward with the attack. You can transition into Homing Attack or jump from this attack as well.

Auto-Spin Charge

DAMAGE 1~6% MAX DAMAGE 13% : 4 HITS

This variation of Spin Charge can be charged by just holding the Special button while holding Down. If you move from Down to the direction opposite of your opponent, it will cancel the charge.The charge time is slightly longer than normal.

Gravitational Charge

DAMAGE 0~6% MAX DAMAGE 11% : 3 HITS

While charging, the force from Sonic spinning in place pulls in opponents in front of him while pushing away opponents behind him. It takes more button presses than usual to charge up to full power.

Final Smash

SUPER SONIC

Sonic transforms into Super Sonic—he is completely gold and able to fly. Flying into your opponents deals damage, and the faster you fly, the stronger the attacks and knockback are. The initial blast of his transformation deals about 18% damage, the least damage you do is around 5%, and the most per hit is around 16%. Though Super Sonic can be difficult to control, you don't have to worry about self-destructing. In this form, you are invulnerable, and you can fly to any edge of the stage without being KO'd. Just be sure to make it back to the stage before transforming back to regular Sonic! Super Sonic starts to glow white when he is about to revert back to regular Sonic, so keep an eye out for this! Finally, note this can't move through platforms or stage walls, so it's much more effective on open stages like Final Destination instead of Reset Bomb Forest.

Strategy

Sonic is the fastest character in the game, so harnessing his full potential certainly takes some time! He has an assortment of attacks in which he balls up and does spin attacks at the opponent. One of the benefits of this is it can be very confusing for opponents to figure out what you're up to. Along with Sonic's speed, his aerial mobility and recovery are good as well. Using his Homing Attack, Spin Dash, and Spin Charge with just his movement speed on the ground will be a challenge for opponents to keep up with. Sonic is fairly lightweight, though, with limited range, so try not to get too carried away with his speed!

Homing Attack is best used from the air against a grounded opponent, as long as the opponent is within range. Sonic automatically flies at them, and you can repeat this same attack once before landing. Generally, your goal with Homing Attack is to make sure your opponent is in range. Spin Dash is another quick spinning attack, one that gives you a little bit more control over your direction. It does have a little bit of invincibility on startup, and it doesn't actually attack while turning. If you're going for a horizontal recovery, Spin Dash is your better choice over Spin Charge. Similar to Spin Dash, Spin Charge has Sonic balled up and speeding back and forth around the floor.

It differs, however, by moving considerably faster and allowing you to cancel its startup. Additionally, the first hit of this knocks opponents up fairly well, so consider using this to surprise opponents for a vertical KO. Spring Jump is mainly a recovery tool, but you can also use it to damage opponents by dropping the spring onto them. On stages with platforms, if you use it from the ground, it can be used for three jumps per fighter, until it expires and disappears.

In the air, Sonic's best options for KOs are Back Air for horizontal KOs and Up Air for vertical KOs. Neutral Air is useful to interrupt opponents, while Forward Air is good to rack up damage in combos. Down Air has a decent meteor effect, so you can use this against opponents' recovery when you're edge-guarding. For KOs on the ground, Forward Smash and Down Smash are your best options. Use Sonic's jabs, Forward Tilt, and Up Tilt from the ground as well.

Recovery

Sonic has some decent vertical recovery but not very well-controlled horizontal recovery. Of course, his Spring Jump is his main vertical recovery tool, and it launches Sonic very high into the air. Horizontally, though, Sonic's options aren't as straightforward. He can use his Spin Dash, but it has very short range to send him forward. If an opponent is close enough, he can use his Homing Attack, but that relies on your opponent's distance from you and your distance from the stage.

TOON LINK

Trophy Description

This cartoonish version of Link is how he appeared in *The Legend of Zelda: Wind Waker* and a few other titles. In *Smash Bros.*, he uses moves much like his older, taller counterpart. His small size gives him extra speed, though, so take advantage of that to send your foes flying.

STATISTICS

MAXIMUM NUMBER OF JUMPS: **2**

CAN WALL JUMP: **Yes**

CAN WALL CLING: **No**

CAN CRAWL: **No**

Alternate Colors

Smash Attacks

SIDE SMASH DAMAGE 10%, 11%

This is a two-hit Smash attack. Toon Link swings down with his sword for the first hit. He then swings horizontally for the second hit. Press the button again to get the second attack.

DOWN SMASH

DAMAGE 6~7% MAX DAMAGE 13% : 2 HITS

Toon Link performs a two-hit low sword attack in front of and then behind him that combos. Opponents are launched away by the second hit.

UP SMASH DAMAGE 10~13%

A spinning sword uppercut that launches your opponent upward.

Basic Attacks

STANDING ATTACK

DAMAGE 3%, 2%, 4%

A series of three sword strikes that combo.

UP TILT **DAMAGE 5%**

Toon Link swings his sword in an arc over his body. This can hit opponents behind Toon Link and launches opponents vertically.

DASH ATTACK **DAMAGE 6~8%**

Toon Link hops forward while attacking with a downward sword strike.

SIDE TILT **DAMAGE 9%**

Toon Link swings his sword downward at your opponent, knocking that opponent away.

DOWN TILT **DAMAGE 7%**

A low sweep attack using Toon Link's sword.

EDGE ATTACK

Toon Link climbs back up to the stage and then attacks low with his sword.

Air Attacks

NEUTRAL AIR ATTACK

DAMAGE 7~8.5% MAX DAMAGE 15.5% : 2 HITS

A two-hit sword attack that attacks in front of and then behind Toon Link.

FORWARD AIR ATTACK

DAMAGE 13%

A horizontal sword slash in front of Toon Link.

DOWN AIR ATTACK

DAMAGE 5~16% MAX DAMAGE 21% : 2 HITS

Toon Link performs a diving sword attack that can meteor smash opponents and deal decent damage. While similar to Link's Down Air, this version will not be canceled or cause Toon Link to bounce on enemy contact. So, be careful not to KO yourself when going for this meteor smash!

UP AIR ATTACK **DAMAGE 11~14%**

Toon Link thrusts his sword upward to hit opponents above him. This move can hit through most of its animation and launches opponents vertically.

BACK AIR ATTACK **DAMAGE 11%**

A horizontal sword slash behind Toon Link. This attack is much faster than his Forward Air Attack.

Special Attacks

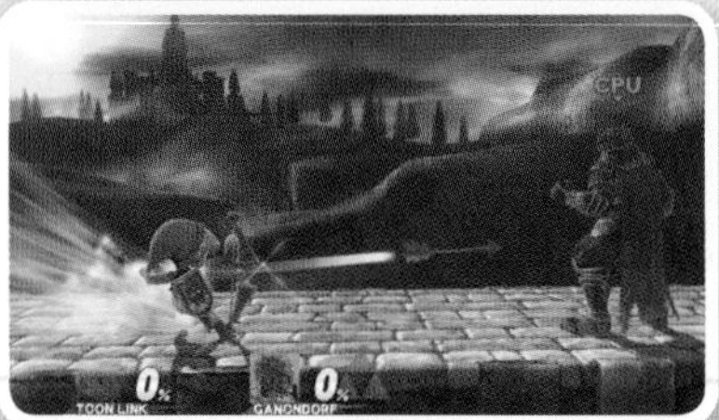

HERO'S BOW (Neutral Special) DAMAGE 4~12%

Toon Link fires an arrow from his bow. Charge it up to shoot it farther and straighter for more damage.

Fire Arrow DAMAGE 2~6%

Shoots a flaming arrow that doesn't travel as far as regular arrows. The arrows stick in the ground and deal damage to anyone who makes contact with them. The startup is slightly faster, but the recovery is longer.

Piercing Arrow DAMAGE 1~6%

These arrows pierce through opponents and shields. They do less damage but can travel farther when fully charged. Charging to maximum takes slightly longer than normal.

BOOMERANG (Side Special)

DAMAGE 3~8%

Toon Link attacks with his boomerang. It can hit opponents on its way out and on its way back. You can also throw it diagonally by hitting Up or Down. If you do not catch it upon its return, you have to wait a while before using it again. Smash your input to throw the boomerang farther.

Floating Boomerang DAMAGE 4%

This boomerang is slower to return, and disappears if it makes contact with anything on its way back. Since it stays on screen longer with its slower return time, the damage it deals is less.

High-Speed Boomerang

DAMAGE 1~3% MAX DAMAGE 4% : 2 HITS

A high-speed boomerang that pierces through multiple opponents as it goes a set distance. On its return, it comes straight back in the direction it was thrown. This means that it doesn't return to Toon Link's current position.

SPIN ATTACK (Up Special)

ON LAND NO CHARGE 1~3%

MAX DAMAGE 12% : 10 HITS

ON LAND MAX CHARGE 1.6~4.8%

MAX DAMAGE 19.2% : 10 HITS

IN AIR 2~4% MAX DAMAGE 14% : 5 HITS

A sword spin attack. When using it on the ground, you can charge it up for additional hits and damage. When using it in the air, Toon Link launches himself very high into the air with the attack. In the air, this only hits in front of Toon Link, but on the ground, it hits in front and behind.

Sliding Spin Attack

ON LAND NO CHARGE 10%

ON LAND MAX CHARGE 16%

IN AIR 1~5% MAX DAMAGE 10% : 5 HITS

Toon Link slides forward while spinning. This only hits once on the ground. In the air, you move more horizontally than vertically. This version takes a little longer to startup than the regular version.

Flying Spin Attack

ON LAND NO CHARGE 1~4%

MAX DAMAGE 14% : 9 HITS

ON LAND MAX CHARGE 1.6~6.4%

MAX DAMAGE 22.4% : 9 HITS

IN AIR 2~4% MAX DAMAGE 14% : 5 HITS

This spinning sword attack ends with an upward sword slash that sends both Toon Link and the opponent high into the air. The upward sword slash occurs even when the move is used on land, and Toon Link has super armor throughout it.

BOMB (Down Special) DAMAGE 4~8.2%

Toon Link pulls out a throwable bomb. It explodes on impact or when its fuse runs out. You can throw it up, forward, or down.

Time Bomb DAMAGE 1~5.2%

This bomb only detonates when its fuse runs out. It doesn't detonate on impact with opponents. The explosion damage is lower, but it launches opponents farther.

Short-Fuse Bomb DAMAGE 10~14.2%

A bomb that quickly explodes, deals a lot of damage, and launches opponents. The bomb also has more range than the regular version; the downside is that it takes longer to pull the bomb out and throw it.

Final Smash

TRIFORCE SLASH

Toon Link sends out a beam of light across the stage directly in front of him. The first opponent it makes contact with is stunned, and Toon Link dashes in to unleash an incredible sword combo that ends with a giant swing. This last hit has more horizontal range than any of the previous hits and catches anyone who stays too close. Though very similar to Link's, this Final Smash has significantly less range than Link's, as it can only reach about halfway across the Final Destination stage.

Strategy

For the most part, Toon Link is very similar to Link except he is smaller, faster, and lighter. He has a great projectile game amplified by his size and mobility. His sword gives him some much-needed range for most of his regular attacks. Similar to Link, his shield also block projectiles that hit him from the front as long as he is not attacking. Toon Link's main weaknesses are his KO potential and his horizontal recovery.

One of Toon Link's main differences from Link is that Toon Link's Boomerang doesn't generate a tornado to pull opponents back. Instead, Toon Link's Boomerang deals damage in both directions of its path. You can still throw it diagonally, but if you don't catch it upon its return, you'll have to wait a bit before you can use it again. His Hero's Bow is still a great harassment projectile. Compared to Link's version, Toon Link's arrows float more and have more range. His Bomb Special doesn't damage him as long as it hits the opponent, making it good for close combat as well. Throwing a bomb up will allow you to pull a second bomb! Using these projectiles while utilizing Toon Link's mobility is key to racking up damage on your opponents.

For grounded attacks, Toon Link's Up Smash is one of his better tools when looking for KOs. His Side Smash deals good damage, and his Down Smash covers both sides of him. Side Tilt is also a good poke tool for its range and damage. When Toon Link is in the air, his Down Air is active for a long time and has a meteor effect at the start that can come in handy for early KOs. Up Air is active for a very long time as well, and it can also be useful for KOs. Neutral Air is different from Link's and is useful for racking up damage. And finally, don't forget to use his grapple in the air, as it is a good keepout tool to help your projectile game. When edge-guarding, use all of the projectiles at your disposable. Boomerang angled downward or Bombs thrown downward at recovering enemies are particularly useful. For enemies with worse horizontal recovery, keep them out with charged-up arrows from the Hero's Bow.

Recovery

Toon Link's recoveries are, for the most part, identical to Link's recoveries. The two options are Spin Attack and grapple/throw. You can use grapple to grab onto the edge, but you have to time it correctly and be facing the right way. Press the throw button again to pull yourself up or hit Up to return to the ledge. Note that Toon Link's Spin Attack leaves him in a fall state. And if you are holding onto a bomb that explodes while you're in fall state, you can use Spin Attack again!

VILLAGER

Trophy Description

An energetic young man from a peaceful town in *Animal Crossing*, he is eager to make his *Smash Bros.* debut! His Balloon Trip recovery lets him fly like a character from *Balloon Fight*. The Villager sets out to answer that age-old question: If a tree falls on the battlefield and foes are beneath it, do they get launched?

STATISTICS

MAXIMUM NUMBER OF JUMPS: **2**

CAN WALL JUMP: **Yes**

CAN WALL CLING: **No**

CAN CRAWL: **No**

Alternate Colors

Smash Attacks

SIDE SMASH DAMAGE 15-17%

Villager drops a bowling ball on the opponent. If he does this on an edge, the bowling ball will drop off the stage, hitting anyone in its path. But beware: this is a projectile and can be reflected!

DOWN SMASH DAMAGE 3-6%

Villager uses his shovel to dig on each side of him. Enemies hit will be temporarily buried.

UP SMASH

DAMAGE 1-4% MAX DAMAGE 11% : 6 HITS

Villager sets off fireworks to blast opponents upward!

Basic Attacks

STANDING ATTACK DAMAGE 3%, 3%

Put on some boxing gloves and swing away. Two punches you can repeat but never goes into rapid jabs.

UP TILT

DAMAGE 5~6% MAX DAMAGE 11% : 2 HITS

Swing a tree branch in a circle above Villager's head. Lifts opponents into the air.

DASH ATTACK DAMAGE 6~10%

Villager stumbles while running and throws a planter forward. The planter acts as a projectile and can destroy other projectiles.

SIDE TILT DAMAGE 9%

Swing an open umbrella horizontally in front of Villager. This attack can destroy projectiles.

DOWN TILT DAMAGE 8~13%

Villager pulls out weeds in front of him. If opponents are above the weeds, they are hit upward.

EDGE ATTACK

Villager pulls himself back up then swings a leg around to kick the opponent away.

Air Attacks

NEUTRAL AIR ATTACK

DAMAGE 5~9%

A mid-air cartwheel attack.

FORWARD AIR ATTACK

DAMAGE 2.5~7%

Use Villager's slingshot to attack your opponent at range!

DOWN AIR ATTACK

DAMAGE 1 TURNIP 4~8%

DAMAGE 2 TURNIPS 5~10%

DAMAGE 3 TURNIPS 6~13%

Villager pulls out between one and three turnips and swings them downward. More turnips mean more damage, and three can have a meteor effect on hit.

UP AIR ATTACK

DAMAGE 1 TURNIP 4~8%

DAMAGE 2 TURNIPS 5~10%

DAMAGE 3 TURNIPS 6~13%

Villager pulls out between one and three turnips and swings them upward. More turnips mean more damage.

BACK AIR ATTACK DAMAGE 3~9%

Villager spins around and uses his slingshot to attack behind him at range.

Special Attacks

POCKET (Neutral Special)

DAMAGE 0%

Villager can use this to pocket items or projectiles for later use. Press the button again to take the item out or to throw the projectile. Villager is invincible when using the Pocket. You can only keep items in your Pocket for 30 seconds before they disappear.

Garden DAMAGE 10%

Villager attacks by planting a flower on the opponent's head every time he misses a Pocket attempt. The Pocket attempt itself has less range and duration.

Pocket Plus DAMAGE 0%

This alternate version of Pocket allows Villager to pocket items much easier. It has more range, faster startup, and longer duration. The trade-off is that the items deal less damage and it takes Villager longer to bring them back out of his pocket.

LLOID ROCKET (Side Special)

DAMAGE 5~7% EXPLOSION 12%

Fires off Lloid like a rocket horizontally. It eventually slows and falls before exploding or it explodes on contact. You can't fire another one until the first one explodes. Hold the button to ride Lloid, causing Lloid to deal 2.3x more damage! Jumping from Lloid leaves Villager in a falling state. Riding Lloid until impact deals much more damage. While riding Lloid, slow his speed by hitting Back and speed up by hitting Forward.

Liftoff Lloid

DAMAGE 5~8% EXPLOSION 14%

After being fired, Lloid shoots upward! Damage is higher, and Villager jumps upward when Lloid explodes. Lloid exploding with Villager aboard deals 2.4x as much damage.

Pushy Lloid DAMAGE 1.5%

MAX DAMAGE 12% : 5 HITS EXPLOSION 6%

A larger Lloid Rocket hits opponents multiple times, pushing them until it explodes. This Lloid Rocket travels slower and less distance. Lloid exploding with Villager aboard deals 1.2x as much damage.

BALLOON TRIP (Up Special)

DAMAGE 0%

Villager puts on a balloon hat and flaps his arms to gain a lot of height. Repeatedly press the button to gain that height. You can also move left or right while recovering, but the balloons can be popped by incoming attacks! Hit the attack button to detach from the balloons and fall.

Extreme Balloon Trip

DAMAGE 6~9% MAX DAMAGE 18% : 2 HITS

These balloons don't rise as high or as fast, but when you press the attack button, it detonates a balloon. Damage is strongest at the center of the balloon when it explodes.

Balloon High Jump DAMAGE 6~10%

These balloons allow Villager to ascend very quickly, damaging any opponents in his path. The balloons pop a lot faster than usual, and you can't move as freely. If one balloon breaks, you continue to ascend. Note you can't detach from these balloons by hitting the attack button.

TIMBER (Down Special)

DAMAGE SEE TIMBER DATA TABLE

This is a three part move. First, Villager plants seeds. This deals no damage and is not an attack in the air. Once seeds are planted, this changes to a watering can that can push opponents around. Watering the seed grows it into a tree, which can hit opponents as it grows. When the tree is grown, the attack becomes an axe swing that deals a lot of damage. If you chop the tree down, it can hit the opponent for a lot of damage. It takes two axe chops on the same side to chop down the tree. You can then Pocket the wood and throw it later!

Timber Counter

DAMAGE SEE TIMBER DATA TABLE

In this alternate Special, the fresh sprouts you plant can trip up opponents for some damage. Additionally, the fully grown tree fights back against opponents! The tree's damage when growing and falling is less than normal.

Super Timber

DAMAGE SEE TIMBER DATA TABLE

Everything is a bit bigger and slower in this version. The tree requires more water to grow, so watering takes longer than usual. Once the tree is grown, the axe is even more powerful than usual, but is also slower. The tree deals more damage and also has more stamina than usual.

POCKET DATA

	STARTUP	DURATION	DAMAGE SCALING
POCKET	8th frame	16 frames	1.9x
GARDEN	11th frame	11 frames	1x
POCKET PLUS	7th frame	25 frames	1.3x

TIMBER DATA TABLE

	TIMBER	TIMBER COUNTER	SUPER TIMBER
SEEDS / SPROUTS	0%	2%	0%
WATERING CAN	0%	0%	0%
TREE GROWING	13~18%	10~12%	16~20%
AXE SWING	14%	6%	16%
TREE FALLING	15~25%	8~12%	18~27%
TREE COUNTER ATTACK	N/A	5%	N/A

Final Smash

DREAM HOME

Villager calls upon Tom Nook and the twin Nook employees to build a house around all opponents within range! The opponents take damage while the house is being built, and when it's finished, the house explodes, dealing additional damage and knocking back opponents up and away from Villager. In total, this deals about 45% damage to all opponents caught in the house. The range on this attack is limited, but you can estimate the range by identifying the farthest puff of smoke when the raccoons appear. Villager is invulnerable while the house is being built, and if anyone runs into the house while it is building, they take damage as well. Using this on airborne opponents is not a great idea unless they are right beside you in the air. The knockback isn't great, so use it closer to the sides of a stage to KO an opponent.

Strategy

Villager is a small, average-weight character with average mobility. Unlike most small characters, however, he has surprisingly good range on most of his attacks, thanks to the large number of things he carries around! For example, his Side Tilt is an umbrella, his Dash Attack throws a planter forward, and his Forward And Back Airs shoot a projectile from his slingshot! The downside to this is, in general, he doesn't deal a lot of damage, and it can be difficult to approach opponents. You can increase Villager's damage by using his Timber attack to get his axe out, but this limits his range and is temporary, as the tree doesn't stick around forever.

Pocket can be very useful against projectile characters, allowing you to return the projectiles at almost double damage! You also have some invincibility while actually capturing projectiles or items. Unfortunately, there are exceptions to what you can Pocket, as you can't use it on Smash Balls or Assists. Villager also has his own massive projectile attack with Lloid Rocket. Use this with your Forward and Back Air attacks to really zone opponents. It doesn't deal much damage by itself, but if Villager is riding it when it explodes, the damage is significantly higher! While Villager is riding Lloid Rocket, you can trick opponents by using Up or Down to control the speed of Lloid Rocket. Timber is Villager's most interesting tool—each step of the process leaves him with a new tool to use for attacking. Once you've planted the seeds, your Down Special becomes Villager using his water can. Use this attack anywhere, even in the air. It doesn't deal damage, but it does push opponents away. Once you water the

seeds and they grow into a tree, your Down Special becomes an axe. This deals good damage but is only available until the tree disappears. "The tree requires two axe swings on the same side before it will fall over. Hitting the tree once on each side will not make it fall over. Note that opponents can attack the tree to destroy it as well. Finally, once you chop down the tree, the falling tree causes massive knockback and damage, so try to place it closer to edges of the stage. Timing this to hit an opponent is very difficult, however, because of the number of steps involved to make it fall. This makes it better suited for a free-for-all scenario or edge-guarding. Balloon Trip isn't an attack, but it is one of the better recoveries in the game. Against projectile-heavy characters, though, it can be very difficult to use because they can pop the balloons!

Villager's throws have decent range, thanks to the handle on the net he swings at opponents. This also makes it slower, so it can be harder to catch opponents. In the air, his Forward Air and Back Air are fantastic to poke opponents while Up Air and Down Air are best for their vertical KO ability. From the ground, Villager's Side Smash is his best option for KOs, but it's very slow to attack. You can drop it off platforms, though, to surprise unsuspecting victims below! Instead of landing Side Smash directly, try to land Down Smash so you can bury opponents to rack up damage on them or to land the Side Smash. Down Smash also becomes extra useful when you have a tree nearby for Timber! Edge-guarding is one of Villager's strengths, thanks to his water can, tree growth, and tree fall from Timber, his slingshot aerials, and his Lloid Rocket.

Recovery

Villager has some of the best recovery tools in the game. First, though, it should be noted he has decent jump height and the ability to wall jump. His Balloon Trip has incredible vertical recovery, but opponents can pop the balloons, so you have to stay alert! You can control the Balloon Trip to recover horizontally as well. Hold the Special button to increase vertical recovery, and hit the Attack button to enter a fall state. For horizontal recovery, Villager can ride Lloid Rocket by holding the Special button. Hit Down to slow down or Up to speed down. If Lloid Rocket hits an opponent, Villager pops off, but if it passes everyone, Villager can jump off by pressing any button. If Villager jumps off the rocket, he enters a fall state.

WARIO

Trophy Description

A living embodiment of gross, this villain hates Mario and loves money. He claims to have known Mario since childhood, but who can tell if that's true? In *Smash Bros.*, he's a seriously agile heavyweight fighter. He can store up his trademark Wario Waft for explosive results. Did I mention he's gross?

STATISTICS

MAXIMUM NUMBER OF JUMPS: **2**

CAN WALL JUMP: **No**

CAN WALL CLING: **No**

CAN CRAWL: **Yes**

Alternate Colors

Smash Attacks

SIDE SMASH DAMAGE 19%

Wario leans back before swinging forward with a giant fist punch!

DOWN SMASH DAMAGE 5~13%

Wario winds up and spins himself on the ground like a sloppy break dancer, hitting anyone around him!

UP SMASH DAMAGE 13~16%

Wario uses his head for this massive headbutt!

Basic Attacks

STANDING ATTACK DAMAGE 4%, 5%

A two-punch attack string that combos.

UP TILT DAMAGE 6~10%

Wario throws both giant hands into the air! His arms and head are invincible during this attack.

DASH ATTACK DAMAGE 4~7%

Wario dives headfirst at his enemies!

SIDE TILT DAMAGE 11~13%

Wario delivers a giant punch attack. You can aim this up or down.

DOWN TILT DAMAGE 4%

Wario uses his a giant finger to poke at his opponent's feet!

EDGE ATTACK

Wario uses a variation of his Back Air attack to return to the stage backward while swinging his arms up over his head.

Air Attacks

NEUTRAL AIR ATTACK

DAMAGE 4~6.5% MAX DAMAGE 10.5% : 2 HITS

Wario strikes a flying pose and uses it as an attack while he spins in the air.

DOWN AIR ATTACK

DAMAGE 1.3~4% MAX DAMAGE 11.8% : 7 HITS

Wario flips himself upside down and drills into his opponent using his own head! This hits multiple times.

BACK AIR ATTACK DAMAGE 12%

Wario lies back horizontally in the air before quickly throwing his arms back.

UP AIR ATTACK DAMAGE 13%

Wario uses his large hands and claps upward to squash anyone above him.

FORWARD AIR ATTACK

DAMAGE 4.5~7%

A quick jump kick attack.

Special Attacks

CHOMP (Neutral Special)

DAMAGE 2~5% MAX DAMAGE 11% : 4 HITS

Wario takes a bite out of his opponents or even eats up items or projectiles! Eating healing items will restore 50% more health than usual. Eating explosive items will cause him some damage, but nearby enemies will also be hurt! The more Wario eats, the gassier he gets and the stronger his Wario Waft becomes!

Inhaling Chomp

DAMAGE 2~4% MAX DAMAGE 10% : 4 HITS

Wario pulls enemies in with a powerful breath before chomping down on them. Power is lower than normal, and you can't speed up Wario's chewing by rapidly hitting the Special button.

Garlic Breath **DAMAGE 6%**

Wario releases his rancid breath, causing opponents to fall over and pass out. There is no chomping in this variation and Wario can't eat projectiles or other items.

CORKSCREW (Up Special)

DAMAGE 1~5% MAX DAMAGE 13% : 6 HITS

This high-reaching recovery jump has Wario spinning to strike opponents. You can hit Left or Tight immediately after inputting this attack to send Wario upward in a diagonal direction.

Widescrew

DAMAGE 0.5~4% MAX DAMAGE 9% : 6 HITS

The angle at which you can send Wario is much wider in this version. The downside is the damage and range are both reduced. Landing recovery is slightly faster, though.

Corkscrew Leap **DAMAGE 0%**

Wario focuses on leaping as high as possible but doesn't attack. Though this is the highest-reaching variation, you can't change the angle Wario ascends. Landing recovery is slightly longer than normal.

WARIO BIKE (Side Special)

RIDING 0~10.5% WHEELIE 5~13%

TURNING 3~7% THROWN 8~26.8%

Wario whips out his bike and tries to crash into his opponents with it. The faster you go, the more damage it does on contact with an enemy. Be ready to jump off in case you ride off an edge! Increase speed by hitting the same direction you are traveling. Turn by hitting the opposite direction you are traveling. Hit Up to pop a wheelie. While doing a wheelie, hit Down to drop back down. The bike can take 18% damage before breaking.

Speeding Bike

RIDING 0~9% WHEELIE 5~10% THROWN 8~26.8%

A much faster bike that gains extra distance when you use it in the air. The bike does less damage and has significantly less stamina, breaking after only 5% damage. Note that you cannot turn around while riding this bike.

Burying Bike

RIDING 0~8.4% WHEELIE 5~10%

TURNING 3~7% THROWN 8~26.8%

This bike is much heavier and can bury opponents it runs over. The speed is much lower, but the bike has more stamina, breaking after 40% damage. Additionally, Wario can jump off the bike much faster to follow up after burying opponents.

WARIO WAFT (Down Special)

DAMAGE SEE WAFT DATA TABLE

Wario unleashes his pent-up gas from his rear! The more he has eaten, the stronger this will be, but it also naturally charges up over time. He will glow and then flash once fully charged. The fully charged attack sends Wario up into the air with super armor.

Rose-Scented Waft

DAMAGE SEE WAFT DATA TABLE

Wario releases gas that causes flowers to grow on the opponent's head. This variation charges up to full power faster than the regular version. At the lowest level, it deals more damage than the regular version, but consistently deals less damage through higher levels.

Quick Waft

DAMAGE SEE WAFT DATA TABLE

With the quickest charge time available, Wario can release gas much more often! The downside is that all levels have lower damage output. From level 2 onward, opponents are knocked back!

WAFT DATA

	WARIO WAFT		ROSE-SCENTED WAFT		QUICK WAFT	
LEVEL	Damage	Charge Time	Damage	Charge Time	Damage	Charge Time
LEVEL 1	0%	-	6%	-	2%	-
LEVEL 2	10~12%	15 sec	10%	12 sec	5%	8 sec
LEVEL 3	20%	55 sec	15%	35 sec	13%	20 sec
LEVEL 4	20~27%	110 sec	18~21%	70 sec	14~18%	30 sec

Final Smash

WARIO-MAN

Wario transforms into his alter-ego, Wario-Man! Wario-Man is much faster, deals more damage, and his Specials have increased ability. Wario-Man's fully charged Wario Waft has incredible damage and knockback! Be careful when using the Wario Bike, especially on smaller stages, as it is incredibly fast. Another significant change for Wario-Man is that his aerial attacks give him some lift and can be done in succession. This works for all aerials except his Down Aerial attack. Use the Up Aerial repeatedly as a vertical recovery or the Forward or Back Aerials to recover horizontally.

Strategy

Wario is a relatively short character, yet he's also one of the heaviest in the game. Further, he has some of the best air mobility, which is quite surprising, given his size and weight. His recovery tools with his Wario Bike, his Corkscrew, and even his fully charged Wario Waft are fantastic. His small size, however, means his range is fairly limited and his impressive air mobility is balanced by relatively slow ground speed. Because his air mobility and aerial attacks are so amazing, use them often. Use his Forward Air, then move Wario back through the air to have a protective hitbox out in front of you. His Up Air and Back Air are good tools to KO opponents, while his Down Air is good to break your bike and refresh your other moves!

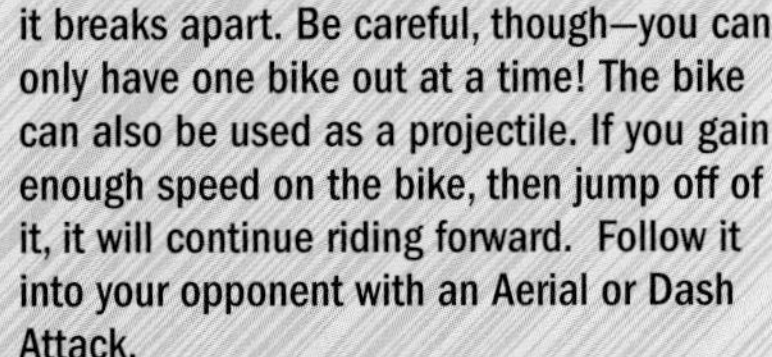

Whether or not Wario has his Wario Bike available will greatly affect your options when playing with him. Hitting an opponent with the bike is obviously good for damage and is great for horizontal recovery, but this only scratches the surface of what this tool can do. The bike itself acts as a shield that absorbs damage for Wario, especially while you pop a wheelie on it. When the bike falls, you can repeat the move to ride it again, or you can throw it at your opponent or up into the air! Once the bike takes enough damage, it breaks apart. Be careful, though—you can only have one bike out at a time! The bike can also be used as a projectile. If you gain enough speed on the bike, then jump off of it, it will continue riding forward. Follow it into your opponent with an Aerial or Dash Attack.

As mentioned before, Wario's range is his main weakness, so you'll have to compensate for this with the Wario Bike whenever possible. Without the bike, however, his Side Smash and his Side Tilt both have good range. His Up Tilt is useful when breaking his bike, and it gives his arms and head some invincibility. During his Up Smash attack, his head is invincible, making this a good defense against opponents approaching from above. And while Wario Waft can be extremely dangerous, it takes a lot of time to charge it up. So, save it until you really need it!

Recovery

For horizontal recovery, use the Wario Bike. It also gives you a bit of lift, so it's a little easier to shorten your horizontal distance. You are able to jump from the bike itself after using your double jump, so you effectively get a third jump with Wario! Since you are not in a fall state after jumping from the Wario Bike, you can also use his Corkscrew attack to recover vertically. The Corkscrew attack does leave you in a fall state, though, so you need to use the Wario Bike first if you need to make up horizontal distance. Don't forget to hit Left or Right immediately after inputting the Corkscrew attack to send Wario diagonally upward. When knocked far away, though, having the Wario Bike available is crucial to most of Wario's recovery. Getting knocked off while the bike is still on stage or during cooldown makes things much more difficult! Also, a fully charged Wario Waft can blast Wario very high!

Wii FIT TRAINER

Trophy Description

The female trainer who helps you in the *Wii Fit* series. She favors a fighting style composed of yoga poses. This makes her a capable close-quarters fighter, but she has ranged attacks as well. She also has a move called Deep Breathing, which can heal you and increase attack power if timed right.

STATISTICS

MAXIMUM NUMBER OF JUMPS: **2**

CAN WALL JUMP: **Yes**

CAN WALL CLING: **No**

CAN CRAWL: **Yes**

Alternate Colors

Smash Attacks

SIDE SMASH DAMAGE 14~15.5%

Wii Fit Trainer strikes the Warrior yoga pose while using it as an attack.

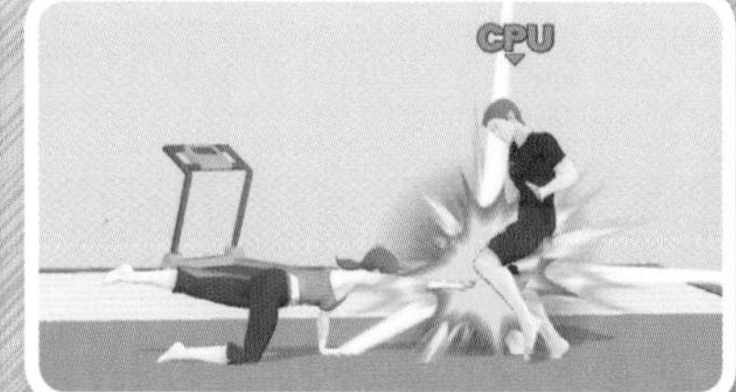

DOWN SMASH DAMAGE 8~10%

Wii Fit Trainer strikes with her fist and foot while doing the Arm & Leg Lift exercise.

UP SMASH DAMAGE 8~18%

Reach up to attack the opponent with the Tree yoga pose. This attack has some invincibility.

Basic Attacks

STANDING ATTACK

DAMAGE 2~3%, 2%, 3%

This advancing attack leads into a three-hit string in which the third hit buries your opponent into the ground, allowing follow-up attacks!

UP TILT DAMAGE 8%

Touch your toe with one hand as you swing the other to the sky in the Triangle pose, knocking opponents upward!

DASH ATTACK DAMAGE 6%

Wii Fit Trainer slides toward the opponent while striking the Gate pose.

SIDE TILT DAMAGE 9%

Wii Fit Trainer strikes forward with her arm while This attack strikes on both sides of Wii Fit Trainer.

DOWN TILT DAMAGE 12%

Wii Fit Trainer scoots forward to attack with her knees while doing the Bridge pose.

EDGE ATTACK

Wii Fit Trainer returns to the stage and kicks the opponent.

Air Attacks

NEUTRAL AIR ATTACK

DAMAGE 5~9% MAX DAMAGE 14% : 2 HITS

Wii Fit Trainer does the Jack Knife pose, hitting below herself then above herself with this two-hit combo.

DOWN AIR ATTACK DAMAGE 8~14%

Wii Fit Trainer uses Mountain pose to stomp down on her opponent. This attack has a meteor effect against airborne opponents.

BACK AIR ATTACK DAMAGE 6~13.5%

Wii Fit Trainer shows her agility and flexibility by doing Cobra pose in the air! This functions much like a dropkick, as both legs extending behind her kick the opponent away.

UP AIR ATTACK DAMAGE 10%

Wii Fit Trainer stretches both arms into the air then leans over to her side to hit the opponent up and away.

FORWARD AIR ATTACK

DAMAGE 6~10%

With the Single Leg Extension pose, Wii Fit Trainer attacks with one arm high in front of her and one leg out behind her. This hits on both sides of Wii Fit Trainer. There is a meteor effect from her foot.

Special Attacks

SUN SALUTATION (Neutral Special)

DAMAGE 5% FULL CHARGE 18%

Charge up a ball of energy. Hit Shield, Left or Right, to store your charge. Tap the button a second time to release the projectile. If charged all the way, this deals more damage and heals Wii Fit Trainer for 1%

Enriched Sun Salutation

DAMAGE 3% FULL CHARGE 20%

This variation charges to full much faster and has a smaller sphere. Compared to the default Sun Salutation, the charged damage is higher, but the uncharged damage is lower. Additionally, there is no healing effect with this alternate Special.

Sweeping Sun Salutation

DAMAGE 1.2% MAX DAMAGE 4.8% : 4 HITS

FULL CHARGE 1.6% MAX DAMAGE 12.8% : 8 HITS

This Sun Salutation hits opponents multiple times and pushes them away. It takes longer to charge up, and it moves slower than the regular version. Using it while fully charged heals Wii Fit Trainer for 2%.

HEADER (Side Special)

DAMAGE 10~15% MAX DAMAGE 23.9% : 2 HITS

BALL DAMAGE 8.9~11.8%

Toss a soccer ball into the air before jumping up to head it at the opponent. Press the button again to head it earlier or press the Shield button to cancel the header. Only one ball can be out at a time, so if you repeat the attack too early, Wii Fit Trainer jumps to do the header portion of the attack without the ball. This header without the ball has a meteor effect.

Huge Header

DAMAGE 10~15% MAX DAMAGE 19.2% : 2 HITS

BALL DAMAGE 4.2~9.8%

A larger ball for Wii Fit Trainer to head. It moves slower, but the ball stays out longer. Rushing to head the ball by hitting the button again quickly doesn't change the angle of the header as it does in the regular version.

Weighted Header

DAMAGE 10~15% MAX DAMAGE 26.6% : 2 HITS

BALL DAMAGE 11.6~16%

This heavier version of the ball does not travel as far but deals more damage. Once headed, the ball doesn't stay out very long and falls faster than the regular version. You can't change the angle of the ball by heading it earlier.

DEEP BREATHING

(Down Special) DAMAGE 0%

Wii Fit Trainer breathes in to relax. During this, an outer circle approaches an inner red circle. Hit the button when they meet to gain additional damage and launching power, reduced damage taken, and slightly increased walk speed. You also recover 2% health. If you don't time this right, you are left vulnerable.

Volatile Breathing DAMAGE 8~15%

This forbidden breathing method causes an explosion! Wii Fit Trainer has super armor during the startup of this variation. None of Wii Fit Trainer's abilities are increased on success.

Steady Breathing DAMAGE 0%

With this alternate Special, Wii Fit Trainer becomes much harder to launch and regains 5% health. but you are not be able to use the attack again for some time. This effect lasts about 6 seconds.

SUPER HOOP (Up Special)

DAMAGE 5%

Wii Fit Trainer hula hoops to safety. Rapidly press the button to rise faster. You can also move Wii Fit Trainer left or right as she ascends. This is also an attack that can hit opponents, but it doesn't knock them back very far.

Jumbo Hoop

DAMAGE 6% MAX DAMAGE 30% : 5 HITS

This larger hoop grants Wii Fit Trainer more horizontal mobility but less vertical mobility. Another important difference is this Jumbo Hoop can hit opponents multiple times.

Hoop Hurricane

DAMAGE 2% MAX DAMAGE 10% : 5 HITS

Wii Fit Trainer's hula hoops pull in opponents as she rises, then knocks them upward when the hoops hit. These hoops can hit multiple times, but they also "prevent Wii Fit Trainer from moving horizontally.

Final Smash

Wii FIT

Wii Fit Trainer emits multicolored yoga pose silhouettes as she attacks. These yoga poses expand as they move outward from Wii Fit Trainer, hitting anyone in their way. Each hit only does about 5% damage. While not dealing the most damage or knockback, this is very effective on both small and large stages because of its incredible range. Look for groups of opponents near the sides of stages, and try to hit them from as close as possible. The more yoga poses that hit, the farther the opponents will be pushed off the stage.

Strategy

While being one of the more unexpected characters, Wii Fit Trainer is quite a capable fighter! Her yoga poses hit surprisingly hard, and she has a few attacks with special properties to increase their usability. Given that she is also able to increase her damage and launching power by using Deep Breathing, it's clear she doesn't have any issue in KOing opponents. Her weaknesses are her average weight and average mobility.

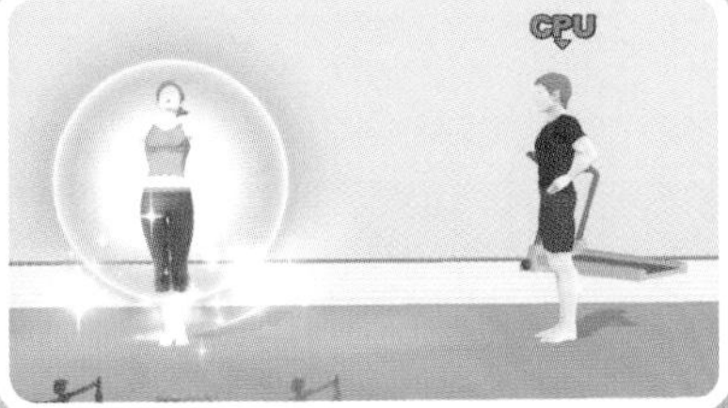

Wii Fit Trainer's Sun Salutation is a great projectile attack you can charge up over time. When charging, use Left, Right, or Shield to retain the charge and either evasive roll or shield. The projectile itself can be rather large, increasing its effectiveness. The larger it gets, the more damage it delivers. Header is a projectile attack in which Wii Fit Trainer headbutts a soccer ball at the opponent. It's strongest when you can get both Wii Fit Trainer's head and the ball to hit the opponent, but you don't have much control of the angle the ball travels, so it isn't too effective. It deals good damage, however, and you have the option to fake it by hitting the Shield button. You can also use this is to slow your horizontal momentum when being knocked off-stage—it doesn't leave you in a fall state and makes you drop vertically. Deep Breathing's main use is to increase damage and knockback. While it can heal you, this is so minimal that the power output and damage reduction are what you're actually trying to gain by using it. But every percent of lower health might mean the difference between surviving or being KO'd!

In the air, Wii Fit Trainer's best options for KOs are Forward Air—if you can sweet-spot it—or Back Air. Forward Air can send opponents downward at high percentages off Wii Fit Trainer's back leg, but Down Air is your main meteor smash. On the ground, Side Smash hits both in front of and behind Wii Fit Trainer and has great KO potential. Note that Up Smash has invincibility, but it's very rare you will hit a grounded opponent with it, so focus your efforts against airborne characters. All of Wii Fit Trainer's tilt attacks are quick with minimal recovery, so incorporate these into your poke game. After a dash attack, the knockback usually gives you enough time to charge up your Sun Salutation. For edge-guarding, use Sun Salutation, Header, Down Smash, and Back Air.

Recovery

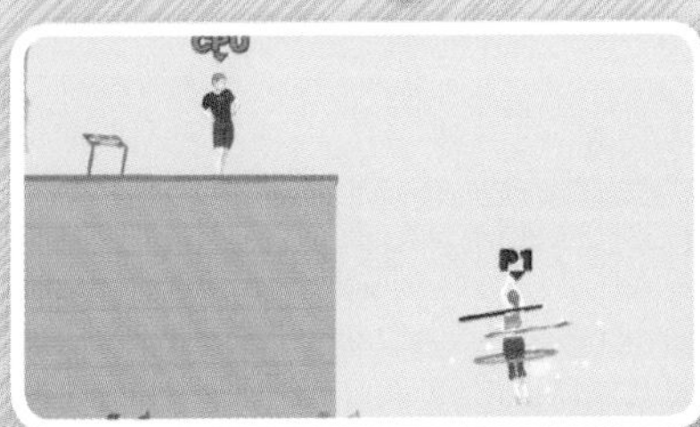

Wii Fit Trainer's main recovery tool is her Super Hoop. This attack can raise Wii Fit Trainer higher if you rapidly press the button. It recovers more vertically than it does horizontally, but it certainly takes you far enough before leaving you in a falling state. Using Header can get you some extra lift while also attacking the opponent. If you cancel the Header by hitting the Shield button, you enter a fall state, but if you don't cancel it, you won't enter a fall state. Additionally, you can slow your fall by using Deep Breathing. This is generally a good idea, as it increases many of your statistics if you time it correctly. If you don't time it right, though, it takes some extra time before you can use the Super Hoop.

YOSHI

Trophy Description

As dependable a partner as one could hope for, Yoshi often aids Mario in his adventures. Yoshi can swallow just about anything and make an egg out of it instantly. He's got some serious airborne power, making launching opponents skyward and then following up with more attacks a wise choice.

STATISTICS

MAXIMUM NUMBER OF JUMPS: **2**

CAN WALL JUMP: **No**

CAN WALL CLING: **No**

CAN CRAWL: **Yes**

Alternate Colors

Smash Attacks

SIDE SMASH DAMAGE 13~15.5%

Yoshi winds back before hurling his head forward. You can aim this slightly up or down. Yoshi's head is invincible during the attack.

DOWN SMASH DAMAGE 10~12%

A double tail sweep that hits on both sides of Yoshi. Good damage on both hits!

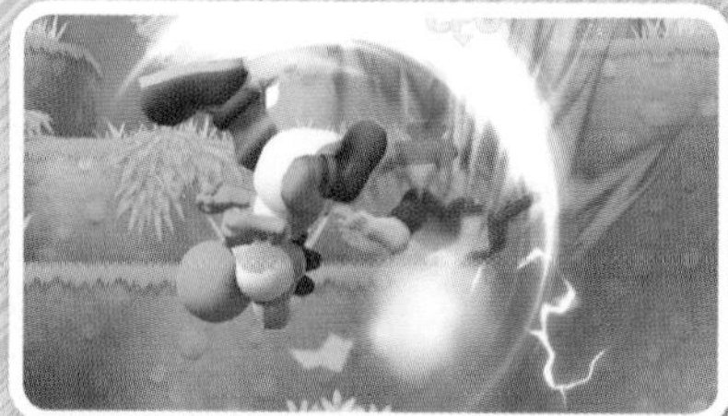

UP SMASH DAMAGE 12~14%

Yoshi performs a standing flipkick, knocking your opponent upward. Yoshi's raised feet are invincible during the attack.

Basic Attacks

STANDING ATTACK DAMAGE 3%, 4%

Yoshi's basic attack is a standing kick that hits nearly over his head. It combos into a short string for a little extra damage and knockback.

UP TILT DAMAGE 7%

Yoshi whips his tail upward to launch your opponent up into the air. Can be followed up with an UP SMASH at lower percentages.

DASH ATTACK DAMAGE 6~9%

Yoshi runs and does a jump kick attack before landing on the floor.

SIDE TILT DAMAGE 7%

This tail whip can be angled up or down and has both good range and knockback potential.

DOWN TILT DAMAGE 4~5%

Yoshi swings his tail around to sweep your opponents off their feet.

EDGE ATTACK

Yoshi leaps onto the stage and strikes with his tail.

Air Attacks

NEUTRAL AIR ATTACK

DAMAGE 5~10%

A quick double-leg kick in the air. This doesn't have a lot of range, but it stays out for a long time.

DOWN AIR ATTACK

DAMAGE 1~3% MAX DAMAGE 32% : 13 HITS

Yoshi goes into a run animation while in the air, stepping and kicking multiple times on anyone he comes in contact with below him. This move is fantastic and can net over 30% damage if all hits connect.

BACK AIR ATTACK

DAMAGE 2.5~5% MAX DAMAGE 10% : 3 HITS

This multi-hit tail whip deals good damage and covers Yoshi's back well.

UP AIR ATTACK DAMAGE 12%

Yoshi strikes upward with his tail. Use this to knock opponents out of the tops of stages. Its forward range is minimal, so your opponent has to be nearly on top of you.

FORWARD AIR ATTACK

DAMAGE 14~15%

Yoshi winds up then performs a headbutt attack. If this hits from above, it can cause a meteor smash.

Special Attacks

EGG LAY (Neutral Special)

DAMAGE 7%

Yoshi sticks out his tongue to grab opponents, swallows them, and turns them into eggs. The higher percentage they have, the harder it will be for them to break free! Opponents take 40% less damage while in the eggs, so attack them as much as possible! Yoshi is invincible between swallowing an opponent and laying an egg.

Lick DAMAGE 10%

Yoshi springs forward and uses his tongue as a weapon. You don't swallow opponents; instead his tongue deals straight damage. This knocks opponents away straight horizontally.

Egg Launch DAMAGE 10%

After swallowing an opponent, Yoshi launches them as powerfully as possible. The distance is predetermined and isn't based on the opponent's accumulated damage. Note the egg breaks earlier and this move is a little slower than the regular version.

EGG ROLL (Side Special)

DAMAGE 4~9%

Yoshi turns into an egg and rolls into battle! The faster you roll, the more damage you do. While rolling, you can also jump once. And though you can start the move while airborne, it won't do any damage until Yoshi is on the ground again.

Heavy Egg Roll DAMAGE 1~15%

Yoshi gains super armor throughout his roll while he's in egg form. This means you don'tflinch from attacks during the roll. The downside to this is it takes longer to recover after you're done.

Light Egg Roll DAMAGE 1~12%

A multi-hop variation of the roll. After the initial hop, all subsequent hops are automatic; however, you have some control over the falling angle of each hop.

EGG THROW (Up Special)

DAMAGE 1~5% MAX DAMAGE 6% : 2 HITS

Throw an exploding egg at your enemy! You can affect its trajectory with directional inputs. To throw the egg straight up, press backward. How long you hold the button determines whether it is a light throw or a heavy throw.

High Jump DAMAGE 0%

Fake throwing an egg and jump. You can use this up to three times to extend your time off the ground. Each jump gains less height, and you don't rise at all after the fourth jump. This also has a bit of invincibility on startup.

TIMED EGG THROW DAMAGE 9%

This throws a slightly larger egg that deals more damage. Only the explosion deals damage, though, not the egg itself. It explodes after a set time or when hitting the ground. It explodes quicker and flies faster than regular eggs, but it takes a bit longer to throw.

YOSHI BOMB (Down Special)

DAMAGE 4~15% MAX DAMAGE 19% : 2 HITS

Yoshi jumps before slamming himself down to the ground, emitting stars on both sides that deal 4% damage each. This is more damaging when used from the ground, as it hits on the way up and on the way down. From the air it only does the second half of the attack.

Star Bomb

DAMAGE 3~4% MAX DAMAGE 7% : 2 HITS

The Yoshi Bomb part of the attack does less damage, but a big star erupts upon landing. These stars can deal 4~8% damage.

Crushing Bomb

DAMAGE 5~18% MAX DAMAGE 23% : 2 HITS

Yoshi uses all his force and braces his legs for impact. No stars are emitted with this version, but the damage is higher. When used from the ground, the jump is higher than usual, but the attack is slower before and after the Yoshi Bomb.

Final Smash

SUPER DRAGON

Yoshi sprouts wings and begins to shoot fireballs! The fireballs fly far away, getting larger but weaker as they travel. You can fly around the stage by using the control stick. Line up as many opponents as possible for your fireball shots. Also, make sure you're back over the stage before Super Dragon runs out!

Strategy

Everyone's favorite dinosaur is back, and he's adjusted his posture a bit! Yoshi now stands up taller but is just as fast as (if not faster than) he used to be! While this makes him more like the rest of the cast, one key difference is that Yoshi's Egg serves as his shield. This lets him be more defensive than everyone else! Yoshi's strengths are his speed, zoning, throws, combo abilities, and above average weight. Yoshi does have some super armor on his Egg Lay and on his double jump but not a significant amount. So, use his speed and Egg Roll to stay away from your opponents so you can harass them with Egg Throw. Yoshi can now move horizontally while performing Egg Throw, so you can use this to close distance on hit or to keep away and harass even more effectively. Try a quick upward Egg Throw while moving horizontally away from your opponent. When your opponent gets close, don't be afraid to shield—now that Yoshi can jump out of shield, you can try to punish with his Down Air attack for lots of damage. Additionally, you can keep opponents from advancing on you by using his Forward Tilt. If opponents jump in at you, keep them out with Yoshi's Up Tilt, UP SMASH, Neutral Air, or Up Air.

Another strength for Yoshi is his throw game. Egg Lay acts as a throw and drops opponents quickly. If you can catch opponents while your back is to the edge, they may not have time to break free before the egg drops them to their doom! This can be a very tricky tactic, especially on stages with slight declines near the edges, like Yoshi's Island. Of course, once an opponent is trapped in an egg, you need to deal as much damage as possible, so be sure to chase and combo afterward! Separately, Yoshi's regular throw has quicker recovery now, while his pivot throw has more recovery but longer range. Use his Down Throw and follow up with a Yoshi Bomb or multiple Egg Throws.

Yoshi Bomb is one of your better knockout moves. It's risky, though, because of its long recovery. In general, use Yoshi's charged SMASH attacks, Back Air, and Up Air attacks for knockouts. Don't forget that his Forward Air can also meteor smash your opponent. When edge guarding, be sure to use his, Egg Throw, Forward Air, Down Tilt, and DOWN SMASH. Additionally, you can cancel his double jump into any special attack, so keep this option in the back of your mind at all times.

Recovery

Compared to how other characters recover, Yoshi may seem like he is lacking in this regard. While most characters' Up Special gives them some kind of vertical recovery, Yoshi's Egg Throw only gives him a little bit of extra height. And while other characters' Side Special helps them recover horizontally, using Yoshi's Egg Roll off stage is basically knocking yourself out of the battle! New to this game, however, is the opportunity for Yoshi to attempt to recover if he flies off the stage while using his Egg Roll; he will no longer be in free-fall after this move. Because those primary options don't work well for Yoshi, his double jump is significantly higher than that of other characters. This makes double jump his main recovery. Additionally, your first Egg Throw gains some height, while subsequent Egg Throws gain less and less vertical height, so be sure to use it, too. In addition to getting some height, you can also move horizontally with Egg Throw and potentially hit your opponent with it! Egg Throw can also be useful when hanging from an edge to attack opponents and regrab the edge. The only other attack useful for recovery is Yoshi's Yoshi Bomb when returning to the stage from high above. Yoshi Bomb snaps to the edge as long as you are lined up correctly.

ZELDA

Trophy Description

This is the namesake of the *Legend of Zelda* games. Her appearance may change, but she always plays an important role. In *Smash Bros.*, she's quick on the draw when it comes to magic, though a bit slow when moving. She has a new move that summons a Phantom to her aid.

STATISTICS

MAXIMUM NUMBER OF JUMPS: **2**

CAN WALL JUMP: **No**

CAN WALL CLING: **No**

CAN CRAWL: **No**

Alternate Colors

Smash Attacks

SIDE SMASH

DAMAGE 1~13% MAX DAMAGE 17% : 5 HITS

Zelda leans forward and casts a large multi-hitting magical blast in front of her.

DOWN SMASH DAMAGE 10~12%

Zelda spins to kick opponents close to her on both sides.

UP SMASH

DAMAGE 0.8~5% MAX DAMAGE 15.4% : 8 HITS

Zelda waves her hand back and forth above her head. Anyone caught by this will be hit multiple times and knocked upward.

Basic Attacks

STANDING ATTACK

DAMAGE 2% MAX DAMAGE 6% : 3 HITS

Zelda lifts one hand and casts magic at her opponent. This hits multiple times but pushes opponents away quickly.

UP TILT DAMAGE 6.5%

Zelda waves her arm overhead in a single swipe.

DASH ATTACK DAMAGE 6~12%

Zelda rushes forward while casting a blast of magic in front of her.

SIDE TILT DAMAGE 10~12%

This arm swipe attack has good range and damage. It can be aimed up or down.

DOWN TILT DAMAGE 4.5%

A crouching kick that has decent range.

EDGE ATTACK

Zelda swoops back on stage with a double leg sweep.

Air Attacks

NEUTRAL AIR ATTACK

DAMAGE 1~3% MAX DAMAGE 11% : 5 HITS

Zelda spins twice in the air with her arms outstretched while casting magic from her hands. Can hit multiple times before knocking opponents away.

DOWN AIR ATTACK DAMAGE 4~16%

Zelda stomps downward with one foot, sending a small blast below her. The blast does minimal damage, but hitting deep will knock opponents down.

BACK AIR ATTACK DAMAGE 4~20%

Zelda goes horizontal and kicks directly behind her. There is a sweet spot just above the tip of her feet, so if you can connect with this properly, the results are shocking!

UP AIR ATTACK DAMAGE 15%

Zelda looks up then casts a fiery blast immediately above her.

FORWARD AIR ATTACK

DAMAGE 4~20%

Zelda lunges forward with a far-reaching jump kick attack. This attack deals a lot of damage when you connect with the sweet spot at the tip.

Special Attacks

NAYRU'S LOVE (Neutral Special)

DAMAGE 1~5% MAX DAMAGE 11% : 4 HITS

Zelda summons a crystal barrier that can reflect projectiles. Unlike most Specials that reflect, this can also do damage by itself! Zelda has temporary invincibility when the crystal appears.

Nayru's Rejection

DAMAGE 1~5% MAX DAMAGE 7% : 3 HITS

Instead of hitting opponents, this variation spins them around. Zelda has some invincibility during this attack. The attack takes a bit longer to startup, but it also has slightly increased range.

Nayru's Passion DAMAGE 15%

As Zelda spins, she pulls opponents in before dealing fire damage to them. Though it has increased damage, this version does not reflect projectiles.

REFLECTION DATA

	REFLECT STARTUP	DAMAGE SCALING	SPEED SCALING
NAYRU'S LOVE	6th frame	1.25x	1.4x
NAYRU'S REJECTION	19th frame	1.25x	1.2x

FARORE'S WIND (Up Special)

DAMAGE 6~12%

Teleport Zelda in any direction by hitting a second directional input after the Up Special. She deals damage to nearby opponents both when she disappears and when she reappears. When reappearing in the air, Zelda is left in a fall state, so be careful near edges!

Farore's Squall DAMAGE 0%

No damage is dealt with this teleport, but a gust of wind from your path pushes opponents away. The startup is slower, but the distance you can teleport is farther. If you land on an opponent, that opponent is sent straight up from the wind, taking no damage.

Farore's Windfall DAMAGE 4~7%

Zelda is able to teleport upward only, but anyone hit when she reappears is meteor smashed. You have some horizontal control over Zelda after she reappears.

PHANTOM SLASH (Down Special)

DAMAGE STAGE 1 6~8.4%

DAMAGE STAGE 2 11.6~15.2%

DAMAGE STAGE 3 11.4~13.4%

MAX DAMAGE 24.8% : 2 HITS

Zelda summons a phantom to attack in front of her. Charging the attack affects both the type of attack the phantom does and how far it travels. If the phantom takes too much damage, Zelda won't be able to summon it for a while. Take care against characters with reflect abilities, as they can reflect the phantom back toward Zelda!

Phantom Breaker

DAMAGE STAGE 1 5~7%

DAMAGE STAGE 2 10~13%

DAMAGE STAGE 3 9~11%

MAX DAMAGE 20% : 2 HITS

This phantom only goes a set distance but significantly wears down shields. Its attack damage is slightly lower, as its primary focus is to break shields.

Phantom Strike

DAMAGE STAGE 1 8~10.4%

DAMAGE STAGE 2 13.6~17.2%

DAMAGE STAGE 3 13.4~15.4%

MAX DAMAGE 28.8% : 2 HITS

This phantom strikes harder, but it doesn't travel as far forward. Compared to the regular version, this phantom charges to full in about half the time.

DIN'S FIRE (Side Special)

DAMAGE 3.5~7% MAX DAMAGE 7~14%

This fireball attack is an extension of Zelda. Although it has limited range, Zelda can direct it toward her opponents with directional input while holding the Special button and also control when it explodes by releasing the Special button. Release the attack right on your opponents for best results! Note, you are in a fall state after using this in the air.

Din's Flare DAMAGE 7~14%

This version can travel farther and faster, but it can't move up or down. The damage is the same regardless of the distance it has traveled.

Din's Blaze

DAMAGE 3.8~7.6% MAX DAMAGE 9~18%

A slow-moving fireball that floats through the air a bit before exploding. It moves at the same speed as the regular version, but you have more control over its vertical movement. The longer the fireball has been out, the more powerful it is. It is most powerful at its center.

Final Smash

LIGHT ARROW

Zelda pulls out a large bow and fires an arrow across the stage. It hits all targets in its path, but the damage and knockback decrease per target. The first opponent receives 40% damage, the second receives 30%, and the third receives 22%. The range is incredible, reaching across Gerudo Valley. The knockback of this Final Smash knocks opponents up at a 45-degree angle at its peak but lower angles for successive targets.

Strategy

Zelda's toolset suggests she should be played in a zoner, campy style, but she actually has some strong attacks up close as well. She has a projectile she can control, a phantom to attack out in front of her, a teleport to attack or run away with, and a reflect tool to return projectiles and attack opponents. Combine this with her being one of the lightest characters in the game who has below-average mobility, and it becomes clear why she has so many tools to keep opponents away. Her Din's Fire, however, can be spot-dodged, so you will need to be ready to fight up close as well. Fortunately, Zelda has some strong attacks up close with multiple hitting Smash Attacks and a strong Throw game. Note that she has above-average throw damage, too, so use throws when possible! You can approach opponents with her Dash Attack or surprise them with her Farore's Wind. Follow either of these up with her basic attacks or short aerial attacks to stack up damage!

During Nayru's Love, the crystal barrier essentially renders Zelda invincible for a moment. Additionally, note that the reflect duration is longer than the attack duration of this move, and any projectiles reflected will be faster and will deal more damage! Yet Din's Fire is still your main ranged attack. Though the blast grows larger the longer you control it, remember you can detonate it early by letting go of the button. You can also try to crash it into parts of the stage to trigger the explosion. Phantom Slash has three different attacks, depending on how long you're able to charge it. The quickest charge causes the phantom to appear immediately in front of you with a quick diagonal upward swing of its sword. At the next level, the phantom comes out quickly and swings downward diagonally with his sword. The longest charge causes the phantom to dash forward before stabbing horizontally, then swinging the sword up for a two-hit combo. The higher-level phantom's attacks have more recovery, so opponents will be able to attack it to get rid of it, but the phantom can also serve as a shield in front of Zelda. Try to protect the phantom by sending out Din's Fire. Coincidentally, after a successful Din's Fire is usually a good time to charge up a phantom! If opponents work their way around your Din's Fire or Phantom Slash, you can try Farore's Wind to escape in an unpredictable direction.

Though she has a lot of ranged attacks, Zelda's normal attacks are fairly strong and useful. Forward Tilt has good range and damage, and you can aim it up or down as well. Her Up Smash hits multiple times for a good chunk of damage to protect her from airborne opponents. While her Up Tilt attack doesn't deal much damage, it can be useful during combos. Down Smash is a good option when looking for a KO because it is only one hit before it launches opponents away. Side Smash and Up Smash both hit multiple times and may be interrupted in a Free For All setting. Farore's Wind is also particularly good for KOs, especially against characters without a counter. Zelda's invincibility throughout helps a great deal here. In the air, Zelda has good single-hit attacks that can deal a ton of damage with her Forward and Back Air attacks. These moves have a wide range of damage, however, depending on where you hit them, so spacing is important. Neutral Air is a good move to keep opponents off of you, and Down Air has a meteor effect to keep in mind.

Recovery

While Zelda's main recovery tool is her Farore's Wind teleport, she also has some interesting ways to stall or protect herself while recovering. Farore's Wind can be used as both a horizontal and vertical recovery tool. It takes some time to master this, though, as it requires very precise placement. For stalling, you can use Nayru's Love—it pauses Zelda's descent while it reflects projectiles. Because it's also an attack, it can be useful to zone out opponents trying to meet you air to air. For much less stalling, Zelda has Phantom Slash, which stalls her as she sends the phantom out to attack and doesn't leave her in a fall state. This can turn a battle by clearing opponents away from using their own edge-guard strategies. So, in one jump, you could potentially use Nayru's Love, Phantom Slash, and Farore's Wind! While this may not be the most effective strategy for recovery, it's important to remember you have all of these options available.

ZERO SUIT SAMUS

Without her Power Suit, Samus Aran may not have her usual strength, special moves or over-powered arm cannon, but her Jet Boots definitely kick things up a notch in their own way. The Paralyzer, her gun, does just what you'd expect it to, but it can also turn into a whip for attacking and grabbing onto edges while falling.

STATISTICS

MAXIMUM NUMBER OF JUMPS: **2**

CAN WALL JUMP: **Yes**

CAN WALL CLING: **No**

CAN CRAWL: **Yes**

Alternate Colors

Smash Attacks

SIDE SMASH

DAMAGE 5~11% MAX DAMAGE 16% : 2 HITS

Zero Suit Samus uses her jet boots as she performs this double-kick attack that advances her forward.

DOWN SMASH DAMAGE 6~8%

Fires Zero Suit Samus's Paralyzer at the ground in front of her. This can temporarily stun your opponent.

UP SMASH

DAMAGE 0.8~4% MAX DAMAGE 11% : 7 HITS

Zero Suit Samus spins her whip above her head, hitting multiple times. While this move is great for hitting opponents above Zero Suit Samus, it can also be used against grounded opponents.

Basic Attacks

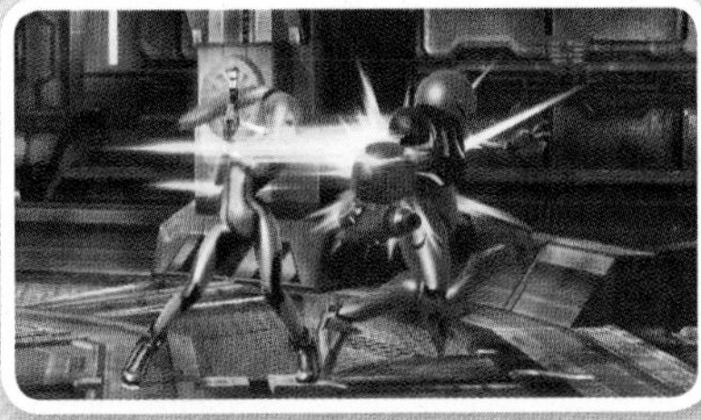

STANDING ATTACK

DAMAGE 1.5%, 1.5%, 3%

An extremely quick jab attack leading into two additional hits that combo and ending with an elbow.

UP TILT

DAMAGE 5~7% MAX DAMAGE 12% : 2 HITS

Zero Suit Samus claps her heels together from a handstand position and spins, hitting opponents around her multiple times. Launches opponents vertically.

DASH ATTACK DAMAGE 5~8%

Zero Suit Samus charges with a running knee attack at your opponent. Though it doesn't have the best range, this isn't an issue, given Zero Suit Samus's speed.

SIDE TILT DAMAGE 6~7%

A spinning horizontal kick attack that can be angled up or down.

DOWN TILT DAMAGE 6~8%

A good ranged sweep attack. This attack launches your opponent diagonally upward.

EDGE ATTACK

Zero Suit Samus swiftly returns to the stage with a long-range sweep kick that sends opponents horizontally away.

Air Attacks

NEUTRAL AIR ATTACK

DAMAGE 10%

Zero Suit Samus spins in the air as she uses her whip. This hits diagonally below in front of her and then diagonally above behind her.

DOWN AIR ATTACK

DAMAGE 5~6% MAX DAMAGE 11.5% : 2 HITS

This attack sends Zero Suit Samus diagonally downward with a fast kick that can meteor smash. Anyone around her as she hits the ground will also take damage.

BACK AIR ATTACK DAMAGE 10~12%

This reverse kick has good KO potential.

UP AIR ATTACK DAMAGE 8%

Using her jet boots, Zero Suit Samus does a quick flipkick attack.

FORWARD AIR ATTACK

DAMAGE 5~7% MAX DAMAGE 12% : 2 HITS

Similar to her Side Smash, this attack has Zero Suit Samus use her jet boots to kick twice in front of her.

Special Attacks

PARALYZER (Neutral Special)

DAMAGE 4% CHARGED 6%

Fires out a paralyzing energy blast that stuns your opponent. You can charge this up to extend its range and increase the stun duration, but the projectile travels slower then.

Blast Shot

DAMAGE 1~2% CHARGED 2.8~3.5%

Fires faster than usual, with charged and non-charged versions traveling about the same distance. It does less damage, but it also doesn't stun the opponent on hit.

Electromagnetic Net

DAMAGE 0.8~1% MAX DAMAGE 5.2% : 6 HITS

CHARGED 1~2% MAX DAMAGE 10% : 7 HITS

This blast travels a much shorter distance but has a larger range. On hit, it connects multiple times, so if there are multiple opponents in range, it hits all of them. Charging up the shot increases the damage and range.

BOOST KICK (Up Special)

DAMAGE 1.3~5% MAX DAMAGE 16.8% : 8 HITS

This attack sends Zero Suit Samus into the air quickly with a swift multi-hitting kick attack followed up by a spinning kick. This attack leaves you in a fall state.

Impact Kick

DAMAGE 6~14% MAX DAMAGE 20% : 2 HITS

Zero Suit Samus kicks the opponent up into the air before finishing that opponent off with a strong spinning kick. This only attacks at the beginning of and at the peak of the jump.

Lateral Kick

DAMAGE 1.3~5% MAX DAMAGE 16.5% : 7 HITS

This version kicks opponents into the air before using the boosters to charge forward with a spinning kick. Knocks opponents away at a lower angle than normal.

FLIP JUMP (Down Special)

STOMP 8% KICK 14%

This flip attack buries an opponent who is grounded or meteor smashes airborne opponents. Hitting the button again during this attack will kick in the direction you started the attack from unless you input the opposite direction. Zero Suit Samus has full invincibility on startup and partial invincibility on her head and lower body while flipping.

Shooting Star Flip Kick KICK 14~17%

In this move, the flip itself does not attack. Pressing the button again does a dive kick attack that deals significant damage.

Low Flip STOMP 4% KICK 6~8%

Zero Suit Samus quickly jumps into a low flip from which you can then do a quick kick attack. She retains her invincibility on startup but does not have any invincibility during the flip. Jumping during the flip helps you land faster.

PLASMA WHIP (Side Special)

DAMAGE 0.8~6% MAX DAMAGE 10.4% : 5 HITS

Zero Suit Samus attacks with her energy whip. Hitting with the tip launches an opponent farther. This can also be used to grab onto edges!

Plasma Dash

DAMAGE 1.2~4% MAX DAMAGE 13.2% : 8 HITS

This is a dashing strike using Zero Suit Samus's gun. Because the whip does not extend, you can't use it to grab onto the edge. You can still use your grapple to grab the edge instead.

Whip Lash DAMAGE 6%

The end of the whip is the only part that can hit opponents. On hit, it knocks opponents toward Zero Suit Samus. The hitbox on the tip is larger than usual.

Final Smash

GUNSHIP

Zero Suit Samus jumps into her gunship as it flies by and an aiming reticle appears on the screen. You control the aiming reticle with your control stick and use any attack button to fire the double laser beams from the ship. While the lasers are firing, you have a tiny bit of control to move them around still. Each hit scores about 15% damage and knocks the opponent away. You have up to 5 shots or about 15 seconds in the gunship, whichever comes first. Once done in the gunship, Zero Suit Samus returns from the top of the stage. This Final Smash is best suited when going up against multiple opponents.

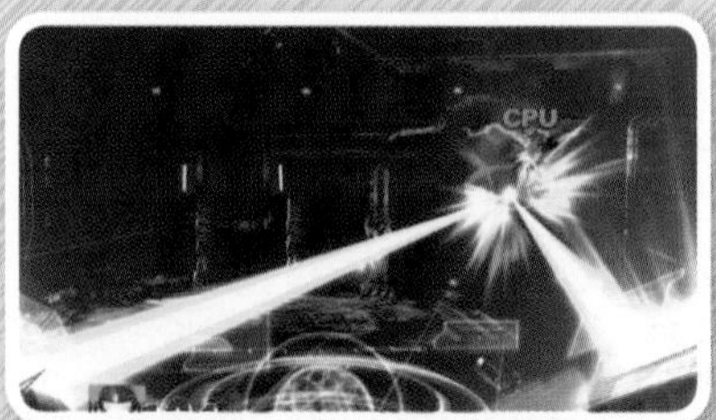

Strategy

Without her Power Suit, you might expect Samus to be less powerful, but this isn't the case. Zero Suit Samus makes up for her Power Suit's absence with her Jet Boots, Paralyzer, and increased mobility. Without that heavy suit, Zero Suit Samus becomes one of the lighter characters in the game—she now has some of the best jumps in the game and increased ground speed as well. Her recovery is good, aided by the height of her jumps and her ability to grab the edge with her Plasma Whip. Compared to Samus with her Power Suit, she doesn't have as strong of a long-range game, but she has a better up-close game. Being a lightweight character fighting up close, though, means you have to rely on your speed and defense a lot more.

Zero Suit Samus has two ways to stun opponents with her Paralyzer weapon. The first is her Down Smash, which is an essential part of her set of moves. Second is her Paralyzer Special. Charging up the Paralyzer Special extends its range but shoots a slower projectile. Opponents hit by the slower projectile will be stunned for a longer period of time. To effectively use her Plasma Whip, hit with just the end of it for the most knockback. This is also a good keepout tool to slow opponents' approaches and control the pace of a match. Don't forget you can also use this for recovery! Her Flip Jump attack takes some getting used to, but once you learn the spacing for it, the kick attack is useful and launches quite far. Flip Jump also has some invincibility, making it a little more usable. Boost Kick is mainly for attacking opponents who are high up or for racking up damage. If you're only looking to hit someone on a platform above you, use Up Smash instead.

In general, you want to set up traps with your stun options while keeping opponents away with Plasma Whip and your grapple. Zero Suit Samus's grapple should not be underestimated with its impressive range matched with her incredible speed. It is extremely effective for following up on long-range Paralyzer shots or Plasma Whip pokes, which tend to force opponents into shielding. Once you land a grapple on an opponent, Down Throw into Forward or Up Air is great for racking up damage at low percentages and even getting a KO at higher percentages. You can also use the grapple in the air as an attack to poke opponents and control space. Use Zero Suit Samus's fast attack speed to punish opponents' mistakes and build up as much damage as possible. Note that her Up Tilt has some invincibility at the tips of her feet, which should help against airborne opponents. Since her Down Tilt pops opponents into the air diagonally, follow this up with something like her Dash Attack. In the air, Neutral Air deals good damage but is awkward to land. Forward Air hits twice for decent damage, but it doesn't knockback very far. For KOs while airborne, your best bet is Back Air attack, though her Up Air is also effective. Down Air on airborne opponents can meteor smash as well, but only if you're willing to KO yourself with it. From the ground, your best bets for KOs are Side Smash, Up Smash, and Flip Jump into kick. When guarding the edge, use Paralyzer, Plasma Whip, and Flip Jump.

Recovery

The main recovery moves for Zero Suit Samus are her Boost Kick and Flip Jump. Boost Kick is her vertical recovery tool, attacking on the way up. You can angle it a little to the left or right during input, and Zero Suit Samus will be in a fall state when it completes. For horizontal recovery, Flip Jump is her best option. If you do Flip Jump by itself, Zero Suit Samus will not be in a fall state. If you extend Flip Jump by hitting the Special button again to do the second kick, however, Zero Suit Samus takes a long time to recover. Don't forget that Zero Suit Samus has a grapple and Plasma Whip to recover to the edge horizontally as well.

CHARACTER WEIGHTS

The weight of a character determines how far the character will be knocked away when hit by attacks. The lighter a character is, the farther they will be knocked away. The heavier a character is, the less they will be knocked away. For this reason, lighter characters can generally be KO'd at lower accumulated damage percentages than heavier characters.

	CHARACTER	ITEM WEIGHT CAPACITY (FOR REFERENCE ONLY)
EXTREMELY LIGHT	JigglyPuff	21
	Kirby	21
	Rosalina and Luma	22
	Zelda	22
	Meta Knight	22
	Falco	22
LIGHT	Peach	23
	Mr Game & Watch	23
	Zero Suit Samus	23
	Palutena	23
	Marth	23
	Little Mac	23
	Pikachu	23
	Duck Hunt Duo	23
	Olimar	23
	Lucina	23
	Sonic	23
MIDDLE	Luigi	24
	Diddy Kong	24
	Sheik	24
	Toon Link	24
	Pit	24
	Robin	24
	Fox	24
	Greninja	24

	CHARACTER	ITEM WEIGHT CAPACITY (FOR REFERENCE ONLY)
MIDDLE	Villager	24
	Wii Fit Trainer	24
	Dark Pit	24
	Mario	25
	Lucario	25
	Ness	25
	Captain Falcon	25
	Dr. Mario	25
	Shulk	25
	PAC-MAN	25
	Mega Man	25
HEAVY	Yoshi	26
	Link	26
	Ike	26
	R.O.B	26
	Bowser Jr	27
	Wario	27
	Donkey Kong	27
	Samus	27
	Charizard	27
	King Dedede	28
EXTREMELY HEAVY	Ganondorf	29
	Bowser	29

Mii FIGHTERS

Use your system's *Mii Maker* application to create Miis, then import them into the game for use as Mii Fighters! Like the game's official characters, Mii Fighters can be customized with equipment and alternate Specials. You can even use any outfits and headgear items you've collected in the game to give your Mii Fighters entirely new looks!

When you create a new Mii Fighter, you're given the choice of three distinct combat styles. It's also important to note that your Mii's height and weight will effect his or her basic stats. Larger characters tend to be slow and strong, while smaller characters are quick and agile. Experiment with different combinations to create your ultimate Mii Fighter!

Mii Fighter Specials don't need to be collected—all of them are available in the game's Custom modes. Unlock new Powers, headgear, and outfits by collecting random drops and completing special Challenges.

Mii Fighters can be used in any game mode that allows customized characters.

Brawler

As an expert in hand-to-hand combat, the Brawler uses powerful strikes and rapid-fire combinations to deal heavy damage at short range.

BRAWLER SPECIALS

INPUT	SPECIAL 1 (DEFAULT)	SPECIAL 2 (ALTERNATE)	SPECIAL 3 (ALTERNATE)
Neutral Special	Shot Put: This iron ball makes an impact, but it doesn't go far.	Ultimate Uppercut: A devastating uppercut charged up with all your might.	Exploding Side Kick: A kick so explosive, it'll set the world on fire (or at least your leg).
Side Special	Onslaught: Rush forward to deliver a flurry of kicks, and then finish with an uppercut.	Burning Dropkick: A fiery dropkick with decent range. Charge it to really turn up the heat!	Headache Maker: Pummel your foes with a swing of your arms as you descend from a jump.
Up Special	Soaring Axe Kick: Hit 'em on the way up while flipping, and hit 'em on the way down with an axe kick.	Helicopter Kick: A series of spin kicks delivered while soaring diagonally into the air.	Piston Punch: A storm of rising punches, carrying both you and your foes into the air for a high-flying combo.
Down Special	Head-On Assault: Crash headfirst into the ground, burying any foes standing nearby.	Feint Jump: An invincible leap out of danger that you can combo into a mighty kick.	Foot Flurry: A flurry of kicks. On the ground you charge forward, but in the air you stay in place.

Swordfighter

The Swordfighter uses his or her weapon to deliver precision attacks. From slashing combos to powerful lunges, this Mii Fighter is an expert at swordplay.

SWORDFIGHTER SPECIALS

INPUT	SPECIAL 1 (DEFAULT)	SPECIAL 2 (ALTERNATE)	SPECIAL 3 (ALTERNATE)
Neutral Special	Gale Strike: A blade technique that sends a tornado hurtling forth.	Shuriken of Light: A small throwing weapon made of light that flies straight forward.	Blurring Blade: A flurry of sword slashes. Charge it longer for extra power.
Side Special	Airborne Assault: Flip forward to strike a foe, and then rebound off of them.	Slash Launcher: Rush through anyone in your path, and launch them upward.	Chakram: A throwing weapon that you can guide with directional inputs.
Up Special	Stone Scabbard: A high jump followed by a firm downward strike with your sword.	Skyward Slash Dash: A flurry of slashes that sends you in the direction of your choice.	Hero's Spin: A spinning sword attack that sends you upward if used in the air.
Down Special	Blade Counter: Counter an enemy attack. The strength of your strike depends on the enemy's attack.	Reversal Slash: Creates a rainbow that reflects projectiles. Can also flip foes around if it hits them.	Power Thrust: A high-speed strike that goes forward on the ground and diagonally down in the air.

Gunner

The Gunner is an expert in long-range projectile combat. If you're looking to attack enemies from a safe distance, this is the Mii Fighter for you!

GUNNER SPECIALS

INPUT	SPECIAL 1 (DEFAULT)	SPECIAL 2 (ALTERNATE)	SPECIAL 3 (ALTERNATE)
Neutral Special	Charge Blast: A straight plasma shot. Charge it for extra firepower.	Laser Blaze: A rapid-fire laser beam that deals damage but won't make foes flinch.	Grenade Launch: A grenade thrown in an arc that explodes on impact.
Side Special	Flame Pillar: Fire a blast diagonally toward the ground, creating a miniature inferno on impact.	Stealth Burst: A stealthy shot that explodes when you release the button.	Gunner Missile: Fires a guided missile. Alternatively, enter the move like a Smash attack for a super missile!
Up Special	Lunar Launch: Shoot downward, and the recoil rockets you into the air.	Cannon Uppercut: An uppercut powered by a downward blast that can dunk airborne foes.	Arm Rocket: Take to the sky using jet propulsion. The direction of flight can be adjusted left or right.
Down Special	Echo Reflector: Reflects enemy projectiles, sending them back even stronger than they were before.	Bomb Drop: A thrown bomb that rolls a short distance on the ground.	Absorbing Vortex: Sucks in enemy projectiles, forming a barrier that also heals your damage.

STAGES

Stage Selection

Some game modes, such as Smash or Training, allow you to select a specific stage before the action begins. *Super Smash Bros.* for the Nintendo Wii U has a different selection of stages than *Super Smash Bros.* for the Nintendo 3DS, and each version of the game offers its own set of available commands during stage selection.

Each selectable stage is inspired by a well-known game or franchise. Most selectable stages are related to one or more of the available fighters, but a few stages are based on separate franchises or ones established by the *Super Smash Bros.* franchise itself.

NORMAL STAGES

On the "normal" setting, most stages contain some combination of animated backgrounds, moving platforms, environmental hazards, and scene transitions. Learning to recognize these scripted events—even in the heat of battle—can give you a noteworthy advantage over less observant players.

> **TIP**
>
> **During stage selection, follow the on-screen commands to toggle between a stage's normal and Final Destination forms.**

FINAL DESTINATION FORMS

Although environmental elements can lead to some particularly exciting matches, players looking to minimize distractions can take advantage of each stage's Final Destination form, indicated by an omega (Ω) near the stage name. These simplified stages incorporate some design elements from their respective normal variants, but they all share the same basic layout—each stage's Final Destination form contains a single large platform. This reduces the need for spacial awareness, making it much easier to focus on your opponents.

Wii U Stages

During stage selection, you can toggle between each stage's normal and Final Destination (Ω) forms. Before you confirm your selection, you can also use the "My Music" command to adjust the chances of a specific song playing during each battle. Any custom stages you've created in the game's Stage Builder mode can be accessed through the "Custom" tab.

UNLOCKING HIDDEN STAGES

Super Smash Bros. for the Nintendo Wii U contains 46 selectable stages, but only 40 of them are available by default. To unlock the six hidden stages, you must complete each of the corresponding Challenges.

HIDDEN STAGES

STAGE	HOW TO UNLOCK
Duck Hunt	KO more than one opponent in a single game of Cruel Smash.
Flat Zone X	Play as Mr. Game & Watch and destroy 100 or more blocks in a single game of Solo Trophy Rush.
Kongo Jungle 64	Clear the Event "The Original Heavyweights."
PAC-LAND	Play all of the maps in Smash Tour.
Pokémon Stadium 2	Clear the Event "When Lightning Strikes."
Smashville	Clear the Event "Playing Tricks."

SECRET STAGE OPTIONS

During stage selection, you can input secret commands to activate special features for Boxing Ring or Orbital Gate Assault.

SECRET STAGE OPTIONS: BOXING RING

The player selecting the stage can choose to battle on special a *Smash Bros.* version of Boxing Ring or a *Punch Out!!* version of the Boxing Ring.

STAGE SELECTION COMMANDS

CONTROLLER	FOR *SMASH BROS.* BOXING RING	FOR *PUNCH OUT* BOXING RING
Standard Controllers	ZL + Ⓐ during stage selection	ZR + Ⓐ during stage selection
Wii Remote:	⊖ + ② during stage selection	⊕ + ② during stage selection
Wii Remote + Nunchuck	Ⓒ + Ⓐ during stage selection	Z + Ⓐ during stage selection
GameCube Controller	Z + L + Ⓐ during stage selection	Z + R + Ⓐ during stage selection
Nintendo 3DS	L + Ⓐ during stage selection	R + Ⓐ during stage selection

SECRET STAGE OPTIONS: ORBITAL GATE ASSAULT

During stage selection, players can vote to trigger special dialogue options on Orbital Gate Assault. All players must input their choice at the same time. Votes that are input too early or too late will not be counted. In the event of a tie, one of the dialogue options will be selected at random.

STAGE SELECTION COMMANDS

CONTROLLER	FOR STAGE-RELATED DIALOGUE	FOR FIGHT-RELATED DIALOGUE
Standard Controllers	ZL + Ⓐ during stage selection	ZR + Ⓐ during stage selection
Wii Remote:	⊖ + ② during stage selection	⊕ + ② during stage selection
Wii Remote + Nunchuck	Ⓒ + Ⓐ during stage selection	Z + Ⓐ during stage selection
GameCube Controller	Z + L + Ⓐ during stage selection	Z + R + Ⓐ during stage selection
Nintendo 3DS	L + Ⓐ during stage selection	R + Ⓐ during stage selection

STAGE DESCRIPTIONS

NOTE

The following descriptions apply to each stage's normal form.

BATTLEFIELD

INSPIRED BY: ***Super Smash Bros.***

Battlefield is one of the game's more straightforward stages. All of the available platforms are static and permanent, offering a few tactical options without the distractions of the more complicated stages. Aside from a subtle (but constant) shift between day and night, this stage remains unchanged for the duration of a battle.

BIG BATTLEFIELD

INSPIRED BY: ***Super Smash Bros.***

Like its smaller counterpart, Big Battlefield offers a few tactical options without the transitions and hazards of more complicated stages. With its sheer size and additional platforms, however, this stage is a great option for larger battles or for fighters who favor a more elusive playstyle.

BOXING RING

INSPIRED BY: *Punch-Out!!*

This stage consists of a boxing ring at the center of an indoor arena. While the ring provides a nice, open space to battle your opponents, this stage offers a surprising number of tactical options.

There are entrance ramps located on both sides of the stage, meaning you'll have to launch an opponent well past the ropes to score a knockout. Jumping on the ropes launches you into the air, allowing you to reach the lights hanging above the ring. These lights can serve as an additional platform or as a fighter-activated hazard—dealing damage to the hanging lights will cause them to break loose and fall on any fighters beneath them.

BRIDGE OF ELDIN

INSPIRED BY: *The Legend of Zelda: Twilight Princess*

Initially, you'll find only a single platform running the length of the stage. Every so often, however, the stage undergoes a temporary transformation.

Each time King Bulblin appears, he charges across through the area and drops an explosive barrel near the center of the stage. Jump out of his path to avoid being trampled, and make sure you stay clear of the barrel he leaves behind. When the barrel detonates, a large section of the bridge is destroyed. The resulting hole is a significant, but temporary, hazard. After a short time, the bridge is patched and the cycle repeats.

CASTLE SIEGE

INSPIRED BY: THE *Fire Emblem* SERIES

This stage features frequent transitions, moving the action through a cycle of three sets. The first set consists of a castle wall. This area contains a simple cluster of fixed platforms, so plan your strategy accordingly.

In the castle hall, fighters are able to affect the available terrain. The statues near the center of the area can be destroyed, clearing the attached platforms from the area. This stage also features an underground area with a large, teetering platform. Transitions occur fairly frequently, so try to adapt your tactics to take advantage of the available platforms.

COLISEUM

INSPIRED BY: THE ***Fire Emblem*** SERIES

This stage uses several mechanical platforms to provide frequently shifting terrain. These transitions aren't as dramatic as those found on some stages, but you'll find new tactical options with each platform arrangement.

DELFINO PLAZA

INSPIRED BY: ***Super Mario Sunshine***

On this stage, fighters are carried to different locations around Delfino Plaza. The platforms provided during each transition vary, so consider the current arrangement and adapt your strategy accordingly.

As the battle moves to each location, use the available terrain to your advantage. You'll only spend a short time in any given area, however. Each time a new cluster of platforms appears, hop on to avoid being left behind.

DUCK HUNT

INSPIRED BY: ***Duck Hunt***

This relatively small stage contains some interesting elements. The bush and tree branches can be used as small platforms, as can the large dog that frequently appears in the background. New patches of tall grass sometimes emerge from the ground—clever fighters can slip behind temporary cover to lay traps or charge powerful attacks to use on distracted opponents.

Attacking the flying ducks increases the score displayed near the bottom of the screen. This score doesn't have any effect on the battle, but attacking a duck sometimes causes it to drop a useful item.

> **Duck Hunt becomes available after you KO more than one opponent in a single game of Cruel Smash.**
>
> **NOTE**

FINAL DESTINATION

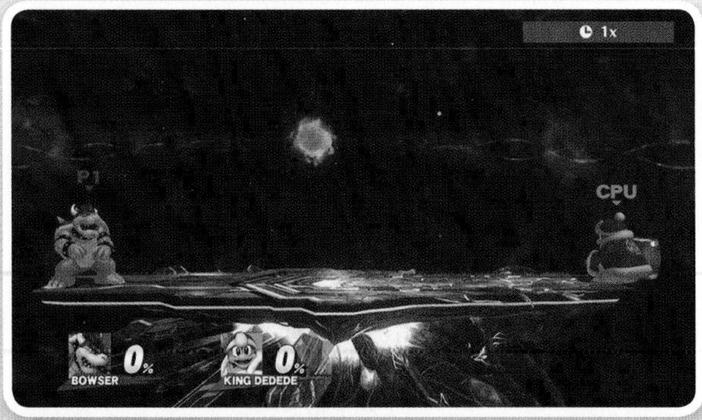

INSPIRED BY: ***Super Smash Bros.***

Final Destination is the game's most straightforward "normal" stage. It features one large platform at the center of the area, eliminating any of the terrain advantages found in other stages. Aside from the cycling background transitions, this stage remains unchanged over the course of a battle.

FLAT ZONE X

INSPIRED BY: THE ***Game & Watch*** **SERIES**

This stage features dramatic scene changes, and each of the available sets is inspired by a different game from the *Game & Watch* series. Over the course of a single battle, the frequent transitions place fighters in various randomly selected environments.

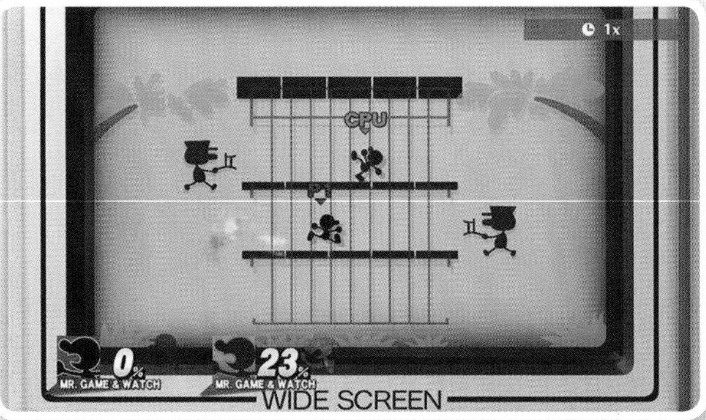

While some sets contain harmless elements like trampolines, shifting platforms, and a slippery oil spill, others feature unique hazards. Be particularly wary of the falling food items found in the kitchen and the chair-wielding animal tamers that guard the lion cages. Each time the battle moves to the kitchen, however, you can defeat the Chef to trigger a faster stage transition!

> **Flat Zone X becomes available after you destroy 100 or more blocks in a single game of Solo Trophy Rush while playing as Mr. Game & Watch.**
>
> **NOTE**

GAMER

INSPIRED BY: ***Game & Wario***

This stage contains a large table with a random selection of platforms. Every so often, a strict mother appears in the room. At the very least, you can expect the mother to emerge from the room's door, the windows along the background, and the nearby television screen. The table occasionally contains a small gaming console on which the mother can also appear.

Each battle is sure to have a few false alarms. When the door opens, for example, there's a chance that a cat will briefly poke its head into the room. When the mother does appear, however, any fighters caught in her gaze will take heavy damage. Each time you spot the mother, move toward one of the available platforms and take cover in the shadows to avoid her wrath.

GARDEN OF HOPE

INSPIRED BY: ***Pikmin 3***

This stage features a tiled bridge and a cracked pot flanked by two suspended tins. The tins are connected to each other—adding weight to one tin will force it toward the bottom of the screen as the opposite tin moves upward. Staying on a tin for too long will cause it to drop clear out of the stage. Fighters can also attack the bridge and the pot. When one of these objects sustains enough damage, it will be destroyed for a short time.

Every so often, a Peckish Aristocrab scuttles through the area. Jump out of this creature's path to avoid being trampled. If the bridge is destroyed, the Peckish Aristocrab simply falls through the gap. Otherwise, it moves across the length of the stage.

TIP

When a shattered pot is repaired, any fighters caught inside it are particularly vulnerable to damage. The effect ends once a fighter breaks free, but a well-timed attack can be devastating to a trapped opponent.

GAUR PLAIN

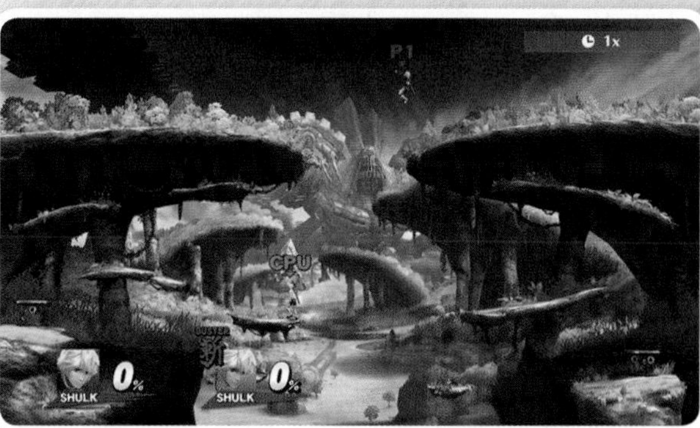

INSPIRED BY: ***Xenoblade Chronicles***

This stage features clusters of small platforms below two large ledges. It can be tricky to traverse the available footholds in the heat of battle, so be careful! When you want to cover a lot of ground quickly, use the spring-loaded platforms to launch yourself toward the top of the stage.

During extended battles, Metal Face will occasionally appear. This large enemy spends most of his time perched near the center of the stage, using his large claws to swipe at nearby fighters. If left to his own devices, Metal Face eventually leaves his perch and charges across the stage, damaging any fighters caught in his path. You can attack Metal Face while he's near the center of the stage, however—if you deal enough damage, Metal Face will be destroyed before he can complete his attack.

THE GREAT CAVE OFFENSIVE

INSPIRED BY: ***Kirby Super Star***

This massive stage features multiple paths between visually distinct areas. Watch your step! You'll find plenty of hazards scattered throughout the stage. Fiery hazards are particularly common, and touching one will result in heavy damage. If your damage is above 100%, touching a fiery hazards results in an instant KO! Keep your distance, but try to knock an opponent or two into a hazard when the opportunity presents itself.

In addition to obvious hazards, this stage contains a few useful—but potentially dangerous—items. Rotating cannons can be great for making a quick retreat, but timing is important. A poorly aimed shot can send you into a hazard or straight out of the stage! Hopping into a mine cart allows you to take a short ride, but remember to jump out before you crash. If one of your opponents beats you to a mine cart, move out of its path to avoid taking damage!

HALBERD

INSPIRED BY: ***Kirby Super Star***

This level features platforms that carry fighters to and from the deck of Meta Knight's ship. Each time the larger of the two platforms appears, hop on to avoid being left behind.

The deck of the Halberd contains additional hazards, so be particularly careful when the battle moves to this area. Keep one eye on the turrets and the mechanical arm in the background. One turret fires a slow-moving projectile; this attack is easy enough to avoid if you're paying attention. When a reticle appears near one of the fighters, it signals an incoming beam attack. Dash away from the reticle to avoid the impending blast. The robotic arm occasionally lunges into the foreground, so look for signs of movement to get clear of the strike.

JUNGLE HIJINXS

INSPIRED BY: ***Donkey Kong Country Returns***

In this stage, fighters can use the available Barrel Cannons to move between the platforms in the foreground and those in the background. Barrel Cannons appear and disappear over the course of a battle, so it's important to plan your movements accordingly. Keep an eye out for columns that sometimes appear between the two areas—launching yourself into one of these columns prevents you from reaching your intended landing spot.

When blue arrows appear in the area, it means the indicated platform is about to vanish. Luckily, each arrow also indicates the future location of an incoming Barrel Cannon. If you find yourself near these arrows, move to a nearby platform or use a Barrel Cannon to launch yourself to safety. After a short time, the missing platform will reappear.

KALOS POKÉMON LEAGUE

INSPIRED BY: ***Pokémon X*** **AND** ***Pokémon Y***

This stage features frequent transitions. Over the course of a single battle, the default platform will incorporate elements of various Pokémon. Along with new platforms, each of these sets contains a hazard related to the type of Pokémon that appears in the area.

The stage shifts between four distinct Pokémon types: Fire, Water, Dragon, and Steel. Each of these types has a standard form and a legendary form. The standard Water-type set, for example, features a powerful stream of water that can carry unsuspecting fighters out of the stage, and the legendary Water-type set transforms the central platform into one large water hazard. Whenever a hazard is in play, it's often best to stick to the smaller platforms—just make sure you hop back off before the next transition!

KONGO JUNGLE 64

INSPIRED BY: ***Donkey Kong Country***

This small stage features several platforms, some of which are constantly moving. The Barrel Cannon hidden below the main platform, however, offers some particularly interesting tactical options.

During battle, the Barrel Cannon slides back and forth across the stage. Most of the time, the Barrel Cannon is out of view, making it fairly difficult to track its position. Still, it can often be used to recover from a sudden fall. Once you've made it into the Barrel Cannon, use it to launch yourself back up to the main platform—a well-aimed shot will even damage any opponents unfortunate enough to be in your path!

Kongo Jungle 64 becomes available after you clear the Event "The Original Heavyweights."

NOTE

LUIGI'S MANSION

INSPIRED BY: ***Luigi's Mansion***

This stage features a variety of platforms within a large, fully destructible mansion. Additionally, the main structure is often flanked by small, slowly moving platforms; occasionally, however, these platforms vanish for a short time.

The mansion's interior contains four columns. Once a column is destroyed, the surrounding area crumbles. The columns on the lower floor can't be damaged while the areas above them are intact. If you intend to level the structure, make sure you destroy the upper columns first. Shortly after the mansion is completely destroyed, it will reappear in the stage.

LYLAT CRUISE

INSPIRED BY: THE *Star Fox* FRANCHISE

This stage features a simple cluster of tilting platforms and some fairly dramatic background elements. The ever-changing scenery doesn't have any effect on the battle, however. As long as you keep your footing, you're free to focus on your opponents.

> **NOTE**
>
> **You can trigger special dialogue events by repeatedly taunting as Fox or Falco. The specific dialogue will vary depending on the timing of the taunts and which character was used to perform them.**

MARIO CIRCUIT

INSPIRED BY: *Mario Kart 8*

On this stage, moving platforms carry fighters to different points along a race track. The terrain varies between locations, but the platforms that appear during each transition are always the same.

Many of the stops along the track contain additional hazards—particularly when the racers speed through the area. Watch for the alerts that signal incoming karts to avoid taking unnecessary damage. Whenever possible, launch your opponents into oncoming racers to deal heavy damage and increase the chances of a fast KO.

MARIO CIRCUIT (BRAWL)

INSPIRED BY: THE *Mario Kart* SERIES

This stage places fighters at the raised intersection of a figure-eight race track. Throughout a battle, racers speed through the area, striking any fighters in their path. Use the monitor in the background to keep track of kart positions, and move to a safe location each time they approach. The racers alternate between the upper and lower paths each time they appear, so you shouldn't have trouble avoiding them as long as you're paying attention.

MARIO GALAXY

INSPIRED BY: *Super Mario Galaxy*

This relatively simple stage features two small platforms above a large, rounded patch of land. There's a special gravity effect that causes most projectiles to follow the stage's curved shape. Some projectiles, however, will still travel in straight lines.

MUSHROOM KINGDOM U

INSPIRED BY: ***New Super Mario Bros. U***

This stage features frequent transitions and various hazards that appear and vanish over the course of a battle. Each set offers a unique platform arrangement, but elements like sprouting beanstalks, falling icicles, and erupting geysers can often be used as temporary platforms.

Kamek appears in the area just before each transition; when you spot him, prepare yourself for the impending change. Once you've found safe footing in a new set, watch out for any new hazards. If you notice falling drops of water, move away to avoid the incoming icicle. Make sure you keep an eye out for Nabbit—this sneaky pest will attempt to capture fighters and toss them off of platforms. Keep your distance, or move in to defeat this pest before he has a chance to attack you.

NORFAIR

INSPIRED BY: THE ***Metroid*** SERIES

This stage contains a cluster of five small platforms in a large, lava-filled cavern. Throughout a battle, waves of lava can rise up from below the platforms or come rushing in from either side, rendering any submerged platforms unusable. During these events, simply move the action away from the lava to avoid being launched.

Occasionally, a giant wave of lava approaches from the background. Each time this happens, a temporary shelter appears on one of the platforms. Attack the shelter to open it, then slip inside to protect yourself from the lava as it passes through the area. Move quickly, though! You won't have much time to react, and it can be difficult to enter a shelter once another fighter has claimed it. In addition, if you fail to get into the shelter in time, a properly timed dodge can be used to avoid damage from the lava wave.

ONETT

INSPIRED BY: ***EarthBound***

This small stage offers enough platforms to accommodate any number of strategies. During a battle, however, the drugstore's sign can come loose, temporarily destroying the awnings below it. The most important feature on this stage, however, is the traffic on the street. Watch for alerts about incoming cars! If you're on the ground when one of these warnings appears, move to an available platform as quickly as possible.

ORBITAL GATE ASSAULT

INSPIRED BY: ***Star Fox Assault***

This stage features frequent transitions, some of which can be fairly confusing for new players. Fighters must use the available ships as temporary platforms. Each ship only stays in the area for a short time, so take note of new vessels as they appear, and watch for signs that existing ships are about to vanish.

Some transitions are harder to navigate than others. Be particularly careful when a ship explodes, scattering the fighters through the area. The blast can make it very difficult to identify an available platform while you still have enough time to reach it.

PAC-LAND

INSPIRED BY: ***PAC-LAND***

This scrolling stage forces fighters to keep pace with the moving scenery. Each area contains its own platforms, obstacles, and hazards, so it's important to pay attention to your surroundings. Near the beginning of the stage, be particularly wary of the fire hydrants scattered along the ground. A small burst of water can be enough to knock a straggling fighter right off of the screen.

As the battle moves through the stage, you'll encounter geysers, crumbling bridges, and hazardous pools of water. If you're not sure whether or not an item or surface is safe, it's usually best to avoid it. Try to stick to solid ground, and hop over any obstacles in your path to keep the battle moving.

> PAC-LAND becomes available after you play all of the maps in Smash Tour.
>
> **NOTE**

PALUTENA'S TEMPLE

INSPIRED BY: ***Kid Icarus: Uprising***

This expansive stage offers enough platforms and paths to accommodate even the largest battles. You'll find varied terrain and plenty of fixed platforms, so try to move the battle to a spot that favors your playstyle. If you need to withdraw from a dangerous situation, look for a nearby ladder or spring-loaded platform.

This stage doesn't feature any actual transitions, but it does contain a large structure that occasionally vanishes. The altar floating near the top of the stage sometimes moves out of the area—make sure you're safely on solid ground when it does!

> Taunting as Pit will sometimes trigger a special dialogue event. The specific dialogue will vary based on the fighters involved in the battle.
>
> **NOTE**

PILOTWINGS

INSPIRED BY: ***Pilotwings***

On this stage, the battle takes place high above the ground, moving back and forth between two different airplanes. While on the biplane, fighters can make use of three separate areas. The upper wings serve as one long platform, while the lower wings are divided by the plane's body. The seaplane offers one main platform, but particularly agile fighters can use its pontoons as hard-to-reach footholds.

Both planes tilt back and forth, often moving in and out of the foreground as they fly through the area. You may have to make small adjustments to maintain your position and avoid slipping off of the available platforms. Over the course of the battle, fighters are automatically moved back and forth between the planes. These transitions are easy to anticipate, however—when one plane flies over the other, fighters are dropped into position.

POKÉMON STADIUM 2

INSPIRED BY: ***Pokémon series***

This stage features frequent transitions. In addition to the default platforms, fighters must deal with various sets inspired by different Pokémon types. Watch the monitor in the background for clues about when a transition is about to occur and which set will appear.

Each alternate set is inspired by one of four Pokémon types. The Flying-type set features heavy winds that add a floating effect to fighters' jumps. The Ground-type set includes additional platforms and obstacles. The Electric-type set offers new platforms and conveyor belts. And the Ice-type set features slick surfaces with minimal traction.

> **Pokémon Stadium 2 becomes available after you clear the Event "When Lightning Strikes."**
>
> **NOTE**

PORT TOWN AERO DIVE

INSPIRED BY: ***F-Zero***

On this stage, fighters are carried to various points on and around an F-Zero track. While the platforms are in motion, any fighters who fall onto the track are launched into the air. Keep your footing to avoid taking unnecessary damage!

Each stop along the route offers different platforms and hazards, so try to use the terrain to your advantage. When the battle stops near the track, it's also important to watch out for any racers that might come speeding through the area.

PYROSPHERE

INSPIRED BY: ***Metroid: Other M***

This relatively small stage features several unique elements—the most important of which is a large dragon-like creature named Ridley. When Ridley appears, he attacks fighters, often destroying smaller platforms in the process. Although it's possible to simply evade this powerful enemy, attacking him can yield some surprising results.

As Ridley takes damage, each fighter's contribution is recorded. If and when Ridley absorbs enough damage, he fights alongside the player who dealt the most damage. After this happens, however, fighters can continue to damage Ridley in an effort to change his allegiance. It's also important to note the slug-like creatures that sometimes appear can be thrown at Ridley to deal heavy damage, attacking floating turrets cause them to fire, and defeating a hovering Joulion causes it to explode.

75 M

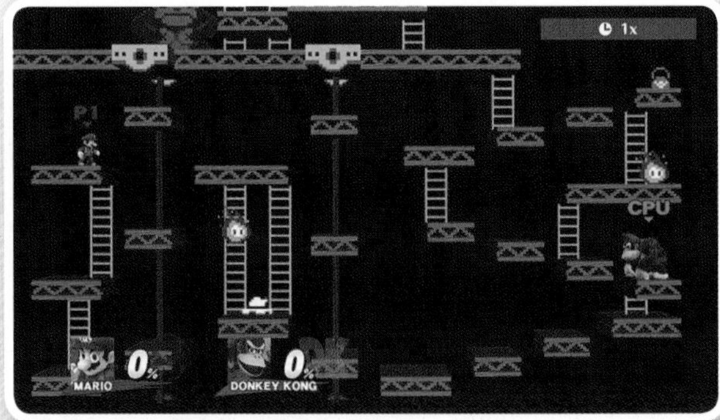

INSPIRED BY: ***Donkey Kong***

This compact level offers climbable ladders and a variety of small platforms, along with a few persistent hazards. It's important to avoid the slow-moving fireballs, but items like the umbrella and purse can be collected. Doing so increases the score displayed near the top of the stage, but it has no effect on the battle.

During battle, watch the Donkey Kong figure near the top of the stage. Soon after the figure steps out of the shadows, fast-moving springs begin bouncing across the stage. Touching a spring is likely to result in a KO, so stay out of the way until the figure steps back into the shadows.

SKYLOFT

INSPIRED BY: ***The Legend of Zelda: Skyward Sword***

This stage features clusters of moving platforms that transport fighters to different spots thought the area. The specific formation of platforms varies during each transition, so adapt your strategies accordingly.

Each time the battle moves to a new location, use the available terrain to your advantage. Whenever a new cluster of moving platforms appears, hop on to avoid being left behind.

SKYWORLD

INSPIRED BY: ***Kid Icarus***

This small stage features a tight cluster of platforms and an additional platform that occasionally moves across the bottom of the area. Each fixed platform is composed of one or more stone segments resting on a cloud. Attacking a stone segment eventually causes it to shatter. Once this happens, fighters can jump or drop through the exposed cloud, making it a bit easier to move around the area. This effect is temporary, however; stone segments regenerate fairly quickly.

SMASHVILLE

INSPIRED BY: ***Animal Crossing***

This simple stage features a large platform floating high above the ground. Smaller platforms frequently float through the area, but they move relatively quickly. Small balloons sometimes appear near the top of the stage. If you like, you can attack them to free any attached items or to clear the area to help ensure that your projectile attacks are able to reach your intended targets.

> Smashville becomes available after you clear the Event "Playing Tricks."
>
> **NOTE**

TEMPLE

INSPIRED BY: ***The Legend of Zelda***

This sizable stage features numerous platforms and a variety of terrain, making it another good choice for larger battles. While the upper platforms provide plenty of open space, the lower platforms are a bit more confined. Whenever possible, move the battle to an area that favors your personal playstyle.

TOWN AND CITY

INSPIRED BY: *Animal Crossing: City Folk*

This stage features a large platform that carries fighters back and forth between two different locations. Each location has its own set of additional platforms, so be sure to take advantage of the available terrain—just make sure you return to the main platform before it moves out of the area.

WII FIT STUDIO

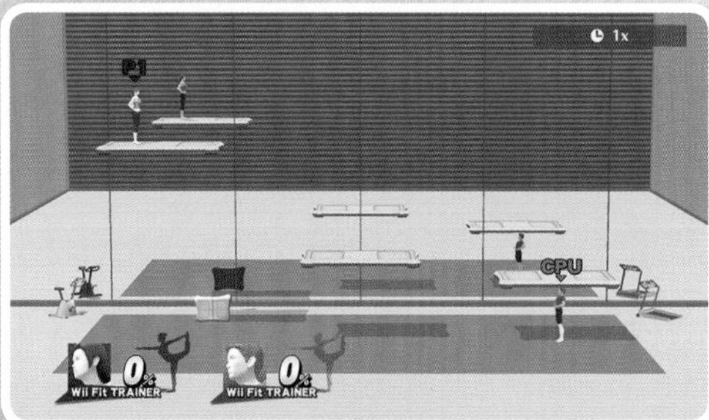

INSPIRED BY: *Wii Fit*

This stage frequently transitions between two relatively simple sets. The first set contains a number of randomly placed platforms floating in front of a mirrored wall. Jumping onto one of these platforms causes it to lower slightly, but all of the platforms remain relatively still until the scene changes.

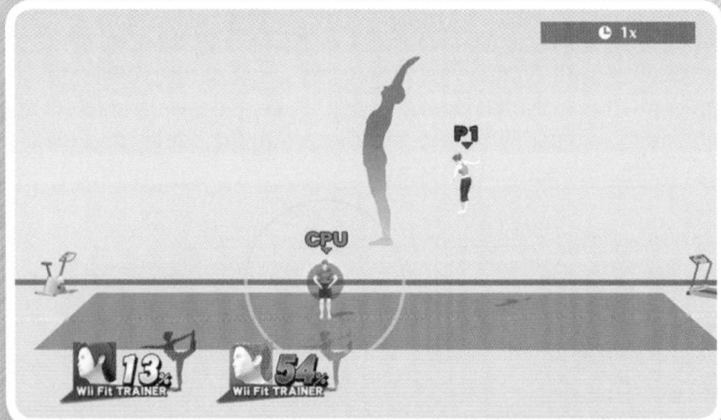

The second set is an empty room with nothing but a yoga pose displayed in the background. Each time you transition back to the first set, you're given a new platform arrangement. Each time you transition back to the second set, a new yoga position appears on the wall.

WILY CASTLE

INSPIRED BY: THE *Mega Man* SERIES

This stage contains a single fixed platform, but additional temporary platforms appear over the course of a battle. These platforms move along visible tracks. When one of these platforms reaches a dotted section of track, it flips down, dropping anyone it might be carrying. More important, however, this stage features the Yellow Devil—a massive robot that occasionally emerges from the castle in the background.

While the Yellow Devil is in the area, it fires a series of projectiles across the stage. After a few attacks, the robot usually moves to the opposite edge of the main platform and fires projectiles in the other direction. Fighters can dodge these projectiles or take cover behind the Yellow Devil until it leaves the area. Alternatively, fighters can attack the robot until it explodes—if you manage to deliver the finishing blow, the resulting explosion counts as your attack, damaging all nearby opponents.

WINDY HILL ZONE

INSPIRED BY: *Sonic Lost World*

This stage features a large, curved mass of land surrounded by a number of smaller platforms. Most of the time, you'll find a spring floating on each side of the main platform. They'll occasionally vanish, however, so make sure you look before you leap! The windmill near the right edge of the stage has a platform attached to each of its blades. Each of these platforms can only be used for a short time, however, before they move out of the area.

WOOLLY WORLD

INSPIRED BY: ***Yoshi's Woolly World***

This stage contains two seemingly separate clusters of suspended platforms. When you interact with these platforms, however, it's clear they're all connected to each other—placing weight on one platform will have a subtle effect on all of them.

Every so often, the floor drops out from the bottom of the stage. Watch for the arrows that signal the impending transition, and move to one of the available platforms to avoid falling off-screen. After a while, the floor returns and the cycle starts over.

WRECKING CREW

INSPIRED BY: ***Wrecking Crew***

This stage features a large building with an endless stack of randomly selected floors. The available ladders can be used to climb between any visible floors, and fighters can slip behind metal cans to reach areas that might otherwise be inaccessible. Most important, however, the bombs scattered throughout the building can be used to destroy nearby supports. With enough damage, the entire floor will collapse, dropping a new selection of platforms into the area. Watch out! Fighters can be caught inside of falling barrels. Attack trapped fighters to deal heavy damage until they manage to free themselves.. To trigger an explosion, simply attack an available bomb.

WUHU ISLAND

INSPIRED BY: ***Wii Sports Resort***

On this stage, moving platforms carry fighters to various spots scattered throughout the area. Different platforms appear during each transition, so be prepared to adjust your tactics as needed.

Wuhu Island offers plenty of exciting locations, and you'll find yourself constantly adjusting to new hazards. You'll never spend long in one spot, however. Each time a set of moving platforms appears, hop on to avoid being left behind.

YOSHI'S ISLAND

INSPIRED BY: ***Super Mario World***

This small stage features relatively little level ground. The sharp inclines on each side of the area can make it difficult to line up effective attacks, and the Turn Block platforms can be rendered temporarily unusable if a fighter attacks them. Of course, you can also use this against your opponents. The Turn Blocks covering the gap at the center of the stage are particularly dangerous, as an unexpected fall could easily result in a KO!

3DS Stages

During stage selection, you can toggle between each stage's normal and Final Destination (Ω) forms. Make sure you've activated your desired form before you confirm your choice.

UNLOCKING HIDDEN STAGES

Super Smash Bros. for the Nintendo 3DS contains 34 selectable stages, but only 27 of them are available by default. To unlock the seven hidden stages, you must complete each of the corresponding Challenges.

HIDDEN STAGES

STAGE	HOW TO UNLOCK
Balloon Fight	Use Villager three or more times in Smash.
Dream Land	Use a Final Smash while playing as Kirby.
Flat Zone 2	Unlock the hidden character Mr. Game & Watch and complete the first Challenge panel.
Magicant	Unlock the hidden character Ness.
Mute City	Win three Smash battles with Captain Falcon.
PAC-MAZE	Use a Final Smash while playing as PAC-MAN.
WarioWare, Inc.	Unlock the hidden character Wario.

STAGE DESCRIPTIONS

The following descriptions apply to each stage's normal form.

NOTE

ARENA FEROX

INSPIRED BY: ***Fire Emblem: Awakening***

At first glance, Arena Ferox appears to be a fairly straightforward battleground. Over the course of a battle, however, this stage cycles through a series of elaborate platform configurations. Some platforms can even be destroyed!

During the battle, watch for the purple mist that signals an incoming set change. If the mist appears while you're standing on a temporary set piece, make sure you're located safely above the main platform before the impending transition.

BALLOON FIGHT

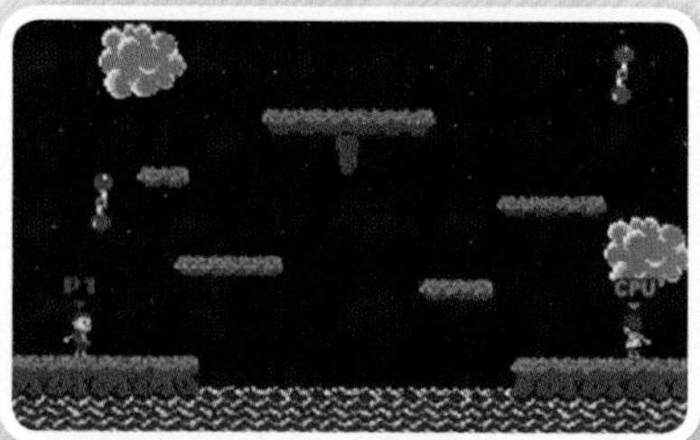

INSPIRED BY: ***Balloon Fight***

This stage contains a randomly selected arrangement of platforms and hazards. Though specific locations will vary, you can expect each variation to include two clouds, at least one flipper, and a water hazard near the bottom of the stage. Touching a flipper will cause it to spin, knocking the player away and resulting in light damage. Getting too close to the water will lure a giant fish out of hidingif this fish grabs you, it will drag you into right into the water hazard.

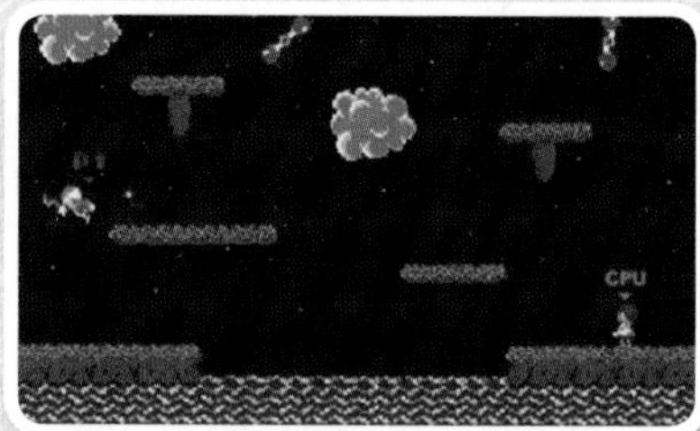

Every so often, a cloud will release a lightning spark—take care to avoid these slow-moving hazards as they bounce around the area. This stage does offer one more unique feature: fighters can move past the screen's left and right edges to appear on the opposite side of the stage!

On this stage, players can actually move past the left or right.

Balloon Fight becomes available after you use Villager three or more times in Smash.

NOTE

BATTLEFIELD

INSPIRED BY: *Super Smash Bros.*

Battlefield is one of the game's more straightforward stages. All of the available platforms are static and permanent, offering a few tactical options without the distractions of more complicated stages. Aside from a subtle (but constant) shift between day and night, this stage remains unchanged for the duration of a battle.

BOXING RING

INSPIRED BY: *Punch-Out!!*

This stage consists of a boxing ring at the center of an indoor arena. While the ring provides a nice, open space to battle your opponents, this stage offers a surprising number of tactical options.

There are entrance ramps located on both sides of the stage, meaning you'll have to launch an opponent well past the ropes to score a knockout. Jumping on the ropes will launch you into the air, allowing you to reach the lights hanging above the ring. These lights can serve as an additional platform or as a fighter-activated hazard—dealing damage to the hanging lights will cause them to break loose and fall on any fighters beneath them.

BRINSTAR

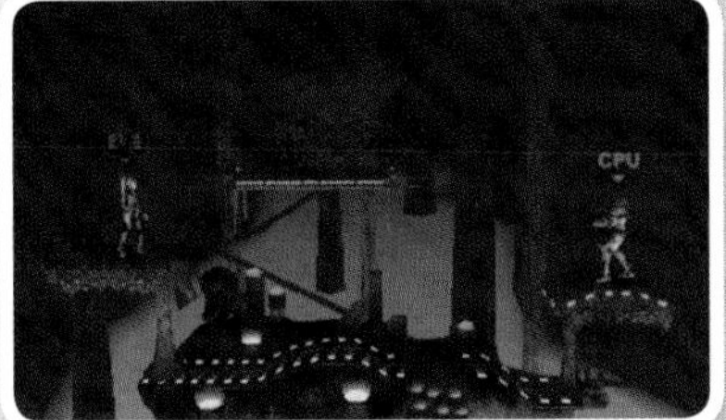

INSPIRED BY: *Metroid*

This stage contains a cluster of platforms suspended within a cavern. Over the course of a battle, the cavern occasionally fills with acid, rendering any submerged platforms unusable. Any fighters who touch the acid will be launched into the air with a damaging attack, so move as needed to keep clear of this environmental hazard. There's a weak spot near the center of the lowest platform—destroying this spot will temporarily split the platform in half.

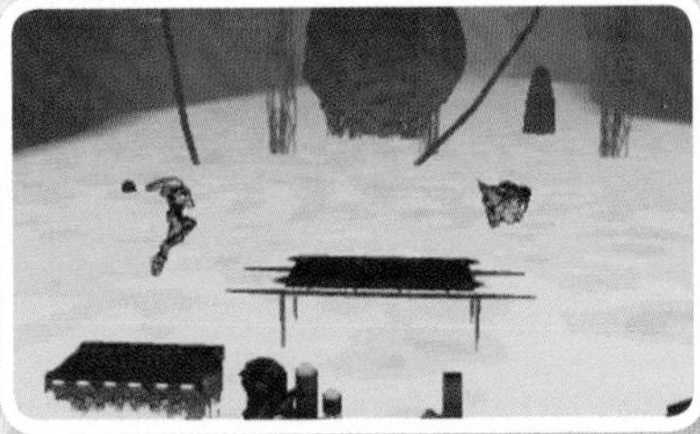

The platforms tremble each time the acid level rises or lowers. At its highest point, the acid covers the three lower platforms, leaving a single platform as the only safe perch.

CORNERIA

INSPIRED BY: *Star Fox*

This stage features a large ship—known as the *Great Fox*—which serves as a mobile battleground. Most of the action will take place along the ship's hull, but in an emergency, the *Great Fox*'s front-mounted cannons can be used as a platform. Be careful, though! You don't want to be anywhere near these weapons when they're fired.

TIP

If you're playing as Fox on Corneria, you can perform Down Taunt multiple times to trigger a secret dialog between Star Fox characters!

Every so often, an Arwing or Wolfen appears in the area. As one of these smaller ships moves through the area, it attacks with a series of laser blasts. These attacks aren't targeted at specific players, so it's generally best to stay out of the line of fire. These smaller ships can also can also be used as platforms while they remain in the area.

DISTANT PLANET

INSPIRED BY: *Pikmin*

As opposed to the rigid platforms found in most areas, the leaves and vines found in this stage sag under heavy weight. More important, however, this stage contains a number of unique items and hazards. Sprouting flowers produce numbered Pellets that can be used in combat. Attack a flower to free its Pellet, then toss the Pellet at an opponent—Pellets with larger numbers deal more damage! You can even throw a loose Pellet into an Onion (one of the onion-shaped vehicles that occasionally appear) to produce useful items.

Every so often, a Bulborb appears to the right of the platforms. While its jaws are open, you can force an opponent into its mouth for a quick KO. While a Bulborb's mouth is shut, the creature's head can be used as a temporary platform—just make sure you return to the relative safety of the leaves and vines before the Bulborb moves off-screen. Standing on the Bulborb's nose is never wise; the creature will eat any fighters who wander too close to its mouth. During heavy rain, try to avoid the slope to the left of the platforms; the runoff is strong enough to carry unprepared fighters right off the stage.

DREAM LAND

INSPIRED BY: ***Kirby's Dream Land***

This stage features a small viewing window, scrolling areas, and multiple set changes. While the scenery is static, use the available platforms and items to your advantage. Whenever a pointing hand appears at the edge of the screen, however, start moving in the indicated direction to avoid slipping off-screen.

During set changes, the existing scenery fades away as new platforms appear in the area. During these transitions, try to identify and avoid any new hazards or pitfalls that materialize beneath you.

> **NOTE**
> Dream Land becomes available after you perform a Final Smash while playing as Kirby.

FINAL DESTINATION

INSPIRED BY: ***Super Smash Bros.***

Final Destination is the game's most straightforward "normal" stage. It features one large platform at the center of the area, eliminating any of the terrain advantages found in other stages. Aside from the cycling background transitions, this stage remains unchanged over the course of a battle.

FIND MII

INSPIRED BY: ***Find Mii***

This stage contains two platforms, one of which is beneath a suspended cage. This cage can be used as a platform, but it can also be destroyed to free the imprisoned Mii. Soon after a battle begins, a large green dragon-like creature known as the Dark Emperor appears.

The Dark Emperor uses magic to temporarily strengthen or weaken affected combatants. More important, the Dark Emperor has the ability to destroy one of the available platforms. When the stage trembles, look for the sparkling lights that appear on one of the platforms—the indicated platform will survive the tremor, while the other platform sinks off-screen. The Dark Emperor only stays in the area while the Mii is imprisoned; destroying the cage will force this enemy out of the stage. When the Dark Emperor is defeated, the fighter who landed the final blow is rewarded with a power-up.

FLAT ZONE 2

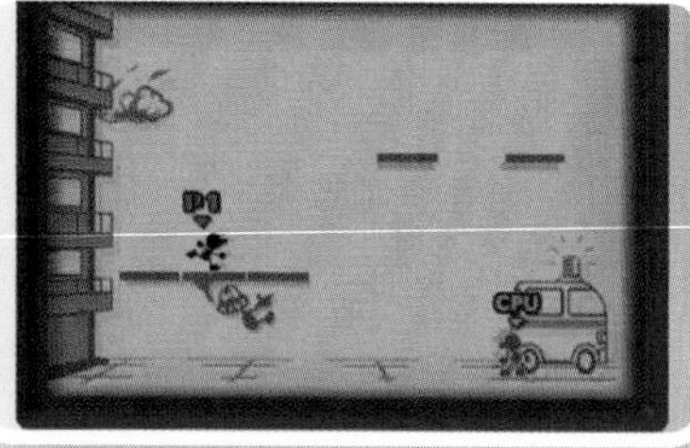

INSPIRED BY: THE ***Game & Watch*** SERIES

This stage features dramatic scene changes, and each of the available sets is inspired by a different game from the *Game & Watch* series. Over the course of a single battle, the frequent transitions place fighters in various randomly selected environments.

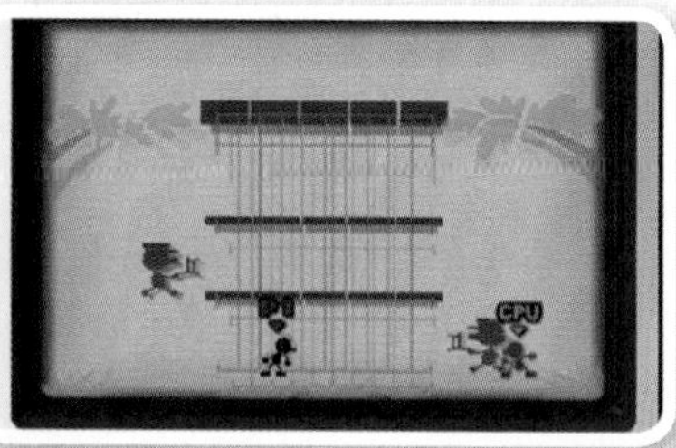

While some sets contain harmless elements like trampolines and shifting platforms, others feature unique hazards. Be particularly wary of the falling food items found in the kitchen and the chair-wielding animal tamers that guard the lion cages. Each time the battle moves to the kitchen, however, you can defeat the Chef to trigger a faster stage transition!

> **NOTE**
> Flat Zone 2 becomes available after you unlock the hidden character Mr. Game & Watch and complete the first Challenge panel.

GAUR PLAIN

INSPIRED BY: ***Xenoblade Chronicles***

This stage features a cluster of small platforms floating beneath two large platforms. The background cycles between day and night, but the stage remains otherwise unchanged over the course of a battle.

GERUDO VALLEY

INSPIRED BY: ***The Legend of Zelda: Ocarina of Time***

The gap at the center of this stage effectively divides the battleground into two separate areas. The bridge over the gap is fragile and can break several times over the course of a single battle. Standing on the bridge (or attacking it) can destroy it fairly quickly, but the ropes holding the bridge together will occasionally snap on their own. There are two small platforms hidden beneath the bridge; they can be handy in a pinch, but they're fairly fragile. Be careful!

Kotake and Koume appear each time the bridge is broken. Shortly after these two circle the area, one of them retreats while the other initiates an elemental attack. If Kotake, Sorceress of Ice, attacks, the right half of the stage is blanketed with shards of ice. If Koume, Sorceress of Flame, attacks, the left half of the stage is set ablaze. Each time one of these characters initiates an attack, move away from the targeted area.

GOLDEN PLAINS

INSPIRED BY: ***New Super Mario Bros. 2***

This colorful stage features moving platforms, scrolling areas, and collectible coins. This area also contains scale-like platforms suspended from pulleys. Standing on one of these platforms will force the attached platform upward. The contraption breaks if either of its platforms touches a pulley, so be careful! During a battle, watch for the arrows that appear near the bottom of the screen—these signal the active area is about to move. Head in the indicated direction to avoid suffering a KO as the current area scrolls off-screen.

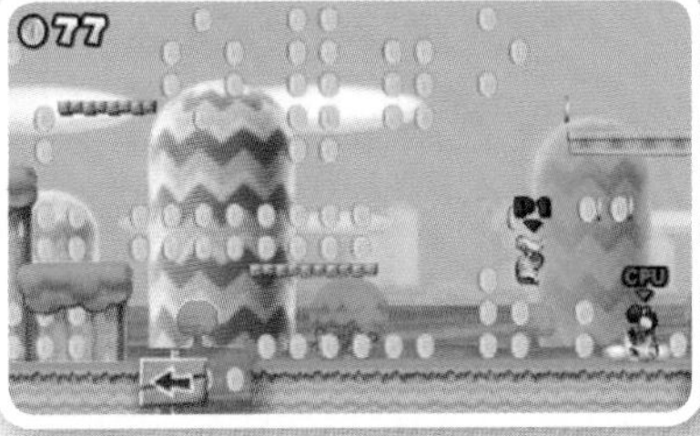

Any coins you collect are added to the tally in the upper-left corner of the top screen. When a fighter collects 100 gold coins, he or she turns to gold. The effect is temporary, but gold fighters enjoy increased power and immunity to flinching. Hit P-Switches to reveal hidden blue coins, and pass through Red Rings to reveal red coins. Collecting a blue coin will add a single gold coin to your tally, but each red coin you collect is worth five gold coins!

GREEN HILL ZONE

INSPIRED BY: ***Sonic the Hedgehog***

This stage features uneven terrain and some unique hazards. Watch for the Point Markers that occasionally emerge from the ground. When a fighter hits one of these objects, it spins around, striking any nearby opponents.

The most severe hazards are the gaps that periodically appear in what appears to be solid ground. If the area under your feet begins to crumble, move quickly to get clear of the newly formed pit. Fighters can also focus their attacks on the ground to create fresh gaps in strategically useful areas.

JUNGLE JAPES

INSPIRED BY: ***Donkey Kong 64***

This stage features a fast-moving river below a cluster of platforms. Any fighter who touches the water will be swept off-screen for a quick KO. The available platforms are fairly close to the river, so it's important to recover from any slips or falls as quickly as possible. Watch out for the fish that sometimes leap out of the water—getting hit by one of these creatures results in an instant KO.

LIVING ROOM

INSPIRED BY: ***Nintendogs + Cats***

At first glance, this large indoor stage may seem like a relatively simple setting. Over the course of a battle, however, fighters must deal with background distractions, falling hazards, and frequent terrain changes.

Watch for the shadows that appear on the floor—these indicate a fresh batch of blocks and household items have appeared above the battleground. Stay clear of these shadows to avoid taking damage from falling objects. As these objects land, they serve as temporary platforms and obstacles. Take advantage of the available terrain until the objects vanish, then watch for more shadows to appear and repeat the process.

MAGICANT

INSPIRED BY: ***EarthBound***

In addition to its fixed platforms, this stage features a variety of moving elements. Over the course of a battle, the mountaintop near the bottom of the screen slides back and forth across the stage, temporary obstacles appear, and a series of Flying Men appear from their tower. Each Flying Man fights for the first player who touches him, so you'll have to be fast to gain these allies. Defeat hostile Flying Men to remove them from the battle. Up to five Flying Men can appear over the course of a single battle.

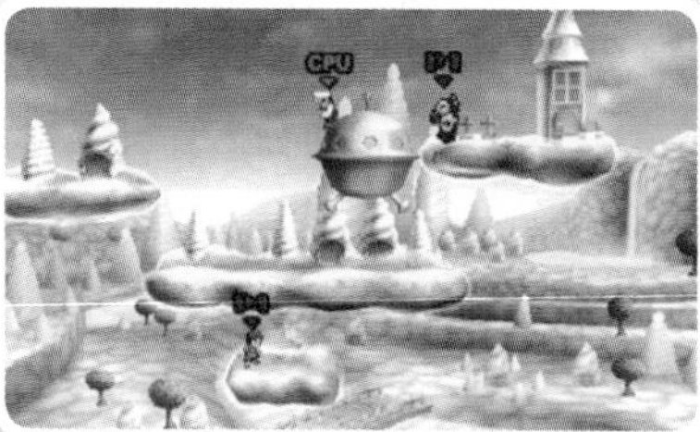

The spaceship that occasionally appears can be used as a temporary platform, but make sure you hop off before it carries you off-screen. After a giant tomato or iron octopus appears on a cloud, it begins sinking through the platform. Standing on one of these objects will speed up the process.

> Magicant becomes available after you unlock the hidden character Ness.
>
> **NOTE**

MUSHROOMY KINGDOM

INSPIRED BY: ***Super Mario Bros.***

This scrolling stage features destructible platforms, hidden items, and a variety of obstacles. Smash through Brick Blocks to destroy them, and hit ? Blocks to free helpful items. Revealed items can be used by any fighter, so move quickly to claim them.

As the stage scrolls, watch out for new obstacles and hazards. Stay alert, and keep pace with the active area to avoid suffering a premature KO.

MUTE CITY

INSPIRED BY: ***F-Zero***

In this stage, fighters must battle atop racing F-Zeros. Falling onto the track results in significant damage and launches the unfortunate fighter into the air.

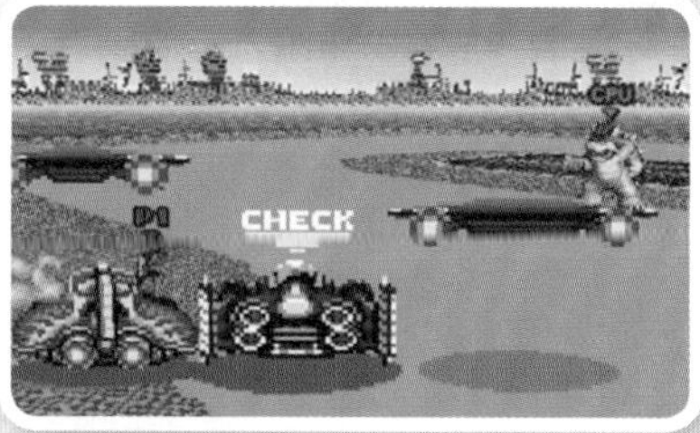

The vehicles on the track can be used as platforms, but watch for the "check" alert that appears when two racers are battling for the lead. This warning means the indicated vehicle is about to be knocked from the track. Abandon a marked F-Zero to avoid taking damage from the impact and to prevent the jostled vehicle from carrying you off-screen.

> Mute City becomes available after you use Captain Falcon to win three or more Smash battles.
>
> **NOTE**

PAC-MAZE

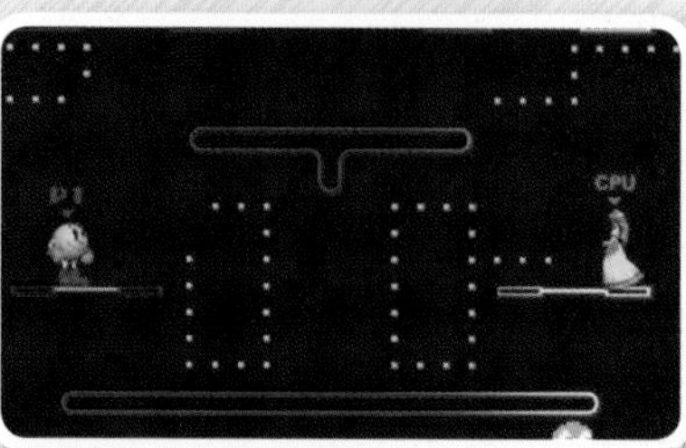

INSPIRED BY: ***PAC-MAN***

This stage is loaded with numerous platforms, roaming ghosts, and—perhaps most important—collectible dots. Steer clear of the ghosts, but try to collect any available dots as you move around the stage.

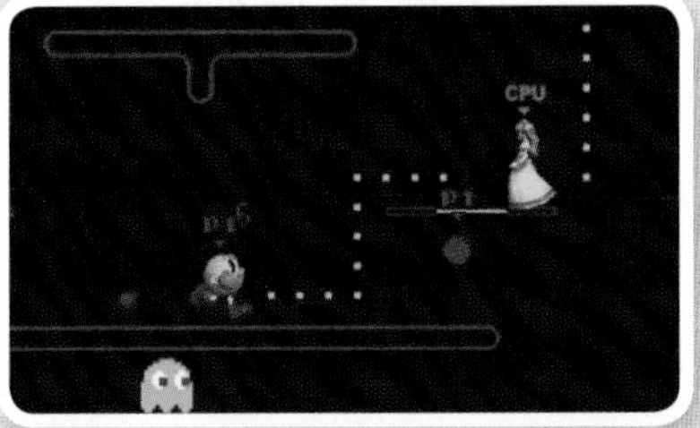

Each time a fighter collects 100 dots, he or she is rewarded with a Power Pellet. Over the course of a battle, earn and collect Power Pellets for temporary boosts to your combat abilities. As an added bonus, the roaming ghosts are vulnerable while any fighter is affected by a Power Pellet. Collecting fruit adds to a fighter's dot count, and unassigned Power Pellets occasionally appear. You can even destroy an opponent's Power Pellet to prevent your foe from collecting it!

NOTE

PAC-MAZE becomes available after you perform a Final Smash while playing as PAC-MAN.

PAPER MARIO

INSPIRED BY: THE *Paper Mario* SERIES

Over the course of a battle, this stage cycles through a series of distinct scenes, each of which contains its own platform arrangements, hazards, and environmental distractions. On the windmill set, for example, watch out for the large fan that appears in the background; once its blades start spinning, the resulting wind pushes fighters across the stage and makes it significantly easier to launch damaged opponents past the stage's right border.

Scene transitions are particularly dangerous, as most sets contain multiple falling hazards. It only takes a short time for a complete transition, so move onto new platforms as soon as they become available.

PICTOCHAT 2

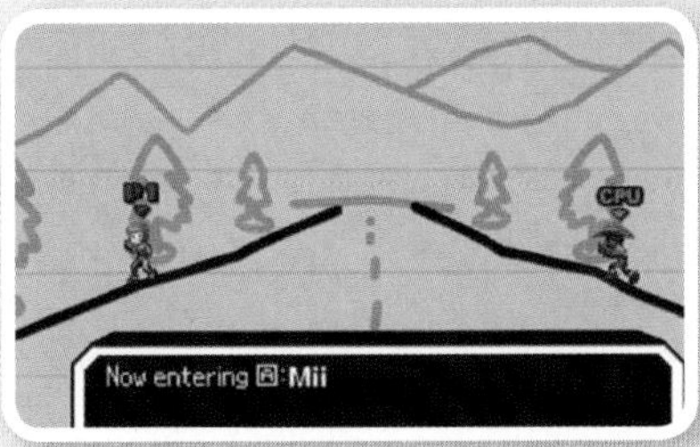

INSPIRED BY: *PictoChat*

This stage features a series of scenes composed of interactive doodles. Each doodle only lasts a short time, but the large platform along the bottom of the stage remains in place for the duration of a battle. Depending on the scene, doodles can serve as platforms, obstacles, hazards, and more.

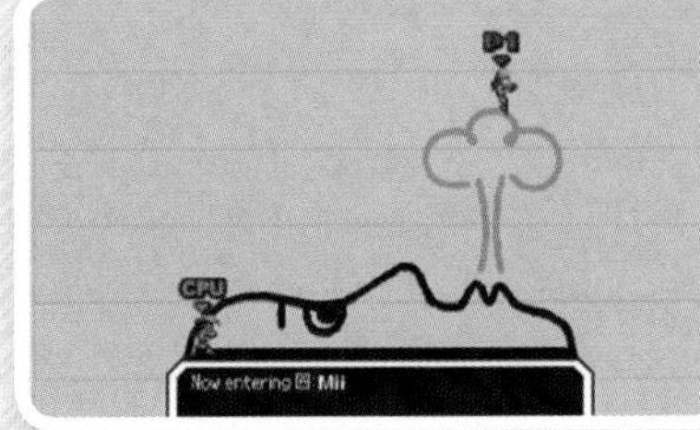

Although some doodles are simply background elements, most of them have very real effects while they are active. Gusts of wind can propel fighters into the air, falling objects can deal damage, precarious platforms can crumble under a fighter's weight. These constantly changing elements offer some interesting gameplay options, but be prepared for sudden scene changes.

PRISM TOWER

INSPIRED BY: *Pokémon X* AND *Pokémon Y*

On this stage, a large platform moves the battle off of the ground and around Prism Tower's exterior. As you're carried around the area, the view can be distracting—make sure you focus on your opponents, and watch for the platform shifts that occur throughout the stage.

The main platform appears shortly after the battle starts. Once it does, hop on to avoid being left behind. The main platform then stops at a several locations, some of which odder additional platforms. Flashing red lights indicate that platform is about to vanish or change shape. When in doubt, move near the center of the main platform to avoid falling.

RAINBOW ROAD

INSPIRED BY: *Mario Kart 7*

On this stage, fighters are carried to various points along an elaborate track. Each location offers unique terrain. Between stops, however, the action is contained to a single large platform.

You spend a relatively short time at each location, so watch for the boost pads that indicate impending transitions. Soon after these animated arrows appear in the background, the main platform returns to the area; hop on to avoid being left behind. Keep in mind this is an active track—a warning sign appears whenever racers approach. Whenever this happens, clear the track to avoid incoming karts. While the platform is moving, any fighters who touch the road will be damaged and launched. Be careful!

RESET BOMB FOREST

INSPIRED BY: ***Kid Icarus: Uprising***

This stage transitions between two very different areas. Each battle starts in the ruins of a castle that contains several platforms and minimal distractions. Soon after Viridi appears in the background, however, an explosion significantly alters the scene.

The second area contains a new cluster of platforms. These irregular platforms offer new tactical options, so adjust your tactics accordingly. In addition to this uneven terrain, the area contains a roaming Lurchthorn—avoid touching this creature as it passes along the bottom of the stage. All but the lowest platforms can be destroyed, so keep track of the available footholds. During prolonged battles, the stage continues to cycle between these two distinct areas.

SPIRIT TRAIN

INSPIRED BY: ***The Legend of Zelda: Spirit Tracks***

This stage features a high-speed train racing along a set of tracks. Over the course of a battle, new platforms and hazards move in and out of the area. Falling onto the tracks is, of course, dangerous—but landing behind the speeding train virtually guarantees a KO.

Each time the train's caboose slips off-screen, it's replaced with a new car. Watch for the arrows that indicate car switches or other potential hazards. Be particularly wary of the Dark Train whenever it appears—soon after the Dark Train leaps off the tracks, it comes crashing down in a random location.

3D LAND

INSPIRED BY: ***Super Mario 3D Land***

This stage features scrolling areas, moving platforms, and a variety of blocks. Keep pace with the active area to ensure you remain on-screen, and try to take advantage of new elements as they appear. Destroy Brick Blocks, hit ? Blocks to reveal hidden items, and use the Note Block to launch yourself high into the air.

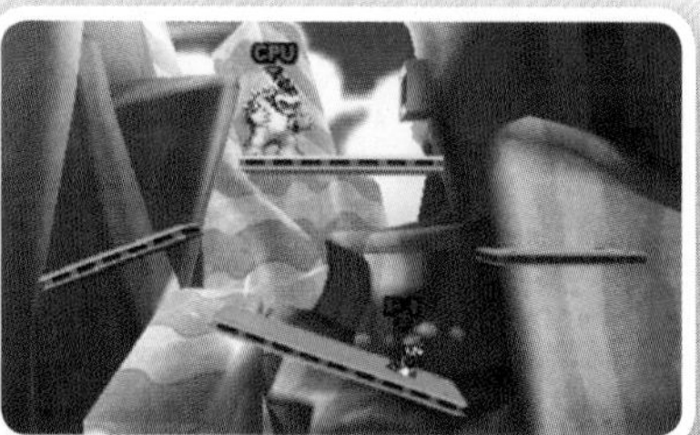

The playfield undergoes dramatic changes as it moves through the stage, so adjust your tactics accordingly. Many platforms rotate or shift while they're on-screen, but all of them eventually vanish. Be sure you take advantage of new terrain as it becomes available.

TOMODACHI LIFE

INSPIRED BY: ***Tomodachi Life***

This stage features four long platforms mounted to a large apartment building. Individual rooms are revealed only when fighters are directly in front of them. The available rooms—and any Miis that inhabit them—are randomly selected for each battle.

TORTIMER ISLAND

INSPIRED BY: ***Animal Crossing: New Leaf***

This stage always features a small island, but the island's specific layout is randomly selected for each battle. Regardless of the specific layout, however, it's important to avoid the water at each edge of the island.

Over the course of a battle, you'll often encounter stage-specific items like coconuts and durians. Most of these items can be thrown at your opponents, so use them wisely! Occasionally, Kapp'n docks his boat at the edge of the island. This vessel can be used as a temporary platform—just keep an eye out for the sharks lurking at the edges of the stage, and remember to abandon the boat before it heads back out to sea.

UNOVA POKÉMON LEAGUE

INSPIRED BY: ***Pokémon Black*** **AND** ***Pokémon White***

This stage features three platforms floating above a large pit. Stairs periodically appear at either edge of the stage, providing additional terrain as long as they remain in the area.

Soon after a battle starts, a randomly selected Pokémon appears in the area. Some Pokémon just sit back and watch the action, but whenever Reshiram or Zekrom appears, they attack the combat area. Reshiram's Fusion Flare ignites various sections of the stage, and Zekrom's Fusion Bolt can knock platforms askew. Both of these Pokémon can also destroy the stairs that appear at the edges of the stage. Stay clear of any Pokémon attacks, then adjust your tactics to deal with the aftermath.

WARIOWARE, INC.

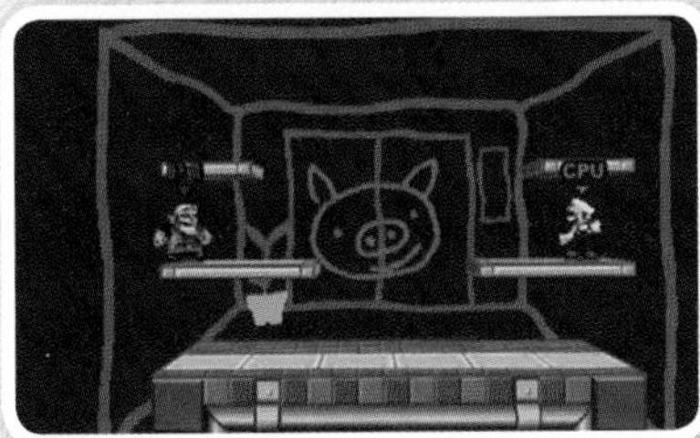

INSPIRED BY: ***WarioWare, Inc.***

This stage features frequent stage transitions, cycling between an elevator set and a collect of randomly selected minigames. While in the elevator, fighters have access to a cluster of platforms. Before long, however, the elevator starts to move, and a minigame begins.

Each time the elevator doors open, look for the instructions that appear on the screen, then move, jump, attack, or taunt to accomplish the goal. Some minigames require precision timing, so watch the background for prompts. Otherwise, simply complete the objective within the allotted time. Fighters who successfully complete a minigame are granted temporary bonuses upon returning to the elevator set.

> **WarioWare, Inc. becomes available after you unlock the hidden character Wario.**
>
> **NOTE**

WILY CASTLE

INSPIRED BY: ***Mega Man 2***

This stage contains a single fixed platform, but additional temporary platforms appear over the course of a battle. This stage also features the Yellow Devil, a massive robot that occasionally emerges from the castle in the background.

While the Yellow Devil is in the area, it fires a series of projectiles across the stage. After a few attacks, the robot usually moves to the opposite edge of the main platform and fires projectiles in the other direction. Fighters can dodge these projectiles or take cover behind the Yellow Devil until it leaves the area. Alternatively, fighters can attack the robot until it explodes—if you manage to deliver the finishing blow, the resulting explosion counts as your attack, damaging all nearby opponents.

YOSHI'S ISLAND

INSPIRED BY: ***Yoshi's New Island***

This stage contains two permanent platforms, the smaller of which tilts back and forth over the course of a battle. Fly Guys (flying Shy Guys) often appear in the area. Attacking Fly Guys forces them to drop any items they might be carrying.

This area also feature's frequent background changes and a small platform that sometimes appears on either edge of the stage. This temporary platform can be useful, but be careful—it never stays in place for long.

ITEMS

Items in Battle

During some game modes, items frequently appear on the battlefield. Fighters can use these items to summon allies, recover health, gain temporary abilities, and more. Some items are activated the moment they're collected or after they've absorbed a certain amount of damage. Most items, however, must be collected and activated manually. Approach such items and press the Attack button (Ⓐ) to grab them. When you're holding an item, press the Attack button to use it.

In the game's Smash modes, players have the option to switch off some or all of the items that might appear over the course of a battle. Use the Item Switch option in the "Rules" menu to determine which items have a chance to appear.

During Training, you're free to practice with any of the game's selectable items; simply use Training menu to select and spawn the item or items you'd like to test.

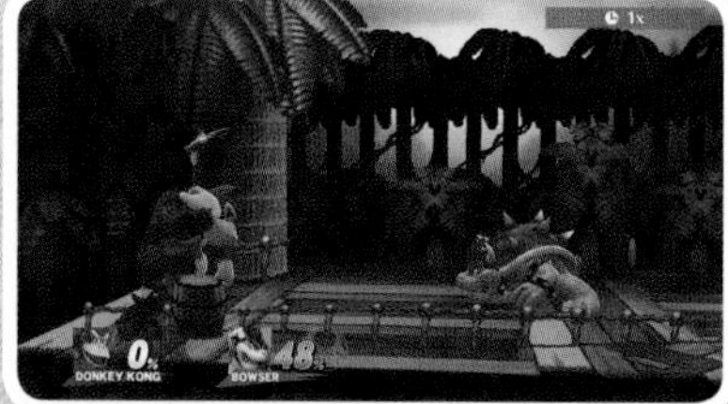

Some items are automatically consumed when they're collected, but many items will be carried until they're activated or depleted. In these cases, press the Grab button to drop an unwanted item.

While discarding an item, you can flick the Left Stick (or Circle Pad) to throw the item in the corresponding direction. Use this ability to clear items from the battlefield or to throw items at other fighters. You can even use this technique while dashing to add a little extra distance to your throw! Be careful, though—fighters can catch thrown items by pressing Ⓐ at just the right time.

Item Categories

FINAL SMASH

The game contains only one item in this category: the Smash Ball. Destroying this item allows a fighter to perform a character-specific Final Smash move.

HELPING

Helping items grant temporary allies to fight alongside the fighters who activate them. The game contains three helping items:

- Assist Trophy
- Poké Ball
- Master Ball

Some stages affect which allies these helping items can summon.

COMBINING

Combining items must be assembled before they're used, but the finished weapons are well worth the effort. The game contains two types of combining items:

- Dragoon Parts
- Daybreak

If a fighter manages to collect all three Dragoon Parts or Daybreak pieces, the corresponding weapon is automatically assembled. Until that time, however, attacking opponents will force the fighter to drop any combining items he or she is holding.

CARRYING

This category applies to various Containers. These heavy items can be carried around the battlefield, but most fighters will struggle to do so. Attacking or throwing these Containers usually reveals additional items, but there's a small chance a Container will explode when it's destroyed.

The selected stage determines the look of available Containers.

PUNCHING

The game contains only one item in this **Category:** Sandbag. Hitting Sandbag forces it to drop items. As it takes damage, Sandbag becomes easier to launch off the ground.

EXPLODING

The game contains only one item in this **Category:** the Blast Box. Blast Boxes explode after absorbing significant damage—this can be achieved with a series of standard attacks, but a fire attack can detonate a Blast Box in a single hit.

Many of the available items can produce powerful explosions. Aside from the Blast Box, however, all of these volatile items belong to other categories.

NOTE

RECOVERY

Items in this category can be collected to heal damage. The game contains four basic recovery items:

- Food
- Maxim Tomato
- Heart Container
- Fairy Bottle

The stage often affects the specific food items that can appear over the course of a battle.

TRANSFORMING

Fighters can collect transforming items to initiate unique attacks and temporary effects. The game contains a wide variety of transforming items:

- Super Mushroom
- Poison Mushroom
- Warp Star
- Super Star
- Metal Box
- Bunny Hood
- Superspicy Curry
- Timer
- Lightning
- Bullet Bill

Some transforming items have negative effects. Before you grab one of these items, weigh the potential benefits against any negative results.

BATTERING

Battering items are, for the most part, best used as short-range weapons. Some of them, however, offer longer range options or additional effects. The game contains a fair selection of battering items:

- Beam Sword
- Lip's Stick
- Star Rod
- Fire Bar
- Ore Club
- Hammer
- Home-Run Bat
- Golden Hammer

Most battering items degrade as they're used, vanishing once their power is depleted. Some battering items, however—like the Hammer—remain active for a set amount of time.

SHOOTING

Fighters can use shooting items to launch projectiles at their opponents. The game contains six basic shooting items:

- Super Scope
- Ray Gun
- Fire Flower
- Gust Bellows
- Steel Diver
- Drill

Shooting have limited ammunition.

THROWING

Fighters can hurl throwing items for a variety of effects. Some throwing items deal direct damage to fighters, while others can be used to create temporary hazards or to trigger unique effects. The game contains a wide variety of throwing items:

- Bob-omb
- Motion-Sensor Bomb
- Gooey Bomb
- Smart Bomb
- Bombchu
- X Bomb
- Hocotate Bomb
- Deku Nuts
- Freezie
- Smoke Ball
- Pitfall
- Hothead
- Mr. Saturn
- Green Shell
- Banana Peel
- Bumper
- Spring
- Unira
- Soccer Ball
- Team Healer
- POW Block
- Spiny Shell
- Boomerang
- Beetle
- Cucco
- Beehive
- Killer Eye
- Boss Galaga

Use the Left Stick (or Circle Pad) to determine the direction of a throw. When throwing an item, flick the Left Stick (or Circle Pad) to cause the item to travel farther than usual.

GEAR

When collected, gear items temporarily augment a fighter's natural abilities. There are five items belonging to this **Category:**

- Franklin Badge
- Back Shield
- Screw Attack
- Super Leaf
- Rocket Belt

Some gear items significantly alter the way a fighter handles

EFFECT

The game contains only one item in this **Category:** the Special Flag. Holding a Special Flag in a timed battle eventually adds a KO to your tally; in a stock battle, holding a Special Flag eventually adds +1 to your stock count. Grabbing this item leaves you vulnerable until the effect triggers, however, so plan ahead!

Item Descriptions

ASSIST TROPHY

Category: Helping

Origin: *Super Smash Bros. Brawl*

Description: Grab this to call on one of various characters to help you in a fight!

BACK SHIELD

Category: Gear

Origin: *Kid Icarus: Uprising*

Description: This shield protects your back from various attacks. It'll break, however, if it takes too much damage.

BANANA PEEL

Category: Throwing

Origin: *Super Mario Kart*

Description: A classic comedy staple: step on one of these, and you'll fall on your rump. It never gets old!

BEAM SWORD

Category: Battering

Origin: *Super Smash Bros.*

Description: This replaces your side attacks and has the farthest reach of any melee weapon! The blade gets longer when you use stronger attacks.

BEEHIVE

Category: Throwing

Origin: *Animal Crossing*

Description: A swarm of bees emerges, mobbing a fighter and dealing damage to that fighter bit by bit.

BEETLE

Category: Throwing

Origin: *The Legend of Zelda: Skyward Sword*

Description: Throw the beetle in any direction to send it flying. It'll grab opponents and drag them upward. The more damage they've taken, the more difficult it'll be to escape. You can also reflect a thrown beetle by attacking it before it hits you.

BLAST BOX

Category: Exploding

Origin: *Super Smash Bros. Brawl*

Description: Watch out—if you hit this with a fire attack, it'll explode!

BOB-OMB

Category: Throwing

Origin: *Super Mario Bros. 2*

Description: Despite their size, these bombs pack a serious punch. Left alone, they'll start wandering around, too...

BOMBCHU

Category: Throwing

Origin: *The Legend of Zelda: Ocarina of Time*

Description: These little fellas run along walls, ceilings, and the ground. They'll explode when they hit someone or when their fuse runs out.

BOOMERANG

Category: Throwing

Origin: *Super Mario Bros. 3*

Description: It goes all the way out and then comes back, even if it hits an enemy along the way. If you catch it, its power increases.

BOSS GALAGA

Category: Throwing **Origin:** *Galaga*

Description: When used, it flies around briefly and then shines a beam on an opponent before whisking that opponent into the air.

BULLET BILL

Category: Transforming

Origin: *Super Mario Bros.*

Description: Use this to turn into a Bullet Bill and charge through enemies! You can even choose your launch direction!

BUMPER

Category: Throwing

Origin: *Super Smash Bros.*

Description: A bumper can be placed in the air or on the ground. Anyone who touches it will be bounced like a pinball.

BUNNY HOOD

Category: Transforming

Origin: *The Legend of Zelda: Ocarina of Time*

Description: Put this on to boost your speed and make great jumps. What long ears it has! Will the power of the wild spring forth?

CONTAINERS

Category: Carrying

Origin: Varies by item

Description: Attack these or throw them to get at the items inside. Or you can throw them at the enemy!

CUCCO

Category: Throwing

Origin: *The Legend of Zelda: A Link to the Past*

Description: Cuccos wander around the stage, minding their own business. If you're heartless enough to attack one, you deserve what's coming to you.

DAYBREAK

Category: Combining

Origin: *Kid Icarus: Uprising*

Description: Construct this huge weapon by collecting its three parts, and then use its powerful beam attack!

DEKU NUTS

Category: Throwing

Origin: *The Legend of Zelda: Ocarina of Time*

Description: These nuts explode on impact. The explosion dazes fighters on the ground and launches those who are airborne.

DRAGOON PARTS

Category: Combining

Origin: *Kirby Air Ride*

Description: Collect all three parts of the Dragoon, and then aim carefully and launch a deadly attack!

DRILL

Category: Shooting

Origin: *Kid Icarus: Uprising*

Description: Fire this to send a drill bit shooting into an enemy, pushing that enemy across the stage for repeated damage. Then you can throw the base!

FAIRY BOTTLE

Category: Recovery

Origin: *The Legend of Zelda: A Link to the Past*

Description: This item will heal only a fighter who has taken more than 100% damage. Don't throw it at an enemy with damage that high!

FIRE BAR

Category: Battering

Origin: *Super Mario Bros.*

Description: This weapon is made of fireballs. It'll get shorter the more hits you land with it.

FIRE FLOWER

Category: Shooting

Origin: *Super Mario Bros.*

Description: Hold this out and unleash a bath of fire on your foes. There's only so much fire, though, so don't waste it.

FOOD

Category: Recovery

Origin: Varies by item

Description: Eat to heal some damage! The amount you recover depends on what kind of food you eat.

FRANKLIN BADGE

Category: Gear

Origin: *EarthBound*

Description: Pick this up and it'll attach itself to you, reflecting all projectile attacks from foes.

FREEZIE

Category: Throwing

Origin: *Mario Bros.*

Description: An item that slowly slides along the stage. Opponents hit with one will be frozen in ice for a time. Attacking a Freezie will have the same result!.

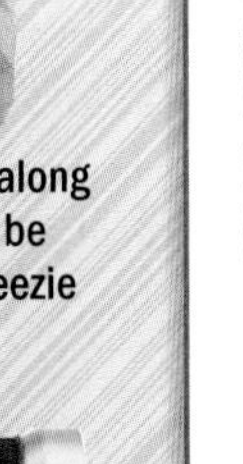

GOLDEN HAMMER

Category: Battering

Origin: *Wrecking Crew*

Description: Attack quickly over and over, and press Jump repeatedly to float in midair. If you don't do any damage, you probably have a squeaky one instead.

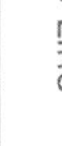

GOOEY BOMB

Category: Throwing

Origin: *Super Smash Bros.*

Description: These bombs stick to almost anything, exploding after a time. If it gets stuck to you, just brush it off onto someone else!

GREEN SHELL

Category: Throwing

Origin: *Super Mario Bros.*

Description: Attack or throw the Green Shell to send it sliding across the ground!

GUST BELLOWS

Category: Shooting

Origin: *The Legend of Zelda: Skyward Sword*

Description: Blow your opponents away with the strong winds of this item. Put it down and it'll blast gale-force winds in random directions!

HAMMER

Category: Battering

Origin: *Donkey Kong*

Description: Once you start, you'll just keep swinging this item to great effect, though the hammer's head can pop off. Oops!

HEART CONTAINER

Category: Recovery

Origin: *The Legend of Zelda*

Description: This heals 100 of the damage you have taken so far! Grab it before your foes get to it!

HOCOTATE BOMB

Category: Throwing

Origin: *Pikmin 2*

Description: Once placed, this bomb soars into the sky...only to return a short time later to explode!

HOME-RUN BAT

Category: Battering

Origin: *Super Smash Bros.*

Description: Use a Side Smash to send a foe flying for the fences. It's a tough attack to land, but it has lots of attack power.

HOTHEAD

Category: Throwing

Origin: *Super Mario World*

Description: This item sticks to the stage and rolls around. The sparks deal damage, and hitting the Hothead will make it grow.

KILLER EYE

Category: Throwing

Origin: *Kid Icarus: Uprising*

Description: Once it touches the stage, it'll stay in place and fire beams in a straight line. Attack a Killer Eye adjust its line of fire.

LIGHTNING

Category: Transforming

Origin: *Super Mario Kart*

Description: Grab this to make other fighters shrink—unless it backfires and shrinks you!

LIP'S STICK

Category: Battering

Origin: *Panel de Pon*

Description: Attacking with this makes an energy-sapping flower bloom on your opponent's head!

MASTER BALL

Category: Helping

Origin: The *Pokémon* series

Description: Throw this to summon a rare or Legendary Pokémon to team up with you against your foes!

MAXIM TOMATO

Category: Recovery

Origin: *Kirby's Dream Land*

Description: A tomato with a big M on it. When eaten, it removes 50% damage from your counter.

METAL BOX

Category: Transforming

Origin: *Super Mario 64*

Description: Turns you into metal. Light attacks won't make you flinch, and you'll be tough to launch—but you'll fall faster.

MOTION-SENSOR BOMB

Category: Throwing

Origin: *Super Smash Bros.*

Description: Once placed on the battlefield, these small bombs go off the moment anyone gets too close.

MR. SATURN

Category: Throwing

Origin: *EarthBound*

Description: Mr. Saturn won't deal much damage when thrown, but he'll decimate any shields he's thrown at.

ORE CLUB

Category: Battering

Origin: *Kid Icarus: Uprising*

Description: Swing this to perform an incredibly strong attack. Side Smash attacks create a whirlwind effect.

PITFALL

Category: Throwing

Origin: *Animal Crossing*

Description: Throw this at the ground to create a pitfall, burying an opponent in the dirt and leaving that opponent vulnerable.

POISON MUSHROOM

Category: Transforming

Origin: *Super Mario All-Stars*

Description: Running into one of these mushrooms shrinks you, making you easier to launch and your attacks less powerful.

POKÉ BALL

Category: Helping

Origin: The *Pokémon* series

Description: Throw this to summon a random Pokémon to team up with against your foes!

POW BLOCK

Category: Throwing

Origin: *Mario Bros.*

Description: Hit it or throw it at something to launch anybody standing on the ground at the time. It'll disappear after the third use.

RAY GUN

Category: Shooting

Origin: *Super Smash Bros.*

Description: Fires a fast blaster shot that can knock enemies backward and into the air.

ROCKET BELT

Category: Gear

Origin: *Pilotwings*

Description: While wearing this, hold Up or hold the Jump button to rocket into the sky. You'll refuel automatically on the ground.

SANDBAG

Category: Punching

Origin: *Super Smash Bros. Melee*

Description: Hit Sandbag to make items fall out! The more you hit it, the easier it will be to launch.

SCREW ATTACK

Category: Gear

Origin: *Metroid*

Description: Pick this up and you'll execute a high-speed Screw Attack every time you jump.

SMART BOMB

Category: Throwing

Origin: *Star Fox*

Description: These bombs create a massive explosion when they detonate, hurting anyone caught in the blast.

SMASH BALL

Category: Final Smash

Origin: *Super Smash Bros. Brawl*

Description: Destroy this floating orb, and then press the Special Move button to unleash your Final Smash!

SMOKE BALL

Category: Throwing

Origin: *Super Smash Bros. Brawl*

Description: After being thrown, this item will roll around on the ground or stick to opponents. The smoke makes it hard to see the battle.

SOCCER BALL

Category: Throwing

Origin: *Super Mario Strikers*

Description: Give it a good kick, and watch the ball burst into flames! You can't pick it up, though—that's a foul.

SPECIAL FLAG

Category: Effect

Origin: *Rally-X*

Description: You'll be vulnerable while holding this , but eventually you'll gain +1 KO (in a timed battle) or +1 stock (in a stock battle). Risk and reward!

SPINY SHELL

Category: Throwing

Origin: *Mario Kart 64*

Description: Once thrown, it floats above someone's head and then explodes after a short while.

SPRING

Category: Throwing

Origin: *Donkey Kong Jr.*

Description: Jump on this to get a boost! If you bump into it while it's laying on its side, though, you'll be sent flying sideways.

STAR ROD

Category: Battering

Origin: *Kirby's Adventure*

Description: Side Smash attacks and Side Tilt attacks will make this item fire star-shaped projectiles. Its ammo is limited, though...

STEEL DIVER

Category: Shooting

Origin: *Steel Diver*

Description: This "sub-machine gun" fires powerful torpedoes that take a second to get going before taking off at high speed.

SUPER LEAF

Category: Gear

Origin: *Super Mario Bros. 3*

Description: After picking this up, hold Up or hold the Jump button to hover in midair with the help of a very fuzzy tail!

SUPER MUSHROOM

Category: Transforming

Origin: *Super Mario Bros.*

Description: Touching this will make you a giant, raising your attack power and making you tough to launch.

SUPER SCOPE

Category: Shooting

Origin: Super Nintendo Entertainment System accessory

Description: This laser rifle can fire rapidly or unleash a power-charged shot. You can even shoot while moving!

SUPER STAR

Category: Transforming

Origin: *Super Mario Bros.*

Description: Touch one of these, and you'll be invincible! Not forever, though—more like for 10 seconds.

SUPERSPICY CURRY

Category: Transforming

Origin: *Kirby's Dream Land*

Description: Eat this spicy dish to send a constant eruption of flame pouring from your mouth! You can still attack, but you can't stand still.

TEAM HEALER

Category: Throwing

Origin: *Super Smash Bros. Brawl*

Description: Only available in team battles. Throw it at teammates to heal their damage. If thrown at an enemy, it will either damage or heal that enemy. It's a roll of the dice!

TIMER

Category: Transforming

Origin: *Super Smash Bros. Brawl*

Description: This item slows down everyone but the player who collects it...except when it backfires.

UNIRA

Category: Throwing

Origin: *Clu Clu Land*

Description: Throw or attack this to reveal its dangerous spikes. Attack it again to make the spikes retract.

WARP STAR

Category: Transforming

Origin: *Kirby's Dream Land*

Description: Grab this to fly up into the air, and then slam back down to the ground in a devastating attack. You can aim slightly to the left or the right.

X BOMB

Category: Throwing

Origin: *Kid Icarus: Uprising*

Description: Once thrown, these bombs hover in the air and then blast fire in four directions. Your throw determines the angle of the fire.

SMASH

Smash Overview

In Smash, you battle for victory against other players or CPU fighters. The game offers a number of exciting Smash modes, and the available settings ensure that every player can find an experience to match his or her tastes.

Smash Menus

The main menu's "Smash" option contains four selections:

- Smash: Battle with up to four players!
- 8-Player Smash: Battle it out with eight players! Wow!
- Special Smash: Battle with special rules.
- Rules: Change settings to customize the battle!
- Controls: Change the button configuration.

Smash

Smash is a straightforward game mode in which up to four players battle for victory. During character selection, the first fighter slot is always occupied. Use additional controllers to add human players to the game, or manually activate the available slots to add CPU fighters to the battle. To add a Figure Player to an empty slot, simply tap the desired amiibo figure on the Wii U GamePad controller.

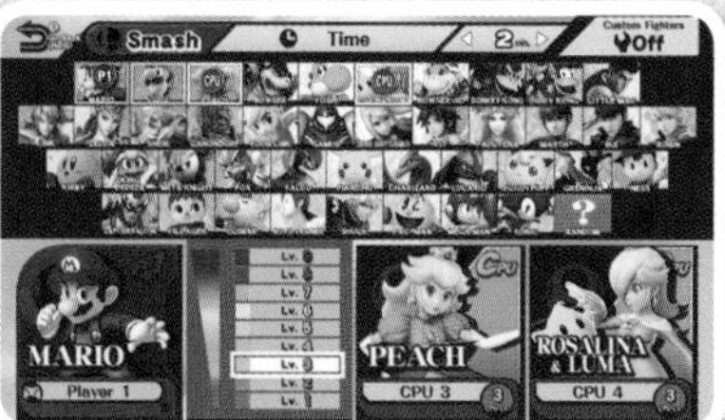

Once you've activated the desired fighter slots, use the available player tokens to select specific characters from your roster. Use the tabs at the top of the screen to make last-minute adjustments to the match rules. You can also use the fighter portraits to cycle through each character's available looks and to change the difficulty levels of any CPU fighters.

TEAM BATTLE

By default, Smash pits players against each other in a free-for-all battle; however, you can use the "Smash" tab at the top of the screen to activate a Team Battle. Once you've done this, use the flag displayed on each fighter portrait to assign that character to a specific team.

TIMED SMASH BATTLES

The winner of a timed Smash battle is determined by which fighter scores the most points within the time limit. The clock in the upper-right corner of the screen shows the remaining time. Fighter damage percentages are displayed along the bottom of the screen. The more damage a fighter has taken, the easier that fighter is to launch. Launch an opponent clear out of the stage to score a KO!

TIP

A fighter with a high damage percentage also has a slightly easier time launching his or her opponents. The effect is minimal, but every bit helps!

In a timed Smash battle, your final score is determined by three factors:

- KOs: You gain one point each time you KO an opponent.
- Falls: You lose one point each time you are KO'd by an opponent.
- Self-Destructs: By default, you lose one point each time you KO yourself or are KO'd by the environment. This setting can be adjusted in the "More Rules" option within the "Rules" menu.

Each fighter's final score is only revealed at the end of the battle, so it's important keep track of KOs as they occur.

SUDDEN DEATH

If a timed Smash battle ends without a clear victor, all fighters tied for the lead enter a Sudden Death round. In Sudden Death, fighters each have one stock life—suffering a single KO will eliminate a fighter from the competition. All fighters start with 300% damage, so the smallest mistake can be very costly.

STOCK SMASH BATTLES

Each fighter begins a stock Smash battle with a set number of lives. Every time a fighter is KO'd, his or her stock count is reduced by one. The battle ends when only one fighter remains.

During a stock Smash battle, each fighter's remaining lives are displayed near the bottom of the screen, near the appropriate fighter portrait.

COIN SMASH BATTLES

During a battle of Coin Smash, attacking players produces currency. Bigger hits result in a better payout, so don't hold back! Be careful, though: suffering a KO will cost you a portion of any money you've managed to collect. Victory goes to the fighter who holds the most coins when time runs out. Check the bottom of the screen to keep track of each fighter's current coins, and remember to grab whatever you earn before an opponent has a chance to snatch it up!

8-Player Smash

As the name implies, 8-Player Smash allows up to eight fighters to battle for victory. When setting up a game, you'll have access to all of the same options and features found in the game's standard Smash mode. Choose your desired rules and compete against any combination of human players, CPU fighters, and amiibo Figure Players!

Many of the game's stages cannot be used in 8-Player Smash. It's important to note, however, that a few more options become available when the stages' Final Destination forms are activated.

Special Smash

Special Smash modifies the established format by adding custom rules you won't find in any other Smash mode! For example, you can change fighter sizes to make them easier or tougher to launch. You can grant special effects or gear that last for the duration of the battle. You can even change the camera angle or adjust the speed at which the fighters move. Experiment with the available rules to find your perfect Special Smash experience!

SPECIAL SMASH RULES

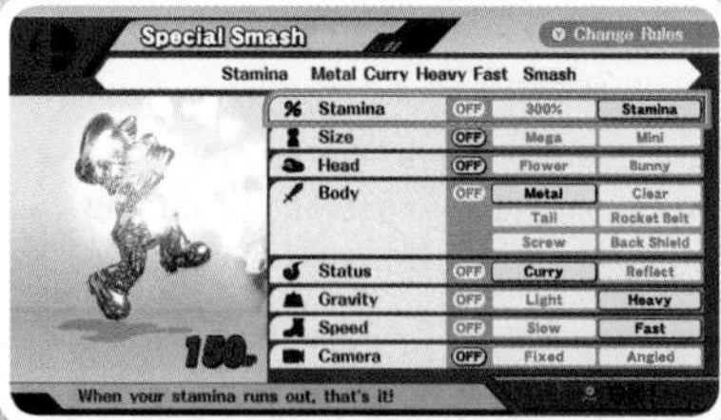

The available special rules are separated into eight categories. To change a rule, highlight the appropriate category and select your desired option. You can also press Ⓨ to access standard Smash rules.

> Some standard rules cannot be changed during Special Smash.
>
> **NOTE**

% STAMINA

- Off: Start with 0% damage.
- 300%: Start with 300% damage! One-hit KOs!
- Stamina: When your stamina runs out, that's it!

SIZE

- Off: Fight at a normal size.
- Mega: All fighters are super-sized!
- Mini: All fighters are itty-bitty!

HEAD

- Off: Fight with nothing weird on your head.
- Flower: Fight with a damage-dealing flower on your head!
- Bunny: Start the battle wearing a Bunny Hood.

BODY

- Off: Fight as normal with no extras.
- Metal: All fighters are metallic, taking less damage.
- Clear: Everyone's invisible!
- Tail: Grow a tail and float around!
- Rocket Belt: Everyone gets a Rocket Belt!
- Screw: Perform a Screw Attack with every jump!
- Back Shield: Start the battle with a Back Shield equipped.

STATUS

- Off: Fight in a normal state.
- Curry: Fight with nonstop fiery curry breath!
- Reflect: Reflect all projectiles.

GRAVITY

- Off: Play at normal weight.
- Light: You'll be much lighter descending in the air.
- Heavy: Jumps are lower; descents are faster.

SPEED

- Off: Play at normal speed.
- Slow: Play at 1/2 normal speed.
- Fast: Play at 1.5× normal speed.

CAMERA

- Off: Use the normal camera position.
- Fixed: Stop the camera from zooming or scrolling.
- Angled: Fight with the camera tilted slightly over you.

Rules

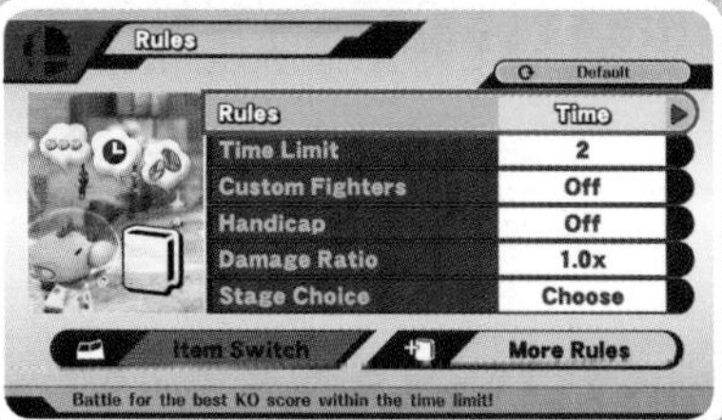

The "Rules" menu contains settings that affect all Smash game modes. To change the options and features of your upcoming matches, highlight a category and cycle through the available settings:

- Rules: This determines the objective of the battle. Select "time" to battle for the best score within a set time limit; choose "stock" to engage in a battle of pure survival; select "coin" for a battle to see which fighter can collect the most coins.
- Time/Stock: Adjust the time limit or stock count (depending on the currently selected objective).
- Customizations: Allow or prohibit the use of customized fighters.
- Handicap: The "off" setting ensures that each player begins the battle with 0 damage. The "on" setting allows players to increase starting damage, making it easier for them to be launched. With the "auto" setting, the results of a battle will affect the starting damage for the following match.
- Damage Ratio: Adjust the damage done by all fighters. A higher number makes it easier for fighters to launch each other.
- Stage Choice: This setting allows you to streamline stage selection. If you prefer, you can choose random stage selections, or you can automatically cycle through the available stages. These options are available for both normal stages and Final Destination forms. You can even choose to let the loser of each match choose the stage for the next battle!

ITEM SWITCH

The "Item Switch" menu allows you to adjust how often items will appear in battle or to prohibit specific items from appearing at all.

MORE RULES

The "More Rules" option offers even more ways to customize your battles:

- Stock & Time: Set a time limit for stock Smash battles.
- Team Attack: Determine whether or not teammates can damage each other.
- Pause Function: Enable or disable pausing during battle.
- Score Display: Determine whether or not fighter scores are displayed during battle.
- Damage Gauge: Show or hide damage percentages during battle.
- SD Penalty: Determine whether a Self-Destruct reduces a fighter's score by one point or two points.

RANDOM STAGE SWITCH

The "Random Stage Switch" options allows you to limit which stages have a chance to appear during random stage selection. This feature only becomes available once you've unlocked all of the game's stages.

Controls

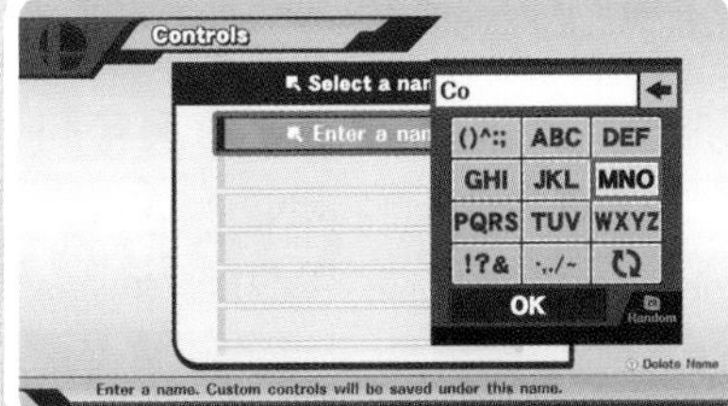

The "Controls" option allows you to customize the game's controls. The first time you use this option, you'll be prompted to create a name for the new control scheme. You can revisit this menu to create additional control schemes or to edit an existing set.

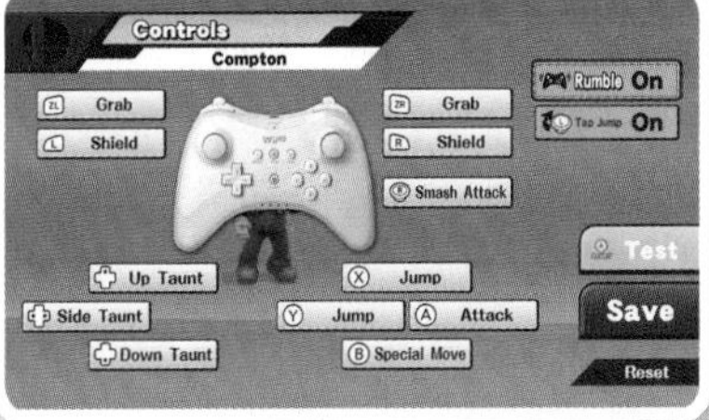

After you select your desired controller type, you're free to remap the game's controls to suit your personal playstyle. Select a button, then scroll through the available commands. When you're finished, you can test your new control scheme, save your changes, or revert to the game's default controls.

Unlocking Hidden Characters in Smash

In addition to the starting roster, the game contains eight hidden characters. Depending on the specific character, you can unlock new fighters through Classic, All-Star, Mulit-Man Smash, and Special Orders. All hidden characters, however, can also be unlocked by playing Smash.

Complete the required number of Smash battles to trigger a one-on-one battle against a hidden character. If you win the battle, the hidden character is unlocked and added to your roster; if you fail, simply complete another Smash battle to try again.

REVEALING HIDDEN CHARACTERS

CHARACTER	SMASH PREREQUISITE	ALTERNATE METHOD
Falco	Play 10 or more matches	Clear Classic
Wario	Play 20 or more matches	Clear 100-Man Smash
Lucina	Play 30 or more matches	Clear Classic at any intensity level above 5.5
Dark Pit	Play 40 or more matches	Complete All-Star on a difficulty of "normal" or above
Dr. Mario	Play 50 or more matches	Clear "hard" or higher in Master Orders
R.O.B.	Play 60 or more matches	Clear more than 8 turns in Crazy Orders
Mr. Game & Watch	Play 80 or more matches	Clear Classic on intensity 2.0 or higher with 5 or more characters.
Duck Hunt	Play 100 or more matches	KO one opponent in Cruel Smash

Completing a match in any Smash mode will contribute to hidden character perquisites; however, any match that ends in a "No Contest" is not counted.

NOTE

SMASH TOUR

Smash Tour Overview

In Smash Tour, four contestants move around a board to collect fighters, stat boosts, and helpful items. Battles are triggered when two or more players bump into each other or when a player lands on a Battle Space. After a set number of turns, all players face off in a final battle to determine the winner of the game.

Smash Tour Options

Use these to determine whether custom fighters are allowed, the size of the Smash Tour board, and how many turns the game will last.

TIP

On average, each turn adds about a minute to the length of a Smash Tour game.

SMASH TOUR BOARDS

Before starting a game of Smash Tour, you must select one of three boards.

The small board ensures that players are never far from one another. This tends to result in frequent battles as players race to grab the available items.

The normal board offers a bit more space, generally resulting in a moderate number of battles.

The big board allows enough room for players to spread out. This usually results in less frequent battles as players scramble to grab uncontested items.

Smash Tour Basics

When the game starts, each player receives two randomly selected fighters. Once the starting fighters have been distributed, four roulette spinners appear. Stop your spinner to determine how many spaces you're permitted to move before the turn ends.

Once you've determined how many spaces you can move, use the Left Stick to select an available path. When choosing a path, consider where your fighter will eventually stop and which items he or she will grab along the way. Subsequent turns will follow a similar format. Instead of receiving randomly selected fighters, however, players will usually be given a randomly selected item at the start of each turn.

If two players bump into each other, all four players leave the board to compete in a battle. When the battle ends, the winner claims a new fighter, the remaining players each lose a fighter, and the next turn begins.

NOTE

If a player has no fighters at the beginning of a turn, there's a chance that he or she will be given a randomly selected fighter instead of an item.

COLLECTIBLE ITEMS

New items appear on the board during each turn. Grab them to add new fighters to your stable, to power up your existing fighters, or to gain single-use items.

FIGHTER PANELS

Collect fighter panels to add the corresponding fighter to your stable of fighters. Fighter panels can be found on Fighter Spaces or are dropped by opponents and certain Smash Tour enemies.

STAT BOOSTS

Collect stat boosts to power up all of your fighters. Different stat boosts affect different fighter abilities. The size of a stat boost determines how much of an effect it has.

There are seven different types of stat boosts in Smash Tour:

Speed

Speed determines how fast your fighter moves on the ground and in the air. Increase this stat by collecting Speed stat bonuses or by running through the battlefield.

Jump

Jump determines how high and how far your fighters can jump.

Attack

Attack determines the damage caused by your fighters' standard attacks, tilt (strong) attacks, and Smash attacks.

Special

Special determines the damage caused by your fighters' Special attacks.

Arms

Arms determines the effectiveness of items and the power of your fighters' throws.

Defense

Defense determines how difficult it is to launch your fighters.

All

Collect special star-shaped stat boosts to improve all of your fighters' stats.

USABLE ITEMS

The game contains a variety of usable, trophy-like items that can be activated at certain points in the game. Each player can only hold four usable items at one time. If a fifth item is collected, that player's oldest item is automatically discarded.

You'll have the opportunity to use an item at the beginning of each turn and each time a battle is triggered. When the inventory wheel appears, use the Left Stick to select one of the available choices and gain the described effect. Once you use an item, it's removed from your inventory, so choose wisely!

Usable items are divided into three categories: board items, battle items, and general items.

BOARD ITEMS

A board item can be identified by its blue base. These items can only be used at the start of a turn before the roulette spinner appears. Board items tend to focus on things like player movement and collectible items.

AVAILABLE BOARD ITEMS

NAME	EFFECT TRIGGER	EFFECT DESCRIPTION
Excitebike	When the roulette outcome is decided	Your roulette result is doubled
Ashley	At the start of roulette	The roulette spins slower
Great Fox	At the start of the movement phase	Warps you to a checkpoint you haven't yet passed
Boss Galaga	At the start of the movement phase	Shuffles all other players
Dillon	When bumping into or moving by an opponent	Launches an opponent out of your path
Doc Louis	At the start of the movement phase	The effect of a power-up you pick up is increased
Riki	At the start of the movement phase	Draws in nearby items as you move
Ghosts (Luigi's Mansion)	When bumping into an opponent	Allows you to move past another player
Isabelle	At the start of the movement phase	All nearby power-ups are increased to their maximum value
Timmy & Tommy	At the start of the movement phase	All nearby items are changed into different items
Tetra	Placement: When entering movement; Activation: When someone moves onto the square it is placed on	Places a trap that steals fighters
Zingers	Placement: When entering movement; Activation: When someone moves onto the square it is placed on	Places a trap that launches a player
Snorlax	When you are launched	Allows you to stay in place if you're launched
Yellow Wollywog	When stepping on a trap	Neutralizes any trap you touch
Chain Chomp	At the start of the movement phase	Launches all nearby opponents
Bus to the City	At the start of the movement phase	All players are warped to your position
POW Block	At the start of the movement phase	All other players lose a fighter
Tingle	At the start of the movement phase	All fighters are shuffled
Super Star	At the start of the movement phase	You become invincible, and your roulette result is doubled

BATTLE ITEMS

A battle item can be identified by its red base. These items can only be used when a battle is triggered. Battle items tend to focus on things like combat items and fighter abilities.

AVAILABLE BATTLE ITEMS

NAME	EFFECT TRIGGER	EFFECT DESCRIPTION
Majora's Mask	Before the start of Battle	Inflicts 50% damage, but doubles your stats
Energy Tank	Before the start of Battle	Recovers 50% damage once when damage is at 100%
Mr. Saturn	Before the start of Battle	Does great damage to an opponent's shield with attacks
Black Knight	Before the start of Battle	Grants a chance that Smash attacks will turn into a one-hit KO
Dixie Kong	Before the start of Battle	Allows +1 mid-air Jump
Phosphora	Before the start of Battle	Grants an instant landing when the Left Stick is flicked downward
Sidesteppers	Before the start of Battle	Increases the speed of dodging to the left and right
Kat & Ana	Before the start of Battle	Minimizes the impact from being launched into walls and ceilings
Daisy (uniform)	Before the start of Battle	Allows you to automatically catch items
Plasm Wraith	Before the start of Battle	Grants health recover when you block an attack with your shield
Mecha-Fiora	Before the start of Battle	Increases your attack power as you take more damage
Wolfen	Before the start of Battle	Adds 100% to the damage of the chosen opponent
Resetti	Before the start of Battle	Reduces the chosen opponent's stats to 0 for a single battle
Poison Mushroom	Before the start of Battle	Shrinks the chosen opponent

AVAILABLE BATTLE ITEMS (CONTINUED)

NAME	EFFECT TRIGGER	EFFECT DESCRIPTION
Darkrai	Before the start of Battle	Puts the chosen opponent to sleep
Boo	Before the start of Battle	Turn invisible for a limited time during the battle
Hammer	Before the start of Battle	Grants a Hammer at the start of the battle
Super Scope	Before the start of Battle	Grants a Super Scope at the start of the battle
Home-Run Bat	Before the start of Battle	Grants a Home-Run Bat at the start of the battle
Bob-omb	Before the start of Battle	Grants a Bob-omb at the start of the battle
Ore Club	Before the start of Battle	Grants an Ore Club at the start of the battle
Steel Diver	Before the start of Battle	Grants a Steel Diver at the start of the battle
X Bomb	Before the start of Battle	Grants an X Bomb at the start of the battle
Metal Box	Before the start of Battle	Turns you metallic for one battle
Super Mushroom	Before the start of Battle	Turns you giant for one battle
Franklin Badge	Before the start of Battle	Grants a Franklin Badge at the start of the battle
Bunny Hood	Before the start of Battle	Grants a Bunny Hood at the start of the battle
Rocket Belt	Before the start of Battle	Grants a Rocket Belt at the start of the battle
Back-Shield	Before the start of Battle	Grants a Back-Shield at the start of the battle
DK Barrel	Before the start of Battle	Allows you to team up with one of your fighters
Latias & Latios	Before the start of Battle	Allows you to team up with one of your opponents
Ultimate Chimera	Before the start of Battle	Causes the last player you KO to lose an additional fighter. This item has no effect if you fail to score a KO during the battle
Magnus	Before the start of Battle	Launches all players that you KO'd during the battle

GENERAL ITEMS

A general item can be identified by its green base. These items can be used at the beginning of a turn or before a battle starts. General items redirect the effects of other players' items.

AVAILABLE GENERAL ITEMS

NAME	EFFECT TRIGGER	EFFECT DESCRIPTION
Proto Man	When an item is used on you	Reflects the effect of an item used on you
Substitute Doll	When an item is used on you	Redirects the effects of a used item from you to one of your opponents
Porky	When the chosen opponent uses an item	Steals an item used by a chosen opponent

BOARD SPACES

The board contains a variety of special spaces. Stopping on one of these spaces will trigger a special event or effect.

Stopping on a Warp Space instantly moves your fighter to another Warp Space across the board.

Warp Space

Stopping on a Stat Boost Space triggers one of three possible effects: your stats are shuffled, your stats are raised, or your stats are lowered.

Stat Boost Space

Stopping on a Battle Space instantly triggers a battle.

Battle Space

Reach a Fighter Space to collect its fighter panel before one of your opponents can claim it!

Fighter Space

CHECKPOINTS

Each Smash Tour board contains five checkpoints. Pass over a checkpoint to receive a small stat boost. Pass over all five of the checkpoints to earn a Checkpoint Bonus for a huge boost to your stats!

NOTE

Each of a map's five checkpoints is a different color. When you pass a checkpoint, it activates a corresponding icon on your stat display. Use this to keep track of which checkpoints you've already claimed.

SMASH TOUR ENEMIES

Occasionally, a special enemy will appear on the Smash Tour board. Some enemies are best avoided, but a few of them offer special bonuses!

ENEMIES

PORTRAIT	NAME	DURATION	EFFECT
	Iridescent Glint Beetle	Lasts 5 turns or until a player bumps into it	Bump into these enemies to collect any fighter panels they might be carrying!
	Tac	Lasts 5 turns or until a player bumps into it	Bump into these enemies to collect large stat boosts!
	Nabbit	Lasts until a player bumps into it	Bump into these enemies to collect any items it has swiped from the board!
	Flying Man	Lasts 3 turns after a player bumps into it, or until it launches an opponent or absorbs damage intended for the player.	Bump into these enemies to convert them into temporary allies!
	Souflee	Lasts 5 turns or until a player bumps into it	Bump into these enemies to earn Checkpoint Bonuses.
	Metroid	Lasts 5 turns or until a player bumps into it two times	Bumping into this enemy costs you several stat boosts! Reclaim lost stat boosts by bumping into it a second time.
	Reaper	Lasts 3 turns	Bump into this enemy to exchange 3 fighters for a Checkpoint Boost. If you don't have enough fighters, bumping into a Reaper will cause it to launch you. Push the Left Stick toward a Reaper to pass it without bumping into it.
	Koffing	Lasts 1 turn	This enemy covers the board in a gas cloud that vanishes at the end of the turn.
	Kamek	Lasts 1 turn	This enemy shuffles all of the board's checkpoints. The effect lasts for the remainder of the game.
	Banzai Bill	Lasts 1 turn	When a Banzai Bill appears, it marks a large section of the board. When the turn ends, the Banzai Bill crashes into the indicated area, releasing stat boosts and launching any players caught in the blast.
	Yellow Devil	Last 3 turns or until it's defeated in battle	Bump into this enemy to trigger a battle. If a player manages to defeat the Yellow Devil, he or she is rewarded a massive boost to all stats. Stat boosts can also be earned if a player wins the battle by scoring KOs against his or her opponents. If the Yellow Devil is not defeated in time, it will retain its remaining stamina and move to another space on the board.
	Metal Face	Lasts 3 turns or until he's defeated in battle	Bump into this enemy to trigger a battle. If a player manages to defeat Metal Face, he or she is rewarded a massive boost to all stats. Stat boosts can also be earned if a player wins the battle by scoring KOs against his or her opponents. If Metal Face is not defeated in time, he will retain his remaining stamina and move to another space on the board.
	Ridley	Lasts 3 turns or until he's defeated in battle	Bump into this enemy to trigger a battle. If a player manages to defeat Ridley, he or she is rewarded a massive boost to all stats. Stat boosts can also be earned if a player wins the battle by scoring KOs against his or her opponents. If Ridley is not defeated in time, he will retain his remaining stamina and move to another space on the board.

BATTLES

Battles are triggered when two players bump into each other or when a player lands on a Battle Space. The game automatically selects a random Smash battle-type, each of which features a special rule. In Pokémon Smash, for example, Poké Balls frequently appear over the course of the battle.

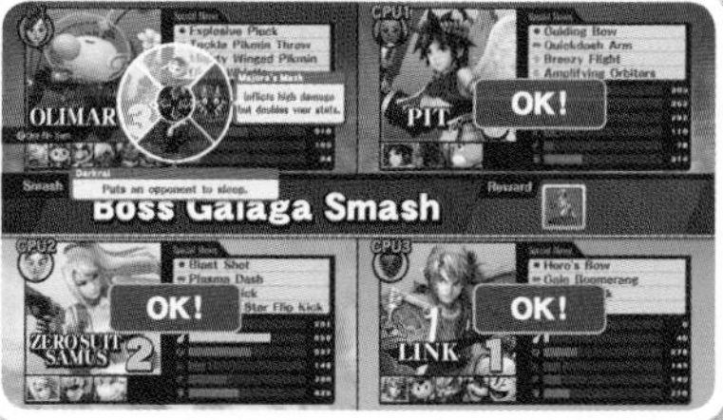

Before a battle starts, each fighter is given the chance to activate one of the usable items in his or her inventory. Most of the Smash Tour items will provide significant benefits, but some of them can even add special rules to a battle. For example, the battle item Latias & Latios causes two fighters to team up for the duration of the battle.

> **TIP**
>
> **Before you activate an item, review each player's remaining fighters and current stat boosts to help form an effective strategy for the upcoming battle.**

In standard Smash Tour battles, each player is given one stock life. KO your opponents to remove them from the battle before time runs out. The winner of the battle is awarded the last fighter he or she managed to KO. The players ranked third and fourth place simply lose their fighters. Each battle also offers a randomly selected usable item to be rewarded to the victor.

> **NOTE**
>
> **You can only participate in a battle if you have at least one fighter in your stable. Otherwise, you must simply wait until the battle ends and all players are returned to the board.**

THE FINAL BATTLE

When the game's last turn ends, all fighters are transported to Stat Boost Bonus. Here, players have the chance receive additional stats and fighters before beginning the final battle.

POSSIBLE STAT BOOST BONUSES

BONUS	EFFECT
Distance Moved	Speed stat is boosted based on the number of spaces moved!
Lucky 7	All stats with a 7 are powered up!
Booby Prize	You get a fighter!
Launched Ace	You get a fighter!
Launching Ace	Your powerful stats will increase even more!

In the final battle, each player uses all of the fighters remaining in his or her stable. When a fighter is KO'd, the next fighter in that player's stable automatically enters the battle. The match ends when the four-minute time limit expires or when only one player remains. Claim first place in the final battle to win the game of Smash Tour!

SMASH TOUR TIPS

Smash Tour contains a wide variety of random elements, so it can be difficult to utilize a specific strategy. Still, there are a few things you can do to improve your chances of victory:

- **Focus on powering up your fighters! It's important to keep at least a few fighters in your stable, but three or four strong fighters will usually be more effective than an army of underpowered combatants.**
- **If you're not sure which path to take, head for the nearest unclaimed checkpoint. Checkpoint Bonuses go a long way to powering up your fighters.**
- **Checkpoint Bonuses are based on your current stat boosts. The more powerful your fighters are, the larger your Checkpoint Bonuses will become.**
- **Remember that you can't choose which fighter you use during a battle. It's sometimes best to avoid collecting any that don't complement your playstyle.**
- **Unless you're running low on fighters, it's often best to avoid unnecessary battles. Bumping into an opponent will cause you to forfeit any remaining movement points. The more spaces you move, the better your chances of powering up your fighter!**
- **Using the appropriate items at the appropriate times can make a big difference over the course of a game. Don't miss a chance to turn the tables on your opponents.**
- **Remember that you can only hold four usable items at a time. If a powerful item is in danger of being dropped from your inventory, activate it as soon as possible.**

GAMES & MORE

Games & More Overview

Games & More contains a wide variety of game modes, galleries, and options. Much of the game's content is located within this menu, so make sure you explore all of the available selections.

Games & More Menu

The main menu's "Games & More" menu contains five selections, most of which contaln additional menus:

- Vault: Check out trophies, music, records, tips, and more!
- amiibo: Train an amiibo to be your own personalized Figure Player!
- Solo: Take on Classic mode, play some minigames, or do some Training.
- Group: Play modes like Classic, Events, and Stadium with friends!
- Custom: Create your own Mii Fighter or customize existing characters.
- Stage Builder: Use the Wii U GamePad to create an original stage!
- Options: Customize Super Smash Bros. to suit you!

Vault

VAULT OVERVIEW

In addition to its galleries and records, the Vault includes the game's Shop and the Trophy Rush minigame.

The specific commands detailed in this chapter correspond to the default scheme for standard controllers. If you're using a customized scheme or a specialty controller, please refer to the game's manual or options for more information.

NOTE

VAULT MENU

The "Vault" menu contains eight options:

- Trophies: Check out trophies showcasing all kinds of Super Smash Bros. characters and items.
- Replays: Manage and watch the replays you've saved.
- Album: Look at the snapshots you've take while playing.
- Movies: Watch some Super Smash Bros. videos.
- Sounds: Listen to your favorite music and sounds from the game.
- Records: Take a look back at your milestones and stats.
- Tips: View all sorts of hints and tips gathered together in one place.
- Masterpieces: Check out some of the original games the fighters came from.

TROPHIES OVERVIEW

Visit the "Trophies" menu for a closer look at your trophy collection, to purchase new trophies from the Shop, or to play a round of Trophy Rush.

GALLERY

Gallery gives you an up-close look at all of the trophies you've collected, as well as information about the objects and characters they represent.

While viewing a trophy, press ⓧ to view the related trophy box. As your collection grows, revisit your trophy boxes to check your progress!

Trophies can be organized by the order in which you obtained them, by series, or by category—use Ⓛ and Ⓡ to switch between these options.

HOARD

Hoard allows you to see all of your trophies in one large group. Use the on-screen commands to control the viewing angle and zoom level.

TROPHY RUSH

In Trophy Rush, you have a limited time to smash blocks for trophies and other prizes—the more gold you invest, the more time you get! Each second costs six gold. You can purchase a minimum of 30 seconds (for 180 gold) up to a maximum of 2 minutes and 30 seconds (for 900 gold). You can play Trophy Rush alone, or you can team up with a friend.

Use your fighter's abilities to shatter the blocks as they appear. Destroying blocks adds to your score and fills the Fever Rush Gauge. Many blocks contain trophies, gold, and customization items, so keep an eye out for any blocks marked with relevant icons. Some blocks explode shortly after they land. Destroy explosive blocks before they detonate or keep your distance to avoid any impending explosions.

Destroy blocks in quick succession to earn chain bonuses for even more points, and fill the gauge near the top of the screen to enter Fever Rush. During Fever Rush, most of the falling blocks contain valuable prizes!

If you remain in one spot for too long, a special hazard will drop down to your position. If you take too much damage, you'll be launched out of the stage—and each time this happens, your remaining time is reduced by 15 seconds. Additionally, allowing the blocks to stack too high will result in a KO! Watch the line near the top of the screen; shortly after a stack reaches that line, the entire platform vanishes. If this happens, the platform won't return until after you've fallen out of the stage.

NOTE

Pause the game during a battle to access the available snapshot functions.

SHOP

In the game's Shop, you can use gold to purchase new trophies. The Shop contains up to eight trophies at a time. Visit the Shop regularly to check for new stock and special sales.

CAUTION

If one of the Shop's offers is labeled "Unlocked," it means that trophy is already in your collection. Buyer beware!

REPLAYS

View and manage your saved replays! Replays can be organized by the order in which they were saved, by creator, by stage, or by game mode. Use Ⓛ and Ⓡ to cycle through these options. Select a replay to view it, add a brief comment, or delete it from your collection.

ALBUM

Album lets you review and manage all of the snapshots you've taken while playing the game. You can view individual images, add brief comments, create albums, and delete unwanted snapshots from your collection.

MOVIES

Movies lets you review a variety of game-related videos. You'll find a nice selection of videos when you start a new game, but new videos will be added to your collection as you unlock them.

SOUNDS

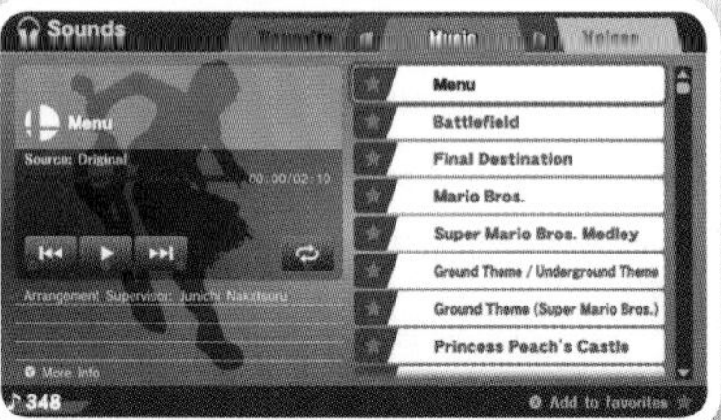

Sounds allows you to listen to all of the music and voice samples you've unlocked. Press Ⓧ to flag a specific track as one of your favorites. Follow the on-screen commands to control playback, and use Ⓛ and Ⓡ to switch between the available tabs.

RECORDS

Records contains information about how you've been playing the game. Review your fighter records, current stats, and all of the milestones you've earned.

FIGHTER RECORDS

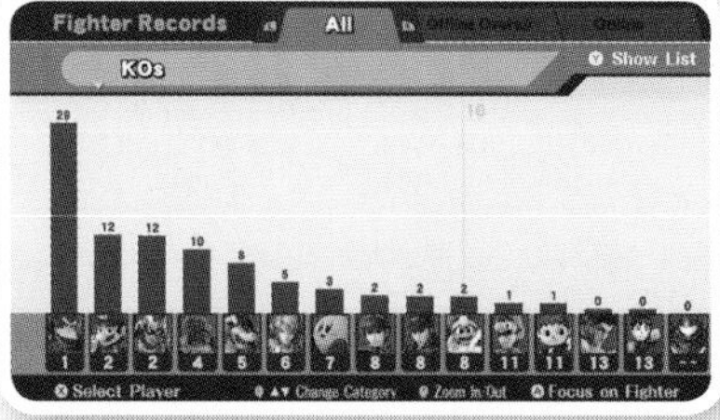

Review extensive records for each of the fighters on your roster! Records for offline and online performances can be combined or viewed separately. Use Ⓛ and Ⓡ to switch between the available tabs.

The game tracks virtually everything each fighter does—from the KOs a character has scored to how many coins he or she has collected. Use the Left Stick to switch categories. Press Ⓨ to show a list of available categories. You'll have all of the information you need to determine just how effective you've been with each fighter.

STATS

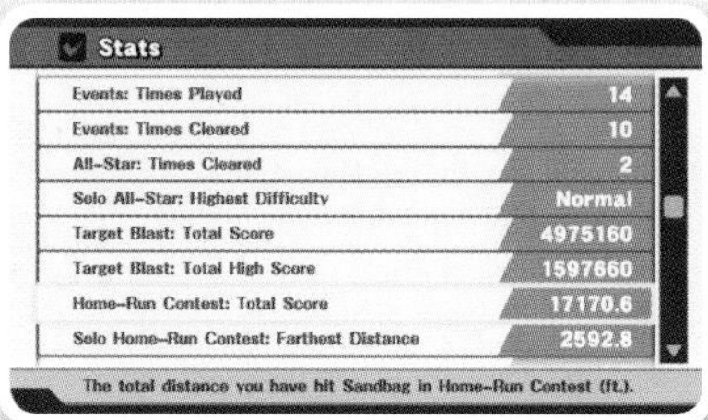

Stats tracks virtually every detail of how you've been playing the game. How many times have you turned on the game? How many total KOs have you scored? How much gold have you spent on trophies? If you're curious about how you've spent your time in-game, this is the section for you!

MILESTONES

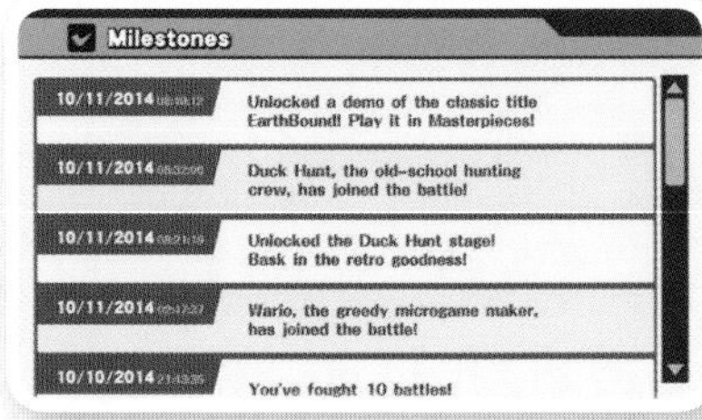

Check all of the milestones you've reached in the game and when you reached them. Use the Left Stick to scroll through your milestones and see how far you've come!

TIPS

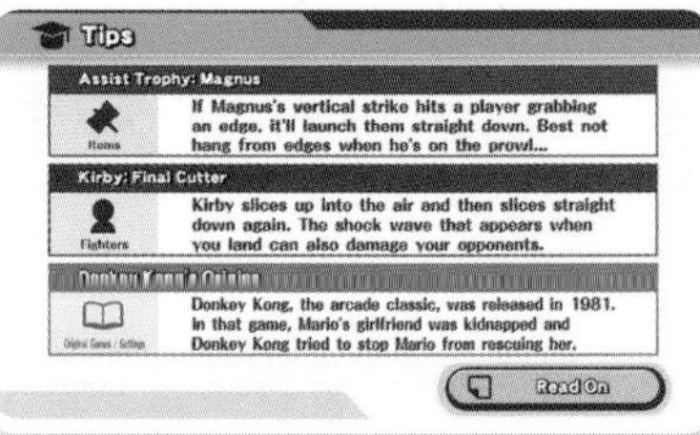

Tips contains loads of helpful information about fighters, game modes, items, and more. When you're looking for something new to try, visit this menu to cycle through pages of randomly selected tips.

MASTERPIECES

Masterpieces contains playable demos featuring many of the characters and items found in *Super Smash Bros.*! Each demo can be played for a short time, but there's no limit to how often you can play. Most of the demos are available by default, but a few must be unlocked by completing corresponding challenges.

UNLOCKING MASTERPIECES

MASTERPIECE	CHALLENGE PREREQUISITE
Dr. Mario	Clear Solo 10-Man Smash without taking any damage while playing as Dr. Mario.
EarthBound	Hit Sandbag 1,968 ft. or more in Home-Run Contest.
Kirby's Adventure	Clear Solo Classic at intensity 5.5 or higher while playing as Kirby.
Punch Out!! Featuring Mr. Dream	Clear the "No Mere Sparring Match" Event on normal difficulty or higher.
Yoshi	Clear Solo Classic while playing as Yoshi.

amiibo

The Games & More "amiibo" feature allows you to create and manage your amiibo Figure Players. When prompted, tap an amiibo figure on your Nintendo Wii U GamePad to create your Figure Player. Select a default look and choose a name to complete a Figure Player creation.

After you create a Figure Player, use the "amiibo" feature to assign alternate Special moves or feed it unwanted equipment. Alternate Specials only become available as you unlock them in the game. Any equipment you feed to a Figure Player will be destroyed, but all stats and bonus effects granted to your Figure Player in the process are permanent.

> **Remember to follow the in-game instructions and prompts to ensure proper use of your amiibo figures.**
>
> **NOTE**

Solo

SOLO OVERVIEW

Solo contains a diverse selection of single-player offerings. You'll find some fairly extensive game modes along with a variety of challenging scenarios and minigames. Exploring these game modes is a great way to hone your skills as you earn gold, trophies, equipment, and more.

SOLO MENU

The "Solo" menu contains six selections:

- Classic: Control a fighter on the battlefield, and keep winning fights! A boss awaits you at the end!
- Special Orders: Clear challenges set by Master Hand and Crazy Hand to win rewards!
- Events: Fight under set conditions to win rewards! (Strict "no-items" policy.)
- All-Star: Take on every fighter in reverse chronological order!
- Stadium: Defeat an army, destroy targets, hit a home run...and beat your high scores!
- Training: Try out a fighter for the first time or brush up on an old favorite!

CLASSIC (SOLO)

CLASSIC OVERVIEW

Compete in a five-round Smash tournament, then put your skills to the test as you face off against some less conventional opponents! You can spend gold to increase the difficulty for a chance to earn better rewards with each battle.

INTENSITY

After choosing a fighter, you can spend gold to adjust the game's intensity. The default intensity of 2.0 is the only no-cost option. Raising the intensity results in a more difficult game with the chance to earn better prizes. Lowering the intensity results in an easier game; doing so costs only a small amount of gold, but it will limit your potential prizes.

INTENSITY THRESHOLDS

Increasing the intensity level has several effects:

- Opponents are harder to launch.
- Opponents are more aggressive and can launch you more easily.
- You have a greater chance to fight team battles without the aid of CPU allies.
- The reward roulette at the start of each battle grants more prizes.

In addition to these gradual effects, some specific elements are only available at or above certain intensity levels:

- At an intensity level between of 2.9 and below, you will face Master Hand in the final match.
- At an intensity level between 3.0 and 5.0, you will face both Master Hand and Crazy Hand in the final match.
- At an intensity level between 5.1 and 5.9, you will face Master Hand, Crazy Hand, and Master Core during the final battle. Master Core will utilize two distinct combat forms.
- At an intensity level between 6.0 and 6.9, you will face Master Hand, Crazy Hand, and Master Core during the final battle. Master Core will utilize three distinct combat forms.
- At an intensity level between 7.0 and 7.9, you will face Master Hand, Crazy Hand, and Master Core during the final battle. Master Core will utilize four distinct combat forms.
- At an intensity level of 8.0 and above, you will face Master Hand, Crazy Hand, and Master Core during the final battle. Master Core will utilize five distinct combat forms.

SELECTING BATTLES

Before each battle, your fighter is represented as a figurine on a large board with opponents clustered at one or more locations. Look at each group to determine the number of participants, as well as any additional customizations rewards that might be involved in the corresponding battle.

Use the Left Stick to direct your fighter's figurine toward a group of enemies to trigger a battle. You have 30 seconds to choose your opponents. Otherwise, you'll be drawn into a randomly selected battle.

After each battle, you're automatically returned to the board to find a new selection of available opponents. Any fighters you've managed to defeat are displayed near the bottom of the screen. In some cases, you'll be prompted to choose one or more of these defeated fighters to aid you in team battles.

Each game of Classic includes a rival figurine. Rivals get stronger as they win battles of their own. Defeat a rival while he or she is more powerful to earn better prizes!

INTRUDER ALERT

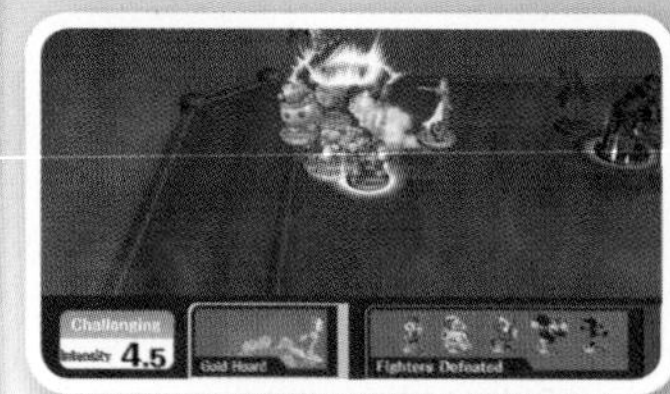

You'll sometimes receive an "intruder alert" after you've selected a battle. This means that a new fighter has unexpectedly joined the fight. Intruders will either be giant or metallic, so be prepared for a tougher battle!

PROGRESSING THROUGH CLASSIC

Each game of Classic consists of seven battles. Before each battle, use the roulette spinner to determine the type of reward you can earn by defeating your opponents. Specific rules will vary, but you'll always be granted two stock lives. This means that you can suffer one KO without being eliminated from the match. Each match also has a five-minute time limit—failing to win a match before time expires will end your game.

The first five battles are randomized versions of Smash and Team Smash. Specific rules are only revealed after the battle is selected, but the basic objective is always the same: survive long enough to KO all of your opponents!

The sixth battle pits you against an army of 20 opponents. These fighters are fairly easy to launch, but their sheer numbers make them fairly dangerous. Use your skills and any available items to clear out the opposition before you're overwhelmed.

The final battle consists of one or more boss fights. Master Hand is always involved in the finale, but depending on your chosen intensity level, you may also face Crazy Hand and Master Core.

MASTER HAND

On his own, Master Hand is a formidable opponent with a wide variety of devastating attacks. Most of these attacks take some time to charge, however, making it simpler to identify and avoid incoming threats. A few of his attacks are fairly quick, though, so it's often best to keep your distance until he commits to a move.

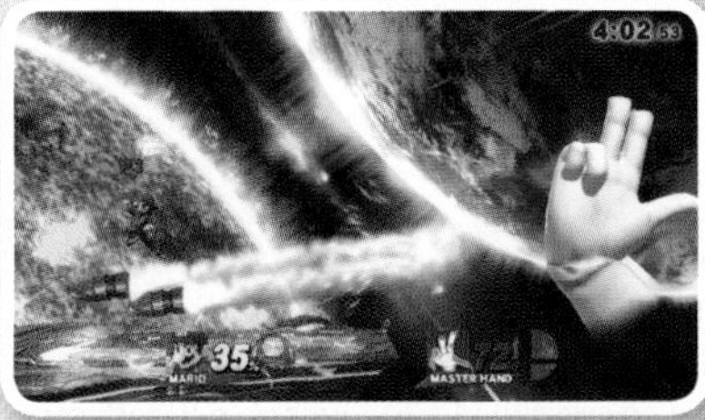

Master Hand's elaborate attacks are easy to identify, so the results are easier to predict. Whether he's snapping his fingers for a short-range attack, clenching his fist to slam down on the platform, or tracking your movements as he charges a projectile attack, you simply need wait until just before he strikes, then activate your shield or dodge the attack.

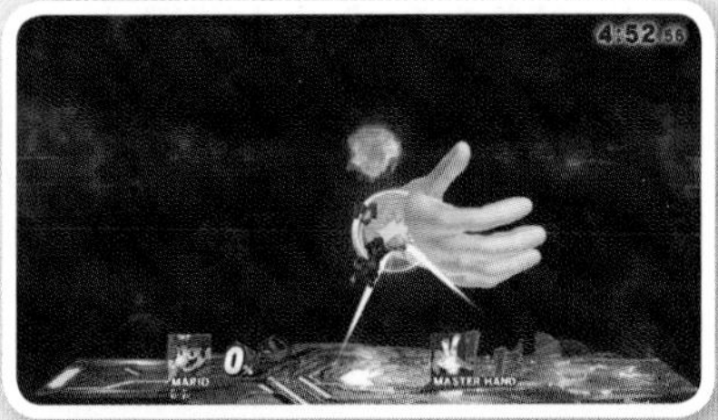

Master Hand is particularly vulnerable immediately after he attacks. This is the best time to go on the offensive, so move in and unleash one or two of your most powerful moves. It's often safe to strike while he's charging one of his moves, but make sure you allow enough time to get clear of the impending attack.

Master Hand is usually idle for several seconds between his attacks. You can deal a lot of damage during this time, but be careful—not all of his moves are easy to anticipate. Try to stick with your quick attacks and watch for any sudden movements; lingering near Master Hand can allow him to grab you right off of the platform. If this happens, flick the Left Stick back and forth until you break free of his grip.

Master Hand's health is displayed near the bottom of the screen. Use this number to gauge your progress over the course of the battle. At an intensity of 2.9 and below, you'll face Master Hand on his own. Defeat him to end the battle and complete your game of Classic.

MASTER HAND AND CRAZY HAND

If your intensity is set to 3.0 or above, Master Hand and Crazy Hand will team up in the final match. These two do more than simply split your attention, however—Master Hand and Crazy Hand often coordinate their attacks, making it difficult to maintain a solid defense.

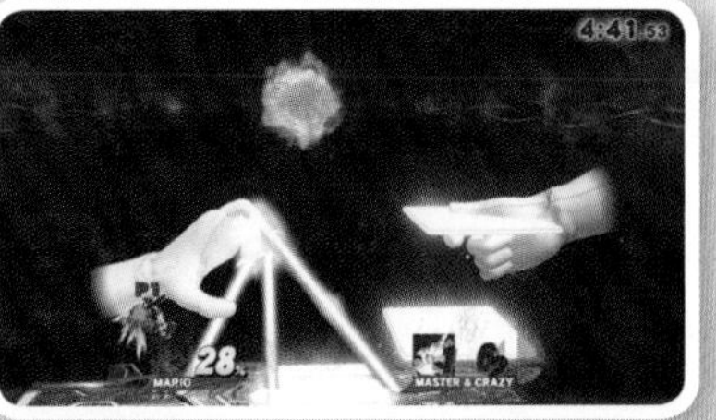

It's important to attack whenever the opportunity presents itself, but make sure you pay attention to the entire battlefield. When one opponent seems vulnerable, there's a good chance his partner is preparing an attack of his own. Avoid committing to slower moves unless you're certain you have enough time to see them through.

Master Hand and Crazy Hand often combine their attacks. Whether they attack simultaneously or in quick succession, the effect is generally the same—it's much more difficult to stay out of harm's way. For example, escaping from one of Master Hand's rising platforms could send you tumbling right into Crazy Hand's flailing attack. Similarly, any attempts to spot-dodge or shield yourself are unlikely to protect you for the duration of a coordinated attack.

Surviving unscathed often means alternating between activating your shield and dodging. If both of your opponents are charging their attacks, use the time to weigh your defensive options. Whether you plan on dodging or relying on your shield, try to be patient. Watch your opponents as they move around the area, and adjust your position as needed. Wait until they commit to their attacks and then react accordingly.

Jumping is an important part of every fight, but remember your defensive options are limited while you're in the air. The more time you spend off of the platform, the more likely it is you'll be caught in an extended attack. Before you commit to a big jump or an aerial attack, make sure you have a safe place to land. When all else fails, try to use the air dodge and fast fall techniques to avoid your opponents' juggling attacks.

Master Hand and Crazy Hand share a single pool of health, and you can deal heavy damage each time you manage to hit both enemies with a single attack. At intensity levels of 5.0 and below, the battle ends when you defeat these opponents. At higher intensity levels, however, Master Core will step in if Master Hand and Crazy Hand fail to stop you. During these battles, it's important to beat Master Hand and Crazy Hand as quickly as possible. Be aggressive!

MASTER CORE

Your intensity level not only determines if you're able to face Master Core, but it also affects exactly which forms Master Core will take during the battle. Regardless of your intensity level, however, you must deal damage to each of Master Core's forms to progress through the battle and eventually defeat your enemy.

To confront Master Core, you must select an intensity between 5.1 and 9.0, and you must choose to face both Master Hand and Master Core in the final match.

NOTE

MASTER GIANT

When the intensity is set to 7.0 and above, Master Core first appears in the form of Master Giant. While in this form, he's capable of several attacks, most of which affect the bulk of the battlefield. When you're not busy defending yourself, move below Master Giant's head and attack upward. It takes a few seconds for Master Giant to recover from its own attacks, so you should have enough time to use your fighter's more powerful attacks.

Soon after Master Giant sweeps its arm through the area, a large beam speeds toward you. This beam moves very quickly, so a well-executed dodge will allow you to avoid taking damage. The beam appears soon after the swipe's shadowy trail vanishes.

Watch for the growths that sometimes appear on top of the Master Giant's head. Soon after they do, Master Giant smashes down on the platform and releases them into the air. Once the shadowy blobs are in place, each of them detonates, releasing horizontal and vertical beams in the process. Position yourself to avoid all of the beams until they fade, or shield yourself to avoid taking damage. Resume your attacks as soon as the beams vanish.

When Master Giant sprouts extra arms, two of its hands begin to glow. Evade these glowing fists to avoid being temporarily absorbed into the shadowy figure. Dodge the glowing fists, or hop off of the platform and grab its edge to help stay out of Master Giant's attack range. Some larger characters can still be grabbed from this position, so be prepared to release the edge and air jump to safety.

When Master Giant releases a swarm of energy orbs, try to deal a bit of damage then activate your shield as the platform is lifted toward the top of the screen. If defense is your priority, you can position yourself directly under a gap between the hazards. This often makes it much easier to avoid taking damage. The orbs roam for the duration of the attack, though, so be prepared to shield or dodge as necessary.

Master Giant sometimes creates a rift in the space near its head. Stand completely still as you're drawn toward the rift—you'll only be pulled into the rift if you're in the air. Stick to the platform and use your shield to defend yourself from the energy orbs that move through the area. If one of the orbs makes contact, you'll be launched into the air and pulled into the rift for heavy damage.

When Master Giant clutches its head and writhes around, this signals an impending burst of energy. Watch for the small waves of energy to appear, then dodge just as the massive foe releases a powerful shriek. Don't bother shielding, as it won't protect you from the pulse's powerful knockback effect. Above all, make sure you stick to the platform. If the blast catches you in the air, it will very likely result in a KO.

> **TIP**
>
> **The Master Giant form has some particularly devious attacks and learning to avoid them is an important part of completing this battle. Remember, however, that you have a relatively short time to win the match. Take every opportunity to attack!**

MASTER BEAST

When the intensity level is set between 6.0 and 6.9, Master Core first appears in the form of Master Beast. At intensity levels of 7.0 and above, this monstrous form appears after you defeat Master Giant. Master Beast has a few distinct attacks. Once you learn to identify each of them, they're fairly easy to avoid. After each of Master Beast's attacks, you should have enough time to deal significant damage with a Smash attack or two.

Soon after Master Beast sprouts spikes on its back, a trail of dark energy appears. When this trail reaches your position, spikes erupt from the platform. If you're on the ground, activate your shield or dodge away from the spikes just before they emerge. If you're caught in the air, use your recovery moves to land safely away from the spikes.

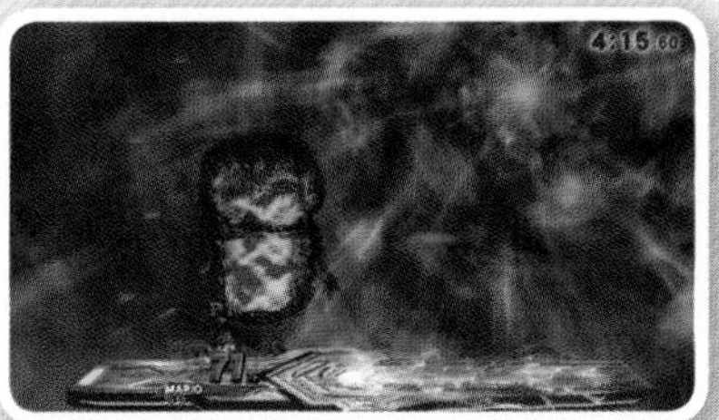

Each time Master Beast leaps into the background, it hooks back and snaps its jaws as it returns to the platform. Activate your shield or dodge away from the attack just before Master Beast reaches you.

Sometimes Master Beast leaps straight into the air and comes crashing down with enough force to tilt the platform. If you are near the point of impact, activate your shield to avoid taking damage. If you manage to get clear of the initial hit, shield or jump to maintain control of your fighter as the platform tilts upward.

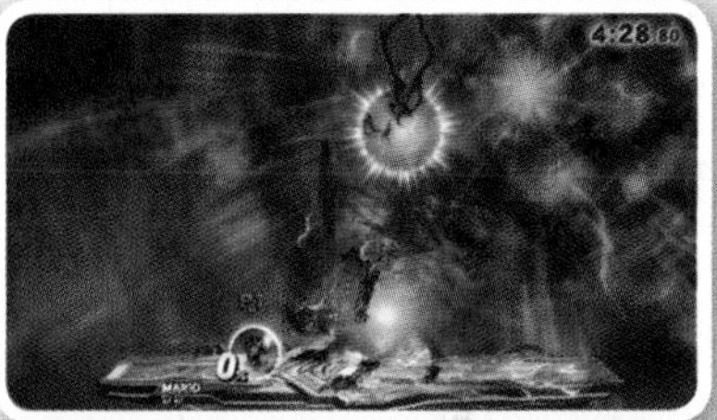

If Master Beast uses its tail to summon a bolt of dark energy, move away to avoid the impending eruption. If that's not possible, activate your shield to avoid taking damage.

MASTER EDGES

If your intensity is set between 5.1 and 5.9, Master Core first appears in the form of five shadowy blades known as Master Edges. At higher intensities, he changes to this form after you've dealt enough damage to his Master Beast. The Master Edges form can attack as individual swords or as a single cluster of blades. Additionally, this form summons dangerous orbs of dark energy. These floating blades often hover high above the platform, so be prepared to use aerial attacks. When Master Edges is within range, though, look for opportunities to use some of your fighter's more powerful attacks.

When facing Master Edges, look for the yellowish shimmer that appears along the blades just before each attack. If the blades shimmer while they're tightly clustered and pointing upward, it means they're about to release a flurry of strikes. This flurry has a fairly long range, so it's often best to simply activate your shield just as the attack begins. Your shield should last until the pause after the initial flurry—deactivate your shield and dodge the final strike to avoid taking damage.

If the blades are pointing downward when they shimmer, it usually indicates some type of quick slash attack. Slashing attacks often produce orbs of dark energy. Use your shield to defend yourself from the initial strike, and then evade the orbs as they move through the area.

Smaller orbs move fairly slowly, but they're very good at homing in on your position. This can make the orbs surprisingly difficult to avoid, so it's important to time your jumps and dodges properly.

The larger orbs have limited homing ability, but they move considerably faster than their smaller counterparts. Their sheer size can also make it more difficult to slip around the larger orbs—so, be prepared to spot-dodge or activate your shield as needed.

Occasionally, Master Edges's blades separate in order to surround you. When this happens, move to the center of the platform and wait for the attack. Spot-dodge each of the smaller blades as they slash through the area. The attack ends when the large blade above you comes crashing down to the platform. Shield yourself from the impact or dodge away and hit the large blade with a Smash attack.

TIP

Master Edges' orbs are considered energy projectiles, so some character-specific moves can be helpful in dealing with either of these orb attacks. For example, Villager can pocket the orbs, and they can be reflected by characters like Fox, Falco, and Mii Gunner. Characters with projectile-absorbing abilities, like Ness and Mii Gunner, can even use these orbs to regain health!

MASTER SHADOW

Whenever you face Master Core—regardless of your intensity level—he creates a shadowy version of your fighter once you've defeated Master Edges. This form is known as Master Shadow. Master Shadow possesses more powerful versions of your fighter's abilities and equipment. This means its attacks do more damage than yours, and any equipment-based bonus effects are more potent than those granted to your fighter.

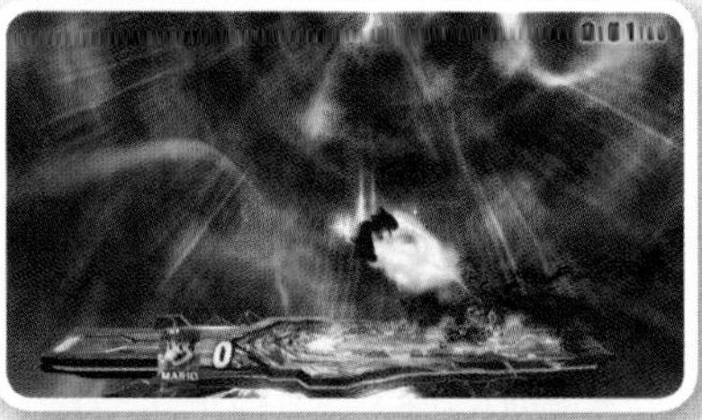

When Master Shadow is first revealed, your shadowy opponent is a considerably larger version of your fighter. Your successful attacks, however, will slowly cut your doppelgänger down to size. Remember that Master Shadow isn't limited to offensive maneuvers—it can shield itself and dodge your attacks as well as any standard opponent. Use your more powerful attacks each time you see an opening, and use plenty of throws to break through Master Shadow's defenses. Continue to deal damage until you destroy Master Shadow or until you're able to launch your opponent out of the stage.

MASTER FORTRESS

At an intensity level of 8.0 and above, Master Fortress appears after you defeat Master Shadow. To defeat Master Fortress, you must find and destroy four glowing cores hidden within the shadowy structure. When Master Fortress appears, you're given a Heart Container, and a little extra time is added to the clock. Unless your damage is above 100%, it's usually best to leave the Heart Container until you've destroyed at least one of Master Fortress's cores. Monitor your health and claim the Heart Container whenever you need it.

When Master Fortress first appears, there's only one path inside. Follow this path to find the first core within a small enclosure. A new path appears each time you destroy a core. Pay attention to your surroundings to ensure you can identify newly accessible areas.

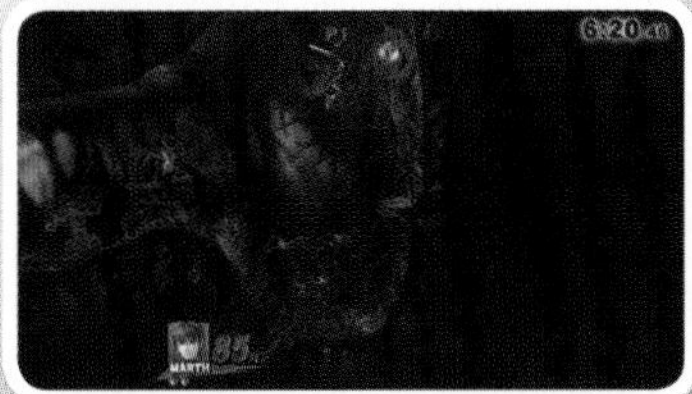

Master Fortress is filled with shadowy enemies intent on impeding your progress. When and if you should engage each enemy depends on your chosen fighter's abilities and equipment and how quickly you aim to complete your playthrough. Learn to identify each of the shadowy enemies to ensure that you can deal with them as needed:

- The flower-like turrets should usually be your highest priority. Attack them quickly to interrupt their beam attacks then finish them off as quickly as possible.
- The shadowy flame-like enemies have a variety of dangerous attacks, so it's often best to deal with them quickly. If possible, use projectile attacks or long-range vertical attacks to stay out of danger as you finish them off.
- The shadowy skeletons use shields to block your attacks. Grab and throw these enemies then attack them before they can recover.
- The wall-crawling enemies aren't particularly tough. Simply attack them until they're defeated.

Remember to dodge and shield as needed, and consider dashing past enemies that don't pose an immediate threat.

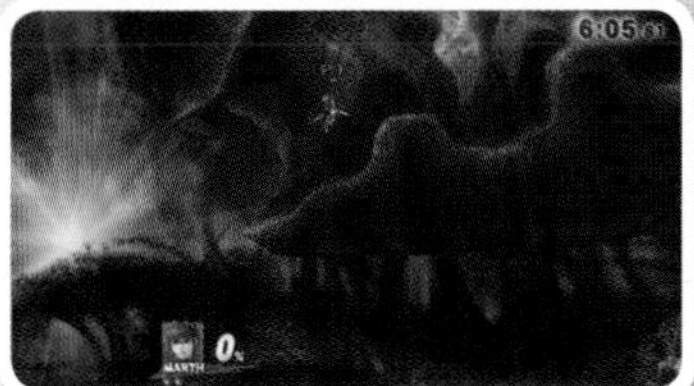

After you destroy the first core, leave the enclosure to find a new path above the original entrance. Defeat or avoid patrolling enemies as you follow the path to the second core.

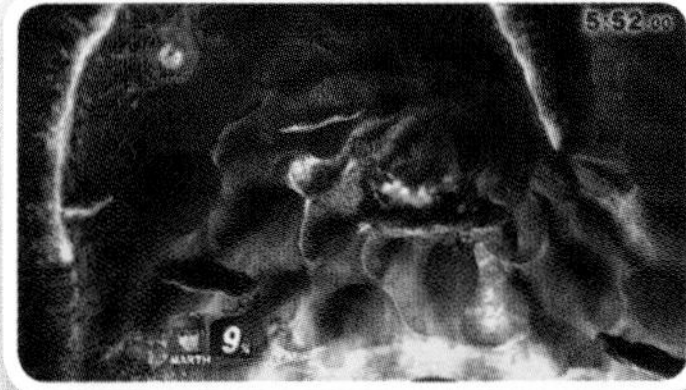

Take care to avoid all of the glowing yellow areas scattered throughout Master Fortress. Touching one of these areas causes heavy damage to you. If your damage is above 125%, touching one of the glowing areas will result in an instant KO. After you destroy the second core, you're automatically ejected from Master Fortress.

Hop back over to Master Fortress and follow the upper path through the area.

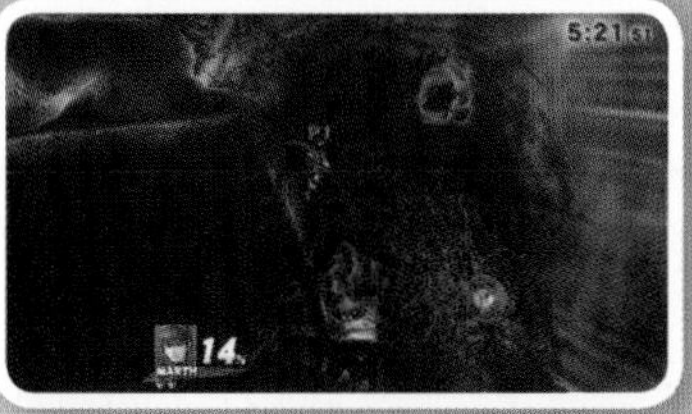

The third core is floating just off the far edge of Master Fortress. If possible, use projectile attacks to destroy the core from the nearby ledge. Otherwise, use aerial attacks to destroy the core—just make sure you return to the nearby ledge after each blow. Once you've destroyed the third core, a large shadow moves through the area. Turn back and jump up to the newly revealed ledge to the left.

Follow the path to the left and drop down into the newly accessible area. Be careful, though! This path contains massive amounts of glowing yellow areas, so it's important to land on one of the available platforms.

Follow the path as it twists its way to the fourth and final core. You'll find plenty of enemies in this area, and incoming attacks are likely to knock you right into a nearby glowing hazard. Clear out the enemies then jump up to the last remaining core and destroy it.

TIP

It's much easier to defeat Master Fortress if your fighter is properly equipped. If you're having trouble with this encounter, consider making your next attempt after you've collected some more powerful equipment.

MASTER CORE

Once you've defeated all of Master Core's shadowy forms, his true form is revealed. When he's exposed, Master Core lacks any defensive abilities. If you remain idle too long, however, Master Core will unleash a powerful attack, resulting in an instant KO! Dash in and perform a series of attacks to prevent this from happening. All of your attacks should prove effective, but you must KO Master Core to finish the battle. Hit Master Core with a series of Smash attacks until you launch him out of the stage.

As Master Core takes damage, he becomes easier to launch. Until you finally score the KO, however, he'll return to the center of the platform after each of your attacks. Luckily, the clock stops once Master Core's true form is revealed, so you're free to hit Master Core as many times as needed.

STAFF CREDITS

During the staff credits, you can attack the individual names to slowly reveal the image on the wall. For a name to contribute to the image, however, you must hit it at the just the right time and in just the right spot. Jump up and use aerial attacks to reveal the top of the image as the names pass in front of any blank areas, then work your way down.

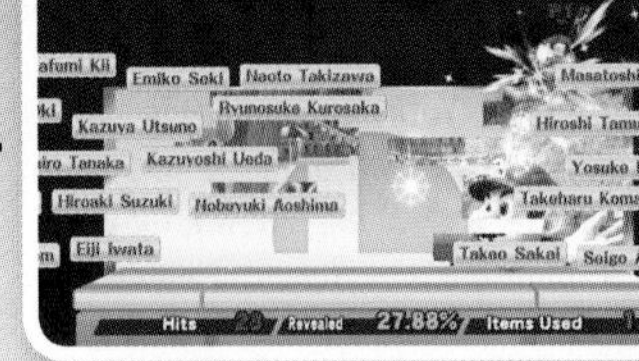

As you reveal more of the image, it becomes important to aim your shots. Look for the sparkles that help identify hidden sections, then strike a name as it passes through the area. Watch for helpful items that sometimes appear, and use them to attack several names at once!

GAME OVER

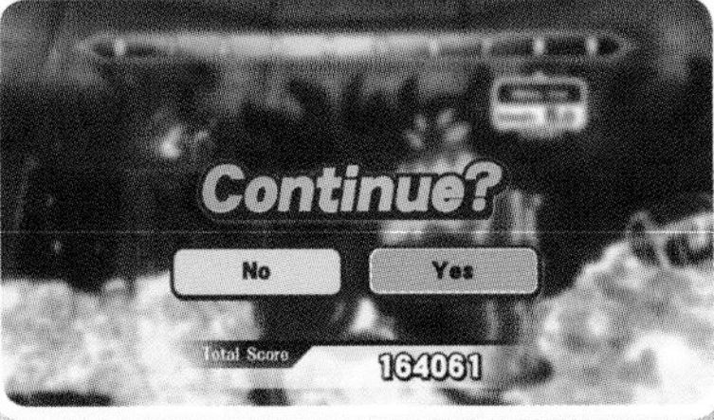
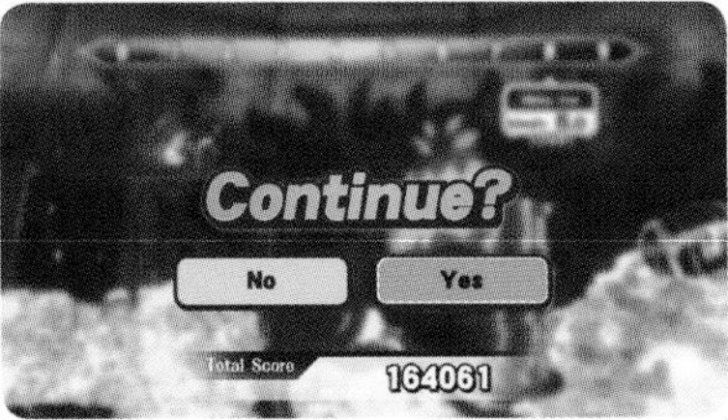

In Classic, you start each match with two stock lives. This means that you can suffer one KO during each battle without losing the match. If you lose both of your stock lives during a match—or if you fail to complete a match within the allotted time—the game ends. This reduces your score and gold, and it usually eliminates at least a few of the rewards you've earned. Each time you lose a match, however, you're given the opportunity to continue. This allows you to resume your playthrough, but any penalties you took remain in place. In most cases, continuing your game also affects the intensity level for the remaining matches.

If you decide not to continue, you're granted whatever score, gold, and rewards are displayed on the results screen.

CLEARING CLASSIC

When you clear a game of Classic, you receive information about your score, as well as any gold and rewards you've earned. Any rewards you might have lost are also displayed. Most important, however, clearing Classic unlocks your fighter's primary trophy and triggers the staff credits!

SPECIAL ORDERS

SPECIAL ORDERS OVERVIEW

There are two different categories of Special Orders: Master Orders and Crazy Orders. Both categories offer randomly selected scenarios that can be completed for rewards, but Master Orders and Crazy Orders each have a number of distinct features.

MASTER ORDERS

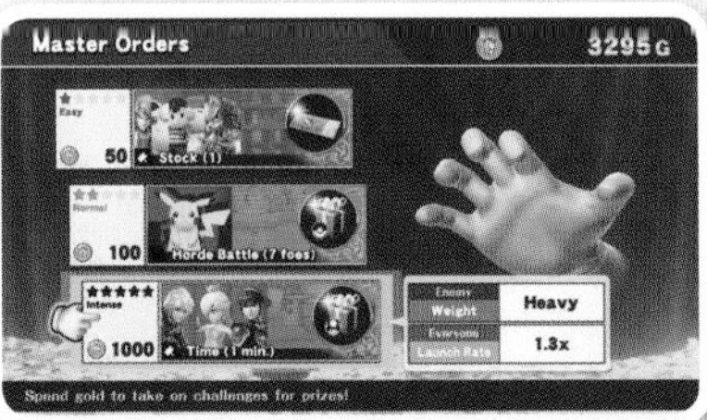

In Master Orders, you can exchange gold for entry into one of three randomly selected scenarios. Check the available tickets for each scenario's cost, difficulty level, and rules. Tickets also include information about the opponents you'll face and potential rewards. Highlight individual tickets to see any special rules that might be in place and which fighters those rules affect.

NOTE

Master Orders are separated into five difficulty levels: easy, normal, hard, very hard, and intense. More difficult Master Orders have larger entry fees.

You're free to use customizations to complete Master Orders. Choosing the right characters, equipment, and Special moves can make difficult scenarios much easier to handle!

CRAZY ORDERS

In Crazy Orders, you can complete a series of matches to earn bigger and bigger rewards. To play, you must invest 5,000G or use a Crazy Orders Pass. Once you've purchased entry into Crazy Orders, you're given one stock life and 10 minutes to clear as many matches as possible. You must then defeat Crazy Hand in a final battle. During each turn, select one of the available tickets to begin a match. Tickets display match types, opponents, and potential rewards, so choose wisely!

After you complete at least one turn, you have the option to face Crazy Hand in the final battle. Complete as many turns as possible before you face Crazy Hand to maximize your rewards. Be warned, though—if you suffer a KO or fail to begin the final battle within the allotted time, you'll lose the bulk of any rewards you've earned!

TIP

Press Ⓨ during ticket selection to review the rewards you've earned during previous turns.

Only the time spent in battle counts against the 10-minute time limit, so try to deal with your opponents as quickly as possible. You'll recover a bit of health during each turn, but damage will accumulate throughout a Crazy Orders playthrough.

You're free to use customized characters during Crazy Orders, and doing so can allow you to finish matches very quickly. Combine equipment with the "Home-Run Bat equipped" and "Quick bat swing" bonus effects to score instant KOs! It can also be helpful to utilize a piece of equipment that grants some form of health recovery.

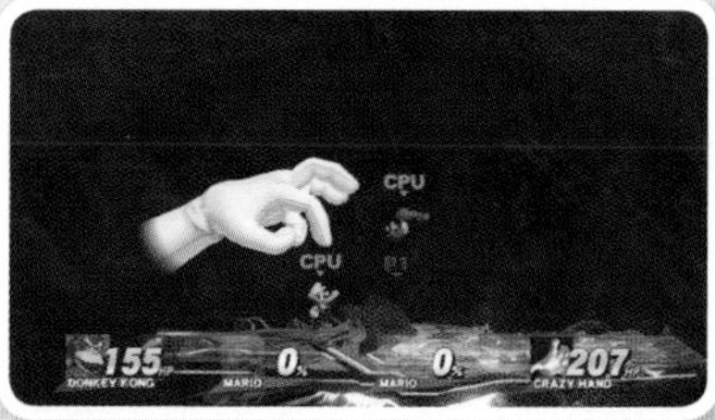

At the start of each turn, check the remaining time and your current damage percentage. Remember that while additional victories will bring greater rewards, failure will cost you the bulk of what you've earned. When you're ready, select the "Crazy Hand" ticket to begin the final battle. While Crazy Hand will always be featured, final battles can contain additional foes. When you face Crazy Hand after 14 or more turns, Master Hand will join the battle! This makes for a tougher fight, but you'll have plenty of chances to earn additional chests..

The final battle is always a stamina battle with no time limit. Your starting HP is determined by how much damage you've taken in previous matches. The higher your damage percentage, the more HP you'll have! Attacking Crazy Hand not only lowers his HP, but it often produces chests with additional rewards. Stay healthy, collect any chests you find, and defeat Crazy Hand to claim all of the rewards you've earned in Crazy Orders!

EVENTS (SOLO)

EVENTS OVERVIEW

In Events, you must complete challenging scenarios under set conditions. Clear Events to record high scores and unlock additional scenarios. Use your skills to complete special objectives to receive useful rewards!

CLEARING EVENTS

Select an available Event tile for a description of the specific scenario, reward conditions, and permitted fighters. Most Events can only be completed with a specified character, but you're free to use any custom sets you've created. Each Event offers three difficulty levels: easy, normal, and hard. Difficulty levels can sometimes play an important role in reward conditions and Event-related Challenges, so choose wisely!

NOTE

During Events, equipment bonus effects that grant items will be nullified. Any stat changes related to those pieces of equipment, however, will still be in effect.

UNLOCKING NEW EVENTS

Make sure you read the Event description for important details about your primary objective. Some Events require that you utilize Special moves, defeat opponents within a certain amount of time, or prevent other fighters from completing objectives of their own. Clearing the "The Falchion's Seal" Event, for example, requires the use of a Final Smash to defeat your opponent.

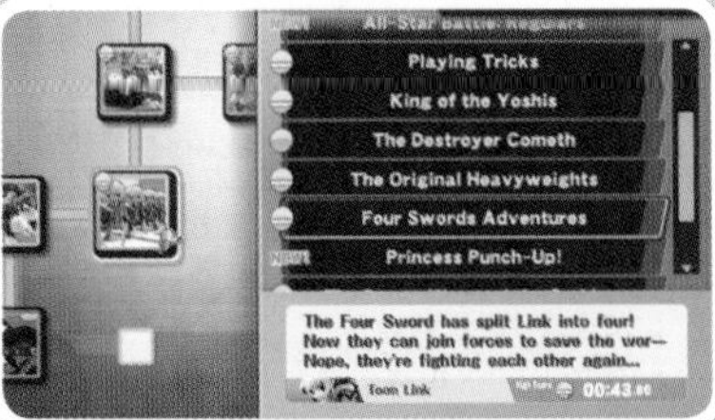

Once you've cleared an Event, an icon appears in the upper-left corner of its tile. The specific icon varies depending on your chosen difficulty level. A gold flag appears in the tile's lower-right corner if you've managed to meet the Event's reward condition. You can also press Ⓡ to activate the Event list. The Event list is a quick and easy way to locate specific Events, review your progress, and identify unfinished tasks.

By default, only one Event tile is available. Clear the "The Original Heavyweights" Event to unlock nearby tiles. Some Events can only be unlocked after specific characters are added to your roster. If an Event description includes a condition for a hidden route, it means one of the connected Events involves a hidden character. A hidden route will appear only after you've cleared the appropriate Event and unlocked the required fighter.

Unlocking paths not only allows access to new Events, it can sometimes grant you additional rewards like gold, trophies, as Crazy Orders Passes. These rewards are automatically collected when the appropriate paths are revealed.

> **NOTE**
>
> The first available Event, "The Original Heavyweights," is located on the tile designated as C6.

EVENT DETAILS

The game includes a total of 55 Solo Events connected by a series of branching paths.

TILE KEY

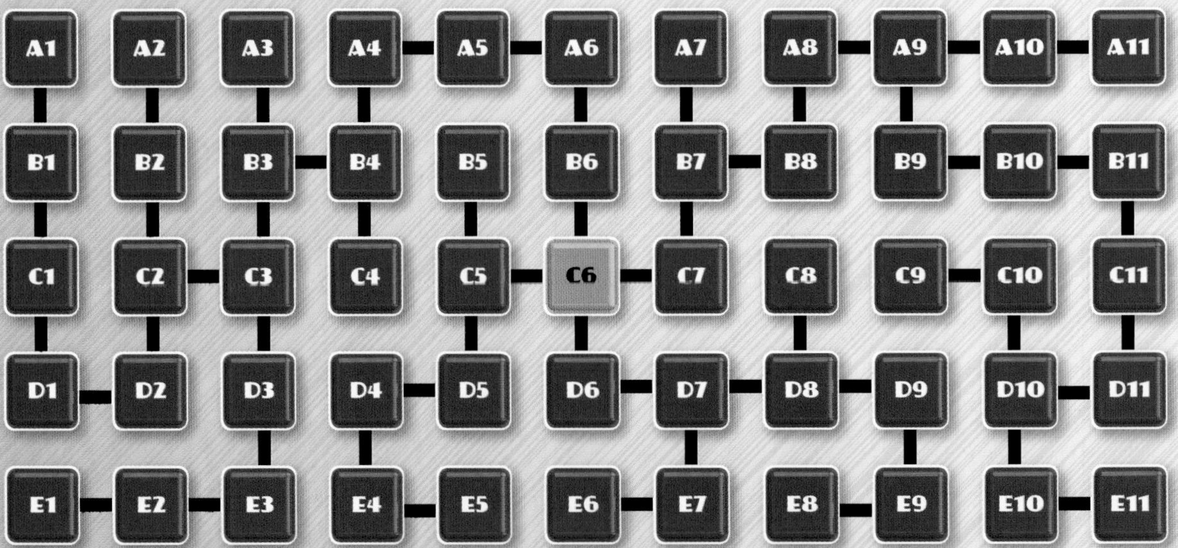

SOLO EVENTS

LOCATION	EVENT NAME	DESCRIPTION	REQUIRED CHARACTER	REWARD CONDITION	HIDDEN ROUTE CONDITION
A1	The FINAL Final Battle	This is it...the true FINAL BATTLE!	Your choice	Clear the stage on hard difficulty.	None
A2	A Fated Battle	The fate of the world hangs in the balance. Ganondorf seems to have something up his sleeve, though...	Link	Clear on normal difficulty or higher within 80 seconds.	None
A3	In the Name of the Hero-King!	"You may have taken my name...but can you match my strength?"	Marth	Clear the stage on hard difficulty.	None
A4	Great Fox Defense	A mysterious group of bandits is invading! Don't let a single one of them on board!	Falco	Clear the stage on hard difficulty.	None
A5	Behind Enemy Lines	Fox has been critically injured in battle. Survive the ongoing skirmish until backup can arrive!	Fox	Clear on normal difficulty or higher after defeating 8 enemies.	Unlock Mr. Game & Watch.
A6	Pokémon Battle	It's a Pokémon battle royal. Gotta beat 'em all!	Greninja	Clear on normal difficulty or higher after defeating 2 enemies.	None
A7	It's Past Your Bedtime!	It's WAY past these kids' bedtime, but they're still playing around! Send them all to sleep with a lullaby!	Jigglypuff	Clear the stage on hard difficulty.	None
A8	When Lightning Strikes	It's Pikachu versus Pikachu in an electrifying battle! Grab the Lightning items to take out the enemies quickly!	Pikachu	Clear on normal difficulty or higher within 60 seconds.	Unlock Wario.
A9	Oh Yeah, Luigi Time!	What do you do when your bro is late for his duel with Wario? Beat Wario yourself, and show the world you're player-one material!	Luigi	Clear within 30 seconds.	Unlock Dr. Mario.
A10	Jackpot Oppor-tunity	Tom Nook has set up a tournament, and the prizes are massive! Collect 1,000G, and pay off your loan!	Villager	Clear on normal difficulty or higher within 100 seconds.	None
A11	Fitness Junkie	These two couch potatoes don't get enough exercise. Time to whip them into shape!	Wii Fit Trainer	Clear on hard difficulty within 45 seconds.	None
B1	The Final Battle	You have overcome many struggles and reached your final destination. Defeat these three bosses and claim victory!	Your choice	Clear the stage on hard difficulty.	None
B2	No Mere Sparring Match	Little Mac has a new training regimen: a 60-second onslaught of walking punching bags!	Little Mac	Clear on normal difficulty or higher within 40 seconds.	None
B3	Beautification	These fighters' faces are a bit...scary. Give them a much-needed makeover by planting beautiful flowers on their heads!	Rosalina & Luma	Clear on hard difficulty within 60 seconds.	Unlock Lucina.
B4	The Falchion's Seal	This fearsome dragon cannot be sealed away without Chrom's help. A Final Smash should do the trick!	Robin	Clear on normal difficulty or higher within 60 seconds.	None
B5	All-Star Battle: Regulars	Take on eight fighters who have been smashing since the very beginning!	Your choice	Clear the stage on normal difficulty or higher.	None
B6	Up to Speed	The quickest fighters in the land have met to do battle! Take out your opponents...if you can catch them!	Sonic	Clear on hard difficulty within 25 seconds.	None
B7	Playing Tricks	Kids sure love to cause trouble, and Ness is no different! Use Pitfalls to bury both of the Villagers at once!	Ness	Clear on normal difficulty or higher within 20 seconds.	None
B8	King of the Yoshis	Only one Yoshi can join Mario on his next big adventure. May the best Yoshi win!	Yoshi	Clear after defeating at least 5 enemies.	None

SOLO EVENTS (CONTINUED)

LOCATION	EVENT NAME	DESCRIPTION	REQUIRED CHARACTER	REWARD CONDITION	HIDDEN ROUTE CONDITION
B9	Doctor Schmoctor	"Ugh...I ain't feelin' so hot. Must be all that raw garlic I munched. Better waft on over to the doctor's office! WAHAHAHA!"	Wario	Clear on normal difficulty or higher within 30 seconds.	None
B10	Wrecking Mario	It's not every day the wrecking crew asks for backup. Better demolish this building lickety-split to help them out!	Mario	Clear the stage on hard difficulty.	Unlock Duck Hunt.
B11	Guardian of the Jungle	"Looks like poachers are hunting in my jungle. Time to teach them a lesson!"	Donkey Kong	Clear within 60 seconds.	None
C1	Mechanical Menace	We knew this day would come. The robots have become self-aware! Take them out quickly or they'll call for backup.	Shulk	Clear within 60 seconds.	None
C2	Bounty Hunter Clash	Two bounty hunters fight over a priceless bounty! But they may not be the only ones looking to make a quick buck...	Captain Falcon	Clear on normal difficulty or higher within 80 seconds.	Unlock R.O.B.
C3	A Situation of Some Gravity	In the far reaches of the galaxy, Samus discovers a planet with unusually strong gravity. Can she withstand it enough to defeat this alien life form?	Zero Suit Samus	Clear on normal difficulty or higher within 50 seconds.	Unlock Dark Pit.
C4	The Ultimate Swordsman	In the middle of a training journey, Ike happens upon a castle under siege! It's the perfect opportunity to test his skills!	Ike	Clear on normal difficulty or higher after defeating 5 enemies.	None
C5	The Destroyer Cometh	The dark king and his brood have come to destroy Skyworld! Take them out before they smash up all of the terrain!	Palutena	Clear within 45 seconds.	None
C6	The Original Heavyweights	Mario's greatest archenemies have joined forces. Take out these two very different heavyweights!	Mario	Clear without taking any damage.	Unlock Falco.
C7	Four Swords Adventures	The Four Sword has split Link into four! Now they can join forces to save the wor—Nope, they're fighting each other again...	Toon Link	Clear on normal difficulty or higher within 45 seconds.	None
C8	A Battle of Scale	They may be small, but they never give up! Prove that the biggest doesn't always mean the best!	Olimar	Clear within 60 seconds.	None
C9	All-Star Battle: Brawl	Take on 10 fighters who've been in the roster since *Super Smash Bros. Brawl*!	Your choice	Clear the stage on normal difficulty or higher.	None
C10	Kirby's Crazy Appetite	Kirby's absolutely starving over here! Feed him until he's all healthy again.	Kirby	Clear the stage on hard difficulty.	None
C11	The Jungle in Chaos	Are they Kongs, or are they bunnies?! Whatever they are, these strange creatures are causing a ruckus. Chase them out quickly!	Diddy Kong	Clear on normal difficulty or higher within 90 seconds.	Unlock Falco.
D1	Unwavering Chivalry	A noble knight raises not his sword against a lady. Therefore, KO no maiden—Marth is your only target!	Meta Knight	Clear the stage on hard difficulty.	None
D2	Robotic Rampage	A new experimental giant robot has gone haywire! If you don't take it out, it might destroy the whole island!	R.O.B.	Clear within 70 seconds.	None
D3	Doppelgänger Duel	Dark Pit has challenged Pit to a duel! Time to decide once and for all which angel is the real deal!	Dark Pit	Clear the stage on hard difficulty.	None
D4	Princess Punch-Up!	It's princess against princess in a royal showdown! Looks like their bodyguards just became obsolete.	Zelda	Clear on normal difficulty or higher within 60 seconds.	None

SOLO EVENTS (CONTINUED)

LOCATION	EVENT NAME	DESCRIPTION	REQUIRED CHARACTER	REWARD CONDITION	HIDDEN ROUTE CONDITION
D5	The Demon King and the Goddess	The Demon King wages battle against his eternal foes. They seem more confident than usual—some trick up their sleeve?	Ganondorf	Clear on normal difficulty or higher within 45 seconds.	None
D6	The Big 7650!	Use PAC-MAN's Final Smash to chomp through six enemies in a row to get a 7,650-point bonus!	PAC-MAN	Clear the stage on hard difficulty.	None
D7	The King Strikes Back	King Dedede has set up a one-on-one prizefight to settle things with his nemesis! Will the king finally prevail?!	King Dedede	Clear without taking any damage.	None
D8	Fire-Type Frenzy	Some rather unlikely Pokémon have turned up the heat! Show them who's the real Fire-type around here!	Charizard	Clear on normal difficulty or higher within 70 seconds.	Unlock Mr. Game & Watch.
D9	That Elusive 9	Defeat the enemy with the number 9 Judge attack! If you use anything else, you'll be here awhile...	Mr. Game & Watch	Clear the stage on hard difficulty.	None
D10	New Challengers 1	Take on seven of the newcomers to the Smash Bros. series!	Your choice	Clear the stage on normal difficulty or higher.	None
D11	Duck Hunt!	Today's target: take out 10 ducks in a row. But there are some extra birds who are determined to get in the way...	Duck Hunt	Clear the stage on hard difficulty.	Unlock Lucina.
E1	New Challengers 2	Take on another seven newcomers to the Smash Bros. series!	Your choice	Clear the stage on normal difficulty or higher.	None
E2	The Break of Day	Collect the three parts required to assemble the Daybreak, then bring the ruin to your opponents with this powerful weapon!	Pit	Clear within 70 seconds.	None
E3	Aura Mastery	A true master of Aura doesn't need eyes to sense the enemy. With your ultimate Aura at the ready, defeat the invisible foes!	Lucario	Clear on normal difficulty or higher within 90 seconds.	None
E4	Identity Crisis	Two fierce heroines, each with her own secrets. Only one will reign victorious!	Sheik	Clear on hard difficulty within 50 seconds.	None
E5	Galactic Avenger	"The time has come to avenge my parents. Anyone in my path will be destroyed!"	Samus	Clear on normal difficulty or higher within 80 seconds.	None
E6	Yellow Devils	"Ah, it's my old foe, the Yellow Devil. But who are these other yellow monsters?! Is this the work of Dr. Wily?!"	Mega Man	Clear on normal difficulty or higher within 90 seconds.	None
E7	Family Ties	Your big, bad dad wants to show you the ropes of being a villain. Back him up as he takes on those pesky brothers!	Bowser Jr.	Clear on normal difficulty or higher within 30 seconds.	None
E8	All-Star Battle: Melee	Take on eight fighters who have been in the roster since *Super Smash Bros. Melee*!	Your choice	Clear the stage on normal difficulty or higher.	None
E9	Below the Belt	The battle is decided...but this contender won't stop attacking! It's up to the referee to intervene!	Mario	Clear on hard difficulty within 60 seconds.	Unlock Falco.
E10	Enough with the Kidnapping!	When you've been kidnapped this many times, maybe it's time to learn some self-defense...	Peach	Clear within 60 seconds.	Unlock R.O.B.
E11	All-Star Battle: Secret	Take on eight fighters who were secret unlockables in previous titles!	Your choice	Clear the stage on normal difficulty or higher.	None

ALL-STAR (SOLO)

ALL-STAR OVERVIEW

In All-Star, you must complete a series of seven matches, each of which contains fighters from various time periods of video game history. To win a match, simply KO all of the available opponents.

You're only given a single life to complete a game of All-Star—if you're KO'd, the game ends, and you must restart from the beginning. You are, however, provided with a limited supply of recovery items that can be used between matches. Knowing when to use each of the available items is an important part of any All-Star strategy.

BETWEEN MATCHES

After you clear a stage, you're given a reward based on your performance. When the results are displayed, use the Left Stick to review all of the rewards you've collected during your All-Star playthrough.

Between matches, your fighter appears in the rest area. The portal floating near the center of the rest area will transport your fighter to the next match, so avoid touching it until you're ready to continue. The portraits that appear near to the left of the portal indicate your opponents in the upcoming match. Sometimes a randomly selected collectible item appears near these portraits, so make sure you check that area before you head out.

Your available recovery items are located to the right of the rest area portal. There's no way to earn additional recovery items, so remember to pace yourself. The figurines that appear in the background indicate the fighters you've already defeated during your playthrough.

TRUE ALL-STAR

True All-Star only becomes available after you unlock all of the game's hidden characters. Until then, you have access to a temporary version of All-Star. This modified game mode is indicated by the small padlock icon that appears on the "All-Star" option within Games & More.

True All-Star is similar to the temporary version, but unlocking the full roster does trigger a few important changes. Some stages will contain a different number of opponents, you'll be provided with different recovery items, and you'll be eligible for different bonus scores.

OPPONENTS PER STAGE

STAGE	TEMPORARY ALL-STAR	TRUE ALL-STAR
Stage 1	5 opponents	7 opponents
Stage 2	7 opponents	7 opponents
Stage 3	7 opponents	7 opponents
Stage 4	5 opponents	7 opponents
Stage 5	6 opponents	7 opponents
Stage 6	5 opponents	7 opponents
Stage 7	5 opponents	6 opponents

DIFFICULTY

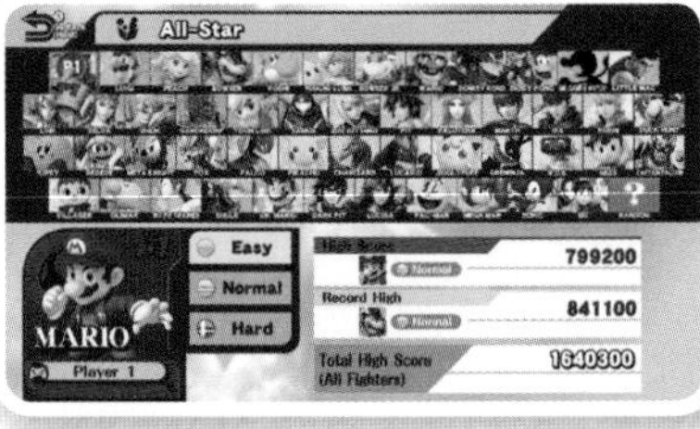

Both the temporary All-Star mode and the true All-Star mode offer three difficulty settings. Choose your desired setting during character selection.

At harder difficulties, your opponents are more aggressive and harder to launch. Playing at higher difficulties, however, also increases your potential score and rewards, and All-Star difficulty is an important part of completing some of the game's Challenges.

TIP

Earn higher scores by completing battles without taking damage and leaving recovery items in the rest area.

REST AREA RECOVERY ITEMS

RECOVERY ITEM	NUMBER AVAILABLE IN TEMPORARY ALL-STAR	NUMBER AVAILABLE IN TRUE ALL-STAR
Maxim Tomato	2	1
Fairy Bottle	1	1
Heart Container	1	2

CLEARING ALL-STAR

Whether your All-Star playthrough ends in victory or failure, you're able to keep all of the gold and rewards you've collected during your playthrough. Highlight specific items for additional details about your rewards. Of course, clearing All-Star does provide additional benefits—ayou'll unlock your fighter's Final Smash trophy, your fighter's alternate trophy will have a chance to appear in the Shop, and you'll trigger the staff credits.

STAFF CREDITS

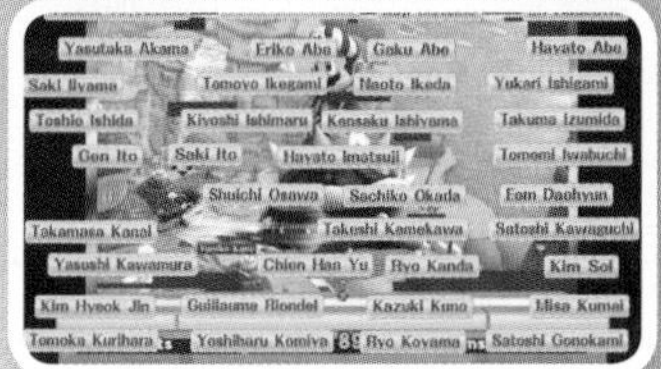

As in the Classic staff credits, you can attack the names in the All-Star staff credits to reveal the hidden image in the background. Jump up and use aerial attacks to reveal the top of the image as the names pass in front of any blank areas, then work your way down. Again, as you reveal more of the image, it becomes important to aim your shots. Look for the sparkles that help identify hidden sections, and then strike a name as it passes through the area.

STADIUM (SOLO)

STADIUM OVERVIEW

Stadium contains a variety of single-player game modes. You'll find several opportunities for combat, but Stadium also allows you to use your fighter's skills in new and interesting ways.

STADIUM MENU

Stadium Menu contains three selections, each of which offers a unique game mode:

- Target Blast!: Launch a bomb, and destroy as many obstacles as you can!
- Multi-Man Smash: Stand strong against an oncoming horde!
- Home-Run Contest: Help Sandbag go the distance! It's a glutton for punishment!

TARGET BLAST!

In Target Blast, you have two bombs to destroy as many targets and obstacles as you can. The bomb begins a brief countdown as soon as you touch it. Use the available time to damage the bomb, then use a Smash attack to launch it from the platform.

TIP

At the start of each round, follow the on-screen commands to zoom out for a better look at the available targets.

Success is based on timing and accuracy, so keep track of all pertinent factors. What was the bomb's damage percentage? How long did you charge your Smash attack? What was your position on the platform? How much time was left on the countdown? Knowing these answers allows you to make small adjustments in future attempts.

Bombs often create falling debris, so it can be very effective to aim for the higher targets during your first round—a well-placed bomb can create chain reactions of loose obstacles. If you're having trouble controlling the angle of your launch, try bouncing one of your bombs off of the nearby wall. This allows you to achieve dramatically different results with the same basic attacks. Utilizing the wall is also an important part of some Challenges.

Target Blast offers three distinct stages, each of which provides a different basic arrangement of targets and obstacles. To maximize your score, make sure you take advantage of any available explosive blocks. These blocks will detonate soon after they're jostled; hit an explosive block with a bomb, catch it in a bomb's blast, or send debris crashing into it! Every game of Target Blast contains at least a few random elements, but the basic layout of each stage remains fairly consistent between playthroughs.

MULTI-MAN SMASH

10-MAN SMASH

Defeat a 10-man army as fast as you can! Your opponents are very easy to launch, so you don't generally need to waste time with extended combos or charged attacks. A quick Smash attack is almost always enough to KO all fighters within range. Dash attacks can be particularly effective—especially when your opponents use projectile weapons to attack from a distance—and aerial attacks are great for dealing with more agile enemies.

100-MAN SMASH

Defeat a 100-man army as fast as you can! Your opponents are still very easy to launch, but their sheer numbers can make it difficult to defend yourself from incoming attacks. Keep an eye on your fighter's damage percentage, and take advantage of the items that occasionally appear near the top of the stage. Be particularly wary of enemies that utilize ranged attacks. Use the available platforms to move the battle away from incoming projectiles—just remember that some enemies can aim their projectiles upward!

3-MINUTE SMASH

Defeat as many enemies as you can within the time limit! You have three minutes and an endless supply of easily launched opponents. You can build a decent score using virtually any techniques, and the items that appear in the area can be very useful. Again, dodging projectile attacks will be an important part of effective defense. Avoid lingering in one spot for too long!

RIVAL SMASH

Defeat more enemies than your rival! Standard enemies are very easy to launch, but this also benefits your rival. There's no time limit, but you are limited to a single stock life—once you're defeated, the final score determines the winner. Your rival, on the other hand, has an infinite supply of stock lives. Scoring a KO on your rival is worth three points, but he or she can absorb much more damage than standard opponents.

> Your rival is always the same character you've selected for Rival Smash.
>
> **NOTE**

ENDLESS SMASH

No time limit! Fight until you can fight no more! Endless Smash lets you put your skills to the test. Like most Multi-Man Smash modes, your enemies are very easy to launch. Given enough time, though, you're sure to sustain enough damage that even the lightest hit will launch you clear out of that stage—so, use your preferred techniques to score points until that happens.

CRUEL SMASH

The elite army is ready to attack! Don't hold back—it's a fight to the end! In Cruel Smash, you opponents are extremely hard to launch. Unfortunately, the same can't be said for your fighter; each of your opponents packs enough of a punch to send you soaring off of the platform. Throwing your opponents is often effective. These powerful foes have minimal fall recovery, so throws can be particularly effective if your fighter is near the edge of the platform.

Characters equipped with a Counter special—like Marth, for example—can be very useful in Cruel Smash. It's often possible to catch several opponents with a single Counter. If you lure them to the end of the stage, you have an excellent chance of scoring multiple KOs with a single Counter.

HOME-RUN CONTEST

In Home-Run Contest, you must launch Sandbag as far as possible. Use your fighter's attacks to increase Sandbag's damage percentage, then grab the Home-Run Bat and use it to launch Sandbag from the platform. It's best to minimize the time you spend chasing Sandbag across the platform. Try using Smash attacks and tilt attacks to bounce Sandbag against the invisible wall that surrounds the platform. Sandbag's damage percentage will change the angle of its bounce, but small adjustments should allow you to land a steady series of hits.

As you pummel Sandbag, watch for the countdown to appear on the screen. With most fighters, you must grab the Home-Run Bat and begin your final attack before time runs out. If you grab the Home-Run Bat too early, you'll sacrifice any additional damage you might have delivered to Sandbag. Grabbing the Home-Run Bat too late, on the other hand, will prevent you from launching Sandbag at all.

Some characters have powerful attacks that can launch Sandbag without using the Home-Run Bat. Ganondorf's turn-around Warlock Punch is particularly effective. For most characters, however, knowing when to grab the Home-Run Bat and start your swing is an important part of maximizing your distance.

TRAINING

TRAINING OVERVIEW

Training is a great way to practice with—and against—specific fighters under a variety of conditions. Select your fighter, your opponent, and your stage just as you would when starting a game of Smash.

DURING TRAINING

By default, useful information is displayed near the screen's right edge. Use these panels to track the damage caused by your attacks and the length of any combos you perform.

Pause the game to adjust the available Training settings at any time during your session:

- Item: Use the Left Stick to cycle through the game's various items. Confirm a selection to spawn the indicated item on the battlefield.
- Speed: Change the game's speed. This includes options for constant effects and speed changes that are triggered by holding L.
- Camera: Choose between normal, zoom, and fixed camera settings.
- No. of CPUs: This setting determines if you face one, two, or three CPU opponents.
- CPU Behavior: Use this setting to determine whether your opponents stand still (stop), walk, run, jump, or attack. You even have the option to control your opponent with an additional controller!
- Damage: Adjust the current damage percentage for all fighters.
- Info: Hide or show the information panels displayed at the screen's right edge.

> **TIP**
>
> **Collectible items such as trophies and equipment sometimes appear on the ground. Any item Sandbag touches is automatically added to your collection!**

Group

GROUP OVERVIEW

Use the "Group" menu to play a variety of cooperative and competitive games—all you need is an extra controller and a nearby friend!

GROUP MENU

The "Group" menu contains four selections, each of which is a modified version of an existing Solo game mode:

- Classic: Work together to win the day!
- Events: Clear the given challenges to win rewards! (Strict "no-items" policy.)
- All-Star: Take on all of the fighters chronologically. No continues allowed!
- Stadium: Defeat an army, destroy targets, hit a home run...and beat your high scores!

CLASSIC (GROUP)

Group Classic works much the same way as Solo Classic. You and your partner must win a series of matches to face off against some combination of Master Hand, Crazy Hand, and Master Core. In Group Classic, Master Shadow always copies the fighter used by Player 1, Master Fortress never appears, and your enemies will always have more HP during the final battle. Employ the same basic strategies you'd use in Solo Classic. Watch each other's backs, and work together to claim victory!

In Group Classic, you'll have all the same options found in the Solo offering. You and your partner can select characters—including any custom sets you might have created—spend gold to adjust the intensity level, and move your figurines around the battlefield to choose your preferred opponents. Keep in mind that your figurines are linked. Struggling against your partner's movements will make it difficult to select a battle. So, work together!

For each battle, you and your partner each receive two stock lives. Work together to win the match before the 5-minute time limit runs out. Keep each other out of danger to help ensure your victory.

Clearing Group Classic will unlock the primary trophies of your respective fighters. Any rewards you and your partner earned along the way will also be added to your collection.

As an added bonus for clearing Group Classic, you and your partner can both attack the staff credits! Be careful, though—attacking your partner with strikes or items will hinder your progress.

EVENTS (GROUP)

The game offers a selection of cooperative Group Events. You and a friend can work together to clear challenging scenarios at various difficulty levels.

Complete Events with your partner to unlock new scenarios, and meet special objectives to earn valuable rewards. As in the game's Solo Events, you'll find some paths can only be unlocked after specific characters are added to your roster. Like Solo Events, Group Events each offer easy, normal, and hard difficulty levels.

EVENT DETAILS

The game contains a total of 24 Group Events connected by a series of branching paths.

TILE KEY

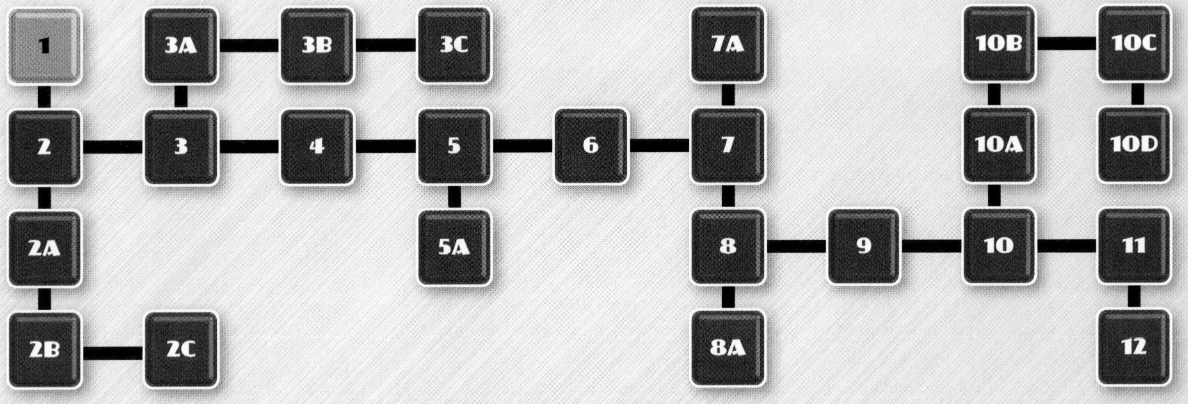

GROUP EVENTS

LOCATION	EVENT NAME	DESCRIPTION	REQUIRED CHARACTER	REWARD CONDITION	HIDDEN ROUTE CONDITION
1	A Lurking Menace	If you work together, taking out Bowser Jr. should be pretty easy. But be quick about it because he's got a surprise planned...	Mario/Luigi	Clear within 15 seconds.	None
2	Pokémon Multi Battle!	It's a two-on-two Pokémon Multi Battle! And it looks like your opponents have the same Pokémon as you!	Pikachu/ Charizard	Clear within 40 seconds.	Unlock the hidden character Falco.
2a	Visiting Onett	The Villager's come to visit, so Ness is giving him a tour of Onett. But suddenly a group of aliens interrupt their tour!	Ness/Villager	Clear on normal difficulty or higher within 60 seconds.	Unlock the hidden character Mr. Game & Watch.
2b	Keep 'Em off the Ship!	A mysterious group of bandits is invading! Don't let a single one of them on board!	Fox/Falco	Clear the stage on hard difficulty.	Unlock the hidden character Dark Pit.
2c	Sky Pirates	You have 60 seconds to dispatch all the guards and take control of the yellow plane.	Meta Knight/ Dark Pit	Clear on normal difficulty or higher within 50 seconds.	None
3	Getting Healthy	These two health nuts just finished a killer burpee sesh, brah! If they can win this battle, they might just treat themselves to some carbs!	Little Mac/ Wii Fit Trainer	Clear within 40 seconds.	Unlock the hidden character Wario.
3a	Wrecking Bros.	No job's too big when two brothers team up. Work quickly to demolish the building!	Mario/Luigi	Clear the stage on hard difficulty.	None
3b	A Royal Errand	Your friend's mother isn't feeling well. Collect 500G on the way to the Bazaar so you can buy her some medicine.	Marth/Robin	Clear the stage on normal difficulty or higher within 80 seconds.	None
3c	Food Fight	There are some baddies in Dream Land eating up everything in sight! Don't let 'em get away with that!	Kirby/King Dedede	Clear on normal difficulty or higher within 60 seconds.	None
4	1988	DK and Diddy have gone back in time. Now Mario's angry at them for kidnapping Pauline...but he's got the wrong guys!	Donkey Kong/ Diddy Kong	Clear within 60 seconds.	None
5	Full Speed Ahead	It's a high-octane battle in a world of high-octane fighters. Don't get left behind!	Sonic/Captain Falcon	Clear on normal difficulty or higher within 25 seconds.	Unlock the hidden character Lucina.
5a	Mirror Magic	Ganondorf's made giant mirror images of you that he's controlling with magic. Take him out—he's the real target!	Lucina/Ike	Clear on normal difficulty or higher within 30 seconds.	None
6	A Fairy Nice Trip	A pair of adventurers set off to find the fairy who once traveled with them. No foe will stand between them and Fairyland!	PAC-MAN/ Link	Clear after defeating at least 20 enemies.	None
7	Scheming Sorcerer	That scoundrel Kamek has sent a pair of tome-wielding magic users against you, and he's got reinforcements at the ready...	Yoshi/Toon Link	Clear on normal difficulty or higher within 90 seconds.	Unlock the hidden character Dr. Mario.
7a	Viral Visitors	These alien visitors are infected with a terrible virus. Send them packing before the whole island's infected.	Dr. Mario/ Peach	Clear within 60 seconds.	None
8	Solidarity	Pikmin and Lumas are all the family you need! Now go show those fancy "blood relative" families who's boss!	Olimar/ Rosalina & Luma	Clear on normal difficulty or higher within 90 seconds.	Unlock the hidden character R.O.B.

GROUP EVENTS (CONTINUED)

LOCATION	EVENT NAME	DESCRIPTION	REQUIRED CHARACTER	REWARD CONDITION	HIDDEN ROUTE CONDITION
8a	Robots vs. Dragons	Dragons have invaded the geothermal power plant! Good thing we've created a pair of combat robots for this very situation.	Mega Man/R.O.B.	Clear within 70 seconds.	None
9	Peach in Peril	"Kidnapping Peach is OUR thing! Anyone who lays a finger on her is getting launched into the next dimension!"	Bowser/ Bowser Jr.	Clear on normal difficulty or higher within 50 seconds.	Unlock the hidden character Dark Pit.
10	An Offering of Coins	Collect 1,000G to give as an offering to Lady Palutena! Just don't expect anything in return...	Pit/Dark Pit	Clear on normal difficulty or higher within 60 seconds.	None
10a	Poisonous Planet	The atmosphere on this planet must contain some sort of poisonous gas. Win the battle before it saps all of your health!	Olimar/Samus	Clear the stage on normal difficulty or higher.	Unlock the hidden character Mr. Game & Watch.
10b	Unlikely Allies	Oh no! Invaders from another dimension! ...But just this once, a goddess and a demon king team up to save us all.	Palutena/ Ganondorf	Clear on normal difficulty or higher within 80 seconds.	Unlock the hidden character Wario.
10c	Flat Fracas	Wario's gone searching for his roots so he can make the best-selling game ever. But...who are those guys? They look familiar...	Wario/Mr. Game & Watch	Clear on normal difficulty or higher within 50 seconds.	Unlock the hidden character Duck Hunt.
10d	Secret Smash	These retro-game heroes are smashing past their bedtime. They'll be in a world of hurt if Mom catches them!	Duck Hunt/ Mr. Game & Watch	Clear the stage on hard difficulty.	None
11	Final Battle Team-Up	It's you against a veritable who's who of villainy! Give it all you've got and win the final battle!	Your choice/ Your choice	Clear the stage on hard difficulty.	Unlock all characters.
12	The Ultimate Battle	They're all here! Defeat every single fighter without a break! If that's not an "ultimate battle," then what is?	Your choice/ Your choice	Clear the stage on hard difficulty.	None

ALL-STAR (GROUP)

Group All-Star works in much the same way as the single-player version. You and your friend must battle through a series of matches as you face every fighter on your roster. Work together to keep each other safe as you KO each of your enemies. As with the Solo offering, the true Group All-Star only becomes available after you've unlocked all of the game's characters.

Cooperation is the key to success; the game ends if either of you suffer a KO or a self-destruct. The rest area recovery items are meant to be shared, and keeping your team healthy should be a priority. Communicate with your partner to determine if and when each item should be used. Battle your way to victory to unlock your respective fighters' secondary trophies and trigger the staff credits!

NOTE

Rival Smash is only available in Solo Multi-Man Smash.

MULTI-MAN SMASH

Multi-Man contains cooperative versions of 10-Man Smash, 100-Man Smash, 3-Minute Smash, Endless Smash, and Cruel Smash. In each game mode, up to four players work together to defeat enemies and meet their chosen Multi-Man objectives.

STADIUM (GROUP)

TARGET BLAST!

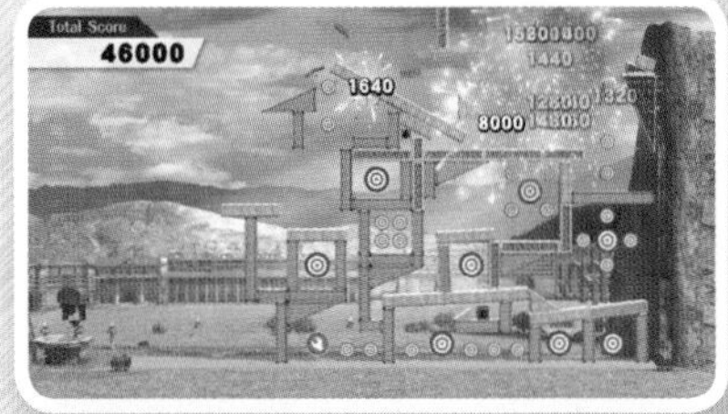

In Group Target Blast, up to four players compete to see who can earn the highest score. All three Target Blast stages are available, so pick your fighters and launch those bombs!

HOME-RUN CONTEST

In Group Home-Run Contest, two players can work together to launch Sandbag as far as possible, or they can take turns to see which player can earn the highest score.

Custom

CUSTOM MENUS

Custom mode separates fighters into two distinct categories:

- Mii Fighters: Create or edit a Mii Fighter.
- Characters: Assign Specials and equipment to the fighters on your roster.

MII FIGHTERS

To create a new Mii Fighter, simply select one of your Miis and choose a basic fighting style:

- Brawler: A fighter skilled in hand-to-hand combat.
- Swordfighter: A warrior versed in the art of swordplay.
- Gunner: An expert in long-range projectile combat.

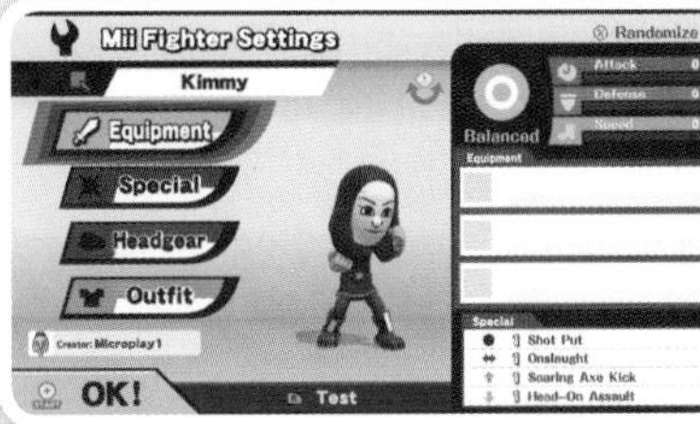

Once you've input a name for your new Mii Fighter, you're free to assign equipment, Special moves, headgear, and outfits to create your ideal warrior. You can even press Ⓧ to randomize. When you're happy with your selections, press R to test your new fighter, or simply save your work to return to the previous menu.

CHARACTERS

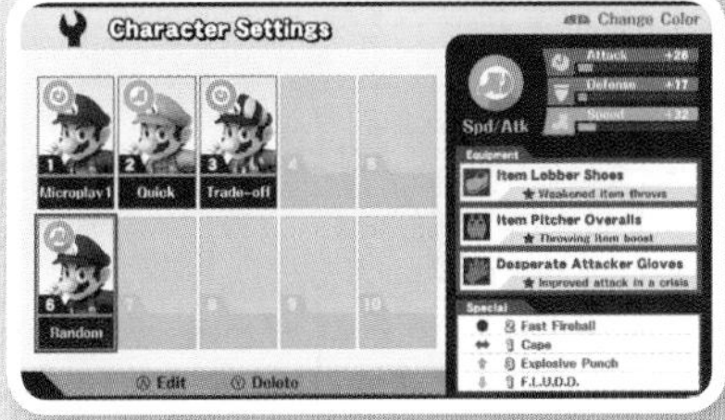

The "Characters" option allows you to select a fighter from your existing roster. You can also choose a new default look and rename your character's custom set to help differentiate it from any existing versions.

You can use the equipment and Special moves you've collected to create up to 10 custom sets for each of the characters on your roster. The right combination of stats and bonus effects can make all the difference in tough battles. Be prepared for every scenario! Press R to test your custom set, or save it to return to the previous menu.

Stage Builder

Use the Stage Builder to create new and unique battlegrounds for a customized Smash experience. You'll find plenty of options to explore, so grab your Nintendo Wii U GamePad and start building!

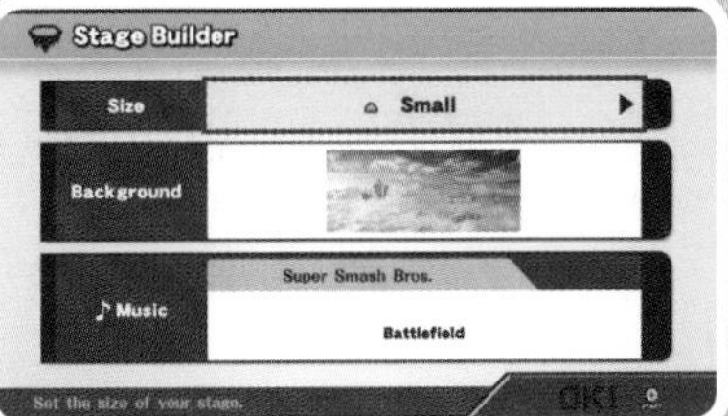

When you create a new stage, you must start by choosing three basic elements:

- Size: Set the size of your stage. You can choose between small, medium, and large.
- Background: Set the background for your stage. The Stage Builder offers five visually distinct backgrounds.
- Music: Set the background music for your stage. You have plenty of options, so pick the track that works for you.

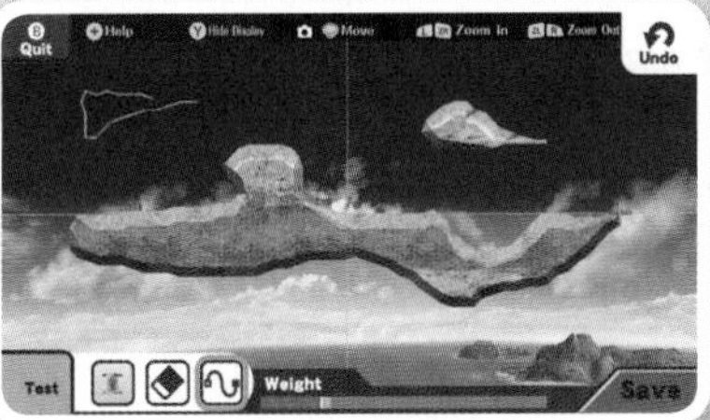

Once you've chosen your basic settings, use the Wii U GamePad to create platforms and access the available menus. You can create custom shapes by drawing on the GamePad's Touch Screen with the stylus, or simply tap two points to create a straight line between them. When two ends of one or more lines meet, the indicated shape becomes a stationary platform. You can even use the available tools to place pre-made elements wherever you like.

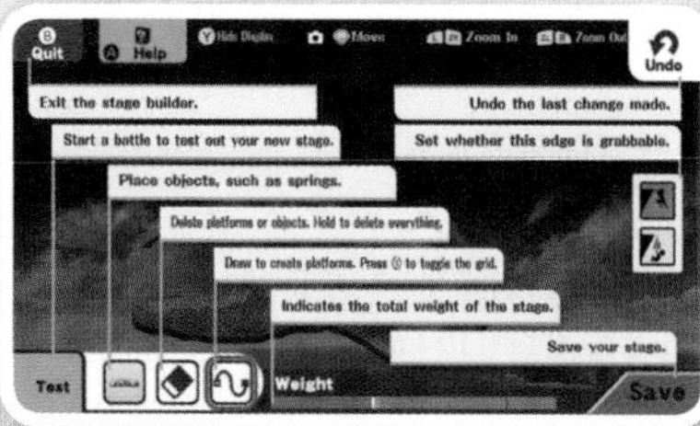

Use the on-screen commands to control the camera or hide the display for a better look at your workspace. Press the + button on the GamePad to open the Help menu. This provides simple descriptions of various Stage Builder menus and features.

Use the available tools to add elements like hazards and moving platforms, erase created objects, or change the texture of existing platforms. The "weight" bar at the bottom of the screen grows as you add elements to the stage. If you fill the bar, you won't be able to add new elements without first erasing part of your creation.

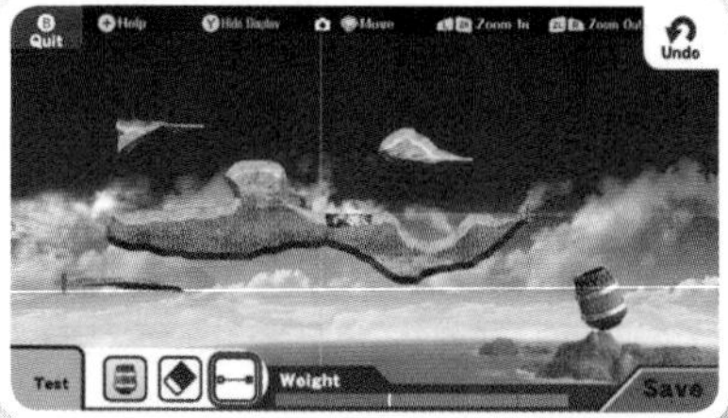

You can even use the GamePad Touch Screen to determine whether or not certain edges can be grabbed. Tap a specific edge with the stylus to change this setting.

It can be helpful to test your stage as you incorporate new elements. Select this option on the GamePad to practice against a CPU opponent. You can then adjust elements that didn't work out quite as you might have hoped. When you're satisfied, save your stage for use in various game modes!

Options

OPTIONS MENU

The "Options" menu is divided into four categories:

- Controls: Change the button assignments.
- Sound: Adjust the volume of music, sound effects, and voices.
- Internet Options: Change your online settings and profile.
- My Music: Manually select the music that will play during battle.

CONTROLS

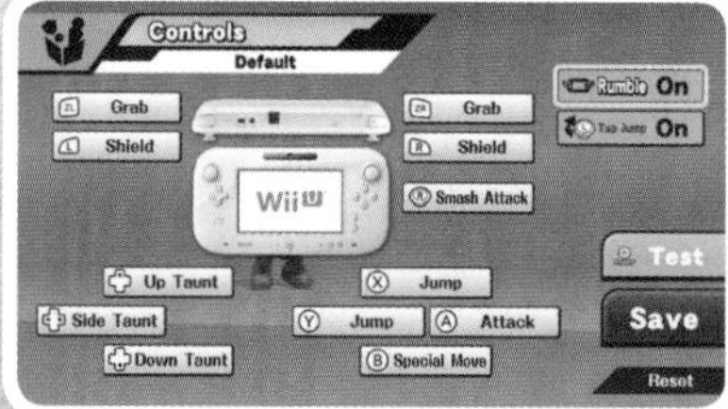

Review the default button assignments for various controllers or create your own custom control schemes. Select an available button, then scroll to the options to assign a new function. You can then test your changes and save for use in battle.

SOUND

Adjust the volume of the game's music, sound effects, and voices to match your tastes. You can preview your settings before you exit, or use the tab near the bottom of the screen to access all of the music and voices you've managed to collect.

INTERNET OPTIONS

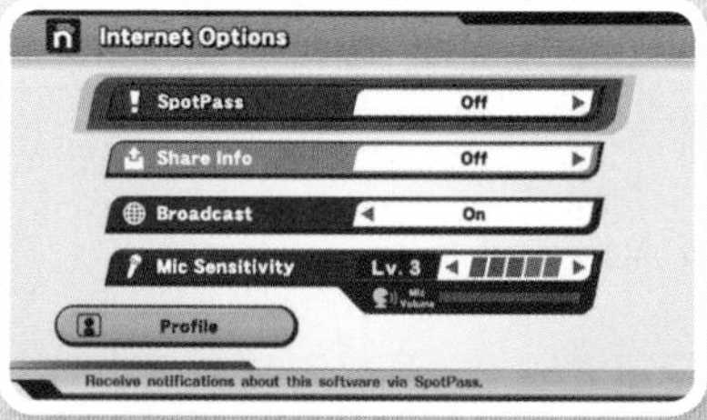

This menu allows you to change your online settings and edit your personal profile:

- SpotPass: This setting determines whether or not you receive SpotPass notifications about the game.
- Share Info: This setting determines whether or not Nintendo will receive information about how you play the game.
- Broadcast: This setting determines whether or not other players will be able to watch your battles in Spectator mode.
- Profile: Select this option to change your profile icon, change your greeting, or edit the short messages assigned to the +Control Pad.

CHALLENGES

Challenges Overview

The game offers a total of 140 Challenges. Complete these tasks to add them to your Challenge panel and unlock the corresponding rewards. You'll unlock many of these Challenges by simply exploring the game's many modes and features. Some of these tasks, however, require a fair amount of time, skill, and determination.

Revealing Challenges

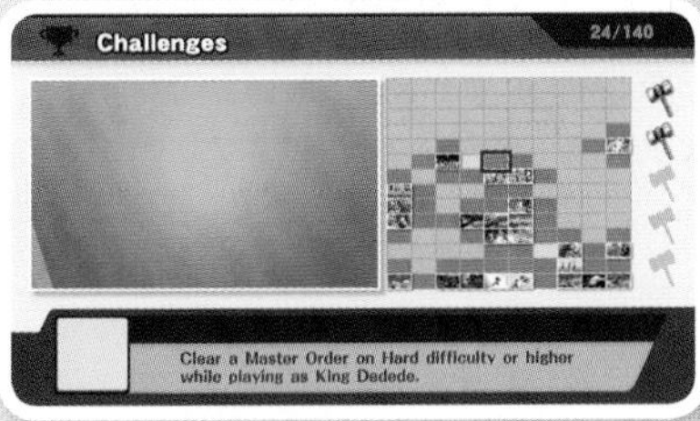

You start the game with a large panel containing 140 gray tiles, each of which holds a hidden Challenge. You must complete at least one of these secret tasks before you are provided any additional information. Once a Challenge is revealed, highlight its tile for details about the related task.

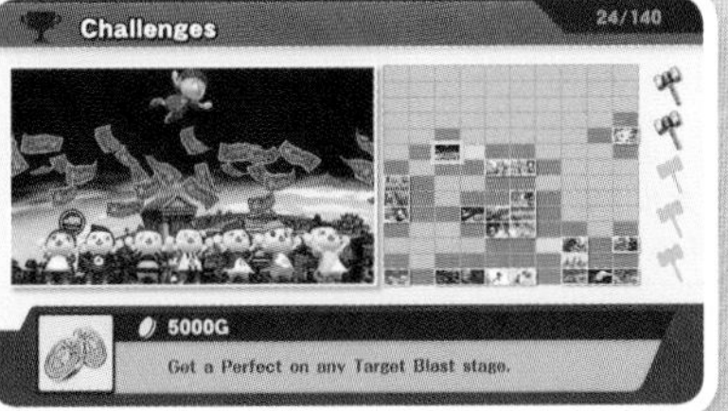

When you successfully complete a Challenge, an image appears on the corresponding tile. Select this image to review the task you've completed and the resulting reward. Additionally, completing a Challenge causes any adjacent tiles to change color. Blue tiles represent revealed (but incomplete) Challenges. If a tile turns light blue, it means that completing the revealed Challenge will grant you a hammer in addition to the standard reward.

There are five hammers hidden within the Challenge panel. When you complete an appropriate Challenge, a single-use hammer appears in one of the slots to the right of the panel. Hammers can be used to unlock Challenges without performing the corresponding tasks.

USING HAMMERS

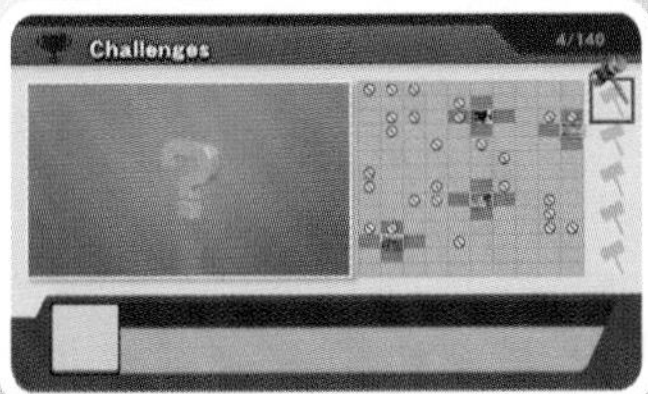

When you use a hammer to open a tile, you gain all the benefits of having completed the corresponding Challenge—you'll gain any rewards or hammers your selected tile contains and reveal the Challenges on any adjacent tiles. This allows you to bypass particularly difficult Challenges or to gain useful rewards fairly early in the game.

It's important to note, however, that not all Challenges can be cracked. When you select a hammer, look for any "no symbols" that appear on the Challenge panel. These tiles are impervious to hammers and can only be unlocked by completing the stated Challenges through gameplay.

Once you've completed the Challenge panel, any unused hammers will go to waste—plan accordingly!

PANEL KEY

1	2	3	4	5	6	7	8	9	10
11	12	13	14	15	16	17	18	19	20
21	22	23	24	25	26	27	28	29	30
31	32	33	34	35	36	37	38	39	40
41	42	43	44	45	46	47	48	49	50
51	52	53	54	55	56	57	58	59	60
61	62	63	64	65	66	67	68	69	70
71	72	73	74	75	76	77	78	79	80
81	82	83	84	85	86	87	88	89	90
91	92	93	94	95	96	97	98	99	100
101	102	103	104	105	106	107	108	109	110
111	112	113	114	115	116	117	118	119	120
121	122	123	124	125	126	127	128	129	130
131	132	133	134	135	136	137	138	139	140

CHALLENGE DETAILS

POSITION	CHALLENGE	REWARD
1	⊘ Clear Classic at intensity 9.0 without losing a single life.	Equipment: Double Final Smasher Protection Badge
2	⊘ Play as Lucina and score 8 or more KOs in a single Solo Cruel Smash	Equipment: Vampire Brawn Badge
3	⊘ Play alone and as Dr. Mario and get a Fever Rush 8 or more times in a single game of Trophy Rush.	Gold: 100,000G
4	Play as Pit and score 4 or more KOs in a single match of Solo Cruel Smash.	Trophy: Reaper
5	Play as PAC-MAN in Stage 3 and score 300,000 or more in Solo Target Blast using the back wall.	Trophy: Whomp
6	Clear Solo Classic in 12 minutes at intensity 9.0 while playing as Marth.	Equipment: Critical Hitter Sword
7	Collect all of the special moves.	Equipment: Smooth Lander Brawn Badge
8	Collect all of the custom outfits.	Trophy: Able Sisters
9	Get 8 or more KOs in a single Cruel Smash.	Trophy: Toadsworth
10	Collect all of the custom headgear.	Trophy: Majora's Mask
11	Clear All-Star on hard difficulty with all the characters.	Trophy: Saki Amamiya
12	Destroy a total of 50,000 or more blocks in Trophy Rush.	Equipment: Moon Launcher Protection Badge
13	Clear the true Solo All-Star mode without recovering health between rounds while playing as Captain Falcon.	Trophy: Deathborn
14	Score at least 450,000 points in a single game of Target Blast on Stage 3.	Trophy: Magolor
15	⊘ Collect over 300,000G	Trophy: Prince of Sablé
16	Collect 700 unique trophies.	Equipment: Item Hitter Agility Badge
17	Get a Perfect on every stage in Target Blast.	Gold: 20,000G
18	Clear Crazy Orders after 20 or more turns while playing as Mario.	Trophy: F.L.U.D.D.
19	Get a score of more than 85 in a single Rival Smash.	Trophy: Waluigi
20	Collect all the CDs.	Trophy: Tac
21	Clear Classic at intensity 9.0 without any customizations.	Trophy: Knuckle Joe
22	⊘ Clear the true Solo All-Star mode within 6 minutes while playing as Jigglypuff.	Trophy: Koffing
23	⊘ Clear Classic at intensity 8.0 with 3 or more characters.	CD: Master Fortress: Second Wave
24	Start the final battle with 10 fighters in Smash Tour.	Trophy: Flying Man

CHALLENGE DETAILS (CONTINUED)

POSITION	CHALLENGE	REWARD
25	Clear the true Solo All-Star mode on hard while playing as Duck Hunt.	Trophy: Samus (Dark Suit)
26	Play as Gonondorf and hit Sandbag at least 3280 ft. in Solo Home-Run Contest.	Trophy: King K. Rool
27	Clear the true Solo All-Star within 6 minutes while playing as Shulk.	Trophy: Mechonis
28	Clear a 3-Minute Smash after getting 120 or more KOs.	Trophy: Kritter
29	Clear the true All-Star mode on normal difficulty or higher without using healing items.	Gold: 15,000G
30	Complete the reward conditions for all of the Solo Events.	Trophy: Galacta Knight
31	Clear the true Solo All-Star mode without recovering health between rounds while playing as Zero Suit Samus.	Trophy: Gunship
32	Clear the "All-Star Battle: Secret" Event on hard difficulty.	Trophy: Shadow
33	Clear Classic at intensity 7.0 or higher with all the characters.	Headgear: Regal Crown
34	Clear the "The FINAL Battle" Event on hard difficulty.	Trophy: Souflee
35	Play as Bowser Jr. in Stage 1 and get a score of 150,000 or more in a single game of Solo Target Blast.	Equipment: Countdown Drill
36	Get a chain of at least 100 in Trophy Rush without taking any damage while playing alone and as Samus.	Equipment: KO Healer Arm Cannon
37	Clear All-Star on hard difficulty with 8 or more characters.	Equipment: Caloric Immortal Protection Badge
38	Clear the true Solo All-Star mode on hard while playing as Ike.	Trophy: Black Knight
39	Play Solo Cruel Smash as Luigi and survive for 1 minute.	Trophy: Mr. L
40	Hit Sandbag 3,280 ft. Or more in Home-Run Contest.	Trophy: Daisy (Baseball)
41	Clear a Master Orders ticket with a difficulty rating of intense.	Equipment: Desperate Specialist Agility Badge
42	Clear Crazy Orders after 12 or more turns.	Trophy: Soda Popinski
43	Use Diddy Kong and get 3 or more KOs on your rival in a single Rival Smash.	Trophy: Dixie Kong
44	Clear the true All-Star mode on hard difficulty.	Equipment: Perfect-Shield Helper Brawn Badge
45	Get 120 or more KOs in a single Endless Smash.	Equipment: Unharmed Attacker Agility Badge
46	Clear Classic at intensity 8.0 with 2 or more characters.	CD: Master Fortress: First Wave
47	Clear the "Kirby's Crazy Appetite" Event on hard difficulty.	Trophy: Fire Kirby
48	Clear 10-Man Smash within 25 seconds with all characters.	Trophy: Wonder-Yellow
49	Clear a Solo 3-Minute Smash after getting 100 or more KOs while playing as Mii Gunner.	Trophy: Birdo
50	Get a chain of 300 or more in a single game of Trophy Rush.	Trophy: CommanderVideo
51	Play as Ness in Stage 3 and get a score of 200,000 or more in a single game of Solo Target Blast.	Trophy: Jeff
52	Play as Meta Knight and score 90 KOs or more in Solo Endless Smash.	Trophy: Substitute Doll
53	Get a Perfect on any stage in Target Blast.	Gold: 5,000G
54	Clear all of the Solo Events.	Trophy: Special Flag
55	Clear a Master Order on hard difficulty or higher while playing as King Dedede.	CD: King Dedede's Theme
56	Clear a Solo 3-Minute Smash after getting 110 or more KOs while playing as Bowser.	Trophy: Banzai Bill
57	Clear Solo 10-Man Smash without taking any damage while playing as Dr. Mario	Masterpiece: Dr. Mario
58	Play alone and as Fox and get a Fever Rush 6 or more times in a single game of Trophy Rush.	Trophy: Krystal

CHALLENGE DETAILS (CONTINUED)

POSITION	CHALLENGE	REWARD
59	KO your rival 4 or more times in a single Rival Smash.	Trophy: Ice Climbers
60	Clear Crazy Orders after 10 or more turns while playing as Greninja.	CD: Battle! (Reshiram/Zekrom)
61	🚫 Clear a Master Order on very hard difficulty or higher.	Equipment: Trade-Off Attacker Protection Badge
62	Get a chain of at least 200 in Trophy Rush while playing alone and as Donkey Kong.	CD: DK Rap
63	Get 3 or more Checkpoint Bonuses in Smash Tour.	Trophy: Bionis
64	Clear Solo 100-Man Smash within 3 minutes while playing as Mii Sword-fighter.	CD: Multi-Man Melee 2 (Melee)
65	Collect 300 unique trophies.	Trophy: Timmy & Tommy
66	Score at least 200,000 points in a single game of Target Blast on Stage 2.	Special Move: Dire Hydrant (PAC-MAN)
67	Defeat 12 or more fighters in a single Smash Tour.	Ticket: Crazy Orders Pass
68	Come in first in 5 or more Smash Tour battles.	Gold: 2,000G
69	View every fighter's Final Smash.	Trophy: Smash Ball
70	Destroy 250 or more blocks in a single game of Trophy Rush.	Ticket: Crazy Orders Pass
71	🚫 Get 1 or more KOs in a single Cruel Smash.	Stage: Duck Hunt
72	Clear Solo Classic within 20 minutes while playing as Olimar.	CD: Mission Mode
73	Play as Zelda in Stage 1 and get a score of 150,000 or more in a single game of Solo Target Blast.	Trophy: Wolf Link
74	🚫 Clear Solo Classic at intensity 5.5 or higher, playing as Wario without any customizations.	CD: Full Steam Ahead (Spirit Tracks)
75	Clear Solo All-Star on normal difficulty or higher while playing as Lucario.	Pokémon: Meloetta
76	Clear Solo 100-Man Smash within 3 minutes while playing as Sonic.	Equipment: Speed Skater Shoes
77	🚫 Hit Sandbag between 1,640 and 1,656 ft. in Home-Run Contest while playing as R.O.B.	Trophy: Dr. Light
78	Play alone and as Robin and get a Fever Rush 4 or more times in a single game of Trophy Rush.	CD: Conquest (Ablaze)
79	Play alone and as Pikachu and destroy 200 blocks in a single game of Trophy Rush.	Pokémon: Xerneas
80	Clear 10-Man Smash within 17 seconds.	CD: Gerudo Valley
81	Play as Sheik and score 50 KOs or more in Solo Endless Smash.	Trophy: Tetra
82	Hit Sandbag between 1,640 and 1,656 ft. in Home-Run Contest.	Trophy: Wonder-Green
83	🚫 Clear the "Fitness Junkie" Event on normal difficulty or higher.	Trophy: Snorlax
84	🚫 Get a chain of at least 150 in Trophy Rush while playing alone and as Falco.	Special Move: Accele-Reflector (Falco)
85	Get a max combo of 50 or more in Training.	Equipment: Unharmed Speed Demon Agility Badge
86	Hit Sandbag 1,968 ft. or more in Home-Run Contest.	Masterpiece: EarthBound
87	Use a Tour Item 18 or more times in Smash Tour.	Trophy: Riki
88	Play as Link and score 50 KOs or more in Solo Endless Smash.	Special Move: Ripping Boomerang (Link)
89	🚫 Play alone and as Mr. Game & Watch and destroy 100 blocks in a single game of Trophy Rush.	Stage: Flat Zone X
90	Clear Solo Classic at intensity 5.5 or higher while playing as Kirby.	Masterpiece: Kirby's Adventure
91	Play as Palutena in Stage 2 and score 80,000 or more in Solo Target Blast using the back wall.	CD: In the Space-Pirate Ship
92	Deal the final blow to a boss in Smash Tour.	Trophy: Ridley

CHALLENGE DETAILS (CONTINUED)

POSITION	CHALLENGE	REWARD
93	Clear Crazy Orders after 5 or more turns.	Equipment: Speed Crasher Agility Badge
94	Get a score of more than 20 in a single Rival Smash.	CD: Star Wolf (Star Fox: Assault)
95	Play as Charizard and get a score of 328 ft. or more in Solo Home-Run Contest without using the bat.	Special Move: Rock Hurl (Charizard)
96	KO your rival 2 or more times in a single Rival Smash.	CD: Super Mario Bros. 3 Medley
97	Clear the "No Mere Sparring Match" Event on normal difficulty or higher.	Masterpiece: Punch-Out!! Featuring Mr. Dream
98	Clear Solo Classic without losing a single life while playing as Little Mac.	CD: Title (Punch-Out!!)
99	Obtain a score of 25 or more ina a single Rival Smash while playing as Dark Pit.	Special Move: Guiding Bow (Dark Pit)
100	Play as Toon Link in Stage 2 and get a score of 120,000 or more in a single game of Solo Target Blast.	Trophy: Lor Starcutter
101	Reveal the entire wall during the credits.	CD: Credits
102	Clear Classic at intensity 5.5 or higher.	CD: Master Core
103	Get a max combo of 30 or more in Training.	CD: Title Theme (Wii Sports Resort)
104	Clear Solo Classic while playing as Yoshi.	Masterpiece: Yoshi
105	Clear 10-Man Smash within 25 seconds.	Outfit: Fancy Suit
106	Play as Peach and hit Sandbag at least 1,049 ft. in Solo Home-Run Contest.	CD: Title/Ending (Super Mario World)
107	Get 50 or more KOs in a single Endless Smash.	Equipment: No-Flinch Smash Protection Badge
108	Clear Classic without losing a single life.	Trophy: Dr. Kawashima
109	Clear All-Star on normal difficulty or higher.	Equipment: Hyper Smasher Brawn Badge
110	Clear 100-Man Smash within 3 minutes.	CD: Wii Fit Plus Medley
111	Clear the "Behind Enemy Lines" Event.	Trophy: Tricky
112	Clear 100-Man Smash.	CD: Tetris: Type B
113	Clear 3-Minute Smash after getting 60 or more KOs.	Gold: 1,000G
114	Have the game on for more than 10 hours.	Trophy: Resetti
115	Clear Classic at intensity 2.0 with 5 or more characters.	Trophy: Master Hand
116	Collect 50 different special moves.	Equipment: Nimble Dodger Agility Badge
117	Recover the stat boosts a Metroid stole from you in Smash Tour.	CD: Vs. Parasite Queen
118	Score at least 150,000 points in a single game of Target Blast on Stage 1.	Special Move: Exploding Popgun (Diddy Kong)
119	Clear the "The Falchion's Seal" Event on normal difficulty or higher.	Special Move: Dashing Assault (Marth)
120	Get a chain of 100 or more in a single game of Trophy Rush.	Headgear: Chomp Hat
121	Clear Solo 10-Man Smash within 35 seconds while playing as Mii Brawler.	Outfit: Fighter Uniform
122	Collect 15 different special moves.	Equipment: Air Attacker Brawn Badge
123	Clear Crazy Orders while playing as Villager.	Trophy: Rover
124	Clear the "When Lightning Strikes" Event.	Stage: Pokémon Stadium 2
125	Collect 50 unique trophies.	Trophy: Celeste
126	Clear the "Playing Tricks" Event.	Stage: Smashville
127	Clear a Master Orders ticket while playing as Mega Man.	Special Move: Tornado Hold (Mega Man)
128	Clear Crazy Orders.	Trophy: Crazy Hand
129	Play all the maps in Smash Tour.	Stage: PAC-LAND
130	Get a chain of at least 50 in Trophy Rush while playing alone and as Wii Fit Trainer.	Trophy: Wii Fit U Trainer

CHALLENGE DETAILS (CONTINUED)

POSITION	CHALLENGE	REWARD
131	Clear 10-Man Smash.	Gold: 100G
132	Clear a Master Orders ticket while playing as Rosalina & Luma.	CD: Rosalina in the Observatory/Luma's Theme
133	Clear a Master Orders ticket.	Ticket: Crazy Orders Pass
134	Bump into an enemy who appears on the board during Smash Tour.	Trophy: Nabbit
135	Create a Mii Fighter in Custom.	Headgear: Peach's Crown
136	Customize a fighter in Custom.	Equipment: Shield Regenerator Protection Badge
137	Create a stage in the Stage Builder.	Trophy: Saharah
138	Bump into every opponent while on the board in Smash Tour.	Outfit: Mecha Suit
139	Clear the "The Original Heavyweights" Event.	Stage: Kong Jungle 64
140	Clear All-Star.	Pokémon: Victini

Challenge Tips

Most of the game's Challenges are straightforward, and many of them can be completed without any special techniques or knowledge. Some of them, however, call for a significant amount of skill and strategy. Here are some tips to help you complete a few of the game's trickier Challenges.

COMBOS

All of the combo Challenges must be performed in Training. This not only makes it easy to monitor the effectiveness of each attempt, but it allows you make each attempt under the ideal conditions.

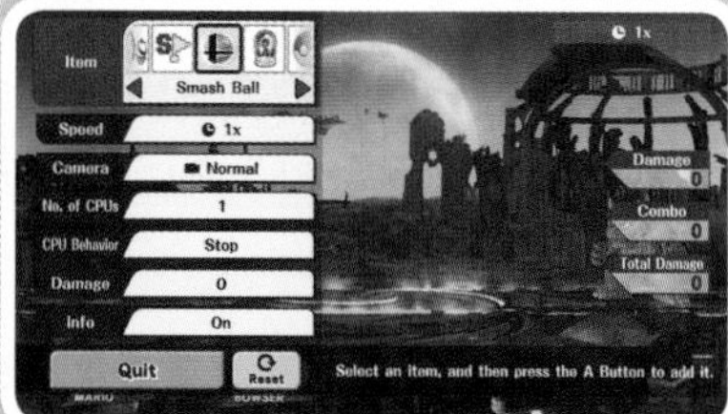

By using the available items, any character should be able to perform combos of at least 50 hits. Stand near your opponent, then activate the Training menu and summon four X Bombs and four Smart Bombs. Grab a Smart Bomb and toss it onto the pile to trigger an explosive combo!

CLASSIC

Many of the available Challenges involve clearing Classic. The best way to complete most of these Challenges is to simply hone your skills with plenty of practice. However, there are few things you can do to gain an advantage as you master Classic.

For Challenges that allow customizations, choosing the right equipment can make all the difference. Remember that equipment with negative bonus effects tend to grant much better stats boosts. If you're attempting to clear Classic at intensity 9.0 without losing a life, consider using a piece of equipment with the "No respawn invincibility" bonus effect. Since respawning would mean failing the Challenge, this negative bonus effect won't be a factor! If a Classic-related Challenge involves a strict time limit, use equipment to build up your fighter's "Attack" rating for faster KOs.

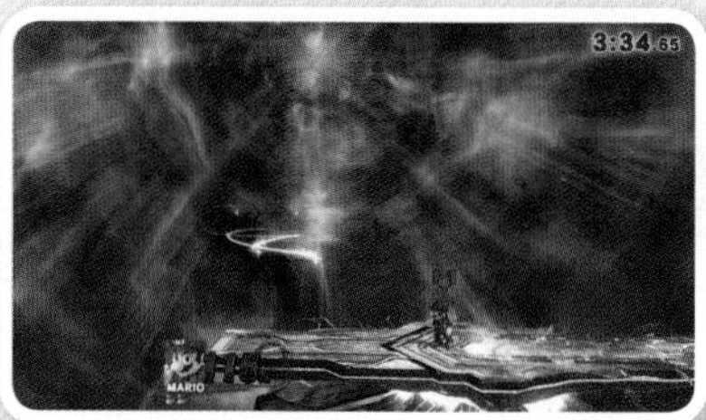

Of course, equipment with positive bonus effects can also be a big help. Anything that grants health recovery, for example, will make it much easier to survive early battles. Just remember that at intensities of 5.1 and above, you'll eventually face Master Core's mirror form. This doppelganger will receive the same stat boosts and bonus effects of any equipment your fighter is using.

NOTE

For more details about clearing Classic, please refer to this guide's Wii U Games & More coverage.

All-Star

All-Star doesn't allow the use of any customizations, and many of the Challenges related to All-Star specify the characters that must be used or the difficulty levels that must be cleared. As such, completing most of these Challenges is simply a matter of developing the required skills.

If an All-Star Challenge doesn't require the use of a specific character, consider choosing Robin for his (or her) Down Special, Nosferatu. This move allows Robin to regain health throughout the game without using the rest area recovery items.

Challenges that specify true All-Star can only be completed after you've unlocked all of the game's hidden characters.

NOTE

Staff Credits

When you complete a game of Classic or All-Star, you can use your fighter to attack the staff credits. When done properly, attacking individual names reveals a image on the back wall. For a name to contribute to the image, however, you must hit it at just the right time and in just the right spot. Jump up and use aerial attacks to reveal the top of the image as the names pass in front of any blank areas, then work your way down.

As you reveal more of the image, it becomes important to aim your shots. Look for the sparkles that help identify hidden sections, then strike a name as it passes through the area.

Crazy Orders

It's much easier to perform well in Crazy Orders once you've collected equipment with specific bonus effects. One of the best ways to stay ahead of the clock is to combine equipment with the "Home-Run Bat equipped" and "Quick bat swing" bonus effects. This can result in remarkably fast KOs, allowing you to speed through many more turns than you might otherwise clear in the 10-minute time limit. To help ensure your fighter stays healthy, use your remaining equipment slot for something that grants a recovery-based bonus effect. Equipment with the "KO Healer" bonus effect is particularly good for fast recovery. Best of all, this strategy works well with any character!

3-Minute Smash

To score 110 KOs within a single round of 3-Minute Smash, you need to stay very active. Luckily, your opponents tend to be very aggressive. It's often best to stick to the main platform and use tilt attacks to score a steady stream of KOs as your enemies approach. If your enemies linger out of reach, use a dash attack to close the distance as quickly as possible.

Mii Gunners are bound to be your most troublesome opponents, so make taking them out your priority. Dodge to the left or right to quickly close short distances. If a Mii Gunner refuses to approach, hop onto one of the available platforms to get clear of incoming projectile attacks. This often forces a Mii Gunner to relocate as you deal with nearby opponents.

Cruel Smash

In Cruel Smash, it can be difficult to score even a single KO before you're eliminated. There are, however, a few things you can do to improve your chances. Some fighters—like Mario and Luigi—spin around while they perform Back Throws. This allows you to strike nearby opponents as you create a little breathing room.

Characters equipped with a Counter special—like Marth, for example—can be very effective. Because your opponents are particularly aggressive, it's often possible to catch several of them with a single Counter. When this happens near the edge of the stage, you have an excellent chance of scoring multiple KOs. No matter which character you use, however, try to move the battle to the edge of the platform. Your opponents have trouble recovering from falls, and the temporary invincibility granted by your own edge moves can sometimes allow you to escape dangerous situations.

TARGET BLAST

HOME-RUN CONTEST

Many of the game's Home-Run Contest Challenges can be completed with standard techniques, but a few require the use of specific characters and attack combos. Completing these Challenges is likely to take a fair amount of practice, but there are some specific strategies that can yield consistent results:

GANONDORF

- Hit Sandbag with two uncharged Side Smash attacks.
- Perform seven Side Tilt attacks.
- Face away from Sandbag and perform a turn-around Warlock Punch (immediately after you begin the Warlock Punch, push the Left Stick toward Sandbag).

CHARIZARD

- Hit Sandbag with an uncharged Side Smash attack.
- Perform six uncharged Down Smash attacks.
- Launch Sandbag with a fully charged Side Smash.

R.O.B.

- Hit Sandbag with an uncharged Side Smash attack.
- Move into range and hit Sandbag with three more uncharged Side Smash attacks. This should cause Sandbag to bounce past you.
- Turn back to the left and hit Sandbag with two more uncharged Side Smash attacks.
- Grab the Home-Run Bat and move as close to Sandbag as possible to deliver one last Side Smash.

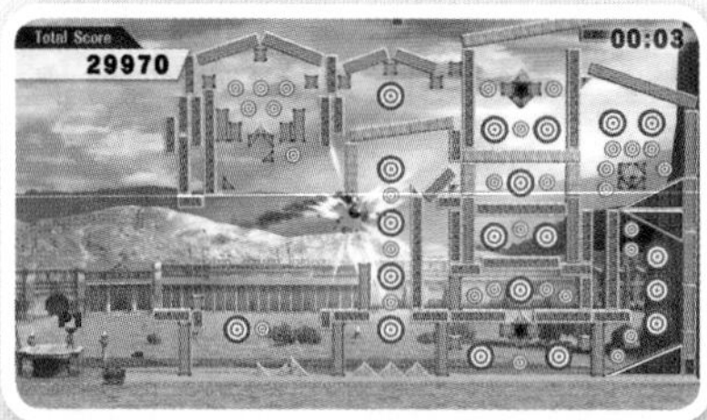

Clearing all of the Target Blast targets is always a little tricky. You have to consider your character's attacks, the position on the platform, and exactly when to launch the bomb. It takes a bit of practice to find the right combination of moves for each situation, but once you've mastered specific sequence of attacks, you'll have a better chance of achieving consistent results with each character.

BOWSER JR. ON STAGE 1

BOMB 1

- Jump over the first bomb and hit it with a Back Air attack (to the left) just before you land. The bomb should now show 14% damage.
- Hit the bomb with one Side Tilt attack (to the left). The bomb should now show 22% damage.
- Jab the bomb with a single neutral standing attack (to the left). The bomb should now show 25% damage.
- Quickly hit the bomb with a Side Tilt attack (to the left). The bomb should now show 33% damage.
- Use a fully charged Side Smash attack to launch the bomb off of the back wall (to the left). The bomb should show 55% damage as it leaves the platform.

BOMB 2

- Approach the bomb and hit it with two Side Tilt attacks (to the right). The bomb should now show 16% damage.
- Launch the bomb with a fully charged Side Smash attack (to the right).

> **Make sure you hit the bomb with the tip of each attack. Use the bomb's damage percentage to ensure that you've properly performed each step, and make sure to avoid accidentally bumping or pushing the bomb.**
>
> **NOTE**

ZELDA ON STAGE 1

BOMB 1

- Bump the bomb to activate it.
- Let the bomb explode without launching it.

BOMB 2

- Jump over the bomb and face back to the left.
- Hit the bomb with a Side Tilt attack (to the left). The bomb should now show 12% damage.
- Approach the bomb and hit it with a Side Tilt attack (to the left). The bomb should now show 24% damage.
- Hit the bomb with two Down Tilt attacks (to the left). The bomb should now show 33% damage.

Use a fully charged Side Smash attack to launch the bomb off of the back wall (to the left). The bomb should show 56% damage as it leaves the platform.

PALUTENA ON STAGE 2

BOMB 1

- Approach the bomb and hit it with the tip of an uncharged Side Smash attack. The bomb should now show 13% damage.
- Hurry in and hit the bomb with an uncharged Up Smash attack. The bomb should now show 29% damage.
- Hit the bomb with another uncharged Up Smash attack. The bomb should now show 45% damage.
- Dash past the bomb, then turn back and perform an uncharged Side Smash attack to launch the bomb off of the back wall (to the left). The bomb should show 61% damage as it leaves the platform.

BOMB 2

- Jump over the bomb and face back to the left.
- Approach the bomb and perform four uncharged Up Smash attacks. The bomb should now show 64% damage.
- Use an uncharged Side Smash attack to launch the bomb off of the back wall (to the left). The bomb should show 80% damage as it leaves the platform.

TOON LINK ON STAGE 2

BOMB 1

- Bump the bomb to activate it.
- Let the bomb explode without launching it.

BOMB 2

- Approach the bomb and hit it with a Down Tilt attack. The bomb should now show 7% damage.
- Follow the bomb and perform a series of 10 Down Tilt attacks. The bomb should now show 77% damage.
- Perform a short hop and use a Forward Air attack to launch the bomb toward the targets. The bomb should show 90% damage as it leaves the platform.

NESS ON STAGE 3

BOMB 1

- Jump over the bomb and hit it with a Back Air attack (to the left) just before you land. The bomb should now show 15% damage.
- Hit the bomb with a Side Tilt attack (to the left). The bomb should now show 24% damage.
- Approach the bomb and use a Side Smash attack to launch it off of the back wall (to the left). When you do, make sure you hit the bomb with the center of Ness' bat. The bomb should show 42% damage as it leaves the platform.

BOMB 2

- Jump over the bomb and face back to the left.
- Approach the bomb and hit it with three Side Tilt attacks (to the left). The bomb should now show 27% damage.
- Use a fully charged Side Smash Attack to launch the bomb off of the back wall (to the left). When you do, make sure you hit the bomb with the center of Ness' bat. The bomb should show 52% damage as it leaves the platform.

Due to some random elements, this series of attacks does not provide consistent results. However, properly executing these steps should allow you to complete the related Challenge within a few attempts.

NOTE

PAC-MAN ON STAGE 3

BOMB 1

- Bump the bomb to activate it.
- Let the bomb explode without launching it.

BOMB 2

- Approach the bomb and hit it with two uncharged Up Smash attacks. The bomb should now show 34% damage.
- Step toward the bomb to get back into range, then hit it with a series of six Up Tilt attacks. When done properly, the bomb should land behind you (to the left). The bomb should now show 76% damage.
- Use a fully charged Forward Smash attack to launch the bomb off of the back wall (to the left). The bomb should show 98% damage as it leaves the platform.

Due to some random elements, this series of attacks does not provide consistent results. However, properly executing these steps should allow you to complete the related Challenge within a few attempts.

NOTE

SMASH

Smash Overview

In Smash, you battle for victory against CPU fighters or nearby players. This game mode has a straightforward format, but the settings provide players with a great deal of flexibility.

Smash Menus

The main menu's "Smash" option contains three Smash menus:

- Solo: Play against AI-controlled opponents!
- Group: Play against people nearby who have their own copy of the game.
- Rules: Change settings to customize the battle!

Solo

Solo Smash is ideal for players who want to test their skills against one or more CPU fighters. During character selection, use the Touch Screen to adjust the match rules or change the number of CPU opponents you'll face. Simply tap each panel to cycle through the available options or—in some cases—to open additional menus.

Tap the panels along the top of the Touch Screen to toggle between Smash and Team Smash, adjust the match rules, or to determine whether or not custom fighters are allowed.

You can adjust match time or stock count without leaving character selection. For larger changes, however, tap the Touch Screen's stock/time panel to access all of the options found in the "Rules" menu.

NOTE

Use the panels above the fighter slots to activate or deactivate opponents and to adjust each CPU fighter's AI level. Tap each fighter's portrait to cycle through the available appearances. During Team Smash, use the panels near the bottom of the Touch Screen to assign fighters to teams.

When you're ready, confirm your settings and choose a stage to begin the match.

TIMED SMASH BATTLES

The winner of a timed Smash battle is determined by which fighter scores the most points within the time limit. The clock in the upper-right corner of the Main Display shows the remaining time, while the Touch Screen shows the current damage percentage of each fighter. The Touch Screen also displays Combinable items the fighters are currently holding, and brief alerts appear each time a fighter gains or loses a point.

In a timed Smash battle, your final score is determined by three factors:

- KOs: You gain one point each time you KO an opponent.
- Falls: You lose one point each time you are KO'd by an opponent.
- Self-Destructs: By default, you lose one point each time you KO yourself or are KO'd by the environment.

Each fighter's final score is only revealed at the end of the battle, so it's important keep track of KOs as they occur.

SUDDEN DEATH

If a timed Smash battle ends without a clear victor, all fighters tied for the lead enter a Sudden Death round. In Sudden Death, fighters each have one stock life—suffering a single KO will eliminate a fighter from the competition. All fighters start with 300% damage, so the smallest mistake can be very costly.

STOCK SMASH BATTLES

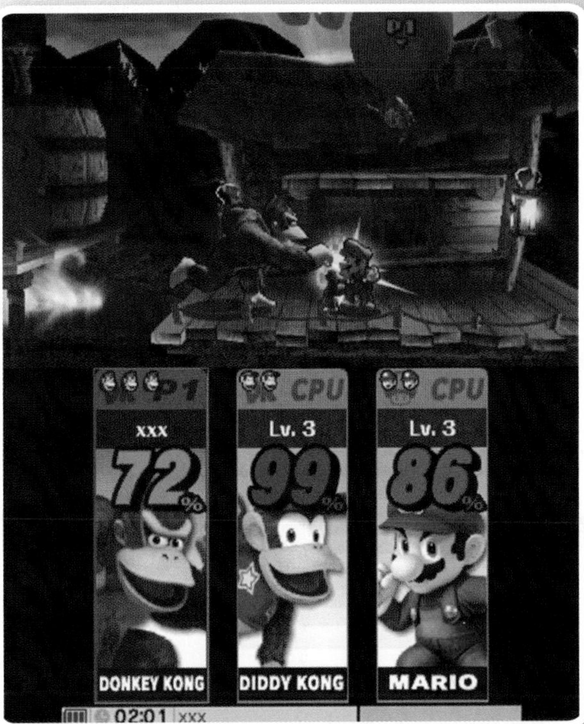

Each fighter begins a stock Smash battle with a set number of lives. Every time a fighter is KO'd, his or her stock count is reduced by one. The battle ends when only one fighter remains.

During a stock Smash battle, the Touch Screen displays each fighter's damage percentage, stock count, and any Combining items the fighters are holding.

Group

Group Smash allows up to four nearby players to battle each other. Use this menu to search for available games or to start one of your own. If you opt to start a Group Smash game, you must then set the game's permissions:

- Anyone: Any nearby player can join your game.
- Friends Preferred: Lets everyone know you'd prefer to have friends join your game.
- Friends Only: Only friends are able to join your game.

Once you start a game, you move to character selection. From this point on, you have access to the same options found in Solo Smash.

RULES

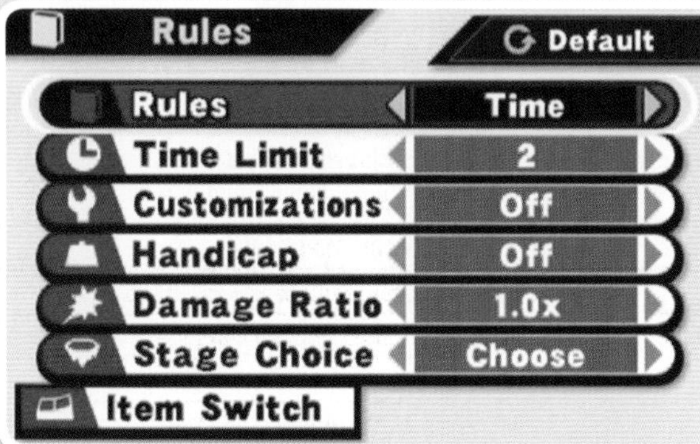

The "Rules" menu contains the available Smash settings. To change the options and features of your upcoming matches, use the Circle Pad to select an item, then cycle through the available settings:

- Rules: This determines the objective of the battle. Select "time" to battle for the best score within a set time limit, or choose "stock" to engage in a battle of pure survival.
- Time/Stock: Adjust the time limit or stock count (depending on the game's objective).
- Customizations: Allow or prohibit the use of customized fighters.
- Handicap: The "off" setting ensures that each player begins the battle with 0 damage. The "on" setting allows players to increase starting damage, making it easier for them to be launched. With the "auto" setting, the results of a battle will affect the starting damage for the following match.
- Damage Ratio: Adjust the damage done by all fighters. A higher number makes it easier for fighters to launch each other.
- Stage Choice: This setting allows you to bypass stage selection. If you prefer, you can choose random stage selections or you can automatically cycle through the available stages. These options are available for both normal stages and Final Destination forms.
- Item Switch: The Item Switch menu allows you to limit which items have a chance to appear during a battle.

MORE RULES

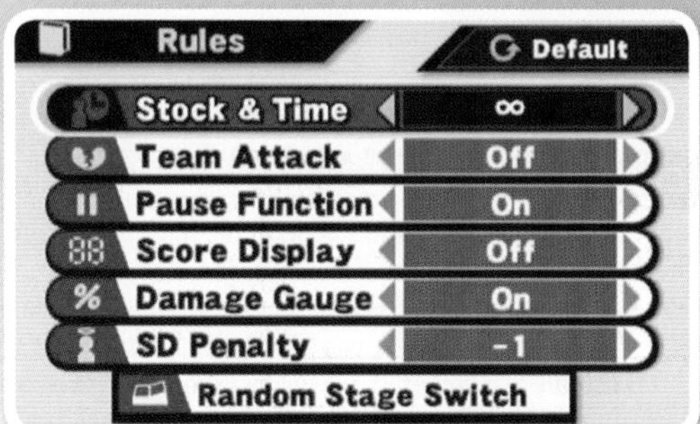

Once you've scored at least 200 KOs in Smash, a new tab appears at the bottom of the "Rules" menu. Select "More Rules" to find even more ways to customize your Smash Battles:

- **Stock & Time: Set a time limit for stock Smash battles.**
- **Team Attack: Determine whether or not teammates can damage each other.**
- **Pause Function: Enable or disable pausing during battle.**
- **Score Display: Determine whether or not fighter scores are displayed during battle.**
- **Damage Gauge: Show or hide damage percentages during battle.**

SD Penalty: Determine whether a Self-Destruct reduces a fighter's score by one point or two points.

Random Stage Switch: Limit which stages have a chance to appear during random stage selection.

Unlocking Hidden Characters in Smash

In addition to the starting roster, the game contains 12 hidden characters. Depending on the specific character, you can unlock new fighters through Classic, Mulit-Man, trophy collection, or equipment collection. All hidden characters, however, can also be unlocked by playing Smash.

Complete the required number of Smash battles to trigger a one-on-one battle against a hidden character. If you win the battle, the hidden character is unlocked and added to your roster; if you fail, simply complete another Smash battle to try again.

> **Solo Smash, Group Smash, and online Smash matches all count toward hidden character Smash prerequisites.**
>
> **NOTE**

REVEALING HIDDEN CHARACTERS

CHARACTER	SMASH PREREQUISITE	ALTERNATE METHOD
Ness	Play 10 or more matches	Clear Classic on any difficulty
Falco	Play 20 or more matches	Clear Classic without any continues
Wario	Play 30 or more matches	Complete 100-Man Smash
Lucina	Play 40 or more matches	As Marth, clear Classic without any continues
Dark Pit	Play 50 or more matches	Clear Classic with three or more characters
Dr. Mario	Play 60 or more matches	As Mario, clear Classic on intensity 4.0 or higher
R.O.B.	Play 70 or more matches	Collect at least 200 different trophies
Ganondorf	Play 80 or more matches	As Zelda or Link, clear Classic on intensity 5.0 or higher
Mr. Game & Watch	Play 90 or more matches	Clear Classic with 10 or more characters
Bowser Jr.	Play 100 or more matches	As Bowser, clear Classic on intensity 6.0 or higher
Duck Hunt	Play 110 or more matches	Clear Classic with 15 or more characters
Jigglypuff	Play 120 or more matches	Collect at least 30 different equipment items

SMASH RUN

Smash Run Overview

In Smash Run, you have five minutes to defeat enemies and search for helpful items scattered across a massive battlefield. Virtually every action you take during this time improves your character's stats! When the clock runs out, use your powered-up fighter to smash your way to victory in one of seventeen final battle types.

Smash Run Menu

The "Smash Run" menu contains four selections:

- Solo: You've got five minutes! Boost your stats, and then face three CPU rivals in battle!
- Group: Collect stat boosts and face off against up to three other people via local wireless!
- Custom: Choose Power and equipment combinations to give your fighter a tactical advantage! Create new custom sets or edit existing combinations.
- Select Music: Select the background music that plays during Smash Run.

Solo

SOLO SMASH RUN BASICS

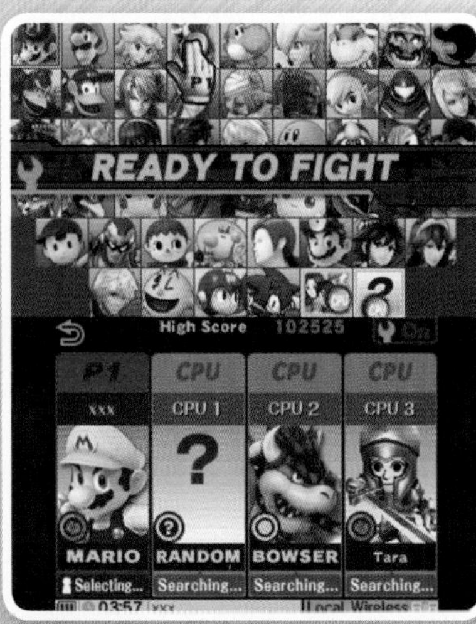

Beginning a game of Solo Smash Run is much like starting a battle in Smash. Select a fighter from your roster, then choose any CPU opponents you'd like to face.

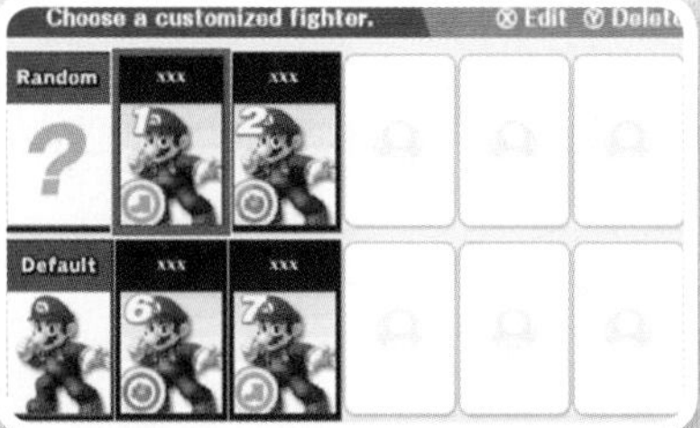

If custom characters are allowed, you'll be asked to select one of your fighter's custom sets. From this screen, you can also choose to edit an existing set or create a new one. By selecting one of these options, you'll enter the Smash Run Custom mode without leaving your current game. Once you're satisfied with your fighter and your CPU opponents, press START to begin the game.

You begin the game at a random location within the Smash Run area. Explore the available paths and platforms to find enemies, treasure chests, challenge doors, and more. While you're in the Smash Run area, a clock in the upper-right corner of the Main Display shows the remaining time. The final battle begins when the clock runs out. The bar above the clock indicates exactly when special events will be triggered; each time the bar reaches a white line, a new event begins.

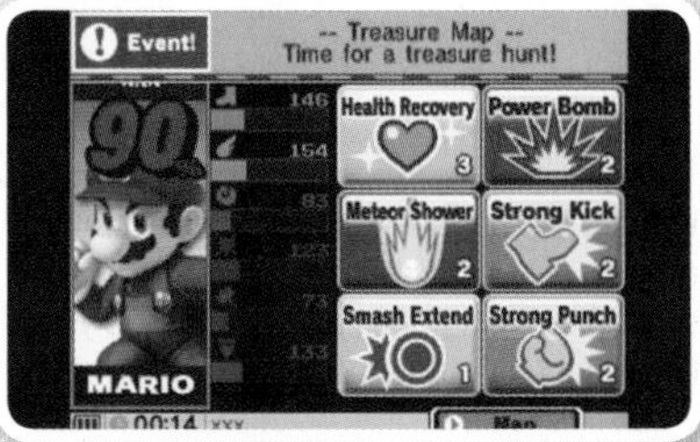

In Smash Run, the Touch Screen displays important information and gives you access to your available Powers. By default, the Touch Screen shows your current damage percentage, stat levels, collected items, and available Powers. Additionally, you'll also receive notifications about active events, and opponent actions appear near the top of the Touch Screen. To activate a Power, tap the corresponding icon. To display a map of the Smash Run area, tap the Touch Screen anywhere other than where the Powers are displayed.

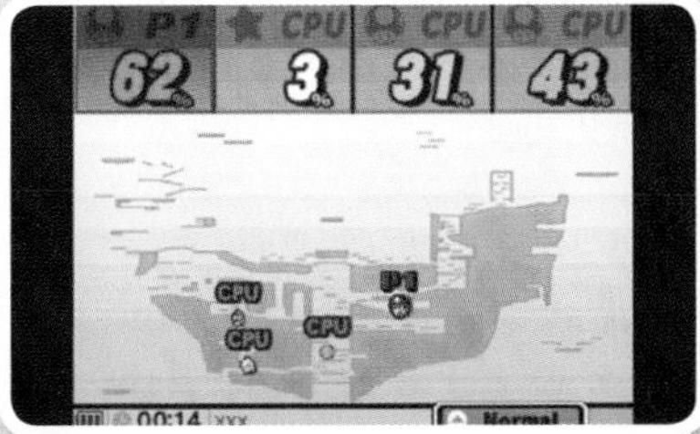

Activate the Touch Screen map to help navigate the Smash Run area, locate event-related items and enemies, and to get a bit of information about how your opponents are faring. The Touch Screen map shows each fighter's current position and damage percentage. During events, objectives appear near the top of the Touch Screen, and important locations are marked on the map. Tap the map at any time to return to the Touch Screen's default mode.

TIP

You will not encounter any of your opponents in the Smash Run area. Tracking fighter locations, however, can give you some insight into how your opponents are using the available time.

POWERING UP YOUR FIGHTER

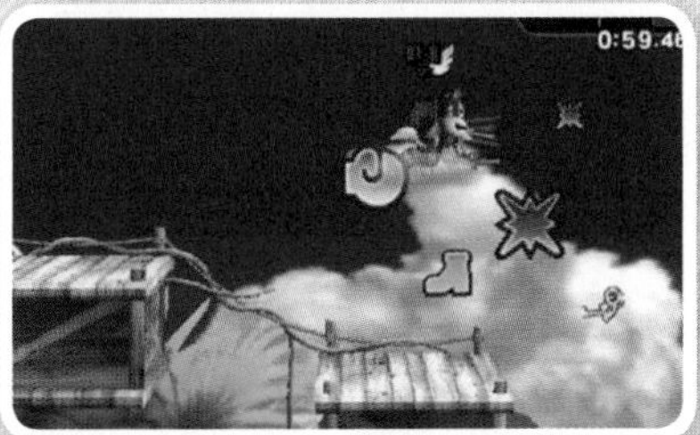

When the game starts, your fighter's stats are very low. You have five minutes to earn and collect stat bonuses that increase your fighter's effectiveness in the coming battle. Virtually every action you take will increase one of your fighter's stats, but stat bonuses can also be found scattered across the battlefield, hidden in treasure chests, or collected from defeated enemies.

Keep an eye on your damage percentage as you power up your fighter. The more damage you take, the more likely it is that an enemy will launch you off-screen. Each time you suffer a KO or fall out of the Smash Run area, you lose a large portion of your fighter's stats. Be careful, or you might find yourself at a severe disadvantage during the final battle!

STAT BOOSTS

SPEED

Speed determines how fast your fighter moves on the ground and in the air. Increase this stat by collecting Speed stat bonuses or by running through the battlefield.

JUMP

Jump determines how high and how far your fighter can jump. Increase this stat by collecting Jump stat bonuses or by jumping around the battlefield.

ATTACK

Attack determines the damage caused by your fighter's standard attacks, tilt (strong) attacks, and Smash attacks. Increase this stat by collecting Attack stat bonuses or by using the related attacks to damage enemies.

SPECIAL

Special determines the damage caused by your fighter's Special attacks. Increase this stat by collecting Special stat boosts or by using Special attacks to damage enemies.

ARMS

Arms determines the effectiveness of items and the power of your fighter's throws. Increase this stat by collecting Arms stat boosts or by using items and throwing enemies.

DEFENSE

Defense determines how difficult it is to launch your fighter. Increase this stat by collecting Defense stat boosts or by taking damage, shielding your fighter from damage, and dodging enemy attacks.

STAR-SHAPED STAT BOOSTS

Look for special star-shaped stat boosts that sometimes appear in Smash Run. Collecting one of these boosts all six of your fighter's stats!

Stat boosts come in four sizes; the larger a stat boost, the greater its effect. Stat boosts dropped by defeated enemies only remain in the area for a short time, so make sure you grab them before they disappear!

SECRET DOORS

As you explore the Smash Run area, keep an eye out for secret doors. Move in front of one of these doors and slide the Circle Pad up to enter a bonus room.

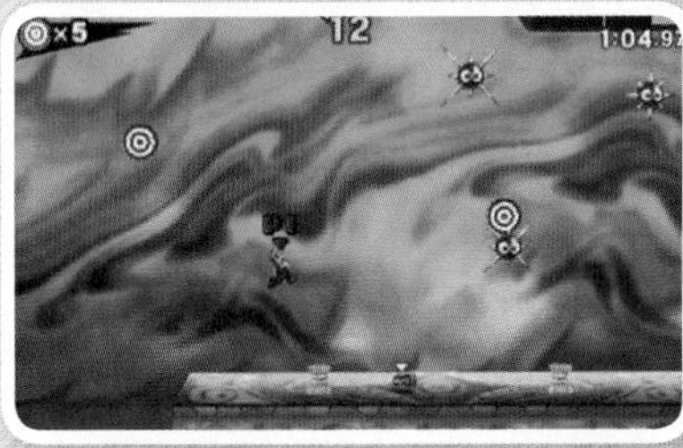

Some rooms simply contain miscellaneous items, but many bonus rooms hold secret door challenges that can be completed for big rewards!

SECRET DOOR CHALLENGES

OBJECTIVE	DESCRIPTION
SURVIVE	Survive in the face of enemies and environmental hazards until time runs out.
DEFEAT THEM ALL!	Defeat all available enemies within the allotted time.
TARGET SMASH	Destroy all available targets within the allotted time.
CRYSTAL SMASH!	Destroy all available crystals within the allotted time.

TREASURE CHESTS

Open treasure chests to find stat boosts, trophies, Powers, and other collectible items! Treasure chests can appear throughout the Smash Run area, so a little exploration can be very rewarding.

POWERS

Powers can be earned or collected in most game modes, but they can only be used in Smash Run. Visit the Smash Run Custom mode to review and equip the Powers you've unlocked. A fighter can hold up to six Powers at a time. Each Power has a predetermined weight, however, so possible combinations are limited by your chosen character's weight limit.

TIP

Assigning equipment to a character can change his or her weight limit. In general, slower characters can carry more than faster characters.

During Smash Run, the Touch Screen's default mode displays an icon for each of your fighter's equipped Powers. Tap an icon to activate the corresponding Power. Many Powers can be used multiple times in a single game; the number in the lower-right corner of each icon indicates a Power's remaining charges.

Using Powers is a great way to maximize your stat boosts or to prevent yourself from losing the bonuses you've already earned. Offensive Powers are great when you're outnumbered or when you encounter a particularly dangerous enemy. It's always wise, however, to bring at least one Power that focuses on damage prevention or health recovery. Knowing when and where to activate each of your Powers ensures your fighter will be as strong as possible by the time the final battle starts.

TIP

Powers can only be used in the Smash Run area. As you get closer to the final battle, look for opportunities to use any of your fighter's remaining Powers.

RECOMMENDED POWERS

Experimenting with Powers is a great way to develop strategies and tactics that complement your personal playstyle. A few Powers, however, deserve a place in almost any custom set.

Spinning Blades, for example, is a surprisingly versatile Power. It lasts longer than most direct attacks, allowing you to clear a large area with ease. Spinning Blades is also a great way to complete many of the objectives found behind challenge doors. Activate this Power to quickly clear a bonus room of enemies or destructible objects!

It's also wise to enter Smash Run with some version of Health Recovery or Warp equipped. You never know when you'll stumble onto a group of particularly tough enemies, and either of these Powers can help you escape dangerous situations intact. Combining one of these Powers with a piece of Auto-Heal equipment makes it much easier to reach the final battle without suffering a single KO.

EVENTS

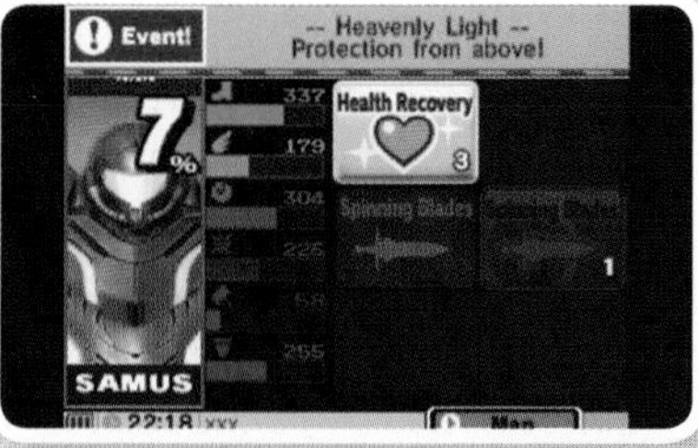

As you explore the Smash Run area, watch the Touch Screen for notifications about a variety of events. Some events offer special objectives that can be completed for valuable rewards; some events introduce new hazards or temporary power-ups. Use the bar in the Main Display's upper-right corner to track upcoming events—a new event begins each time the bar reaches a white line.

Once an event begins, a clock appears in the upper-left corner of the Main Display. This clock indicates the duration of the event; when the event ends, the clock disappears. If a small arrow appears on the screen, it indicates a special target or location related to the event.

While an objective marker is active, you can use the Touch Screen's Smash Run map to identify key locations. This is especially handy if you need to plot a route through multiple objectives.

You'll frequently receive News Smash updates about various fighters. Like special event notifications, these updates appear along the top of the Touch Screen. Unlike events, however, News Smash updates are not indicated on the bar in the Main Display's upper-right corner.

NOTE

EVENT TYPES

NAME	DESCRIPTION
Heavenly Light	You gain Heavenly Light.
Fast Learner	It's easier to increase a randomly selected stat.
Bonus Time	More stat boosts appear.
Warp	You are teleported to a random location.
Wanted	Defeat the marked enemy for rewards.
Treasure Trove	A new door appears in the area.
Treasure Map	Treasure chests appear throughout the area.
Otherworldly Door	A new door appears in the area.
Big Haul	Treasure chests yield more loot.
Doors Galore	Doors appear throughout the area.
Amped Up!	Your Speed and Jump stats are maxed out.
[?] Fest	A randomly selected enemy appears more often.
Gale	You are pushed by a strong wind.
Dirty Trick	An enemy spawns bombs.
Final Battle Forecast	You're given a hint about the final battle match type.

THE SMASH RUN AREA

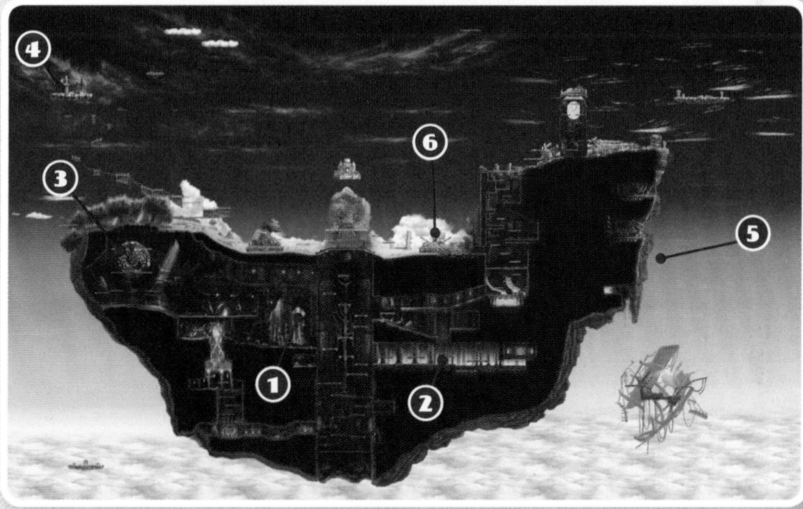

The Smash Run area always has the same basic layout, but it includes enough random elements to keep you guessing during each playthrough. Enemies vary during each visit, and you never know where you'll find secret doors, treasure chests, and specific stat boosts. The cannons that launch you between platforms are limited to certain locations, but not all of them will be present during every playthrough. Each time you play Smash Run, you'll have to adapt to any number of small changes.

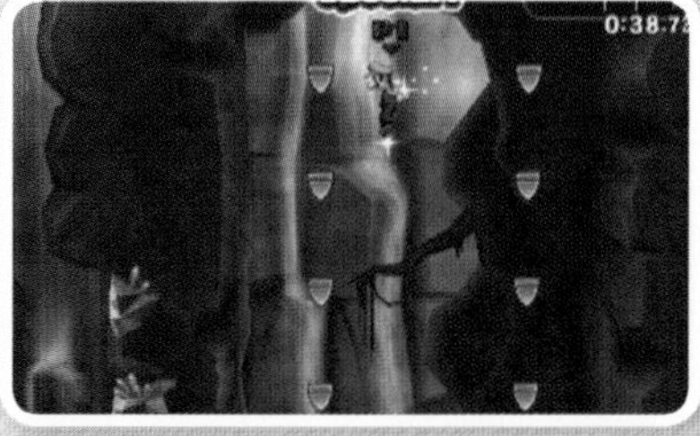

1 When you start a game of Smash Run, you may have some trouble reaching certain platforms and collectible items. Early in the game, try to focus on weaker enemies and smaller jumps. As your stats improve, you'll find it much easier to move through the area.

2 The Smash Run area contains plenty of enemies and falling hazards, but you'll encounter a few additional dangers. One section of the map, for example, features a scorching hot floor that can damage and launch fighters and enemies while it's glowing. Watch your step!

3 Moving platforms can make it tough to reach elusive enemies, and they can sometimes carry you away from hard-earned stat boosts. Keep track of available footholds to ensure you always have a safe place to land.

4 In general, you're likely to find bigger stat boosts and more powerful enemies as you move to the outer edges of the Smash Run area. The most rewarding locations are often hard to reach, however, and an untimely fall can undo minutes of hard work. When choosing a strategy, remember to weigh the potential risks against the possible rewards.

5 You'll usually find clusters of valuable stat boosts floating well off the edge of the Smash Run area's central mass. If you attempt to collect these, remember to watch for cannons that might launch you back to solid ground. If all else fails, use the Touch Screen map to look for any platforms that might catch you before you fall out of the area.

6 Suspiciously empty areas usually contain a surprise or two. You might find a Mimicutie disguised as a treasure chest, or an abandoned platform might whisk you away to an enemy ambush. Stay alert, and be prepared to adjust to new developments.

FINAL BATTLES

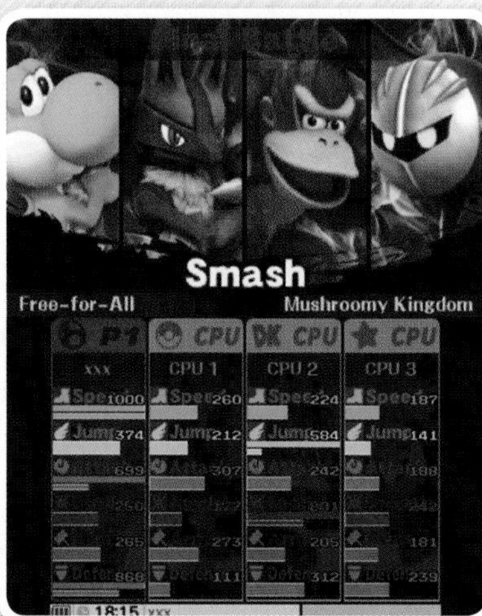

After five minutes in the Smash Run area, the screen displays the stats for each fighter, and the final battle match type is revealed. Use this time to develop a basic strategy for the upcoming battle. Different match types favor different stats, so identifying the strengths and weaknesses of your opponents can help improve your chances of victory.

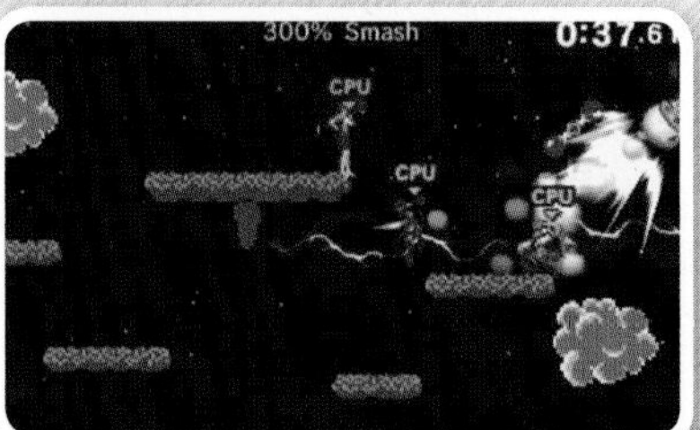

Most final battles offer some sort of Smash variation. Fighters might be divided into teams, specific items might be provided, or special rules might be in effect. You'll sometimes find that the final battle match type neutralizes your fighter's highest stats, so adjust your tactics as needed.

In some final battle match types, competitors never even cross paths. Vs. Enemy Team, for example, pits each fighter against waves of Smash Run enemies. You might even find yourself in a round of Multi-Man Smash, battling Mii Fighters and other characters rather than your opponents.

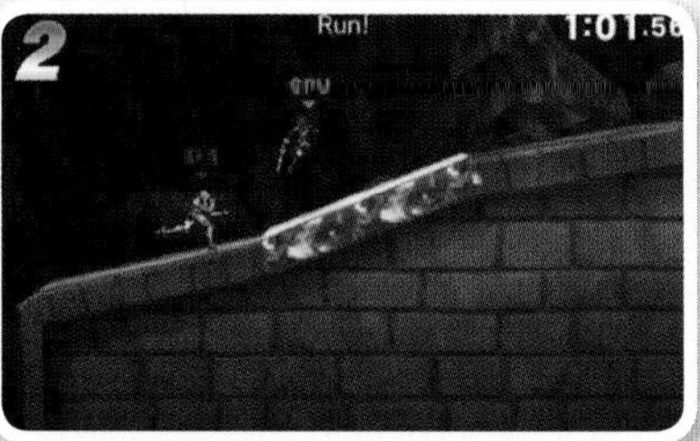

The Run and Climb match types focus on mobility rather than combat. In a Run final battle, all fighters race to a finish line. The Run course is packed with fiery hazards—touching one will cost you valuable time.

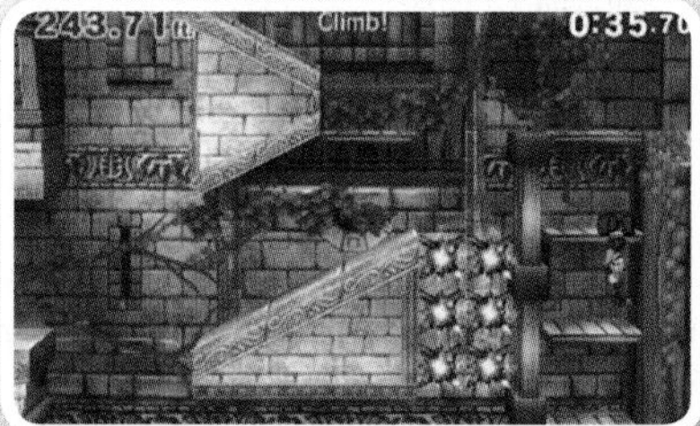

In a Climb match, fighters race each other through a vertical course. Avoid fiery hazards and detonating bombs to improve your chances of victory. A stumble or two can be enough to knock even the speediest fighter out of the lead. Familiarize yourself with all of the possible final battle match types and plan for every contingency.

FINAL BATTLE MATCH TYPES

NAME	DESCRIPTION
Smash	Smash is as simple as it gets! Use the available time to score more points than your opponents.
Mega Smash	All fighters are granted increased size and power.
High-Launch Smash	All fighters are easier to launch.
Flower Smash	All fighters are afflicted by flowers, causing their damage percentages to increase over time.
300% Smash	All fighters start with 300% damage. Be careful!
Reflect Smash	All fighters are given a Franklin Badge, which reflects incoming projectiles.
Stamina Smash	Instead of damage percentages, each fighter starts out with a set amount of health.
Stock Smash	Each fighter has a limited amount of stock lives.
Glorious Smash	The battle takes place on a stage's Final Destination form.
Explosive Smash	Explosive items appear throughout the battle.
Mushroom Smash	Super Mushrooms and Poison Mushrooms appear throughout the battle.
Mr. Saturn Smash	Mr. Saturns appear throughout the battle. Use these items to take out your opponents' shields.
Warp Star Smash	Warp Stars appear throughout the battle.
Multi-Man Smash	Each fighter faces a team of Mii Fighters and other characters. Score more points than your opponents!
Vs. Enemy Team	Each fighter faces a team of Smash Run enemies. Score more points than your opponents!
Run	Fighters compete in a footrace. Make sure you avoid those fiery hazards on your way to the finish line.
Climb	Fighters jump along a series of platforms in this vertical race. Stay clear of the hazards scattered throughout the course!

SMASH RUN ENEMIES

Defeating Smash Run enemies is a great way to earn stat boosts, and tougher foes tend to drop more rewards. Most of the enemies you'll encounter can be damaged with items, attacks, and throws, but some creatures have significant strengths and weaknesses. You never know which enemies you'll encounter, so remember to equip your fighter with a few versatile Powers before you start a game of Smash Run.

BANZAI BILL

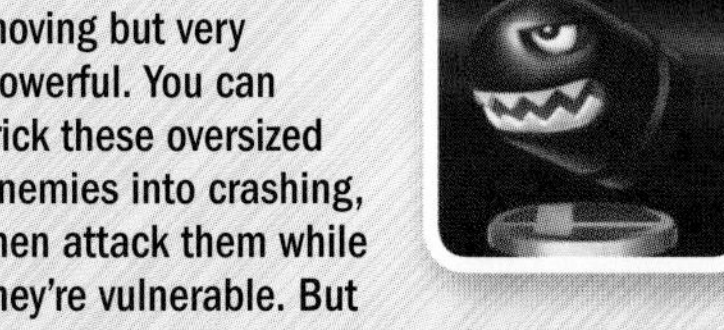

Banzai Bills are slow moving but very powerful. You can trick these oversized enemies into crashing, then attack them while they're vulnerable. But this strategy is risky! Soon after a Banzai Bill gets stuck in a wall, it explodes! Whenever possible, try to slip under a Banzai Bill and deliver an Up Smash attack for heavy damage.

BIG GOOMBA

Much like their smaller counterparts, Big Goombas usually attack by charging toward their targets. They can also stomp with enough force to knock you right off your feet. These enemies have a lot of health, but you can jump on them to deal heavy damage.

BILL BLASTER

Bill Blasters usually fire Bullet Bills, but they'll also launch the occasional Koopa or Shy Guy. On rare occasions, a Bill Blaster can even launch a Poppant into the area! Destroy any Bill Blasters you see to help keep the skies clear.

BONKERS

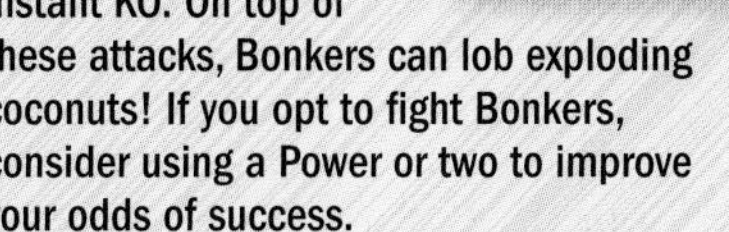

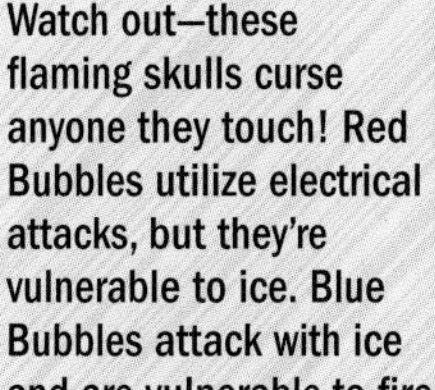

This ape-like creature uses its massive hammer to launch its foes. If you're hit by its Hammer Flip attack, you'll suffer an instant KO. On top of these attacks, Bonkers can lob exploding coconuts! If you opt to fight Bonkers, consider using a Power or two to improve your odds of success.

BOOM STOMPER

Once a Boom Stomper spots you, it follows you through the area, trying to stomp you right into the ground. Defeating one of these troublesome enemies can yield big rewards. Attack the leaf on a Boom Stomper's head to deal significant damage and consider using a Power or two to speed up the process.

BRONTO BURT

Bronto Burts aren't particularly dangerous, but they can be a real nuisance! In Smash Run, a Bronto Burt can take one of three actions: it can flee from a fighter, it can attack by flying in a straight line, or it can follow a fighter around the area.

BUBBLE

Watch out—these flaming skulls curse anyone they touch! Red Bubbles utilize electrical attacks, but they're vulnerable to ice. Blue Bubbles attack with ice and are vulnerable to fire. When possible, use the appropriate elemental attack to defeat these enemies with ease.

BULBORB

These large creatures can use their massive jaws to snap at you, or they can trample you underfoot. If you spot one in a group of enemies, try to take the Bulborb out as quickly as possible. A defeated Bulborb can damage nearby enemies as it bounces through the area.

BULLET BILL

These flying enemies can be very persistent, but they aren't particularly tough. Attack an incoming Bullet Bill to defeat it before it reaches you. If you find yourself swarmed by Bullet Bills, consider a strategic retreat.

BUMPETY BOMB

This explosive enemy can move fairly quickly, and its front-mounted armor can absorb a lot of damage. Attack a Bumpety Bomb from behind to defuse it or seek higher ground to escape its blast radius.

CHAIN CHOMP

These territorial enemies are very tough, so it's usually best to avoid them. Chain Chomps you encounter in Smash Run will always be anchored to the ground, so you'll be safe if you keep your distance. If you're itching for a fight, however, focus your attacks on the wooden stake at the end of the creature's chain.

CHANDELURE

This Ghost/Fire-type Pokémon attacks in bursts of three, so don't drop your guard. Attacking a Chandelure with fire-based moves and items will only make it stronger!

CLUBBERSKULL

When you encounter one of these enormous enemies, it will usually be trapped in one spot. Attacking a Clubberskull will set the beast free, however. Clubberskulls are very dangerous—they can't be grabbed or launched, and they can absorb an incredible amount of damage. It's often best to avoid these enemies, but defeating one will earn you an impressive selection of stat boosts and other prizes.

CRYOGONAL

This Ice-type Pokémon utilizes freezing attacks. Watch out for Cryogonal's Ice Beam! This attack comes in two forms: one that travels in a straight line and one that can bend to pursue its target.

CUCCO

When a Cucco feels threatened, it summons an entire flock to even the odds. It's best to just avoid these enemies. Engaging a Cucco will result in an extended fight with no rewards.

DAPHNE

These deceptively dangerous enemies scatter mines throughout an area. Daphnes have very little health, so try to take them out quickly. The mines they drop are surprisingly powerful—detonate them from a distance to stay clear of the resulting blasts.

DARKNUT

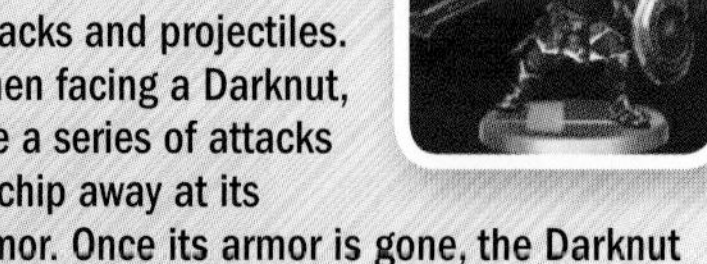

This powerful, slow-moving enemy uses its sword to block attacks and projectiles. When facing a Darknut, use a series of attacks to chip away at its armor. Once its armor is gone, the Darknut becomes more agile, but it also becomes more vulnerable to your attacks.

DEVIL CAR

Devil Cars attack by speeding back and forth, damaging fighters with each hit. Their exhaust fumes can cause paralysis. Stay clear of an attacking Devil Car until you see an opportunity to dash in and take it out.

EGGROBO

These robotic enemies tend to hang back, attacking their foes from a distance. When you spot an Eggrobo, slip around any incoming beams, then dash in and quickly defeat this enemy.

FLAGE

These gelatinous enemies use their blades to deliver slashing combo attacks. Dash in and hit a Flage when it pauses between attacks. Whenever a Flage vanishes, use its shadow to keep track of its location.

FLAME CHOMP

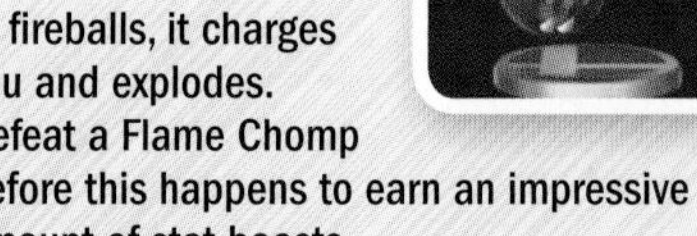

Flame Chomps use their fiery tails to fuel their projectile attacks. Once a Flame Chomp runs out of fireballs, it charges you and explodes. Defeat a Flame Chomp before this happens to earn an impressive amount of stat boosts.

FLY GUY

Fly Guys aren't particularly tough, but they'll occasionally carry useful items. Defeating a Fly Guy at just the right time can yield a valuable reward!

GASTLY

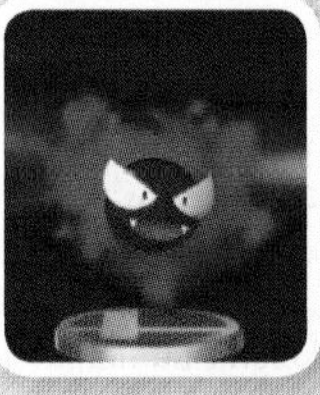

Due to its cloud of noxious gasses, this Ghost/Poison-type Pokémon is very dangerous at close range. When you encounter a Gastly, stick to projectile attacks to take it out from a distance. If that's not an option, then it's time to retreat—your melee attacks have no effect! These enemies are often stationary, but occasionally one will follow you through an area.

GEEMER

Geemers can cling to any surface, so check an area's floors and ceilings for these spiked enemies. Whenever possible, use projectile attacks to take Geemers out from a distance.

GENERATOR

This mysterious entity acts as a portal, spitting out Mites and other enemies to attack nearby fighters. Destroy Generators as quickly as possible; the faster you defeat one, the more stat boosts it's likely to drop!

GHOST

When one of these floating enemies appears in Smash Run, it uses a small shield to protect itself and any nearby allies. Hit a Ghost from behind or grab and throw it to put it out of commission.

GLICE

If you wander too close to this spinning enemy, it will attack with a blast of icy damage. When a Glice freezes you, slide the Circle Pad back and forth to break out of the ice. If possible, attack this enemy with fire-based attacks to deal increased damage.

GLIRE

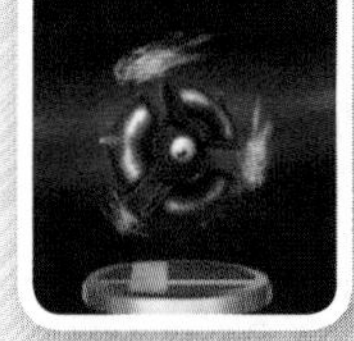

Approaching this enemy causes it to release a blast of fire. The Glire has more stamina than the Glice and the Glunder, but it's very slow. Glires are particularly vulnerable to ice-based attacks; keep that in mind when you encounter one of these enemies.

GLUNDER

When a fighter is in range, the Glunder releases a blast of lightning. A single surge doesn't do much, but consecutive attacks can lead to serious damage. When you spot a Glunder, it's usually best to attack it from a distance.

GOOMBA

Goombas attack by charging fighters, but they aren't particularly powerful. Jump up and stomp a Goomba to defeat it with minimum effort.

GORDO

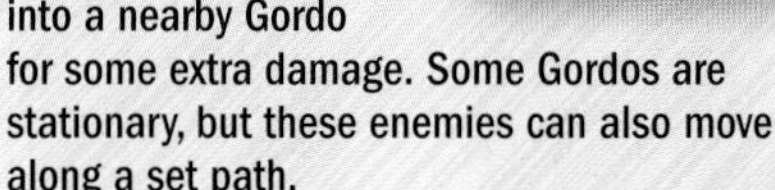

Don't bother attacking these spiked enemies—they can't be defeated. It's usually best to keep your distance, but you can also knock enemies into a nearby Gordo for some extra damage. Some Gordos are stationary, but these enemies can also move along a set path.

HAMMER BRO

These enemies attack by lobbing hammers. A Hammer Bro will occasionally jump to a new location, so use caution when approaching these enemies.

IRIDESCENT GLINT BEETLE

These rare enemies can be tough to chase down, but attacking an Iridescent Glint Beetle can grant you a fair amount of gold.

KAMEK

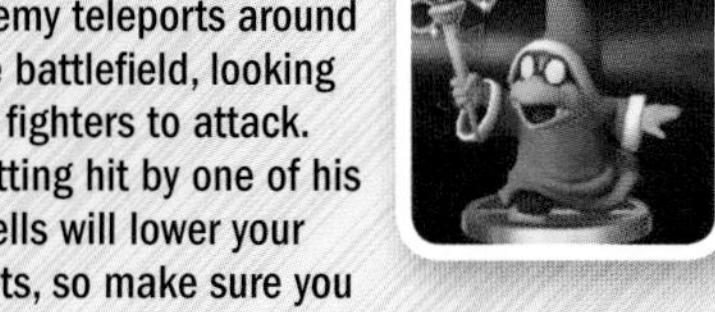

This magic-wielding enemy teleports around the battlefield, looking for fighters to attack. Getting hit by one of his spells will lower your stats, so make sure you protect yourself. Kamek can absorb a lot of damage, so use your more powerful attacks to take him out as quickly as possible.

KIHUNTER

Kihunters can dash right into foes or spit acid to attack from a distance. Acid can go through your shield, and it will stun you if it makes contact. Be ready to dodge! Defeated Kihunters drop stat boosts, so your effort is sure to be rewarded!

KOFFING

This Poison-type Pokémon releases stat-lowering gas! Defeat this enemy while its body is deflated to avoid its attacks, then collect all of the items it leaves behind!

KOOPA PARATROOPA

Stomp or damage a Koopa Paratroopa to knock it out of the air. Doing so will turn it into Koopa Troopa, so keep attacking to finish it off. Red-shelled Koopa Paratroopas are slightly more agile than their green-shelled counterparts, but all Koopa Paratroopas exhibit the same basic behaviors.

KOOPA TROOPA

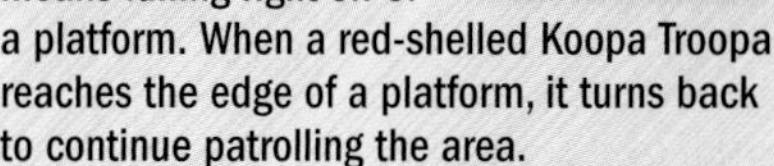

After you defeat a Koopa Troopa, you can throw its shell at nearby enemies. Green-shelled Koopa Troopas will march straight ahead, even if it means falling right off of a platform. When a red-shelled Koopa Troopa reaches the edge of a platform, it turns back to continue patrolling the area.

KRITTER

Kritters are fairly straightforward enemies—they'll march right up to you and attack. Green Kritters will deliver a series of bites, the last of which delivers extra damage. Blue Kritters will use their claws to swipe at you. Kritter attacks don't have much of a knockback effect; if you're caught by a Kritter's opening attack, you're likely to stay in range for the full duration of the combo.

LAKITU

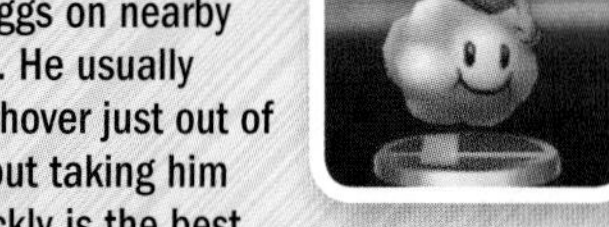

Lakitu floats around the battlefield, dropping Spiny Eggs on nearby fighters. He usually tries to hover just out of reach, but taking him out quickly is the best way to limit the number of Spinies you'll have to deal with.

LETHINIUM

These flower-like enemies fire wide beams that are capable of penetrating walls. While a Lethinium is attacking, however, its back is vulnerable. Slip behind an attacking Lethinium and use a Special or a Smash attack to defeat it.

LURCHTHORN

These massive enemies shoot projectiles as they fly around the battlefield. Each of a Lurchthorn's segments attacks separately. You can destroy individual segments, but attack its head to defeat a Lurchthorn as quickly as possible.

MAHVA

This flying, fishlike enemy uses a large, spherical barrier to protect itself. This barrier also protects the Mahva's nearby allies. The barrier changes color as it takes damage; keep attacking until you shatter the barrier and expose the Mahva. A vulnerable Mahva will try to flee; move quickly to defeat it and earn some Defense stat boosts.

MEGONTA

This giant enemy attacks by curling into a ball and rolling across the battlefield. Don't bother trying to break through its shell; instead, use a Down Smash attack (or a similarly powerful low attack) to knock a Megonta onto its back, then aim your attacks at its stomach while the Megonta struggles to recover.

METROID

When this enemy spots you, it attempts to latch onto your head! You'll take damage while a Metroid is attached; slide the Circle Pad to the left and right until you shake it loose. Metroids are extremely vulnerable to cold. If possible, use ice-based attacks to quickly defeat these enemies.

METTAUR

A Mettaur will spend most of its time hiding inside of its helmet, emerging just long enough to fire off a few projectiles. While a Mettaur is hunkered down, its helmet deflects all of your strikes; grab and throw these timid enemies to break through their defenses.

MIMICUTIE

This crafty enemy disguises itself as a treasure chest! When you approach a Mimicutie, it unleashes a flurry of powerful kicks. These enemies are very aggressive—once you've engaged a Mimicutie, it will follow you virtually anywhere. Dodge its kicks and defeat a Mimicutie to collect its stat boosts.

MITE

These small enemies use jumpkicks to attack nearby fighters. A single Mite doesn't pose much of a threat, but they can be very troublesome in large groups. When you spot a Mite on the battlefield, check the area for a nearby Generator. Quickly destroying Generators will limit the number of Mites you'll have to deal with.

MONOEYE

Once a Monoeye spots you, it usually follows you around the area. This enemy attacks by firing projectiles from its large eye. These enemies are fairly weak, so it's usually best to take them out quickly.

NUTSKI

These fast-moving enemies tend to fly in unpredictable patterns. If you get too close to a Nutski, it flips over and fires three seeds.

OCTOROK

These enemies tend to hide underground, firing projectiles each time they emerge. Grab and throw an Octorok to defeat it quickly.

ORNE

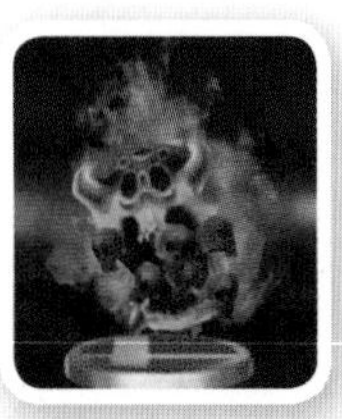

This powerful enemy is immune to your attacks, and it will instantly KO any fighter it touches. If you spot an Orne, don't even try to fight it—just leave the area as quickly as possible!

PARASOL WADDLE DEE

These enemies use their parasols to float down on unsuspecting fighters. A Waddle Dee will sometimes release its parasol before landing on the ground, so don't linger below these enemies! Parasol Waddle Dees aren't particularly tough, though, so you shouldn't have much trouble clearing them from an area.

PEAHAT

This enemy spawns Peahat Larva whenever a fighter gets too close. Additionally, Peahats use their spinning attacks to deal damage as they keep their foes at bay. Defeating one of these enemies, however, is almost always worth the effort!

PETILIL

This Grass-type Pokémon releases purple Sleep Powder when a fighter gets too close. This attack has a considerable range, so it's easy to get caught by it while you're engaged with other enemies. If you spot a Petilil, try to defeat it as quickly as possible.

PLASMA WISP

Plasma Wisps float up to fighters and fire off energy attacks once they're in range. There are three different levels of Plasma Wisp attacks. Level-one attacks deal standard damage, level-two attacks can stun you, and level-three attacks deal increased damage.

POLAR BEAR

This seemingly laid-back enemy will occasionally jump into the air, only to come crashing down with enough force to shake the entire area. These tremors damage anyone unlucky enough to be standing on the ground during each attack. This enemy is vulnerable to heat, however, so try to use fire-based attacks to quickly defeat a Polar Bear.

POOKA

These little creatures can burrow underground to avoid incoming attacks. If you manage to hit a Pooka, however, it puffs up. Land additional attacks to inflate a Pooka until it bursts. This not only defeats the Pooka, it can also damage any nearby enemies!

POPPANT

Attack these elusive enemies to earn items and food. A Poppant will flee the moment it spots you, dropping a few items as it does. Catching a Poppant can yield serious rewards, so don't give up without a fight!

REAPER

Reapers use their scythes to deliver powerful short-range attacks. They're also capable of summoning Reapettes to aid them in battle. It's usually best to use Powers or projectile attacks to deal with a Reaper from a safe distance.

REDEAD

These slow-moving enemies use spine-chilling howls to temporarily incapacitate nearby foes. Dash in and take them out between attacks or hang back and use projectile attacks to defeat them from a safe distance.

REO

A Reo's attack has a significant knockback effect, but this enemy's predictable movements make it fairly easy to deal with. Use strikes, projectile attacks, or throws to defeat them.

ROTURRET

This enemy uses its two cannons to fire projectiles at nearby fighters. Roturrets fire in bursts of three—with two cannons, that's a total of six projectiles per attack. Each attack's final shot has improved launching power, so be careful. Hitting a Roturret between its cannons can disrupt its attack as you inflict heavy damage.

SHOTZO

Some Shotzos fire at a fixed angle, while others can aim their shots at nearby fighters. Either way, it's best to avoid these cannons. Shotzos can't be defeated, so don't bother trying to attack one.

SHY GUY

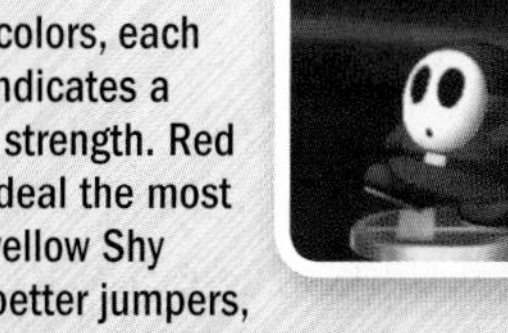

Shy Guys come in a variety of colors, each of which indicates a particular strength. Red Shy Guys deal the most damage, yellow Shy Guys are better jumpers, green Shy Guys are a bit faster, and blue Shy Guys are slightly more difficult to launch. Additionally, the color of a Shy Guy usually indicates which stat it will drop when it's defeated.

SKUTTLER

Skuttlers use their clubs to deliver vicious attacks—the bigger the swing, the more damage it deals. These enemies have a fair amount of health, but your stronger attacks should send them stumbling. When you encounter a Skuttler, try to attack it from behind.

SKUTTLER CANNONEER

These enemies use ranged weapons to attack from a distance. The color of a Skuttler Cannoneer's weapon determines which type of projectile you can expect: green cannons cause explosions, blue cannons can fire through obstacles, and red cannons launch homing missiles. Occasionally, a Skuttler Cannoneer's weapon stops working—use this time to strike back!

SKUTTLER MAGE

These troublesome enemies specialize in magic attacks. Skuttler Mages can attack at close range or grab distant fighters and do magical damage. A Skuttler Mage's close-range attacks decrease your fighter's stats, so be careful!

SNEAKY SPIRITS

These rare enemies can sometimes be found popping in and out of the ground. This movement follows a set rhythm, so time your attacks to land each time a Sneaky Spirit shows itself. This enemy will flee after a short time, but defeating one will yield a star-shaped stat boost.

SOUFLEE

The Souflee uses its erratic movements and unpredictable attacks to confuse its foes. Fortunately, they aren't that tough and defeating one can yield some impressive stat boosts! Swat them out of the air to put an end to their mischief.

SPIKE TOP

Spike Tops can sometimes be found crawling along floors, ceilings, and walls. These enemies are immune to projectiles, so you'll have to get in close if you want to defeat one.

SPINY

These creatures emerge from the Spiny Eggs Lakitu throws. Once a Spiny hatches, it heads straight toward the nearest fighter. They're easy enough defeat, but consider moving to a new area if you find yourself surrounded by these spiked creatures.

STALFOS

These enemies use their shields to block incoming attacks. When possible, try to hit a Stalfos from behind or jump over the enemy and come crashing down from above. If these options aren't viable, consider using a Power or moving to a new area.

STARMAN

Starman uses its PSI attacks to keep its foes at bay. Dash in and defeat a Starman between its attacks or use projectile attacks to defeat it from a safe distance.

TAC

These sneaky enemies will attempt to steal your stat boosts. The amount they take is determined by how much you've managed to improve your stats. Move quickly to chase down a fleeing Tac and reclaim any stat boosts he took from you.

TIKI BUZZ

Passing under one of these flying enemies will cause it to dive-bomb down onto you; however, hopping onto a Tiki Buzz gives your jump some extra bounce.

WADDLE DOO

This enemy uses a short-range energy attack to stun and damage fighters. Waddle Doos aren't particularly powerful, but they're fairly aggressive. Use projectile attacks to damage them from a distance or dash in to strike them between their attacks.

ZUREE

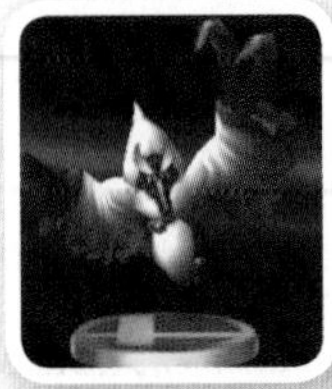

From a distance, a Zuree looks like a small cloud of mist. When you approach one, however, it springs into action with a swipe of its claws. Use your most powerful attacks to defeat a Zuree while it's vulnerable.

Group

GROUP SMASH RUN BASICS

In Group Smash Run, you can face off against nearby players. Use the "Group" menu to host or join a game, then select your desired character and custom set. CPU opponents will automatically fill any vacant slots.

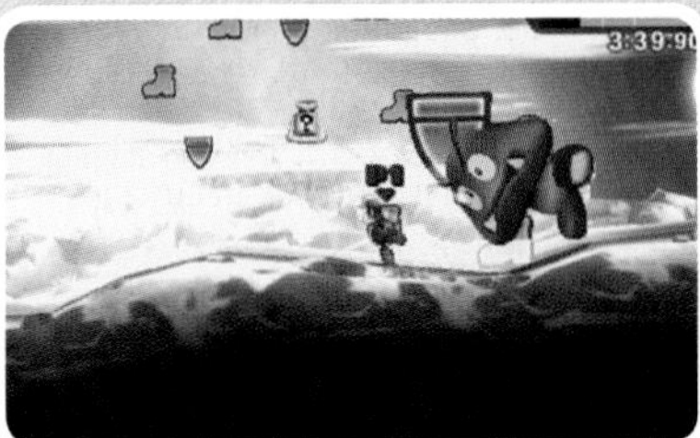

Once the game starts, Group Smash Run is virtually identical to the Solo version. Each player has five minutes to defeat enemies and collect stat boosts before the final battle begins.

The enemies, events, and final battle match types found in Solo Smash Run also appear in Group Smash Run. Use the same tactics to power up your fighter and improve your chances of victory!

TIP

In Group Smash, treasure chests have a chance to drop Bomb Buttons. Hit one of these buttons to spawn giant Bob-ombs on or near each of your enemies!

Custom

CUSTOM OVERVIEW

The Smash Run Custom mode and the Games & More Custom mode share many of the same features. Both modes can be used to assign new Specials and equipment to your available characters. This menu, however, also allows you to review your collected Powers and assign them to your fighters' custom sets.

CUSTOM SETS

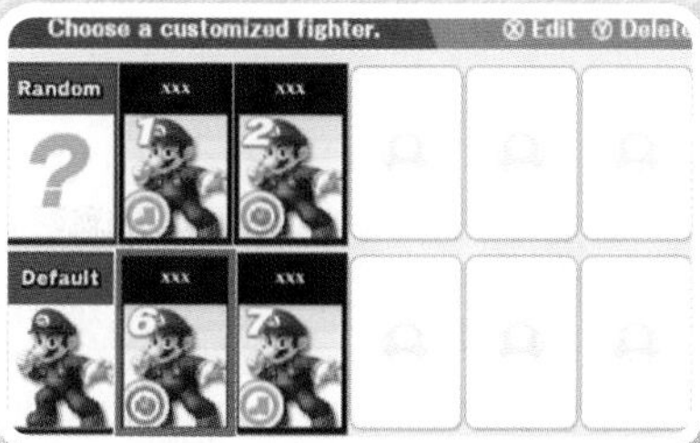

Select any fighter on your roster to create or edit a custom set. Each fighter can have up to 10 custom sets for use in various game modes. Experiment with different combinations of equipment, Specials, and Powers to ensure that you have a fighter for every occasion!

> **NOTE**
>
> Mii Fighters are only represented on your roster once you've created one. If you haven't already done so, you can create a Mii Fighter by visiting the Games & More Custom mode.

EQUIPMENT

Use equipment to modify a fighter's attack power, defensive abilities, or movement speed. Many pieces of equipment even offer special bonus effects.

Each custom set can hold up to three pieces of equipment. As you play through the game's various modes, you'll collect a wide variety of equipment, so remember to update your custom sets as more powerful items become available. Equipment that raises one stat will generally lower another; this can have a dramatic effect on a fighter's performance.

Equipment can be organized by category, by the order in which they were collected, or with recently used equipment placed at the top of the list. No matter how you choose to organize your equipment, however, you can use the colored icons to identify each piece's category:

- Orange: Orange icons indicate a piece of equipment that raises a fighter's attack power. These items usually lower defensive abilities.
- Blue: Blue icons indicate a piece of equipment that raises a fighter's defensive abilities. These items usually lower movement speed.
- Green: Green icons indicate a piece of equipment that raises a fighter's movement speed. These items usually lower attack power.

> **TIP**
>
> As you review your collected equipment, you can press Ⓨ to trade unwanted items for gold!

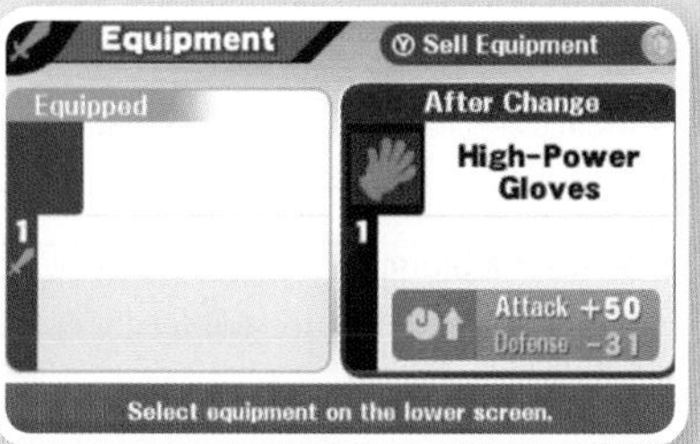

Some equipment can only be used by certain characters. These items can be identified by special icons, and they'll only appear when you're creating or editing a custom set for an appropriate character.

CHARACTER-SPECIFIC EQUIPMENT

EQUIPMENT TYPE	APPLICABLE CHARACTERS
Badge of Might	All characters
Gloves	Mario, Luigi, Captain Falcon, Wario, Sonic, Dr. Mario, PAC-MAN, Mii Fighter Brawler
Banana	Donkey Kong, Diddy Kong
Sword	Link, Toon Link, Marth, Meta Knight, Ike, Lucina, Mii Fighter Swordsman, Shulk
Arm Cannon	Samus, Mega Man, Mii Fighter Gunner
Egg	Yoshi
Lollipop	Kirby
Blaster	Fox, Falco
X Attack	Pikachu, Lucario, Jigglypuff, Greninja
Bat	Ness
Toad	Peach
Fake Nails	Bowser, Charizard
Dark Stone	Zelda, Ganondorf
Needle	Sheik
Hammer	King Dedede
Torch	Mr. Game & Watch
Zapper	R.O.B., Duck Hunt
Sacred Treasures	Pit, Dark Pit
Drill	Bowser Jr.
Beam Whip	Zero Suit Samus
Pikmin	Olimar
Staff	Palutena, Rosalina & Luma
Protein	Wii Fit Trainer
Boxing Gloves	Little Mac
Lloid	Villager
Tome	Robin
Badge of Protection	All characters
Overalls	Mario, Luigi, Wario
Tie	Donkey Kong, Dr. Mario
Shield	Link, Toon Link, Palutena
Suit	Captain Falcon, Samus, Sheik, Zero Suit Samus
Saddle	Yoshi

EQUIPMENT TYPE	APPLICABLE CHARACTERS
Hat	Kirby, Ness, Diddy Kong
Jacket	Fox, Falco, Shulk, Mii Fighter Brawler, Mii Fighter Swordsman, Mii Fighter Gunner
X Defend	Pikachu, Lucario, Charizard, Jigglypuff, Greninja
Cape	Marth, Ike, Lucina, Ganondorf
Dress	Peach, Zelda, Rosalina & Luma
Shell	Bowser, Bowser Jr.
Coat	King Dedede, Robin
Plumage	Pit, Dark Pit
Watch Battery	Mr. Game & Watch
Mask	Meta Knight
Space Suit	Olimar
Block	R.O.B.
Ring	Sonic the Hedgehog
Clothes	Villager, Wii Fit Trainer, Little Mac
Collar	Duck Hunt
Helmet	Mega Man, PAC-MAN
Badge of Agility	All characters
Shoes	Mario, Luigi, Ness, Sheik, Wario, Sonic the Hedgehog, Dr. Mario, Wii Fit Trainer, Villager, Shulk
Boots	Captain Falcon, Yoshi, Link, Toon Link, Mii Fighter Brawler, Mii Fighter Swordsman, Mii Fighter Gunner, Little Mac, PAC-MAN, Marth, Ike, Lucina, Robin, Olimar, Zelda
X Speed	Pikachu, Lucario, Charizard, Jigglypuff, Greninja
Booster	Samus, Zero Suit Samus, R.O.B., Mega Man
Pumps	Peach, Rosalina & Luma
Shin Guards	Fox, Falco, Ganondorf
Sandals	Pit, Dark Pit, Palutena
Dash Mushroom	Donkey Kong, Bowser, Bowser Jr.
Rocketbarrel Pack	Diddy Kong
Microchip	Mr. Game & Watch
Wings	Duck Hunt
Shooting Star	Kirby, King Dedede, Meta Knight

BONUS EFFECTS

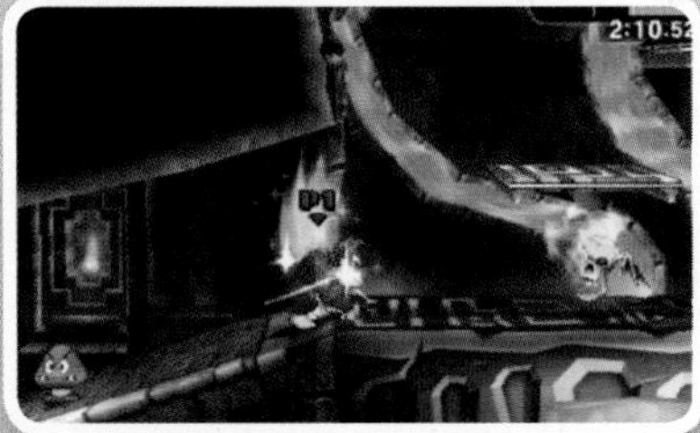

Depending on your playstyle, the bonus effects granted by some equipment can be even more important than stat changes. Some equipment can heal you over the course of a battle, provide you with a special item, or grant a variety of other effects.

Keep in mind that not all effects are advantageous. Some equipment items include negative effects to offset significant bonuses.

TIP

Auto-Heal is particularly helpful in most game modes, but it can be difficult to find a piece of equipment with that effect. Once you've unlocked the second Challenge panel, however, you can earn the Auto-Healer Brawn Badge by clearing 100-Man Smash.

SPECIALS

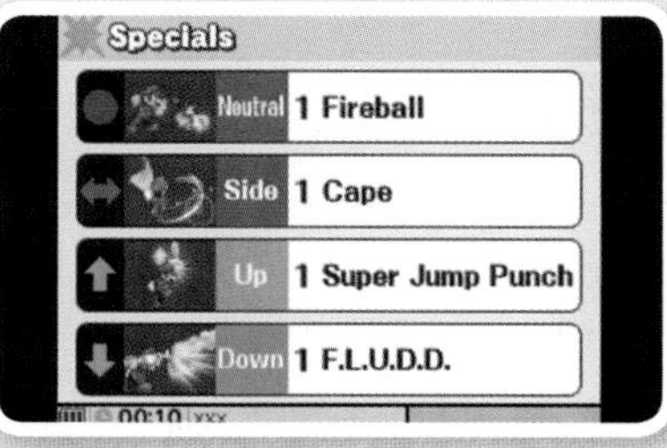

Each fighter is equipped with four default Special moves. As you play through the game's various modes, however, you'll discover alternate Specials for each of the characters on your roster. You can then use custom sets to assign new Specials to your fighters.

Each Special move is limited to a specific input:

- Neutral Special
- Side Special
- Up Special
- Down Special

Use the Touch Screen to select an input, then choose one of the available Specials.

Alternate Specials can dramatically change a fighter's offensive abilities. Before you save your custom set, press R to test your current loadout against Sandbag. This option provides all the information you'll need to familiarize yourself with a Special's unique elements.

POWERS

As you collect Powers from the game's various modes, you can assign them to your fighters' various custom sets. Press L and R to change the way they're organized. Press Y to mark the highlighted Power as one of your favorites. This ensures that the Power will remain near the top of the list each time.

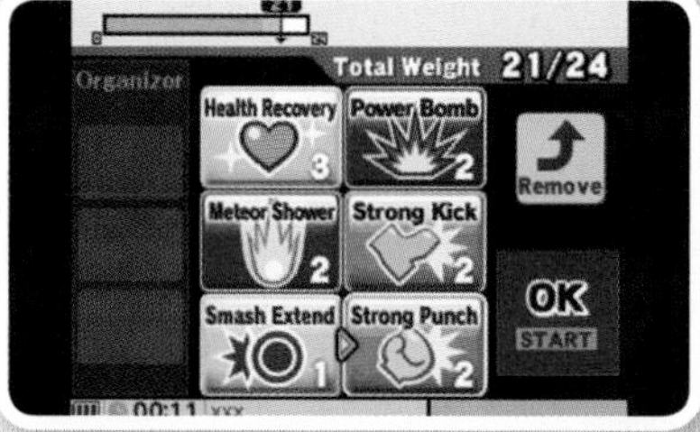

When you select a Power, it appears on the Touch Screen. Touch and drag the Power's icon to move it to a different slot or to place it in the Organizer for easy access. Near the top of the Touch Screen, you'll see the combined weight of the equipped Powers. This number cannot exceed your fighter's weight limit.

TIP

Remember that slower characters can bear more weight than faster characters. If your fighter can't handle the desired combination of Powers, try using equipment to reduce your fighter's movement speed.

MII FIGHTERS

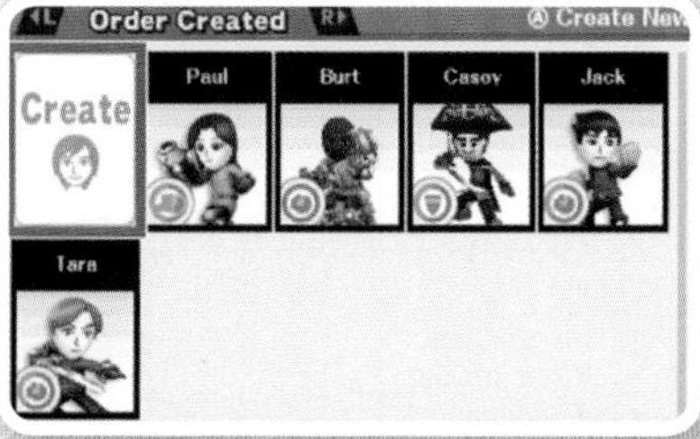

If you've already created a Mii Fighter in the Games & More Custom mode, you can use the Smash Run Custom mode to edit or create Mii Fighter custom sets. To do so, simply select the Mii Fighters from your roster.

Like the every other character on your roster, Mii Fighters can utilize equipment, Specials, and Powers; however, you can also use the headgear or outfits you've managed to collect to alter your Mii Fighter's appearance. Headgear and outfit items are purely cosmetic—they don't have any effect on your fighter's stats or abilities.

The body type of an imported Mii has a dramatic effect on the resulting Mii Fighter. Larger Miis tend to be slower and stronger, while smaller Miis are faster and harder to hit. Experiment with different height and weight combinations to find a Mii Fighter that complements your playstyle!

Select Music

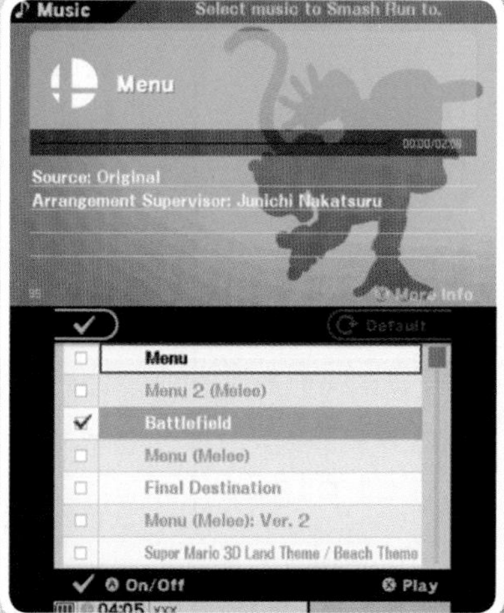

Use the "Select Music" option to determine which songs have a chance to play in the Smash Run area. The available tracks are displayed on the Touch Screen. Press X to listen to the highlighted track, and press A to add or remove that track from your playlist. Refer to the Main Display for more information about a selected track.

SMASH RUN POWERS

NAME	WEIGHT	DESCRIPTION
Auto-Recovery Lv. 1	3	Automatically heals damage bit by bit.
Auto-Recovery Lv. 2	5	
Auto-Recovery Lv. 3	7	
Auto-Recovery Lv. 4	9	
Back Shield Lv. 1	1	Equips you with a Back Shield.
Back Shield Lv. 2	2	
Back Shield Lv. 3	3	
Back Shield Lv. 4	4	
Beam Sword Lv. 1	3	Equips you with a beam sword.
Beam Sword Lv. 2	5	
Beam Sword Lv. 3	7	
Beam Sword Lv. 4	9	
Bob-omb Lv. 1	2	Equips you with a Bob-omb.
Bob-omb Lv. 2	3	
Bob-omb Lv. 3	4	
Bob-omb Lv. 4	5	
Boomerang Lv. 1	2	Boomerang.
Boomerang Lv. 2	3	
Boomerang Lv. 3	4	
Boomerang Lv. 4	5	
Brief Invincibility Lv. 1	3	Prevents you from taking damage, just for a moment.
Brief Invincibility Lv. 2	4	
Brief Invincibility Lv. 3	5	
Brief Invincibility Lv. 4	6	
Devil's Pact Lv. 1	2	Temporarily boosts your stats and increases your damage to 300.
Devil's Pact Lv. 2	4	
Devil's Pact Lv. 3	6	
Devil's Pact Lv. 4	8	
Dual Cyclone Lv. 1	6	Generate two cyclones, one on each side of you, that ensnare enemies.
Dual Cyclone Lv. 2	8	
Dual Cyclone Lv. 3	11	
Dual Cyclone Lv. 4	13	
Evershield Lv. 1	2	Prevents your shield from decreasing in size.
Evershield Lv. 2	3	
Evershield Lv. 3	4	
Evershield Lv. 4	5	
Extra Jump Lv. 1	3	Increases the number of times in a row you can jump in midair.
Extra Jump Lv. 2	5	
Extra Jump Lv. 3	8	
Extra Jump Lv. 4	10	
Hammer Lv. 1	4	Equips you with a Hammer.
Hammer Lv. 2	6	
Hammer Lv. 3	8	
Hammer Lv. 4	10	

NAME	WEIGHT	DESCRIPTION
Healing Shield Lv. 1	3	Shield against enemy attacks to heal yourself.
Healing Shield Lv. 2	4	
Healing Shield Lv. 3	6	
Healing Shield Lv. 4	7	
Health Recovery Lv. 1	3	Heals damage you have taken.
Health Recovery Lv. 2	5	
Health Recovery Lv. 3	7	
Health Recovery Lv. 4	9	
Heavenly Light Lv. 1	2	Call down a pillar of light that damages nearby enemies.
Heavenly Light Lv. 2	3	
Heavenly Light Lv. 3	4	
Heavenly Light Lv. 4	5	
High Jump Lv. 1	3	Increases the height of your jumps.
High Jump Lv. 2	5	
High Jump Lv. 3	8	
High Jump Lv. 4	10	
Homing Foe Lv. 1	3	Increases the chance that a launched opponent will collide with another enemy.
Homing Foe Lv. 2	4	
Homing Foe Lv. 3	6	
Homing Foe Lv. 4	7	
Homing Missiles Lv. 1	7	Fire two homing missiles at enemies.
Homing Missiles Lv. 2	10	
Homing Missiles Lv. 3	13	
Homing Missiles Lv. 4	17	
Horizon Beam Lv. 1	5	Fire a giant laser beam straight ahead.
Horizon Beam Lv. 2	9	
Horizon Beam Lv. 3	12	
Horizon Beam Lv. 4	15	
Instant Drop Lv. 1	3	Let's you perform a fast, downward attack by pressing down while airborne.
Instant Drop Lv. 2	5	
Instant Drop Lv. 3	7	
Instant Drop Lv. 4	9	
Launch Ring Lv. 1	4	Create a ring of light that launches enemies.
Launch Ring Lv. 2	7	
Launch Ring Lv. 3	10	
Launch Ring Lv. 4	12	
Meteor Shower Lv. 1	7	Call down meteors in front of you.
Meteor Shower Lv. 2	10	
Meteor Shower Lv. 3	13	
Meteor Shower Lv. 4	16	
Ore Club Lv. 1	8	Equips you with an Ore Club.
Ore Club Lv. 2	11	
Ore Club Lv. 3	14	
Ore Club Lv. 4	17	

SMASH RUN POWERS

NAME	WEIGHT	DESCRIPTION
Payback Lv. 1	2	Converts damage you take into a one-time boost to your next attack.
Payback Lv. 2	4	
Payback Lv. 3	6	
Payback Lv. 4	8	
Power Bomb Lv. 1	4	Drop a bomb that deals damage to enemies in the blast radius.
Power Bomb Lv. 2	7	
Power Bomb Lv. 3	10	
Power Bomb Lv. 4	13	
Rage Lv. 1	3	The more damage you've taken, the stronger you'll be.
Rage Lv. 2	5	
Rage Lv. 3	6	
Rage Lv. 4	8	
Random Lv. 1	3	Triggers the effect of a random Power.
Random Lv. 2	5	
Random Lv. 3	7	
Random Lv. 4	9	
Ray Gun Lv. 1	2	Equips you with a ray gun.
Ray Gun Lv. 2	4	
Ray Gun Lv. 3	6	
Ray Gun Lv. 4	8	
Reflector Lv. 1	3	Deflects incoming projectiles for a time.
Reflector Lv. 2	5	
Reflector Lv. 3	8	
Reflector Lv. 4	10	
Rocket Belt Lv. 1	3	Equips you with a Rocket Belt.
Rocket Belt Lv. 2	5	
Rocket Belt Lv. 3	7	
Rocket Belt Lv. 4	9	
Shinespark Lv. 1	5	Increases your running speed. When you start to shine, you can also deliver a body blow.
Shinespark Lv. 2	7	
Shinespark Lv. 3	9	
Shinespark Lv. 4	11	
Shocking Taunt Lv. 1	4	Taunt to fire lightning in the direction pressed on the +Control Pad.
Shocking Taunt Lv. 2	6	
Shocking Taunt Lv. 3	9	
Shocking Taunt Lv. 4	11	
Shuffle Lv. 1	3	Randomly reassigns the power of your stats.
Shuffle Lv. 2	5	
Shuffle Lv. 3	7	
Shuffle Lv. 4	9	
Smart Bomb Lv. 1	4	Equips you with a smart bomb.
Smart Bomb Lv. 2	6	
Smart Bomb Lv. 3	8	
Smart Bomb Lv. 4	10	

NAME	WEIGHT	DESCRIPTION
Smash Extend Lv. 1	3	Allows you to charge a smash attack longer, increasing its power.
Smash Extend Lv. 2	5	
Smash Extend Lv. 3	7	
Smash Extend Lv. 4	9	
Spinning Blades Lv. 1	5	Summon swords that spin around you, harming nearby enemies.
Spinning Blades Lv. 2	8	
Spinning Blades Lv. 3	12	
Spinning Blades Lv. 4	15	
Strong Head Lv. 1	2	Increases the power of head-based attacks, such as headbutts.
Strong Head Lv. 2	3	
Strong Head Lv. 3	5	
Strong Head Lv. 4	7	
Strong Body Lv. 1	2	Increases the power of torso-based attacks, such as tackles.
Strong Body Lv. 2	3	
Strong Body Lv. 3	5	
Strong Body Lv. 4	7	
Strong Kick Lv. 1	2	Increases the power of leg-based attacks, such as kicks.
Strong Kick Lv. 2	3	
Strong Kick Lv. 3	5	
Strong Kick Lv. 4	7	
Strong Punch Lv. 1	2	Increases the power of arm-based attacks, such as punches.
Strong Punch Lv. 2	3	
Strong Punch Lv. 3	5	
Strong Punch Lv. 4	7	
Strong Throw Lv. 1	2	Increases the distance and strength of throws.
Strong Throw Lv. 2	3	
Strong Throw Lv. 3	5	
Strong Throw Lv. 4	7	
Super Armor Lv. 1	4	Prevents you from flinching when you take damage.
Super Armor Lv. 2	7	
Super Armor Lv. 3	10	
Super Armor Lv. 4	13	
Super Leaf Lv. 1	2	Equips you with a Super Leaf.
Super Leaf Lv. 2	3	
Super Leaf Lv. 3	4	
Super Leaf Lv. 4	5	
Super Scope Lv. 1	4	Equips you with a Super Scope.
Super Scope Lv. 2	6	
Super Scope Lv. 3	8	
Super Scope Lv. 4	10	
Warp Lv. 1	4	Instantly transports you to a random location.
Warp Lv. 2	6	
Warp Lv. 3	8	
Warp Lv. 4	10	

GAMES & MORE

Games & More Overview

Games & More contains a wide variety of game modes, galleries, and options. Much of the game's content is located within this menu, so make sure you explore all of the available selections.

Games & More Menu

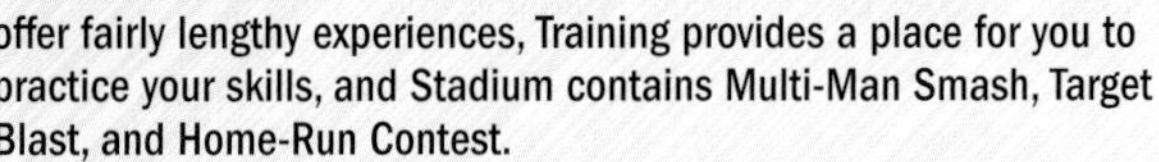

The main menu's "Games & More" menu contains five selections, most of which contain additional menus:

- Solo: Access a variety of single-player game modes. Classic and All-Star offer fairly lengthy experiences, Training provides a place for you to practice your skills, and Stadium contains Multi-Man Smash, Target Blast, and Home-Run Contest.
- Group: Team up with nearby players for All-Star or various Multi-Man Smash modes.
- Custom: Create or edit new Mii fighters, or customize any of the characters on your roster. This menu contains most of the options found in the Smash Run Custom menu.
- Vault: The bulk of the Vault is committed to various galleries and records, but it does contain a few additional features. The "Trophies" menu allows you to review the trophies you collected and gain new items through the Shop or the Trophy Rush minigame. Use the other menus to access your saved snapshots and replays, available game sounds and music, fighter and player records, and a random selection of loading screen tips.
- Options: Adjust the game's controls and sound settings, as well as important display and Internet options.

Solo

SOLO OVERVIEW

Solo contains a diverse selection of single-player offerings. You'll find some fairly extensive game modes along with a variety of challenging minigames. Exploring these game modes is a great way to hone your skills as you earn gold, trophies, equipment, and more.

SOLO MENU

The "Solo" menu contains four selections:

- Classic: Choose your own path to victory! Classic pits you against familiar foes as well as a few enemies you won't find anywhere else!
- All-Star: Time to fight everyone! In All-Star, you have one stock life to defeat every fighter on your roster.
- Training: Try out new fighters or hone your skills with an old favorite. Training includes enough options to explore every aspect of combat.
- Stadium: Defeat armies, destroy targets, or hit home runs as you explore the game modes found in Stadium.

CLASSIC

CLASSIC OVERVIEW

Choose your own path to victory in the Classic game mode! To clear Classic, you must win a series of six matches—the last of which pits you against one or more particularly powerful enemies. Each match has a five-minute time limit, so keep an eye on that clock! With plenty of opportunities to earn gold, equipment, trophies, and more, Classic is a great way to discover many of the game's hidden elements.

INTENSITY

After choosing a fighter, you can spend gold to adjust the game's intensity. The default intensity of 2.0 is the only no-cost option. Raising the intensity results in a more difficult game with the chance to earn better prizes. Lowering the intensity results in an easier game; doing so costs only a small amount of gold, but it will limit your potential prizes.

INTENSITY THRESHOLDS

Increasing the intensity level has several effects:

- Opponents are harder to launch.
- Opponents are more aggressive and generally more effective.
- You have a greater chance to fight team battles without the aid of CPU allies.
- The reward roulette at the start of each battle grants more prizes.

In addition to these gradual effects, some specific elements are only available at or above certain intensity levels:

- If the intensity is set to 3.0 or above, you have the option to face both Master Hand and Crazy Hand in the final match.
- If the intensity is set to 5.1 or above, you have the option to face Master Core.
- If the intensity is set to 6.0 and above, Master Core cycles through three hostile forms.
- If the intensity is set to 7.0 and above, Master Core cycles through four hostile forms.
- If the intensity is set to 8.0 and above, you don't have the option to avoid facing Master Core.
- Some hidden characters can be unlocked by using specific fighters to clear Classic at various intensity levels.

SELECTING STAGES

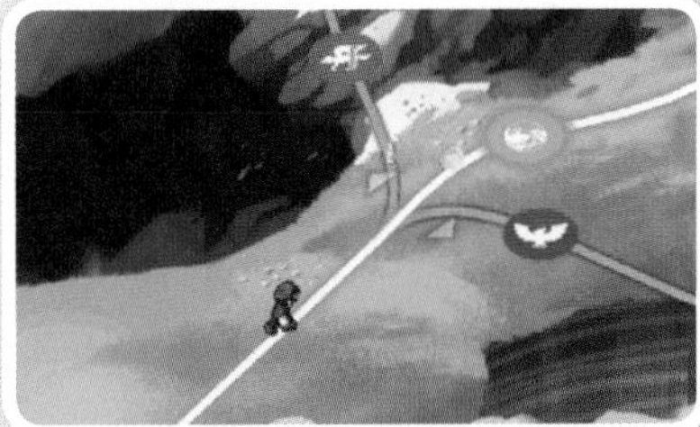

In a game of Classic, the available stages are connected by a series of branching paths. The color of each path usually indicates the relative difficulty of the next match:

- Blue paths often lead to the easier options.
- Green paths often lead to options of standard difficulty.
- Red paths often lead to the most difficult matches.

TIP

When in doubt, look for gold and other rewards that appear on the map—the more lucrative path is generally the more difficult one.

At intensity 3.0 and above, the black path near the end of the game leads to a stage containing both Master Hand and Crazy Hand. At intensities of 5.1 and above, this path also leads to Master Core.

Between matches, your fighter automatically follows the highlighted path to the next stage. To choose to change course, use the Circle Pad to highlight an alternate path before your fighter reaches the intersection.

PROGRESSING THROUGH CLASSIC

The matches that appear in Classic are, for the most part, randomly selected at the start of the game. In a given match, you might fight alone or with CPU allies; you might face a single opponent or a team of enemies; or you might stumble upon a giant or metallic variation of a familiar opponent.

Whenever the reward roulette appears on the Touch Screen, check the Main Display for details about the upcoming match.

In a game of Classic, the fifth match always pits you against 10 enemies. These matches often feature the Fighting Mii Team, but there's a chance you'll face other characters from your roster. You're clearly outnumbered during these battles, but compared to other match types, your opponents are significantly easier to launch.

The sixth and final match always features Master Hand.At intensity 3.0 and above, you have the option to enter more difficult battles. Choose wisely!

MASTER HAND

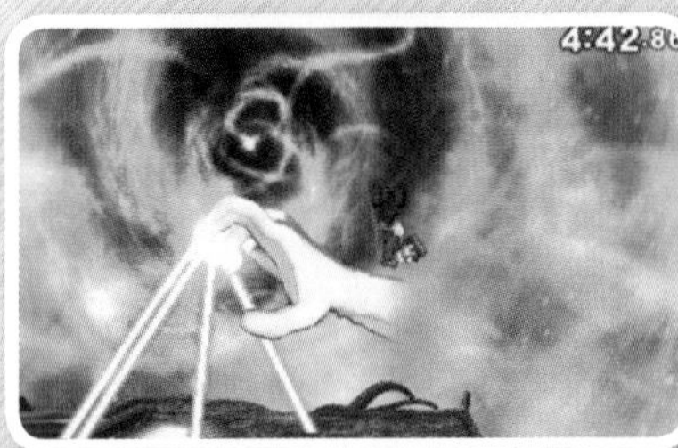

On his own, Master Hand is a formidable opponent with a wide variety of devastating attacks. Most of these attacks take some time to charge, however, making it fairly easy to identify and avoid incoming threats. A few of his attacks are fairly quick, though, so it's often best to keep your distance until he commits to a move.

Master Hand's elaborate attacks are easy to identify, so the results are fairly easy to predict. Whether he's snapping his fingers for a short-range attack, clenching his fist to slam down on the platform, or tracking your movements as he charges a projectile attack, you simply need wait until just before he strikes, then activate your shield or dodge the attack.

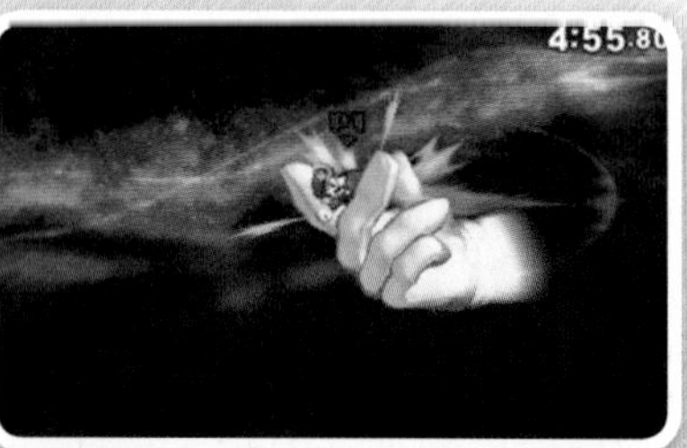

Master Hand is particularly vulnerable immediately after he attacks. This is the best time to go on the offensive, so move in and unleash one or two of your most powerful moves. It's often safe to strike while he's charging one of his moves, but make sure you allow enough time to get clear of the impending attack.

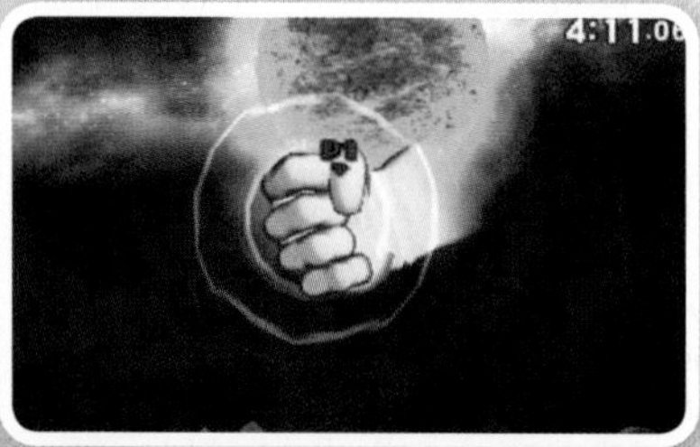

Master Hand is usually idle for several seconds between his attacks. You can deal a lot of damage during this time, but be careful—not all of his moves are easy to anticipate. Try to stick with your quick attacks and watch for any sudden movements; lingering near Master Hand can allow him to grab you right off of the platform. If this happens, quickly slide the Circle Pad back and forth until you break free of his grip.

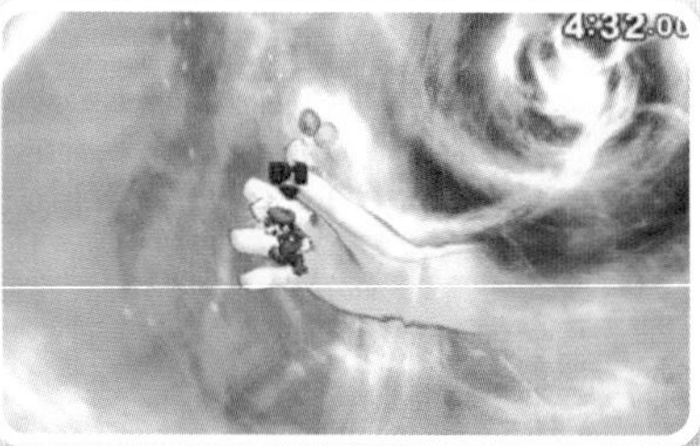

Master Hand's health is displayed on his Touch Screen portrait. Use this number to gauge your progress over the course of the battle. If you've opted to face Master Hand on his own, you must defeat him to end the battle and complete your Classic playthrough.

MASTER HAND AND CRAZY HAND

If your intensity is set to 3.0 or above, you'll have the option to face both Master Hand and Crazy Hand in the final match. Master Hand and Crazy Hand do more than simply split your attention, however—these foes often coordinate their attacks, making it difficult to maintain a solid defense.

It's important to attack whenever the opportunity presents itself, but make sure you pay attention to the entire battlefield. When one opponent seems vulnerable, there's a good chance his partner is preparing an attack of his own. Avoid committing to slower moves unless you're certain you have enough time to see them through.

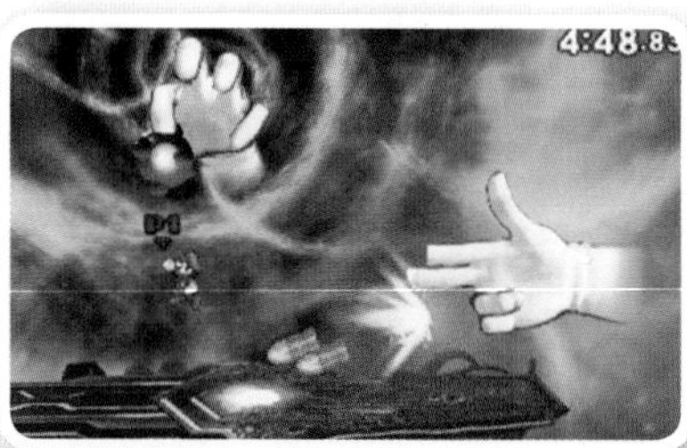

Master Hand and Crazy Hand often combine their attacks. Whether they attack simultaneously or in quick succession, the effect is generally the same—it's much more difficult to stay out of harm's way. Jumping away from Master Hand's projectile attacks, for example, can put you right under Crazy Hand's bombs. Any attempts to spot dodge or shield yourself, on the other hand, are unlikely to protect you for the duration of a coordinated attack.

Surviving unscathed often means alternating between activating your shield and dodging. If both of your opponents are charging their attacks, use the time to weigh your defensive options. Whether you plan on dodging or activating your shield, try to be patient. Watch your opponents as they move around the area, and adjust your position as needed. Wait until they commit to their attacks, and then react accordingly.

Jumping is an important part of every fight, but remember your defensive options are limited while you're in the air. The more time you spend off of the platform, the more likely it is you'll be caught in an extended attack. Before you commit to a big jump or an aerial attack, make sure you have a safe place to land. When all else fails, try to use the air dodge and fast fall techniques to avoid your opponents' juggling attacks.

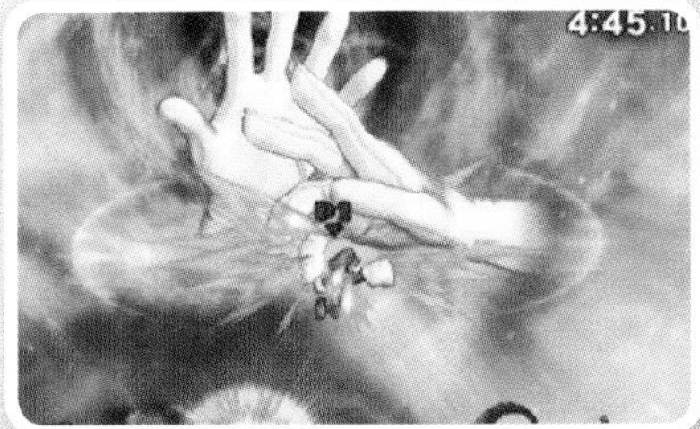

Master Hand and Crazy Hand share a single pool of health, so use the Touch Screen to monitor your progress over the course of the battle. At intensity levels of 5.0 and below, the battle ends when you defeat these opponents. At higher intensity levels, however, Master Core will step in if Master Hand and Crazy Hand fail to stop you.

MASTER CORE

Your intensity level not only determines if you're able to face Master Core, but it also affects exactly which forms Master Core will take during the battle. Regardless of your intensity level, however, you must deal damage to each of Master Core's forms to progress through the battle and eventually defeat your enemy.

> **To confront Master Core, you must select an intensity between 5.1 and 9.0, and you must choose to face both Master Hand and Master Core in the final match. When playing at an intensity of 8.0 or above, you have no choice but to face Master Hand, Crazy Hand, and Master Core in the final match.**
>
> **NOTE**

MASTER GIANT

When the intensity is set to 7.0 and above, Master Core first appears in the form of Master Giant. Master Giant is capable of several attacks, most of which affect the bulk of the battlefield. When you're not busy defending yourself, move below Master Giant's head and attack upward. It takes a few seconds for this massive enemy to recover from its own attacks, so you should have enough time to use your fighter's more powerful attacks.

Soon after Master Giant sweeps its arm through the area, a large beam speeds toward you. This beam moves very quickly, so a well-executed dodge should allow you to avoid taking damage. Until you have the timing down, however, it's best to simply shield yourself from the attack.

Watch for the growths that sometimes appear on top of Master Giant's head. Soon after they do, Master Giant smashes down on the platform and releases them into the air. Once the shadowy blobs are in place, each of them detonates, releasing horizontal and vertical beams in the process. Position yourself to avoid all of the beams until they fade, and then resume your attacks.

When Master Giant sprouts extra arms, two of its hands begin to glow. Evade these glowing fists to avoid being temporarily absorbed into Master Giant. Shielding yourself also prevents the giant from grabbing you, but just make sure your shield is only active when you're in imminent danger.

When Master Giant releases a swarm of energy orbs, try to position yourself directly under one of the available gaps. This improves your chances of avoiding damage when the Master Giant lifts the platform into the air. The orbs roam for the duration of the attack, though, so be prepared to shield or dodge as necessary.

The Master Giant sometimes creates a tear in the space near its head. Move away as soon as this happens, then activate your shield to avoid being pulled into the tear. During this attack, energy orbs travel through the area. Allowing even one of these orbs to touch you will significantly weaken your shield—if you're forced to dodge an orb, reactivate your shield as soon as you're clear.

When Master Giant clutches its head and writhes around, this signals an impending burst of energy. Watch for the small waves of energy to appear, then activate your shield to avoid the incoming attack.

> **TIP**
>
> **Master Giant has some particularly devious attacks, and learning to avoid them is an important part of completing this battle. Remember, however, that you have a relatively short time to win the match. Take every opportunity to attack!**

MASTER BEAST

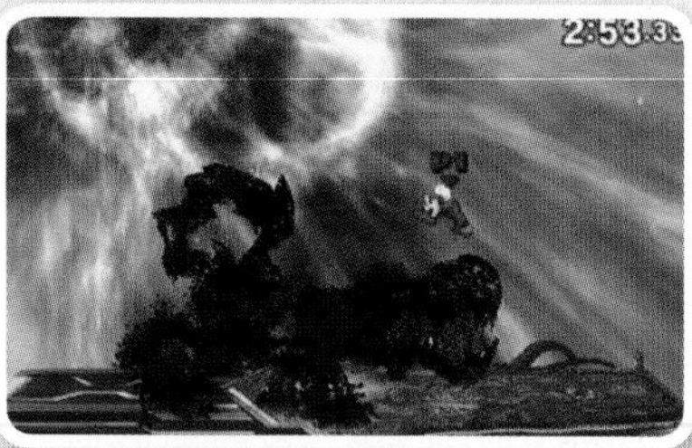

When the intensity level is set between 6.0 and 6.9, Master Core first appears in the form of Master Beast. At intensity levels of 7.0 and above, Master Beast appears after you defeat Master Giant. This monstrous form has a few distinct attacks. They're fairly easy to identify, but they can sometimes be difficult to avoid. Between Master Beast's attacks, however, you should have enough time to deal significant damage.

Soon after Master Beast sprouts spikes on its back, a trail of dark energy appears. When this trail reaches your position, spikes erupt from the platform. If you're on the ground, activate your shield or dodge away from the spikes just before they emerge. If you're caught in the air, use your recovery moves to land safely away from the spikes.

Each time Master Beast leaps into the background, it hooks back and snaps its jaws as it returns to the platform. Activate your shield or dodge away from the attack just before Master Beast reaches you.

Sometimes Master Beast leaps straight into the air and comes crashing down with enough force to tilt the platform. If you are near the point of impact, activate your shield to avoid taking damage. If you manage to get clear of the initial hit, jump up or shield to maintain control of your fighter as the platform tilts upward.

If Master Beast uses its tail to summon a bolt of dark energy, move away to avoid the impending eruption. If that's not possible, activate your shield to avoid taking damage.

MASTER EDGES

If your intensity is set between 5.1 and 5.9, Master Core first appears in the form of five shadowy blades known as Master Edges. At higher intensities, he changes to this form after you've defeated Master Beast. Master Edges can attack as individual swords or as a single cluster of blades. Additionally, this form summons dangerous orbs of dark energy. These floating blades often hover to high above the platform, so be prepared to use aerial attacks. When Master Edges is within range, though, look for opportunities to use some of your fighter's more powerful attacks.

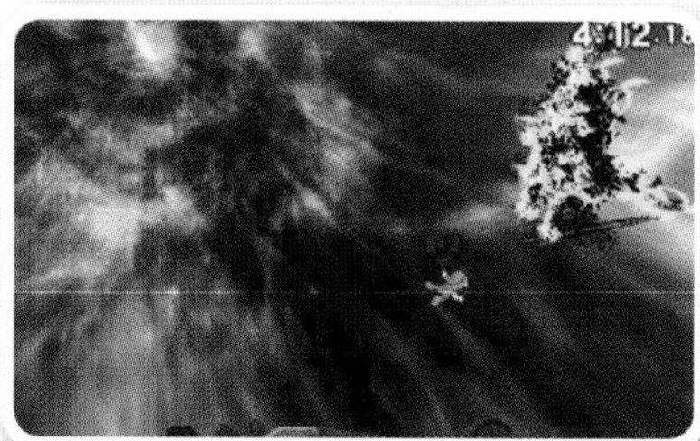

When you face Master Edges, look for the yellowish shimmer that appears along the blades just before each attack. If the blades shimmer while they're tightly clustered and pointing upward, it means they're about to release a flurry of strikes. This flurry has a fairly long range, so it's often best to simply activate your shield and wait it out. If the shimmer appears while you're airborne, use your fast fall to return to the platform as quickly as possible.

If the blades are pointing downward when they shimmer, it usually indicates some type of quick slash attack. Such attacks almost always produce orbs of dark energy. Use your shield to defend yourself from the slashing blades, and then evade the orbs as they move through the area.

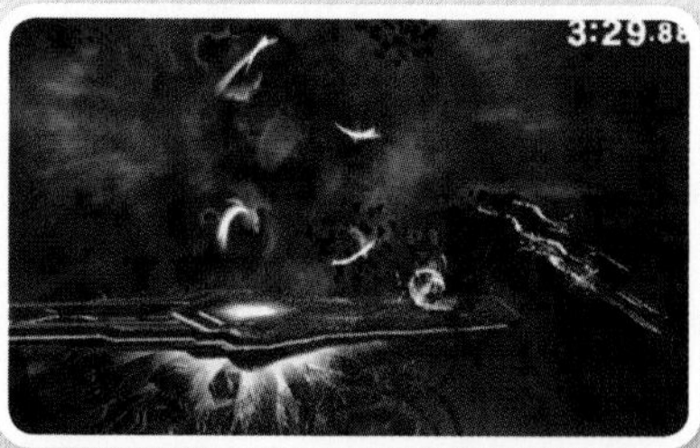

Smaller orbs move fairly slowly, but they're very good at homing in on your position. This can make the orbs surprisingly difficult to avoid, so it's important to time your jumps and dodges properly.

The larger orbs have limited homing ability, but they move considerably faster than their smaller counterparts. Their sheer size can also make it more difficult to slip around the larger orbs—so, be prepared to spot dodge or activate your shield as needed.

Occasionally, Master Edges separates its blades in order to surround you. When this happens, move to the center of the platform and wait for the attack. Spot dodge each of the smaller blades as they slash through the area. The attack ends when the large blade above you comes crashing down to the platform. Spot dodge or shield yourself from the impact, then hit the large blade with a few counterattacks.

MASTER SHADOW

Whenever you face Master Core—regardless of your intensity level—Master Shadow appears once Master Edges is defeated. This mysterious clone possesses more powerful versions of your fighter's abilities and equipment. This means Master Shadow's attacks do more damage than yours, and any equipment-based bonus effects are more potent than those granted to your fighter.

When Master Shadow is first revealed, your shadowy opponent is a considerably larger version of your fighter. Your successful attacks, however, will slowly cut your doppelgänger down to size. Remember that while Master Shadow isn't limited to offensive maneuvers—Master Shadow can shield and dodge as well as and standard opponent. Use your more powerful attacks each time you see an opening, and use plenty of throws to break through Master Shadow's defenses. Continue to deal damage until you destroy or KO Master Shadow.

MASTER CORE

Once you've defeated all of Master Core's shadowy forms, his true form is revealed. When he's exposed, Master Core lacks any defensive abilities. If you remain idle too long, however, Master Core will unleash a powerful attack, resulting in an instant KO! Dash in and perform a series of attacks to prevent this from happening. All of your attacks should prove effective, but you must KO Master Core to finish the battle. Use any combination of attacks to get Master Core's damage percentage well above 100, then perform Smash attacks until you launch him out of the stage.

As Master Core takes damage, he becomes easier to launch. Until you finally score the KO, however, he'll return to the center of the platform after each of your attacks. Luckily, the clock stops once Master Core's true form is revealed, so you're free to make as many attempts as you need to launch him out of the stage.

GAME OVER

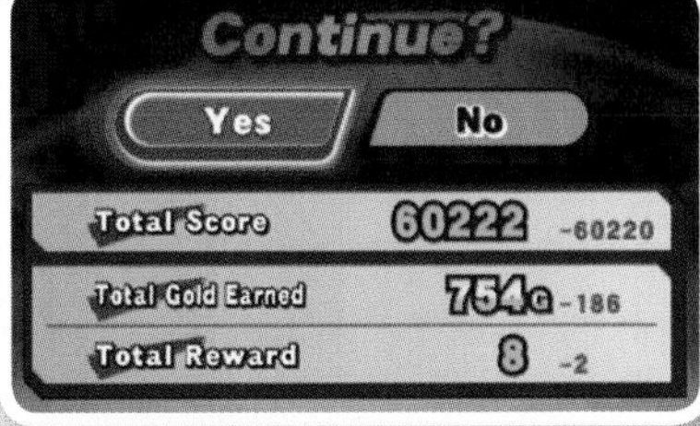

In Classic, you start each match with two stock lives. This means that you can suffer one KO during each battle without losing the match. If you lose both of your stock lives during a match—or if you fail to complete a match within the allotted time—the game ends. This reduces your score and gold, and it usually eliminates at least a few of the rewards you've earned. Each time you lose a match, however, you're given the opportunity to continue. This allows you to resume your playthrough, but any penalties you took remain in place. In most cases, continuing your game also affects the intensity level for the remaining matches.

If you decide not to continue, you're granted whatever score, gold, and rewards are displayed on the results screen.

CLEARING CLASSIC

When you clear a game of Classic, you receive information about your score, as well as any gold and rewards you've earned. Tap the icons on the Touch Screen for details about your final rewards. This screen also displays any rewards you might have sacrificed by continuing the game.

Most important, however, clearing Classic unlocks your fighter's primary trophy and triggers the staff credits.

ALL-STAR

All-Star can be found in both the "Solo" menu and the "Group" menu within Games & More. Make sure you select the desired version before you start the game.

NOTE

STAFF CREDITS

During the staff credits, you can attack the individual names to slowly reveal the image on the wall. For a name to contribute to the image, however, you must hit it at the just the right time and in just the right spot. Jump up and use aerial attacks to reveal the top of the image as the names pass in front of any blank areas, then work your way down.

As you reveal more of the image, it becomes important to aim your shots. Look for the sparkles that help identify hidden sections, then strike a name as it passes through the area.

HIDDEN CHARACTERS

All of the game's hidden characters can be unlocked by playing Smash, but many of them can also be unlocked in Classic. Different characters have different prerequisites, so make sure you select the correct fighter and intensity before you start a playthrough.

UNLOCKING HIDDEN CHARACTERS IN CLASSIC

CHARACTER	PREREQUISITE
Ness	Clear Classic on any difficulty.
Falco	Clear Classic without using any continues.
Lucina	As Marth, clear Classic without using any continues.
Dark Pit	Clear Classic with three or more characters.
Dr. Mario	As Mario, clear Classic on intensity 4.0 or higher.
Ganondorf	As Zelda or Link, clear Classic on intensity 5.0 or higher.
Mr. Game & Watch	Clear Classic with 10 or more characters.
Bowser Jr.	As Bowser, clear Classic on intensity 6.0 or higher.
Duck Hunt	Clear Classic with 15 or more characters.

ALL-STAR OVERVIEW

In All-Star, you must complete a series of seven matches, each of which contains fighters from various time periods of video game history. To win a match, simply KO all of the available opponents.

You're only given a single life to complete a game of All-Star—if you're KO'd, the game ends and you must restart from the beginning. You are, however, provided with a limited supply of recovery items which can be used between matches. Knowing when to use each of the available items is an important part of any All-Star strategy.

BETWEEN MATCHES

After you clear a stage, you're given a reward based on your performance. When the results are displayed, use the Touch Screen to review all of the rewards you've collected during your All-Star playthrough.

Between matches, your fighter appears in the Rest Area. The portal near the center of the Rest Area will transport your fighter to the next match, so avoid touching it until you're ready to continue. The portraits that appear in the background indicate your opponents in the upcoming match. Sometimes a randomly selected collectible item appears to the left of the portal, so make sure you check that area before you head out.

Your available recovery items are located to the right of the Rest Area portal. If necessary, jump over the portal and consume a desired item before you proceed to the next match.

The Touch Screen displays your fighter's current health and all of the opponents you've defeated during your All-Star playthrough.

TRUE ALL-STAR

True All-Star only becomes available after you unlock all of the game's hidden characters. Until then, you have access to a temporary version of All-Star. This modified game mode is indicated by the small padlock icon that appears on the Touch Screen when All-Star is selected.

True All-Star is similar to the temporary version, but unlocking the full roster does trigger a few important changes. Some stages will contain a different number of opponents, you'll be provided with different recovery items, and you'll be eligible for different bonus scores.

OPPONENTS PER STAGE

STAGE	TEMPORARY ALL-STAR	TRUE ALL-STAR
Stage 1	5 opponents	5 opponents
Stage 2	5 opponents	7 opponents
Stage 3	6 opponents	7 opponents
Stage 4	5 opponents	7 opponents
Stage 5	4 opponents	7 opponents
Stage 6	6 opponents	7 opponents
Stage 7	5 opponents	7 opponents

REST AREA RECOVERY ITEMS

RECOVERY ITEM	NUMBER AVAILABLE IN TEMPORARY ALL-STAR	NUMBER AVAILABLE IN TRUE ALL-STAR
Maxim Tomato	1	1
Fairy Bottle	1	1
Heart Container	1	2

DIFFICULTY

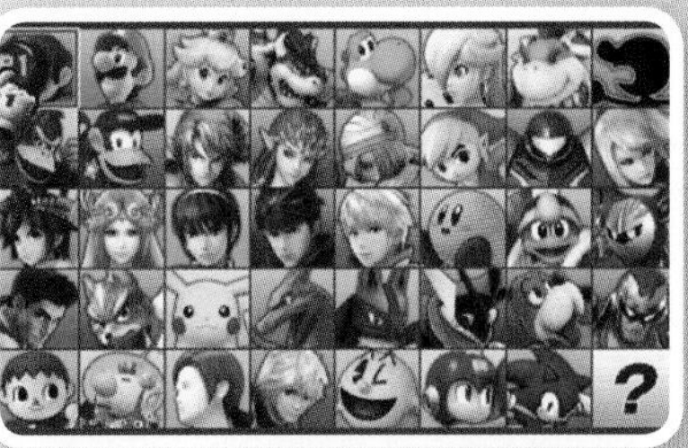

Both the temporary All-Star mode and the true All-Star mode offer three difficulty settings. During character selection, use the tabs near the top of the Touch Screen to select your desired difficulty.

At harder difficulties, your opponents are more aggressive and harder to launch. Playing at higher difficulties, however, also increases your potential score and rewards, and All-Star difficulty is an important part of completing some of the game's Challenges.

BONUS SCORE

In addition to your base score, you can earn a bonus score by meeting a number of conditions. Your potential bonus score is affected by your chosen difficulty and whether or not you've unlocked true All-Star mode.

TEMPORARY ALL-STAR BONUS SCORE

CONDITION	VALUE ON EASY	VALUE ON NORMAL	VALUE ON HARD
Mode Cleared	30,000	60,000	90,000
Maxim Tomatoes remaining in the Rest Area	2,500 (each)	5,000 (each)	7,500 (each)
Fairy Bottles remaining in the Rest Area	3,500 (each)	7,000 (each)	10,500 (each)
Heart Containers remaining in the Rest Area	5,000 (each)	10,000 (each)	15,000 (each)
Cleared without taking damage	150,000	300,000	450,000

TRUE ALL-STAR BONUS SCORE

CONDITION	VALUE ON EASY	VALUE ON NORMAL	VALUE ON HARD
Mode Cleared	60,000	120,000	180,000
Maxim Tomatoes remaining in the Rest Area	5,000 (each)	10,000 (each)	150,000 (each)
Fairy Bottles remaining in the Rest Area	7,000 (each)	14,000 (each)	21,000 (each)
Heart Containers remaining in the Rest Area	10,000 (each)	20,000 (each)	30,000 (each)
Cleared without taking damage	300,000	600,000	900,000

CLEARING ALL-STAR

Whether your All-Star playthrough ends in victory or failure, you're able to keep all of the gold and rewards you've collected during your playthrough. Tap the icons on the Touch Screen for additional details about your rewards. Of course, clearing All-Star does provide additional benefits—a successful All-Star playthrough unlocks your fighter's alternate trophy and triggers the staff credits!

STAFF CREDITS

As in the Classic staff credits, you can attack the names in the All-Star staff credits to reveal the hidden image in the background. Jump up and use aerial attacks to reveal the top of the image as the names pass in front of any blank areas, then work your way down. Again, as you reveal more of the image, it becomes important to aim your shots. Look for the sparkles that help identify hidden sections, and then strike a name as it passes through the area.

TRAINING

TRAINING OVERVIEW

Training is a great way to practice with—and against—specific fighters under a variety of conditions. Select your fighter, your opponents, and your stage just as you would when starting a game of Smash. Once Training begins, use the Touch Screen to adjust the available settings and create your desired scenario.

DURING TRAINING

By default, the Main Display shows helpful information in the bars above the action. Use these bars to track the damage caused by your attacks and the length of any combos you perform.

Use the Touch Screen to adjust the available Training settings at any time during your session:

- Item: Use the arrows to cycle through the game's various items. Tap the selection to spawn the indicated item on the battlefield.
- Speed: Change the game's speed. This includes options for constant effects and speed changes that are triggered by holding L.
- No. of CPUs: This setting determines if you face one, two, or three CPU opponents.
- CPU Behavior: Use this setting to determine whether your opponents stand still (stop), walk, run, jump, or attack.
- Damage %: Adjust the current damage percentage for all fighters.
- Camera: Choose between normal, zoom, and fixed camera settings.
- Info: Hide or show the information bars at the top of the Main Display.

TIP

Use the player/settings tab near the bottom of the Touch Screen to switch between fighter portraits and Training settings.

STADIUM

STADIUM OVERVIEW

Stadium contains a variety of single-player game modes. You'll find several opportunities for combat, but Stadium also allows you to use your fighter's skills in new and interesting ways.

STADIUM MENU

Stadium Menu contains three selections, each of which offers a unique game mode:

- Multi-Man Smash: Stand alone against an oncoming horde of enemies in a variety of Multi-Man Smash game modes.
- Target Blast!: Launch bombs to destroy an arrangement of targets and obstacles.
- Home-Run Contest: Use a Home-Run Bat to knock Sandbag as far as you can.

MULTI-MAN SMASH

> Multi-Man variants can be found in both the "Solo" menu and the "Group" menu within Games & More. Make sure you select the desired version before you start the game.
>
> **NOTE**

10-MAN SMASH

Defeat a 10-man army as fast as you can! Your opponents are very easy to launch, so you don't generally need to waste time with extended combos or charged attacks. A quick Smash attack is almost always enough to KO all fighters within range. Dash attacks can be particularly effective—especially when your opponents use projectile weapons to attack from a distance—and aerial attacks are great for dealing with more agile enemies.

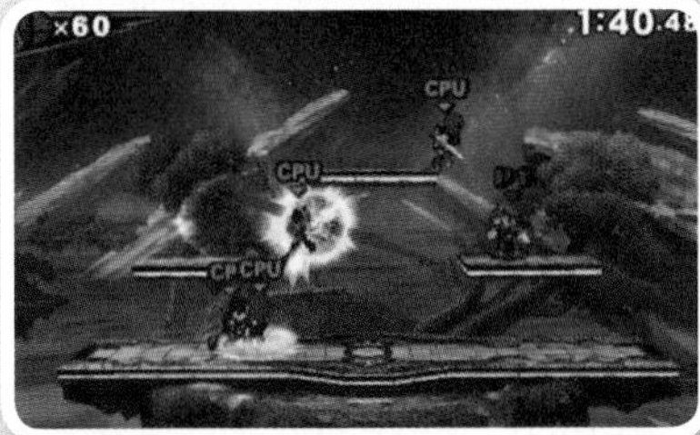

100-MAN SMASH

Defeat a 100-man army as fast as you can! Your opponents are still very easy to launch, but their sheer numbers can make it difficult to defend yourself from incoming attacks. Keep an eye on your fighter's damage percentage, and take advantage of the items that occasionally appear near the top of the stage. It's often helpful to stand on the highest platform—simply launch your opponents as they move into range.

3-MINUTE SMASH

Defeat as many enemies as you can within the time limit! You have three minutes and an endless supply of easily launched opponents. You can build a decent score using virtually any techniques, and the items that appear in the area can be very useful. Again, standing on the highest platform is a great way to control the battlefield. Use Up Smash attacks and Up Tilt attacks to launch your opponents as they jump up to you.

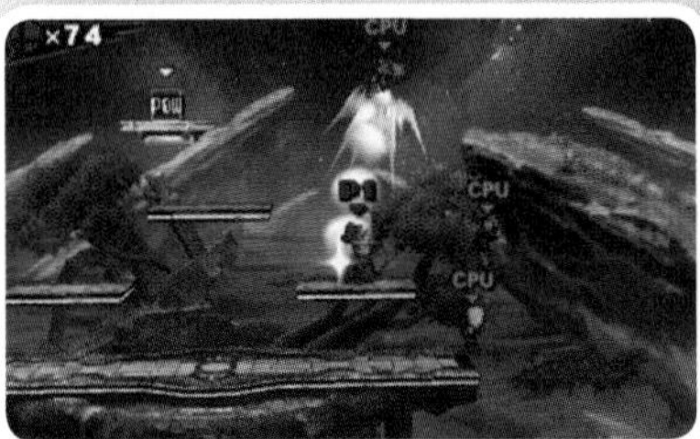

RIVAL SMASH

Defeat more enemies than your rival! Standard enemies are very easy to launch, but this fact also benefits your rival. There's no time limit, but you are limited to a single stock life—once you're defeated, the final score determines the winner. Your rival, on the other hand, has an infinite supply of stock lives. Scoring a KO on your rival is worth three points, but he or she can absorb much more damage than the standard opponents.

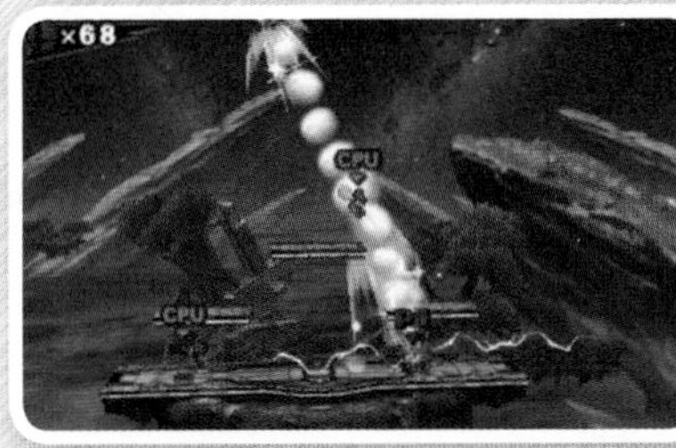

ENDLESS SMASH

No time limit! Fight until you can fight no more! Endless Smash lets you put your skills to the test. Like most Multi-Man modes, your enemies are very easy to launch. Given enough time, though, you're sure to sustain enough damage that even the lightest hit will launch you clear out of that stage—so, use your preferred techniques to score points until that happens.

CRUEL SMASH

The elite army is ready to attack! Don't hold back—it's a fight to the end! In Cruel Smash, you opponents are extremely hard to launch. Unfortunately, the same can't be said for your fighter; each of your opponents packs enough of a punch to send you soaring off of the platform. Throwing your opponents if often effective, particularly if your fighter is near the edge of the platform.

Characters equipped with a Counter special—like Ike, for example—can be very effective in Cruel Smash. It's often possible to catch several opponents with a single Counter. If you lure them to the end of the stage, you have an excellent chance of scoring multiple KOs with a single Counter.

TARGET BLAST!

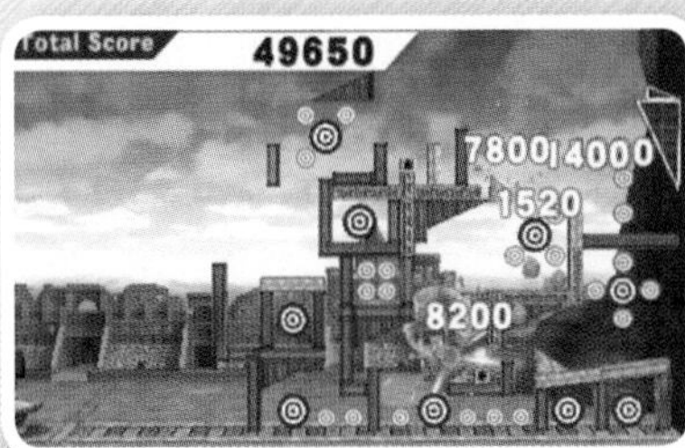

In Target Blast, you have two bombs to destroy as many targets and obstacles as you can. During each round, touch the bomb to start its countdown. Use the available time to damage the bomb, then use a Smash attack to launch it from the platform. Success is based on timing and accuracy, so keep track of all pertinent factors. What was the bomb's damage percentage? How long did you charge your Smash attack? What was your position on the platform? How much time was left on the countdown? Knowing these answers allows you to make small adjustments in future attempts.

Bombs often create falling debris, so it can be very effective to aim for the higher targets during your first round—a well-placed bomb can create chain reactions of loose obstacles. If you're having trouble controlling the angle of your launch, try bouncing one of your bombs off of the nearby wall. This allows you to achieve dramatically different results with the same basic attacks.

TIP

Use the Touch Screen to zoom in and out for a better look at the area. Identify the available targets before you begin each countdown!

HOME-RUN CONTEST

In Home-Run Contest, you must launch Sandbag as far as possible. Use your fighter's attacks to increase Sandbag's damage percentage, then grab the Home-Run Bat and use it to launch Sandbag from the platform. It's best to minimize the time you spend chasing Sandbag across the platform. Try using Smash attacks to bounce Sandbag against the invisible wall that surrounds the platform. Sandbag's damage percentage will change the angle of its bounce, but small adjustments should allow you to land a steady series of hits.

As you pummel Sandbag, watch for the countdown to appear on the screen. You must grab the Home-Run Bat and begin your final attack before time runs out. If you grab the Home-Run Bat too early, you'll sacrifice any additional damage you might have delivered to Sandbag. Grabbing the Home-Run Bat too late, on the other hand, will prevent you from launching Sandbag at all.

TIP

Collectible items such as trophies and equipment sometimes appear on the ground. Any item Sandbag touches is automatically added to your collection!

Group

GROUP OVERVIEW

Use the "Group" menu to play cooperative games with a nearby friend. Your success depends on working together!

GROUP MENU

The "Group" menu offers two selections:

- All-Star: Team up with a friend to face every fighter on your roster. The game ends if either of you are KO'd, so watch your partner's back.
- Multi-Man: Face an army with a friend by your side. This selection offers multiplayer versions of most Multi-Man Smash types.

ALL-STAR

All-Star can be found in both the "Solo" menu and the "Group" menu within Games & More. Make sure you select the desired version before you start the game.

NOTE

Group All-Star works in much the same way as the single-player version. You and your friend must battle through a series of matches as you face every fighter on your roster. Work together to keep each other safe as you KO each of your enemies.

Cooperation is the key to success; the game ends if either of you suffer a KO or a self-destruct. The Rest Area recovery items are meant to be shared, and keeping your team healthy should be a priority. Communicate with your partner to determine if and when each item should be used.

MULTI-MAN

Multi-Man contains cooperative versions of 10-Man Smash, 100-Man Smash, 3-Minute Smash, Endless Smash, and Cruel Smash. In each game mode, you must work with your partner to defeat enemies and work toward your chosen Multi-Man objectives.

> Rival Smash is only available through the "Solo" menu.
>
> **NOTE**

Custom

CUSTOM OVERVIEW

> The Games & More Custom mode and the Smash Run Custom mode share many of the same features. Powers cannot be reviewed or assigned from this menu, but the Games & More Custom mode is the only way to create your first Mii Fighter. For more details about Custom options, please refer to the guide's Smash Run section.
>
> **NOTE**

CUSTOM MENUS

The Games & More Custom mode separates fighters into two distinct categories:

- Mii Fighters: Create or edit a Mii Fighter.
- Characters: Assign Specials and equipment to the fighters on your roster.

CHARACTERS

The "Characters" option allows you to select a fighter from your existing roster, just as you would in the Smash Run Custom mode. You can also rename your character's custom set to help differentiate it from existing versions. You can use the equipment and Specials you've collected to create up to 10 custom sets for each of the characters on your roster.

MII FIGHTERS

To create a new Mii Fighter, simply select one of your Miis and choose a basic fighting style:

- Brawler: A fighter skilled in hand-to-hand combat.
- Swordfighter: A warrior versed in the art of swordplay.
- Gunner: An expert in long-range projectile combat.

Once you've input a name for your new Mii Fighter, you're free to assign equipment, Specials, headgear, and outfits to create your ideal warrior. When you're happy with your selections, press R to test your new fighter, or press START to save your work and return to the previous menu.

Vault

VAULT OVERVIEW

In addition to its galleries and records, the Vault includes the game's Shop and the Trophy Rush minigame.

VAULT MENU

The "Vault" menu contains six options:

- Trophies: Inspect your trophies, or check in for a chance to add new trophies to your collection.
- Album: Review the snapshots you've taken while playing the game.
- Replays: Manage the replays you've saved while playing the game.
- Sounds: Listen to the music and sounds you've unlocked.
- Records: Review records for each fighter, game stats, and earned milestones.
- Tips: Cycle through randomly selected loading screen tips.

TROPHIES OVERVIEW

Visit the "Trophies" menu for a closer look at your trophy collection, to purchase new trophies from the Shop, or to play a round of Trophy Rush.

GALLERY

Gallery gives you an up-close look at all of the trophies you've collected, as well information about the objects and characters they represent.

Trophies can be organized by the order in which you obtained them, by series, or by category—use Ⓛ and Ⓡ to switch between these options. Tap the small icon in the Touch Screen's upper-right corner to change the background on the Main Display. Once you've selected a trophy, use the on-screen commands to make additional adjustments.

HOARD

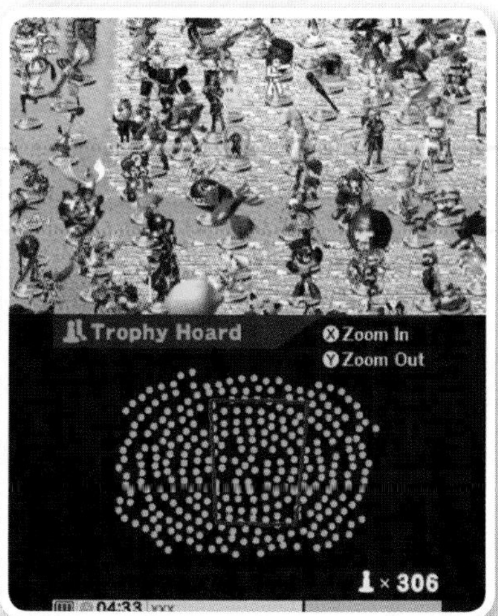

Hoard allows you to see all of your trophies in one large group. Use the Circle Pad to move the camera, and use the on-screen commands to zoom in and out. The Touch Screen shows the trophy locations and how much of the area is caught by the camera.

SHOP

In the game's Shop, you can use gold or Play Coins to purchase new trophies. Press Ⓨ to toggle between currencies. The Shop contains up to six trophies at a time, and it features regular sales.

Seven minutes after leaving the Shop, the inventory updates if any of the following conditions have been met:

- You've purchased all six of the Shops available trophies.
- You've reached a result screen in Smash, Smash Run, Solo, or Trophy Rush.

- You've reached the result screen in StreetSmash.

If none of these conditions have been met, the inventory updates after 30 or more minutes of total run time has passed since you last exited the Shop.

CAUTION

If one of the Shop's offers includes a "Got it!" checkmark, it means that trophy is already in your collection. Buyer beware!

TROPHY RUSH

In Trophy Rush, you have a limited time to smash blocks for trophies and other prizes—the more gold you invest, the more time you get! Each second costs six gold. You can purchase a minimum of 30 seconds (for 180 gold) up to a maximum of 2 minutes and 30 seconds (for 900 gold).

Use your fighter's combat skills to shatter the blocks as they appear. Destroying blocks adds to your score—earn higher scores to earn more prizes. Many blocks contain trophies, gold, and customization items, so keep an eye out for any blocks marked with relevant icons. Some blocks explode shortly after they land. Destroy explosive blocks before they detonate, or keep your distance to avoid any impending explosions.

Destroy blocks in quick succession to earn chain bonuses for even more points. Fill the gauge in the upper-left corner of the Main Display to enter Fever Rush. During Fever Rush, most of the available blocks contain additional prizes. If you remain in one spot for too long, a special hazard will drop down to your position. If you take too much damage, you'll be launched out of the stage—and each time this happens, your remaining time is reduced by 15 seconds. Additionally, allowing the blocks to stack too high will result in a KO! Watch the line near the top of the Main Display; shortly after a stack reaches that line, the entire platform vanishes. If this happens, the platform won't return until after you've fallen out of the stage.

ALBUM

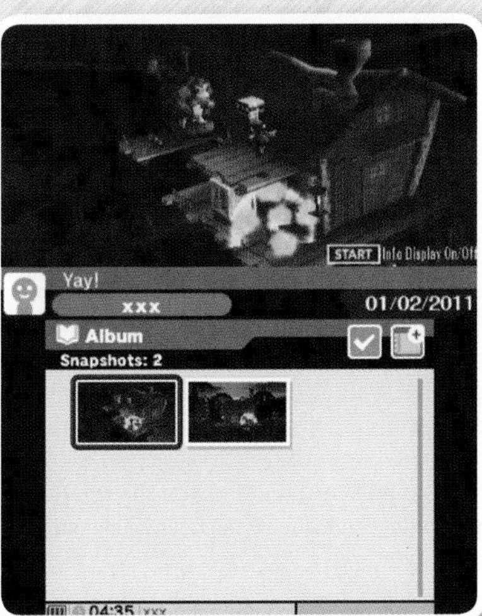

Album lets you review and manage all of the snapshots you've taken while playing the game. You can view individual images, add brief comments, and delete unwanted snapshots to save space on your SD card.

Press START during a battle to take a snapshot through the pause menu.

NOTE

REPLAYS

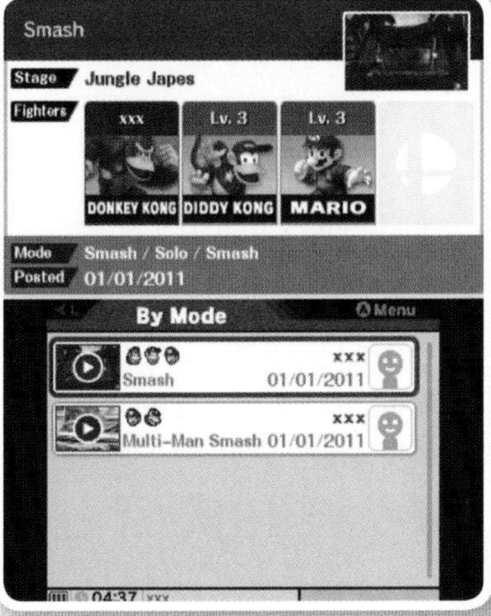

View and manage your saved replays! Replays can be organized by the order in which they were saved, by stage, by creator, or by game mode. Use L and R to cycle through these options. Select a replay to view it, add a brief comment, or delete it from your SD card.

SOUNDS

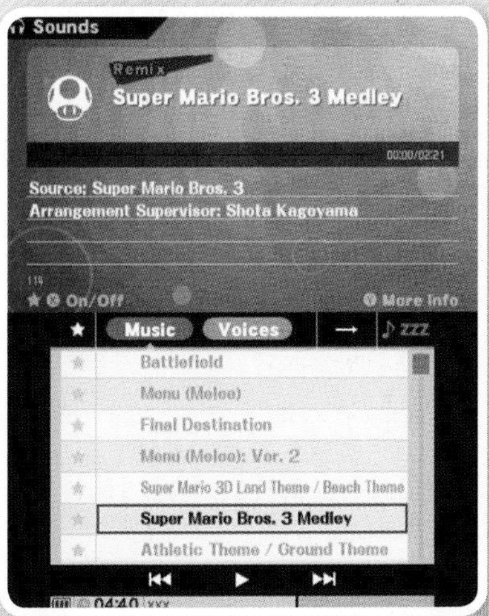

Sounds allows you to listen to all of the music and voice samples you've unlocked. Use the Touch Screen to select tracks, toggle between music and voices, mark your favorite songs, or activate the Play in Sleep Mode option (found in the Touch Screen's upper-right corner).

TIP

When Play in Sleep Mode is active, you can use headphones to listen to music while your system is in Sleep Mode. You can then use L to skip to the previous song and R to skip to the next song.

RECORDS

Records contains information about how you've been playing the game. Review your fighter records, current stats, and all of the milestones you've earned.

FIGHTER RECORDS

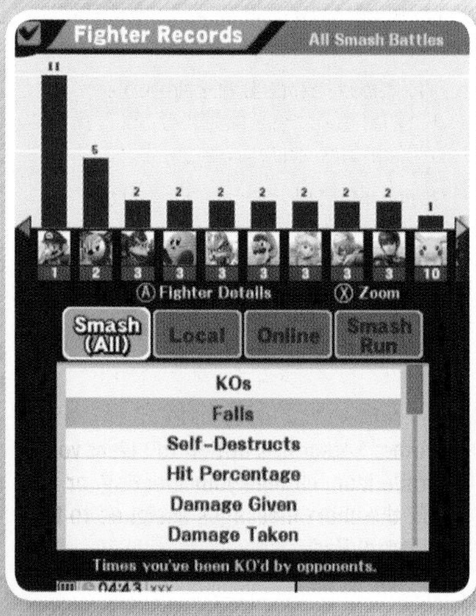

Review extensive records for each of the fighters on your roster! Use the Touch Screen to select specific records, then check the Main Display for each fighter's current rank. The game tracks virtually everything each fighter does—from the KOs a character has scored to how many items he or she has collected. You'll have all of the information you need to determine just how effective you've been with each fighter.

Fighter records are arranged by game mode; use the Touch Screen to select one of the available options.

STATS

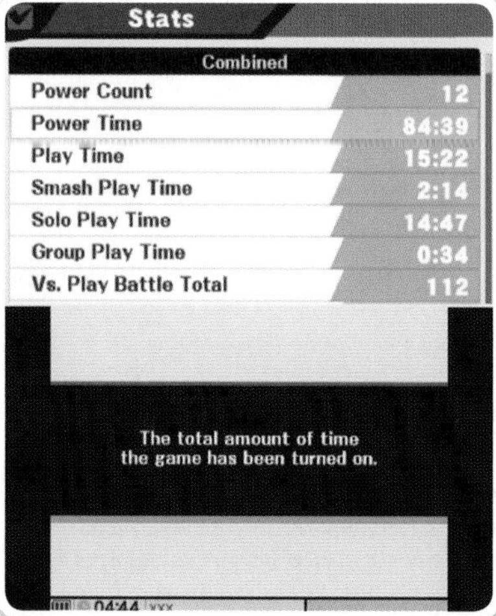

Stats tracks virtually every detail of how you've been playing the game. How many times have you turned on the game? How many total KOs have you scored? How much gold have you spent on trophies? If you're curious about how you've spent your time in-game, this is the section for you! Select an item on the Main Display, then refer to the Touch Screen for a more detailed description of the statistic.

MILESTONES

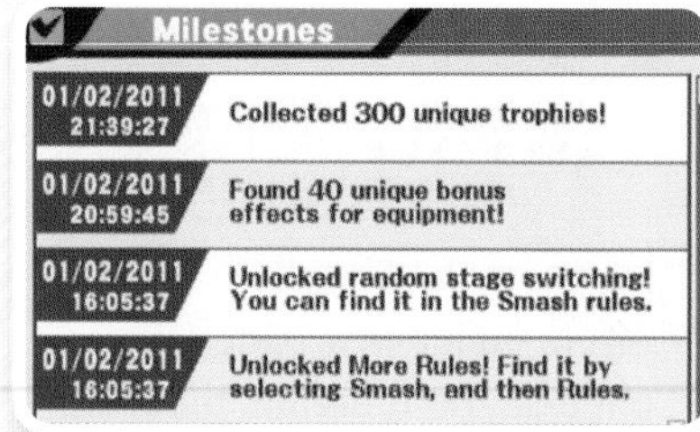

Check all of the milestones you've reached in the game and when you reached them. Use the Circle Pad to scroll through your milestones on the Main Display and see just how far you've come!

TIPS

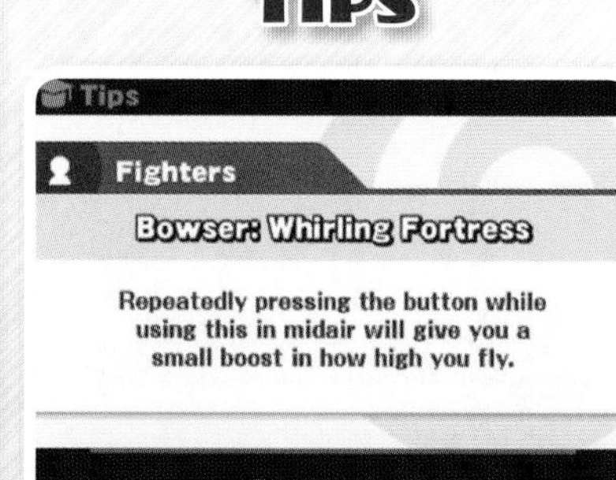

Review this handy collection of helpful tips. Tap the icon on the Touch screen to load a randomly selected tip about fighters, stages, items, game modes, and more!

Options

Options Overview

Customize your experience by adjusting the game's default settings. The choices you make here affect nearly every mode in the game, so return to here anytime you need to make a change.

Options Menu

The "Options" menu is divided into five categories:

- Controls: Change the button configuration.
- Sound: Adjust the volume of music, sound effects, and voices.
- Character Outline: Change the thickness of the outlines surrounding the fighters.
- Damage Display: Change the location of the damage percentages displayed on the Touch Screen.
- Internet Options: Change your online settings and edit your profile.

Controls

Your current control scheme is displayed on the Touch Screen. To adjust the controls, touch one of the available functions and slide it to the desired button.

Sound

The current sound levels are displayed on the Touch Screen. Adjust the volume of the game's music, sound effects, and voices to match your tastes. You can preview your settings before you exit, or use the tab near the bottom of the Touch Screen to access all of the music and voices you've managed to collect.

Character Outline

Adjust the outline that appears around the fighters. You can choose between a thick outline and a thin outline, or you can eliminate the outline altogether.

Damage Display

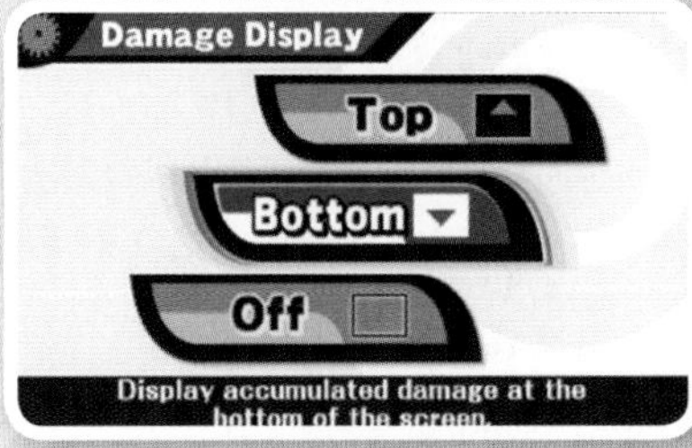

Use this setting to determine where damage percentages will be displayed during battle. You can display this information at the top or bottom of each fighter's portrait, or you can prevent this information from being displayed at all.

Internet Options

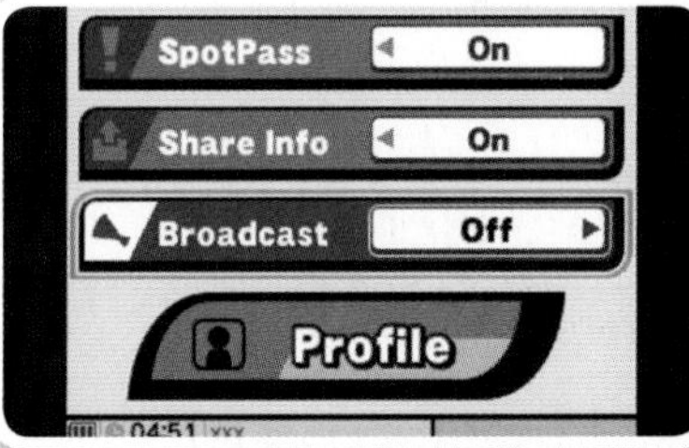

This menu allows you to change your online settings and edit your personal profile:

- SpotPass: This setting determines whether or not you receive SpotPass notifications about the game.
- Share Info: This setting determines whether or not Nintendo will receive information about how you play the game.
- Broadcast: This setting determines whether or not other players will be able to watch your battles in Spectator mode.
- Profile: Select this option to select your profile icon, change your greeting, or edit the short messages assigned to the +Control Pad.

CHALLENGE

Challenge Overview

The game offers a total of 105 Challenges. Complete these tasks to add them to your Challenge panels and unlock the corresponding rewards. You'll unlock many of these Challenges simply by exploring the game's many modes and features. Some of these tasks, however, require a fair amount of time, skill, and determination.

USING HAMMERS

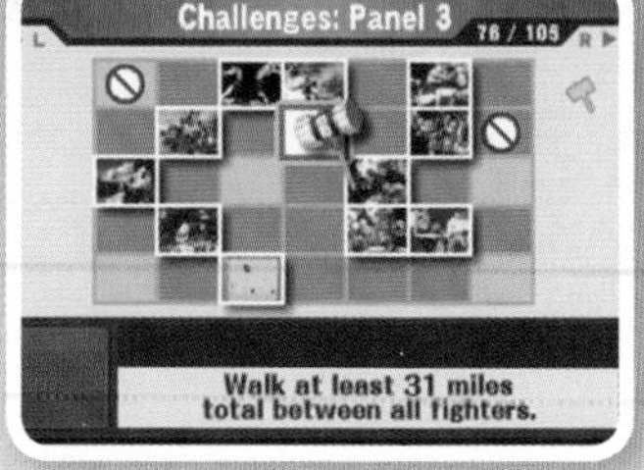

When you use a hammer to open a tile, you gain all the benefits of having completed the corresponding Challenge—you'll gain any rewards or hammers your selected tile contains and reveal the Challenges on any adjacent tiles. This allows you to bypass particularly difficult Challenges or to gain useful rewards fairly early in the game.

It's important to note, however, that not all Challenges can be cracked. When you select a hammer, look for any "no symbols" that appear on the Challenge panel. These tiles are impervious to hammers and can only be unlocked by completing the stated Challenges through gameplay.

Each hammer can only be used within its panel of origin. You can't, for example, use a hammer earned from the first Challenge panel to crack a tile on one of the subsequent panels. This means when you complete a Challenge panel, any unused hammers will go to waste. So, plan accordingly!

Revealing Challenges

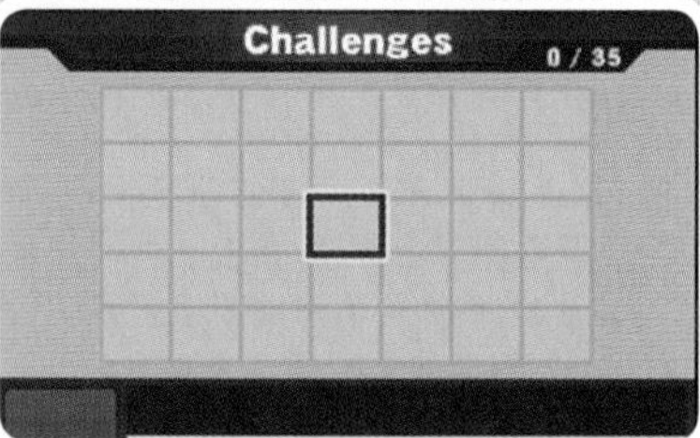

You start the game with a single panel containing 35 gray tiles, each of which holds a hidden Challenge. You must complete at least one of these secret tasks before you are provided any additional details.

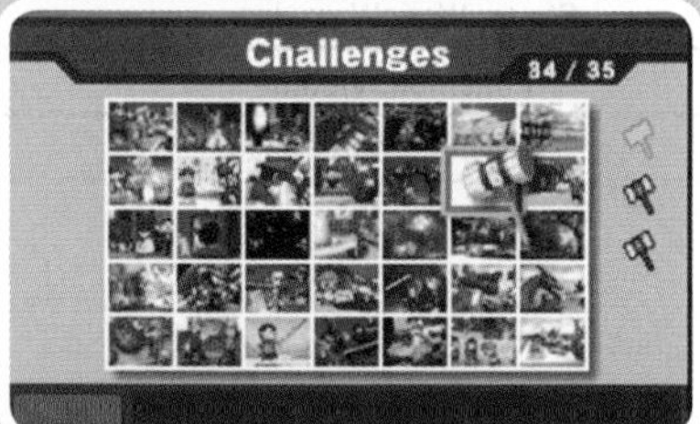

There are three hammers hidden within each Challenge panel. When you complete an appropriate Challenge, a single-use hammer appears near the Touch Screen's right edge. Hammers can be used to unlock Challenges without performing the corresponding tasks.

When you successfully complete a Challenge, an image appears on the corresponding tile. Select this image on the Touch Screen to review the task you've completed and the resulting reward. Additionally, completing a Challenge causes any adjacent tiles to change color. Blue tiles represent revealed (but incomplete) Challenges. If a tile turns light blue, it means that completing the revealed Challenge will grant you a hammer in addition to the standard reward.

Completing Challenge Panels

To complete a Challenge panel, you must open all 35 of its tiles. The second Challenge panel only becomes available once you've completed the first. The third Challenge panel becomes available once you've unlocked all available characters and stages.

If you completed any of the new Challenges before they became available, your progress will be applied to the panel as soon as it's unlocked. Completing each Challenge panel also unlocks a special reward.

Challenge Panel 1

The first Challenge panel is always available.

PANEL 1 KEY

A1	A2	A3	A4	A5	A6	A7
A8	A9	A10	A11	A12	A13	A14
A15	A16	A17	A18	A19	A20	A21
A22	A23	A24	A25	A26	A27	A28
A29	A30	A31	A32	A33	A34	A35

PANEL 1 DETAILS

POSITION	CHALLENGE	REWARD
A1	Collect 30 or more unique trophies.	Trophy: Toad
A2	Place first in 1 or more Smash Run final battles.	Power: Lv. 1 Horizon Beam
A3	Clear All-Star on Easy.	Trophy: Epona
A4	Create 1 or more Mii Fighters in Custom.	Headgear: Football Helmet
A5	Battle 3 or more times on the Rainbow Road stage in Smash.	Trophy: Peach + Birthday Girl
A6	Use a Final Smash while playing as Kirby.	Stage: Dream Land
A7	Hit Sandbag 984 ft. or more in Home-Run Contest.	Trophy: Bonkers
A8	Get a max combo of 10 or more in Training.	Special: Huge Header (Wii Fit Trainer)
A9	Unlock the hidden character Ness.	Stage: Magicant
A10	Collect 5 unique custom headgear items.	Power: Lv. 1 Strong Head
A11	Play Target Blast for the first time.	Pokémon: Xerneas
A12	Play Rival Smash for the first time.	Headgear: Super Mushroom Hat
A13	Play StreetSmash for the first time.	Special: Lightning Falcon Kick (Captain Falcon)
A14	Battle 2 or more times on the Tortimer Island stage in Smash.	Special: Liftoff Lloid (Villager)
A15	Obtain 10 types of Smash Run Powers.	Power: Lv. 2 Reflector
A16	Play Trophy Rush for the first time.	Trophy: Timmy & Tommy
A17	Use a Final Smash while playing as PAC-MAN.	Stage: PAC-MAZE
A18	Play Home-Run Contest for the first time.	Trophy: Home-Run Bat
A19	Battle 3 or more times on the Reset Bomb Forest stage in Smash.	Trophy: Cragalanche the Mighty
A20	Win 3 Smash Battles with Captain Falcon.	Stage: Mute City
A21	Unlock the hidden character Dark Pit.	Trophy: Dark Pit Staff
A22	Clear Classic on intensity 3.0 or higher.	Music: Master Hand
A23	Unlock the hidden character Wario.	Stage: WarioWare, Inc.
A24	Play 100-Man Smash for the first time.	Pokémon: Victini
A25	Use Villager 3 or more times in Smash.	Stage: Balloon Fight
A26	Play Endless Smash for the first time.	Pokémon: Genesect
A27	Clear 10-Man Smash.	Pokémon: Zoroark
A28	Get at least 20 KOs in 3-Minute Smash.	Trophy: Karate Joe
A29	Destroy 300 blocks in Trophy Rush.	Special: Giant Bomb (Link)
A30	Win 3 Smash battles with Luigi.	Headgear: Luigi's Cap
A31	Win 2 Smash battles with Ness.	Trophy: Mr. Saturn
A32	Play Cruel Smash for the first time.	Headgear: Spiny Hat
A33	Collect 3 unique custom outfits.	Power: Lv. 1 Strong Body
A34	Win 2 Smash battles with Zelda.	Headgear: Princess Zelda Wig
A35	Score 100,000 or more in Target Blast.	Trophy: Blast Box

Open all 35 of the first Challenge panel's tiles to earn the Super Star trophy and unlock the second Challenge panel.

Challenge Panel 2

The second Challenge panel becomes available only when the first Challenge panel is complete.

PANEL 2 KEY

B1	B2	B3	B4	B5	B6	B7
B8	B9	B10	B11	B12	B13	B14
B15	B16	B17	B18	B19	B20	B21
B22	B23	B24	B25	B26	B27	B28
B29	B30	B31	B32	B33	B34	B35

PANEL 2 DETAILS

POSITION	CHALLENGE	REWARD
B1	Place first in Smash Run final battles with 5 different characters.	Power: Lv. 2 Spinning Blades
B2	Get a max combo of 40 or more in Training.	Equipment: Beam Sword Agility Badge
B3	Unlock all playable fighters.	Music: Menu 2 (Melee)
B4	Create 3 custom characters in Custom.	Equipment: Sprinter Agility Badge
B5	Destroy 1,000 blocks in Trophy Rush.	Special: Close Combat (Ike)
B6	Get 100 KOs in Smash.	Equipment: Hyper Smasher Brawn Badge
B7	Collect 150 or more unique trophies.	Trophy: Redd
B8	Have a total score of over 2,000,000 between all fighters in Target Blast.	Trophy: King Bob-omb
B9	Get a total of 5 hits in StreetSmash.	Power: Lv. 2 Shinespark
B10	Get 10 or more KOs in a single Rival Smash.	Equipment: KO Healer Protection Badge
B11	Battle 3 or more times on the Living Room stage in Smash.	Trophy: Golden Retriever
B12	Get 10 KOs by knocking foes into other foes in StreetSmash.	Trophy: Mugly
B13	Obtain 25 types of Smash Run Powers.	Power: Lv. 2 Instant Drop
B14	Clear 100-Man Smash.	Equipment: Auto-Healer Brawn Badge
B15	Reveal 99% of the wall during the staff credits.	Music: Credits
B16	Clear Classic with five fighters.	Trophy: Master Hand
B17	Battle 3 or more times on the Find Mii stage in Smash.	Trophy: Dark Emperor
B18	Win 5 Smash battles with Meta Knight.	Special: High-Speed Drill (Meta Knight)
B19	Unlock the hidden character Mr. Game & Watch.	Stage: Flat Zone 2
B20	Defeat Master Core.	Music: Master Core
B21	Get 20 or more in KOs by countering in StreetSmash.	Equipment: First Striker Agility Badge
B22	Hit Sandbag 1,968 ft. or more in Home-Run Contest.	Equipment: Home-Run Bat Agility Badge
B23	Get 30 or more KOs in Endless Smash.	Trophy: Fire Stingray
B24	Play Smash Run 5 times.	Power: Lv. 2 Horizon Beam
B25	Unlock every stage.	Trophy: Tortimer Island
B26	Play 10 collective hours of Smash. (Total gameplay × participants.)	Trophy: Knuckle Joe
B27	Win 10 Smash battles with Samus.	Headgear: Samus's Helmet
B28	Collect 15 unique special moves.	Equipment: Smash Ball Attractor Agility Badge
B29	Collect 5 unique custom outfits.	Headgear: Spartan Helmet
B30	Get 300 KOs in Smash.	Equipment: Critical Hitter Brawn Badge
B31	Play Home-Run Contest with 15 or more fighters.	Equipment: Quick Batter Brawn Badge
B32	Create 8 or more Mii Fighters in Custom.	Headgear: Top Hat
B33	Collect 10 unique custom headgear items.	Outfit: Plate Armor
B34	Clear All-Star on Normal.	Trophy: Medusa, Queen of the Underworld
B35	Have the game on for more than 8 hours.	Pokémon: Meloetta

Open all 35 of the second Challenge panel's tiles to earn the Tutorial Pig trophy.

Challenge Panel 3

The third and final Challenge panel becomes available once you've unlocked all available characters and stages.

PANEL 3 KEY

C1	C2	C3	C4	C5	C6	C7
C8	C9	C10	C11	C12	C13	C14
C15	C16	C17	C18	C19	C20	C21
C22	C23	C24	C25	C26	C27	C28
C29	C30	C31	C32	C33	C34	C35

PANEL 3 DETAILS

POSITION	CHALLENGE	REWARD
C1	Clear Classic on intensity 9.0 or higher.	Trophy: Guardian
C2	Hit Sandbag 3,280 ft. or more in Home-Run Contest.	Power: Lv. 3 Ore Club
C3	Place first in 20 or more Smash Run final battles.	Power: Lv. 3 Dual Cyclone
C4	Create 10 custom characters in Custom.	Equipment: Air Defender Protection Badge
C5	Get 50 or more KOs in a single Rival Smash.	Power: Lv. 3 Health Recovery
C6	Get at least 110 KOs in 3-Minute Smash.	Equipment: Crouch Healer Protection Badge
C7	Obtain all custom outfits, headgear, and Special moves.	Trophy: Michaela
C8	Destroy 3,000 blocks in Trophy Rush.	Special: Exploding Popgun (Diddy Kong)
C9	Clear Classic with all fighters.	Trophy: Crazy Hand
C10	Clear 100-Man Smash within 3 minutes.	Special: Effortless Blade (Marth)
C11	Walk at least 31 miles total between all fighters.	Equipment: Speed Walker Brawn Badge
C12	Clear 10-Man Smash within 20 seconds.	Equipment: Quick Smasher Protection Badge
C13	Get a max combo of 400 or more between all fighters in Training.	Equipment: Leaper Agility Badge
C14	Clear All-Star with all fighters.	Headgear: Regal Crown
C15	Destroy all red targets in Target Blast.	Outfit: Steampunk Getup
C16	Reach a total of 49,212 ft. in the Home-Run Contest between all fighters' high scores.	Trophy: Sandbag
C17	Collect 500 or more unique trophies.	Trophy: Luigi (With Poltergust 3000)
C18	Clear Solo 10-Man Smash with all fighters.	Trophy: Kat & Ana
C19	Score 200,000 or more in Target Blast.	Special: Explosive Punch (Mario)
C20	Clear Solo 100-Man Smash with all fighters.	Trophy: Shadow
C21	Play 50 collective hours of Smash. (Total gameplay × participants.)	Trophy: Color TV-Game 15
C22	Place first in Smash Run final battles with all fighters.	Power: Lv. 3 Shuffle
C23	Jump at least 6 miles total between all fighters.	Power: Lv. 3 High Jump
C24	Play Target Blast with all fighters.	Trophy: Dark Train
C25	Get 20 KOs by knocking foes into other foes in StreetSmash.	Trophy: Koopa Troopa (Green)
C26	Get a max combo of 100 or more in Training.	Outfit: Protective Gear
C27	Have the game on for more than 20 hours.	Headgear: Princess's Crown
C28	Get 4 or more KOs in Cruel Smash.	Headgear: Lion Hat
C29	Clear All-Star on Hard.	Trophy: Nintendoji
C30	Get 1,000 KOs in Smash.	Equipment: Moon Launcher Brawn Badge
C31	Get 2 or more KOs in Cruel Smash.	Equipment: Shield Exploder Protection Badge
C32	Get 200 or more KOs in Endless Smash.	Power: Lv. 3 Launch Ring
C33	Collect all Smash Run Powers.	Headgear: Prince's Crown
C34	Clear All-Star with 15 fighters.	Music: All-Star Rest Area
C35	Collect 600 or more unique trophies.	Trophy: Wentworth

Open all 35 of the third Challenge panels' tiles to earn the Gold Bone trophy.

Challenge Tips

Most of the game's Challenges are straightforward, and many of them can be completed without any special techniques or knowledge. Some of them, however, call for a significant amount of skill and strategy. Here are some tips to help you complete the game's more difficult Challenges.

COMBOS

All of the combo Challenges must be performed in Training. This not only makes it easy to monitor the effectiveness of each attempt, but it allows you make each attempt under the ideal conditions.

Many fighters can achieve 10-hit combos simply by performing a steady stream of jabs. By using the available items, however, any character should be able to perform combos of at least 50 hits. Stand near your opponent and summon four X Bombs. Grab one and toss it into the pile. Repeat the process with various characters to build up the max combos across your roster.

The easiest way to perform a 100-hit combo is to use Lucario's Aura Sphere. Select Fox as your opponent, and choose to face him on Corneria. Force Fox against the Great Fox's vertical stabilizer, then turn your back to him without moving away. Charge Lucario's Aura Sphere to begin building your combo. Fox's fall-speed should keep him within range of each pulse, making it easy to build your combo. Simply hold your attack until you've completed the Challenge or until Fox sustains enough damage to be launched out of range.

CLASSIC

Several of the game's Challenges require clearing Classic at different intensity levels or with different fighters. Some of these tasks, however, are a bit easier to accomplish with a bit of preparation.

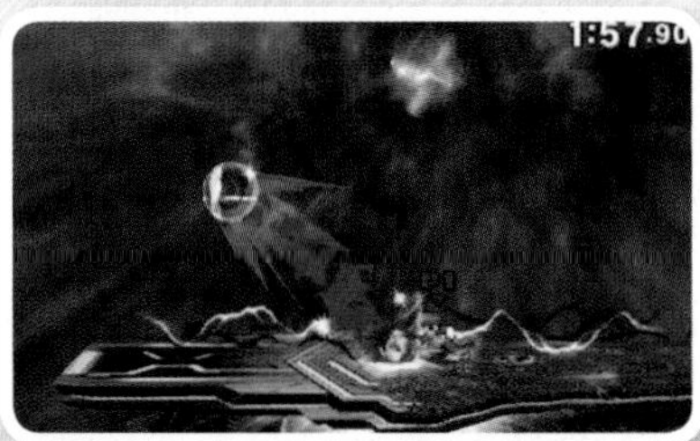

Master Core is only available in Classic when the intensity is set to 5.1 or above. Additionally, you must select the final battle that contains both Master Hand and Crazy Hand (indicated by the black path on the Classic map). The fight changes a great deal between an intensity of 5.1 and an intensity of 9.0, but the goal is always the same: damage each of your opponent's shadowy forms until Master Core is revealed, then defeat the orb to end the battle.

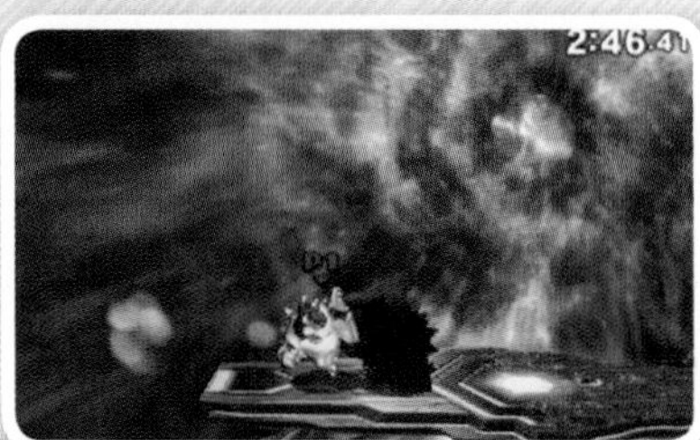

For most players, clearing Classic on an intensity of 9.0 is likely to be one of the more difficult Challenges. It's generally best to use whatever fighter best suits your skills, but Bowser's high defense allows him to survive at least a few attacks that would launch lighter characters. It can also be very helpful to customize your character with stat-altering equipment—particularly any items with an Auto-Heal effect. It's important to note, however, that during the Master Core battle, your shadowy doppelgänger will receive the same benefits your equipment grants you.

STAFF CREDITS

When you complete a game of Classic or All-Star, you can use your fighter to attack the staff credits. When done properly, attacking individual names reveals a image on the back wall. For a name to contribute to the image, however, you must hit it at just the right time and in just the right spot. Jump up and use aerial attacks to reveal the top of the image as the names pass in front of any blank areas, then work your way down.

As you reveal more of the image, it becomes important to aim your shots. Look for the sparkles that help identify hidden sections, then strike a name as it passes through the area.

3-MINUTE SMASH

To score 110 KOs within a single round of 3-Minute Smash, it's best to avoid chasing your opponents around the battlefield. Instead, hop onto the stage's highest platform—most of your opponents will spawn near you, and those that don't shouldn't take long to move into range.

It can be helpful to select a fighter with heavy attacks—Donkey Kong is a particularly good choice. Focus on using Up Smash and Up Tilt attacks, but don't shy away from any heavy attacks that have a chance to connect. You're bound to be knocked from your position every so often. When this happens, hurry back up to the platform and resume your attacks.

Cruel Smash

In Cruel Smash, it can be difficult to score even a single KO before you're eliminated. There are, however, a few things you can do to improve your chances. Some fighters—like Mario and Luigi—spin around while they perform Back Throws. This allows you to strike nearby opponents as you create a little breathing room.

Characters equipped with a Counter Special—like Ike, for example—can be very effective. Because your opponents are particularly aggressive, it's often possible to catch several of them with a single Counter. When this happens near the edge of the stage, you have an excellent chance of scoring multiple KOs.

Home-Run Contest

With a little practice, you shouldn't have much trouble consistently hitting Sandbag more than 1,000 feet, and particularly good efforts should yield more than 2,000 feet. Launching Sandbag more than 3,280 feet, however, requires a solid strategy. The key to success is to play to the strengths of your chosen fighter. Little Mac, for example, can use Smash attacks to deal heavy damage as he follows Sandbag back and forth across the platform. Many fighters can simply stand in one spot and use Smash attacks to juggle Sandbag off of the invisible wall surrounding the platform. Choose attacks that deal heavy damage, but make sure you're in a position to land your next blow as quickly as possible.

It's usually best to put off grabbing the Home-Run Bat until you're ready to use it. If you grab it a bit early, however, you can still use aerial attacks to juggle Sandbag for the remainder of the countdown. This strategy requires precision timing—and it isn't suitable for all fighters—but it can be very effective under the right circumstances. Choose the tactic that allows your fighter to deal the most damage to Sandbag, and remember to begin your swing just before the countdown ends!

Target Blast

Clearing all of the Target Blast targets is always a little tricky. You have to consider your fighter's attacks, the position on the platform, and exactly when to launch the bomb. For most characters, however, you'll find it's fairly easy to reach the higher targets when you launch the bomb off of the wall to the left. It's often best to do this during your first attempt, increasing the chance that at least a few of the lower targets will be destroyed by falling debris.

SUPER SMASH BROS.™ TIME LINE

1999: SUPER SMASH BROS.™

The game that started it all, *Super Smash Bros.*, debuted on the Nintendo 64 in 1999. It featured 12 fighters and 9 stages. It also included a 4-player Versus mode and a selection of single-player game modes.

2001: SUPER SMASH BROS.™ MELEE

Super Smash Bros. Melee was released on the Nintendo GameCube in 2001. It featured 26 fighters and 29 combat stages, as well as a variety of new game modes. It also introduced trophies for players to earn and collect.

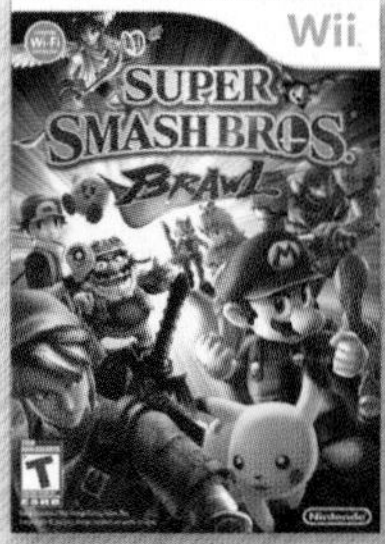

2008: SUPER SMASH BROS.™ BRAWL

Released in 2008, *Super Smash Bros. Brawl* featured 39 fighters and 41 combat stages. This was the first game in the series to include third-party characters as playable fighters. It also introduced online play and a variety of new game modes.

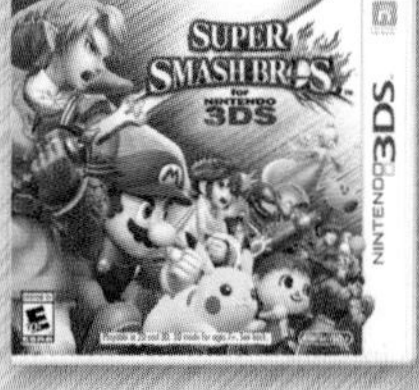

2014: SUPER SMASH BROS.™ FOR NINTENDO 3DS

In 2014, *Super Smash Bros.* for Nintendo 3DS launched with 48 fighters (51 including the three Mii Fighter classes) and 34 stages. It featured a variety of single player, multiplayer, and online game modes. Most significantly, however, this game marked the series' debut on a handheld system.

2014: SUPER SMASH BROS.™ FOR WII U

Super Smash Bros. for Wii U was released in 2014. At launch, it featured 48 fighters (51 including the three Mii Fighter classes) and 46 combat stages. This game offered a wide variety of game modes and customization options. Additionally, it introduced amiibo functionality to the series, featuring the ability to create and train amiibo Figure Players.